ESSAYS ON WOMEN
IN EARLIEST CHRISTIANITY

VOLUME ONE

Edited by

Carroll D. Osburn

*Virgil –
Best wishes –
Carroll 2/94*

ESSAYS ON WOMEN
IN EARLIEST CHRISTIANITY

VOLUME ONE

Edited by

Carroll D. Osburn

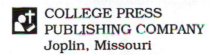
COLLEGE PRESS
PUBLISHING COMPANY
Joplin, Missouri

Contents

Contents

Participants

Frederick Aquino, M.Div., Abilene Christian University

Allen Black, Ph.D., Emory Univ.; Associate Professor of New
Testament, Harding Graduate School of Religion

Mark C. Black, Ph.D., Emory Univ.; Assistant Professor of
New Testament, David Lipscomb University

Barry L. Blackburn, Ph.D., University of Aberdeen (Scot.);
Professor of New Testament, Atlanta Christian College

Randall D. Chesnutt, Ph.D., Duke University; Associate Professor
of Religion, Pepperdine University

Jeffrey W. Childers, M.A., M.Div., Abilene Christian University;
D.Phil. student, Oxford University

Larry Chouinard, Ph.D., Fuller Theological Seminary; Assistant
Professor of New Testament, Kentucky Christian College

Everett Ferguson, Ph.D., Harvard University; Lewis Distinguished
Professor of Church History, Abilene Christian University

Thomas C. Geer, Jr., Ph.D., Boston University; Walling
Professor of New Testament Language and Literature,
Abilene Christian University

Jan Faver Hailey, M.A. (cand.), Abilene Christian University

Stanley Helton, M.S., M.A. (cand.) Abilene Christian University

Brian McLemore, M.S., Abilene Christian University; Instructor
of Missions, Abilene Christian University

Marcia Moore, M.Div., Harding Graduate School of Religion;
Instructor of Greek, Abilene Christian University

Kenneth V. Neller, Ph.D., University of St. Andrews (Scot.);
Assistant Professor of New Testament, Harding University

v

Participants

Curt Niccum, M.Div., M.A. (cand.), Abilene Christian University; Ph.D. student, University of Notre Dame

Carroll D. Osburn, Ph.D., University of St. Andrews (Scot.), D.Min., Vanderbilt University; Carmichael Distinguished Professor of New Testament, Abilene Christian University

Paul Pollard, Ph.D., Baylor University; Associate Professor of New Testament, Harding University

Kathy Pulley, Ph.D., Boston University; Assistant Professor of Religious Studies, Southwest Missouri State University

Greg Sterling, Ph.D., Graduate Theological Union, Berkeley; Assistant Professor of New Testament, University of Notre Dame

James Thompson, Ph.D., Vanderbilt University; Associate Professor of New Testament, Abilene Christian University

James Walters, Ph.D., Boston University; Associate Professor of New Testament, Harding University

John Willis, Ph.D., Vanderbilt University; Coffman Distinguished Professor of Old Testament, Abilene Christian University

Abbreviations

AJP	*American Journal of Philology*
ANF	The Ante-Nicene Fathers
ANRW	*Aufstieg und Neidergang der römischen Welt*
AR	*Ancient Records of Assyria and Babylonia*
ASNU	Acta serminarii neotestamentici upsaliensis
ASV	American Standard Version
ATR	*Anglican Theological Review*
AusBR	*Australian Biblical Review*
BA	*Biblical Archaeologist*
BAGD	W. Bauer, W. F. Arndt, F. W. Gingrich, and F.W. Danker, *Greek-English Lexicon of the NT*
BAR	*Biblical Archaeologist Reader*
BCE	Before Common Era
BETL	Bibliotheca ephemeridum theologicarum lovaniensium
BFCT	Berträge zur Förderung christlicher Theologie
Bib	*Biblica*
BibLeb	*Bible und Leben*
BJRL	*Bulletin of the John Rylands University Library of Manchester*
BJS	Brown Judiac Studies
BSac	*Bibliotheca Sacra*
BT	*The Bible Translator*
BTB	*Biblical Theological Bulletin*
BWANT	Beiträge zur Wissenschaft vom Alten und Neuen Testament
BZNW	Beihefte zur *ZNW*
CBQ	*Catholic Biblical Quarterly*
CBQMS	Catholic Biblical Quarterly Monograph Series
CE	Common Era
CH	*Church History*
CII	*Corpus inscriptionum iudaicarum*
CP	*Classical Philology*
CQ	*Church Quarterly*
CSCO	Corpus scriptorum christianorum orientalium
DJD	Discoveries in the Judaean Desert
Ebib	Etudes bibliques
EKKNT	Evangelische-katholischer Kommentar zum Neuen Testament
ETL	*Ephemerides theologicae lovanienses*
EPRO	Etudes prélimininaries aux religions orientales dans l'empire Romain
ExpTim	*Expository Times*
GNB	Good News Bible
Greg	*Gregorianum*
GRBS	*Greek, Roman and Byzantine Studies*
HeyJ	*Heythrop Journal*
HKNT	Handkommentar zum Neuen Testament
HNTC	Harper's NT Commentaries
HR	*History of Religions*

Abbreviations

HTR	*Harvard Theological Review*
ICC	International Critical Commentary
IDB	G.A. Buttrick (ed.) *Interpreter's Dictionary of the Bible*
IEJ	Israel Exploration Journal
Int	*Interpretation*
ISBE	G. W. Bromiley (ed.) International Standard Bible Encyclopedia, rev.
JAAR	*Journal of American Academy of Religion*
JAC	Jahrbuch für Antike und Christentum
JB	Jerusalem Bible
JBL	*Journal of Biblical Literature*
JEH	*Journal of Ecclesastical History*
JETS	*Journal of the Evangelical Theological Society*
JJS	*Journal of Jewish Studies*
JNES	*Journal of Near Eastern Studies*
JR	*Journal of Religion*
JSNT	*Journal for the Study of the New Testament*
JSNTSup	*Journal for the Study of the New Testament Supplement Series*
JSOT	*Journal for the Study of the Old Testament*
JSP	*Journal for the Study of the Pseudepigrapha*
KJV	King James Version
LCL	Loeb Classical Library
LSJ	Liddell-Scott-Jones, *Greek-English Lexicon*
MNTC	Moffatt NT Commentary
NAB	New American Bible
NedTTs	*Netherlands theologisch tijdschrift*
NEB	New English Bible
NICNT	New International Commentary on the New Testament
NIV	New International Version
NKJB	New King James Bible
NTD	Das Neue Testament Deutsch
NovT	*Novum Testamentum*
NPNF	Nicene and Post-Nicene Fathers
NRSV	New Revised Standard Version
NTS	*New Testament Studies*
ÖBS	Österreichische biblische Studien
PG	J. Minge, *Patrologia graeca*
PSTJ	*Perkins (School of Theology) Journal*
PW	Pauly Wissowa, *Real Encyclopädie der classischen Altertumswissenschaft*
QD	Quaestiones disputatae
RAC	*Reallexikon für Antike und Christentum*
RevExp	*Review and Expositior*
RHPR	*Revue d'historie et de philosophie religieuses*
RNT	Regensburger Neues Testament
RQ	*Restoration Quarterly*
RSV	Revised Standard Version

Abbreviations

RTL	*Revue théologique de Louvain*
SBLBSNA	SBL Biblical Scholarship in North America
SBLDS	SBL Dissertation Series
SBLMS	SBL Monograph Series
SBLSBS	SBL Sources for Biblical Study
SBLSP	SBL Seminar Papers
SBM	Stuttgarter biblische Monographien
SNTSMS	Society for New Testament Studies Monograph Series
ST	*Studia theologica*
StEv	*Studia Evangelica*
TBT	*The Bible Today*
TAPA	*Transactions of the American Philological Association*
TDNT	G. Kittel and G. Friedrich (eds.) *Theological Dictionary of the New Testament*
TEV	Today's English Version
THKNT	Theologischer Handkommentar zum Neuen Testament
TQ	*Theologische Quartalschrift*
TS	*Theological Studies*
UBSGNT	United Bible Societies *Greek New Testament*
VC	*Vigiliae christianae*
VT	*Vetus Testamentum*
WBC	Word Biblical Commentary
WTJ	*Westminster Theological Journal*
ZAW	*Zeitschrift für die alttestamentliche Wissenschaft*
ZNW	*Zeitschrift für die neutestamentliche Wissenschaft*

Editor's Preface

Not unique to any particular religious heritage, problems regarding women in the church are set within the larger context of societal changes. Alternative views abound and unfortunate polarizations have occurred, even among Christians. Not only do understandings of biblical texts which pertain to the topic vary considerably, but even the role of these texts in current discussion is debated. Some opt to accept new definitions of women in the church based upon societal perspectives rather than biblical norms. Among those who take the Bible seriously, this very complex situation raises major questions about women in earliest Christianity.

Precisely what was the understanding of women in the early church? And how does one arrive at the import of that understanding for determining today's view? There exists an obvious need for a careful approach to these questions in terms of controlled exegesis and responsible hermeneutic.

Accordingly, the fresh analyses of the various texts and topics in this volume present thorough and balanced discussions of essential components of the problem. The contributors are some of the best-known scholars from among the churches of Christ, but also include a few younger scholars, both male and female, who will help–it is hoped–to continue the rich tradition of scholarship from the Restoration perspective. While a few are "biblical feminists," most would feel uncomfortable with that nomenclature and would fit more comfortably in what might be called a "complementarian" perspective. The purpose of the book is not to argue a particular viewpoint, but to approach the text carefully to see what results from controlled exegesis.

Not all contributors would agree on all aspects of the volume. However, writing independently and free to arrive at their own conclusions, each attempts to follow a common exegetical method which places firm literary and historical controls upon interpretation. The views expressed do yield a rather uniform perspective that is neither fundamentalist nor radical feminist.

Now it is to be expected that some readers will find their views to be confirmed, while others will find challenges to certain preferred understandings. Undoubtedly, some will think the essays take the matter much too far, while others will be of the opinion that they do not take matters far enough. However, the reader may hope to gain from these essays 1) a clearer perspective of the contours and complexity of the question which disallows simplistic answers, 2) a methodologically responsible way to approach biblical texts in their literary and historical contexts, 3) a hermeneutically responsible procedure for arriving at doctrinal conclusions based upon the results of controlled exegesis, and 4) biblical perspectives vital to any attempt to arrive at a valid understanding of women in contemporary Christianity.

A second volume, now in progress, will treat other texts and topics not covered here, e.g., Gen. 1-3, Prov. 31, Deborah, Huldah, women in the Fourth Gospel and Acts, Prisca and Aquila, Col. 3:18-19, 1 Pet. 3:7, women in the Restoration heritage, special essays on the hermeneutical problem, and a theology of women in the church.

I am indebted to Mrs. Lucille Carmichael of Dallas, TX, for her special interest in bringing biblical research to bear upon contemporary faith and practice. It is a special privilege to thank Ms. Jo Ann Walling Halbert of Dallas, TX, and Mrs. S. V. Varner of Wichita, KS, for their assistance in bringing this volume to completion. To my secretary, Mrs. Charme Robarts, and my graduate assistant, Chris Benjamin, I express thanks for the preparation of a complicated manuscript. The editorial staff at College Press have been most helpful, especially Mr. John M. Hunter. Finally, to my wife, Linda, I am thankful for uncommon patience.

Carroll D. Osburn

Abilene, TX
1 June 1993

Corrigenda

page	line	
vi.	13	Omit Associate
vii	3	Read *Niedergang*
vii	20	Read Judaic
2	37	Read Ruether
3	21	Read Ruether
26	24	Read incident *because*
26	25	Read condemned *because*
31	20	Read OT accounts
147	19	Read 2:4
190	31	Read Ruether
227	1	Omit comma
239	22	Read God of disorder
271	39	Read Elisabeth Schüssler
273	28	Omit " before The
370	4	Read Caesar's
376	36	Read derives
389	19	Read distinguishing
433	34	Read *Evangelium*
445	25	Read Elisabeth
531	11	Read *Epistulae*
533		Lactantius and Origen should appear under Early Christian Sources, p. 541
535	2	Read *Institutiones*
540	13	Augustine, for 26=7, read 26.7
540	35	Add Epiph. *Pan.* 49.2: 511
540	40	Read *1 Clement*
541	18	Read *Apostolic Tradition*
549	20	Read Ruether

(6:4).[22] If the doctrinal concepts of the false teachers were Paul's primary concern, one would expect such concepts to be specifically refuted, but this occurs only once (4:3-5). Instead, the concern which Paul repeatedly expresses is the *effect* of such constant controversy on the life of the church: their obsession with debating these matters has resulted in the rejection or neglect of what is *really* important—faith, moral integrity, and especially, love (1:5,6 and 19; 4:1; 6:21)). The false teaching also brings about endless speculation rather than the οἰκονομίαν of God (1:4).[23] If the meaning is "stewardship,"[24] the Ephesian church[25] is

---

[22]Many have tried to identify the content of the "false teaching." See, for example, John J. Gunther, *St. Paul's Opponents and their Backgrounds* (Leiden: E. J. Brill, 1973). One explanation for such "vague" descriptions is given by Robert J. Karris, "The Background and Significance of the Polemic of the Pastoral Epistles," *JBL* 92 (1973): 549-564, who argues that one of the main weapons of the Pastorals' author was "name-calling polemic," based on a traditional schema used by philosophers to criticize sophists, and that all such "stock" charges should not be understood as reflecting the actual situation, "unless there is a clear indication in other sections of the Pastorals to the contrary." However, if 1 Tim. was actually written by Paul to a specific colleague in a specific location about the conduct and teaching of specific individuals (two of whom he names), the usage of a traditional schema which did not reflect the actual situation would surely backfire and discredit Paul instead of the false teachers.

[23]Though many translate οἰκονομίαν as the "training" of God or "God's plan of salvation," it can also mean "stewardship, commission, administration." See Walter Bauer, *A Greek-English Lexicon of the New Testament and Other Early Christian Literature* (trans. by W. F. Arndt and F. W. Gingrich; 2nd ed. rev. F. W. Gingrich and F. Danker; Chicago: Univ. of Chicago Press, 1979): 559-60. This word is used in 1 Cor. 9:17, Eph. 3:2, 9, and Col. 1:25, and a similar word (οἰκονόμος; steward) is used in 1 Cor. 4:1 and Tit. 1:7, in each instance referring to a person being entrusted with sharing the message of God's grace.

[24]See Markus Barth, *Ephesians* (AB, 34; Garden City, NY: Doubleday, 1974): 86-88, 358-359; Walter Lock, *A Critical and Exegetical Commentary on the Pastoral Epistles* (ICC; Edinburgh: T. & T. Clark, 1924): 9-10; and Ronald A. Ward, *Commentary on 1 and 2 Timothy and Titus* (Waco: Word, 1974): 30.

Chapter One

WOMEN IN THE CHURCH IN RECENT DISCUSSION

Kathy J. Pulley

Because the Bible is viewed as authoritative, discussion of "women in the church" in conservative churches has centered largely around texts such as Gal. 3:28; 1 Cor. 14:34-35; Eph. 5:22; and 1 Tim. 2:12. But discussion in conservative churches is surrounded by many other complex issues, one of which is the changing role of women in our society. The vast amount of literature that is being and has been written about women and theology–most often referred to as "feminist theology"–has focused certain concerns and issues germane to any responsible discussion of the topic.

1. *The Emergence of Feminist Concerns and Issues*

What is "feminist theology?" In the early 1960's, the Women's Movement began to draw national attention. In the same decade that Betty Friedan would write *The Feminine Mystique* (1963), Mary Daly wrote *The Church and the Second Sex* (1968). Daly, credited by most to be the earliest formulator of a feminist critique of religion, initially drew attention to the discrimination of women by the church and called for the church to be more attentive to women's issues. Other feminists began to explore the biblical images of women and to investigate the history of how women were regarded in religious communities.

Lerner,[1] a social historian, claims that Western culture, including some culturally-driven teachings in churches, is

---

[1]Gerda Lerner, *The Creation of Patriarchy* (New York: Oxford Univ. Press, 1986): 220, 236-37.

marked by what she calls "a conceptual error of vast proportion." It has been assumed that male experiences and viewpoints represent the experiences and viewpoints of all humanity, and simply "adding women" is not enough to change this distorted view of reality. For example, adding anecdotes about women as well as men to sermons is not enough. Minnich,[2] a contemporary philosopher, believes that when women are moved from the margin to the center, it is a major change, not just an addition. It is comparable to adding "the earth is round" to the world view that "the earth is flat"—it changes everything.

In feminist thought, what is called for is a radical change in human perception. An accurate perception of reality is that both men's and women's experiences and viewpoints must be recognized and counted equally if society is to have a complete picture of humankind. In Western history, for the most part, only half the story has been acknowledged.

Today feminist theology encompasses a variety of topics and is a field of study in its own right. The best way to define the subject for this essay may be in a broad way, which attempts to embrace all the above, rather than by narrowly characterizing specific areas within the field. Reuther, one of the best-known Christian feminists, offers such a broad definition when she states that the critical principle of feminist theology is "the promotion of the full humanity of women. Whatever denies, diminishes, distorts the full humanity of women is, therefore, appraised as not redemptive."[3] This working definition allows both men and women who are interested in promoting the full humanity of women in regard to religious and/or theological issues to "do" feminist theology, regardless of their own religious tradition, and regardless of whether they perceive themselves to be theologically liberal or theologically conservative.

---

[2]Elizabeth Minnich, *Transforming Knowledge* (Philadelphia: Temple Univ. Press, 1990): 14, 27-28.

[3]Rosemary Radford Reuther, *Sexism and God-Talk* (Boston: Beacon, 1983): 18-19.

It is more than interesting that the study of women in the church is continuing to flourish across denominational lines and for such an extended period of time. Mainly, it is because for many a variety of debates about the issues have not been satisfactorily resolved. There remains a gnawing suspicion that certain Scriptures, at least in the ways that they have been most often interpreted, are prejudiced against women. There is also the belief that, whether intentionally or not, many religious institutions promote a second-class status for women. Many women ask themselves whether they can maintain a life-long commitment to their Christian tradition, considering the lack of resolution of these issues. Such suspicions and questions are not small matters. They do, in fact, deal with the very core of a woman's sexual and spiritual identity. So until these several issues are resolved, religious institutions will continue to struggle in various ways with women in the church.

Given the breadth of this field of study, it will not be possible to examine all the material or all the significant spokespersons. Pioneer feminist theologians such as Daly, Reuther, Russell, Fiorenza, and Trible, continue to provide challenging ideas for discussion in the area of Christian theology and changing roles in Western society. However, not all these feminist writers view the Bible as authoritative.

2. *Biblical Feminism*

The primary focus in this essay will be the feminist writers emerging out of conservative Christian traditions and the issues that exist in those circles. Although some conservative feminists are scholars in the fields of religion and theology, others are not. These scholars bring their expertise to the church from such diverse fields as psychology, history, sociology, anthropology, philosophy, and literature. Despite multi-disciplined approaches and representing different church traditions, what they seem to share in common is two-fold: 1) a commitment to "the promotion of the full humanity of women," and 2) a commitment to the authority of the Bible.

Because the Bible is believed to be authoritative, and foundational to any study of the topic, it is not surprising that a variety of methodologies concerning biblical interpretation are employed by conservative feminists. What is involved in a re-examination of biblical texts? Two matters, at least, are foundational. First, any attempt at reexamination of an ancient text involves a clear recognition of what are one's own presuppositions regarding the Bible. Second, it involves critiquing and closely scrutinizing how ancient texts have been interpreted. Sakenfeld[4] suggests that there are three interpretive styles that feminists have brought to the Bible, and the three styles mentioned below have been adapted from her work:

1. Look specifically at selective texts about women with the presupposition that the Bible is an authoritative guide for how to live and for how to understand gender roles.

2. Look generally at the biblical texts, not as specific instructions but as teachings and stories which guide the reader to an overall theological perspective on such matters as justice, patriarchy, and human liberation.

3. Look specifically at all texts about women, to point out patriarchal narratives, and to learn from them, allowing the Bible to serve as a means of showing women their true position in ancient cultures, and yet still giving hope that it might be different.

If one investigates what might be included in each of these approaches, it is easy to recognize that the first approach would be of great interest to those who would call themselves conservative feminists because it is the only one of the three which works primarily under the presupposition that the biblical text is authoritative in its entirety. This does

---

[4]The styles, although somewhat revised, are taken from Katherine Doob Sakenfeld, "Feminist Uses of Biblical Materials," *Feminist Interpretation of the Bible* (ed. Letty Russell; Philadelphia: Westminster, 1985): 56. The styles are not mutually exclusive and overlapping is common.

not mean that scholars who use this approach do not benefit from the writings of those who use the second and third approaches mentioned. It does mean, however, that they share a common biblical hermeneutic, even if it is shared loosely. So, the common ground for debate is established— ultimately, whatever the role of women in the church is to be, it is declared to be such because it is what is perceived to be biblically correct. And being biblically correct is the ultimate standard for judging all human roles and relationships.

Those conservative scholars who approach the text and the role of women in the church from this perspective are most commonly referred to as either "biblical feminists" or "evangelical feminists," because of their understanding of the high priority that must be given to the Bible.

For those who wish to use the first approach, referred to by some as a "loyalist hermeneutic," what are the specific ways in which selective biblical texts can be used to address women's role?[5] Again, there is overlapping, but it seems possible to describe at least four alternatives.

A. *Reinterpretation of Problematic Scriptures.* Biblical texts that have been traditionally used against women, when reinterpreted in terms of rigorous literary and historical controls, may become supportive of women. Fresh information from historians, linguists, textual critics and others often brings new insights and understandings to problematic passages. E.g., 1 Cor. 14:34-35 would involve careful exegesis of every word, including an evaluation of historical-critical issues, text-critical issues, and any social

---

[5]For more information about this hermeneutical interpretation and the ways in which it is used by biblical feminists, see Sakenfeld, "Feminist Uses of Biblical Materials," *Feminist Interpretation of the Bible*, 55-64; Anne E. Carr, *Transforming Grace* (San Francisco: Harper and Row, 1988): 7-14; and Carolyn Osiek, "The Feminist and the Bible: Hermeneutical Alternatives," *Feminist Perspectives on Biblical Scholarship* (ed. Adela Yarbro Collins; Chico, CA: Scholars Press, 1985): 93-106.

issues that might shed new light on the interpretation of the passage. This approach would address the question of whether the text, properly understood apart from traditional exegesis, mandates sexist attitudes and practices.

B. *Counter Negative Passages about Women with Positive Passages.* Biblical texts that might suggest a negative view of women in leadership positions, for example, could be countered with passages that point out biblical characters who were female and who also are portrayed positively in positions of leadership. E.g., 1 Tim. 2:11-15 has been taken by some to mean that women are by their very nature inferior to men and thus not suited to leadership positions over men. This might be countered with reference to Deborah, who according to Judges, was a judge herself, presiding over men and women. Also, Phoebe has been used to show that whatever leadership roles "deacons" had in the first century, Phoebe was called "deacon" by Paul. Too, some have concluded that references to Miriam in the OT indicate that she may have been as important to the Exodus as her brother Aaron.[6]

The intention of this approach is to demonstrate that one cannot assume that God does not intend for women to be in leadership positions based upon a select group of passages seeming to support that assumption, while ignoring other passages that counter that assumption. In fact, other texts may be used to make just the opposite point, i.e., that the Bible itself evidences that some women were indeed capable of leadership and that they exercised that leadership in a manner acceptable to the biblical writers telling their stories.

C. *Focus on Jesus' Treatment of Women and the Roles They Had in His Ministry.* The presupposition of this approach is rather obvious. Since Jesus is God incarnate, his life and teachings serve as the ultimate "norm" or "model" for how God intended God's people to relate to one

---

[6]Alice L. Laffey, *An Introduction to the Old Testament: A Feminist Perspective* (Philadelphia: Fortress, 1988): 51-55, and Mic. 6:4.

another. Therefore, the attitudes and values practiced by Jesus have priority over other texts that may appear to be in conflict with the teachings of Jesus. Those who approach the texts in this way compare Jesus' treatment of women, in first-century Israel, with the average Jewish or Roman male's treatment of women. The differences are vast, and all seem to point to Jesus' representing a radical change from the "norm."[7] Unlike other men of his day, Jesus showed an attitude of great respect toward women.[8]

For example, in the story of Jesus talking to the Samaritan woman at the well (John 4), two points are usually made: 1) Jesus engages in a long conversation with a woman despite cultural taboos against such interactions, and 2) the story indicates that the woman was the primary spokesperson who took the message back to the Samaritan villagers. The value of this approach from the perspective of biblical feminists is that a case can be made for Jesus taking an "anti-status-quo" stance on women's issues, i.e., that he advocated both in his ministry and his teachings an elevation of the status of women, . . . an elevation to the place of equality with men, which would have been then and still is today considered radical.

D. *Use Exegesis and Textual Criticism to Do Background Studies and Word Studies which May Not Directly Deal with Women.* This approach is similar to the first one mentioned above; however, it differs in that the exegesis may or may not deal with texts specifically pertaining to women. E.g.,

---

[7]Two authors who develop Jesus' treatment of women in detail are Elisabeth Moltmann-Wendell, *The Women Around Jesus* (New York: Crossroad, 1992), and Leonard Swidler, *Biblical Affirmations of Woman* (Philadelphia: Westminster, 1979): 163-290.

[8]Leonard Swidler, "Jesus Was a Feminist," *Southeast Asian Journal of Theology* 13 (1971): 102-110, although it is unlikely that Swidler would consider himself as an evangelical. Others, such as Evelyn Stagg and Frank Stagg, *Woman in the World of Jesus* (Philadelphia: Westminster, 1978), continue to advocate that Jesus neither viewed nor treated women in an inferior way and that his model should be followed by his followers.

Rom. 16 is presently receiving careful attention by exegetes and others. Superficially, it appears to be a list of greetings. Upon closer study, those to whom Paul sends greetings include one named "Junias" or perhaps "Junia." Is the person male or female? Many have assumed that since this person was referred to as an apostle, the person must have been a male. Recent scholarship, however, has concluded that this person was female.[9] On the basis of this, biblical feminists claim that the Bible itself mentions a woman in the highest leadership position available to a follower of Jesus in the first century. Other studies merit the attention of biblical feminists, such as the household code in Titus and the roles of "deacon," "evangelist," "prophet," "elder," and "teacher" in the early church.

All four of these hermeneutical alternatives are critical in conservative scholarship. Yet critiquing selective biblical texts is not the only criterion used by biblical feminists.

3. *Controversy Among Conservatives*

Despite agreement that the Bible is the final authority on all matters, conservatives are still divided on the role of women. Often the debate seems to be much more centered around a presuppositional difference than on methodologies used to study the texts. The presuppositional issue involves this question: what is the biblical model for human relationships, specifically those between women and men?

A. *The Hierarchical Paradigm.* Some claim that the Bible advocates a hierarchical paradigm. Based primarily on the order of creation (Gen. 2-3), woman is secondary to man. She was created second. She was created from the man. She was created to be his "helper." Other biblical texts are used to support the view that this concept of a hierarchy in human relationships was continued in the early church (Eph. 5:22-24; Col. 3:18; 1 Tim. 2:11-15).

---

[9]See Bernadette Brooten, "'Junia . . . Outstanding Among the Apostles' (Romans 16:7)," *Women Priests* (ed. L. Swidler and A. Swidler; New York: Paulist, 1977): 141-44.

Theologically, the conclusion is reached that God, from the moment of creation, intended that at least a functional hierarchy would exist between men and women in the church and home. Therefore in practice, hierarchicalists advocate male leadership in both the church and home, with the woman being submissive to the man's authority, which is perceived to be given to him by God. In order to be theologically "correct" in one's relationship to God, both the individual and the church must accept and practice this hierarchical model.

Recent hierarchicalists are quick to point out the vast contributions of women in both church and home arenas. They contend that this approach does promote true dignity and liberation for women.[10] And it is a less structured and certainly less demeaning hierarchy than the traditional model of male domination and female subjection, which cannot under any circumstances be considered Christian. One major criticism against hierarchicalism is that in the past such a model of male leadership and female submission has contributed to abusive behavior against women in both the church and the home.[11] Nevertheless, the hierarchical model is viewed by some as the one intended by God.

The internal issues faced by hierarchicalists center around where the specific boundaries should be drawn for women's participation. Various conservative traditions draw their lines in different places, depending to some extent upon their organizational structures and their own biblical hermeneutic. Regardless, hierarchicalists are always working with the presupposition that God intends man to be the primary human leader, and the woman to be submissive to him. Essentially, any change in women's role would come under the rubric of her work still being done in submission to male authority.

---

[10]See John Piper and Wayne Grudem, ed., *Recovering Biblical Manhood and Womanhood: A Response to Evangelical Feminism* (Wheaton: Crossway, 1991): xiv.

[11]See Osiek, "The Feminist and the Bible," *Feminist Perspectives on Biblical Scholarship*, 100.

One of the leading proponents of the hierarchical model is Susan Foh.[12] Her work is a comprehensive critique of biblical feminism and primarily challenges the hermeneutical positions taken by such biblical feminists as Paul Jewett, Virginia Mollenkott, Nancy Hardesty, and Letha Scanzoni. After treating the major exegetical issues in the difficult biblical passages, Foh concludes that the Bible does not advocate equality or role interchangeability between men and women; rather, she believes the hierarchical model taught in the Bible is one in which structures of authority do exist and the submission of women to men is one of those structures.

Piper and Grudem, whose recent work contains twenty-two essays addressing textual and theological questions, also advocate the hierarchical model. The editors reject the label of "hierarchicalists," preferring instead to be called "complementarians" because they view the traditional understanding of hierarchy as over-emphasizing structured authority. Still, their conclusion is that women should be excluded from being preachers and elders, since those would be the positions of ultimate authority in most traditions.[13]

Another hierarchicalist is Jack Cottrell, in whose recent work is given a concise definition of hierarchicalism:

> It is the belief that there are inherent differences between the sexes that go beyond anatomy. These differences are such that, either by chance or God's design, it is natural or intended for men to be "in charge" and for women to follow, at least in certain crucial roles. Thus role distinctions must be maintained, including relationships of authority and submission.[14]

---

[12]Susan Foh, *Women and the Word of God: A Response to Biblical Feminism* (Phillipsburg, NJ: Presbyterian and Reformed Pub., 1979): esp. 39-41.

[13]Piper and Grudem, *Recovering Biblical Manhood and Womanhood*, 60-61.

[14]Jack Cottrell, *Feminism and the Bible* (Joplin, MO: College Press, 1992): 14.

His book surveys secular feminism, goddess feminism, liberal Christian feminism and biblical feminism and contains an exhaustive bibliography that is most helpful to those wanting to get an overview of the various types of feminism. Like Foh, Piper and Grudem, Cottrell rejects an egalitarian model. While he concludes that hierarchicalism is the model that represents the will of God, he does acknowledge that the issue is a complicated one (340).

It seems inaccurate to characterize the scholarship of those who advocate the hierarchical model as "feminist theologians," especially considering that feminist theology is most commonly understood as the promotion of the full humanity of women in all aspects of religion and spirituality. It is also inaccurate to do so because those who advocate the hierarchical paradigm would be the first to say that they are not feminists. This does not negate the importance of their scholarship, which does make a contribution to the ongoing dialogue in conservative groups about theology and hermeneutical issues, including those about women's roles.[15]

B. *The Egalitarian Paradigm.* Biblical feminists claim that the Bible supports an egalitarian model. The basic premise is that it is contrary to the nature of God, as revealed throughout the entirety of the Bible, and against the spirit of Judaism and Christianity overall, that God would have created a human type which was intended to live in an inherently second-class status to the other type. A more positive way to state the position would be to say that God

---

[15]On the possible relationship between modern American history and the hierarchical model, see Betty DeBerg, *Ungodly Women: Gender and the First Wave of American Fundamentalism* (Minneapolis: Fortress, 1990): 149. DeBerg claims that the hierarchical paradigm came back strongly in America's conservative churches in the 1930's because many were threatened by the public roles women had come to play both in the church and society during the urbanization and industrialization of the late 19th and early 20th centuries. There was fear that the churches had become too "feminized" and the men needed to reclaim them.

created all humankind fully human and fully equal. Osiek
puts it this way:

> Men and women are intended to live in true happi-
> ness and mutual respect with that divine plan, not in
> the oppressive patterns of domination and struggle
> against one another, which are sinful manifestations
> of the disorder of human nature and without divine
> grace.[16]

Egalitarians reject the notion that Gen. 2 necessarily supports
a hierarchy in the created order itself. One argument used is
that hierarchicalists seem to ignore Gen. 1, which does not
indicate that woman came after the man, or that she was a
"helper." Bilezikian,[17] a biblical feminist, concludes that
hierarchicalists read too much into Gen. 2 and 3. He makes
a distinction between what God intended for human relations
at the time of the creation as opposed to what happened as a
result of "the Fall."

Egalitarians use NT passages to support their interpretations of Gen. 2-3, concluding that true Christian servant-
hood requires all to submit to one another, with mutual
submission being the expectation. Gal. 3:28 is the major
NT text in terms of which other texts are interpreted. One of
the more recent works presupposing an egalitarian model by
examining ancient cultural issues is that of Richard and
Catherine Clark Kroeger.[18] Combining exegesis and
historical analysis of religion and culture in ancient Ephesus,
the Clark Kroeger's claim that women have been denied
equality on the basis of 1 Tim. 2:11-15 more than any other
passage, observing that "Many evangelicals view all biblical
passages about the role and ministry of women through the

---

[16]Osiek, "The Feminist and the Bible," *Feminist Perspectives on
Biblical Scholarship*, 99.

[17]Gilbert Bilezikian, *Beyond Sex Roles* (Grand Rapids: Baker,
1985): 50-58.

[18]Richard Clark Kroeger and Catherine Clark Kroeger, *I Suffer
Not a Woman: Rethinking 1 Timothy 2:11-15 in Light of Ancient
Evidence* (Grand Rapids: Baker, 1992).

lens of 1 Tim. 2:12" (p. 12). Their work attempts to demonstrate, on the basis of Scripture, that both men and women are equally called to serve and that 1 Tim. 2:11-15 should not be a hindrance to egalitarian service.

The egalitarian paradigm advocates that the Bible supports an equal relationship between men and women, and that the oppression of women is not the intention of God. Therefore, in the context of the church, women and men should relate as "partners" or in "mutual submission" to each other, regardless of the specific task or role.

C. *Cultural Concerns.* Since a vast amount of feminist literature which is on the market today does not take biblical studies seriously, another legitimate concern is the disagreement that exists between hierarchicalists and biblical feminists. Both groups claim to rely upon biblical authority, yet they argue inconclusively with each other about the meaning of the most significant texts.

Hierarchicalists claim that egalitarians want to assume that all the texts about women are culturally determined and are not necessarily divine norms and mandates. They go on to say that egalitarians want human experience, particularly women's experience, to be the final judge in determining biblical meaning. Cottrell states:

> . . . this is the real source of disagreement between Biblical feminists and non-feminists: the Biblical feminists have never been able to escape the seductive power of women's experience. . . . Hermeneutics is adapted to experience. The passages that must be labeled cultural or descriptive are selected first on the basis of *women's experience*, and then rules are sought to justify this selection.[19]

Egalitarians have responded to the hermeneutical positions of hierarchicalists by pointing out that there are indeed different hermeneutical principles being applied by each group.

---

[19]Cottrell, *Feminism and the Bible*, 262.

Basically, the issue is whether interpretation should be based solely upon the presumed role of the biblical author, or whether the interpretation ought not also include the role of the present-day reader. Johnston suggests,

> It is the reader who uses incomplete knowledge as the basis of judgment. It is the reader who chooses between equally valid possibilities based on personal preference. It is the reader who develops criteria for what is universal and what is culturally specific, what is translatable and what is transcultural. . . . Yet evangelicals, in their desire to escape the supposed relativity of such reader-oriented perspectives, have too often attempted to hide themselves behind the veneer of objectivity.[20]

Contrary to what Cottrell would argue, egalitarians would acknowledge that unqualified or complete objectivity is not a possibility, for the very reasons mentioned by Johnston. When pressed, hierarchicalists recognize that there is some cultural conditioning in the biblical texts, but believe that egalitarians have assumed that far too many texts are culturally conditioned.[21] Egalitarians hold out for a final interpretation that considers both the cultural conditioning of the biblical writers and the cultural conditioning of the present-day reader. So, despite the fact that both rely upon biblical authority, neither side has convinced the other to accept its presuppositional differences concerning hermeneutics.[22] As thorough as this in-house conservative hermeneutical-cultural debate may be, it points to a larger cultural issue.

---

[20]Robert K. Johnston, "Biblical Authority and Interpretation: The Test Case of Women's Role in the Church and Home Updated," *Women, Authority and the Bible* (ed. Alvera Mickelsen; Downers Grove, IL: IVP, 1986): 35.

[21]See George W. Knight, *"The Role Relationship of Men and Women* (rev. ed.; Chicago: Moody, 1985): 5.

[22]See Graham Stanton, "Presuppositions in New Testament Criticism," *New Testament Interpretation: Essays on Principles and Methods* (ed. I. H. Marshall; Grand Rapids: Eerdmans, 1977): 60-71.

D. *Conceptual Concerns.* Minnich's discussions about a culture's presuppositions may have something to contribute to the evangelical debate about the role of the present-day reader in matters of interpretation. She points out that the modern reader is not just exposed to his/her immediate cultural experiences but also to the "encoding" of all the presuppositions of Western civilization. One such lingering presupposition has been that woman is inferior to man. Aristotle assumed the inferiority of woman in his writings, and other early church leaders did the same. In the Middle Ages, the words of Thomas Aquinas continued to carry an inferior view: "woman is defective and misbegotten."[23] In the eyes of many, women have ranked higher than animals but lower than men. Minnich believes that such a generalization has contributed to woman's being perceived as "Other" than man. She says, ". . . man is what it means to be human; woman is his Other (as, in different but related ways, slave is Other to master, and the 'primitive' is Other to 'civilized man')."[24]

How might this discussion impact the evangelical debate regarding hermeneutics and paradigms? It is instructive to compare Minnich's understanding of femininity and masculinity with the hierarchical understanding evidenced by Piper and Grudem. Minnich claims that, based on the faulty generalization regarding women's inferiority, it has been left to the dominant male culture to define what the terms "feminine" and "masculine" mean in our culture. However, definitions of those terms in the Western world are cultural-specific, not universal attributes of manhood and womanhood. E.g., in describing her own understanding of "feminine," Minnich says,

---

[23]For a historical review of church leaders' views on women, see the collected essays in *Religion and Sexism* (ed. Rosemary Radford Reuther; New York: Simon and Schuster, 1974).

[24]Minnich, *Transforming Knowledge*, 54. Simone de Beauvoir, *The Second Sex* (trans. & ed. H. M. Parshley; New York; Vintage, 1974): xv-xxxiv, was one of the earliest feminists to point out that woman was "Other" than man.

Feminine *adds* something to the idea of woman; it
doesn't just restate it. It tells us that a woman enacts
her gender in obvious ways (for example, she
"enjoys being a girl" and may not even mind being
called one when she is well past adolescence because
"feminine" has been defined in ways that entail enact-
ment of weakness and dependency.[25]

Over time, these non-universal attributes gradually become
universal attributes of womanhood and manhood. The result
is that a woman who is "unfeminine," based on how the
dominating culture has defined "feminine," becomes "not so
much socially as spiritually suspect."[26] That is, there is very
little room for a woman to be acceptable in the eyes of the
dominating culture if she does not carry with her the right set
of "feminine attributes," even though those attributes are
non-universals to the authentic nature of womanhood.

On the other hand, Piper and Grudem use "masculine"
and "masculinity" and "feminine" and "femininity" inter-
changeably with manhood and womanhood. Manhood and
womanhood are essential to one's personhood.[27] They
begin their development of biblical manhood and womanhood, then switch to the terms "masculine" and "feminine."
Masculinity is then defined: "At the heart of mature
masculinity is a sense of benevolent responsibility to lead,
provide for and protect women in ways appropriate to a
man's differing relationships" (36). Men, they say, have a
"God-given" responsibility to protect women because,

he is a man and she is a woman. . . . Women and
children are put into the lifeboats first, not because
the men are necessarily better swimmers, but because
of a deep sense of honorable fitness. It belongs to
masculinity to accept danger and to protect women
(43).

---

[25]Minnich, *Transforming Knowledge*, 55.
[26]*Ibid.*
[27]Piper and Grudem, *Recovering Biblical Manhood and Womanhood*, 32-35.

Regarding femininity, Piper says,

> A significant aspect of femininity is how a woman responds to the pattern of initiatives established by mature masculinity. This is why I have discussed masculinity first. . . . Much of the meaning of womanhood is clearly implied in what I have already said about manhood. . . . Mature femininity is a freeing disposition to affirm, receive and nurture strength and leadership from worthy men in ways appropriate to a woman's differing relationships (pp. 45-46).

He goes on to say, ". . . she is to be his [man's] partner and assistant. She joins in the act of strength and shares in the process of leadership. She is, as Gen. 2:18 says, 'a helper suitable for him'" (pp. 48-49).

Piper and Grudem do not define the woman apart from the man. Man is the central character; woman is a response to the defining category of "man." Are Piper's and Grudem's definitions of masculinity and femininity characteristic of universal attributes of maleness and femaleness? Probably not. E.g., does the Bible always portray man as the "protector"? In the story of Adam and Eve (Gen. 2-3), which is so often used to establish what God intends the roles of men and women to be, where was Adam when the serpent tempted Eve? The narrative itself places Adam in the garden, not as protector, but as a silent complier. Considering that hierarchicalists believe that there is a clear biblical prescription for masculinity/manhood and femininity/womanhood and that these prescriptions are universal, it is possible to see that hierarchicalists would be suspicious of an "unfeminine woman." Minnich, reflecting an egalitarian viewpoint, argues that such feminine or masculine attributes as mentioned by Piper and Grudem are not universals. From the egalitarian perspective, such attributes may be culturally determined by a society already "encoded" with an understanding of woman as "Other." With such differing presuppositions, resolution is difficult, even between groups who share a commitment to biblical authority.

3. *Compendium of the Development of Biblical Feminism*

In addition to the importance of hermeneutical and
cultural issues, it may be useful to provide an overview of
the foundational supporters of biblical feminism and some
observations about the irresolutions and the contributions of
conservative scholarship on this topic.

To understand the development of this area, one must
go back to the early 1970's when some evangelicals began to
meet formally and to write about issues concerning women.
In 1974, The Evangelical Women's Caucus was formed as
an international organization of women and men who believe
that the Bible supports the equality of the sexes. Since that
time the Caucus has continued and another organization has
emerged. "Christians for Biblical Equality" was organized
in 1987. Two evangelical feminist publications also deserve
mention: *Priscilla Papers* and *Daughters of Sarah.*

Between 1974 and 1976, three books were published
by Paul Jewett, Virginia Mollenkott, Nancy Hardesty and
Letha Scanzoni, which have served as foundational texts for
biblical feminism. Jewett's first book sets the "woman
question" in terms of the hermeneutical issues raised above.
Do the biblical texts support a hierarchical model of male-
female relationships or a "model of partnership," as he refers
to it? He sought to answer the question by rooting it in what
the Bible had to say about the doctrine of the "image of
God." Much of his discussion centers around Gen. 1 and 2
in light of NT passages. The following excerpts illustrate
his argument:

> In framing a theology of the man/woman relation-
> ship, the basic issue that has to be faced is this: Is the
> woman, according to the ordinance of creation, sub-
> ordinate to the man? While the first creation
> narrative, which includes the fundamental affirmation
> that Man in the divine image is male and female
> (Gen. 1:27), contains no hint of such a hierarchical
> view, the second narrative (Gen. 2:18-23), which we
> have treated as supplementing the first, allows, if it

does not actually imply, that the woman was created *from and for* the man. . . . Does the fact that the man was created first imply the headship of the male?[28]

Jewett concludes that,

Since the Creator has given us our humanity as a fellowship of male and female, it is only as we achieve the ideal of partnership that we achieve the ideal of humanity. And this partnership is not simply an abstract "ideal," but a concrete reality, since God in Christ has actually begun the creation of a new humanity in which there is no male and female. The historic rivalry between the sexes which has characterized fallen human history, a rivalry in which the man has subjugated the woman, treating her as an inferior, and in which the woman has taken her subtle revenge is done away in Christ (p. 171).

From this perspective, he views the model of partnership as a more biblical model for the Christian community to follow than the hierarchical model. As do many other feminists, he believes that the hierarchical view is inconsistent. Although hierarchicalists claim that the woman is only *different* from the man, but not *inferior* to the man, they insist that the woman must be subordinate to the man. However, in a dualism of true equality, subordination would not be present.

Jewett closes his work with discussions of misogyny, the ordination of women, and the idea of God as feminine. In a subsequent work, Jewett argues that sexual hierarchy is the basis for much discrimination shown against women in the church. He goes so far as to say that, "an affinity between maleness and divineness remains the basic assumption behind every argument from the nature of God for the exclusion of women from the office of the

---

[28]Paul K. Jewett, *Man as Male and Female* (Grand Rapids: Eerdmans, 1975): 50.

ministry."[29] If the issue is to be resolved satisfactorily, both male and female must be perceived as made in the image of God.

Mollenkott, a professor of English skilled in literary critique, expands Jewett's ideas and takes the case of the egalitarian model in a new direction.[30] While referring to the egalitarian model as one of "mutual submission," she challenges the metaphor of a masculine God. Essentially, her argument is that the biblical male metaphor of God should not be taken literally; rather, she advocates that the Bible supports God's nature as both male and female. She illustrates with passages, primarily from the OT, that refer to God by using female imagery.[31] E.g., she uses Isa. 46:3-4, which refers to God carrying Israel as a mother would carry a child in her womb, to point out that although God may be referred to with masculine pronouns a majority of times in biblical passages, there are other examples in which feminine traits and metaphors are used of God. She concludes that the metaphors point to the reality that God is not to be understood literally as male. In her view, humanity, made in the image of God, is fully equal in both male and female personhood. The implication of this view is that, "the Christian way of relating achieves male-female equality through mutual submission."[32]

Hardesty and Scanzoni also stress an egalitarian model for relationships based upon equality before God.[33] Both free-lance writers (and Hardesty has held a professorship in Church History at Emory), they are among the earliest to

---

[29]Paul K. Jewett, *The Ordination of Women* (Grand Rapids: Eerdmans, 1980): 35.

[30]Virginia Mollenkott, *Women, Men and the Bible* (New York: Crossroad, 1989).

[31]Virginia Mollenkott, *The Divine Feminine* (New York: Crossroad, 1988). On the uses of metaphors in the OT, see Phyllis Trible, *God and the Rhetoric of Sexuality* (Philadelphia: Fortress, 1978).

[32]Mollenkott, *Women, Men and the Bible*, 33.

[33]Nancy A. Hardesty and Letha Dawson Scanzoni, *All We're Meant To Be* (Nashville: Abingdon, 1986).

offer alternative explanations of the word κεφαλή (head) as it is used in NT texts about marriage (e.g., Eph. 5:23, "for the husband is head of the wife"). They emphasize that Christian marriage is one of mutual partnership and submission to each other, and that Eph. 5:23 has been misinterpreted throughout most of Western history. If κεφαλή were translated "source" instead of "authority over," there would be greater reciprocity of mutual respect and less self-destructive behaviors on the part of both the wife and husband.[34] The interpretation of this Greek term for "head" has become a source of controversy between biblical feminists and hierarchicalists. Biblical feminists translate the term as "source" or "origin."[35] Piper and Grudem reject such an interpretation and conclude that the traditional translation of κεφαλή as "authority over" is more accurate.[36]

It is, therefore, understandable why biblical feminists aggressively seek to apply their interpretations of Scripture to ecclesiastical matters. As might be expected, biblical feminists advocate the full participation of women in all forms of ministry. Therefore, much biblical feminist literature discusses specific roles in ministries, and the discussions encompass a large number of religious traditions.[37]

---

[34]Hardesty and Scanzoni, *All We're Meant To Be*, 122-24.

[35]See Berkeley and Alvera Mickelsen, "What Does Kephale Mean in the New Testament?" *Women, Authority and the Bible*, 97-110. See also pp. 111-132.

[36]Piper and Grudem, *Recovering Biblical Manhood and Womanhood*, 425-468.

[37]See further, Mary J. Evans, *Woman in the Bible* (Downers Grove, IL: IVP, 1984); Patricia Gundry, *Neither Slave Nor Free* (San Francisco: Harper and Row, 1987); David Scholer, "Feminist Hermeneutics and Evangelical Biblical Interpretation," *JETS* 30 (1987): 407-20, and *Women in Ministry* (Chicago: Covenant Press, 1984); Ruth Tucker and Walter Liefeld, *Daughters of the Church: Women and Ministry from New Testament Times to the Present* (Grand Rapids: Zondervan, 1987); and Mary Stewart Van Leeuwen, *Gender and Grace* (Downers Grove, IL: IVP, 1990).

Conclusion

Biblical feminists have made significant contributions to both feminist theology and to conservative biblical scholarship. One such contribution is that the Bible, which has been viewed by some feminist theologians as completely sexist and irredeemable for women, has been shown to have redeemable qualities. The reinterpretation of certain texts and inclusion of positive as well as negative passages results in a strong challenge to the traditional view of women as inferior. The very book which historically has been used against women is now being used as the foundation to justify their full humanity.

A second contribution is the emphasis placed upon Jesus as the model for egalitarian relationships.[38] Biblical feminists, along with other feminist theologians, have raised the consciousness of their audiences. By looking at Jesus' egalitarian teachings and life-style, they have emphasized the ideal for human relationships. They believe that in the life of Jesus both the true nature of God and the true spirit of Christianity are illustrated. And based upon this overview, they have proceeded to make a strong case against patriarchy as the norm for biblical authors, at least in the Gospels.

Historical-critical scholarship and feminism are not mutually exclusive.[39] Each needs the other. Historical-critical methods have been of primary importance to a large number of conservative scholars because such methodology has claimed to be unbiased and value neutral. Biblical feminist thought can bring creative dialogue to historical criticism because feminist thought challenges the notion that exegesis is value-neutral.

However, certain concerns and irresolutions linger and demand attention.

---

[38]See Jacquelyn Grant, *White Women's Christ and Black Women's Jesus: Feminist Christology and Womanist Response* (Atlanta: Scholars Press, 1989).

[39]Collins, ed., *Feminist Perspectives on Biblical Scholarship*, 9.

A. *Irresolutions in Biblical Scholarship.*   The first systemic issue is that despite a desire to be "biblically correct" in their scholarship, and to reexamine the texts thoroughly, controversy continues. Among conservatives, the question is one of how much some biblical feminist authors adhere to biblical correctness. Do they give adequate attention to the function of experience in theology and hermeneutics? Other questions arise: Are biblical feminists taking too much liberty with the texts? Do biblical feminists believe that all the Bible is the word of God, or are they guilty of selectively choosing what they think will support their own assumptions? These questions indicate suspicion and a lack of trust in some feminist hermeneutics. Such questions are not easily resolved because, for the most part, biblical feminists are coming from diverse religious backgrounds and their training in theology and hermeneutics is varied. Both factors will probably continue to contribute some uneasiness in accepting the egalitarian model. There is a definite need to reexamine the biblical texts pertaining to women, rigorously following literary-historical method.

In the larger arena of feminist theology, there is broader concern about the reexamination of biblical texts. Some recognize that texts regarding women are indeed diverse. Thus, they question whether the Bible has an explicit theology on the role of women. If there can be no "biblical" resolution to the question of what the role of women is to be, then it seems to defeat the purpose of doing biblical feminist study. However, this argument has its origins in a theology that discounts the primacy of biblical texts. Neither biblical feminists nor conservative scholars concede that the biblical texts are too dissimilar to be pertinent.

B. *Irresolution of Hierarchical/Egalitarian Debate.*   A second concern is the lack of a satisfactory resolution to the hierarchical versus egalitarian debate. Is it possible to assess completely the cultural conditioning that has gone into the presuppositions of each perspective? The essential question is whether it is possible for women and men to live in the world and be ontologically equal, yet functionally unequal; or in essence, equal—in practice, unequal. Hierarchicalists

would support such a thesis. Egalitarians would support the
opposite. There is a definite need for critical reexamination
of presuppositions underlying each school of thought.

C. *Concern with Narrow Focus of Biblical Feminist
Literature.* A third concern is the narrow focus of biblical
feminist literature. With the majority of the attention
centered around biblical texts and hermeneutical issues, there
has been little analysis of church tradition as important to
women's issues. Little attention has been given to the
relevance of church history or American religious history
from a feminist perspective. Also little effort has been
expended on the reformulation of Christian doctrines based
upon feminist methodology. Much of what has been done in
this area is being done by scholars outside biblical feminism.

There are also the unresolved socio-cultural questions
that affect all theologies. If Western culture has indeed
assumed that male conceptualization represents the whole of
humanity, what are the implications for women and men
who are committed to the Christian tradition but still desire to
promote the full humanity of women? What are the images
of femaleness and maleness in any religious context? How
do these projected images affect a given individual's worth,
her/his participation with, and the institutional support she/he
receives from others within a particular religious community? Issues about the importance of the public life
versus the private life must also be taken into consideration.

Biblical feminist study is guilty of that which most
feminist study (as well as most academic disciplines) has
been guilty to date: it is narrow. Many concerns that are
addressed are class and race specific. Biblical feminism is
most relevant to middle-class white women and men. It has
very little to say to the poor or women and men of color.
Feminist theology generally is already expanding to meet the
needs of women outside the white middle-class and it is
likely that biblical feminism will expand in that direction as
well. There is a definite need for the re-examination of
cultural and theological concerns regarding women beyond
the narrow focus of biblical and hermeneutical issues.

Chapter Two

WOMEN IN THE OLD TESTAMENT

John T. Willis

The OT records a wide variety of attitudes toward women.[1] Some of these attitudes are expressed by men (e.g., Amnon's feelings first of lust, then of repulsion, toward his half-sister Tamar [2 Sam. 13:1-2, 4, 15-17]); some are exhibited by women (e.g., Peninnah's haughty and scornful attitude toward Hannah [2 Sam. 1:6-7]); others are seen in a woman's own children (e.g., the childrens' praise of their mother in the description of the "good wife" [Prov. 31:28]); and yet others are evidenced by society in general (e.g., the high respect for Deborah by the Israelites who came to her for judgment [Judg. 4:4-5]). In light of this fact, it is *absolutely imperative* that one who is attempting to determine what the OT teaches about women deal with each statement about women in its own context, using the best exegetical tools of which one is capable.

1. *Setting the Parameters*

First, the fact that an OT writer records an event or statement in which a man (or men) harbors a negative feeling toward a woman (or women) or treats a woman (women) in a negative way does not mean that that writer condones such

---

[1]The volume of literature on biblical views of women and the role of women in religion is staggering. For rather extensive lists of books and articles on this subject, see e.g., C. J. Vos, *Woman in Old Testament Worship* (Delft: Judels & Brinkman, 1968): 213-219; and I. Ljung, *Silence or Suppression: Attitudes toward Women in the Old Testament* (Acta Universitatis Upsaliensis. Uppsala Women's Studies. A. Women in Religion, 2; Stockholm: Almqvist & Wiksell, 1989): 130-44.

a feeling or treatment or evidences a bias against women. If this were the case, when an OT writer records an event or statement in which a man (or men) harbors a negative feeling toward a man (or men) or treats a man (or men) in a negative way, one would have to conclude that that writer condones such a feeling or treatment, or has a bias against men! The biblical portrayal of Ahab and Jezebel is one of many illustrations of this point. E.g., when Naboth of Jezreel refuses to sell or trade his property to Ahab, the king of Israel, Jezebel, his Phoenician queen, sends letters to the elders and nobles of Jezreel, instructing them to have two base fellows accuse Naboth of cursing God and the king (1 Kgs. 21:1-14). Elijah the prophet announces that as a punishment for Jezebel's treatment of Naboth, the dogs will eat Jezebel at Jezreel (1 Kgs. 21:23). This occurs later when Jehu storms Jezreel (2 Kgs. 9:30-37). Similarly, when Ahab goes to take possession of Naboth's vineyard upon learning that Naboth had been executed, Elijah the prophet meets him there and announces that in the place the dogs had licked up Naboth's blood, they will lick Ahab's blood (1 Kgs. 21:15-22). This occurs later when Ahab's soldiers return his body to Samaria in his chariot after he is killed at Ramoth-gilead (1 Kgs. 22:29-38). Obviously, Jezebel is not condemned by the writer of the Naboth incident*because she is a woman* any more than Ahab is condemned*because he is a man*. Rather, he condemns them both because of their unjust and unloving treatment of Naboth.

Another instructive biblical account along these lines is that of Abraham and Sarah. Perhaps two examples will suffice. Sarah is listening at the tent door when the Lord tells Abraham she will have a child in her old age (ninety), and she laughs in unbelief (Gen. 18:10-15). Does the biblical writer record this because he is biased against women, assuming, perhaps, that a woman is weaker in trust in God than a man? Certainly not! In the previous chapter, the narrator states that when the Lord told Abraham he would have a son by Sarah in his old age (one hundred), Abraham laughed in unbelief (Gen. 17:15-19). The biblical author's reproach of Sarah and Abraham is not due to her/his prejudice against women or men, but to their lack of trust in

God. Again, after several years had passed from the time God had first told Abraham that he would have a son, Sarah urged Abraham to go in to her handmaid Hagar and to have a child by her. "And Abram hearkened to the voice of Sarai" (Gen. 16:1-2). Is the writer here revealing his bias against women by subtly saying to his readers: "Look what terrible things happen to a man if he makes the mistake of listening to a woman?" Not at all! One finds a situation which is just the reverse to this in Genesis 20:9-13 (see 12:11-13). When Abraham and Sarah come to the land of Gerar, Abraham urges Sarah to tell anyone who asks that Abraham is her brother, not that he is her husband. In fact, he urges Sarah to lie about their relationship wherever they go (20:13). Is the writer here revealing his bias against men by subtly saying to his readers: "Look what terrible things happen to a woman if she makes the mistake of listening to a man?" Nothing suggests such a thing!

Second, the fact that an OT writer records an event or a statement in which a man (or men) exercises power over a woman (or women) does not mean that that writer approves of such activities, or that he/she is biased against women. The same line of reasoning would force one to conclude that if an OT writer records an event or statement in which a man (or men) exercises power over a man (or men), that writer approves of such activities or is biased against men! An illustration of this appears in the story of Esther. King Ahasuerus has unquestioned authority over both Vashti (Esth. 1:10-22) and Esther (Esth. 2:16-17; 5:1-8; 7:1-6; 8:3-8). Even though Esther is Ahasuerus's queen, she must approach the inner court of his palace with all caution, and wait to see if he will hold out his golden scepter to her, indicating that she may come into his presence (Esth. 5:1-2; 8:3-5). Now this account indicates that the Persians of the fifth century BC believed that their male king had authority over the women of his empire, including his own queen. But it does not follow from this that *all Israelites* in OT times believed that God's will was for men to have authority over and dominate women. Nor can one infer from it that God's will for all times is that men rule over and control women, no questions asked.

But the story of Esther also shows that, as queen, Esther has authority over and dominates men in the Persian Empire. She "orders" one of the king's eunuchs to go to Mordecai and find out why he would not take off the sackcloth he was wearing and put on the clothing she had sent him (Esth. 4:4-5); she "orders" her own (older) uncle Mordecai to gather all the Jews at Susa and to hold a fast in preparation for her going to the king (Esth. 4:15-17); and Haman the Agagite, who has a very high official position in the Persian government, falls before Esther on her couch to beg her to spare his life (Esth. 8:6-8). Is the reader to deduce from this that the OT is teaching that women have authority over and are to dominate men in all places throughout human history?

But again, the book of Esther records that King Ahasuerus "commanded" all his servants to bow down and do obeisance to Haman the Agagite, whose seat he had set above all the princes of the empire (Esth. 3:1-2). Should one conclude from this that the OT is biased against men and teaches that certain favored men are to have authority over and dominate all men in every age at every place?

Third, the fact that an OT writer depicts woman in a *subjective* or *dependent* role does not mean that that writer either considers woman *inferior* to man or evidences a male chauvinistic attitude toward womankind.[2] OT writers consistently speak of God as *husband* and Israel (or Judah) as his *wife* (Hos. 2:2-15; Isa. 1:21; Jer. 3:1-11; Ezek. 16:1-43b; 23), never the reverse. However, they do not do this out of a feeling that women are inferior to men, but in order to emphasize God's love for his people and his desire to provide their every need, as a caring husband does for his wife. That this is indeed the intention is clear from parallel figures which OT writers use to describe the relationship between God and his people.

---

[2]One should recall that Paul teaches *both* that the wife is *submissive to* her husband *and* that the husband is *submissive to* his wife— 1 Cor. 7:4; Eph. 5:21 expanded and explained in vv. 22-33.

One of the most pervasive OT figures for the relationship between God and his people is that of a king and his kingdom or subjects (see e.g., Exod. 19:6; Num. 23:21; Deut. 33:5; Judg. 8:23; 1 Sam. 8:7; 12:12; Isa. 33:22). God is always the king, and his people (male and female) are his subjects, never the reverse. Is one to conclude from this that OT writers were biased against all human beings except kings? On the contrary, they use this figure to emphasize that God cares for his people, protects them from enemies and dangers, and supplies their needs; for these were the widely accepted responsibilities of kings in ancient Near Eastern societies.

OT writers also frequently portray the relationship between God and human beings under the figure of a father and his son. God is father and Israel is his son (Exod. 4:22-23; Deut. 1:31; Hos. 11:1; Jer. 31:9, 20); and again, God is father and the king of Israel (or Judah) is his son (2 Sam. 7:14; 1 Chron. 22:10; 28:6; Psa. 2:7; 89:26-27); never the reverse. Would the reader be justified in concluding from this that OT writers were biased against male children or against kings? Just the opposite is true! They are trying to emphasize the great concern and love which God has toward his people and toward the king. Those who used this figure had no intention of "putting down" the Israelites (male and female) or the king by using it. In a similar way, it is a fundamental mistake to conclude that OT writers were biased against women and considered them to be inferior to men *because* they used the figure of God as a husband and Israel as a wife to depict the relationship between God and his people.

2. *Outstanding Women of the Old Testament*

Space allows mention of only a few of the outstanding women portrayed in the OT and brief comments are possible about only select ones of these. Now one cannot expect sinlessness or perfection from any of these women. But the same is true of men!

The statements:

> There is none that does good,
>   no, not one (Psa. 14:3=53:3),

and

> Enter not into judgment with thy servant;
>   for no man (generic) living is righteous before thee
>   (Psa. 143:2),

apply to all human beings, male and female alike. Accordingly, when OT writers make observations about women which indicate they are sinners or that they fail in some way, one is not justified in inferring from this that they were biased against women, or that they assumed or affirmed that women are inferior to men.

Miriam, the older sister of Moses and Aaron, was held in very high esteem in Israel. She was a "prophetess" (Exod. 15:20). Like Moses and the people of Israel (Exod. 15:1), she praised God in song for delivering his people from Egypt by parting the waters of the Sea of Reeds and letting them pass over on dry land (Exod. 15:21). When God rehearsed some of his mighty acts to Israelites in the days of Micah, he said:

> I brought you up from the land of Egypt,
>   and redeemed you from the house of bondage;
> and I sent before you Moses,
>   Aaron, and Miriam (Mic. 6:4).

Here God declares that Miriam held a role of equal importance with Moses and Aaron when he brought his people out of Egyptian bondage. The same God who spoke to the Israelites through Moses spoke to them also through Miriam and Aaron (Num. 12:1-2).

Deborah was an outstanding and respected leader of the Israelites in the period of the judges. She was a prophetess (Judg. 4:4). She was a judge, and the people of Israel (male and female alike) came to her for judgment (Judg. 4:4-5). She was a "mother in Israel" (Judg. 5:7), not in the physical sense, but in the sense of being a courageous leader of her people when the Canaanites attacked them. She summoned Barak (a man), and told him that the Lord "commanded" him to lead the Israelites against Sisera and the Canaanites (Judg. 4:6-7). Barak refused to go unless Deborah went with him. So she went with Barak and actually accompanied him in leading the Israelites to the battle front (Judg. 4:8-10). And she made it very clear that Barak would not be exalted for Israel's victory over Sisera, "for," she said, "the Lord will sell Sisera into the hand of a woman" (Judg. 4:9). This occurred when Jael killed Sisera by driving a tent-peg through his skull while he slept in her tent (Judg. 4:17-22; 5:24-27). At the right moment, Deborah charged Barak to lead his army against the enemy (Judg. 4:14). When the Lord gave Israel the victory, Deborah and Barak sang a song, praising the Lord for what he had done (Judg. 5). Thus Deborah is the author of a song which now composes an entire chapter of Scripture. As in all OT accounts of Israel's victories over her enemies, in the story of Deborah the Lord is the one and only central hero. But in this set of events, he works through two women to carry out his purposes: Deborah and Jael; indicating the biblical text presents these women in the highest possible situations.[3]

In a similar way, Naomi (a Judean) and Ruth (a "foreigner," a Moabitess) are clearly the major individuals through whom Yahweh works out his purposes in the book of Ruth. Naomi and her family so influence Ruth by their unwavering faithfulness to Yahweh even while living in a foreign land that when Naomi's husband and two sons (one of whom, Mahlon, had married Ruth—see 4:10) die, Ruth

---

[3]For excellent and suggestive interpretations of the biblical account of Deborah in Judges 4-5, see Y. Amit, "Judges 4: Its Content and Form," *JSOT* 39 (1987): 89-111; H.-D. Neef, "Der Sieg Deboras und Baraks uber Sisera. Exegetische Beobachtungen zum Aufbau und Werden von Jdc 4, 1-24," *ZAW* 101 (1989): 28-49; and A. Brenner, "A Triangle and a Rhombus in Narrative Structure: A Proposed Integrative Reading of Judges IV and V," *VT* 40 (1990): 129-138.

forsakes her people and their gods to become a member of God's people and worship their God, Yahweh (1:16).[4] The main purpose of the book of Ruth is to present a concrete example of Yahweh's work through "common people" (in this case, primarily a woman, Naomi) within his own chosen people to convert "foreigners" to himself (see 1:15-17; 2:10, 12; 4:9-12), in order to admonish its readers to follow this example. Thus its purpose is strikingly similar to that of the book of Jonah, Isaiah 19:18-25, the prophet's presentation of the "servant of Yahweh" (Israel, the remnant of Israel) in Isaiah 40-55, and several psalms (e.g., Psa. 47 and 66).[5] Yahweh works through Ruth to comfort Naomi when she returns to Bethlehem after having lost her husband and two sons in a foreign land (Ruth 1:19-22), to support Naomi in the land of Judah (2:1-3, 11, 17-18, 23), to marry Boaz, a kinsman of Elimilech, Naomi's deceased husband (2:19-20; 3:1-14), and to bear a son by Boaz, whom they name Obed, who in due time becomes the grandfather of David (4:13-22).

---

[4]Most scholars agree that the author of the book of Ruth presents Naomi as an outstanding example of unselfish concern for others, especially for Ruth. See P. Trible, *God and the Rhetoric of Sexuality* (Philadelphia: Fortress, 1978): 166-169. Recently, however, D. N. Fewell and D. M. Gunn, "'A Son is Born to Naomi!': Literary Allusions and Interpretation in the Book of Ruth," *JSOT* 40 (1988): 99-108, and "Is Coxon a Scold? On Responding to the Book of Ruth," *JSOT* 45 (1989): 39-43, have argued at length that this author portrays Naomi as embittered and self-centered. It seems to me that P. W. Coxon, "Was Naomi a Scold? A Response to Fewell and Gunn," *JSOT* 45 (1989): 25-37, is correct in taking Fewell and Gunn to task for this interpretation, and defending the traditional viewpoint.

[5]See G. A. F. Knight, *Ruth and Jonah* (second impression; Torch Bible Commentaries; London: SCM, 1956): 9-10, 20-21, 37, 41 (against Knight, however, I am not convinced that the author of the book of Ruth intended to be writing a polemic against Ezra's policy of having the Jews of his day put away their foreign wives—Ezra 10); D. Harvey, "Ruth, Book of," *IDB* 4 (1962): 133; and J. L. McKenzie, "Ruth," *Dictionary of the Bible* (New York: Bruce Publishing Co., 1965): 750.

The author of 1 Samuel 1-2 displays a very lofty view of Hannah. In her deep distress, she prays that Yahweh give her a son and vows to give him to Yahweh all the days of his life (1:10-11). She chides the priest of Shiloh, Eli, for accusing her of being intoxicated when in reality she was praying quietly to Yahweh (1:12-18). Yahweh empowers her to have a child; she gives birth to Samuel; and after he is weaned she brings him to Shiloh so that Eli may train him to become a priest (1:20, 24-28). Before returning home from Shiloh, she sings a beautiful prayer of praise to Yahweh for his wisdom in ruling his world, which the author of the book of Samuel records with highest approval, so that 1 Sam. 2:1-10 is one of several pieces of Scripture which come from a woman.[6]

The author of 1-2 Kings held the prophetess Huldah in very high esteem. In the eighteenth year of Josiah, king of Judah (623 BC), the priest Hilkiah finds the book of the law in the temple while it is being repaired (2 Kgs. 22:8). He gives it to Shaphan the secretary, who reads it before king Josiah. Josiah then commands Hilkiah and Shaphan and three of their associates to "inquire of the Lord" concerning the words of this book. So (naturally!) they go to Huldah the prophetess! She tells them to report to Josiah that the disasters recorded in this book of the law will come upon God's people in Judah and Jerusalem because of their sins, although Josiah himself will have died by the time this happens (2 Kgs. 22:12-20). This text makes it quite clear that Huldah was highly respected as an important religious leader of God's people in the days of Josiah. 2 Kings 23

---

[6]The content of Psalm 113 and its similarities to the Song of Hannah in 1 Samuel 2:1-10 suggest that this psalm also could have been originally composed or written by a woman. Proverbs 31:2-9, if not vv. 2-31, contains "the words of Lemuel, king of Massa, *which his mother taught him*" (v. 1). Of numerous other biblical passages which originated with women, one may mention in the NT, Elizabeth's blessing of Mary as the appropriate expression of her (Elizabeth) being "filled with the Holy Spirit" (Luke 1:39-45), and Mary's exaltation to the Lord (the Magnificat) for choosing her to be the mother of Jesus (Luke 1:46-55).

indicates that Josiah carried out his religious reform of Judah
and Jerusalem as a result of the message Huldah sent to him.
Indeed, as with Hannah and the mother of Lemuel, Huldah
originated the words which the writer of Kings sets forth to
his readers as genuine Scripture.

The author of the book of Esther presents Esther with
the highest possible esteem. In the eyes of the Persians,
including the Persian king and her husband Ahasuerus,
Esther was subject to the king in every way. In fact, she had
to wait for his summons to enter his presence (Esth. 5:1-2;
8:3-5). (However, the same was true of all males as well,
4:11.) But in the eyes of the biblical writer, God used
Esther as his instrument to deliver his people living in the
Persian empire from the plot of Haman the Agagite to put
them to death (4:14; 7:3-10; 8:3-9:28). Esther orders her
older cousin Mordecai to hold a fast with all the Jews in
Susa in her behalf, and they obey her (4:15-17). Haman
falls on the couch before Esther to beg for his life (7:6-8).
Esther commands the Jews to keep the Feast of Purim on the
fourteenth and fifteenth days of the month Adar each year,
and they do so (9:20-32).

3. *The High View of Women in the Old Testament*

There are many texts in the OT which reflect a high view
of women. Here we call attention to a few of these and
make brief comments on them. The creation account in
Genesis 1-2 affirms that God created both "male and female"
in his image, after his likeness (1:26-27). He created
animals inferior to man (2:19-20), but woman as his equal,
for the phrase "a helper fit for him" (2:18, 20) "does not
denote inferiority, but rather man's incompleteness without
woman; the making of Eve from Adam's rib symbolizes
their essential unity."[7] God caused sexuality to occur
simultaneously for male and female when he brought the
woman to the man (2:23). Both the man and the woman are

---

[7]R. B. Edwards, "Woman," *ISBE*, 4 (1988): 1091. See also C.
Westermann, *Genesis 1-11: A Commentary* (trans. J. Scullion;
Minneapolis: Augsburg, 1984): 227, 232.

completely indebted to God alone for their existence and for the life they enjoy. Adam's rule over Eve (3:16) was not God's original design in creation, but the curse God placed on Eve for her disobedience. It is a perversion of God's intentions for the relationship between a man and wife, and never has been his real desire.[8]

This truth appears in the bold contrast between Israel's attitude toward her relationship to Yahweh and Yahweh's desire as to how Israel should feel about that relationship in the book of Hosea. Israel thought of Yahweh as "my master" (Hebrew *ba ali*), a term which signifies the rule of one person over another (Judg. 19:22, 23, 27). Yahweh declares that this is an incorrect understanding of the relationship between a husband and a wife. Instead, it is announced that Israel will come to call him "my husband" (Hebrew *'ishi*; Hos. 2:16), the term Adam used of himself when God first brought the woman to him (Gen. 2:23) to signify the harmony between the two. Since male and female are both created in God's image and thus stand equal before him, God emphatically denounces the double standard being practiced in Israel in the days of Hosea, according to which the people condemned a female for practicing cult prostitution as an act of worship to Baal, but not a male who went aside with harlots and sacrificed with cult prostitutes (Hos. 4:13-14).

The author of The Song of Solomon (The Song of Songs, Canticles) describes a harmonious equality between a male and a female who are lovers, probably newlyweds. The young wife uses a phrase of deep intimacy in defining their relationship: "My beloved is mine and I am his" (Cant. 2:16; 6:3). This thought is strikingly similar to that of Paul in his portrayal of the marriage relationship: "The wife does not rule over her own body, but the husband does; likewise the husband does not rule over his own body, but the wife does" (1 Cor. 7:4). In The Song of Solomon, the male does not dominate, and the female is not subordinate.

---

[8]See especially the remarks of P. Trible, "*Woman in the OT,"*IDB Sup* (1976): 965.

Among other things, the female seeks out the male for love-making (3:1-4). And as an interesting variation on her phrase of deep intimacy, once she says:

> I am my beloved's
> and his desire is for me (7:10).

This statement stands in bold contrast to the curse God placed on Eve because of her disobedience: "your desire shall be for (to) your husband" (Gen. 3:16).[9]

One of the most extensive exalted pictures of woman in the OT appears in Prov. 31:10-31. This text describes the "good wife" as priceless, faithful to her husband, industrious, generous, courageous, creative, strong, poised, kind, instructive, one who provides well for her household, praiseworthy, and one who fears God. There is no hint in this passage that she takes second place to her husband or anyone else. Indeed, because of her godly nature and character, her husband trusts in her and has no lack of gain (v. 11), she does him good all the days of his life (v. 12), and he is known in the gates (v. 23), i.e., he is respected as an outstanding, upright citizen of the community. But these observations do not reflect a male-dominated point of view. On the contrary, the woman described here is independent. On her own initiative, she develops a widespread mercantile business (vv. 13-14, 18, 24) and engages in very successful agricultural ventures (v. 16). And everyone praises her for her significant role in her home, in the community and in the world: her husband (v. 28), her children (v. 28), and her

---

[9]C. L. Meyers, "Gender Roles and Genesis 3:16 Revisited," *The Word of the Lord Shall Go Forth. Essays in Honor of David Noel Freedman in Celebration of His Sixtieth Birthday* (ed. C. L. Meyers and M. O'Connor; Winona Lake, IN: Eisenbrauns, 1983): 337-354, thinks Genesis 3:16 announces an increase in the strength of the woman's feeling for the man to share with him in sexual love and agricultural tasks, and declares that although woman will assume a significant portion of the work-load (approximately 40%), man will "predominate" (not "rule") over her as he will assume approximately 60% of the work-load.

community (v. 31). E. L. Lyons is surely correct in arguing that "the high level of respect (for a mature, experienced, godly woman) evident in Prov. 31:10-31 is consistent . . . with the general attitude toward women in premonarchic Israel . . . ."[10]

The author of Proverbs holds women in such high regard that he personifies Wisdom as a woman. God "created" her as his first work and she existed alongside him for numerous eons before he created the heavens and the earth (Prov. 8:22-23). When he created the universe, she "was beside him, like a master workman" (Prov. 8:30). Now she calls on human beings to listen to her instruction and keep her ways in order that they may receive riches and honor, walk in righteousness and justice, find life and obtain favor from Yahweh (Prov. 8:1-21; 8:32-9:6).

A most compelling piece of evidence that OT writers had a high regard for women is that they describe God as a mother. Yahweh promises the discouraged exiles who have recently returned to Jerusalem:

> As one whom his mother comforts,
>   so I will comfort you;

---

[10]E. L. Lyons, "A Note on Proverbs 31:10-31," *The Listening Heart. Essays in Wisdom and the Psalms in Honor of Roland E. Murphy* (ed. K. G. Hoglund, E. F. Huwiler, et al.; JSOT Sup 58; Sheffield: JSOT Press, 1987): 240. The entire essay covers pages 237-245. Lyons thinks this acrostic poem was originally written in the premonarchial period when women played a major role in the development of Israel and Judah. Later the redactor of the book of Proverbs incorporated it into his book in the postexilic period, because at that time women again played a major role in the restoration of Israel in the land of Canaan. She also contends that the woman being described here is the wise matriarch of the household, who has had vast experience that has taught her much wisdom. Her children who praise her (v. 28) are grown children with families of their own in the extended household. For the view that the woman depicted in this text is young (a view which is hardly compelling in light of the statements made about her), see M. B. Crook, "The Marriageable Maiden of Prov 31:10-31," *JNES* 13 (1954): 137-140.

you shall be comforted in Jerusalem (Isa. 66:13).

When Zion laments that Yahweh has forsaken her, he responds:

> Can a woman forget her suckling child,
>   that she should have no compassion on the son
>   of her womb?
> Even these may forget,
>   yet I will not forget you (Isa. 49:15).

These passages call to mind the words of Jesus over Jerusalem's refusal to come to him:

> O Jerusalem, Jerusalem, killing the prophets and stoning those who are sent to you! How often would I have gathered your children together *as a hen* gathers her brood under her wings, and you would not! (Matt. 23:37=Lk. 13:34).

Jesus does not hesitate to compare his concern for the inhabitants of Jerusalem with a hen's (not a rooster's) care for her chicks. To be sure, OT writers frequently compare God with a father (e.g., Deut. 32:6; Jer. 3:4, 19; Psa. 103:13), but God is not a sexual being. "Father" is simply one of many human figures which may appropriately be used to denote certain attributes or characteristics of God. Among others are "shepherd," "potter," "physician," "husband," and—"mother"![11] There are ways in which God is like a father; there are also ways in which God is like a mother. The OT writers do not hesitate to call attention to these latter, but in doing so, they indicate their highest regard for woman.

---

[11]On the use of the idea of "mother" to depict God, see U. Winter, *Frau und Gottin. Exegetische und ikonographische Studien zum weiblichen Gottesbild im Alten Israel und in dessen Umwelt. Orbis Biblicus et Orientalis* 53 (Göttingen: Vandenhoeck & Ruprecht, 1983): 530-538.

Concluding Observations

The OT presents several views of women. The biblical interpreter must first strive to understand the view of women as it is presented in each OT context. In doing so, he must apply the best principles of exegesis to the text and seek to be as unbiased as he can in trying to determine the biblical writer's meaning and intention. This is admittedly very difficult in many instances. Thus, one is not surprised by various interpretations which have been suggested.

Some have asserted or concluded, for one reason or other, that the OT writers consistently display a low view of women. They cite the law which allows a man to divorce his wife but does not allow a woman to divorce her husband (Deut. 24:1-4), the differences between the length of a mother's uncleanness depending on whether she has a son or a daughter (Lev. 12:1-5), the limitation of the priesthood to males (Exod. 28:1; etc.), and various other OT texts in support of this position. In opposition to this view, the present essay has attempted to demonstrate that, whatever other views of women appear in the OT, there are certainly ample passages which show that certain biblical writers held a very high view of women.

Chapter Three

WOMEN IN THE HELLENISTIC AND ROMAN WORLDS (323 BCE-138 CE)

Gregory E. Sterling

On the other hand there are a good number of customs which are proper for us which are considered disgraceful among the Greeks. For what Roman thinks it shameful to take his wife to a banquet? Or whose matron does not occupy the front rooms of the house and move about in public? It is far different in Greece. For a woman is only allowed to attend a banquet of relatives and reside in the inner part of the house which is called the "women's quarter" where only a near relative may enter.

Cornelius Nepos, *Praefatio 6-7* [1]

The Feminist Movement has made an impact not only on political structures within our society but intellectual ones as well. For the first time in Western culture, scholars have made women the object of serious historical inquiry.[2] The

---

[1] All translations are mine and are based on LCL unless noted. I want to thank Professor Elizabeth P. Forbis of the Classical and Oriental Languages and Literatures Department of the University of Notre Dame for her comments on an early draft of this chapter.

[2] The first major effort to consider the place of ancient Greek women from a contemporary perspective is W. K. Lacey, *The Family in Classical Greece* (Ithaca: Cornell Univ. Press, 1968). The standard comprehensive treatment of women in the Greco-Roman world continues to be Sarah B. Pomeroy, *Goddesses, Whores, Wives, and Slaves: Women in Classical Antiquity* (New York: Schocken, 1975). While the work is somewhat dated and offers interpretations which are

task of writing the story of women in the ancient world is, however, complicated by three major factors. The first is the silence of our sources, i.e., women were the subject of ancient writings only in exceptional instances.[3] This is compounded by the fact that we have very few texts written by women.[4] The result is that our sources are largely oblique observations about women written by men. Perhaps readers will forgive another male for attempting to put these masculine pieces of information together. The second is that the bulk of the evidence is restricted socially. Most data are from authors of the upper class who have their own

---

disputed, it provides a collection of the major sources with a critical analysis. Her later *Women in Hellenistic Egypt: From Alexander to Cleopatra* (Detroit: Wayne State Univ. Press, 1984, 2nd ed. 1990 [All references are to the second edition]) is a helpful treatment of women in the period we are considering. There are collections of important essays in *Arethusa* 6 (1973) and 11 (1978) which have appeared together as John Peradotto and J. P. Sullivan, *Women in the Ancient World: The* Arethusa *Papers* (Albany: SUNY Press, 1984). A more recent collection is Sarah Pomeroy, ed., *Women's History and Ancient History* (Chapel Hill: Univ. of North Carolina Press, 1991).

[3]A useful collection of pertinent texts is Mary R. Lefkowitz and Maureen B. Fant, *Women's Life in Greece and Rome* (Baltimore: Johns Hopkins Univ. Press, 1982[1], 1992[2] [All references are to the first edition]). I have cross-referenced citations to this work throughout this essay. There is also a helpful collection of Greek epigraphic evidence relating to women by H. W. Pleket, *Epigraphica*, Vol. 2: *Texts on the Social History of the Greek World* (Textus Minores, 41; Leiden: Brill, 1969). The fact that until recent years historical works were written principally by and about men has led modern feminists to reject the term history since history means the history of men. Some prefer Herstory and others Prehistory. See Mary Daly, *Gyn/ecology: The Metaethics of Radical Feminism* (Boston: Beacon, 1978): 24. Elise Boulding, *The Underside of History: A View of Women through Time* (Boulder, CO: Westview, 1976), offers another possibility within a more conventional framework.

[4]Jane McIntosh Snyder, *The Woman and the Lyre: Women Writers in Classical Greece and Rome* (Carbondale/Edwardsville: Southern Illinois Univ. Press, 1989), has collated, translated, and commented on these texts. See also Sylvia Barnard, "Hellenistic Women Poets," *The Classical Journal* 73 (1978): 204-13, who deals with Erinna, Anyte, and Nossis–three Hellenistic poets.

agendas. This means that we can not assume that what is true for the upper class is necessarily true for the lower. It also means that texts often reflect the social values of the author rather than the reality of ancient society.[5] The third is that it is extremely difficult for us to keep our own values from coloring our reading of the ancient material since the place of women is such a volatile contemporary issue. As with the ancient authors, modern analyses sometimes reflect twentieth-century interests rather than ancient practice.[6]

This study offers a social description of the roles and status of women in the Hellenistic and Roman worlds from the emergence of the Hellenistic world c. 323 BCE to the end of Hadrian's reign in 138 CE. It attempts particularly to show how that world is reflected in NT texts and to raise the issue of how an understanding of the larger world affects our assessment of NT texts. I have used sources principally from this period, but have also incorporated others from each end which are either important for or reflective of this period. I have refrained from citing Jewish texts or entering into detailed discussions of NT texts since other essays in this collection address those concerns. The data is organized along the lines of a woman's life, from birth to adulthood.

---

[5]An excellent example of this is the view of the Roman elegists. See Judith P. Hallett, "The Role of Women in Roman Elegy: Counter-Cultural Feminism," *Arethusa* 6 (1973): 103-24, and the entire issue of *Helios* 17 (1990): 161-261, which is devoted to Ovid.

[6]This can take various forms. For example, it may be reflected subtly in the selection of sources. A famous illustration of this is the varying assessments of Athenian women. A. W. Gromme, "The Position of Women in Athens in the Fifth and Fourth Centuries B.C.," *CP* 20 (1925): 1-25, relied upon the tragedians to question whether Athenian women were secluded. On the other hand, W. K. Lacey, *The Family in Classical Greece*, 151-76, rejected the tragedians and used the evidence of the orators to argue they were secluded. See Michael Shaw, "The Female Intruder," *CP* 70 (1975): 255-66. In other instances, modern ideological points of orientation openly become the norm by which the ancient evidence is assessed, e.g., Elisabeth Schüssler Fiorenza, *In Memory of Her: A Feminist Theological Reconstruction of Christian Origins* (New York: Crossroad, 1983).

1. *Female Infanticide*

In the twenties of this century, classicists debated the extent of infanticide in the ancient world and concluded that while it was not widespread in fifth and fourth century Athens the practice expanded in the Hellenistic world.[7] More recently, the issue of gender has become the fulcrum of the debate. Most have argued that female infanticide was more widespread than male.[8] Others, however, have argued that widespread female infanticide was demographically impossible[9] or that the positive evidence for it is not substantial.[10] The demographic arguments are inconclusive in my judgment: the data are too meagre and the range of

---

[7]La Rue van Hook, "The Exposure of Infants at Athens," *TAPA* 51 (1920): 134-45, and H. Bolkestein, "The Exposure of Children at Athens and the ἐγχυτρίστριαι," *CP* 17 (1922): 222-39, who both argue it was not a prevalent practice in classical Athens. H. Bennett, "The Exposure of Infants in Ancient Rome," *Classical Journal* 18 (1922-23): 341-51, and A. Cameron, "The Exposure of Children and Greek Ethics," *Classical Review* 46 (1932): 105-14, extended the issue to include Rome and the origins of Christian opposition to infanticide respectively. For a collection of the main evidence, see E. Weiss, "Kinderaussetzung," *PW* 11 (1921): 463-71. One good indication of its widespread practice is the fact that the Stoic philosopher Musonios Rufus delivered a tractate on the issue, "Should Every Child that is Born Be Raised?" (F 15). He answered affirmatively.

[8]Sarah Pomeroy has addressed the issue in several publications, including *Goddesses, Whores, Wives, and Slaves*, 164-65; "Infanticide in Hellenistic Greece," *Images of Women in Antiquity* (ed. Averil Cameron and Amélie Kuhrt; Detroit: Wayne State Univ. Press, 1983): 207-22; and *Women in Hellenistic Egypt*, 44-45, 111, 128, 135-39. See also Anthony Preus, "Biomedical Techniques for Influencing Human Reproduction in the Fourth Century B.C.," *Arethusa* 8 (1975): 237-56.

[9]Donald Engels, "The Problem of Female Infanticide in the Greco-Roman World," *CP* 75 (1980): 112-20, and "The Use of Historical Demography in Ancient History," *CQ* 34 (1984): 386-93, argues that a rate of only a few per-cent of females was possible for a short period of time demographically.

[10]Cynthia Patterson, "'Not Worth the Rearing': The Causes of Infant Exposure in Ancient Greece," *TAPA* 115 (1985): 103-23, esp. 119-21.

possible explanations too great.[11] We are left, therefore, to survey the ancient evidence.

The third-century BCE poet Poseidippos is reported to have said, "Everyone raises a son even if he happens to be poor, but exposes a daughter even if he is rich."[12] The first-century BCE historian Dionysios of Halikarnassos voiced a similar sentiment in a statement that reminds us of Augustus when he wrote that Romulus, the mythical founder of Rome, built up the population of the city by requiring all inhabitants to raise every male child and the firstborn of the female.[13] Preference for male children is even more explicit in an unforgettable letter of the first century BCE. A certain Hilarion who had gone to Alexandria wrote home to his wife Alis and two other females, stating in a matter-of-fact way, "If you have a child and it is a male, let it live; if it is a female, expose it."[14] It is tempting to make a connection between these statements and the observation of the Roman historian Cassius Dio that during Augustus' principate there were more men than women among the upper classes in Rome.[15]

---

[11]Engels has been answered by Mark Golden, "Demography and the Exposure of Girls at Athens," *Phoenix* 35 (1981): 316-31, who contends that up to ten per-cent of female infants could have been exposed as a result of concerns over the number of marriageable females. William V. Harris, "The Theoretical Possibility of Extensive Infanticide in the Greco-Roman World," *CQ* 32 (1982): 114-16, maintains that exposure was common.

[12]F 11K=Stobaios 4.24.40. All references to Stobaios are from Curtius Wachsmuth and Otto Hense, *Ioannis Stobaei: Anthologii* (5 vols.; 1884-1912 [repr., Weidmann, 1974]).

[13]*AR* 2.15.1-2.

[14]*P.Oxy.* 744. I have not translated the problematic πολλα-πολλῶν. See Adolf Deissmann, *Light from the Ancient East: The New Testament Illustrated by Recently Discovered Texts of the Graeco-Roman World* (repr., Grand Rapids: Baker, 1978): 167-70, and George Milligan, *Selections from the Greek Papyri* (Cambridge: Cambridge Univ. Press, 1910 [repr., Chicago: Ares, 1980]): 32-33.

[15]54.16.2 (Fant, *Women's Life in Greece and Rome*, 192).

The Latin evidence is no less ambiguous.[16]   In
Terence's (190-159 BCE) play the *Self-Tormentor*, taken
from Menander, he presents a wife defending herself for dis-
obeying her husband in these words: "Do you remember
when I was pregnant and you expressly informed me if I had
a girl you did not want it raised?"[17]   The elegaic poet Ovid
(43 BCE-17 CE) reversed the situation and had the husband
address his wife: "What I want are these two things: that you
are free from complications and that you have a male; the
other kind is more burdensome and fortune denies us the
means."[18]   Apuleius (born c. 123 CE), addressing the theme
of maternal instinct triumphing over the wishes of a
husband, presents a husband leaving the house and ordering
his pregnant wife "that if she gave birth to a newborn of the
inferior sex, what she had delivered should immediately be
killed."[19]   But she secretly preserved the daughter she had.

Two things impress me about the credibility of this
evidence.   First, it comes from a wide spectrum of social
levels–from litterateurs in Rome to insignificant husbands in
Egypt.   Second, none of the texts appear to consider the
practice to be shocking or unusual; this is our reaction, not
that of the ancients.   I do not mean to imply that infanticide
was frivolous; the fact that in two of the Roman texts cited
above the mother preserved the daughter against the wishes
of the father indicates that it was not.   However, I do think it
likely that this was a common practice both in the Hellenistic
and Roman worlds.   According to the texts, the motivation
behind the practice was economic: girls do not continue the
family line and need a dowry.   Economic concerns are also
the conclusion of Polybios, who attributed the depopulation
of second-century BCE Greece to infanticide.   He wrote,

> Men have degenerated into such a state of pre-
> tentiousness, greed, and laziness that they do not

---

[16]See Gillian Clark, "Roman Women," *Greece and Rome* 2nd
ser., 28 (1981): 194-97.

[17]*Heaut.* 620-630, esp. 626.

[18]*Met.* 9.675-77.

[19]*Met.* 10.23.

want to marry or, if they do, to raise the children which are born—except possibly one or two at most so that they can leave them rich and raise them to be spoiled brats . . . .[20]

Thus, whether it was out of a sense of poverty or a desire to maintain a certain standard of living, infanticide was a reality. It is not important for our purposes to determine the extent to which the ancients practiced it in any specific community, but to recognize that in their practice economic concerns sometimes led to a distinction between male and female newborns.[21]

2. *Female Anatomy and Physiology*

Greek science contributed to the differentiation of males and females in ancient society. The classical world produced two schools of biology: the Hippokratic and the Aristotelian. Although there were significant differences between their assessments of the female body, both considered it inferior to the male.[22] While the later Alexandrian school made advances on their work through the practice of dissection, it did not overturn the basic perspective of the female body developed by their predecessors.[23]

---

[20]36.17.7. Peter Green, *Alexander to Actium: The Historical Evolution of the Hellenistic Age* (Hellenistic Culture and Society; Berkeley/Los Angeles: Univ. of California Press, 1990): 389, argues that Polybios' analysis was correct.

[21]The problem of female infanticide has not disappeared. See Nicholas D. Kristof, "Stark Data on Women: 100 Million Are Missing," *New York Times* 5 Nov. 1991, sec. B5, 9.

[22]So Lesley Dean-Jones, "The Cultural Construct of the Female Body in Classical Greek Science," *Women's History and Ancient History*, 111-37, esp. 114.

[23]On early Alexandrian medicine, see Heinrich von Staden, *Herophilus: The Art of Medicine in Early Alexandria* (Cambridge: Cambridge Univ. Press, 1989).

The Hippokratic corpus (c. 425-350 BCE) contains the first treatises dealing with gynecology.[24] The Hippokratics maintained that both males and females had seed. In the context of explaining the gender of an embryo, the now anonymous author(s) of the tractate *On Generation* wrote, "there is in the male female seed and male seed; and the same in the female. The male is stronger than the female. It is therefore necessary that it came from stronger seed." The author goes on to recount the combinations of seed which produce male or female embryos.[25] Aristotle (384-322 BCE) took exception to the Hippokratic position that both males and females emit seminal fluid. He maintained that only males emit seed: "A woman is like a sterile male. For the female is defined by a certain incapacity, namely the inability to produce seed from the final state of the nourishment (this is either blood or its equivalent in bloodless animals) because of the coldness of her nature."[26] The distinction in sexes is due to the need of reproduction. Aristotle is unambiguous about the relative worth of each gender: the male "is better and more divine since it is the beginning of movement for the things which have come into existence, while the female is the matter."[27] So he can speak of females as deviations from the norm which is the male.[28] The influence of both

---

[24]On the relationship of the Hippokratic corpus to society, see Ann Ellis Hanson, "Continuity and Change: Three Case Studies in Hippocratic Gynecological Therapy and Theory," *Women's History and Ancient History*, 73-110.

[25]*On Generation* 6.1. I have used the edition of Robert Joly, *Hippocrate* (Budé; Paris: Société d'Édition 'Les Belles Lettres,' 1970). For ET, see Fant, *Women's Life in Greece and Rome*, 93.

[26]*GA* 1.20 (728a.18-20). Aristotle recognized that females emitted fluid, but denied that their fluid was seminal. See *GA* 1.20 (727b.34-729a.34) in Fant, *Women's Life in Greece and Rome*, 92.

[27]*GA* 2.1 (732a.9). This is the distinction between form and matter which is so important for Aristotle's work.

[28]*GA* 4.3 (767b.6-10). On the issue of whether Aristotle's biology was prejudiced by the social conditions operative in Athens, see Maryanne Cline Horowitz, "Aristotle and Woman," *Journal of the History of Biology* 9 (1976): 183-213, who calls the inferiority of the female "a value-ridden premise" (205), and Johannes Morsink, "Was

the Hippokratics and Aristotle is evident in the work of Galen (c. 129-199 CE) who concurred in their judgment: "The female is less perfect than the male, for one principal reason—because she is colder." He then added a second reason: "All the parts . . . that men have, women have too, the difference between them lying in only one thing . . . that in women the parts are within [the body], whereas in men they are outside, in the region called the perineum."[29]

The biological premise that the female was inferior to the male had significant social ramifications. There are two areas where these connections surface in the NT. The first is the observation that women are physically weaker than men mentioned above in the Hippokratic text.[30] Aristotle associated the weakness of women with their subordination to men. The Stagirite wrote: "For the divine made one stronger and the other weaker so that the latter would be more protective as a result of her timidity and the former more ready to defend as a result of his manliness." He then assigned each a corresponding place: "the one provides the things from the outside; the other preserves the things inside."[31] Aristotle's basic views became commonplace in the Hellenistic world through their incorporation in *Haustafeln*.[32] It is, therefore, not surprising to find an exhortation in a NT household code which urges husbands

---

Aristotle's Biology Sexist?" *Journal of the History of Biology* 12 (1979): 83-112, who denies that a sexist presupposition taints *GA*.

[29]*UP* 14.6. I have cited the ET of Margaret Tallmadge May, *Galen: On the Usefulness of Parts of the Body* (2 vols; Ithaca: Cornell Univ. Press, 1968). See also Fant, *Women's Life in Greece and Rome*, 211.

[30]Plato, Aristotle's teacher, had mentioned the weakness of females several times: *Rep.* 455e.1-2; 456a.11, and *Leg.* 781a. See Fant, *Women's Life in Greece and Rome*, 87-88. There were some protests in the ancient world, e.g., Euripides, *Med.* 250-51: "I would much rather stand in battle three times than to give birth once."

[31]*Oec.* 1.3 (1343b.30-1344a.3). Xenophon, *Oec.* 7.22-23, makes the same point. See Fant, *Women's Lives in Greece and Rome*, 106.

[32]See below under Philosophy.

to "show honor to your wife as a weaker vessel."[33] Nor is
it unexpected to find statements enjoining wives to be submissive in the same code.[34]

The second area is related to the first. Aristotle
maintained that the fitness of the male to rule over the female
extended to the rational capacities of each. He explained the
nature of subordination in different relationships on the basis
of the capacities of the subordinate member of the relationship: "The slave does not have any deliberative faculty at all;
the female has it, but without authority;[35] the child has it, but
it is undeveloped."[36] Only the mature male has this
capacity. Aristotle was by no means alone in this assessment.[37] Menander (342/1-293/89 BCE), a leading writer of
New Comedy, presented a daughter's efforts to persuade her
father not to dissolve her present marriage and force her to
marry a wealthier man: "Yet, father, even if a woman is a
silly creature when it comes to judging other matters, about
her own affairs perhaps she has some sense."[38] While it
might appear offensive even to suggest, it is at least
conceivable that this view could lie behind the NT statement:
"Adam was not deceived, but the woman was deceived and
fell into transgression."[39]

---

[33]1 Pet. 3:7.

[34]1 Pet. 3:1-6. See also Col. 3:18; Eph. 5:22-24; Titus 2:5.

[35]On the meaning of ἄκυρον in this text, see Horowitz, *Journal of the History of Biology* (1976): 207.

[36]*Pol.* 1.5.6 (1260a.12-14). See Fant, *Women's Lives in Greece and Rome*, 86.

[37]For the evidence that women were considered more gullible and less intelligent than men in classical Athens, see Kenneth J. Dover, *Greek Popular Morality: In the Time of Plato and Aristotle* (Berkeley/ Los Angeles: Univ. of California Press, 1974): 98-100. There were objections to this notion, e.g., Agathon F 14: "A woman as a result of the inactivity of the body, possesses a not inactive mind within her soul." Bruno Snell, et al., ed., *Tragicorum Graecorum Fragmenta* (4 vols.; Göttingen: Vandenhoeck & Ruprecht, 1971-85): 1.165.

[38]Fant, *Women's Life in Greece and Rome*, 38.

[39]1 Tim. 2:14.

What the evidence points to is the widespread conviction that females were biologically inferior to males. Whether those who performed medical research began with sexist presuppositions or attempted to work with intellectual objectivity, the results of their observations were the same: females did not have the same capacities as males. They only needed to take a short step to connect biological and social judgments.

3. *Childhood*

A. *Nourishment.* The discrimination which is evident in the practices of infanticide and in Greek medicine became an inherent dimension of a woman's experience as a human being. One way in which this became obvious in the ancient world was the practice of feeding females. In his opening observations about the unique conditions at Sparta, Xenophon described the basic fare for girls in the remainder of classical Greece: "For the others nourish the girls who are going to bear children and who are selected to be raised correctly with as moderate an amount of food as is practical and with as little fish as possible." Their beverage was no better: "They make them refrain from wine entirely or drink it diluted with water."[40] Presumably conditions did not improve in Greece during the Hellenistic world, when economic conditions actually worsened.

The Roman evidence also indicates that gender could determine diet among the poor. This is evident in the administration of the *alimenta*, a system which arose in the first century CE to provide sustenance for poor children in the Empire.[41] At first this was a private system, but during

---

[40]Xenophon, *Lac.* 1.3.

[41]See A. R. Hands, *Charities and Social Aid in Greece and Rome* (Ithaca: Cornell Univ. Press, 1968): 108-15, and Pomeroy, *Goddesses, Whores, Wives, and Slaves*, 202-04. Hands has a very useful collection of the primary documents in English translation, 175-209. All references are to this collection. For Italy, see 16-19 and 21; for North Africa, 20; and for Asia Minor, 22.

the reign of Trajan (98-117 CE) it became state supported.[42]
Some inscriptions indicate the provisions are for children
without specifying the gender.[43] Others, however, make a
distinction, e.g., at Veleia in northern Italy, Trajan supported
18 boys at 16 *sesterces* each per month and 1 girl at 12
sesterces. Subsequently, he expanded the numbers to 245
boys and 34 girls (and two illegitimate children at a different
rate).[44] It is not clear whether this was designed to promote
the birthrate of boys who could be future soldiers[45] or if
families were only allowed to file for one child and consequently opted to file for the higher allowance if they had
children of both sexes. A number of other inscriptions
stipulate the same number of boys and girls, but give a larger
allowance to the boys.[46] The common assumption is that
boys should be fed more or better than girls. This may have
contributed to the shorter life-span of women.[47] We should

---

[42]On Trajan's benefactions to children, see Pliny, *Paneg.* 26.1-7.

[43]Hands, *Charities and Social Aid in Greece and Rome*, 16-18,
41.

[44]*Ibid.*, 19. It is worth remembering that Augustus is credited
with extending support to boys under eleven. Nothing is said of girls.
See Suetonius, *Aug.* 41.2.

[45]So Pliny, *Paneg.* 28.1-7.

[46]At Tarracina in Italy during the second century, Caelia Macrina
left 1,000,000 *sesterces* to support 100 boys (up to age 16) at five
denarii per month and 100 girls (up to age 14) at four *denarii* per
month. During the second century, P. Licinius Papirianus gave
1,300,000 *sesterces* to the residents of Sicca in North Africa to support
300 boys (from ages 3-15) and 300 girls (from ages 3-13) at the rate of
two and one-half and two *denarii* per month respectively. See Pliny,
Paneg. 20-21.

[47]J. Lawrence Angel, "Ecology and Population in the Eastern
Mediterranean," *World Archaeology* 4 (1972): 88-105, estimated that
the average life-spans for males in Hellenistic Greece (300 BCE) was
42.6; for females it was 36.6. During the Roman period (120 CE),
longevity dropped to 40.2 and 34.3 respectively. While childbirth is
certainly one of the major reasons for the shorter lifespan of women,
they would have done better if they had eaten better and exercised more.
For difficulties in using the epigraphic evidence to compute ages at
death, see Keith Hopkins, "On the Probable Age Structure of the
Roman Population," *Population Studies* 20 (1966-67): 245-64, esp.

remember that the *alimenta* were for the impoverished. Distinctions probably faded as the family resources increased.

B. *Childhood.* Not all of life was hard for every girl in the Hellenistic world, as is clear in several poems written by Hellenistic female poets celebrating aspects of their childhood, e.g., the elusive Erinna (late fourth century BCE) of the island of Telos. Her fame rests on the *Distaff*, a poem of 300 hexameters composed in memory of her childhood friend Baukis.[48] Although fragmentary, her reflections on games she played with Baukis as a girl are clear enough.

> I shouted loudly . . . tortoise
> Leaping up . . . the yard of the great court.
> These things, O poor Baukis, . . . in mourning
> These traces . . . lie in my heart
> warm still . . . embers now
> of dolls . . . in the bedrooms
> . . . Once at dawn
> Mother . . . to the woolworkers
> She came to you . . . salted.
> O for little (girls) . . . Mormo brought fear
> . . . it went around on feet
> four . . . changing its appearance.[49]

Even though the lines are broken, we can still feel the bond of friendship between two little girls playing tag in the yard,[50] dolls in the bedrooms, the roles of adults in the game

---

260-64, where he argues that the commemorative nature of the epigraphic evidence disqualifies the early death rate of women.

[48]On Erinna, see Barnard, *Classical Journal* (1978): 205-08, and Snyder, *The Woman and the Lyre*, 86-97.

[49]See D. L. Page, *Greek Literary Papyri* (LCL; Cambridge: Harvard Univ. Press, 1941): 1.486-89.

[50]Tortoise was an ancient form of tag. The girls sat in a circle with the "tortoise" in the middle. After a series of questions the tortoise leaped up and tagged another girl who became the next "tortoise." See Pollux 9.125.

known today as "house,"[51] and the common fear of a childhood "bogy" (Mormo).

We catch another glimpse in a couple of poems of Anyte (c. 300 BCE) who drew on the mountainous landscape around her native Tegea in Arkadia (a district in the Peloponesos) to create the bucolic-landscape epigram and the animal epitaph.[52] In one, she describes children at play:

> The children put purple reigns on you, billy-goat,
> and a noseband around your shaggy snout.
> They train you in equestrian contests around the
>   god's temple
> so that he can watch them enjoy their childish joys.[53]

In another, she captures the pathos of a girl who has lost her pets:

> For her grasshopper, the singer of the field, and her
>   oak-dwelling
> cicada,[54] Myro made a common grave.
> The girl shed maidenly tears, for both of her
> pets unyielding Hades came and took away.[55]

These poems afford a rare window into the lives of young aristocratic girls.

---

[51]Page, *Greek Literary Papyri*, 1.487, n. b, understood "Mother" to refer to Erinna. Barnard, *Classical Journal* (1978): 205, thought it referred to Baukis' mother. Since the context is that of recalling childhood games, the former seems more likely.

[52]On Anyte, see Barnard, *Classical Journal* (1978): 208-10, and Snyder, *The Woman and the Lyre*, 67-77. The texts are conveniently printed in W. R. Paton, ed., *The Greek Anthology* (5 vols.; LCL; Cambridge: Harvard Univ. Press, 1916-18[1], 1971[2]).

[53]*PA* 6.312. See Paton, *Greek Anthology*, 1.468-69.

[54]The cicada (τέττιξ) is a winged insect whose males make a chirping sound.

[55]*PA* 7.190. See Paton, *Greek Anthology* 2.108-09.

C. *Education.* Girls did more, however, than play. They also learned to take care of the house. In Xenophon's *Oeconomicus*, Sokrates asked Ischomachos: "But this is the point which I would like to learn from you . . . whether you trained your wife yourself to be what she should be or whether when you received her from her father and mother she already knew how to manage her duties?" Ischomachos replied that she knew how to spin wool and to distribute the tasks of spinning to the maids, but that was all that could be expected.[56] In classical Athens, girls were educated in their homes and only in exceptional circumstances did they enjoy the opportunities of their male counterparts.[57] Papyri suggest that opportunities expanded in the Hellenistic world, but hardly in the sense of equal opportunity.[58] Most impressive pieces of evidence in the Hellenistic world are inscriptions left by the benefactors of private elementary schools which were set up so that all free children might be educated. There are several second-century BCE examples from Asia Minor.[59] Elementary education was not, however, an admission to advanced education or a profession. There are a number of stories about women who circum-

---

[56]*Oec.* 7.4-8. See also 3.11-14. Sheila Murnaghan, "How a Woman Can Be More Like a Man: The Dialogue between Ischomachus and His Wife in Xenophon's *Oeconomicus*," *Helios* 15 (1988): 9-22, has pointed out some of the difficulties of moving directly from this work to social *realia.* There is other evidence for the husband as the teacher of the wife, e.g., Hesiod, *Op.* 695-705, and Plutarch, *Mor.* 145c-d.

[57]On the education of girls in classical Athens, see Lacey, *The Family in Classical Greece*, 163. There is some evidence for female education beyond household duties. Frederick A. G. Beck, *Greek Education 450-350 B.C.* (New York: Barnes & Noble, 1964): 85-88, and idem., *Album of Greek Education: The Greeks at School and at Play* (Sydney: Cheiron, 1975): 55-62 and plates 69-88, has collected some of the evidence.

[58]See Pomeroy, *Goddesses, Whores, Wives, and Slaves*, 136-39, and *Women in Hellenistic Egypt*, 48, 59-72, 119, 121.

[59]See the inscriptions in ET in M. M. Austin, ed., *The Hellenistic World from Alexander to the Roman Conquest: A Selection of Ancient Sources in Translation* (Cambridge: Cambridge Univ. Press, 1981): 119-20.

vented custom by attiring themselves in male clothing.
Hyginos (2nd century BCE) relates efforts of one maiden to
learn and practice medicine in the third century BCE:

> A certain young girl, Hagnodike, wanted to learn
> medicine. Having so decided, she cut her hair, put
> on masculine attire, and delivered herself to a certain
> Herophilos for instruction. After she had learned the
> skill, when she heard that a woman was in labor, she
> used to go to her. When the woman didn't want to
> entrust herself (to her) because she thought she was a
> man, she hiked her tunic and showed that she was a
> woman. So she used to cure women.[60]

A significant shift for women with high social status
took place in the late Republic and early Empire of Rome. A
sizeable number of women received a fine education.[61]
Several became famous through their literary and rhetorical
skills, e.g., Cornelia (2nd century BCE), Laelia (1st century
BCE), and Hortensia (1st century BCE).[62] Cicero was
impressed by the rhetorical qualities of Cornelia's letters and
attributed the skill of her famous sons, Tiberius and Gaius,
to their mother. He thought that Laelia's rhetorical skills
were a result of paternal influence. She in turn trained both
her daughters and granddaughters to speak impressively.[63]
The injunction within a NT household code for fathers to
raise their children (both male and female) "in the discipline

---

[60]*Fab.* 274. See text and translation in von Staden, *Herophilus*,
53, 61, 38-41. One major problem with this *fabula* is that it presupposes an Athenian setting, while Herophilus was active in Alexandria.
An earlier example of a female student attiring herself in male clothing
is Plato's student, Axiothea of Philus. See Diogenes Laertios 3.46,
who does not, however, explain why she clothed herself this way.

[61]See Edward E. Best, Jr., "Cicero, Livy and Educated Roman
Women," *Classical Journal* 65 (1969-70): 199-204.

[62]Cicero, *Brut.* 58.211; Quintillian, 1.1.6; and Appian, *BC* 4.32-
34. See Fant, *Women's Life in Greece and Rome*, 204, 206, 220.

[63]*Brut.* 58.211.

and instruction of the Lord" is very appropriate in a Greco-Roman setting.[64]

Parents were not, however, the only educators of young girls. Tutors instructed members of both sexes. One of the most touching pieces of evidence we have for the education of girls in the Roman world is a letter Pliny the Younger (c. 61-112 CE) wrote describing the death of a friend's young daughter: "I never saw a girl so happy and loveable . . . she loved her nurses, her attendants and her teachers, each one for the service given her; she applied herself intelligently to her books . . . ."[65] The changes are also evident in Greece. In the first century CE, we have epigraphic examples of female athletes–a practice foreign to the classical age.[66]

4. *Marriage*

One of the major limitations in a girl's education was the fact that she married at an earlier age than her male counterparts: she normally married at the age a boy entered his secondary education.[67] Plato thought that women should marry between the ages of 16-20 and men between 30-35.[68] Aristotle recommended marriage for females at 18 and for males at 37.[69] Xenophon is closer to Athenian practices when he informs us that Ischomachos' wife was fourteen at

---

[64]Eph. 6:4.

[65]*Ep.* 5.16.

[66]Pleket, *Epigraphica*, 9. See ET in Fant, *Women's Lives in Greece and Rome*, 169. H. A. Harris, *Sport in Greece and Rome* (Ithaca: Cornell Univ. Press, 1972): 40-41, suggested that the development of sport as entertainment and the need to titillate the crowds were factors in the entrance of females into athletics. He provides visual evidence of female participation in athletics in plates 41-45, 48, 58.

[67]Philostratos, *VA* 1.7, says that Apollonios of Tyana began his secondary education at fourteen.

[68]*Leg.* 785b. See also 721b-e and 772d. In the latter, he mentions 25-35 as the most suitable time for males.

[69]*Pol.* 7.14.6 (1335a.28-30). Hesiod, *Op.* 695-701, recommended 19 and 30.

their marriage.[70] This is the general pattern for Greeks in Athens and the Hellenistic world: girls in their early teens and men around thirty.[71] Augustus passed legislation establishing the minimum age of marriage for girls at twelve and for boys at fourteen.[72] In both traditions, the males were older than the females.

The importance of marriage for a woman of the Hellenistic and Roman worlds is hard to overestimate. A fragment attributed to Hipponax (*fl.* 540-537 BCE) states it perversely: "Two days in a woman's life are sweet, when someone marries her and when he carries her corpse to the grave."[73] There are a number of inscriptions which explicitly lament the death of a young girl prior to marriage. An epigram of Anyte which probably served as a sepulchre inscription poignantly reveals the importance of marriage:

> Often in tears on this tomb of her daughter Kleina did her mother call for her dear child prematurely taken, summoning the soul of Philainis which before marriage crossed the pale flow of the river Acheron.[74]

---

[70]*Oec.* 7.5.

[71]Lacey, *The Family in Classical Greece*, 106-07, 162-63, 212, and Pomeroy, *Goddesses, Whores, Wives, and Slaves*, 41, 64, 85. The Cynic Diogenes is credited with the following statement: "Asked at what time one ought to marry, he said, 'Young men not yet; old men never'" (Diogenes Laertios 6.54).

[72]For texts and discussion of the relationship between menarche and marriage laws, see Darrel W. Amundsen and Carol Jean Diers, "The Age of Menarche in Classical Greece and Rome," *Human Biology* 41 (1969): 125-32.

[73]F 68. See Fant, *Women's Lives in Greece and Rome*, 31. I have used the edition of M. L. West, ed., *Iambi et Elegi Greci (Ante Alexandrum Cantati)* (2nd ed.; Oxford: Clarendon, 1989 [vol. 1]). On Hipponax, see Oliver Masson, *Les Fragments du Poète Hipponax* (Paris: C. Klincksieck, 1962 [repr. New York: Garland, 1987]).

[74]*PA* 7.486. See Paton, *Greek Anthology*, 2.264-65. See other examples in *PA* 7.490, 649 (Paton, 2.266-67, 346-47). For an earlier Athenian example, see Fant, *Women's Lives in Greece and Rome*, 21.

One of the difficulties which complicates a summary of Hellenistic and Roman marriage laws is that there were multiple codes. The Romans considered marriage to be a matter of personal law. Roman citizens were subject to *ius civile*, but *peregrini* (non-Romans) were obligated to follow their own laws.[75] This means that marital practices varied within a single community according to the citizenship of the people.[76]

A. *Greek Practices*. In Greek law, a woman was under the authority of a male κύριος [lord] throughout her life.[77] A famous example of this is the will of Aristotle in which the philosopher gave explicit instructions about the κυρεία of Herpyllis and their children.[78] The result was that a female did not marry, but was married. In Athenian law, there were three basic steps in marriage. First, when the respective parties decided on the marriage, the girl's κύριος–normally her closest male relative–"pledged" (ἐγγυᾶν) her to her future husband. This pledge (ἐγγύησις or ἐγγύη) entrusted the girl to the prospective groom. Second, at the time of the pledge, the girl's κύριος either gave the husband a dowry (προίξ) or promised one. The dowry was for the support of the wife.[79] Third, at a convenient time, the woman moved into her husband's house (ἔκδοσις). At this

---

[75]So Wolfgang Kunkel, *An Introduction to Roman Legal and Constitutional History* (2nd ed.; Oxford: Clarendon, 1973): 75-77. For Roman recognition of native traditions, see Gaius, *Inst.* 1.92. I have used the edition of W. M. Gordon and O. F. Robinson, *The Institutes of Gaius* (Ithaca: Cornell Univ. Press, 1988).

[76]For a convenient collection of the major laws, see Fant, *Women's Lives in Greece and Rome*, 64-85 (Greek) and 187-202 (Roman).

[77]Lacey, *The Family in Classical Greece*, 21-22. I have found the work of Raphael Sealey, *Women and Law in Classical Greece* (Chapel Hill: Univ. of North Carolina Press, 1990) to be particularly helpful in explaining the legal status of women in Greek law. My discussion is indebted to him.

[78]Diogenes Laertios 5.11-16.

[79]Demosthenes 30.7; 41.5-6; Menander, *Dysk.* 842-44 and *Pk.* 1013-15.

point, her husband became her κύριος. He then had the full right to administer her property and represent her at law.

A woman's legal status in marriage is best illustrated by divorce laws. A husband could divorce his wife simply by sending her away.[80] A wife, on the other hand, had to file with the magistrate. Plutarch (c. 50-120 CE) relates a famous story about Alkibiades (c. 450-304 BCE) which illustrates this. Alkibiades liked prostitutes. His wife, Hipparete, left in dismay and moved into her brother's home. When Alkibiades continued, she went to the magistrate and filed for divorce. When she appeared according to the law, Alkibiades grabbed her and physically led her back to his home where she lived until she died– which was only a short time later! Perhaps even more dumbfounding to us is Plutarch's editorial comment: "For the law that requires a woman who is separating from her husband to go to court herself, seems to be for the purpose of providing the husband the opportunity to meet and take possession of her."[81] If a man divorced his wife, he had to return the dowry to her former κύριος. A large dowry thus served to encourage the stability of the marriage. While practices in other Greek cities varied in details, virtually all recognized the role of the κύριος and the dowry.[82]

The Egyptian papyri of the Hellenistic world present several significant changes. The three central elements of a marriage were cohabitation, the dowry, and a contract. The following is a typical marriage contract of the Hellenistic world. It is dated 13 BCE.

To Protarchos from Thermion the daughter of Apion with her κύριος, Apollonios the son of Chaireas, and from Apollonios the son of Ptolemaios. Thermion and Apollonios the son of Ptolemaios agree to live

---

[80]Demosthenes 59.63, 83.

[81]*Alc.* 8.3.5. See also Isaios 3.78; Demosthenes 30.17, 26.

[82]See Sealy, *Women and Law in Classical Greece*, 151-60, esp. 154-56.

with one another for partnership in life. The same Apollonios the son of Ptolemaios has received from Thermion by hand from the house as a dowry a pair of gold earrings of three quarters weight and silver . . . From now on Apollonios the son of Ptolemaios will furnish Thermion all necessities and clothing appropriate to a married woman in keeping with his financial ability. He will not abuse her nor throw her out nor treat her outrageously nor bring home another wife or he will immediately return the dowry plus an additional fifty per cent. This will be taken from the same Apollonios the son of Ptolemaios and from all of his property as if by a legal sentence. Thermion shall do what is right for her husband and their shared life. She shall not sleep away or spend a day away from home without the permission of Apollonios the son of Ptolemaios. She shall not ruin or injure their shared home nor have sexual relations with another man. If she has done any of these things, after a trial, she shall be deprived of her dowry and besides the male violator shall be liable to the stipulated fine. 17th year of Caesar, Pharmouthi 20.[83]

The document has a rough parallel in modern pre-nuptial agreements. Like contemporary agreements, the major point of concern is economic, i.e., in this case the fate of the dowry if the marriage dissolves. The stipulations for the husband and wife are formulary as the parallels in other marriage contracts make clear.[84] Two points underscore the subordinate role of the woman: first, in keeping with Greek law, Thermion is represented by her κύριος;[85] second, Thermion was required to stay home unless she had her husband's permission while Apollonios could be away at his

---

[83]BGU. 1052. Text in A. S. Hunt and C. C. Edgar, ed., *Select Papyri* (LCL; Cambridge: Harvard Univ. Press, 1932-41): 3 (1:10-11). For other marriage contracts, see 1, 2, 4, 5 (1:1-23).

[84]The same stipulations with minor modifications appear in 1, 2, 5 (*ibid.*).

[85]Cicero, *Flac.* 71-72, attests the continuing presence of κύριοι.

own will.[86] Other papyri, however, indicate some shifts. In *P. Elephantine* 1 (311 BCE), both the father and mother give the bride away.[87] The wife still has a κύριος, but also has a role that she would not have had in the classical period.

Divorce was relatively easy and could be initiated by either party. The following is a typical divorce document which also dates to 13 BCE:

> To Protarchos from Zois the daughter of Herakleides with her κύριος, her brother Eirenaios the son of Herakleides and from Antipater the son of Zenon. Zois and Antipater agree that they have separated (κεχωρίσθαι)[88] from one another and dissolved the bond which they had entered by agreement through the same court in Hathur of the current 17th year of Caesar. Zois certifies that she has received from Antipater by hand from the house what he held as a dowry, clothes worth 120 *drachmai* and a pair of gold earrings. The agreement of the marriage shall from this point on be considered void. Neither Zois nor another acting on her behalf shall bring charges against Antipater for restitution of the dowry. Neither shall bring charges against the other in regard to their cohabitation or any other matter at all up to the present day. From this day on, it shall be lawful for Zois to marry another man and for Antipater to marry another woman; both are unaccountable to the other. In addition to the validity of the terms of this agreement, the one who violates it will be liable to

---

[86]Plutarch, *Mor.* 139c, advised wives to remain home when their husbands were away.

[87]Hunt and Edgar, *Select Papyri*, 1 (1:2-5). See also 5 (1:16-23) where a woman acting with a man gives away her daughter. It is dated 260 CE. See other examples in Pomeroy, *Women in Hellenistic Egypt*, 89-91.

[88]This term appears in several NT divorce texts: Matt. 19:6; 1 Cor. 7:10, 11, 15.

damages and to the stipulated fine. 17th year of
Caesar, Pharmouthi 2.[89]

Once again, the concern of the document is with the dowry.
It certifies that it has been returned and prohibits any further
legal recourse to either party.

B. *Roman Practices.* Like the Greeks, the Romans practiced
betrothal and gave dowries. The aspect of Roman law
which sets it apart is the *potestas patria*, the right of the
farthest male ancestor to control his descendents. Girls, like
boys, were born *in poteste patria*.[90] As with the Greeks,
marriage was one of the places where authority could be
transferred. There were two types of marriage among
Romans: *ius matrimonium*, a legally valid marriage, and
iniustum matrimonium, cohabitation without a legal
marriage.[91] A legal marriage required *conubium* (the right to
marry), age (both parties must have reached puberty), and
the consent of both parties. The traditional form of Roman
marriage involved *manus* [lit., hand] which denotes the
passage of the woman from the authority of the father to that
of her husband.[92] This was uncommon by the first century

---

[89]B.G.U. 1103. I have used the edition of Hunt and Edgar, *Select
Papyri* 6 (1:22-25). See also 7 (1:24-27) and from a later period 8
(1:26-29).

[90]For examples of the extent of the power of the *pater familias*,
see Publius Horatius and Horatius in Livy 1.26 and the famous story of
Verginia in Livy 3.44-48; Dionysios of Halikarnassos, *AR* 11.28-37;
and Diodoros Sikelos 12.24.

[91]On Roman marriage, see P. E. Corbett, *The Roman Law of
Marriage* (Oxford: Clarendon, 1930) and Susan Treggiari, *Roman
Marriage: Iusti Coniuges from the Time of Cicero to the Time of
Ulpian* (Oxford: Clarendon, 1991). On women in Roman marriage,
see Jane F. Gardner, *Women in Roman Law and Society* (Bloomington/
Indianapolis: Indiana Univ. Press, 1986): 31-65 (marriage), 81-95
(divorce).

[92]There were three forms of marriage *in manum*: *usus*, a man and
a woman lived together as man and wife for one year; *confarreatio*, an
elaborate religious ceremony restricted to patricians and priests; and
coemptio, the fictitious purchase of a wife by her husband. See Gaius,
Inst. 1.108-13.

BCE. Most Romans preferred free marriage which included
two elements: *in domum deductio*, the conducting of the
bride into the husband's house; and *affectus maritalis*, the
consent of both parties. Ulpian (d. 223 CE) wrote: "Living
together does not form marriages, but consent."[93] In this
marriage, the woman remained either *in potestate patria* or
was *sui iuris* (of her own authority). In either case, she did
not pass into the *manus* of her husband.

Since the marriage was based on *affectus maritalis*,
either party could dissolve it.[94] This could be accomplished
by a bilateral agreement or by unilateral repudiation,
repudium. An example of a woman taking the initiative
appears in a letter of Caelius to Cicero (50 BCE): "Paula
Valeria the sister of Triarius, divorced her husband without
cause."[95] There was no particular form for this divorce in
the late Republic.[96] The party dismissing the other simply
sent them away with a statement like, "Keep your things
yourself" or "Look out for your own things."[97] Augustus
tried to curb the practice among Roman citizens in a series of
legislative acts which transformed a personal matter into a
civil one. The first law was the *Lex Julia de adulteriis* (18
BCE), which made adultery a crime and compelled a husband
to divorce an unfaithful wife or face charges of serving as a
pimp.[98] At the same time, it forbade a wife to accuse a
husband of adultery.[99] He also stipulated a procedure for
divorce: "No divorce is valid unless seven adult Roman

---

[93]*The Digest of Justinian* 50.17.30. I have used the edition of
Theodor Mommsen, Paul Kreuger, and Alan Watson, *The Digest of
Justinian* (4 vols; Philadelphia: Univ. of Pennsylvania Press, 1985).

[94]Treggiari, *Roman Marriage*, 435-82, has a useful summary.

[95]Cicero, *Fam.* 8.7.2. See also Plautus, *Men.* 722-23; *Mil.*
1164-67, 1277-78; and *Rud.* 1046-47.

[96]Cicero, *De Or.* 1.183, 238.

[97]*Tuas res tibi habeto* and *Tuas res tibi agito* respectively. On
the formulae, see Gaius, *The Digest of Justinian*, 23.2.1. See also
Plautus, *Amph.* 928; Cicero, *Phil.* 2.28.69; and Martial, *Ep.* 10.41.

[98]*The Digest of Justinian*, 48.5.

[99]*The Digest of Justinian*, 9.1.

citizens are present in addition to the freedman of the individual making the divorce."[100]

Augustus passed two other major pieces of legislation removing the restrictions on marriage and encouraging parenthood: *Lex Julia de maritandis ordinibus* (18 BCE) and *Lex Papia Poppaea* (9 CE). A major focus of this and subsequent legislation was the dowry (*dos*). If the divorce was by mutual consent, the dowry went with the wife. If the husband repudiated his wife without cause, he forfeited all rights to the dowry. If, on the other hand, the wife was at fault (e.g., adultery) or there were children, part of the dowry remained with the husband.

In spite of Augustus' efforts, the divorce rate remained high and was a staple of the satirists and moralists. Seneca (4 BCE/1CE–65 CE) asked sarcastically, "Is there any woman who blushes at divorce (*repudium*) now that certain famous and high-standing women compute their years not by the number of consuls, but by their husbands and leave home to marry and marry to divorce?"[101] Granting the hyperbolic character of the moralist's jab, we must still conclude that the rate was high or there would have been no edge to his knife. On the other hand, we need to point out that divorce was not the ideal. Epitaphs praise women for their domesticity, including loyalty to their husbands.[102]

---

[100]*The Digest of Justinian*, 24.2.9. See Suetonius, *Aug.* 34.2.

[101]*Ben.* 3.16.2-3. See also Martial 6.7; Juvenal 6.142-48, 224-30. The sixth satire of Juvenal is "the largest single example of invective against women remaining from antiquity." See Amy Richlin, *The Garden of Priapus: Sexuality and Aggression in Roman Humor* (New Haven: Yale Univ. Press, 1983): 202-07, esp. 202.

[102]So Richard Lattimore, *Themes in Greek and Latin Epitaphs* (Urbana: Univ. of Illinois Press, 1942): 293-300 and the examples in Jane F. Gardner and Thomas Wiedemann, *The Roman Household: A Sourcebook* (London/New York: Routledge, 1991): 47-55 (nn. 51-59). Since these epitaphs were written by their husbands, they reflect a male perspective.

C. *Summary*. Women who lived under Greek law were thus more limited than their Roman counterparts in the late Republic and early Empire. Even so, the papyri suggest that the legal standing of Greek women increased. This expansion is also evident in the NT. There are three different versions of Jesus' logion on divorce: 1) 1 Cor. 7:10-11, 2) Mk. 10:11-12; Matt. 19:9, and 3) Matt. 5:32; Lk. 16:18). The latter version pre-supposes that only a man may divorce his wife. This is in keeping with the general practice among Jews in Palestine and probably represents the language but not the position of the historical Jesus who forbade all divorce.[103] The Pauline and Markan versions both presume the right of a woman to divorce her husband. This reflects, in all likelihood, an application of the dominical logion to the larger world where women could initiate divorce.

5. Adulthood

A. *Motherhood*. The most important role of a woman in Greek and Roman societies was to bear legitimate offspring. Tacitus wrote, "In the good old days, every citizen's son who was born of a chaste mother was brought up (*educabatur*) not in the chamber of a hired nurse, but on his mother's lap and breast." He explained, "Her greatest praise was to oversee the house and serve her children."[104] Among the Romans there were several famous mothers: Cornelia, the mother of the Gracchi; Aurelia, the mother of Caesar; Atia, the mother of Augustus; and Julia Procilla, the mother of Agricola.[105] Authors who mention these women

---

[103]The most important texts stipulating that only males may initiate divorce are Josephus, *AJ* 15.259 and *m. Yebam.* 14:1. There is a divorce document in which the wife apparently took the initiative among the finds at Wadi Murabba'at. See P. Benoit, ed., *Les grottes de Murabba'at* (DJD 2; Oxford: Clarendon, 1961): 2.108, ll. 7-8. For a different assessment, see Bernadette Brooten, "Konnten Frauen im alten Judentum die Scheidung betreiben?" *EvT* 42 (1982): 65-80.

[104]*Dial.* 28. See also *Germ.* 20, where he praises German mothers who breastfeed their offspring themselves.

[105]Tacitus, *Dial.* 28 and *Agric.* 4.

often do so with a sense of nostalgia, looking back to an age where virtue was lived, not praised. Therefore, we should read statements about these women as idealistic descriptions.

The paragon of Roman motherhood was Cornelia.[106] The second daughter of Scipio Africanus (236-184/83 BCE), the conqueror of Hannibal, Cornelia married Tiberius Sempronius Gracchus, with whom she had twelve children. Although only three of these survived to adulthood, two of her sons became famous: Tiberius and Gaius Gracchus. She turned down a marriage proposal by one of the Ptolemies in order to devote herself to her children.[107] For such efforts, she earned the praise of later generations. Plutarch said, "She raised those who survived so carefully that although they were admittedly the most naturally gifted of all Romans, they appeared to owe their virtue more to training than to nature."[108]   This portrait provides a useful picture of a mother who trained her children.

Cornelia was by no means the only mother credited with providing her children a fine education. All of the mothers mentioned above were singled out for their educational roles. We also have examples of women in this role who were contemporaries with the writers. In his efforts to console his mother for his exile, Seneca imagined Helvia asking, "Where are the studies in which I participated more readily than a woman and more intimately than a mother normally does?"[109] *In nuce*, the ideal Roman mother was a firm disciplinarian who trained her children in the ideals of Rome.[110]

---

[106]Some of the most important *testimonia* include: Cicero, *Brut.* 211; Seneca, *Cons. Helv.* 16; Quintilian, *Inst.* 1.1.6; Tacitus, *Dial.* 28. She appears in the Greek tradition in Plutarch, *TG* 1.2-5; *CG* 19.1-3. See Fant, *Women's Life in Greece and Rome*, 146-149, 204.

[107]Plutarch, *TG* 1.4.

[108]Plutarch, *TG* 1.5. See also Cicero, *Brut.* 211.

[109]*Cons. Helv.* 15.1.

[110]This is the thesis of Suzanne Dixon, *The Roman Mother* (Norman: Univ. of Oklahoma Press, 1988), who bases it partly on a Roman wife's right to dispose of her own property.

This was not limited to Roman women with high social status. Plutarch, for instance, mentions an illiterate Illyrian woman (Euridike) who learned to read as an adult in order to educate her children.[111] The papyri furnish examples of mothers who took active roles in making arrangements for their children's education.[112] It, therefore, does not come as a surprise to find the following advice for young widows in the NT: "I wish that younger widows would marry, have children, and manage their houses . . . ."[113]

B. *Occupations*. The traditional occupation for Greek and Roman women within the home was weaving their family's clothes. Even Augustus saw to it that his daughter and granddaughters were taught weaving.[114] Some women, however, earned incomes. In Asia, for example, there is epigraphic evidence for female physicians from the first century CE and onward.[115] Lefkowitz and Fant collected epitaphs for freedwomen and slave women in Rome from the first century BCE to the second century CE which include the following occupations: seven examples of midwives;[116] six examples of physicians;[117] three examples each for pedagogues, wool-weighers, seamstresses, hairdressers; and one each for stenographer, secretary, dressmaker, weaver, fish dealer, grain and vegetable dealer, portress, attendant, and a slave of a slave.[118] Wet-nurses[119] and

---

[111]*Mor.* 14b-c.

[112]E.g., *P. Oxy.* 930. See Hunt and Edgar, *Select Papyri*, 130 (1:334-35).

[113]1 Tim. 5:14.

[114]Suetonius, *Aug.* 64.2.

[115]Pleket, *Epigraphica* 12 (Tlos, Lycia, 1st cent. CE), 20 (Pergamum, 2nd cent. CE), 26 (Neoclaudopolis, Asia, 2nd-3rd centuries CE). ET in Fant, *Women's Life in Greece and Rome*, 170-71, 175.

[116]Fant, *Women's Life in Greece and Rome*, 177.

[117]*Ibid.*, 172-74.

[118]*Ibid.*, 183. See also the evidence for occupations among the women in the imperial household on p. 182.

[119]Soranos of Ephesus (*fl.* 98-138 CE), who studied in Alexandria and practiced in Rome, devoted a large section of book one

painters[120] also occur. Egyptian papyri indicate that women
worked in clothing, food-preparation, and wet-nursing
industries.[121] This evidence does not mean that these were
independent professional women. Many worked at home or
with their husband as Priskilla did with Aquila (Acts 18:2-
3). Perhaps the closest analogue to an independent woman
in the ancient world was the *hetaira*.[122]

Another way to approach the status of women in
financial matters is to address their legal rights. The
Athenian orator Isaios (c. 420-350 BCE) bluntly stated the
economic options for a woman in classical Athens: "For the
law expressly forbids the legal right of a child or woman to
enter a contract (for anything worth) more than a bushel of
barley."[123] The epigraphic material sustains this claim: there
is very little evidence of women entering into major transactions—even with a κύριος. The same is true for Hellenistic
Athens. However, once we move elsewhere, the picture
changes. There are a number of inscriptions which present
women transacting business, e.g., they manumitted slaves
and entered contractual relationships.[124] The Egyptian
papyri likewise furnish examples of women transacting

---

of his *Gynaikeia* to the topic of wet-nurses. See Fant, *Women's Life in
Greece and Rome*, 178.

[120]Pliny, *HN* 35.40.

[121]See Pomeroy, *Women in Hellenistic Egypt*, 160-73. See also
Hunt and Edgar, *Select Papyri*, 16 (1:46-51).

[122]On prostitutes in Athens and Greek literature see Roger Just,
Women in Athenian Law and Life (London/New York: Routledge,
1989): 52-53, 64-66 and Josephine Massyngbaerde Ford, "The 'Call
girl' in Antiquity and her Potential for Mission," *Proceedings of the
Eastern Great Lakes and Midwest Biblical Societies* 12 (1992): 105-16.
Thomas A. J. McGinn has dealt with some of the issues relating to
prostitutes in the Roman world in "Prostitution and Julio-Claudian
Legislation: The Formation of Social Policy in Early Imperial Rome,"
(Ph.D. dissertation; Univ. of Michigan, 1986) and "The Taxation of
Roman Prostitutes," *Helios* 16 (1989): 79-110.

[123]10.10. See Fant, *Women's Life in Greece and Rome*, 70.

[124]Pomeroy, *Goddesses, Whores, Wives, and Slaves*, 130.

business.[125] The difficulty we have in assessing this evidence is that most of the data we have for sites other than Athens comes from the Hellenistic world. We do not know if conditions changed or if women always had more economic rights in these locales. Κύριοι are common in these inscriptions, but it is not clear whether they are functional or fictional. Greek women in Egypt could opt to follow Egyptian law, which did not require a κύριος.[126] Whether the κύριος was a vestigial reminder of a former system or an essential legal figure, women did engage in significant business transactions in the Hellenistic world.

C. *Benefactors.* Some of these women became wealthy enough to become public benefactors and receive honorary inscriptions from communities. For example, Junia Theodora, a Roman citizen in Corinth, was honored by the Lykioi of Asia Minor c. 43 CE for her benefactions to their citizens.[127] In the Greek East, the honorary inscriptions praised women benefactors for both their munificence and their virtues as wives and mothers. In Roman Italy, inscriptions concentrate more on the former. The importance of these inscriptions is that they demonstrate the presence of women who controlled significant sums of money and who used those funds for public purposes–a role previously restricted to men.[128] In the NT, Luke-Acts repeatedly presents women in the role of benefactors to the Christian community: the women who supported Jesus in his ministry

---

[125]Hunt and Edgar, *Select Papyri*, provide examples of business contracts (16, 18, 19, 20), as well as real estate transactions (27 [sale], 41 and 354 [lease]). Pomeroy, *Women in Hellenistic Egypt*, 148-60, has a helpful discussion of women's ownership of land.

[126]See David M. Schaps, *Economic Rights of Women in Ancient Greece* (Edinburgh: Edinburgh Univ. Press, 1979): esp. 96-98, and Sealy, *Women and Law in Classical Greece*, 38, 89-95.

[127]Pleket, *Epigraphica*, 8.

[128]The two most important treatments of women in honorary inscriptions are Riet Van Bremen, "Women and Wealth," *Images of Women in Antiquity*, 223-42, and Elizabeth P. Forbis, "Women's Public Image in Italian Honorary Inscriptions," *AJP* 111 (1990): 493-512.

(Lk. 8:2-3; 23:55-56), Mary who opened her home to the Jerusalem community (Acts 12:12), Lydia who was the patron for the church in Philippi (Acts 16:14-15, 40), and Priskilla who with her husband was a significant figure in Corinth and Ephesus (Acts 18:2-3, 26). The author made it a point to note women of substance.[129] The same pattern is present in the Pauline corpus. Paul called Phoebe a "benefactor" of the church in Cenchreae (Rom. 16:2). Similarly, Paul or one of his disciples urged the Colossians to greet "Nympha and the church in her house."[130] While it would be a mistake to think that Phoebe, Lydia, Nympha, and other female Christian patrons enjoyed the same status in society as the women who were honored with inscriptions, they were women of substance who stood in an analogous relationship to the churches they assisted as their wealthier counterparts did to the communities who received their benefactions.

D. *Limitations.* There were, however, limits to the public roles women could take. The greatest initial challenge to the traditional roles was the gauntlet thrown down by the Hellenistic queens–women like the Ptolemaic queens Arsinoë II (c. 316-270 BCE), Berenike II (c. 273-221 BCE), and Kleopatra VII (69-30 BCE).[131] The public roles of these

---

[129]Acts 17:4, 12, 34. See also 13:50.

[130]Col. 4:15. There are two problems which complicate the understanding of this verse. First, it is not clear whether Nympha is a name for a male (Nymphas as an abbreviation for Nymphadoros) or a female. Second, the manuscript tradition has several different pronouns in the following phrase ("in her house" [B]; "in his house" [D]; "in their house" [‎‎א]). The feminine has the strongest claim to be the original reading. Both the plural and the masculine look like attempts to replace the feminine with a masculine name. It is hard to see why a scribe would replace the masculine or plural pronoun with a feminine pronoun when the masculine form of the name Nymphas was a clear option. Therefore, I consider the feminine (her house) to be original and understand Nympha to be a woman's name.

[131]See Grace Harriet Macurdy, *Hellenistic Queens: A Study of Woman-Power in Macedonia, Seleucid Syria and Ptolemaic Egypt* (Baltimore: Johns Hopkins Univ. Press, 1932), and Pomeroy, *Women in Hellenistic Egypt*, 3-40.

women set a precedent for other women of the aristocracy
and much the same was true for Roman women. The
leading women of Roman society set a pattern for wealthy
women outside of the inner circles in Rome.[132] Their ability
to influence public affairs was, however, limited in a very
significant way: generally, women did not address public
assemblies. To be sure, there are some exceptions to this
practice, e.g., the famous speech of Hortensia in 42 BCE
when she argued against the imposition of a tax on herself
and the other wealthy women of Rome.[133] Such speeches
were, however, not the rule. The norm was that women
could be seen in public, but not heard. Women exercised
their influence through men and not over them.[134] It is,
therefore, not surprising to find injunctions in the NT which
attempt to impose silence on women in public assemblies (1
Cor. 14:34-36; 1 Tim. 2:9-15).

6. The Philosophical Tradition

There were, however, voices which challenged the
traditional assessments of women. Some of the most significant came from within the philosophical tradition.[135]

---

[132]See Ramsay MacMullen, "Women in Public in the Roman
Empire," *Historia* 29 (1980): 208-18. The leading women during the
Trajanic and Hadrianic periods did not, however, exercise much
autonomy. See Mary T. Boatwright, "The Imperial Women of the
Early Second Century A.D.," *AJP* 112 (1991): 513-40.

[133]Quintilian 1.1.6; Appian *BC* 4.33. See Stephen J. Simon,
"Women Who Pleaded Causes Before the Roman Magistrates,"
Classical Bulletin 66 (1990): 79-81.

[134]So Mary Lefkowitz, "Influential Women," *Images of Women
in Antiquity*, 49-64, esp. 55-56.

[135]See Gilles Ménage, *The History of Women Philosophers*
(trans. and intro. B. Zedler; New York: Univ. Press of America, 1984
[1960[1]]), an uncritical but useful collection of sixty-five women philosophers in antiquity modeled on the work of Diogenes Laertios; J. M.
Rist, *Human Value: A Study in Ancient Philosophical Ethics* (Leiden:
Brill, 1982): 133-41, a brief but helpful overview; Mary Ellen Waithe,
ed., *A History of Women Philosophers 1:   Ancient Women
Philosophers 699 B.C.-500 A.D.* (Dordrecht: Martinus Nijhoff, 1987),
the best comprehensive treatment; Ethel M. Kersey, ed., *Women*

A. *Plato.* Plato (429-347 BCE) launched the discussion in book five of the *Republic*. Drawing inspiration from the practices of Sparta, but going beyond them, Sokrates argues, "There is then no task of those who administer the state that belongs to a woman because she is a woman nor to a man because he is a man; rather the natures are similarly distributed in both living beings." He concludes, "A woman participates in all tasks according to nature as does a man; however, in everything a woman is weaker than a man."[136] If there are to be both male and female guardians, both must receive the same training.[137] The final step in this argument is that wives and children are to be held in common.[138] Plato's assessment, therefore, appears to be paradoxical: on the one hand, he assigns equal roles and training to women; on the other, he clearly states that they are weaker than men. Complicating the discussion even more is the fact that this is a discussion about the guardian class, the highest class in Plato's ideal state.[139] The best explanation of this paradox is that Plato's views of women are not driven by a concern for women per se, but from a political perspective.[140] He is not as interested in bringing *women* into the state as he is in

---

Philosophers: A Bio-Critical Source Book (New York: Grunwood, 1989), a collection arranged in alphabetical order of women philosophers from antiquity to 1920; and Snyder, *The Woman and the Lyre*, 99-121.

[136]*Rep.* 455d. See also 451c-456a and *Men.* 71e-73c.

[137]*Rep.* 456c. See also 456b-457b and *Leg.* 804c-806c.

[138]*Rep.* 457c-461e.

[139]Rist, *Human Value*, 27-28, 133-34, questions whether Plato would extend his policies here to all groups.

[140]So Sarah Pomeroy, "Feminism in Book V of Plato's *Republic*," *Apeiron* 8 (1974): 33-35, and her treatment in *Goddesses, Whores, Wives, and Slaves*, 115-19, where she attributes Plato's emancipation of women to his elimination of private property. See also Julia Annas, "Plato's *Republic* and Feminism," *Philosophy* 51 (1976): 307-21 and Susan Moller Okin, *Women in Western Political Thought* (Princeton: Princeton Univ. Press, 1979): 15-70. *Contra* Harry Lesser, "Plato's Feminism," *Philosophy* 54 (1979): 113-17, and Dorothea Wender, "Plato: Misogynist, Paedophile, and Feminist," *Arethusa* 6 (1973): 75-90, who states the paradox forcefully and argues Sokrates was the source of Plato's feminism (82-85).

bringing the *state* to women.[141] This does not, however, negate the fact that Plato assigned a much more significant role to women than did his contemporaries. There is some evidence that this is more than theoretical. Diogenes Laertios tells us that Plato had two women disciples: Lastheneia of Mantinea and Axiothea of Phias, although the latter disguised herself in male attire.[142] The best-known female Platonist was the much later Hypatia, who was active in Alexandria (370-415 CE).[143]

B. *Aristotle.* Plato's most famous pupil had a different understanding. In the first book of his *Politics*, Aristotle treated the family as the smallest unit of the state. He argued that the superiority of the male made him a fit ruler over slaves, females, and children. He stated bluntly, "So stands the male in relation to the female on the basis of nature: he is superior, she is inferior; he is the ruler, she is the ruled."[144] He extended this distinction to their participation in virtue. The male possesses complete intellectual virtue, while slaves, females, and children have only a share of it which is appropriate to their subordinate roles. The same is true of moral virtues: "the same self-control does not belong to a woman and a man, nor the same courage or justice, as Sokrates thought;[145] rather the one is the courage to rule, the other courage to submit."[146] He did, however, argue that women should be educated on the basis of the common good of the state.[147]

---

[141]*Leg.* 780d-781d.

[142]3.46. See n. 60 above.

[143]See J. M. Rist, "Hypatia," *Phoenix* 19 (1965): 214-25; Snyder, *The Woman and the Lyre*, 113-20; and Waithe, "Hypatia of Alexandria," in *A History of Women Philosophers*, 1:169-95.

[144]*Pol.* 1254b. See also 1259a, 1260a; *NE* 1160b.

[145]*Men.* 71e-73c.

[146]*Pol.* 1260a. See also 1259b-1260a.

[147]*Pol.* 1260b. For analyses of Aristotle's view see Okin, *Women in Western Political Thought*, 73-96 and Stephen R. L. Clark, "Aristotle's Woman," *History of Political Thought* 3 (1982): 177-91.

C. *Epicureans.* One of the first Hellenistic schools to include women was the Epicurean. Epikouros (341-270 BCE) formed close connections with Themista, the wife of Leonteos,[148] but his relationships to the *hetairai*, associated with his garden in Athens (306-270 BCE), are more famous. These included the well-known Leontion, who earned the praise of Cicero for her work against Theophrastos, Aristotle's successor,[149] as well as the lesser known Boidion, Demetria, Mammarion, Hedeia, Erotion, and Nikidion.[150] Their presence in the garden and Epikouros' own ethical views led to exaggerated charges by opponents. Important for our purposes is the fact that Epikouros accepted women for their philosophical abilities. His views did not always have authority for his future disciples—at least not in the case of Lucretius (c. 94-55 BCE).[151]

D. *Cynics.* A much more radical approach appears among the Cynics.[152] The first Cynic, Diogenes (c. 400-c. 325 BCE), preferring nature (φύσις) to convention (νόμος),[153] advocated common wives. He held that "there was no marriage except for the man who persuades and the woman who is persuaded to embrace sexually."[154] One of his

---

[148]Diogenes Laertios 10.5. See J. M. Rist, *Epicurus: An Introduction* (Cambridge: Cambridge Univ. Press, 1972): 1-13, esp. 7, 10-11, and Snyder, *The Woman and the Lyre*, 101-05.

[149]Diogenes Laertios 10.5. See Cicero, *ND* 1.93, and Pliny *NH praef.* 29.

[150]They are mentioned in Philodemos, *P. Hercul.* 1005 v.15-17; Plutarch, *Mor.* 1097d, 1089c; and Diogenes Laertios 10.7. It is possible that Mammarion, Hedeia, Nikidion, and Boidion are the same women mentioned in inscriptions to healing gods at the time Epikouros founded the School. See Catherine J. Castner, "Epicurean Hetairai As Dedicants to Healing Deities?," *GRBS* 23 (1982): 51-57.

[151]Jane Snyder, "Lucretius and the Status of Women," *Classical Bulletin* 53 (1976): 17-20.

[152]Diogenes Laertios 6.13 credits his teacher, Antisthenes, with the statement, "Virtue is the same for a man and a woman."

[153]E.g., Diogenes Laertios 6.38.

[154]Diogenes Laertios 6.72. See J. M. Rist, *Stoic Philosophy* (Cambridge: Cambridge Univ. Press, 1969): 60.

disciples, Krates (c. 365-285 BCE), married one of his own students, Hipparchia. According to Diogenes Laertios, "after she adopted the same form of appearance, she used to go around with her husband, publicly engage in sexual embrace, and go out to dinners."[155] Apparently some Cynics not only argued for the equality of women, but at times actually practiced it by deliberately shattering the norms of society. Krates and Hipparchia became the author and recipient of pseudonymous correspondence dating from the first and second centuries CE.[156] In these letters, the husband tells his wife that she is by nature equal to him: "Women are not inferior to men by nature,"[157] and "for you are not inferior to us by nature."[158] He urges her to give up the standard duties of a woman for the pursuit of philosophy,[159] indicating that Cynic ideals were not lost.

E. *Stoics.* The Cynic's more respectable offspring, the Stoics, held different views on women. The founders of the Stoa, Zeno (335-262 BCE) and Chrysippos (280-207 BCE), shared Diogenes' position that wives should be held in common.[160] The former also argued that men and women should wear the same apparel.[161] His immediate successor,

---

[155]Diogenes Laertios 6.97. See Snyder, *The Woman and the Lyre*, 105-08.

[156]Abraham J. Malherbe, ed., *The Cynic Epistles: A Study Edition* (SBLSBS 12; Missoula, MT: Scholars Press, 1977): nn. 1, 28, 29, 30, 31, 32, 33. See also the letter from Diogenes (n. 3). There are other letters from Diogenes addressed to women: Olympias (n. 4) and Melesippe (n. 42). In another group, women are the authors: Xanthippe to several Sokratics (n. 21) and Arete to several Sokratics (n. 27). Stories about Sokrates and Xanthippe are less than flattering. For a Cynic account, see Teles 18h-20h, in Edward O'Neil, *Teles [The Cynic Teacher]* (SBLTTS 2; Missoula, MT: Scholars Press, 1977).

[157]Malherbe, *Cynic Epistles*, n. 28.

[158]*Ibid.*, n. 29.

[159]*Ibid.*, nn. 30, 32.

[160]Diogenes Laertios 7.131. On Zeno's view of sexuality, see Rist, *Stoic Philosophy*, 65-68. According to Diogenes, he was sensitive to the charge of misogyny (7.13).

[161]Diogenes Laertios 7.33.

Kleanthes (331-232 BCE), was said to have written a work defending the thesis that virtue is the same in both men and women.[162] The need to educate women became a common position of the Stoics.[163]

The radical views of the early Stoa did not, however, pass intact to the middle and later Stoa. We can illustrate the late period through four representatives of the first and second centuries CE. Seneca (c. 4 BCE-65 CE), the Roman philosopher and statesman, presents the tension between continuity and transition clearly. In good old Stoic fashion, he wrote to Marcia: "Who, however, has said that nature dealt stingily with the constitution of women and confined their virtues to a narrow sphere? Believe me, they have equal power and equal capacity for moral integrity, if they want . . ."[164] In a similar vein, he expressed regret that his father's old-fashioned severity had curtailed his mother's philosophical interests and he encouraged her to return to them.[165] In contrast to the norms of the ancient world, Seneca thought that husbands and wives should practice the same sexual mores.[166] On the other hand, Seneca regularly uses the adjective "feminine" (*muliebris*) in opposition to virtue. For example, he began his consolation of Marcia with the statement, "If I did not know that you, Marcia, had withdrawn so far from the weakness of the feminine mind (*ab infirmitate muliebria animi*) as from the rest of the vices . . . I would not dare to oppose your grief."[167] Such state-ments–they are not infrequent–are in clear tension with his affirmations of equality. The old Stoa has been merged with more conventional standards.[168]

---

[162]Diogenes Laertios 7.175.

[163]Ioannes von Arnim, *Stoicorum Veterum Fragmenta* (Leipzig: B. G. Teubner, 1905-24): 3.253-254.

[164]Seneca, *Cons. Marc.* 16.1.

[165]Seneca, *Cons. Helv.* 17.3-5.

[166]Seneca, *Ep. 94.26.*

[167]Seneca, *Cons. Marc.* 1.1. See also *Cons. Helv.* 14.2.

[168]Charles Favez, "Les Opinions de Sénèque sur la Femme," *Revue des Études Latines* 16 (1938): 335-45, thought that the contra-

This is even more evident in the works of Epiktetos (c. 55-c. 135 CE). The former slave addressed directly the principle of the old Stoa: "Are not women common by nature?" Of course, he replied. They are common in the same way that food at a banquet is common: it belongs to all of the guests, but each is only to enjoy the assigned portion.[169] Rather than emphasizing the similar nature of male and female, Epiktetos accentuated their difference: males should have beards, females should be smooth.[170]

Another second-century Stoic who demonstrates conventional wisdom is Hierokles (fl. 117-38 CE). Best known for his comments on the *Haustafel*, he made the following assignments: "To the man should be assigned matters relating to the field, marketplace, and city; to the woman matters relating to spinning and food-preparation, and, generally speaking, the matters relating to the house." He goes on, however, to qualify this: "Nor is it fitting for each to be unexperienced in the work of the other . . . . For in this way, they would solidify even more their partnership, if they share in one another's necessary concerns."[171]

---

diction was not absolute, but that the severe statements about women were due to the fact that Seneca placed women in the same category as the ignorant. They could improve their situation through philosophy. C. E. Manning, "Seneca and the Stoics on the Equality of the Sexes," *Mnemosyne* 26 (1973): 170-77, argued that the development of the concept of καθήκοντα or *officia* led the Stoics of the late period to accept a more conventional assessment, i.e., what was appropriate for a man is different than what is appropriate for a woman, even though both are equal by nature. Anna Lydia Motto, "Seneca on Women's Liberation," *Classical World* 65 (1971-72): 155-57, places too much weight on the evidence for equality.

[169] 2.4.8-11. See also F 15, where he mentions Plato's *Republic* in this connection. In 3.7.21, he argues that a man should find only his wife attractive.

[170] 1.16.9-14; 3.1.27-35.

[171] Stobaeos 4.28.21. See ET in A. J. Malherbe, *Moral Exhortation: A Greco-Roman Sourcebook* (Philadelphia: Westminster, 1986): 85-104.

Not all Stoics followed this line. The most impressive exception is Musonios Rufus (c. 30-c. 100 CE). In one of the most remarkable statements advocating equal training preserved from the ancient world, Epiktetos' teacher said:

> As for reason, women . . . have received from the gods the same reason as men, which we use in dealing with one another and by which we consider each thing whether it is good or bad, right or shameful. Similarly, with regard to sense-perception capabilities, the female has the same sense-perceptions as the male: sight, hearing, smelling, and the others. Similarly, the parts of the body are the same for each: neither has more than the other. Further, a desire and natural propensity for virtue is not only in men, but also in women. Women no less than men are by nature pleased with good and just deeds and inclined to reject the opposite. Since these things are true, why would it ever be proper for men to inquire and examine how to live well–this is what philosophy is–but not women?[172]

He was aware that his case would not pass unchallenged. Using the diatribe, he addressed his interlocutors:

> But by Zeus, some say that it is inevitable that women who associate with philosophers will be self-willed for the most part and arrogant when they abandon their duties at home and spend their time with men practicing discourses, speaking subtly, and analyzing syllogisms. They ought to be at home spinning! I would not expect that the women who practise philosophy–any more than the men–would abandon their appropriate tasks to deal only with discourses; rather, I maintain that whatever

---

[172]F 3. See O. Hense, ed., *Musonii Rufi Reliquae* (Leipzig: B. G. Teubner, 1905), and Cora E. Lutz, "Musonius Rufus: The Roman Socrates," *Yale Classical Studies* 10 (1947): 3-147.

discourses they pursue ought to be about the deeds
they pursue.[173]

On another occasion, he advocated training for daughters as
well as sons. Unlike Aristotle's view of virtue, he said:

> In the case of humans, there seems to be a perceived
> need for the males to have something special in
> training and education but not for females, as if it
> were not necessary for the same virtues to be in both
> in the same way, in man and woman, or that it was
> possible to arrive at the same virtues not through the
> same training but through different training. That
> there are not some virtues for a man and others for a
> woman is easy to recognize.[174]

He goes on to argue that the only real difference is in the
strength of each. A male is stronger and should therefore be
assigned the heavier tasks; a woman is weaker and should
receive the lighter duties. In matters of virtue, however,
there is no distinction. Both should have the same training.

> If someone asks me what branch of knowledge is in
> charge of this training, I will say to him that just as
> no man is properly educated without philosophy,
> neither would any woman be. I do not mean that it is
> necessary for clarity and extraordinary skill in
> argumentation to be present in women, since they
> practise philosophy as women–neither do I praise
> this all that much in men–but because it is necessary
> for women to acquire goodness of character and
> nobility of conduct. After all, philosophy is the
> cultivation of nobility and nothing else.[175]

It comes as no surprise that Musonios advocated
identical standards of sexual behavior for women and

173F 3.
174F 4.
175F 4.

men.[176] His views appear to move away from the conventional views of women to a position much closer to Plato.[177] He differed from Plato by applying explicitly his views to all women and not just to an elite group.

F. *Pythagoreans.* Women are commonly mentioned among the Pythagoreans. Diogenes Laertios relates the tradition from Hermippos that when Pythagoras (sixth-fifth centuries BCE) came to Italy, he spent some time in a cave. Later, he claimed that he had visited Hades. Men were so affected that they sent their wives to study with him, becoming known as "Pythagorean women."[178] Diogenes goes on to introduce Pythagoras' wife, Theano, and daughter, Damo.[179] Disregarding the legendary character of this story, there is little doubt that women were associated with the Pythagoreans. Figures within Middle and New Comedy lampooned them, e.g., Kratinos the Younger (fourth cent. BCE) and Alexis (c. 375-275 BCE) each wrote works entitled *Pythagorean Woman.*[180] When Iamblichos (c. 250-c. 325 CE) listed the known Pythagoreans, he included the names of seventeen women.[181] Whether the Pythagoreans actually had communities along the lines Iamblichos describes is a matter of dispute.[182] What is certain is that there were women among the adherents of Pythagoras.

---

[176]F 12. See A. C. van Geytenbeek, *Musonius Rufus and Greek Diatribe* (Wijsgerige Teksten en Studies 8; Assen: Van Gorcum, 1963): 51-77.

[177]Geytenbeek, *Musonius Rufus and Greek Diatribe*, 54-56, argues that Musonios was influenced by Plato.

[178]Diogenes Laertios 8.41.

[179]Diogenes Laertios 8.42.

[180]John M. Edmonds, *The Fragments of Attic Comedy: After Meineke, Bergk, and Kock (Augmented, Newly Edited with Their Contexts, Annotated, and Completely Translated into English Verse)* (Leiden: Brill, 1957-61): 2.4-5, 468-71.

[181]*VP* 267. See ET in John Dillon and Jackson Hershbell, *Iamblichus* On the Pythagorean Way of Life: *Text, Translation, and Notes* (SBLTT 29; Atlanta: Scholars Press, 1991).

[182]See Dillon and Hershbell, *Iamblichus*, 14-16. References in Middle and New Comedy which suggest the possibility of communities

Perhaps the most significant development is the presence of a group of tractates and letters attributed to women authors. These texts date from different centuries within the Hellenistic and Roman periods.[183] There are at least twenty-three works ascribed to six different women. I am very skeptical that these tractates and letters were actually written by women for two reasons. First, the names of the authors are the names of famous women within the philosophical tradition, e.g., Arignote, a daughter of Pythagoras;[184] Myia, a daughter of Pythagoras;[185] Periktione, the mother of Plato;[186] Phintys, a daughter of Pythagoras;[187] and Theano, the wife or a daughter of Pythagoras.[188] While it is possible that parents in the Hellenistic world named their daughters after these women, I think it probable that they are pseudonyms. Second, the perspective of the tractates and letters is conventional; women philosophers were anything but conventional. A

---

include the jabs of Antiphates, Alexis (*the Tarentines*), and Aristophon (*the Pythagoreaner*). For the fragments, see Edmonds, *The Fragments of Attic Comedy*, 2.282-85, 478-81, 524-27.

[183]See Holger Thesleff, *The Pythagorean Texts of the Hellenistic Period* (Acta Academiae Aboensis, Series A: Humaniora 30.1; Åbo: Åbo Akademi, 1965); idem, *An Introduction to the Pythagorean Writings of the Hellenistic Period* (Åbo: Åbo Akademi, 1961): 30-116, and the treatments of the specific letters in Alfons Städele, *Die Briefe des Pythagoras und der Pythagoreer* (Beiträge zur klassischen Philologie 115; Meisenhiem: A. Hain, 1980): 251-353. For ET of some of these texts, see Malherbe, *Moral Exhortation*, 82-85, Kenneth Guthrie and Thomas Taylor, *The Pythagorean Writings: Hellenistic Texts from the 1st Cent. B.C.-3rd Cent. A.D.* (Kew Gardens, NY: Selene Books, 1986): 70-75; and Waithe and Vicki Lynn Harper, *A History of Women Philosophers*, 1:11-58, who also provide discussions. See also Pomeroy, *Women in Hellenistic Egypt*, 61-71, and Snyder, *The Woman and the Lyre*, 108-13.

[184]Porphery, *VP* 4.

[185]*Ibid.*

[186]Diogenes Laertios 3.1. See K. von Fritz, "Periktione," *PW* 19.1 (1937): 794.

[187]Stobaios 4.23.61. Cf, however, Iamblichos, *VP* 267, who mentions a Phintys, the daughter of Theophrios.

[188]See Diogenes Laertios 8.42, and Suidas, *Theano* 2.

case can be made that these documents represent the inter-section of conventional views with women philosophers; however, I think it more likely that most are the compositions of males writing under female pseudonyms for the "benefit" of women adherents.[189] Even so, these documents attest the presence of a significant group of women within Pythagorean circles.

The works deal with specific areas of concern to women: virtue for a woman,[190] child-raising,[191] apparel,[192] advice on how to deal with a faithless husband,[193] and how to handle maids.[194] Two examples dealing with the husband-wife relationship will illustrate the nature of these documents. The first is Theano's letter to Euridike.[195]

> Theano to admirable Euridike. What grief occupies your soul? You are despondent for no other reason than the fact that the man you live with goes to a *hetaira* and finds pleasure of the body with her. You shouldn't feel this way, admirable woman. For don't you see that the ear when it is filled with the pleasure from the musical instruments and is full of musical songs, that when satiety comes from these, it loves the flute and gladly listens to the reed? And yet what does a flute have to do with musical strings and

---

[189]So also K. von Fritz, "Periktione," *PW* (1937): 795; *contra* Pomeroy, *Women in Hellenistic Egypt*, 64 and Waithe, "Authenticating the Fragments and Letters," in *A History of Women Philosophers*, 1:59-74, who argues that the letters embody the ideas of the named authors.

[190]Periktione, *On the Harmony of a Woman*; Phintys, *On the Moderation of a Woman*; Theano, *Feminine Exhortations*.

[191]Myia, *Letter to Phyllis*; Theano, *Letter to Eubule*.

[192]Melissa, *Letter to Kleareta*; Theano, *Letter to Eubule*.

[193]Theano, *Letter to Eurydike*, *Letter to Nikostrate*.

[194]Theano, *Letter to Kallisto*.

[195]See Thesleff, *The Pythagorean Texts of the Hellenistic Period*, 197. The translation is mine. See Städele, *Die Briefe des Pythagoras und der Pythagoreer*, 335-41. Note an ET in Snyder, *The Woman and the Lyre*, 110-11.

with the admirable sound of honey-sweet quality of a musical instrument? In this way you should think of yourself and the *hetaira* with whom your husband lives. For your husband will think of you from habit, nature, and reason, but whenever he receives his fill (of these), he will live with the *hetaira* for a while. Because in those in whom[196] a destructive juice is stored up, there is a certain desire for foods that are not good.

Although this text does not indicate explicitly what sexual standards apply to the wife, it recognizes double standards that are explicit in other texts within this corpus, e.g., Periktione's treatise, *On the Harmony of a Woman*.[197]

She ought to live with her own husband lawfully and honorably, considering nothing as her own property, but keeping and guarding their marriage-bed since everything depends on this. She should endure everything with respect to her husband: if misfortune befalls him; if he makes a mistake through ignorance, distress, or drunkenness; if he lives with other women. For this fault (ἁμαρτίη) is permitted to men, but not at all for women for whom there is a penalty. She ought to keep the law and not by pretense. She ought also to endure his anger, tight control of money, faultfinding, jealousy, abusive language, and any other fault he may have from his nature. She will prudently do everything as it pleases him. For a wife who is dear to her husband and acts honorably toward him is in harmony.

---

[196]Städele, *Die Briefe des Pythagoras und der Pythagoreer*, 180, emends οἷς to αἷς and translates: "Denn auch für diejenigen Speisen, in denen ein verderbenbringender Saft enthalten ist, gibt es eine gewisse Vorliebe von seiten der Leute, die nicht gut sind."

[197]See Thesleff, *The Pythagorean Texts of the Hellenistic Period*, 144 (142-45 for the full text). See ET in Guthrie and Taylor, *The Pythagorean Writings*, 73 (72-74 for the full text).

G. *Summary*. This philosophical material is evident in the *Haustafeln* (Eph. 5:22-6:9; Col. 3:18-4:1; Titus 2:1-10; 1 Pet. 2:13-3:12) and moral instruction of the NT. Household codes took their impetus from Aristotle and became popular among Stoics.[198] When reading NT household codes, we are reading conventional views of popular moral philosophy modified through early Christian reflection. The alterations do not lie in the exhortations as much as they do in the rationale offered, e.g., "Wives submit yourselves to your husbands, *as is proper in the Lord*" (Col. 3:18).

7. Religion

The sphere where women enjoyed the greatest degree of public freedom in the Hellenistic and Roman worlds was religion. The evidence for their participation in religion is extensive.[199]

A. *Priestesses and Prophetesses*. Religion was the one state-sanctioned sphere where women were allowed to take leading public roles throughout this period. Among the Greeks, the priestesses/prophetesses at Delphi were famous. Diodoros Sikelos (1st cent. BCE) related the legend of the origin of the oracle. A herdsman noticed that his goats began leaping around in an extraordinary fashion after peering into a chasm. Soon word spread and people found that the chasm had the same effect on them.

---

[198]David L. Balch, *Let Wives Be Submissive: The Domestic Code in 1 Peter* (SBLMS 26; Chico, CA: Scholars Press, 1981), has demonstrated the importance of Aristotle for the development of the *Haustafel* in three pairs of relationships (master/slave, husband/wife, father/children) and the subsequent influence of his views.

[199]See especially Ross S. Kraemer, *Maenads, Martyrs, Matrons, Monastics: A Sourcebook on Women's Religions in the Greco-Roman World* (Philadelphia: Fortress, 1988) and *idem., Her Share of the Blessings: Women's Religions among Pagans, Jews, and Christians in the Greco-Roman World* (Oxford/New York: Oxford Univ. Press, 1992). See also Fant, *Women's Lives in Greece and Rome*, 113-28, 242-47; and Antoinette Clark Wire, *The Corinthian Women Prophets: A Reconstruction through Paul's Rhetoric* (Minneapolis: Fortress, 1990): 237-69.

For some time, those who wanted to prophesy approached the chasm and made their prophecies to one another; but later, since many were jumping into the chasm as a result of their inspired state–and all (who did) vanished, the local residents (so that no one would be placed in danger) decided to appoint one woman as a prophet for all and that the utterance of the oracle was to come through her. A mechanism was constructed for her which she mounted and safely entered an inspired state and prophesied to those who wanted (to consult her).[200]

Plutarch claimed that in an earlier day three prophetesses used to serve Delphi, but that in his day one sufficed.[201] His comments mark the esteem of the oracle in an earlier age.[202]   Delphi was by no means the only site where prophetesses served as the official oracular spokespersons. We know they were also active at places like Dodona, a sanctuary of Zeus at Epiros,[203] and at the temple of Apollo in Corinth.[204]   Honorary inscriptions attest the esteem in which a number of the priestesses/prophetesses were held by their communities.[205]   One second-century BCE example from Delphi will suffice.

---

[200]Diodoros Sikelos 16.26.4. See 16.26.1-6.

[201]Plutarch, *Mor.* 414b. He describes the prophetess at 405c-d.

[202]See also Cicero, *Div.* 1.19.37-38. On the Delphic oracle see H. W. Parke and D. E. W. Wormell, *The Delphic Oracle* (2 vols.; Oxford: Basil Balckwell, 1956).

[203]Strabo 7.7.12. For details see H. W. Parke, *The Oracles of Zeus: Dodona, Olympia, Ammon* (Cambridge: Harvard Univ. Press, 1967), esp. 1-163.

[204]Pausanias 2.24.1, notes that the temple was historically linked to Delphi. We also have evidence for the "prophetess" at Didyma in Asia Minor. For a description from a later period see Iamblichos, *Myst.* 3.11 and the discussion of H. W. Parke, *The Oracles of Apollo in Asia Minor* (London: Croom Helm, 1985): 210-19.

[205]E.g., Tata in Aphrodisias (2nd cent. CE); and Berenice in Syros (2nd-3rd centuries CE). See Pleket, *Epigraphica* 18, 25.

With good fortune, it was voted by the city of Delphi to praise Chrysis, daughter of Niketes, and to crown her with the god's crown that is customary among the Delphians. It was voted also to give *proxenia* to her and to her descendants from the city, and the right to consult the oracle, priority of trial, safe conduct, freedom from taxes, and a front seat at all the contests held by the city, the right to own land and a house, and all the other honours customary for *proxenoi* and benefactors of the city.[206]

Not all prophetesses were connected with specific sanctuaries. The most famous prophetesses who were not were the sibyls, old women whose prophecies were mostly of future calamities.[207] Although it is problematic to identify individual historical figures with the sibyls, the oracles are attributed to women. There were several collections of these hexameter poems in the ancient world. The most famous was the Roman collection which according to legend Tarquinius Priscius, the fifth king of Rome (616-579 BCE), purchased from an old woman.[208] Numerous other nations also had their claimants.[209] Nor are the sibyls the only example. There were a significant number of prophetesses scattered throughout the Hellenistic and Roman worlds.[210]

---

[206]*IG* II^2 1136. ET from Kraemer, *Maenads, Martyrs, Matrons, Monastics*, 78.

[207]See Ovid, *Met.* 14.129-53. For a detailed treatment see H. W. Parke, *Sibyls and Sibylline Prophecy in Classical Antiquity* (London/New York: Routledge, 1988).

[208]Dionysios of Halikarnassos, *AR* 4.62.1-6; *Sib. Or.* Prologue. I have used John J. Collins, "Sibylline Oracles," *The Old Testament Pseudepigrapha* (2 vols.; J. Charlesworth, ed.; Garden City, NY: Doubleday, 1983-85): 1.317-472. See also *Sib. Or.* 3.809-29.

[209]See catalogues in *Sib. Or.* Prologue and Lactantius, *Div. Inst.* 1.6, whose reported source is Marcus Varro (116-27 BCE). According to both lists, there were ten. Varro mentions sibyls from Persia, Libya, Delphi, Cimmeria, Erythraea, Samos, Cumae, the Hellespont, Phrygia, and Tibur. See also Pausanias 10.12.1-9.

[210]Plutarch, *Mar.* 17.1-3, and Arrian, *Anab.* 4.13.4-6 (Syrian); Strabo 7.2.3, and Tacitus, *Germ.* 8 (German).

We should point out that not all priestesses were primarily concerned with oracular functions. The most famous priestesses of the Roman world were the vestal virgins, who were responsible for the sacred flame of Vesta.[211] These women enjoyed extraordinary privileges; yet they were subject to the *pontifex maximus*. Again, while these were the most celebrated, they were not unique. We have literary and epigraphic evidence establishing the presence of women priestesses throughout the Roman world.[212]

B. *Cults.* We have evidence for the participation of women in a wide range of cults. Some of the more notable are the *Bona Dea* or *Gynaikeia*,[213] and Demeter.[214] The most famous, however, is that of Dionysos.[215] Euripides described the rites of the cult in the *Bacchae* (first performed in 405 BCE). Diodoros Sikelos described the practice of the first century BCE in these terms:

> Therefore among many Greek cities, every other year bands of women devoted to Bacchus come together. It is customary for the young girls to carry the *thyrsos* and to join in the frenzied shouts of "Euai"

---

[211]See Plutarch, *Num.* 10.1-7, and Aulus Gellius, *NA* 1.12.

[212]E.g., Strabo 4.1.3-4. The epigraphic evidence collected in Fant, *Women's Life in Greece and Rome*, and Kraemer, *Maenads, Martyrs, Matrons, Monastics*, gives the following spread for the relevant centuries of the Roman period: Pompeii, Phocacea (1st cent. CE); Athens, Aphrodias (2nd cent. CE). For a broader treatment of women in religious offices see Kraemer, *Her Share of the Blessings*, 80-92.

[213]Worshiped exclusively by women. See Cicero, *Att.* 1.13; Plutarch, *Cic.* 19.3-20.2; 28.1-3; *Caes.* 9.1-10.7.

[214]Worshiped by women and men, but of particular importance to women. See Kallimachos, *Cer.* , and Pausanias, 2.35.4-8 (Corinth); 4.17 (Messenia); 7.27.9-10 (Achaia).

[215]See Marvin W. Meyer, *The Ancient Mysteries: A Sourcebook: Sacred Texts of the Mystery Religions of the Ancient Mediterranean World* (San Francisco: Harper & Row, 1987): 61-109, and Kraemer, *Her Share of the Blessings*, 36-49.

and honors for the god. The women, on the other hand, sacrifice to the god in groups, celebrate the Bacchic rites, and for the most part celebrate the presence of Dionysos in hymns.[216]

The importance of this cult for women is that it afforded them an opportunity to assert themselves outside of a male-dominated context.[217] Nor is this only a modern deduction. In a remarkable prayer preserved on a papyrus celebrating the power of Isis, we read, "You have made women equal in power with men."[218]

It will come as no surprise that men were not always comfortable with such activities.[219] Male anxieties increased as Oriental cults made their way west and won adherents.[220] The best-known incident along these lines occurred in 186 BCE in connection with Bacchic rites. According to Livy, the celebration of these rites began exclusively among females.[221] Soon, however, males began to participate also. The result was that no form of behavior was left untried.[222] When these matters were brought before the Senate, the

---

[216]Diodoros Sikelos 4.3.3.

[217]See Ross S. Kraemer, "Ecstatics and Ascetics: Studies in the Functions of Religious Activities for Women in the Greco-Roman World," (Ph.D. dissertation; Princeton Univ., 1976): 9-123.

[218]*P. Oxy.* 1380, 214-15. See Diodoros Sikelos 1.27.1-2, where a wife's authority over her husband is connected to Isis. Texts regarding Isis and Osiris are in Meyer, *The Ancient Mysteries*, 155-96. Kraemer, *Her Share of the Blessings*, 71-79, provides a summary of the evidence and concludes that, "at the explicit level" the Isis cult was more favorable to women than any other (79).

[219]Early examples of male suspicions are attested in Euripides' *Bacchae* and Aristophanes' *Women at the Thesmophoria.*

[220]On the penetration of these cults into Italy, see Anne Roullet, *The Egyptian and Egyptianizing Monuments of Imperial Rome* (Leiden: Brill, 1972); and Michael Malaise, *Les Conditions de Pénétration et de Diffusion des Cultes Égyptiens en Italie* (EPRO 22; Leiden: Brill, 1972).

[221]Livy 39.13.8.

[222]Livy 39.13.10.

patres were alarmed, "lest those alliances and nocturnal meetings might produce some secret crime or danger."[223] The Senate then restricted the rites in Rome and Italy.[224] The attitude evidenced in this incident lingered for centuries. Juvenal reserved some of his most bitter bile for the secret religious practices of the women of Rome.[225] Plutarch advised the new bride:

> A wife should not acquire her own friends, but should make her husband's friends her own. The gods are the first and most significant friends. For this reason, it is proper for a wife to recognize only those gods whom her husband worships and to shut the door to superstitious cults and strange super-stitions. The performance of clandestine and secret rites by a woman do not ingratiate her to any of the gods.[226]

All of these statements suggest that men realized that religion was a potential area where women could, and in fact did, exercise autonomy. The warnings are attempts to prevent that from happening outside the sphere of male control.

C. *Summary.* While the presence of prophetesses in the NT may strike us as strange, it is exactly what we should expect in the Greco-Roman world. This is true not only of the slave girl with a Pythian spirit (Acts 16:16-18), but of the prophetesses within early Christianity, such as Elisabeth (Lk. 1:41-45), Anna (Lk. 2:36-38), Philip's four virgin

---

[223]Livy 39.14.4.

[224]*CIL* I[2] 581. Fant, *Women's Life in Greece and Rome*, 243.

[225]Juvenal 6.314-41.

[226]Plutarch, *Mor.* 140d. See also the warning in Phintys, *On the Moderation of a Woman*, in Thesleff, *The Pythagorean Texts of the Hellenistic Period*, 152. See also Apuleius, *Met.* 9.14. Aconia Fabia Paulina, the wife of Vettius Agorius Praetextatus (c. 320-84 CE), is an excellent example of a woman who followed her husband's religious preferences. See *ILS* 1259=*CIL* 6.1779 with an English translation in Gardner and Wiedemann, *The Roman Household*, 66-67.

daughters (Acts 21:9), the Corinthian women prophets (1 Cor. 11:2-16), and Jezebel (Rev. 2:20-23). The same may be said for the apparent roles of leadership which some women exercised, e.g., Phoebe as deacon (Rom. 16:1), and probably female deacons in 1 Tim. 3:11.[227] In all probability, a significant number of women in the Roman world were attracted to Christianity because they found it liberating.

Conclusions

How does this data affect our understanding of the role of women in churches today? We can answer by synthesizing some of our findings. 1) Our survey has illustrated the different roles and assessments of women in different periods and geographical locales of the Hellenistic and Roman worlds. Simplistic generalizations which assume that the place of women was static in Greco-Roman culture are at odds with the evidence we have examined, e.g., texts from classical Athenian authors should not be considered normative for the larger and later world without support from the particular geographical region and chronological period. We should, therefore, not be surprised to discover different understandings within the NT itself, e.g., Paul and the Corinthian women prophetesses. 2) A knowledge of the larger world illuminates some of the NT texts we find perplexing, e.g., women as "designated servants" in early Christianity. 3) The ancient world is not our current world: we either snarl or smile in amazement at ancient biology; we would think it shocking for a parent to feed or educate children differently on the basis of gender; our daughters do not marry at puberty; women now have access to public life. In short, the patriarchy that dominated the Hellenistic and Roman worlds is receding. 4) Religion now has a different function for women. In the ancient world, it frequently offered women a vehicle in which they could assert themselves; today it functions as the sphere which most restricts women. Why?

---

[227]Pliny, *Ep.* 10.96, says that the two Christian female slaves he examined were called "*ministrae.*"

There are indeed NT texts which impose restrictions on certain women. Yet there are also texts which affirm the equality of women with men within the NT. This same tension characterizes a number of the philosophical texts we noted, especially those of Plato and the Stoics. Like them, the issue we face is whether to emphasize principle or practice. NT texts which accentuated convention or practice did so within the cultural context of patriarchy. Since we no longer live in such a context, we must ask whether we should maintain the same convictions. The issue is not whether we should dismiss the NT; we should not. The issue is, how can we be true to it? I, for one, think that loyalty to the NT requires us to give priority to principle rather than to practice.

Chapter Four

JEWISH WOMEN IN THE GRECO-ROMAN ERA

Randall D. Chesnutt

Fiorenza's[1] comment a decade ago that "historical darkness" obscures our vision of the roles and status of Jewish women in the Greco-Roman world remains true today. Although intense recent interest in the subject has led to the recovery and analysis of much new data (both archaeological and literary), the application of insightful new methods (especially from the social sciences), and a proliferation of published studies, the available information has yet to be synthesized fully. "Writing the history of Jewish women in the Roman period," Brooten correctly insists, "is an urgent task for Christian theology."[2]

Obstacles to this "urgent task" are enormous. Reference to four such barriers at the outset will serve to clarify the methodological parameters of the present study. First, progress has been impeded by the persistent tendency to give primary, or even exclusive, attention to the rabbinic sources as representative of early Jewish thought and practice. Although popularized in such monolithic reconstructions of early Judaism as Moore's "normative Judaism,"[3] and in

---

[1]Elisabeth Schüssler Fiorenza, *In Memory of Her: A Feminist Theological Reconstruction of Christian Origins* (New York: Crossroads, 1983): 108-110.

[2]Bernadette J. Brooten, "Jewish Women's History in the Roman Period: A Task for Christian Theology," *HTR* 79 (1986): 22.

[3]G. F. Moore, *Judaism in the First Centuries of the Christian Era: The Age of the Tannaim*, 3 vols. (Cambridge, MA: Harvard Univ. Press, 1927-30): *passim*. See Jacob Neusner, "'Judaism' After Moore: A Programmatic Statement," *JJS* 31 (1980): 141-56.

countless studies of individual topics, including women's roles,[4] this approach founders on the extreme pluralism now known to have characterized Judaism around the turn of the eras. Rabbinic efforts after AD 70 to standardize Jewish thought and practice were only partially successful, and even this limited standardization must not be read back into the pre-70 period. Neither the rabbinic literature nor any other single body of data should be considered "representative" or "normal." Not only must the rabbinic materials be sifted critically to distinguish late traditions from those early enough to elucidate Christian origins,[5] but it is necessary to take fully into account such diverse literary sources as the OT Apocrypha and Pseudepigrapha, the works of Philo and Josephus, and the Qumran scrolls. The fact that subsequent Jewish tradition did not accord the same authoritative status to these non-rabbinic materials as to the Mishnah and Talmud does not alter the historian's obligation to incorporate them fully into the discussion. Most of these works, in fact, date much closer to the period of our interest than do the rabbinic sources, and some reflect images of women radically different from rabbinic stereotypes.

Second, literary works, by their very nature, present formidable barriers to historical reconstruction. The interpreter must perceive and decode subtle gender symbols as well as analyze explicit references to women. Extrapolating social reality from literary texts is complicated even in cases of detailed portrayals of women. One must ask whether a given portrayal of women is descriptive or prescriptive; that is, did the author mean to describe things as they actually

---

[4]Ben Witherington III, *Women and the Genesis of Christianity* (Cambridge: Cambridge Univ. Press, 1990): 3-9, is only one example.

[5]The earliest rabbinic materials date from around AD 200 in their written form. This fact alone demonstrates the need for caution in using rabbinic literature in the study of Christian origins. See Jacob Neusner, "The History of Earlier Rabbinic Judaism: Some New Approaches," *History of Religions* 16 (1977): 216-36; and "The Use of Rabbinic Sources for the Study of Ancient Judaism," *Approaches to Ancient Judaism* (ed. W. S. Green; BJS 11; Chico, CA: Scholars Press, 1981): 1-17.

were, or things as he (she?) wanted them to be?[6] The
possibility that some Jewish portrayals of women were
shaped more by Greco-Roman literary conventions and
social patterns than by the social realities of Jewish life must
also be considered. Even if social realities can be legitimately extrapolated from literary portrayals, one must not
generalize across social classes, geographical boundaries,
and cultural settings. Reconstruction of women's roles from
scattered literary representations is therefore hazardous.

Third, insufficient attention has been given to extensive
non-literary data, primarily inscriptions and papyrus documents.[7] These diffuse records are often difficult to interpret.
Even such basic matters as dating the materials, distinguishing Jewish from non-Jewish ones, and distinguishing
male from female names are problematic. Nevertheless,
non-literary records lack the tendentiousness which characterizes literature and which so complicates historical
reconstruction. They provide unbiased testimony to the way
things actually were. Moreover, the non-literary evidence
for Jewish women's lives constitutes a surprisingly large
body of evidence, the potential of which for supplementing
or even correcting literary representations is considerable.

Fourth, political, religious, and social agendas too often
have dictated the outcome of scholarly investigation of
women's status and roles in antiquity. Some have been

---

[6]The feminine pronoun is supplied here to suggest the possibility
of female authorship of at least some of the literature. See on this
Ross S. Kraemer, "Women's Authorship of Jewish and Christian
Literature in the Greco-Roman Period," *'Women Like This': New
Perspectives on Jewish Women in the Greco-Roman World* (A.-J.
Levine, ed.; Septuagint and Cognate Studies, Studies in Early Jewish
Literature, 1; Atlanta: Scholars Press, 1991): 221-43; and in the same
volume, Mary Lefkowitz, "Did Ancient Women Write Novels?" 199-
220. Unknown authors of early Jewish literature are hereafter referred to
with masculine pronouns, but only to avoid cumbersome forms such as
"he/she" and "his/her." This accommodation to grammatical convention
implies neither a decision about authorship nor a sexist bias.

[7]See Ross S. Kramer, "Non-Literary Evidence for Jewish Women
in Rome and Egypt," *Helios* 13 (1986): 85.

predisposed to give one-sided emphasis to the misogyny of ancient cultures, while others have exaggerated the extent to which women occupied favorable or even dominant positions in antiquity. For our purposes, it is especially important to note that Christian scholars have contributed often to distorted portrayals of Jewish women in an effort to present early Christian attitudes toward women in a more favorable light. Thus, to exalt Jesus as the great liberator of women from a repressive patriarchal system, many have exaggerated the repression of women in the world of Jesus.[8] Similarly, to mitigate Paul's apparent male chauvinism, or to set his apparent egalitarian ideal in sharper contrast, Christian theologians have delighted in pointing to the more pronounced chauvinism of Paul's Jewish contemporaries while ignoring Jewish evidence for more progressive roles for women.[9] Until such agendas are set aside, progress toward reconstructing the place of women in early Judaism will be seriously impaired. Jewish sources need to be examined on their own terms rather than selectively cited to provide contrasting background against which to present appealing images of early Christianity.[10]

In view of the extensive and diverse data and the methodological complexity of reconstructing social reality

---

[8]E.g., Ben Witherington III, *Women in the Ministry of Jesus* (SNTSMS, 51; Cambridge: Cambridge Univ. Press, 1984); *idem*, *Women in the Earliest Churches* (SNTSMS, 59; Cambridge: Cambridge Univ. Press, 1988); and *idem*, *Women and the Genesis of Christianity*.

[9]E.g., Robin Scroggs, "Paul and the Eschatological Woman," *JAAR* 40 (1972): 283-303; *idem*, "Paul and the Eschatological Woman: Revisited," *JAAR* 42 (1974): 532-37; and Robert Jewett, "The Sexual Liberation of the Apostle Paul," *JAAR* (Suppl. Vol.) 47 (1979): 55-87.

[10]On the tendency of Christian feminists to project onto Judaism what they cannot bear to acknowledge in their own heritage, see further Judith Plaskow, "Christian Feminism and Anti-Judaism," *Cross Currents* 28 (1978): 306-09; *idem*, "Blaming the Jews for the Invention of Patriarchy," *Lilith* 7 (1980): 11-12; Bernadette Brooten, "Jüdinnen zur Zeit Jesu: Ein Plädoyer für Differenzierung," *TQ* 161 (1981): 281-85; Fiorenza, *In Memory of Her*, 107-07; and Susannah Heschel, "Anti-Judaism in Christian Feminist Theology," *Tikkun* 5 (1990): 25-28.

from the data, this essay will simply illustrate the broad range of attitudes toward and roles of Jewish women in the Greco-Roman period. By no means does this approach yield a comprehensive picture of Jewish women's lives in antiquity, but perhaps it sheds some light on the broad contours of such a picture.

1. *Literary Images: The Patriarchal Model*

Modern caricatures typically present ancient Jewish women as repressed, denigrated, and relegated to inferior status and exclusively domestic roles in a male-dominated world. Although this caricature is exaggerated (as will be shown below), it is not without considerable support from early Jewish literature. Texts illustrating such denigration of women and their limited status and function abound.

Most notorious is *Ecclesiasticus*, also known as the *Wisdom of Jesus ben Sirach*, an apocryphal book of wisdom from the early second century BC. Ben Sirach has such a negative estimate of women that he values a man's wickedness over a woman's goodness (42:14). Indeed, he considers woman to be the cause of all evil: "From a woman sin had its beginning, and because of her all will die" (25:24).[11] Though well aware of the blessing of a good wife, this author seems rather obsessed with the curse of a bad one:

Any wickedness, but not the wickedness of a wife!

. . . .

I would rather dwell with a lion and a dragon
    than dwell with an evil wife.

. . . .

---

[11]The chauvinism of this distich is even more pronounced if, as John R. Levison, "Is Eve to Blame? A Contextual Analysis of Sirach 25: 24," *CBQ* 47 (1985): 617-23, argues, "woman" here refers not to Eve but to the evil wife. On this interpretation, the sinfulness of men is directly attributable to the evil influence of their wives. Unless otherwise noted, quotations of the Apocrypha are from the RSV.

Any iniquity is insignificant compared to a wife's
    iniquity; may a sinner's lot befall her!
A sandy ascent for the feet of the aged--
    such is a garrulous wife for a quiet husband.
. . . .
A dejected mind, a gloomy face, and a wounded heart
    are caused by an evil wife.
Drooping hands and weak knees are caused by the wife
    who does not make her husband happy.
. . . .
An evil wife is an ox yoke which chafes;
    taking hold of her is like taking hold of a scorpion.
(25:13, 16, 19-20, 23, 26:7).

Not even the passages in which ben Sirach extolls the
"good wife" (7:19; 25:8; 26:1-4, 13-18, 26; 36:22-26;
40:23) reflect a positive estimate of woman as woman. The
"good wife" functions exclusively within the domestic
sphere (see esp. 25:22), and she is not valued in her own
right, but in terms of the benefits she brings to her husband
(26:1-4). Moreover, she must be held in constant check
because she has the potential at any moment to ruin her
husband's financial security and honor.[12] A wife who
cannot be controlled must be divorced (25:26). Not
surprisingly, among the most desirable traits in a wife are
submissiveness, silence, and modesty (26:13-16; 36:22-24).

If ben Sirach's misogyny is not mitigated by his praise
of the good wife, neither is it vitiated by the female imagery
he uses for personified Wisdom. His placement of Lady

_____

[12]Claudia V. Camp, "Understanding a Patriarchy: Women in
Second Century Jerusalem Through the Eyes of Ben Sira," *'Women
Like This'*, 1-39, has shown that ben Sirach reflects the well-known
Mediterranean "shame/honor" complex in which maintaining male
honor and status was considered the highest good. Because women rank
high on ben Sirach's list of forces which threaten that honor and status,
various groups of women receive considerable attention in this book,
and control over each of them is considered crucial. Note the language
of "control" in the discussion of loose women, singing girls, virgins,
prostitutes, attractive women, daughters, married women, and women
generally (9:1-9; 25:21-26; 26:7-12; 33:19-23; 42:9-14; 47:19-21).

Wisdom on a pedestal stands in marked contrast to his attitude toward women in the flesh, and may even be a means of repressing women through negative comparison.[13]

Because ben Sirach considers all females lustful and sexually indiscriminate (26:10-12), daughters—even more so than wives—represent a threat to a man's ability to control his household and hence maintain his honor. While the undisciplined son is a disgrace to the father, the mere "birth of a daughter is a loss" (22:3). A man who educates his son brings honor to himself (30:3), but in the case of a daughter all a father can hope for is to avoid being publicly shamed by her promiscuity before marriage, her failure to marry in her youth, or her unfaithfulness or barrenness after she is married (42:9-11). Fathers should keep their unmarried daughters secluded, not even allowing them to converse with married women (42:12).[14] The numerous warnings about prostitutes, the promiscuity of daughters, and the unfaithfulness of wives focus not on the evil deeds themselves or their effect on the woman involved, but on their impact on the honor and status of the male. In the patriarchal world view of ben Sirach, a woman had no autonomous status or function and was not valued in her own right; rather, at every stage of life her existence was determined by her relationship to a man.[15]

---

[13]Claudia V. Camp, "The Female Sage in Ancient Israel and in the Biblical Wisdom Literature," *The Sage in Ancient Israel* (ed. J. Gammie and L. Perdue; Winona Lake, IN: Eisenbrauns, 1990): 199.

[14]This advice appears in P. W. Skehan's translation in P. W. Skehan and A. A. DiLella, *The Wisdom of Jesus Ben Sira* (AB, 39; New York: Doubleday, 1987): 478-83. In the RSV it is the wise man who is advised to avoid the company of women. In either case, the reason given in v. 13 is that wickedness comes from women as moths come from garments.

[15]See also Kenneth E. Bailey, "Women in Ben Sirach and in the New Testament," *For Me To Live: Essays in Honor of James Leon Kelso* (ed. R. A. Coughenour; Cleveland: Dillon/Liederbach, 1972): 56-73; Henry McKeating, "Jesus ben Sira's Attitude to Women," *ExpTim* 85 (1973): 85-87; Maurice Gilbert, "Ben Sira et la femme," *RTL* 7 (1976): 426-42; and W. C. Trenchard, *Ben Sira's View of Women: A Literary Analysis* (BJS 38; Chico, CA: Scholars Press, 1982).

Ben Sirach's attitude toward women is expressed with unusual frequency and poignancy, but it does not differ in kind from that expressed in numerous other early Jewish works. According to the *Letter of Aristeas*, a pseudepigraphon probably dating from the late second century BC, "the female sex is bold, positively active for something which it desires, easily liable to change its mind because of poor reasoning powers, and of naturally weak constitution" (248).[16] Of kindred spirit is the sentiment expressed in the *Testament of Reuben*:[17]

> For women are evil, my children, and by reason of their lacking authority or power over man, they scheme treacherously how they might entice him to themselves by means of their looks. . . . women are more easily overcome by the spirit of promiscuity than are men. . . . Accordingly, my children, flee from sexual promiscuity, and order your wives and your daughters not to adorn their heads and their appearances so as to deceive men's sound minds (5:1-5).

Here, as in *Ecclesiasticus* and numerous other ancient sources dealing with sexual misconduct, women are presented as the lustful ones, and men as the innocent ones seduced by them.[18]

In other texts, it is the naiveté of women rather than their sexual aggressiveness which brings men down. In the

---

[16]Quotations of the so-called Pseudepigrapha are from James H. Charlesworth, *The Old Testament Pseudepigrapha* (Garden City, NY: Doubleday, 1983-85): 2 vols.

[17]The larger work of which the *T. Reub.* is a part, the *Testaments of the Twelve Patriarchs*, is of uncertain date and has Christian as well as Jewish components. These testaments probably reached a form recognizably similar to their present form by 100 BC, though there were later reworkings and interpolations by both Jews and Christians.

[18]The pseudonymous author of *T. Reub.* reinforces this point in 5:6 by blaming women for the illicit and disastrous union of sons of God and daughters of men narrated in Gen. 6:1-4.

Testament of Job, an embellishment of the biblical story of Job which probably dates to the first century AD, women function as foils to highlight Job's superior insight into heavenly reality.[19] Although men as well as women serve as foils for Job, this work suggests that women—precisely because they are women—are so spiritually imperceptive that they become easy prey for Satan and lead men astray as well.[20] Thus, in 26:6, Job's wife is described as "one of the senseless women who misguide their husband's sincerity."

If the *Wisdom of Jesus ben Sirach* is less than explicit about Eve's role in bringing sin and death into the world, no such ambiguity exists in the *Life of Adam and Eve*. In this first century AD interpretive expansion of Gen. 1-4, responsibility for sin in the world is consistently placed on Eve rather than Adam. Thus, Adam claims that he and the angels prevented Eve from being deceived at first and that only in their absence was Satan able to take advantage of the unguarded female and persuade her to sin (32-33; and the parallel account in another recension of the same book, mis-named *Apocalypse of Moses* 7:1-2). Elsewhere in the *Life of Adam and Eve*, Adam says to Eve: "What have you done? You have brought upon us a great wound, transgression and sin in all our generations" (44:2; see also *Apoc. Mos.* 14:2; 26:1). In *Apoc. Mos.* 32:1-2, Eve herself is depicted as acknowledging full responsibility for the human situation. Nine times in her short prayer of confession she admits, "I have sinned," and her prayer always ends with "all sin has come about through me."[21] Although it is impossible to

---

[19]See John J. Collins, "Structure and Meaning in the Testament of Job," *SBLSP 1974* (ed. G. MacRae; Cambridge, MA: SBL, 1974): 40.

[20]This observation applies only to *T. Job* 1-45. In chapters 46-53, as will be shown below, a much more positive estimate of women's spiritual capacities appears.

[21]See also *Life of Adam and Eve* 3:1; 5:2; 18:1, 35, 37, and *Apoc. Mos.* 9:12 and 10:12, where Eve accepts full blame for the human predicament. In *Life of Adam and Eve* 38 and *Apoc. Mos.* 11:1-3, the beast who attacks Seth also reminds Eve that the blame for sin and its consequences rests squarely on her. The view that *Apoc. Mos.*

reconstruct the actual status of women from this theological use of traditions about the first woman, there is little doubt that the portrait of Eve as one constantly weeping, ignorant, perplexed, vulnerable to sin, and dependent upon the males around her for insight bears some relation to the way women were actually perceived and treated in the authors' and redactors' own times and places.[22]

Philo of Alexandria has little to say about individual women in real life—so little, in fact, that it is unclear from his writings whether he was married. Nevertheless, his elaboration of the relationship between gender and the characteristics of the soul, together with his frequent insistence on female inferiority (often in quite gratuitous insults), clearly place his assessment of women among the most deprecatory that we have seen thus far. For Philo the soul's rational quality (νοῦς, mind or intellect) is masculine, while its irrational quality (αἴσθησις, sense-perception) is feminine. The rational part of the soul is the superior and immortal part, made in the image of God. Woman, who was fashioned from the inferior mortal aspect, has no part in the soul's rational quality, but only its irrational quality.[23] In explaining the Genesis account of the fall, Philo, like others we have seen, cites woman's intellectual inferiority and vulnerability to sin:

> . . . woman is more accustomed to be deceived than
> man. For his judgment, like his body, is masculine
> and is capable of dissolving or destroying the

15-30 exculpates Eve and originated independently from the rest of the work is discussed below. Also blaming Eve for the origin of evil is II Enoch, the original of which probably dates prior to AD 70. See II Enoch 30:18; 31:6.

[22]It is significant in this connection that Eve is not the only one who calls Adam "Lord." In *Life of Adam and Eve* 2:1, the narrator refers to Adam as "her [Eve's] Lord."

[23]*On the Creation* 21-29, 46, 59; *The Worse Attacks the Better* 23; *Allegorical Interpretation* 2.11, 14; *Questions and Answers on Genesis* 1.37; and see further Richard A. Baer, Jr., *Philo's Use of the Categories Male and Female* (Leiden: Brill, 1970).

designs of deception; but the judgment of woman is more feminine, and because of softness she gives way and is taken in by plausible falsehoods which resemble the truth (*Questions and Answers on Gen.* 1.33; see also 1:37 and *On the Creation* 59).[24]

Woman is thus responsible for the origin of sin, while man, who was the first to repent, initiated the atonement (*Questions and Answers on Gen.* 1.43).

Numerous contrived excuses to depreciate women appear in Philo's exegetical writings. Thus, he explains the biblical prescription of a male animal for the paschal sacrifice as follows:

> ... the male is more perfect than the female. . . . the female is nothing else than an imperfect male. . . . progress is indeed nothing else than the giving up of the female gender by changing into the male, since the female gender is material, passive, corporeal, and sense perceptible, while the male is active, rational, incorporeal and more akin to mind and thought (*Questions and Answers on Exodus* 1.7-8).

Another example is Philo's ingenious explanation why Zelophehad (Num. 27:1-11) had produced only daughters and no sons:

> Do you not notice, that the five daughters of Zelophehad, whom we take to be a figure of the senses . . . are of the tribe of Manasseh, . . . for his name means "from forgetfulness" . . . "and he had no sons" (Numb. 27:3) but only daughters, for whereas the faculty of memory, being naturally wide awake, has male progeny, forgetfulness, wrapt in a slumber of reasoning power, has female offspring; for it is irrational, and the senses are daughters of the

---

[24]Quotations of Philo are from F. H. Colson et al, *Philo* (LCL; Cambridge, MA: Harvard Univ. Press, 1929-53): 12 vols.

irrational portion of the soul (*On the Migration of Abraham* 37).

Philo rarely comments on the legal and social status of women, but he does make clear that "wives must be in servitude to their husbands, a servitude not imposed by violent ill-treatment but promoting obedience in all things" (*Hypothetica* 7.3), and that women are best kept secluded:

> The woman is best suited for the indoor life which never strays from the house. . . . A woman, then, should not be a busybody, meddling with matters outside her household concerns, but should seek a life of seclusion (*On the Special Laws* 3.31).

His assumption that a marriageable girl is virtually the property of her father (*On the Special Laws* 3.11) and the metaphors he uses for intercourse and childbearing (*On the Special Laws* 3.6) indicate that he perceived women more as chattel than as persons.[25]

Although Josephus expresses the highest admiration for the matriarchs of Israel and for certain prominent women in his own time, his motives for this are transparent,[26] and when his true colors come out he clearly shares the condescending attitudes toward women that we have seen in other

---

[25]See further Judith R. Wegner, "The Image of Woman in Philo," *SBLSP 1982* (ed. K. Richards; Chico, CA: Scholars Press, 1982), 551-63; and *idem*, "Philo's Portrayal of Woman–Hebraic or Hellenic?" *'Women Like This'*, 41-66.

[26]The hellenized and idealized portraits of Sarah, Rebekah, Rachel, and Leah are clearly designed to win Roman admiration for these heroines of Israel and thus for the Jewish people. See James L. Bailey, "Josephus' Portrayal of the Matriarchs," *Josephus, Judaism, and Christianity* (ed. L. Feldman and G. Hata; Detroit: Wayne State Univ. Press, 1987): 154-79. With regard to Josephus' favors from and favorable comments about royal women such as Poppaea, the consort and later the wife of Nero, and Domitia, the wife of Domitian, Bailey notes that "although he was part of a male dominated society, Josephus understood the advantage of knowing women who had access to powerful men" (156).

sources. Thus, in *Antiquities* 4.8.15 he writes: "From women let no evidence be accepted, because of the levity and temerity of their sex."[27] In *Against Apion* 24 he grounds the inferiority of women in Scripture: "The woman, says the Law, is in all things inferior to the man. Let her accordingly be submissive, not for her humiliation, but that she may be directed; for the authority has been given by God to the man." Such a view of women is implicit even amid Josephus' exalted portrayals of the matriarchs. He typically deletes or downplays assertiveness and initiative on the part of these biblical women, stresses their submissiveness, allows them no direct speech in the narrative, and eliminates suggestions of their receiving direct communication from God.[28] Similarly, he cannot bring himself to express unqualified admiration for a woman survivor at Masada, but only to say that she was "superior in sagacity and training to most of her sex" (*Jewish War* 7.9.1). Even Josephus' references to his family betray the assumption that males are more important than females. Although he includes the names of his sons in his rather detailed domestic history, he never names any of his wives, even the third wife whom he regarded highly (*Life* 76).

---

[27]Quotations of Josephus are from H. St. John Thackeray, et al., *Josephus* (LCL; Cambridge, MA: Harvard Univ. Press, 1926-65): 9 vols.

[28]E.g., in Gen. 16 Sarah is impatient because of her barrenness and suggests that Abraham father a son by Hagar, whereas in *Antiquities* 1.10.4 Abraham is the one who is distressed over Sarah's sterility, and the plan for redressing the problem is launched by divine initiative; and in Gen. 25:23 the oracle concerning Jacob and Esau is given by God directly to Rebekah, but in *Antiquities* 1.18.1 it is Isaac who receives this divine communication. See also Bailey, "Josephus' Portrayal of the Matriarchs," *Josephus, Judaism, and Christianity* 154-79; Betsy Halpern-Amaru, "Portraits of Biblical Women in Josephus' Antiquities," *JJS* 39 (1988): 143-70; L. H. Feldman, "Josephus' Portrait of Deborah," *Hellenica and Judaica: Hommage à V. Nikiprowetzky* (ed. A. Caquot, M. Hadas-Lebel, and J. Riaud; Leuven and Paris: Peeters, 1986): 115-28; and *idem*, "Hellenizations in Josephus' Version of Esther," *Transactions of the American Philological Association* 101 (1970): 143-70.

The Essenes shunned marriage and sexual intercourse according to Philo (*Hypothetica* 11.14-17), Josephus (*Jewish War* 2.8.2; *Antiquities* 18.1.5), and Pliny (*Natural Hist.* 5.15), although Josephus says that a second branch of Essenes did marry (*Jewish War* 2.8.13) and that even the celibate Essenes did not condemn marriage in principle (*Jewish War* 2.8.2). Documents which most scholars consider to have been written by Essenes confirm this duality of practice: the rule for the Essene camps in the *Damascus Document* assumes marriage and family life, while the Qumran *Community Rule* makes no provisions for women in the community and leaves the impression of a wholly masculine society.[29] The Essene's motive for celibacy is explained by Philo as follows:

> For no Essene takes a wife, because a wife is a selfish creature, excessively jealous and adept at beguiling the morals of her husband and seducing him by her continued impostures. . . . and casting off all shame she compels him to commit actions which are all hostile to the life of fellowship (*Hypothetica* 11.14-16).

The view of women expressed in this diatribe is quite consistent with what Philo says about women elsewhere, and there is little doubt that it reveals more about his own personal convictions than about Essene attitudes towards women.[30] A more likely explanation for celibacy at Qumran

---

[29]The only time the *Community Rule* even uses the word אשה (woman) is in the cliché, "one born of woman" (11.21). The graves thus far opened in the large cemetery at Qumran have all contained male skeletons. Although the bones of a few women and children have been found on the periphery of the cemetery, and although the brief *Rule for the End of Days* (an appendix to *Community Rule*) provides for sexual relations when a man has reached the age of twenty, most scholars would agree that the Qumran sectarians were celibate. So Geza Vermes, *The Dead Sea Scrolls: Qumran in Perspective* (Cleveland: Collins and World, 1978): 96-97, 193.

[30]The same can be said of Josephus' explanation that the Essenes "wish to protect themselves against women's wantonness, being per-

is that the priestly self-identity of these sectarians and their conception of the life of the community as a substitute for the Temple cult required a constant state of ritual purity which would be interrupted by sexual intercourse, involuntary emission, or any contact with a menstruating woman.[31] On the other hand, the non-Qumran Essenes, who were not so obsessed with priestly purity, married and had children.

In rabbinic literature,[32] the roles and status ascribed to women are very much in line with the patriarchal patterns of contemporaneous eastern Mediterranean cultures. Compiled by men and for men, the rabbinic corpus considers woman primarily in her relationship to man, as she comes under the authority of man and can contribute to his well-being.[33]

---

suaded that none of the sex keeps her plighted troth to one man" (*Jewish War* 2.8.2).

[31]Vermes, *The Dead Sea Scrolls: Qumran in Perspective*, 181-82, 217-18.

[32]Under this heading are included the Mishnah (compiled around AD 200), the Tosefta (slightly later than the Mishnah), the Palestinian and Babylonian Talmuds (compiled around AD 400 and 500, respectively), and numerous midrashic or commentary materials of varying age. As noted above, one can never be sure that a tradition embodied in one or more of these late collections actually dates back to the time of Christian origins. Our study will draw primarily upon the earliest of these texts, the Mishnah, although even here there are tremendous methodological problems. In addition to the question of date, it is difficult to know whether rabbinic reflections on women represent things as they actually were, or idealized views of the way things should be, or even projections of fears about things that could come about.

[33]Jacob Neusner, "Thematic or Systematic Description: The Case of Mishnah's Division of Women," *Method and Meaning in Ancient Judaism* (BJS 10; Missoula, MT: Scholars Press, 1979): 93-100. Drawing on anthropologists' research on "anomalous women," Neusner shows that the division of the Mishnah dealing with women (*Nashim*) concerns itself largely with those points at which women become anomalous in rabbinic society, i.e., when their relationships to men are in transition: when they reach the age for marriage, are divorced or widowed, or engage in illicit sexual relationships. The rabbis sought to work out these anomalies by assuring orderly transition of women from one man's domain to another, "to bring under control and force into

Woman is placed in a domestic role in which her mind and
energies are directed to fulfilling a man's needs so that the
man's mind and energies can be devoted to worship, study,
and work outside the home.[34] Women who fulfilled these
domestic obligations were held in high esteem.[35] Moreover,
elaborate measures were enacted to protect the dignity and
basic rights of women.[36] These facts alone suffice to dis-
prove the frequent claim that women were mere chattels of
their patriarchal owners.[37] On the other hand, the positive

---

stasis all the wild and unruly potentialities of sexuality" (ibid., 99).
See also idem, A History of the Mishnaic Law of Women (Leiden:
Brill, 1980): 5 vols.

[34]Judith Hauptmann, "Images of Women in the Talmud,"
Religion and Sexism: Images of Women in the Jewish and Christian
Traditions (ed. R. Reuther; New York: Simon & Schuster, 1974): 200.

[35]See Babylonian Talmud Yebamot 62b and Baba Mezia 59a for
praise of the supportive and resourceful wife.

[36]E.g., Mishnah Ketubot 5:5-9 describes a reciprocal arrangement
of matrimonial entitlements and obligations in which the wife performs
specified household chores and produces a prescribed amount of cloth in
return for maintenance at a standard that befits her social class. A wife
retains title to any property she brings into her marriage, but she cannot
sell it without her husband's consent and vice versa (Mishnah Gittin
5:6). She can appoint agents to transact her business (Mishnah Gittin
6:1) and can act as her husband's agent to sell his goods (Mishnah
Ketubot 9:4). She even has the right of action against her husband and
in certain situations can petition the court for a divorce (Mishnah
Ketubot 7:10). A woman not under the authority of a man (an
unmarried adult daughter, a divorcée, a widow whose deceased husband
has a male heir) has even greater autonomy. She may keep anything
she finds, makes, or earns, in contrast to the minor daughter or married
woman, who must turn such things over to her father or husband
(Mishnah Baba Mezia 1:5; Ketubot 4:4; 6:1). She can bring suit for
damages (Mishnah Baba Kamma 1:3) or for the return of her marriage
portion upon being widowed or divorced (Mishnah Ketubot 2:1; 11:2).
In such cases she can even testify in court (Mishnah Ketubot 1:6-7;
2:5-6; cf. Shebuot 4:1). She can swear certain business-related oaths
(Mishnah Shebuot 5:1; Ketubot 9:4), and she can arrange her own
marriage (Mishnah Kiddushin 2:1). In rabbinic law, minor daughters do
not normally inherit property, but are entitled to "maintenance" from
the father's estate (Mishnah Baba Batra 9:1).

and affectionate rabbinic statements about women and the laws protecting their rights must not obscure the fact that a patriarchal ideal is everywhere promoted. Not only is reverence for women predicated upon their submissiveness and their fulfillment of domestic obligations, but women are repeatedly characterized as lazy, frivolous, excessively talkative, nosy, greedy, temperamental, involved in witchcraft, and more prone than males to immorality.[38]

The subordinate legal status of women in the rabbinic system is most evident in the treatment of their sexual and reproductive function. The biological function of a minor daughter is considered the legal property of her father, who literally sells this function for a bride-price (Mishnah *Ketubot* 4:4).[39] If the bride is not a virgin, the bridegroom can claim damages because the goods did not meet specifications (Mishnah *Ketubot* 1:1). When a minor daughter is raped or seduced, her father is entitled to damages because her market value is thereby reduced (Mishnah *Ketubot* 4:1). When a girl is married, the legal right to benefit from her sexuality is transferred from father to husband (Mishnah *Ketubot* 4:5); thus the husband can revoke any vows the wife makes, because these may impair conjugal relations (Mishnah *Nedarim* 11:11-12; *Nazir* 4:5). Woman's social identity is linked to ownership of her sexuality.[40]

---

[37]See Judith R. Wegner, *Chattel or Person? The Status of Women in the Mishnah* (Oxford: Oxford Univ. Press, 1988): and *idem*, "The Image and Status of Women in Classical Rabbinic Judaism," *Jewish Women in Historical Perspective* (ed. J. R. Baskin; Detroit: Wayne State Univ. Press, 1991): 68-93.

[38]See Mishnah *Sotah* 3:4; *Abot* 2:7; Jerusalem Talmud *Kiddushin* 4, 66b; *Soferim* 41a; Babylonian Talmud *Kiddushin* 49b; 80b; *Sanhedrin* 67a; *Pesahim* 111a; *Shabbat* 33b; 152a; *Ketubot* 65a; *Genesis Rabbah* 18:2; 45:5.

[39]However, as Wegner, "The Image and Status of Women in Classical Rabbinic Judaism," *Jewish Women in Historical Perspective*, 71, notes, by the time of the Mishnah it had become customary to assign the bride-price to the bride herself as part of the marriage deed. See Mishnah *Ketubot* 4:7.

[40]Wegner, "The Image and Status of Women in Classical Rabbinic Judaism," *Jewish Women in Historical Perspective*, 72,

The inferiority and limited roles of women in the
rabbinic system are evidenced in other ways as well.
Women are not normally eligible to testify in court (Mishnah
Shebuot 4:1). In this instance, as in many others, women
are consigned to the same category as slaves and children
(Mishnah *Berakot* 3:3; *Sukkah* 2:7). Women are exempt
from most religious observances, especially those for which
there is a set time.[41] This exemption, together with some
rabbis' objections to women's studying the Torah at all
(Mishnah *Sotah* 3:4; Jerusalem Talmud *Sotah* 3:4; Babylonian Talmud *Yoma* 66b; *Baba Kamma* 29b-36a), the ban
on mothers' carrying their infants outside the home on the
Sabbath (Mishnah *Shabbat* 18:2), male fears of female sexuality as a source of both temptation and cultic pollution,[42]
and the principle that a person not bound by a particular
precept cannot perform it on behalf of others who are so
obligated (Mishnah *Rosh Hashanah* 3:8), effectively disqualified women from leadership roles in synagogues and
houses of study.[43] The Mishnah affords only occasional

---

correctly argues that although women were treated as chattel in this one
area, in all other aspects of Mishnaic law they are unequivocally
persons, not chattel.

[41]E.g., Mishnah *Kiddushin* 1:7; *Berakot* 3:3; *Hagigah* 1:1. That
in this system men have more opportunities to fulfill divine commandments than do women may explain the prayer (found in several rabbinic
sources and still part of traditional Jewish liturgy today) in which one
thanks God for not creating him a woman (Tosefta *Berakot* 6:18;
Jerusalem Talmud *Berakot* 9, 13a; Babylonian Talmud *Menahot* 43b).

[42]See Judith Baskin, "The Separation of Women in Rabbinic
Judaism," *Women, Religion, and Social Change* (ed. Y. Haddad and E.
B. Findly; Albany, NY: State Univ. of New York Press, 1985): 11-12.

[43]Babylonian Talmud *Moed Katan* 18a, in discussing the super-
stition that stepping on discarded nail parings could cause a woman to
miscarry, notes that this is not a problem in a house of study because
women so rarely come there. Tosefta *Megilla* 3:11 says that women
were not invited to read Scripture publicly. Babylonian Talmud
Megilla 23a lists women among those eligible to read the Torah in the
synagogue but indicates that they were expected to decline. Babylonian
Talmud *Hagigah* 3a assumes that women merely listen. At least one
rabbi sought to vitiate this exclusion of women from the central
intellectual and spiritual experiences of rabbinic Judaism by suggesting

glimpses of limited social contacts for women outside the home (*Sotah* 6:1; *Ketubot* 7:4-5; *Gittin* 5:9). The Talmud seeks to minimize and carefully regulate women's appearances in public (Babylonian Talmud *Yebamot* 76b-77a; *Berakot* 3a-b; *Gittin* 12a; 90a-b; see also *Genesis Rabbah* 8:12; 18:1). A woman who ventured into the public domain was presumed to be up to no good, and conversation with her was strongly discouraged (Mishnah *Abot* 1:5; *Ketubot* 7:6; Babylonian Talmud *Berakot* 43b). When a woman did go out in public, she was expected to have her head covered. Failure to do so was considered so shameful that it was grounds not just for divorce, but divorce without payment of the marriage settlement (Mishnah *Ketubot* 7:6; Babylonian Talmud *Gittin* 90a-b; *Erubin* 100b).

2. Literary Images: Cracks in a Patriarchal Structure

The images thus far drawn from literary sources all point to an ideological norm and social pattern in which Jewish women were confined to domestic roles and considered intellectually and spiritually inferior to men. As widely documented as such a patriarchal model is, and though many modern studies have left the impression that all the evidence fits such a rigid model, considerable evidence points in other directions. Some literature evaluates women more positively and portrays them in more public and autonomous roles.

That women occasionally played prominent roles in public life in the Hasmonean and Herodian periods is clear from Josephus. Most notable is Queen Salome Alexandra, monarch over the Hasmonean Jewish state from 76 to 67 BC. Even before becoming queen, she showed considerable boldness and initiative in governmental affairs. During the reign of her first husband, Aristobulus I (104-103 BC), she conspired to kill his brother and rival, Antigonus

---

that while men acquire merit by diligent study, women earn merit "by making their children go to the synagogue to learn Scripture and their husbands to the Beth Hamidrash [rabbinical school] to learn Mishnah, and waiting for their husbands till they return from the Beth Hamidrash" (Babylonian Talmud *Berakot* 17).

(*Jewish War* 1.3.3; *Antiquities* 13.11.2). Upon the death of
Aristobulus I, she took charge and appointed another of his
brothers, Alexander Jannaeus, to the throne, and became his
wife (*Jewish War* 1.4.1; *Antiquities* 13.12.1). That she
wielded considerable political power during the reign of
Alexander Jannaeus (103-76 BC) is suggested by Josephus'
statement that "Alexander *and his wife* appointed [Herod's
grandfather] governor of the whole of Idumaea" (*Antiquities*
14.1.3; emph. mine).[44] Upon the death of Alexander
Jannaeus, Alexandra herself assumed the throne and named
her son, Hyrcanus II, high priest (*Jewish War* 1.5.1;
Antiquities 13.16.1-2). Although Josephus preserves
contrasting evaluations of her nine-year reign as queen, he
makes clear that she exercised considerable administrative,
diplomatic, and military initiative and skill.[45] Several other
Hasmonean women were also active in political matters.[46]

Jewish sources from the Greco-Roman period assign
autonomous and public roles not only to historical women,
but to women in quasi-historical and fictional tales. Thus in
the second-century BC fictional work bearing her name,

---

[44]Rabbinic sources also attribute considerable political activity to
Salome Alexandra, but Jacob Neusner, *The Rabbinic Traditions About
the Pharisees before 70* (Leiden: Brill, 1971): I, 86-141, has shown that
these stories are not reliable indicators of her actual role.

[45] Compare the positive evaluation in *Jewish War* 1.5.1-3 with
the criticisms in *Antiquities* 13.16.1-3. Even amid criticism, Josephus
praises her administrative ability. Rabbinic literature preserves both
positive evaluations of her reign as a golden age (Babylonian Talmud
Taanith 23a) and strong objections to a woman's having royal power
(*Sifre to Deut.* 157.12).

[46]The daughter-in-law of Salome Alexandra and wife of Aristobulus II bargained with a Roman proconsul on behalf of her family
after Pompey's conquest of Jerusalem (*Jewish War* 1.8.5; *Antiquities*
14.5.4). With courage and skill, the daughter of Aristobulus II delayed
Herod's capture of the fortress of Hyrcania for years (*Jewish War* 1.19.
1). Alexandra, daughter of Hyrcanus II, was a trusted advisor of Herod,
later ingeniously saving her family from Herod (*Antiquities* 14.13.6;
15.2-7). See J. Sievers, "The Role of Women in the Hasmonean
Dynasty," *Josephus, the Bible, and History* (ed. L. H. Feldman and G.
Hata; Detroit: Wayne State Univ. Press, 1989): 132-46.

Judith single-handedly averts a major catastrophe for the Jewish people, overshadowing all the males in the story in intelligence, piety, resourceful leadership, and bravery.[47] She even assembles the chief magistrate and elders of her home city of Bethulia and censures them for lack of faith and initiative (*Judith* 8-9). In contrast to these helpless male leaders, she cleverly devises and courageously executes a plan which calls to mind some of the boldest and most ingenious exploits of Israel's heroes and heroines (10:6-13:10).[48] Judith is also exemplary in her piety.[49] To celebrate the deliverance of her people from oppression, Judith and a choir of dancing women lead the men in a triumphant procession to Jerusalem, the High Priest and the supreme council in Jerusalem join the people in lavishing praise and gifts upon her, and Judith leads the assembly in a hymn of praise and thanksgiving which is a reprise of the major theological affirmations of the book (chaps. 15-16). Judith then retires to Bethulia, where she grows even more famous and declines many proposals to marriage (she needs no male to protect her!). If this fictional story mirrors social reality to any significant degree, then the world of *Judith* was one in which a competent and aggressive woman, independently of her relationship to a man, could assume an active role of

------

[47]A.-J. Levine, "Character Construction and Community Formation in the Book of Judith," *SBLSP 1989* (ed. D. Lull; Atlanta: Scholars Press, 1989): 564, states, "Only the text's females act in a fully efficacious manner; only Judith displays well-directed initiative; only her maid competently follows instructions. The men are weak, stupid, or impaired." Though there are notes of male chauvinism in the account of Judith's manipulative use of her sexuality, for the author Judith was no weakling, but skillful in the use of weapons in her arsenal that best exploited her enemy's weakness.

[48]G. W. E. Nickelsburg, *Jewish Literature Between the Bible and the Mishnah* (Philadelphia: Fortress, 1981): 106-108, 152 n. 10, suggests that Judith is a personification of several biblical heroes and heroines. In view of a likely date of composition in the Hasmonean period, the very name "Judith" suggests a parallel with Judas Maccabeus.

[49]She prays and fasts regularly (8:6; 9:1-14; 12:6; 13:10), immerses herself daily (12:7-9), and keeps Jewish dietary laws even when she is in the enemy camp (10:6; 12:1-4).

leadership in political, military, and religious matters, and could be respected for so doing.[50]

Extra-biblical works which develop the portraits of women known from the Bible provide especially illuminating case studies of the perceptions of and roles occupied by Jewish women in the Greco-Roman period. Josephus' treatment of Rebekah has already been cited as an example of a woman whose role in Genesis has been reduced and made to conform to contemporary ideals. However, in other works biblical women receive greatly expanded roles and exalted portrayals. An example is the portrayal of Rebekah in *Jubilees*, a second-century BC rewriting of Gen. 1 through Exod. 12. Rebekah, not Isaac, assumes the mantle of leadership in this marriage and provides the bridge between Abraham and Jacob in the drama of salvation history. The exhortation to Jacob not to marry a Canaanite woman (25:1-3) and the lengthy parental blessing for Jacob (25:11-23) are given not by Isaac, but by Rebekah.[51] Not only is the matriarchal blessing without precedent in the biblical text, but Rebekah is said to have been inspired to utter it by the descent of a "spirit of truth" upon her mouth (25:14). Moreover, in her words to Jacob, she addresses some of the very problems which were of greatest concern to the author: assimilation (esp. intermarriage) with gentiles, and the contamination of the Jerusalem temple. Later, her admonitions to familial harmony become the author's means of addressing the internecine strife of the contemporary Jewish community (chap. 35). Further divine revelations to Rebekah not mentioned in the biblical text legitimate her function as the bridge from Abraham to Jacob, as a link in the all-important chain of levitical tradition, and as a spokesperson for the author's ideals (27:1; 35:6). Other alterations

---

[50]The most recent research on *Judith* is James VanderKam, ed., *"No One Spoke Ill of Her": Essays on Judith* (Early Judaism and Its Literature 2; Atlanta: Scholars Press, 1992), which I have not yet seen.

[51]Because Abraham had offered the blessing and warned against exogamy earlier (22:10-30), Rebekah's functions here parallel those of Abraham and suggest that she, not Isaac, is the crucial link in salvation history.

of the Gen. narrative confirm Rebekah's role as the more imperious partner in her marriage,[52] exonerate her from any charge of ethical impropriety, and establish her as an example for the Jewish community to emulate.[53] In every way, Rebekah is for the author of *Jubilees* "the matriarch *par excellence* of the Jewish people."[54]

In the patriarchal narratives in Genesis, Aseneth is mentioned only in passing as the wife of Joseph (Gen. 41:45, 50; 46:20), but in *Joseph and Aseneth*, an apocryphal romance from the first century BC or AD, Aseneth—not Joseph—is the leading character. In the first part of the story (chaps. 1-21), Joseph appears at the beginning and end but is absent throughout the heart of the story, where Aseneth occupies center stage. In the second part (chaps. 22-29), Aseneth again eclipses Joseph, not only by the frequency of her appearances, but also by her role alongside Levi as a prime example of and advocate for the ethical ideals which the text promotes.[55] Carefully-designed parallels between her portrayal and that of Joseph,[56] and others between her portrayal and that of Levi,[57] demonstrate that she is in no way inferior to these revered patriarchs. She

---

[52]Even Isaac's "fatherly" actions of pronouncing a blessing upon Jacob, giving a deathbed speech, and sharing a final meal with his sons, all replicate actions already taken by Rebekah (chaps. 25, 35).

[53]E.g., her preference for Jacob over Esau is no longer arbitrary favoritism, as in Gen., but a choice shared by Abraham, grounded in Jacob's moral superiority, and ordained from heaven (19:13-31; 25:14-23; 26:18).

[54]John Endres, *Biblical Interpretation in the Book of Jubilees* (CBQMS 18; Washington, D.C.: Catholic Biblical Association, 1987): 217, who also provides a much fuller discussion of Rebekah's portrait in *Jubilees*. See also Randall D. Chesnutt, "Revelatory Experiences Attributed to Biblical Women in Early Jewish Literature," *'Women Like This'*, 108-111, 119-25.

[55]See Randall D. Chesnutt, "The Social Setting and Purpose of Joseph and Aseneth," *JSP* 2 (1988): 21-48; and *idem*, "Revelatory Experiences," *'Women Like This'*, 114-15.

[56]See Chesnutt, *JSP* (1988): 31-32.

[57]*Ibid.*, 32.

rebukes the sons of Jacob for their vengefulness and becomes the leading spokesperson for the author's own ideal of clemency and non-retaliation (28:7, 10, 14). Dramatic heavenly revelations to Aseneth strengthen her ethical admonitions, her role as purveyor of revealed knowledge, and the exemplary character of her conduct (chaps. 14-17; 22:13).

As has been acknowledged above, it is impossible to determine the actual social roles and status of women from literary embellishments of biblical characters. Nevertheless, if exalted and influential positions for women such as those assumed by Rebekah in *Jubilees* and Aseneth in *Joseph and Aseneth* had been out of the question in the social environments from which these two works came, the stories could not have been expected to serve the authors' purposes. Moreover, these two authors do not throw social convention to the wind, but demonstrate great concern for proper familial and social patterns.[58] Since it is within a context of respect for proper familial and social patterns that these women are assigned significant—even dominant—roles of leadership in both home and community, and since both works present the lives of the forebears as examples for their respective Jewish communities to emulate, it appears that in the social world of these works it was possible and even desirable for a capable woman to speak out for the principles central to the life of the community and to assume an aggressive role of leadership as the situation demanded.[59]

------

[58]E.g., *Jubilees* 29:14-20, and in *Joseph and Aseneth* the recurring formula, "it is not proper for the man (woman) who worships God to . . . ." (8:5, 7; 21:1; 23:9, 12; 29:3). See further Chesnutt, "Revelatory Experiences," *'Women Like This'*, 123-24.

[59]Pseudo-Philo's *Biblical Antiquities*, an interpretive expansion of Genesis through 2 Samuel which probably dates to the first century AD, is another work which expands the portraits of certain biblical women in interesting ways. This text's expansion of Deborah's role, for example, stands in marked contrast to Josephus' downplaying of Deborah's judicial, political, and military leadership. See Cheryl A. Brown, *No Longer Be Silent: First Century Portraits of Biblical Women* (Louisville, KY: Westminster/John Knox, 1992).

The possibility of such prominent religious and social roles for women is assumed rather than argued in the two works just considered; it is a premise from which the authors proceed to deal with other concerns. However, other authors and redactors may have been more self-consciously attempting to counter the denigration of women. Thus, while *Testament of Job* 1-45 depicts and even promotes such denigration, *Testament of Job* 46-53 presents women much more positively, whether by the same author or a later redactor. As in chaps. 1-45, there is a premium on insight into heavenly reality, but here it is Job's three daughters--not the sons--who are heirs to this insight. When Job dies, his seven sons and his brother are distraught and can only weep and lament. On the other hand, Job's daughters see his soul gloriously conveyed into heaven and are therefore able to look beyond earthly afflictions to take comfort in heavenly reality and worship ecstatically in the language of angels (48:2-3; 52:6-53:4). In a reversal of the stereotypes prominent in the earlier chapters, these women become the leading characters in chaps. 46-53 who embody the author's most cherished values, while the helpless male characters are presented in most unflattering terms.[60] *Testament of Job* 46-53 projects an image of women which contrasts sharply not only with that in chaps. 1-45, but also with prevalent stereotypes of Jewish women in the Greco-Roman world.

If Levison[61] is correct that *Apocalypse of Moses* 15-30 originated independently from the remainder of the *Apocalypse of Moses*, we have yet another work which preserves divergent views of womankind. As we have seen, the *Life of Adam and Eve* and the closely-related *Apocalypse of Moses* blame Eve for the primeval sin and the human predicament. However, as Levison shows, in *Apocalypse of Moses* 15-30, which gives Eve's own testamentary account of the primeval deception, Eve's actions are explained in

---

[60]See further Chesnutt, "Revelatory Experiences," *'Women Like This'*, 115-19, 124-25; and P. W. van der Horst, "The Role of Women in the Testament of Job," *NedTTs* 40 (1986): 273-89.

[61]John R. Levison, "The Exoneration of Eve in the Apocalypse of Moses 15-30," *JSJ* 20 (1989): 135-50.

ways that are sympathetic to her. Blame is placed on Adam, and Eve is exonerated. She is no longer the ignorant, weeping, perplexed, uncontrollably enervated character of chaps. 1-14 and 31-43 who is entirely dependent upon the males in the story for insight. Levison concludes that Eve's testament in 15-30 originated independently and that a later editor obscured the exoneration of Eve by incorporating it into the larger indictment of the first woman. It is, of course, possible that the same author who wrote 1-14 and 31-43 also composed Eve's testament as a literary device by which to give the woman's perspective on the primeval fall, if only to discredit that perspective by including it in the larger work. In either case, the extant form of the *Apocalypse of Moses* reflects an awareness of the denigration of the first woman (and, through her, of womankind) and some concern to voice a more sympathetic view.

Even rabbinic literature provides one glaring example of a woman who did not conform to rabbinic stereotypes of women but whose memory was nevertheless preserved and cherished. Beruriah, wife of the second century sage, Rabbi Meir, is depicted as a scholar and teacher of Jewish law whose knowledge and skills in disputation exceeded those of the most learned and renowned rabbis of her time.[62] Recent studies have shown that the Beruriah traditions are not all of

---

[62]E.g., Babylonian Talmud *Pesahim* 62b. Specific stores about Beruriah indicate that her views were convincing to comtemporary male sages and were passed along in the tradition (Tosefta *Kelim Baba Mezia* 1:6), that she sternly rebuked a rabbi whose knowledge was defective and a student who was not studying properly (Babylonian Talmud *Erubin* 53b-54a), and that she easily refuted challenges from heretics (Babylonian Talmud *Berakot* 10a). Her reputation for studiousness spawned fantastic legends, e.g., that she studied three hundred laws from three hundred teachers in one day (Babylonian Talmud *Pesahim* 62b). In the medieval period, it also spawned attempts to defame her, as in the eleventh-century Talmudic scholar Rashi's comment on the Babylonian Talmud *Avodah Zarah* 18a, that Beruriah was caught in adultery and committed suicide. However, this late attempt to undermine her reputation is itself evidence of the high esteem in which she had been held in rabbinic circles.

equal age and historical reliability,[63] but the mere fact that
the compilers of the Talmud allowed the traditions about her
to stand and presented them in a complimentary light shows
that the rabbinic strictures on women discussed above did
not always obtain, even in the strictest rabbinic circles.

Although it is commonly assumed that women played
no public role in ancient Jewish worship, Neusner[64] notes
correctly that only three known Jewish groups denied
women such roles: the Essenes, the Temple priesthood, and
the rabbis. In other Jewish circles, there is evidence of
women's presence and even prominence in public worship.
Thus, the NT assumes the presence of women in synagogues (Matt. 13:56; Acts 16:13-15; 18:26), and epigraphic
materials considered below evidence prominent positions for
women in synagogal life. Moreover, in at least one community of Egyptian Jewish worshippers described approv-
ingly by Philo, women participated fully.[65] Members of the
Therapeutic community, both men (Therapeutae) and women
(Therapeutrides), lived rigorously ascetic lives but broke
their solitude for a weekly Sabbath assembly. Although
Philo assumes that the senior member who offered the
Sabbath discourse was a male, and although men and
women sat apart, separated by a wall that extended partway
to the ceiling so that they could hear but not see each other,
women participated "with the same ardour and with the same

---

[63]Thus David Goodblatt, "The Beruriah Traditions," *JJS* 26
(1975): 68-85, argues that the traditions about Beruriah's formal
education and those suggesting that she was the wife of Rabbi Meir
and/or the daughter of Rabbi Hananiah ben Teradyon all belong to the
latest strata of Talmudic tradition. These elaborations by the Amoraic
sages have the effect of sanitizing Beruriah's surprising independence by
giving her a venerable rabbinic genealogy and a formal education
appropriate to her authoritative station.

[64]Jacob Neusner, "From Scripture to Mishnah: The Origins of
Mishnah's Division of Women," *JJS* 30 (1979): 138-53.

[65]The following description summarizes the pertinent points of
Philo's lengthy description in *On the Contemplative Life*, our only
source of information on this intriguing monastic community near
Lake Mareotis in lower Egypt.

sense of their calling" (*On the Contemplative Life* 3). In the gathering for the Feast of Weeks, individuals in turn sang favorite hymns, many of which they had composed themselves, while the whole community of men and women joined in the closing lines and refrains. Finally, the men's and women's choirs sang, sometimes together, sometimes antiphonally, to commemorate the exodus from Egypt. Filled with ecstasy, they sang until dawn, when they returned to their individual houses to resume the life of solitude, Scripture study, prayer, contemplation, and composition of hymns (*On the Contemplative Life* 8-11). Like their male counterparts, the female members of this monastic community seem to have been well-educated and to have had considerable financial resources (*On the Contemplative Life* 3, 8-9). In fact, the principal difference between the male and female Therapeutics seems to have been that while the men had left their wives to join the community, most of the women were virgins who had chosen Wisdom as a spouse (*On the Contemplative Life* 8).[66]

In addition to developed literary portraits of Jewish women who break the patriarchal mold, brief and often incidental references to women in numerous and diverse literary sources likewise reveal cracks in the patriarchal system which is often assumed to have been watertight. Thus, the Gospels and Acts in the NT depict various Jewish women, even married ones, as quite mobile and active in public, as initiating litigation and pursuing their legal rights independently of any man, as managing complicated financial affairs, and even as serving in positions of leader-

---

[66]This last fact explains why Philo could write so favorably about the Therapeutrides when, in general, he wrote so disparagingly about women. Because most of the women in this monastic community were unmarried, childless, and post-menopausal, they lacked all of the feminine qualities which for Philo symbolized the lower, sensate part of the soul. Having transcended these feminine traits, they had achieved the higher (i.e., masculine) state of the soul requisite to mystical union with the divine. See further Ross Kraemer, "Monastic Jewish Women in Greco-Roman Egypt: Philo on the Therapeutrides," *Signs: Journal of Women in Culture and Society* 14 (1989): 342-70.

ship.[67] The gender-determined roles assigned to the characters in the second century BC apocryphal book of *Tobit* largely conform to the patriarchal model, but once again there are significant variations which lead Bow and Nickelsburg[68] to speak of "patriarchy with a twist": in the parallel prayers of Tobit and Sarah, Tobit prays in a self-centered and whining tone, while Sarah emerges as the wiser, more unselfish, and more admirable of the two (3:1-6, 10-15); Tobit's grandmother teaches the Law to her grandson (1:8); Anna ventures into the public sphere and becomes the family wage-earner when her husband is incapacitated (2:11-14), and she freely speaks her mind and rebukes her husband when his priorities are misplaced (2:14; 5:17-19; 10:7). In *IV Maccabees*, the mother of seven martyred sons is accorded a status comparable to that of Abraham in the spiritual history of Israel. She is acclaimed "mother of the nation, champion of the Law, defender of true religion . . . more noble than men in fortitude and stronger than heroes in endurance . . . guardian of the Law" (15:29-31). Even Philo recognized that his ideal of secluding women was not realized in actual practice; his castigation of women for their behavior in public presupposes that they did regularly appear in public (*On the Special Laws* 3.31). Rabbinic anecdotes about other learned and resourceful women besides Beruriah likewise suggest at least some variation in women's status and functions.[69] The non-literary records to which we now turn reveal even more cracks in the patriarchal model.

---

[67]See Mk. 5:25-34 (and par); Matt. 13:56; 14:21; 15:38; Lk. 1-2; 8:1-3; 18:1-8; and Acts 16:13-15. Neusner, "Thematic or Systematic Description," *Method and Meaning in Ancient Judaism*, 92, comments, "The women of Jesus' day and country seem to have had great liberty of movement and action."

[68]Beverly Bow and G. W. E. Nickelsburg, "Patriarchy with a Twist: Men and Women in Tobit," *'Women Like This'*, 127-143.

[69]See Hauptmann, "Images of Women in the Talmud," *Religion and Sexism*, 200-205, for a discussion of rabbinic anecdotes in which women display superior knowledge or other admirable traits. In addition to the cases cited by Hauptmann, Babylonian Talmud *Shabbat* 62a refers to a woman who is a *gizbarit* (treasurer) who makes disbursements from charity funds.

3. Non-Literary Data

Reconstructing a comprehensive picture of ancient Jewish women out of brief and disparate epigraphical and papyrological records is impossible. Nevertheless, these and other archaeological data deserve careful study as our only unbiased testimony to the way Jewish women actually lived. The following survey of the non-literary data focuses on two types of materials: inscriptions related to women's roles in ancient synagogues and the archive of Babata. Miscellaneous other non-literary items are cited only summarily to show that the surprising roles and activities of women in these sources are not at all unusual once one moves beyond the literary evidence to consider other data.

The non-literary materials bearing on our subject which have received the greatest attention are several inscriptions which imply prominent roles for women in ancient synagogues.[70] A second-century AD inscription from Smyrna in western Asia Minor reads,

> "Rufina, a Jewess, head of the synagogue, built this tomb for her freed slaves and the slaves raised in her house. No one else has the right to bury anyone (here). Anyone who dares to do (so) will pay 1500 denaria to the sacred treasury and 1000 denaria to the Jewish people. A copy of this inscription has been placed in the (public) archives."[71]

Rufina is not the only woman to be designated ἀρχισυνάγωγος, "head" or "president of the synagogue." Sophia of Gortyn is called "head of the synagogue"

---

[70]See the pivotal study of B. J. Brooten, *Women Leaders in the Ancient Synagogue* (BJS 36; Chico, CA: Scholars Press, 1982).

[71]J.-B. Frey, ed., *Corpus Inscriptionum Judaicarum*, 2 vols. (Rome: Pontificio Instituto di Archaeologia Cristiana, 1936-52): no. 741. Vol. 1 has been reprinted (NY: KTAV, 1975). The translation of this and other inscriptions follows that of Ross S. Kraemer, *Maenads, Martyrs, Matrons, Monastics: A Sourcebook on Women's Religions in the Greco-Roman World* (Philadelphia: Fortress, 1988).

(ἀρχισυναγώγισσα) at Kissamos on Crete in an inscription from the fourth or fifth century AD,[72] as is Theopempte of Myndos in western Asia Minor in an inscription from the same period.[73] Women are also referred to as "elders" in inscriptions from Crete, Thrace, Malta, North Africa, and Italy in the early centuries AD.[74] The title "mother of the synagogue" is applied to women in inscriptions from Italy (Rome, Venetia, and Venosa).[75] Jewish "priestesses" are named as early as the first century BC in epitaphs from Rome, Leontopolis (Egypt) and Beth Shearim (Palestine).[76] An inscription from Thebes names a woman "leader" or "founder" (ἀρχήγισσα) of a synagogue.[77]

What these titles suggest about women's roles in synagogue life is difficult to determine. Ἀρχήγισσα may designate a female "founder" of a synagogue rather than a woman "leader" with actual administrative responsibilities.[78] Similarly, the title "mother of the synagogue" may be merely honorific and not indicative of any official function.[79] However, not all of the titles can be restricted to honorific rather

---

[72]CII, no. 731c.

[73]CII, no. 756.

[74]CII, nos. 400, 581, 590, 597, 731c; and *Supplementum Epigraphicum Graecum* 27 (1977), no. 1201. In addition to these seven inscriptions examined by Brooten, *Women Leaders in the Ancient Synagogue*, 41-55, Ross S. Kraemer, "A New Inscription from Malta and the Question of Women Elders in the Diaspora Jewish Communities," *HTR* 78 (1985): 431-38, calls attention to two others, one yet unpublished. See also Kraemer, *Her Share of the Blessings: Women's Religions Among Pagans, Jews, and Christians in the Greco-Roman World* (New York: Oxford Univ. Press, 1992): 118, and n. 76.

[75]CII, nos. 496, 523, 639; possibly also nos. 166, 606, 619d. See Brooten, *Women Leaders in the Ancient Synagogue*, 57-72.

[76]CII, nos. 1514, 315, 1007. See Brooten, *Women Leaders in the Ancient Synagogue*, 73-99.

[77]CII, no. 696b. See Brooten, *Women Leaders in the Ancient Synagogue*, 35-39.

[78]So Brooten, *Women Leaders in the Ancient Synagogue*, 38-39.

[79]So Shaye J. D. Cohen, "Women in the Synagogues of Antiquity," *Conservative Judaism* 34 (1980): 26.

than functional significance. There is no reason to think that "elder" and "head of the synagogue" were merely titles transferred to women whose fathers or husbands functioned in these capacities, that they date from a period when the titles had lost their functional significance, or that they were functional only when applied to men. The inscriptions rather suggest that Jewish women, at least in some times and places, acted as bona fide heads of and elders of synagogues, filling all the roles filled by men who bore the same titles. These roles would include teaching, collecting the half-shekel tax, serving as a patron of building activities, arranging the services, fulfilling certain liturgical responsibilities, and perhaps dealing with outsiders.[80] Moreover, even if other titles such as "founder" and "mother of the synagogue" are honorific, they nevertheless indicate that the woman named had sufficient financial resources, influence, and prestige to play the kind of patronage role that would earn her such a title.[81]

Besides employing titles suggestive of leadership roles for women in ancient synagogues, numerous epitaphs and other inscriptions commemorate women's financial contributions to synagogues, often without reference to a husband. Women donors to synagogues are documented in Asia Minor, Syria, Cyrenaica, North Africa, and Judea.[82] The donative inscriptions on the mosaic floor of the synagogue in Apamea in Syria suggest that the bulk of the contributions there were made by women.[83] In Jewish synagogues, as in the Greco-Roman system of benefaction generally, major donors—whether male or female—may be presumed to have had considerable prestige and influence, which their contributions both reflect and enhance.[84] This

---

[80]Brooten, *Women Leaders in the Ancient Synagogue*, 27-33, 46-55.

[81]Kraemer, *Her Share of the Blessings*, 121.

[82]Texts and translations of these inscriptions are conveniently collected in Brooten, *Women Leaders in the Ancient Synagogue*, 157-65.

[83]*Ibid.*, 158-59.

[84]Kraemer, *Her Share of the Blessings*, 119.

fact is especially evident in an inscription from Phocaea in Ionia which announces the gift of a woman named Tation. Tation is said to have paid for the construction of an assembly hall and the enclosure of an open courtyard with her own funds. In appreciation, the synagogue honored her with a golden crown and the privilege of sitting in the seat of honor.[85] This important inscription not only reveals the substantial wealth and prestige of a female donor;[86] it also contradicts the common assumption that women were separated from men in the ancient synagogue as they are in modern Orthodox Judaism.[87]

Admittedly, the inscriptional evidence is too scattered geographically and chronologically for us to conclude that women regularly sat in the seat of honor or functioned as heads and elders of synagogues at the time of Christian beginnings. Even so, it must be remembered that the rabbinic texts in which women's roles are much more restricted are likewise very late and of dubious applicability to the way Judaism was actually practiced in most places in the Greco-Roman world. Neither the rabbinic deprecation of women nor the inscriptional evidences of more active and public roles for women should be taken as representative. Rather, these divergent images testify to the extreme

---

[85]*CII*, no. 738.

[86]This is true even if it is less than certain that Tation was Jewish. See Ross S. Kraemer, "Hellenistic Jewish Women: The Epigraphical Evidence," *SBLSP 1986* (ed. K. Richards; Atlanta: Scholars Press, 1986): 197-98.

[87]Even though this assumption is still quite common, there is not a shred of evidence from antiquity that women sat in an upstairs gallery or other separate section. See Brooten, *Women Leaders in the Ancient Synagogue*, 103-38. The gender segregation in the Therapeutic assemblies (Philo, *On the Contemplative Life* 3) was probably rooted in the ascetic ideals of this group and provides no evidence for synagogue practice. That Philo even mentions the physical separation of men from women in this case may imply that such was unusual. The existence of the Women's Court in the Herodian Temple is also cited often in this connection, but this arrangement was obviously not motivated by a desire to segregate the sexes, since various events took place in the Women's Court that involved both men and women.

pluralism which characterized Judaism in the Greco-Roman era. Notwithstanding the rabbinic consensus, prominent roles of leadership for women in ancient synagogues are clearly, if sparsely, documented in inscriptional sources. To ignore these sources and consider only the more familiar patriarchal model attested in rabbinic literature would be to impose upon ancient Judaism a uniformity which never actually existed.

Rufina's inscription illuminates women's roles not only in synagogal life, but in the larger social and economic arenas as well. In addition to being the head of the synagogue, Rufina is a woman of considerable independence, wealth, and social and legal authority in both Jewish and non-Jewish circles. She is head of a large household. She owns real property and slaves. She has sufficient resources to commission a costly inscription on marble. She acts publicly and autonomously without reference to a father, husband, son, or any other male. She has sufficient authority to prescribe penalties for anyone violating the tomb.[88] On virtually all these points, additional inscriptional and papyrological evidence can be cited for comparable positions of Jewish women in economic and social life. Thus, epitaphs from Asia Minor represent other women besides Rufina as owners of family burial sites.[89] Like Rufina, other women had connections and influence in the non-Jewish community.[90] The wealth and independence of many Jewish women throughout the Mediterranean world is shown by the widely-attested and generous benefactions of women to synagogues. Egyptian papyri attest Jewish women's ownership of land and livestock,[91] engagement in

---

[88]See Ross S. Kraemer, "Jewish Women in the Diaspora World of Late Antiquity," *Jewish Women in Historical Perspective*, 43-67.

[89]*CII*, nos. 762, 763, 775, 776.

[90]*CII* nos. 606, 619d (inscriptions from Venosa, Italy) may indicate that Jewish women held public office there.

[91]V. A. Tcherikover and A. Fuks, *Corpus Papyrorum Judaicarum*, 3 vols. (Cambridge, MA: Harvard Univ. Press, 1957-64): nos. 28, 41, 47. See further Sarah B. Pomeroy, "Women in Roman Egypt (A Preliminary Study Based on Papyri)," *Reflections of Women*

litigation,[92] payment of the Jewish tax,[93] arrangement of an even-handed divorce agreement,[94] and involvement in various commercial transactions such as leasing land (more often as lessor than lessee),[95] buying a house,[96] and contracting and settling debts.[97] Fifth-century BC papyri from Elephantine in upper Egypt reveal that women in this Aramaic-speaking Jewish community participated in religious ceremonies,[98] owned property and transacted business independently of father or husband,[99] and had the right to terminate a marriage.[100]

The second major group of materials mentioned at the beginning of this section, the Babata archive, will be treated only cursorily, not at all because it is lacking in importance, but because scholarly investigation of it is still in the early stages. These thirty-five papyri in Greek, Aramaic, and Nabatean, document the life of a Jewish woman and her family and associates in the Judean Desert near the Dead Sea from AD 93 to 132. The bulk of these documents, although

---

in Antiquity (ed. H. B. Foley; New York: Gordon and Breach, 1981): 303-22; and idem, Women in Hellenistic Egypt (New York: Schocken, 1984).

[92]CII, no. 19.

[93]Ibid., nos. 223, 227.

[94]Ibid., no. 144.

[95]Ibid., no. 453; and see editorial note, vol. 3, p. 10, n. 17.

[96]Ibid., no. 483.

[97]Ibid., nos. 26, 148. See further Kraemer, Helios (1986): 94-97.

[98]A. E. Cowley, Aramaic Papyri of the Fifth Century B.C. (Oxford: Clarendon Press, 1923): no. 30.

[99]See esp. the personal archive of Mibtahiah, daughter of Mahseiah (Cowley, Aramaic Papyri, nos. 5, 6, 8, 9, 13, 14, 15). See also nos. 1, 20, 25, 28, 43, and the discussion in Bezalel Porten, Archives from Elephantine: The Life of an Ancient Jewish Military Colony (Berkeley: Univ. of California Press, 1968): 235-63.

[100]Cowley, Aramaic Papyri, no. 15; and E. G. Kraeling, The Brooklyn Museum Aramaic Papyri: New Documents of the Fifth Century B.C. from the Jewish Colony at Elephantine (New Haven: Yale Univ. Press, 1953): nos. 2, 7.

found in 1961,[101] were not published until almost three decades later.[102] Gradually, studies are beginning to appear,[103] but conclusions are preliminary and tentative. All that can be attempted here is a brief description of these materials as they relate to our topic.

Babata's archive reveals a sad and complicated family history.[104] Widowed twice, she spent most of her life in litigation. However, Babata's misfortune is the modern historian's fortune, for Babata did not discard the documents recording her marriages, lawsuits, and property transactions, but meticulously arranged them in four bundles and packed them in a leather pouch, which she wrapped in sackcloth and tied with ropes. The result is "the largest single collection of ancient documents ever found in the Holy Land"[105] and a priceless source of legal, historical, geographical, and linguistic information on Palestinian Jews in the Greco-Roman period. Especially fortunate for purposes of the present study is the fact Babata and other women figure prominently in the social and legal maneuverings reflected dramatically in these documents.

---

[101]See Yigael Yadin, "The Expedition to the Judean Desert, 1961: Expedition D—The Cave of Letters," *IEJ* 12 (1962): 227-57; and H. J. Polotsky, "The Greek Papyri from the Cave of Letters," *IEJ* 12 (1962): 258-62. See also Yigael Yadin, "The Life and Trials of Babata," *Bar Kokhba: The Rediscovery of the Legendary Hero of the Last Jewish Revolt Against Imperial Rome* (London: Weidenfeld and Nicolson, 1971): 222-53.

[102]Naphtali Lewis, *The Documents from the Bar Kokhba Period in the Cave of Letters: Greek Papyri* (JDS 2; Jerusalem: Israel Exploration Society, 1989). A few texts are in Baruch Lifshitz, "Papyrus grecs du désert de Juda," *Aegyptus* 42 (1962): 240-56; Naphtali Lewis, "Two Greek Documents from Provincia Arabia," *Illinois Classical Studies* 3 (1978): 100-14; and N. Lewis, R. Katzoff, and J. C. Greenfield, "Papyrus Yadin 18," *IEJ* 37 (1987): 229-50.

[103]E.g., A. Wasserstein, "A Marriage Contract from the Province of Arabia Nova: Notes on Papyrus Yadin 18," *JQR* 80 (1989): 93-130.

[104]See Yadin, *Bar Kokhba*, 233-53.

[105]*Ibid.*, 225.

Women's ownership and management of property is well-documented in the Babata archive. In a deed dated AD 120, Shimeon (Babata's father) endows Miriam (his wife and Babata's mother) with his property in Mahoza, a village at the southern end of the Dead Sea in the Nabatean region, although Shimeon retains the use of the property during his lifetime.[106] Later Babata inherits this property from her mother.[107] A document from AD 127 has Babata, accompanied by her second husband, going to the capital of Moab to register her extensive holdings of property before the Roman district commander.[108] By AD 130, Babata's wealthy second husband, who owned property in both En-Gedi and Mahoza, has died and Babata has become the owner of several palm groves which had belonged to him. A record of her selling crops of dates from these orchards is preserved,[109] as are records of litigation over the rightful ownership of the grove in Mahoza.[110]

Babata's incessant involvement in litigation spans the entire period covered by the Greek and Aramaic documents from her archive. In court, she defends her interests against claims from various members of her late husband's family,[111] including the other wife of her second husband and the guardians of her son by her first husband.[112] The legal capabilities and initiative of Babata and other women in these documents are striking.

Among Babata's documents is also the *kethuba* (marriage contract) of her second marriage,[113] which is important as one of very few such contracts from Palestine in

---

[106]*Ibid.*, 235-37. See also Lewis, *Documents from the Bar Kokhba Period*, no. 19.

[107]Yadin, *Bar Kokhba*, 236-37, 245-46.

[108]Lewis, *Documents from the Bar Kokhba Period*, no. 16.

[109]*Ibid.*, nos. 21-22.

[110]*Ibid.*, nos. 23-26.

[111]*Ibid.*; see further Yadin, *Bar Kokhba*, 247-49.

[112]Lewis, *Documents from the Bar Kokhba Period*, nos. 12-15.

[113]Yadin, *Bar Kokhba*, 237-39.

the pre-Mishnaic period[114] and therefore a rare first-hand record of a Jewish woman's legal status. This and the other remains of the Babata trove will be the subjects of intensive study for many years. In the meantime, it is safe to say with Neusner[115] that "any picture of the Israelte [sic] woman of the second century as chattel and a dumb animal hardly accords with the actualities revealed in the legal documents of Babata."

Conclusion

Considerable diversity existed in attitudes toward and roles of Jewish women in the Greco-Roman period. Patriarchal patters predominated among the Jews as among Mediterranean peoples generally. Yet, not all Jewish women were as oppressed and repressed as some stereotypes, both ancient and modern, suggest. Significant instances of active and public involvement of Jewish women in social, economic, political, and religious life are known.

Any study of women in the NT and early Christianity which proceeds on the assumption of a monolithic model of ancient Judaism is misinformed and distortive. Judaism existed in the Greco-Roman era in countless local varieties. Before comparing or contrasting ancient Jewish belief and practice with regard to women and some NT text on the subject, one must specify *which* Jewish text, or *which* group of Jews, is meant. This means, among other things, that the complimentary images and prominent roles of women in certain early Christian texts can no longer be considered radical departures from the Jewish heritage, for such can be documented in Jewish sources as well.

---

[114]See Lewis, *Documents from the Bar Kokhba Period*, no. 18; P. Benoit, J. T. Milik, and R. de Vaux, *Les grottes du Murabbaat* (DJD 2; Oxford: Oxford Univ. press, 1961): nos. 20, 21, 115; and Léonie J. Archer, *Her Price is Beyond Rubies: The Jewish Woman in Graeco-Roman Palestine* (JSOTSup 60; Sheffield: Sheffield Academic Press, 1990): 291-99.

[115]Neusner, "Thematic or Systematic Description," *Method and Meaning in Ancient Judaism*, 93.

Chapter Five

"NEITHER MALE AND FEMALE" (GAL. 3:28)

Jan Hailey

Thoughout the history of the church, Paul's statement in Gal. 3:28 has provided impetus for religious and social change. Rooted in this common source are acceptance of Gentiles into the first century church,[1] elimination of anti-Semitism,[2] abolition of slavery in Western civilization,[3] and liberation of women from political and religious strictures.[4] Often taking the form of a slogan, e.g., "Magna Carta of Humanity,"[5] this text is the exhordium for Christians who seek to resolve social, racial, and gender distinctions, as well as a problem to those who seek to retain them. It is not without good reason that Snodgrass[6] calls it "the most socially explosive statement in the New Testament."

Admittedly, Gal. 3:28 is a crucial text in the study of male and female in Christian thought, but the fervor with which the verse has been embraced is reason for caution in its use. Johnson observes that, "the vigorous debate over sex roles has, in effect, lifted it from its exegetical under-

---

[1]Hans Dieter Betz, *Galatians: A Commentary of Paul's Letter to the Churches in Galatia* (Philadelphia: Fortress, 1979): 186.

[2]Richard Longenecker, *New Testament Social Ethics for Today* (Grand Rapids: Eerdmans, 1984): 39-47.

[3]Krister Stendahl, *The Bible and the Role of Women* (FBBS 15; trans. E. T. Sander; Philadelphia: Fortress, 1966): 34; Paul K. Jewett, *Man as Male and Female* (Grand Rapids: Eerdmans, 1975): 144.

[4]Susie C. Stanley, "Response," *Women, Authority & The Bible* (ed. A. Mickelsen: Downers Grove, IL: InterVarsity, 1986): 185-89.

[5]Paul K. Jewett, *Man as Male and Female*, 142.

[6]Klyne Snodgrass, "Galatians 3:28: Conundrum or Solution?" *Women, Authority & The Bible*, 161.

pinnings and set it as a lonely text, a kind of proof-text, in the midst of swirling theological debate."[7] Now, the primary purpose of Gal. 3:28 is not really at issue. Common exegesis understands Paul here to be advocating that access to God is open to all through faith in Christ, without regard to race, social standing, or gender. The principal question which arises, however, is whether the disregard for these categories extends beyond spiritual salvation into social and ecclesiastical dimensions. For instance, is there an implied equality of roles and functions in the church? Do social implications necessarily follow from the spiritual implications of the passage? Can accommodations to cultural roles within the church be observed without violating Paul's call to unity? In view of the bewildering variety of uses to which this verse has been put, an examination of the text in its literary and historical contexts is warranted.

1. *The Diversity of Interpretation of Gal. 3:28*[8]

Few interpreters are as candid in their approach to the contextual study of Gal. 3:28 as Snodgrass, who says frankly "the context gives little help in interpreting these

---

[7]S. Lewis Johnson, "Role Distinctions in the Church: Galatians 3:28," *Recovering Biblical Manhood & Womanhood: A Response to Evangelical Feminism* (ed. J. Piper & W. Grudem; Wheaton: Crossway, 1991): 154. Snodgrass, "Gal. 3:28," *Women, Authority & The Bible*, 161, refers to this text as "a hermeneutical skeleton key by which we may go through any door we choose."

[8]The brief nature of this study precludes a comprehensive review of Gal. 3:28 in the literature of male-female relationships. Although Wayne Meeks, "The Image of the Androgyne: Some Uses of a Symbol in Earliest Christianity," *HR* 13 (1974): 165-208, has some degree of influence in egalitarian literature, it will not be addressed. Also excluded from consideration here will be the works of those whose primary purpose is the establishment of a feminist hermeneutic rather than a consideration of Gal. 3:28 in context, e.g. Elisabeth Schüssler Fiorenza, *In Memory of Her: A Feminist Reconstruction of Christian Origins* (New York: Crossroad, 1983); Mary Daly, *Beyond God the Father: Toward a Philosophy of Women"s Liberation* (Boston: Beason, 1973).

words."[9] A review of the literature, however, reveals that more often than not, the meaning of Gal. 3:28 is determined by an array of historical and cultural influences external to the Galatian letter. This diversity of outlook has so colored the meaning of the passage that interpretation ranges from an "absolute statement that abrogates all differences and governs the interpretations of all other New Testament texts on women"[10] to the mere indication that religious "justification is without regard to racial, social, or sexual differences."[11]

Both those who see Gal. 3:28 as a mandate for the removal of gender role distinctions (henceforth referred to as egalitarians) and those who take the more traditional view that gender restrictions are valid in church and society (hierarchicalists) bring at least four things to bear on the interpretation of "neither male and female." Each group has a hermeneutic shaped by one or more of the following: 1) a cultural orientation; 2) a view of the inspiration of the Scriptures; 3) a particular view toward the function of Gal. 3:28 in the biblical literature of male-female relationships; and 4) a set of theological priorities concerning creation and redemption. Each area provides hierarchicalists and egalitarians alike a network of supporting texts and method of dealing with problematic texts.

A. *The Egalitarian Approach*

1. *Cultural Orientation.* Most writers who seek to broaden the availability of leadership roles to women come to the passage with a sense of urgency to right an injustice, begun after the church of Paul's day and perpetuated by the institutional church for succeeding centuries. The subordination of women is viewed as parallel to the

---

[9]Snodgrass, "Gal. 3:28," *Women, Authority & The Bible*, 161.

[10]Ruth A. Tucker and Walter L. Liefeld, *Daughters of the Church* (Grand Rapids: Academie Books, 1987): 453.

[11]H. Wayne House, *The Role of Women in Ministry Today* (Nashville: Thomas Nelson, 1990): 101.

institution of slavery[12] and with much the same disdain, influenced to some degree, no doubt, by a sympathy for the women's movement of recent years. Longenecker says, "Though it is unpleasant to confess, it must in all honesty be said that there still exists among Christians today an attitude toward women which is, for the most part, a put-down."[13] He urges Christians individually and collectively to hear the "clear cultural mandate" of Gal. 3:28 as the "Magna Carta of the New Humanity."[14] The denial of ecclesiastical equality to women, along with social and civil equality, is seen as wrong because the door Paul has opened for women, Gentiles, and slaves is a door "no man can shut without severely hurting the church's life and witness to the world."[15] While these distinctions between Christians have not ceased to exist in the world, egalitarians stress that they have become inappropriate in the church.[16]

2. *Theological Orientation.* Along with this cultural orientation sympathetic to broader roles for women is a theological perspective toward creation and redemption stressing that what has happened in history through Christ and what happens in the believer in baptism supercedes every other reality. Early Christians, including Paul, worked with questions of sexual roles from two points: what God has done in creation and what God has done in redemption.[17] Gal. 3:28 is seen as the affirmation that Man will always be male and female because God created him so, but what happens in baptism "transcends the Law itself and thereby even the order of creation."[18] Longenecker notes:

---

[12]See Krister Stendahl, *The Bible and the Role of Women,* 34; also Mary Stewart Van Leeuwen, *Gender and Grace* (Downers Grove, IL: IVP, 1990): 237-239.

[13]Longenecker, *New Testament Social Ethics,* 92.

[14]*Ibid.,* 46-47.

[15]Barbara Hall, "Church in the World: Paul and Women," *TToday* 31 (1974): 52.

[16]G. B. Caird, "Paul and Women's Liberty," *BJRL* 54 (1972): 274.

[17]Snodgrass, *Women, Authority & The Bible,* 82.

[18]Stendahl, *The Bible and the Role of Women,* 34.

At the heart of the problem as it exists in the Church is the question of how we correlate the theological categories of creation and redemption. Where the former is stressed, subordination and submission are usually emphasized—sometimes even silence; where the latter is stressed, freedom, mutuality, and equality are usually emphasized. [Paul attempted] to keep both categories united—though, I would insist, with an emphasis on redemption. Because of creation there are differences between the sexes which exist for the blessing of both men and women and for the benefit of society. . . . Yet Paul also lays emphasis on redemption in such a way as to indicate that what God has done in Christ transcends what is true simply because of creation.[19]

Witherington basically agrees, but adds that rather than transcending creation, Christ transforms it. What is done in him is a fulfillment of God's original purpose.[20] Men and women are redeemed from false stereotypes which inhibit their true relationship intended by God.[21] Rather than viewing creation through the accounts in Gen. 2 or Gen. 3, some egalitarians, noting the unusual wording in Gal. 3:28, believe it indicates a tie to Gen. 1:27 and a restoration of the original relationship before the Fall.[22]

---

[19]Longenecker, *New Testament Social Ethics*, 92.

[20]Ben Witherington, *Women and the Genesis of Christianity* (Cambridge: Cambridge Univ. Press, 1990): 244.

[21]Jewett, *Man as Male and Female*, 143-144.

[22]Jewett, *Man as Male and Female*, 142; Snodgrass, "Gal. 3:28," *Women, Authority & the Bible*, 176; F. F. Bruce, *Commentary on Galatians* (Grand Rapids: Eerdmans, 1982): 189. In most translations the phrase is rendered "neither male *nor* female," but literally what Paul says is closer to "not 'male *and* female'," reflecting the wording in the Septuagint translation of Gen. 1:27. The words for man and woman are not used together by Paul in any other place. The only other NT usage is by Jesus in Mark 10:6. Jewett believes that this indicates Paul is deliberately differentiating from the second creation narrative, which he uses exclusively when speaking of women's subordination.

3. *The Eschaton and the Function of Scripture.*
Egalitarians see Paul's view of eschatological reality as a
corollary of the primacy of redemption. Scripture, then,
functions to advance the new world order in which the male-
female relationship has been changed. As time passed
without Christ's return, Paul saw with increasing clarity that
the new age, while still in the future, had already begun.
The future world has broken into the present old world and
manifests itself in a new creation, in disjunction from the old
but in conjunction with the pre-Fall creation: "This new
world is not bound to the mores, the laws, or the societal
roles of the old world."[23] Egalitarian thought attributes
seeming contradictions in Paul's thought to the fact that he is
dealing with two worlds that are operating concurrently.
The new age has begun in Christ's body of redeemed
believers, but the the old age is still operative in the world
and cannot be ignored.[24]

3a. *Gal. 3:28 as Basic Principle.* The concept of
"realized eschatology" influences the manner in which Gal.
3:28 functions in the body of Scriptures dealing with male
and female. It is the vision of the new age, the "eschaton."
With its broad, universal tone, Gal. 3:28 refers to standing
on equal terms before God in the age of redemption. Roles
and functions which are based on the distinctions of the old
age are not operative in the new community. Therefore, for
those who would broaden the availability of leadership roles
and participation in public worship to women, Gal. 3:28 has
served as a *locus classicus.*[25] The verse is taken to be
Paul's programmatic statement about male-female relationships.[26] Bruce, for instance, holds that restrictions on
women elsewhere in Paul's writings are "to be understood in
relation to Gal. 3:28, and not vice versa."[27] Thus, Paul's

---

[23]Robin Scroggs, "Paul and the Eschatological Woman," *JAAR*
40 (1972): 287.

[24]Caird, "Paul and Women's Liberty," *BJRL,* 274.

[25]Fiorenza, *In Memory of Her,* 205.

[26]Witherington, *Women and the Genesis of Christianity,* 7.
Gasque, "Response," *Women, Authority & The Bible,* 189.

[27]Bruce, *Galatians,* 190.

Galatian declaration of freedom should be understood as the universal principle, while passages which might seem to be contradictory (1 Tim. 2:12 and 1 Cor. 14:34-35) are correctives for a particular situation.

3b. *Other Texts as a Support Network.* Other pertinent texts that are placed "alongside Galatians" by egalitarians as a kind of support network fall into two groups. First are the many NT references to women which illustrate Paul's respect and concern for many women with whom he has worked.[28] Also included are those women who, with Paul's apparent blessing, may have served in some kind of official role or participated in public worship or teaching to a degree not characteristic of traditional church practice.[29] These texts highlight Paul's commitment to his statement of equality in Gal. 3:28. While some of his writings sound more restrictive, Paul's treatment of women in the early church was consistent with Gal. 3:28. Paul is not to be categorized as a misogynist.[30]

Second, parallel texts[31] are offered in support of the suggestion that Gal. 3:28 is part of a baptismal formula commonly used in the early church because the baptismal context is present in each instance and the wording is similar except that "male and female" is omitted in the former references.[32] Taken together with Gal. 3:28, these texts indicate that the early church was committed to the understanding of radical equality in Christ.

3c. *Problematic Texts.* The passages in 1 Tim. 2 and 1 Cor. 14 which seem to be in direct contradiction to the freedom from discrimination in Galatians are the most troublesome to the egalitarian interpretation of Gal. 3:28.

---

[28]E.g., Romans 16; Acts 16:13; Acts 18:24-26; Acts 17:4, 12.

[29]Phoebe, Priscilla, the daughters of Philip, Lydia and others.

[30]Jewett, *Man as Male and Female,* 145.

[31]Col. 3:9-11 and 1 Cor. 12:13.

[32]Snodgrass, "Gal. 3:28," *Women, Authority & The Bible,* 173; Witherington, *Women and the Genesis of Christianity,* 163.

Some egalitarians assume that Paul wrote neither of the passages in question, classifying 1 Tim. as pseudo-Pauline and 1 Cor. 14:34-35 as an interpolation.[33] Others, noting the developmental nature of Pauline thought and biblical theology,[34] view Paul as inconsistent. As he was both a Jew and a Christian, Paul's thinking about women simply reflects both of these experiences.[35] Too, Paul is cautious in his implementation of his own Christian insight. As Longenecker suggests, "his perception was not anywhere as clear nor his action anywhere as decisive in this area as it was with respect to the principle 'neither Jew nor Greek'."[36] Jewett[37] observes,

> So far as woman's role in the partnership of life is concerned, it can hardly be the degree of implementation in the New Testament church to which we should look for authoritative guidance in our present moment of history. . . . We should look to the passages which point beyond these first century attitudes toward women to the ideal of the new humanity in Christ.

Snodgrass points to another concern that may be responsible for seeming inconsistencies in Paul's writings, noting, "That Paul did not spell out the implications for slaves and women more than he did is not too surprising if one allows for his concern for missions."[38] Since Paul is a

---

[33]Robin Scroggs, "Paul and the Eschatological Woman: Revisited," *JAAR* 42 (1974): 533; Gordon D. Fee, *The First Epistle to the Corinthians* (Grand Rapids: Eerdmans, 1987): 699-708; Derwood C. Smith, "Paul and the Non-Eschatological Women," *Ohio Journal of Religious Studies* 4 (1976): 15.

[34]Longenecker, *New Testament Social Ethics*, 26. For an introduction to the developmental nature of Pauline theology, see Victor Paul Furnish, "Development in Paul's Thought," *JAAR* 38 (1970): 289-303.

[35]Jewett, *Man as Male and Female*, 112.

[36]Longenecker, *New Testament Social Ethics*, 68.

[37]Jewett, *Man as Male and Female*, 92.

[38]Snodgrass, "Gal. 3:28," *Women, Authority & The Bible*, 179.

missionary, discrepancies between Gal. 3:28 and other passages should be seen as accommodations to culture which are necessary so that the primary focus of the gospel will remain on Christ, rather than on any upheaval radical social change might cause.[39] So, Paul set his theology of women on this principle and acted in accordance with it as much as possible while still making some accommodations to the prevailing culture of his target audience.

By allowing Gal. 3:28 to function as universal principle and more restrictive passages as correctives to specific situations, Paul's strategy has flexibility, yet is consistent with his treatment of women. Gasque[40] writes, "It is hermeneutically illegitimate to set up as theologically normative passages such as 1 Cor. 14:34-35 and 1 Tim. 2:11-12 where Paul is dealing with concrete local situations," when they set aside the theological thrust of Gal. 3:28.

B. *The Hierarchicalist Approach.* Those who take a traditionalist stance prohibit any application of Gal. 3:28 beyond the realm of salvation. Hurley[41] states that Paul is not "reflecting upon relations within the body of Christ" but is only "thinking about the basis of membership in the body." Thus, the only question addressed by the passage is "Who may become a son of God, and on what basis?" To go beyond this context, House objects, would be to "violate the meaning of the text by drawing illogical conclusions . . . [it is] *non sequitor* reasoning."[42]

1. *Appreciation of Tradition.* The interpretation of Gal. 3:28 is restricted, first of all, by a cultural alignment with centuries of church teaching. Johnson includes in his study

[39]James G. Sigountos and Myron Shank, "Public Roles for Women in the Pauline Church; A Reappraisal of the Evidence," *JETS* 26 (1983): 293, note, "Paul is more concerned with the success of the mission than in abstract social progress."

[40]Gasque, "Response," *Women, Authority & The Bible,* 189.

[41]James B. Hurley, *Man and Woman in Biblical Perspective* (Grand Rapids: Zondervan, 1981): 126.

[42]House, *The Role of Women in Ministry Today,* 106.

of the passage a review of the teaching of early church
fathers, stressing the fact that hundreds of years of
prayerful, earnest scholarship have gone into the study of
this passage with the same result: "None of the major
teachers in the history of the church thought Gal. 3:28
abolished the male-female role distinctions in marriage or the
church."[43] Calling into question the motives of those who
promote a new interpretation, he argues that the burden of
proof should be on the new theory rather than on traditional
church teaching.[44]

2. *Social Orientation.* In accord with this appreciation
of tradition is a lack of sympathy toward correcting any
social problems dealing with male-female roles. Hierarchicalists eagerly point out the great advances Christianity
brought in the humane treatment of women, and also are
quick to decry the controversies in modern churches caused
by the women's movement.[45] They stress that distinctions
in role function do not equate to lesser value and that
subordination does not equal inferiority. The inclusion of
the male-female category with Jew-Greek and slave-free
serves only to illustrate the superiority of the spiritual
privileges in the body of Christ through the equality of the
initiatory ordinance. Circumcision, the rite of membership
in the covenant of Judaism, is limited only to men, but
baptism, the symbol of acceptance of Christianity, is open to
women as well.[46] Thus, as Madeleine Boucher puts it:

-----

[43]Johnson, "Role Distinctions in the Church: Gal. 3:28,"
Recovering Biblical Manhood & Womanhood, 163-164. See also
Charles Caldwell Ryrie, *The Place of Women in the Church* (New
York: Macmillan, 1958): 156; see also 97-137. George W. Knight,
The Role Relationship of Men & Women: New Testament Teaching,
(rev. ed.; Chicago: Moody, 1985): 5, mentions the affirmation of the
historic Christian tradition by a number of denominational synods and
boards.

[44]Johnson, "Role Distinctions in the Church: Gal. 3:28,"
Recovering Biblical Manhood & Womanhood, 164.

[45]E.g., House, *The Role of Women in Ministry Today*, 11, 17.

[46]Ryrie, *The Place of Women in the Church*, 70-71.

. . . Paul was not calling for any social reforms: inequalities would continue to exist in the Church. Paul fully intended that women and slaves remain in the subordinate place in which he thought God had put them. The only practical change demanded by Paul—and this is the thrust of Gal. 3:28—was the admission of Gentiles, law-free, into the Church.[47]

3. *View of Scripture.* By far, however, the weightiest argument that hierarchicalists bring to this study is a view of biblical inerrancy which precludes any suggestions of deteuro-Pauline authorship or interpolation. Nor can there be an acceptance of a developmental nature of Paul's theology or the idea that Paul's writing might contain human elements that demonstrate inconsistency or bias on his part. The issue takes on the scope of much greater proportions than the interpretation of one verse. As House states, "The Bible is inspired—infallible, entirely true and without error in original manuscript. The women's issue touches the believeability and applicability of portions of God's word."[48] In a similar vein, Hurley believes that to give in to one point of apostolic authority is to open all points to question. "The authority of Scripture is the issue which is finally under debate."[49]

The practical effect of this view is a compelling need to harmonize all Scriptures which teach about women's roles in family and church. Johnson asserts, "Scripture cannot contradict Scripture. . . . It is the view of our Lord and his apostles."[50] Thus the passage is necessarily viewed through the lens of texts outside of the Galatian letter.

---

[47]Madeleine Boucher, quoted in House, *The Role of Women in Ministry Today*, 101.

[48]House, *The Role of Women in Ministry Today*, 13.

[49]Hurley, *Man and Woman in Biblical Perspective*, 204.

[50]Johnson, "Role Distinctions in the Church: Gal. 3:28," *Recovering Biblical Manhood & Womanhood*, 162.

4. *Order of Creation.* Another point in determining contextual meaning is the theological argument that the male-female relationship has its foundation in the order of creation. That Paul bases other passages that deal with the subject on the order of creation[51] is viewed as incontrovertible proof of the argument. All the creation accounts are seen to have an important place in the relevation of the relationship between man and woman. Genesis 1 demonstrates their joint role, Genesis 2 the formation of man and his exercise of authority over woman, and Genesis 3 shows the headship of man reflected in his being called to account in the Fall.[52] Since God created man first and then woman from man, man's leadership is based on his role as the first-born. Since Adam names woman, a prerogative of one who has authority, man is to be the primary leader. Woman's function is to be man's helper, but this is not a role which indicates she is of lesser (or greater) value. By the creation of man and woman as image bearers of God, and by the redemption "that renews that created image quality, the unity and equality of male and female are most fundamentally affirmed."[53] According to Ortlund, "nothing can change the fact that God created male headship as one aspect of our pre-fall perfection. . . . Christian redemption does not redefine creation: it restores creation . . . ."[54]

5. *Women in the NT.* The difficult passages for hierarchicalists to reconcile are those where women may have functioned in official roles or public worship such as Phoebe, Priscilla, Junia, and the women who prayed and prophesied in Corinth. Hierarchicalists counter that although women were visible and greatly valued by Jesus and Paul,[55] they were still limited in the roles they held and these limits were God-ordained.

---

[51]1 Tim. 2:12-14; 1 Cor. 11:8; Eph. 5:22ff.

[52]Hurley, *Man and Woman in Biblical Perspective,* 202-219.

[53]Knight, *The Role Relationship of Men & Woman,* 8.

[54]Raymond C. Ortlund, Jr., "Male-Female Equality and Male Headship," in *Recovering Biblical Manhood & Womanhood,* 109.

[55]Knight, *The Role Relationship of Men & Women,* 35-36; Hurley, *Man and Woman in Biblical Perspective,* 116.

Johnson, in reply to Snodgrass, insists that it does not follow that the church *must* grant women, who are fully equal in Christ, the office of elder and the freedom to teach in the gathered church any more than these functions must be granted to all men. When dealing with two passages which seem to be contradictory with roles Paul affirmed for women (such as 1 Cor. 11 and 1 Cor. 14), Ryrie would make the more prohibitive passage normative and the less restrictive the exception, because "Paul's basic principle was not something which was simply forged on the spur of the moment because of the particular situation in one local church of the first century."[56] Thus, the women who are mentioned by name as Paul's co-workers or singled out in some way for their service must have served in an *unofficial* capacity. Phoebe, then, was not a deacon in this view, but only "served in a diaconal area."[57]

With regard to the prayers and prophecy of women in Corinth, these actions either did not occur in a public worship setting, or Paul mentions them but doesn't condone them, or these were approved by Paul because there was no implication of headship or authority.[58] Obviously, the more specific passages are seen as carrying the greater force in determining role relationships, and whatever Gal. 3:28 means to hierarchicalists, the meaning is limited in the areas of church and family, for this is the primary area of man's headship.[59]

To the argument posed by egalitarians that sociological changes were brought about between Jews and Gentiles and slaves and free on account of Gal. 3:28, hierarchicalists counter that the order of creation necessitates a difference in

---

[56]Ryrie, *The Place of Women in the Church,* 78-79.

[57]Knight, *The Role Relationship of Men & Women,* 36. It should be noted that Hurley (*Man and Woman in Biblical Perspective,* 232-233) disagrees and would open this role, cautiously, to women, provided that the church did not see this as an authoritative office.

[58]Knight, *The Role Relationship of Men & Women,* 38; Hurley, *Man and Woman in Biblical Perspective,* 187.

[59]Knight, *The Role Relationship of Men & Women,* 41, 86.

the male-female relationship from the other two categories in the verse. While social changes may have been a natural consequence of Paul's teaching in Galatians for the other two parts of the triad, it should not be a natural consequence of the male-female component.

Swartley, commenting on the problem of determining interpretation of scripture on controversial issues, says, "It is striking to note how one's position affects and even determines what one sees in the text."[60] It is precisely this problem which makes the careful study of the passage within its entire context so important.

2. Gal. 3:28 in its Literary Context

A. Preliminary Considerations.

1. *Superiority of Christ.* Fundamental to the understanding of Gal. 3:28 are two elements which are inextricably tied to the arguments Paul makes to the Galatians throughout the epistle. The first is the thematic insistence on the superiority of Christ—the point which undergirds what most commentators see as the central theological treatise of the book, faith vs. law.[61] Paul's lengthy response to his opponents concerning justification by faith in Christ rather than works of the law (especially

---

[60]Willard Swartley, *Slavery, Sabbath, War & Women* (Scottdale, PA: Herald, 1983): 183.

[61]See J. B. Lightfoot, *The Epistle of St.Paul to the Galatians* (Grand Rapids: Zondervan, 1957): 65-68; F. F. Bruce, *Commentary on Galatians*, 2. An alternative view is presented by James D. G. Dunn in "The Theology of Galatians," *SBLSP* (Atlanta: Scholars Press, 1988): 1-16, who sees the book as Paul's first dealings with covenantal nomism, or the understanding of the relationship between God and Israel as an exclusive sense of privilege and prerogative against all other peoples. This led to a national identity of ethnic pride and a sense of exclusiveness. Paul argues against this exclusiveness rather than a system of "works salvation." Richard Longenecker, *Galatians* (Dallas: Word, 1990): 219, agrees on the use of the term nomism, but concedes that any nomistic position can also be legalistic because the two can be intertwined and confused.

circumcision) make up the heart of his argument. Gaventa calls attention, however, to a broader theme which helps to put Gal. 3:28 within the framework of a larger purpose. "The theology reflected in Galatians is first of all about Jesus Christ and the new creation God has begun in him (1:1-4, 6:14-15), and only in the light of that christocentrism can Paul's remarks concerning the law be understood."[62]

Galatians is not so much a treatise on faith vs. law, but on Christ vs. *anything else.* Gaventa notes correctly, "The governing antithesis in Galatians is between Christ/new creation and the cosmos, and the antitheses between Christ and the law, and between the cross and circumcision, follow from this central premise."[63] Christ is the exclusive priority. This is the essential principle that stands behind the book as a whole. Paul alternates between the superiority of Christ and the weaknesses of the law, but any other teaching (i.e., elements of syncretism or behavior) could easily be substituted for the law. It is not that the law is inherently bad, but it is inherently inferior to Christ. "Zeal for tradition, maintenance of the Law, ethnic and social barriers, and observance of feast are alike insofar as they threaten to undermine the exclusive claim of gospel."[64] And compromise of the gospel of Christ in any way is disastrous.[65] There are authority issues and lifestyle/

---

[62]Beverly Roberts Gaventa, "The Singularity of the Gospel: A Reading of Galatians," *SBLSP* (Atlanta: Scholars Press, 1988): 17-26.

[63]*Ibid.*, 19.

[64]Beverly Roberts Gaventa, "Galatians 1 and 2: Autobiography as Paradigm," *NovT* 28 (1986): 319.

[65]W. D. Davies, *Jewish and Pauline Studies* (Philadelphia: Fortress, 1984): 92-93, distinctions between the various meanings of the term "law" should be noted: 1) the commandments which are to be obeyed; 2) the history of the people of Israel in various stages; 3) the wisdom which is the means of expressing the divine activity in creation, morality and knowledge; and 4) the whole of the revealed will of God in the universe, in nature, and in human society. Paul most often uses the term "works of law" in Galatians, referring to the

behavior issues in Galatians which are not directly dependent upon the teaching of faith and law, but rather come from the principal question, Is Christ adequate for every area of the life of the believer?

Growing out of this priority is an emphasis on the community "in Christ."[66] Longenecker sees this as "the essence of the Christian proclamation and experience. One may discuss legalism, nomism, and even justification by faith, but without treating the 'in Christ' motif we miss the heart of the Christian message."[67] It is the "in Christ" teaching which suggests whether (and in what way) Paul intends to influence social and religious relationships, or whether he is concerned only that his Gentile readers have a cognitive understanding that they are not bound to comply with the Jewish law in order to be saved. An enhanced relationship "in Christ" is what Paul's opponents would have the Galatians gain through circumcision.[68] It is the corporate nature of the body that sheds light on the interpretation of "not male and female" by establishing the

---

commandments which Israel was to obey, hence more specifically designated "legalism."

[66]Bruce J. Malina, *The New Testament World: Insights From Cultural Antropology* (Louisville: John Knox, 1981): 54-55, points to the necessity of viewing the first century culture as one oriented around group identity rather than individual, in contrast to modern American culture. "In our culture we are brought up to stand on our own two feet, as distinctive wholes, distinctive individuals. . . . When we relate to other people, we feel that they are as distinct and unique beings as we ourselves. In additional to being unique and distinct persons, each of us lives within our unique social and natural environments. This is individualism, and this sort of individualism is rare in the world's cultures today. It was perhaps totally absent from the New Testament." He maintains that people in that culture, as in all cultures which organize themselves around the values of honor and shame, always perceive themselves to be interrelated to others within horizontal and vertical social positions.

[67]Longenecker, *Galatians*, 151.

[68]Elinor M. Rogers, *The Semantic Structure Analysis of Galatians* (Dallas: Summer Institute of Linquistics, 1989): 103.

nature of union in Christ—the oneness that exists among all who have responded through faith and "clothed themselves" with Christ through baptism (3:27).

   2. *Context of Conflict.* The pervasive element of conflict in the epistle is the second consideration the interpreter should bear in mind. The principle of the authoritative preeminence of Jesus is worked out in a context bound from beginning to end by multifaceted conflict. Disagreement exists over spiritual doctrine, intellectual arguments, and conflict from differing traditions and backgrounds. But the seldom-noticed conflict that permeates the epistle is *the power struggle which arises out of relationships that are unequal.* Oppression, coercion, deceptive persuasion, and manipulation are mentioned either in word or in situation more than twenty times in the letter, excluding the works of the flesh in the vice list of chapter five (and at least half of those mentioned easily fall within these categories).[69] Words and phrases like "kept you from obeying the truth" (5:7); "enslaved" (4:9; 2:40); "compelled" (2:3; 6:12); "forced" (2:14); and "alienate" (4:17; 5:4) weave a common thread through the context.

   Paul is concerned with two groups in this letter. One group attempted to manipulate, or perhaps coerce, Gentile Christians into accepting a "different gospel"[70] and the other group allowed themselves to be so compelled. Neither group perceive themselves to be on the same level as the other, so Paul uses words and examples which characterize

---

   [69]Although Longenecker, *Galatians*, 253, takes the list as a random collection, he notes that Lightfoot and Burton categorize these eight sins as vices having to do with interpersonal conflict.

   [70]While there has been much speculation about the identity of Paul's opponents, it is not critical to the understanding of Gal. 3:28 to know whether they were Jewish Christians (with or without the sanction of Jerusalem) or Gentile Christians. The point is that they acted out of a selfish desire to force behavior in conformance with their wishes. See Loyd Gaston, "Paul and the Law in Galatians 2-3," *Paul and the Gospel, Anti-Judaism in Early Christianity I* (Wilfrid Laurier Univ. Press, 1986): nn. 8, 39.

coercive relationships in order to speak to their situation. He establishes the authority of Jesus and defines the proper mode of Christian behavior within the parameters of community and conflict.

Paul marshals his arguments to convince the Gentile Christians that they must stand firm against this intrusive and incorrect teaching, this perverted gospel. There are three things he does to accomplish this goal. First, he speaks to them from an authoritative position. He impresses upon his audience that his teaching is not on the same level as his opponents. His background and understanding are particularly pertinent for their situation. Second, he gives them a sense of their true value "in Christ." They are not subject to viewing one another through the same set of cultural lenses as their society in general. Their nature and standing must be clearly understood to be a real and significant reason for resistance to the temptation of seeking worth or righteousness by other means. Third, Paul describes how such value is made manifest in community relationships by answering the questions, How should people of such high value treat one another? Are they to be arrogant and manipulative, taking advantage of one another? He tells them what freedom in Christ looks like.

B. Discourse Analysis of Galatians

1. *Gal. 1:1-9.* Paul begins his letter with the typical epistolary salutation, establishing the legitimacy of his authority (which has evidently been called into question by the troublemakers) through his identification as an apostle by making his appeal on the basis of the authority of Jesus, *sent from God the Father.* Longenecker[71] notes the oddity of the reversal of the order in which the divine names are mentioned. Paul commonly refers to God the Father first

---

[71]Longenecker, *Galatians*, 4. See Rom. 1:7; 1 Cor. 1:3; 2 Cor. 1:2; Eph. 1:2; Phil. 1:2; 1 Thess, 1:1; 2 Thess. 1:1; 1:12; 1 Tim. 1:2; 2 Tim. 1:2; Titus 1:4; Phlm. 3. Betz, *Galatians*, 41, attaches no significance to the order, saying only that it is done because of the modifying clause, "who raised him from the dead."

and Jesus Christ second. Also unusual is the additional mention of Jesus and the Paul's highlighting the fact of his saving sacrifice by "the will of our God and Father" (1:4). The basis for Paul's authority is the direct revelation from Christ himself, whose mission and sacrifice is in turn linked directly with the Father and the Father's will. There is no intermediary nor is there any intermediate teaching . . . only Jesus himself, his death and his resurrection.

Paul's direct statement of the problem in Galatia without his customary prayer of thankfulness lends a sense of urgency to this intense, emotional letter. The Galatians are in critical danger. They are turning away from the gospel of Christ to another gospel, resulting in their having "fallen from grace" (5:4). As Paul makes clear through the course of the letter, they have lost their focus on Christ because they have allowed other people to persuade them that their righteousness is not quite complete. Certain elements of the law (i.e., circumcision) and Jewish rituals based on the observance of special days are perceived as beneficial to these new Christians, either as a means of completing their salvation, helping them to gain a more complete religious awareness,[72] or making themselves more desirable.[73] And, as usually is the case, having replaced Christ as the central core of their faith, their relationships with each other have become marked by disharmony, backbiting, arrogance, and other "acts of sinful nature" (5:19-21).

2. *Gal. 1:10-2:21.* Paul follows his introductory salvo with a series of arguments, beginning with historical examples from his background in which he elevates Christ

---

[72]William M. Ramsay, *A Historical Commentary on St. Paul's Epistle to the Galatians* (London: Hodder & Stoughton, 1900): 324-325, the Galatians were accustomed through their pagan background in mystery religions to the idea of a lower and higher stage of religious life, "reaching perfect knowledge through an imperfect knowledge."

[73]Bruce, *Galatians*, 133, notes, "If Gentile Christians were not fit company for Jewish Christians, it must be because their Christianity was defective: faith in Christ and baptism into his name were insufficient and must be supplemented by something else."

and his gospel as authoritative and himself as the bearer of this authority (1:10-2:21).[74] In contrast to those who are trying to pervert the gospel of Christ (6:12), Paul declares his own motive to serve Christ rather than men (1:10). He takes pains to disassociate his conversion and early ministry from Jerusalem and its leaders (1:11-17). Maintaining his independence from any other man, Paul has been chosen by God to receive a revelation from Jesus Christ. The first brief trip to Jerusalem to "get acquainted with Peter" (1:18) accentuates the separate nature of Paul's early Christian experience, except to point out that his turning from Judaism was a source of praise to God in the churches of Judea (1:24). Conspicuously absent is the mention of instruction given to Paul from any source other than the Lord himself.

The emphasis on the sufficiency of his individual revelation continues in the second historical example (2:1-10). His trip to Jerusalem with Barnabas and Titus to inform the leaders there about his mission to the Gentiles provides a sharp contrast to the manipulative nature of the troublemakers. Of special importance in this brief encounter is the attempted coercion on the part of the "false brothers" to force the circumcision of Titus. Paul, unlike the Galatians, does not give in for a minute, so that the truth of the gospel will not be changed.[75] His comment about the appearances of men not being important to God (or to Paul) underscores

---

[74]It should be noted that the purpose of Paul's historical retrospective is not primarily the apologetic defense of his apostleship, but rather it functions as a part of the polemical teaching of the book as a whole. See Gaventa, *NovT* (1986): 309-326; John Schutz, *Paul and the Anatomy of Apostolic Authority* (SNTSMS 23; Cambridge: Cambridge Univ. Press, 1975): 28; Bernard Lategan, "Is Paul Defending His Apostleship in Galatians?" *NTS* 34 (1988): 311-430; D. J. Verseput, "Paul's Gentile Mission and the Jewish Christian Community," *NTS* 39 (1993): 36-58.

[75]It should be noted that there is a textual problem at this point. The Western text as well as Tertullian and Irenaeus omit οἷς οὐδέ, which changes the meaning to "we gave in for a moment." However, as Longenecker, *Galatians*, 52, notes, all the Greek uncial mss (except D*), all the versions (except it[d, e]) and most of the other church fathers retain the negative reading. See also Bruce, *Galatians*, 114.

the authority issue, which is further confirmed by the acceptance by the Jerusalem leaders of God's work in Paul's ministry. The request that Paul "remember the poor"[76] establishes a principle of remembrance and interrelatedness between Christians of differing backgrounds that will reappear again and again as a motif (especially in Gal. 3:28).

Paul's confrontation with Peter at Antioch (2:11-21) is paradigmatic for the Galatian situation as well as Gal. 3:28-29 in particular. In this concrete situation, the conflicts present in Galatia are at work.[77] A coercive situation has arisen in which theological principle conflicts with behavioral consequences of culture.[78] Peter has no question about the Christian status of the Gentiles at Antioch. Since his vision at Joppa at the house of Simon the tanner, he has accepted Gentile participation in the church. The question has to do with the adequacy of Jesus to overcome cultural barriers erected by the deepest of divisions. The acceptance of Gentiles into the table fellowship of the Jewish Christians is not a matter to be decided on the basis of personal preference. Nor is the possible motive of protection of the Jewish Christians in Jerusalem from their zealous countrymen sufficient reason for Paul to overlook the danger of theological consequences.[79] Some things are worth the tension of confrontation and resolution. Cousar writes,

---

[76]The term "poor" is used to mean either the financially impoverished or suggests not only financial impoverishment but also "nuances of 'humility,' 'obedience,' and 'piety' before God." See Longenecker, *Galatians*, 59. Most accept the view that the Jewish Christians of Jerusalem are to be understood as the referent.

[77]Charles B. Cousar, *Galatians* (Louisville: John Knox, 1982): 49, observes, "The alternative facing the Gentiles in Galatia is the same alternative faced by the Gentiles at Antioch who had been forsaken by Peter and Barnabas: become a Jew or remain an inferior member . . . ."

[78]Betz, *Galatians*, 116-117, writes, "The first word of v. 16 states the basis for being a Christian in distinction from being a Jew. This basis is 'theological conviction' (εἰδότες) [we know] over against birth. . . . For the Jewish Christian, this 'theological conviction' has had consequences."

[79]See Bruce, *Galatians*, 130; and Cousar, *Galatians*, 49.

The context [of 2:11-21] is a social setting. The specific point Paul wants to make in that context is that God's favorable judgment in Christ means by its very nature that Gentiles are included in the Christian community on no different level or no different terms than Jews. Both belong at the same table. To put it in negative terms, treating Gentiles as second-class citizens by withdrawing from the common meals is a form of justification by works and thus a denial of the gospel.[80]

Again, Paul is unyielding in his position. The answer to his question to Peter, "How is it, then, that you force Gentiles to follow Jewish customs?" (2:14), sets the theological stance which is crucial for the Galatians. Paul initiates the importance of faith in Jesus (rather than observance of law) in his response to his own question. Peter and the others know that man is not justified by the law, but by faith in Christ (2:15-16). Rejecting the implied argument that Christ promotes sin because Christians who are justified by faith in Christ still sin, Paul connects the death of Christ to Paul's own death to the law. Turning back to the law as the source for righteousness is equal to robbing Christ's sacrificial death of its meaning.

3. *Gal. 3:1-5:12.* The development of Paul's argument for the exclusive dependency on Christ continues in 3:1-5:12, but with an emphasis on the nature of those who have "clothed themselves with Christ"(3:27). Paul temporarily sets aside his own authority to direct attention completely toward the authoritative work of Christ (already confirmed as the source of righteousness in 2:16 and 2:21). He builds his case by presenting Christ as the source of the promised Spirit (3:1-25); the source of sonship (3:26-4:7); the source of freedom (4:21-5:1); and the source of grace and value (5:2-12). All of these are available to the Galatians through faith in Christ, apart from additional requirements of the law or identification with Judaism.

---

[80]Cousar, *Galatians*, 57-58.

This is Paul's attack on the heart of the "different gospel," which appears to be a combination of different aspects of legalism or nomism.[81] At times he seems to refer to the Mosaic law (3:10; 3:23; 4:21) and to the practice of circumcision in particular (5:3-6). Other references to "works or law" are reminiscent of the kind of pagan rituals which have been a part of Phrygian religious background, particularly the specific reference to the observance of special days (4:8-10) in the context of στοιχεῖα (the fundamental elements or principles of the natural world or forms of religion).[82]   Lightfoot explains, "Their [the Galatians] religious temperament, fostered by long habit, prompted them to seek a system more external and ritualistic."[83]   The Galatians appear to have substituted Jewish observances for pagan rituals, all the while keeping the idea that they could "attain their goal by human effort" (3:3). Particularly crucial is the refutation that circumcision be allowed to function as integral to Christian identity. All of these aspects of law come together to result in a "yoke of slavery," (5:1) which alienates from Christ those who accept this yoke and removes them from grace (5:4).

The teachings from Scripture (3:6-3:14; 3:16-22), everyday experience (3:15), and allegory (4:21-31) all contribute to the primary effort Paul makes to convince the Galatians of their value in Christ. They are not dependent upon rituals, observance of the law, or circumcision—their "ascribed honor" [84]comes through Christ. In exalting Jesus

---

[81]Nomism is defined by Longenecker, *Galatians*, 91, as a "Torah-centered lifestyle in expressing their faith."

[82]Walter Bauer, *A Greek–English Lexicon of the New Testament and Other Early Christian Literature* (trans. W. F. Arndt and F. W. Gingrich; 2nd ed. rev. F. W. Gingrich and F. W. Danker; Chicago: Univ. of Chicago Press, 1979): 768-69.

[83]Lightfoot, *The Epistle of St. Paul to the Galatians*, 12.

[84]Bruce J. Malina and Jerome H. Neyrey, "Honor and Shame in Luke-Acts," *The Social World of Luke-Acts* (ed. J. Neyrey; Peabody, MA: Hendrickson, 1991), 27-28, note, "Ascribed honor comes from kinship and family background or by endowment from an honorable person."

as the one through whom the promise and the covenant of Abraham are derived, Paul not only elevates Jesus but also the Galatians because of their relationship with him. Through their baptism they have received the sonship God has willed from the beginning of the covenant with Abraham. Even Paul's exasperated cry, "You foolish Galatians," is not as harsh as might appear at first glance, as affronts such as this verbal insult are only addressed from one equal to another.[85]   It should be noted that he never speaks directly to the troublemakers.

The first century world was a society dominated by the concepts of honor and shame, according to Malina and Neyrey. Honor is the positive value of a person in his or her own eyes and the positive appreciation of that person within his or her social group. In that respect, honor is a claim to positive worth along with the social acknowledgement of that worth by others.[86] "Unlike Western culture, cultures in which honor is a dominant value depend totally for their sense of worth upon this acknowledgement by others as 'honorable.'"[87] And, as far as the culture of the day is concerned, it is understandable why the Galatians would need such encouragement from Paul. Taking the position that the South Galatians of Phrygian ancestry are the more likely recipients of Paul's epistle,[88] Ramsay makes the following observation: they were, along with the Thracians, the "least honoured of mankind" by the Greeks.[89] To be Phrygian was, he says, to be "rude, ignorant, unintelligent, slavish."[90] He explains Paul's purpose in Galatians as ". . . not to frame an argument against Judaism [but to] elevate and ennoble the mind of the Galatians."[91]

---

[85]*Ibid.*, 30.

[86]Bruce J. Malina, *The New Testament World*, 28.

[87]Malina and Neyrey, "Honor and Shame in Luke-Acts," *The Social World of Luke-Acts*, 26.

[88]Ramsay, *St. Paul's Epistle to the Galatians*, 180.

[89]*Ibid.*, 30.

[90]*Ibid.*, 183.

[91]*Ibid.*, 442.

Paul's purpose in this ties back to his concern that the Galatians not be misled (1:6-9). It is necessary that they understand the full implications of their sonship as heirs of the promise (3:26-29). They must not return to weak and miserable principles (4:9-10) or submit again to slavery. While they perceive themselves to be on the lesser side of an unequal relationship, their weak sense of their own honor or value makes them vulnerable to Paul's opponents, who would like to boast in their domination.

Paul shifts from his own history to the history of the Galatians (3:1-5ff) in order to put Christ in his proper place and the law in perspective. He challenges them with something he doesn't expect them to deny—the action of the Holy Spirit in their lives. By basing his argument on their experience,[92] he leads them from the action of the miracles performed by the Spirit (3:5) to the origin of the gift of the Spirit in Abraham (3:6-14). Abraham was given the blessing of promise because of his faith, but it was always God's plan to pass those blessings on to the Gentiles. Christ is the one appointed to do this and his sacrificial death is the means by which the Spirit is given.

In the second example (Abraham; 3:15-25), Paul shows that God made the covenant of promise through Abraham and Christ, i.e., the "seed" of Abraham mentioned in Scripture. The law came after this covenant was made; it is therefore rendered obsolete by the coming of Christ. Paul disposes of the law as 1) the source of righteousness and 2) the source of the Spirit by rooting their experience first in the promise God made to Abraham well before the law was given and second in the work of Jesus in securing that promise for them. In so doing, he elevates Jesus and their faith in him. The law is only an interim guardian with well-marked boundaries, beginning after the covenant and ending before the gift of the Spirit.

---

[92]Longenecker, *Galatians*, 104, advocates translating πάσχω as "to experience" rather than "to suffer" because of the context. See Bauer, *A Greek-English Lexicon of the New Testament*, 633-34.

Whereas 3:19-25 deals negatively with the law, 3:26-29 gives the positive reason for Christian living. The richness of what the promise entails is the focus of 3:26-4:7. It means nothing less than full sonship to those who are in Christ. It is *belonging* in the highest degree. Whatever distinctions have been made in the physical realm are no longer operative in Christ. Unequal relationships and oppression in community are redefined in Christ. "Christ's death as a means of salvation excludes all other means; he creates one community, not many; thus there can no longer be barriers separating otherwise disparate groups."[93]

Paul carefully connects being under law (4:3-5) to the former pagan state of the Galatians (4:8-11) through the use of slavery terminology, imagery which was particularly relevant to the Galatians. They carried the stigma in the ancient world as a people who were "born and intended for slaves," and one ancient writer reports that they were accustomed to selling their children into foreign slavery.[94] Their description as "slaves by nature" probably referred to their "simple, easy-minded, contented, good-humoured, submissive temperament."[95]

The Jews ("we were slaves" before Christ came) were under law because they needed a guardian from the basic principles of the world (στοιχεία), the same weak and ineffective principles (στοιχεία) to which the Galatians are returning in their acceptance of a different gospel. The Gentiles in Asia Minor, who had no such guardian, seem to have been attracted to such basic principles since antiquity for their religious focus. Paul's association of their former pagan worship with observance of the law shows their crucial misunderstanding. Being under the στοιχεία has the same result whether a guardian is present or not: it is still slavery.

---

[93]Cousar, *Galatians*, 85.

[94]Philostr. *Apoll.* 8. See Ramsay, *St. Paul's Epistle to the Galatians*, 31.

[95]*Ibid.*, 444.

In the intensely personal, emotional plea of 4:12-20, Paul renews his bid for authority: "Be like me because I became like you "(4:12). Though this is often understood as Paul's encouragement for them to become free from the law like Paul himself [96] or to become as open to the feelings of friendship as Paul,[97] another interpretation is possible. What follows next in Paul's line of reasoning is a picture of how he came to them in his physical weakness. They were stronger than he, and not only did they not harm him, but they welcomed him and would have assisted him in any way. Now their positions are reversed. They are weak spiritually and Paul is the strong one (he has stood firm, not giving in for a minute to those who would have devalued him or them, 2:4; 2:11; 2:14) and pleads for them to become strong like him (5:1). He will not hurt them—he is still their friend even though he is forced to reprimand them. In contrast to the troublemakers, he has no desire to manipulate them. He tells them the truth: if they wish to be righteous, they must start all over again to have Christ formed in them.

Paul next ties their desire to practice law observance to slavery through a third argument using the example of Abraham (4:21-5:1). So that they can see themselves as the sons of the promise in Christ, Paul contrasts Hagar, the slave woman, and her son to Sarah, the free woman, and her son (a comparison they have probably already heard), but with a completely different twist. Those who followed the law (the covenant on Mr. Sinai) and lived in present city of Jerusalem are the descendants of the slave woman. It is those in the "new Jerusalem" who are the true descendants of "our mother." Pointedly Paul says, "you, brothers" are like Isaac, the children of promise. Of special note is the reference to the persecution of those "born by the power of the spirit"(4:29). Cousar suggests that this is Paul's direct reference to the "aggressive efforts of the opponents in Galatia who are pressuring his readers to be circumcised." [98]

---

[96] Longenecker, *Galatians*, 189; also Cousar, *Galatians*, 100.

[97] Bruce, *Galatians*, 208.

[98] Cousar, *Galatians*, 104.

The imperative to "stand firm" and not allow themselves to be burdened gives evidence to the strong motive underlying all of Paul's arguments. The Galatian readers should not allow themselves to be manipulated by those who have no authority. They are "sons" and "heirs" who need no additional practices or information to move them to a higher plain of religious understanding. Submission on this point is tantamount to slavery.

Paul's final charge is the most serious of all (5:2-12). The consequences of giving in to those who would require circumcision means falling from grace. Jesus, from whom they received the Spirit, righteousness, their inheritance of sonship, and freedom, will be of no value to them. It is an either/or choice. Those who coerce them by persuasion and confusing teachings of a different gospel must be rejected.

4. *Gal. 5:13-6:10.* The results of trusting in external observances rather than walking in the spirit become apparent in 5:13-6:10, as Paul addresses the ethical and relational problems that have begun to affect the church. Acceptance of a lifestyle in which primary identity relies on something other than Christ has logical consequences. Their relationships with each other are obviously out of focus and in need of a common corrective throughout the practical matters of their life in community. Paul supplies that corrective in the concept of mutuality. The reciprocal pronoun ἀλλήλων (one another or each other) is used with marked frequency. Mutual assistance is a hallmark of the church. Paul offers a vision for community life shaped by a pattern of obedience that follows the sacrificial faithfulness of Christ. Hays has noted that Paul cannot be read as a witness for the "privatized religion of soul-salvation."[99] Paul stresses personal responsibility in the area of testing oneself and carrying one's own burden, but it is the concern for others "in Christ" which is the central theme in the ethical considerations of 5:13-6:10.

---

[99]Richard B. Hays, "Postscript: Further Reflections on Galatians 3," *Conflict and Context* (ed. Mark Lau Branson and C. Rene Padilla; Grand Rapids: Eerdmans, 1984): 279.

There are two guidelines for the use of their freedom in Christ: loving service of one another (5:13) and keeping in line with the Spirit (5:26). Paul gives contours to the directive of walking in the Spirit by contrasting the sinful nature and the spiritual nature. He makes a significant distinction: the conflict is between the sinful nature and the Spirit rather than the sinful nature and the nature directed by the law. Longenecker believes that this is in response to teaching from the agitators who have in all likelihood stressed that there is a lifestyle governed by license and the sinful self and a lifestyle governed by the Torah.[100] Paul makes clear, however, in 5:18, that the Spirit is not an adjunct to law, but a replacement for it.

Again Paul brings to the forefront the crucifixion of Christ, already identified by Paul as incompatible with legalism (2:19-20). In 5:24, it is incompatible with the sinful nature previously spelled out. Paul urges the Galatians to keep in step with the Spirit, avoiding the kinds of sins which set brother against brother: conceit, envy, and provocation. They are to do good to all men, but especially to one another.

The mutuality of those in Christ is made even clearer with the admonitions in 6:1-10. The spiritual are instructed to gently restore those who are overtaken by a transgression. And, lest the stronger brothers be tempted to think more highly of themselves than they ought, they are keep a realistic perspective of themselves. Added to this are the injunctives to bear one another's burdens to share "all good things," painting a picture of an interlocked people.[101] If Paul is using the term "law" in 6:2 in the same sense as the

---

[100]Longenecker, *Galatians*, 246.

[101]John G. Strelan, "Burden Bearing and the Law of Christ; A Re-Examination of Galatians 6:2," *JBL* 94 (1975): 266-276, makes a case for Paul's admonition to "bear one another's burdens" to be understood in the sense of financial responsibility to one another. While this might be involved at some point within the broad scope of meaning, to limit the meaning specifically to financial dimensions does not harmonize with the context of the letter.

"guardian" of 4:2 (and indeed, there is much disagreement among scholars as to the precise meaning of the term "law of Christ") perhaps this sense of community and mutual responsibility for one another acts as guardian over the whole in much the same way as the law acted as a guardian for those under it until Christ would come and free them.

5. *Gal. 6:11-18.* The salutation of the Galatian letter (6:11-18) is not, for the most part, in the standard form of Paul's other letters. Betz[102] calls it "most important for the interpretation of Galatians" in that it contains clues to the major concerns of the whole letter. He understands it to function as a "hermeneutical key" to Paul's intention. Cousar says it epitomizes the heart of the letter.[103] The mention of the "large letters" with which Paul writes underscore his message.[104] He makes clear the motive behind those who have tried to compel the Galatians to accept circumcision and certain law observances. They are not really concerned that the whole law be kept; they want only to avoid trouble for themselves and to boast about their power over these new Christians. For the final time, Paul's answer is in christology and the work of the cross. Longenecker states, "The nub of Paul's purpose and the focal point is to be found here in vs. 15."[105] What is of highest importance has nothing to do with circumcision. Only through Christ comes the new creation—and as Paul has said before, herein lies value. "All that matters for the Christian is the fact of being a new creation with that newness of creation reflected externally in culturally relevant lives of worship and service."[106] The implications are clear. "The new creation is a corporate reality, a community whose members are characterized by their accepting attitudes and

---

[102]Betz, *Galatians*, 313.

[103]Cousar, *Galatians*, 148.

[104]Longenecker, *Galatians*, 290, mentions Schlier, Mussner, Betz, and Bruce among others who follow this view. See also Cousar, *Galatians*, 148.

[105]Longenecker, *Galatians*, 295.

[106]*Ibid.*, 296.

actions toward each other."[107] It means no longer using people for selfish reasons. Rather, brothers (and their burdens) are accepted with no barriers, to be served with love.

With his final words in 6:17-18, Paul closes as he began, his authority firmly rooted in Jesus, whose marks he bears on his body. This is plea neither for pity nor self-glorification, but Paul's statement of primary identification.

C. *A Reconsideration of Gal. 3:28*

The same theme of primary identification is the focus of the passage in Gal. 3:28. The nature of identification[108] and the resulting operative principles are best understood from a close examination of the three couplets "neither Jew nor Greek, neither slave nor free, not male and female." Only through establishing a primary identity in Christ can Paul answer a resounding *yes* to the question of adequacy for every area of the lives of these believers.

First, the three sets in 3:28 must be seen through the conflict of opposition which has been a central motif throughout the epistle. Paul has a dual audience, neither of whom have allowed Christ to be their organizing system of theology or behavior. He addresses directly those who identify themselves as "in Christ" but still deficient; those who picture themselves as superior in understanding or status are addressed indirectly, but just as clearly. Paul's remarks to the two groups do not deal specifically with roles but with something much deeper—*worth*.

Another important factor is the corporate identity of Paul's audience. Staying within Malina's picture of first

---

[107]Cousar, *Galatians*, 156.

[108]Rogers, *Semantic Study of Galatians*, 104, writes that Paul has already made the point that the Gentiles are sons of God with his reference to the work of the spirit in their lives. The point he is here trying to make is that being sons of God comes through identification with Christ rather than Abraham.

century society indicates that the imperatives arising from the verse should be understood first of all in a corporate context rather than the one-on-one relationship between individuals. Groups which might take an adversarial stance within the community of Christ should treat one another as equally valuable. Paul's teaching in Galatians is a corrective to the way groups of believers are treating one another.

The origin of the three couplets has been the subject of much discussion. Whether one accepts the view that Paul is countering the threefold prayer[109] or is quoting a part of a baptismal formula,[110] the important thing is not the origin of Paul's examples but what he does with them. The three pairs are so closely connected that whatever is common to all of them should receive priority in interpreting meaning.[111] It is helpful, therefore, to consider their points of similarity and dissimilarity.

---

[109]Bruce, *Galatians*, 187, writes, "Paul's threefold affirmation corresponds to a number of Jewish formulas in which the threefold distinction is maintained, as in the morning in which the male Jew thanks God that he was not made a Gentile, a slave or a woman." This threefold thanksgiving can be traced back as far as R. Judah ben Elai, c. AD 150, or his contemporary R. Me'ir. Both have rather than "slave" the phrase "brutish man." The formula may go back even farther to a Greek formula from the 6th century in which the wording was "human being and not a beast, man and not woman, and a Greek and not a barbarian." Bruce would see this not as any positive disparagement of Gentiles, slaves, or women as persons but indicative of the fact that they were disqualified from several religious privileges that were open to free Jewish males.

[110]Meeks, *HR* (1974): 181, asserts, "We may therefore speak with some confidence of a 'baptismal reunification formula' familiar in congregations associated with Paul and his school." E. Earle Ellis, *Pauline Theology: Ministry and Society* (Grand Rapids: Eerdmans, 1989): 79, n. 84, rejects as "problematic" the idea that 3:26-29 was a baptismal ritual as that reflects a reading back into the text form patristic and Gnostic usage from a later time. He cites Hippolytus, *Apostolic Tradition* 21.

[111]Caird, *BJRL* (1972): 272, observes correctly, "Paul clearly intends the three pairs in his list to be treated in parallel. His meaning must be located in that which is common to all three."

The obvious points of similarity at the outset are, 1) they are all pairs, and pairs of polarity; 2) all signify an unequal relationship with potential for oppression, because each has a stronger and a weaker partner in terms of power; and 3) there are distinctions within each couplet that lead to either social or religious consequences or both. The gulf between Jew and Gentile was perhaps as deep and wide as could be imagined. While an individual Gentile could become a Jewish proselyte, the gulf separating the "chosen people" and everyone else remained. Social inferiority of slaves was a fact of life in Jewish culture and even more marked in the general society under Roman law. While there were some improvements for women under Roman and Jewish law in contrast to primitive pagan cultures, women were seen as men's inferiors in any significant category.[112]

To maintain accuracy in interpretation, the differences among the three couplets must also be taken into account. To view all these as positions from birth is somewhat misleading. While this is obviously true with respect to male and female, the other relationships were not permanent. A Gentile could, by becoming a proselyte, enter the same relationship to God as the rest of the Jews. Movement from slave to free was not uncommon.

The second difference concerns salvation. The salvation of the Gentiles is evidently in question to some Jews as well as the Gentiles in Galatia. In Galatians, Paul's insistence that God has called him to preach salvation to the Gentiles, his reminders of the activity of the Spirit among the Gentile Christians, and his assurance of their freedom from enslavement to the στοιχεῖα are obviously directed to this issue. The question of salvation for women or slaves seems not to have been an issue, however. The use of the slave-free, male-female examples may have been intended to strengthen Paul's arguments for Gentile salvation.

---

[112]See Meeks, *HR* (1974): 186, 174-180; Raphael Jospe, "The Status of Women in Judaism: From Exemption to Exclusion," *Illif Review* 35 (1978): 29-39; also Adela Yarbro Collins, "The Ministry of Women in the Apostolic Generation," *Women Priests*, 159-166.

A third difference is in the way the examples are worded. The construction of the third couplet is slightly different, using καί rather than οὐδέ to separate the polarities, and the words for male and female, ἄρσεν and θῆλυς, are not those usually chosen. Ellis points out that is appears only in this verse and in Jesus' biblical exposition against divorce from Gen. 1:27 and Gen. 2:24. Consequently, he infers that the idea of marriage relationship in the present creation is done away, not in the sense that marriage is abolished but that the "conditions and attitudes of the marriage relationship are transcended in Christ."[113]

The epistolary context indicates that the meaning of Gal. 3:28 has both theological and behavioral significance. The illustrations from Paul's retrospective, and the incident in Antioch in particular, function with the ethical teaching in chapters five and six to connect the theological principles of Paul's message to social interactions.[114] The imperatives to carry one another's burdens and serve one another, to share all good with those who teach, and to do good especially to the family of believers have social consequences. There is no reason to exclude the possibility of ecclesiastical dimensions. Paul is not here sermonizing in the abstract; he is dealing with actual behavior in the life of the church.

Three principles are evident in the passage on both theological and behavioral levels. The first of these is that Christ is the defining point of life for the people of faith. Christ and Christ alone is the source of righteousness, freedom, and relationship with God. There can be no other gospel. Whatever is done through him supercedes all other actions, and whatever one becomes through union with him supercedes all other categories of being before God and mankind. Differing points of identity are not erased or eliminated, but they are subordinated to the identity of the

---

[113]Ellis, *Pauline Theology*, 78.

[114]Caird, *BJRL* (1972): 272, writes, "The idea that the new life in Christ was simply 'religious' and must not be allowed to interfere with existing social patterns was precisely the line adopted by James of Jerusalem and accepted by Peter and Barnabas."

believer with Christ. Thus, what happens in redemption is more important than what happened in creation.

A second principle is the importance of value. Union with Christ means value, and all those so united are equally valuable. Equality of value, however, does not necessarily correspond with equality of roles. It does not follow that there are no unequal roles in the community of faith. Paul himself is claiming an authoritative role as an apostle. Nor would one suggest that the unequal roles of parent-child relationships be considered illegitimate in Christ. Following Paul's model, the point of distinction would involve within the boundaries of his discussion only roles which are perceived by one group as indicative of diminished worth or oppression by another group.

In view of the context of the Galatian letter, a significant point is that *perceived* worth is as important as actual worth, though actual value is the basis for cognitive assent to Paul's theological point.   The actual value of the Gentile Christians at Antioch was not in question, but their perception of their value was the impetus for Paul's intervention on their behalf. Throughout his letter, Paul tries to build a rational theology of worth while at the same time requiring behavior which reinforces the perception of that worth.

The recognition of equality of value is vital to the spiritual well-being of both sides of the social, racial, and gender duos. To the "superiors" Paul implies that every effort should be made to make unity in Christ real in practice as well as principle without hypocrisy or arrogance. To the "inferiors" Paul hammers away at their desire to build themselves up by human means. He demands that they stand firm in the understanding of the value Christ's crucifixion has brought them, avoiding the backbiting and fighting that go on in power struggles. Paul acknowledges that this takes strength, persistence, and "awaiting through the Spirit" by faith (5:5). Indeed, the difficulty of fighting against the feeling of weakness or inferiority has occasioned the letter.

A third principle derived from this study is that of unity. Paul presents two facets to unity: 1) the elimination of barriers and unnecessary distinctions, and 2) reconciliation and mutual responsibility. Being one with Christ means being part of a unified diversity in which "Self-asserting practices that jeopardize the unity of the community are a de facto denial of Christ and the reality of grace (5:4)."[115] The ideal is not the "eradication of these groups nor their distinctives" but the eradication of hostility between them.[116]

Christian love and service provide the power to erode the barriers of unnecessary distinctions, but the "in Christ" community must accept the responsibility for one another's burdens through mutuality. If some perceive themselves as less saved, less important, or less acceptable, the others must address that perception in every possible way to change it. Those with higher status may not simply expect their counterparts to have a cognitive understanding of their true worth in the Lord; actions must make that understanding real. According to Paul, that may mean table fellowship, it may mean allowing treasured and sacred cultural customs to go by the wayside, it may mean financial assistance or gentle intervention without arrogance to correct sinful behavior.

Failure to take such actions renders those less powerful at risk of seeking another gospel to raise their standing. Indeed, what the Galatians were doing has a contemporary parallel in the developments of feminist theology, liberation theology, or any of the various other "theologies" which have at their heart another agenda than the crucified Christ.[117] In such cases, the perception of inequality or oppression, not addressed satisfactorily, has changed the gospel of Christ to a different gospel.

---

[115]Hays, "Jesus' Faith and Ours: A Rereading of Galatians 3," *Conflict and Context*, 268.

[116]Ellis, *Pauline Theology*, 80.

[117]Mary Ann Tolbert, "Defining the Problem: The Bible and Feminist Hermeneutics," *Semeia* 28 [1983]: 114, is illustrative: "I have a clear commitment to feminism and its critique of all oppressive cultural structures, including Christianity."

Chapter Six

"PHOEBE" AND "JUNIA(S)"—ROM. 16:1-2, 7

James Walters

The references to women in Romans 16 are intriguing.[1] Richardson[2] observes, "The effect of this list is startling, since more dramatic roles are attributed to women than are attributed to men, despite their smaller number." While certain terms are used for both men and women (fellow-worker, apostle, first-fruit, fellow-countryman, fellow-prisoner, beloved), two terms are applied to men that are not applied to women (genuine, chosen), and five others—three of them very significant descriptions—are applied only to women (deacon, protectress, hard-worker, sister, mother). Although some detect in these terms "dramatic roles," others find "positions of great authority." This essay does not treat the Rom. 16 list nor does it purport to be an exhaustive exegesis of Rom. 16:1-2, 7. Rather, it focuses particular attention upon the descriptions of Phoebe and Junia(s) that bear on the understanding of women in early Christianity.[3]

---

[1]Although traditionally treated as a misplaced appendage, Rom. 16 is now accepted by an increasing number of scholars as genuine. See H. Gamble, *The Textual History of the Letter to the Romans* (Grand Rapids: Eerdmans, 1977), and more recently, Peter Lampe, "The Roman Christians of Romans 16," *The New Romans Debate* (ed. K. Donfried; Peabody, MA: Hendricksen, 1990): 216-30.

[2]Peter Richardson, "From Apostles to Virgins: Romans 16 and the Roles of Women in the Early Church," *Toronto Journal of Theology* 2 (1986): 239.

[3]For general discussions of women in antiquity with recent and extensive bibliographies, see Ross Kraemer, "Women in the Religions of the Greco-Roman World," *Religious Studies Review* 9 (1983): 127-39; Susan Pomeroy, "Selected Bibliography on Women in Classical

1. *Phoebe*

Prior to the greetings in Rom. 16, Paul commends a woman named Phoebe to the recipients. Although it has been speculated due to the position of the recommendation that she carried the letter to Rome, this must remain conjectural because the letter itself is silent about her reason(s) for traveling to Rome or the time of her arrival in the capital vis-a-vis that of the letter.[4] What the text is not silent about are the reasons why Phoebe should be treated respectfully. In his study of the letter of recommendation, Kim[5] summarized the fundamental character of Paul's commendations, observing that "For Paul the act of introducing or commending someone actually meant sending credentials to the recipient on behalf of the recommended." Structurally, the recommendation of Phoebe may be understood as beginning with an introduction (A), followed by the credentials of the recommended person (B), to which the desired action (C) is appended.[6] Paul then elaborates the credentials (B′) in order to strengthen the recommendation.

Antiquity," *Women in the Ancient World: The Arethusa Papers* (ed. J. Peradotto and J. P. Sullivan; Albany: State Univ. of New York Press, 1984): 343-77; and Eva Cantarella, "The Principate and the Empire: the Emancipation of Women?" *Pandora's Daughters* (trans. M. Fant; Baltimore: Johns Hopkins Univ. Press, 1987): 135-217.

[4]James Dunn, *Romans* (Dallas: Word, 1988): 2.888, thinks that Paul's use of the term πρᾶγμα suggests that Phoebe was travelling to Rome on account of a lawsuit and that Paul seized the opportunity to dispatch a letter to the Roman Christians. Dunn grants that πρᾶγμα is often unspecific, i.e., undertaking, task, matter, affair, but he thinks the more specific sense of lawsuit/dispute (see 1 Cor. 6:1) is preferable here since women often acted as independent litigants. This is possible, but there are too many reasons why someone might travel to Rome to restrict unnecessarily the meaning of πρᾶγμα to "lawsuit."

[5]Chan-Hie Kim, *The Familiar Letter of Recommendation* (Missoula, MT: Scholars Press, 1972): 119. That letters of recommendation were common in early Christianity is evident from the several references to the practice (Acts 9:2; 18:27; 22:5; and 1 Cor. 16:3).

[6]Paul's letter to Philemon includes these same three parts in the same order (see Philemon 8-17).

Our ability to estimate Phoebe's position and activities in this brief commendation depends upon the interpretation of the two key terms διάκονος and προστάτις. The common approach to Rom. 16:1-2 and the interpretation of Phoebe's role in early Christianity has been to enter the analysis via the term διάκονος (deacon). This procedure is not without difficulty, however, because the decision one makes regarding whether or not διάκονος is used as a technical term informs the entire passage. Because the evidence for the existence of women deacons in earliest Christianity has been known for years and because the reading of the evidence is open to only two or three possible interpretations, this avenue of investigation follows a predictable course of statement and restatement.

Alternatively, προστάτις (patron; masc. προστάτης), used to describe Phoebe, has received considerable attention from classical historians in recent years. The discovery of numerous honorific inscriptions using the term coupled with fresh analyses of literary texts has yielded important results that suggest προστάτις as the preferable place to begin.

A. *Phoebe as* προστάτις

The reluctance of translators to render προστάτις as "patron" or "protector" results from an overly-rigid view of patronage in the Roman empire, and an unfounded assumption that a Christian woman would have been an unlikely candidate for such a title.[7] Saller[8] has attempted to broaden the meaning of patronage by describing the characteristics of the relationship as follows:

---

[7]RSV, "a helper of"; NEB, "a good friend to"; NJB, "come to the help of"; NIV, "a great help to." Because προστάτις is feminine, some would favor the translation "patron(ess)" or "protector(ess)." However, because such feminine endings are becoming archaic in English and because the translation may (mistakenly) imply that the activity of patronage for women differed from that of men, the translation "patron" or "protector" is preferred.

[8]Richard Saller, *Personal Patronage under the Early Empire* (Cambridge: Cambridge Univ. Press, 1982): 1.

First, it involves the reciprocal exchange of goods and services. Secondly, to distinguish it from a commercial transaction in the marketplace, the relationship must be a personal one of some duration. Thirdly, it must be asymmetrical, in the sense that the two parties are of unequal status and offer different kinds of goods and services in the exchange—a quality which sets patronage off from friendship between equals.

Further, Saller encourages a pragmatic approach to the subject that pays more attention to the way people behaved in the relationship than to supposed legal bases that defined or regulated it.[9] He writes,

Patently, the Romans applied the language of patronage to a range of relationships, with both humble dependents and their junior aristocratic colleagues labelled *clientes*: usage was more fluid than usually supposed, and the connotations of *amicus*, *cliens*, and *patronus* were subtly and variously manipulated in different circumstances.[10]

Elliott[11] lists Luke 7:2-5 as an example of patronage in the NT even though the term προστάτης does not appear, for the Jewish elders sent by the centurion to appeal to Jesus to heal his slave stress that, "He is worthy to have you do this for him, for he loves our nation, and he built us our synagogue." Rom. 16:2, however, presents the opposite

---

[9]Saller, "Patronage and Friendship in early Imperial Rome: Drawing the Distinction," *Patronage in Ancient Society* (ed. Andrew Wallace-Hadrill; London: Routledge, 1989): 50, questions whether "anything in imperial law, linguistic usage, or social behavior suggests a 'technical' definition in the minds of the Romans." In contrast to Saller's approach, the *Oxford Classical Dictionary* (Oxford: Clarendon Press, 1949): 655, entry for *patronus* offers seven rather narrow categories of usage that make patronage irrelevant to most Romans.

[10]Saller, *Patronage in Ancient Society*, 57.

[11]John H. Elliott, "Patronage and Clientism in Early Christian Society," *Forum* 3 (1987): 40.

circumstance: Paul does not recount the behaviors that occasioned the honor Phoebe is shown, but he does use the vocabulary of patronage.

While Graeco-Roman inscriptions that identify women as patrons are common, those recounting activities of patronage performed by women are even more numerous.[12] Following are typical examples from Rome in which this terminology appears.   In one inscription, a Jewish woman sets up an epitaph to her client in a Jewish catacomb in Rome and in the other a pagan client honors his patron.[13]

To Nicetas, proselyte worthy and well-deserving, his patron(ess) Dionysias set up (this stone).[14]

Gaius Fulvius Eutyches, freedman and manager (honors) NN his patron(ess), wife (daughter?) of Gaius Fulvius Pius my patron.[15]

The inscriptions honoring Junia Theodora illustrate clearly that women were honored often by describing behaviors of patronage without necessarily calling them "patrons."   In fact, traditional patterns for showing honor to women so affected the way honorific inscriptions were composed that,

---

[12]An extra-biblical example of the feminine form προστάτις used in the sense of "protector" has been located in a second-century AD papyrus.   See O. Montevecchi, "Una donna 'prostatis' del figlio minorenne in un papiro del IIa," *Aegyptus* 61 (1981): 103-15.

[13]Women not only served as patrons for individual clients, but also for groups.   R. MacMullen, "Women in Public in the Roman Empire," *Changes in the Roman Empire* (Princeton: Princeton Univ. Press, 1990): 164, estimates that 10% of the protectors and donors that *collegia* sought in the west, Italy and the provinces, were women.

[14]CIJ 256 in H. H. Leon, *The Jews of Ancient Rome* (Philadelphia: Jewish Publication Society, 1961): 301.

[15]The woman's name is missing from the inscription (NN).   The freedman who set up the stone was apparently the common property of Pius and his wife prior to his manumission.   For the inscription with commentary, see G. H. R. Horsley, *New Documents Illustrating Early Christianity* (Melbourne: Macquarie Univ., 1977): 60f.

especially in Greek cities, women who acted as patrons tended to be honored as matrons. Consequently, a woman who made a donation to the city might be praised for her domestic virtues. Forbis[16] has demonstrated this tendency by contrasting honorific inscriptions to women in Italian municipalities with their Greek counterparts. The Italians characteristically honored women with the same terms that were used for men.

The content of Paul's commendation corresponds to that of the Italian honorific inscriptions noted by Forbis.[17] It is rather obvious that the terms Paul used to commend Phoebe are no different from those he would have used if he had been commending a man. He presents her to his readers as a προστάτις worthy of their kindness and cites no familial relationships nor domestic virtues when he honors her. Paul mentions only her actions in behalf of the church at Cenchrea and her patronage of Christians, including himself.

Although Paul does not detail the particular actions of Phoebe performed on behalf of himself and others,

---

[16]Elizabeth P. Forbis, "Women's Public Image in Italian Inscriptions," *AJP*111 (1990): 493-512. The contrast is illustrated by two of her examples (pp. 496-97). The first is from Lycia (c. AD 100):
> The people of Arneae and vicinity, to Lalla daughter of Timarchus son of Diotimus, their fellow citizen, wife of Diotimus son of Vassus; priestess of the Emperor's cult and gymnasiarch out of her own resources, honored five times, chaste, cultivated, devoted to her husband and a model of all virtues, surpassing in every respect. She has glorified her ancestors' virtues with the example of her own character. (Erected) in recognition of her virtues and good will.

The other is a second-century AD inscription from Formiae:
> The citizens of Formiae publicly (give honor to) Cassia Cornelia Prisca, the daughter of Gaius, a woman of senatorial rank, the wife of Aufidius Fronto the consul, pontifex, proconsul of Asia, and patron of our colony, a priestess of the Augusta and the fatherland, in return for the magnificence of her generosity.

[17]Forbis, *AJP* (1990): 499.

inscriptions honoring a contemporary of Phoebe who lived in nearby Corinth offer tangible evidence of what the actions of a female patron might include in that region. Junia Theodora was a resident of Corinth who acted as a benefactor of Lycians in Corinth and who cultivated the goodwill of officials toward the Lycians. Decrees honoring her were gathered, probably at her death, and inscribed on a stele that was found by a French archaeological team in 1954.[18] On the basis of the script of the inscription, a first-century AD date is likely, and because of internal evidence one of the decrees can be dated either to AD 43 or AD 57.[19]

Although each of the five decrees included on the stele honor Junia Theodora for behaviors readily associated with patronage, the following decree uses a form of the word that Paul used to describe Phoebe:

> In the fourth year, under the priest Dionysphanes, . . . the council and people of Telemessos decreed . . . : since Iunia Theodora, a Roman, a benefactress of the greatest loyalty to the Lycian federation and our city has accomplished numerous benefits for the federation and our city . . . welcomes in her own house Lycian travellers and our citizens . . . supplying them with everything; displaying her patronage (*prostasian*) of those who are present . . . her own love of fame and assiduousness: it is decreed that our city in its turn testify to her according to her deserts; by good fortune it pleases the demos of Telmessos to give honour and praise for all the above reasons to the above-mentioned Iunia Theodora and to invite her,

---

[18]See discussion and bibliography in R. A. Kearsley, "Women in Public Life in the Roman East," *Ancient Society* 15 (1985): 124-28 and 132-34.

[19]The specific dates are based on a reference to exiles from Lycia that Junia Theodora housed. D. Pallas, et al., "Inscriptions lyciennes trouvèes à Solômos près de Corinthe," *Bulletin de correspondance hellénique* 83 (1959): 505-06, favors the earlier date. Kearsley, *Ancient Society* (1985): 125, favors the later date.

living with the same intentions, to always be the
author of some benefit towards us, well knowing
that in return our city recognizes and will
acknowledge the evidence of her goodwill.[20]

Of the "numerous benefits" Junia Theodora occasioned for
Telmessos, it is her hospitality to Lycian travellers and
Lycians residing in Corinth that is specified. In addition to
lodging, she supplied "everything" they needed.

It is easy for the modern reader with stereotypical views
of women's roles in antiquity to conclude from this decree
that Junia Theodora's activities in behalf of the Lycians were
nothing more than domestic service. Yet, it should be noted
that a woman of her status and wealth managed a large
household where the needs of those who were under her
care were met by servants who discharged the actual tasks.
A clearer indication of the scope of her activity is found in a
letter from the federal assembly of the Lycians—inscribed on
the stele—which links her hospitality with what sounds
more like international diplomacy:

[She] hasn't ceased to show her zeal and
generosity towards the nation and is full of
goodwill to all travellers whether private
individuals or ambassadors sent by the nation or by
various cities; and has procured the gratitude of all
of us by assuring the friendship of the authorities
which she seeks to win by every means.[21]

In addition to caring for Lycian travellers, Junia Theodora
sought to procure the goodwill of Roman officials
(ἡγεμόνες) for Lycia, and the honors that were returned by
the Lycians suggest that she did so with success.
Apparently, she served as an agent for Lycian interests in

---

[20]The inscription is published in Pallas, *Bulletin de
correspondence hellénique* (1959): 496-508. Kearsley's translation is in
Ancient Society (1985): 134.

[21]See Kearsley, *Ancient Society* (1985): 134.

Corinth, a city whose location and commercial importance recommend why her services were so prized.[22]

It should be noted that the decrees and letters honoring Junia Theodora nowhere suggest that her activities were directed by a man, either her husband or father.[23] Rather, it is evident that she acted independently. Further, she exerted her influence without holding an office. Marshall[24] has observed correctly that attempts to estimate the power of women under Roman rule focus too much attention on the question of whether women were able to hold civic offices. This, he claims, misunderstands how power was exercised:

> In Roman eyes, the influence and prestige of these wealthy women was not really based upon, or expressed by, the degree of actual political power vested in whatever civic offices they might hold. Vis-a-vis the Roman governor, city magistracies probably afforded little effective political "power" whether held by men or women. The real leverage was of the kind exerted by Junia Theodora in Corinth . . . . Money and social standing secured office, but not vice versa, and it was the realities of the former which earned Roman respect (p. 125).

The interplay between wealth and status afforded the power that women like Junia Theodora were able to exercise. MacMullen, in a comment explaining Junia Theodora's accomplishments, describes the relationship succinctly:

---

[22]Kearsley, *Ancient Society* (1985): 127, observes that the gifts which were dedicated by the Lycians for Junia for her funeral were those normally reserved for federal officials upon their retirement from office or to other persons of similar importance who benefitted the nation.

[23]The letter from Myra mentions that she is the daughter of Lucius, but suggests nothing of her father's activities. It is not possible to determine whether her father was still alive or whether she was married or if married whether her husband was deceased.

[24]A. J. Marshall, "Roman Women and the Provinces," *Ancient Society* 6 (1975): 125.

. . . she never accomplished all this with money alone, she never 'bought the leaders,' nor did she content herself with formal appearances on balconies or the like. No, what she was able to bring to bear, from (of course) a naturally favored social position, can have been nothing but a network of connections woven and made to work for the objects of her interest, in the way politicians of both sexes and every period in history have done since time began.[25]

Clearly, Junia Theodora's behaviors correspond well to Saller's definition of patronage. Moreover, her actions in behalf of the Lycians could be grouped easily under the descriptives Paul utilizes for Phoebe. Although Phoebe's deeds are not described so fully, there is no reason to doubt that she also acted as a patron according to Saller's definition and engaged in activities analogous to those of Junia Theodora.[26] Furthermore, it is apparent that Greco-Roman women who acted as patrons were able to exert considerable influence irrespective of any official office they might have held.

Nonetheless, the term προστάτης has within its possible range of meanings the sense of one who "rules over" or "governs" (i.e., the πρύτανις of a city), or in a more general usage, the "leader" or "presider" of a club or guild.[27] Although it is apparent from the lack of mention on the inscription that Junia Theodora did not hold public office, Phoebe is thought by some to have held an office in the church at Cenchrea. Did Paul intend by the use of προστάτις to recommend Phoebe as the one who "ruled" or "governed" the church at Cenchrea?

---

[25]MacMullen, *Changes in the Roman Empire*, 168.

[26]The omission of Phoebe and any discussion of the term προστάτις by F. W. Danker, *Benefactor: Epigraphic Study of a Graeco-Roman and New Testament Semantic Field* (St. Louis: Clayton, 1982), is more than curious.

[27]Wayne Meeks, *The First Urban Christians* (New Haven: Yale Univ. Press, 1983): 60.

This question is complicated by the long-standing debate over the nature and development of "offices" in the early church.[28] It is generally agreed that in Pauline communities functional roles (*charismata*) were recognized early on as the consequence of God's distribution by the Spirit. "Offices" emerged as these charismatic roles gave way to a developing institutionalization.[29] The problem of interpretation is that of avoiding anachronisms when reading terms that ultimately represented office-holders but only identified roles granted by the Spirit in the early stages or in particular locations.

Analysis of Paul's use of προΐστημι (a verb related to προστάτις) in 1 Thess. 5:12 and Rom. 12:8 may provide some assistance in clarifying the early relationship between patronage and leadership. During the NT period, the semantic range of the participial form προιστάμενος included one who "rules" or "leads," as well as one who "is concerned about" or "cares for" or "gives aid to."[30] Hence, it could identify a ruling official or describe a patron's activities. In 1 Thess. 5:12, the RSV has Paul instructing the Thessalonians to acknowledge "those who labor among you and are over you in the Lord and admonish you." The three parallel participles occurring in the phrase do not designate three roles, but three functions of one role. The middle term, our term προιστάμενοι, is understood by the RSV in the former sense of "ruling" or "leading."

---

[28] An introduction to this debate is Karl Kertelge, *Das kirchliche Amt im Neuen Testament: Wege der Forschung* (Darmstadt: Wissenschaftliche Buchgesellschaft, 1977). See also H. von Campenhausen, *Ecclesiastical Authority and Spiritual Power in the Church of the First Three Centuries* (trans. J. Baker; Stanford: Stanford Univ. Press, 1969), as well as the general discussion of the question in relation to the Pauline churches in Meeks, *First Urban Christians*, 134ff.

[29] The contrast is often illustrated by comparing 1 Cor. 12:8-10, 28-30, Rom. 12:6-8, and Eph. 4:11 with 1 Tim. 3:1-13.

[30] For the former sense, see Herodotus 1.69; Thucydides 2.65.5, 8.75.2, or in the LXX 2 Sam. 13:17; Prov. 23:5; Amos 6:10. The latter meaning is attested in Euripides, *Heracl.* 1036; Demosthenes, *Or.* 10.46; Polybius 5.5.8. For other references, see Bo Reicke, "προΐστημι," *TDNT* 6.700.

Malherbe[31] rejects the RSV reading as "incorrect and [one that] is rejected by the vast majority of commentators." He emphasizes that in the introduction to the paragraph where 5:12 is found, Paul makes pastoral care the duty of every member of the church (5:11). Instructions follow, then, regarding the conduct of pastoral care, particularly the proper attitude toward those exercising it (5:12-13)[32] and the manner in which it should be exercised (5:14-15). Malherbe accounts correctly for the translation error in the RSV at 5:12 by emphasizing how assumptions regarding "offices" in the early church affect the inquiry:

> The interpretation of this passage has been bedeviled by attempts to discern in it the earliest New Testament evidence of the institutional organization of the church. Paul does not, however, mention any particular office, nor does he have in mind two clearly defined groups, one that has assumed the responsibility for pastoral care and another that habitually receives it (pp. 88-89).

In Rom. 12:8, προιστάμενος occurs in a list of gifts (*charismata*) which clearly correspond to roles that are to be carried out within the Christian community rather than presiding or governing offices. Decisive for the interpretation of προιστάμενος is its position between two other forms of giving aid (μεταδιδούς and ἐλεῶν). The προιστάμενος is not one who "governs" but one who "protects" the interests of those who are socially vulnerable, a patron.[33] Inevitably, persons who could benefit the church by virtue of their status and wealth would be viewed as leaders in some sense. This, however, is not equivalent to a situation

---

[31] Abraham Malherbe, *Paul and the Thessalonians* (Philadelphia: Fortress, 1987): 90.

[32] Meeks, *First Urban Christians*, 134, agrees that in 1 Thess. 5:12 the role of the patron is in view, but suggests that if the patron can "admonish" then he or she is certainly being accorded authority of some sort. But this does not necessitate "governing leadership."

[33] Dunn, *Romans* 2.731.

where formal processes lead to the selection of leaders whose ostensible responsibilities are to govern the group.[34]

Nonetheless, Fiorenza[35] argues that Phoebe's leadership must be understood in "the more juridical, technical sense of *patrona*," suggesting a governing officer or president. She takes issue with Käsemann,[36] who favors "personal care" because "Women could not take on legal functions." Both are working with assumptions, however, that interpret patronage in the Roman world too narrowly as a legal phenomenon. Hence, with regard to Phoebe's "position" in the church at Cenchrea, *prostatis* implies more than Käsemann allows, but less than Fiorenza demands.[37]

Junia Theodora of Corinth and Phoebe of Cenchrea were contemporaries who lived only a few miles apart. Given the steep social pyramid of Graeco-Roman cities, it is possible that these women knew, or were aware of, each other. The description of Phoebe as a προστάτις to many and to Paul himself is quite parallel to the description of Junia Theodora. Although Phoebe's status and activities may not have matched the scope of Junia's, they were surely analogous. By virtue of wealth and status, she was able to make connections that benefitted Paul and other Christians residing in or passing through Corinth. Hospitality was likely a key element of her patronage; however, we must be careful not to confuse Phoebe's activities with those of a domestic servant. Elliott[38] noted the significance of the contributions that patrons like Phoebe made toward the growth and expansion of early Christianity, stating that,

---

[34]Meeks, *First Urban Christians*, 134.

[35]Elisabeth Schüssler Fiorenza, *In Memory of Her* (New York: Crossroad, 1983): 181.

[36]E. Käsemann, *Romans* (trans. G. Bromiley; Grand Rapids: Eerdmans, 1980): 411.

[37]The idea of "presiding over" or "governing" is, as Meeks, *The First Urban Christians*, 60, notes, "rendered impossible by the context, for it is difficult to imagine what Paul could have meant by describing Phoebe as 'also presiding over me'."

[38]Elliott, *Forum* (1987): 46.

This rapid expansion was due in no small part to the social networks which its (Christianity's) members 'worked' for personal advantage as well as for the good of the movement: protection, material support, legal aid, hospitality, opportunities for employment and trade, places for assembly and worship.

B. *Phoebe as* διάκονος

Of the descriptives Paul used for Phoebe, the term διάκονος has generated the most interest and controversy among interpreters through the centuries.[39] Did Paul use διάκονος here in a technical sense to refer to a church "office" or did he employ it in the sense of "servant" or "minister"? If taken technically, should it be understood as the office of a "deaconess" (as defined in later sources) or as that of a "deacon" according to earliest Christian sources?

On one hand, it is well-known that Paul often uses the word διάκονος in the general sense of "servant" or "minister" (1 Cor. 3:5; 2 Cor. 3:6; 6:4; 11:15, 23; Gal. 2:17).[40] He refers to himself as a servant/minister of Christ or God and addresses co-workers in the same manner (2 Cor. 6:4; 1 Cor. 3:5). In none of these cases, however, is there any suggestion that the person so identified is being presented as an office-holder in a congregation by virtue of the description διάκονος.

On the other hand, the salutation of Paul and Timothy to the saints at Philippi with the ἐπίσκοποι and διάκονοι and

---

[39]Although διάκονος is masculine, it can refer either to a man or a woman because no feminine form of the noun was in use during the early Christian period. See W. Bauer, *A Greek-English Lexicon of the New Testament and Other Early Christian Literature* (trans. W. F. Arndt & F. W. Gingrich; 2nd ed. rev. F. W. Gingrich and F. W. Danker; Chicago: Univ. of Chicago Press, 1979): 184.

[40]In Rom. 13:4, it is used of civil magistrates and in Rom. 15:8 it is used of Christ. The general sense of "servant" is also common in the so-called "disputed" letters (see Eph. 3:7; 6:21; Col. 1;7, 23, 25).

the qualification list for the διάκονοι in 1 Tim. 3:8-13—
which follows immediately a similar list for the ἐπίσκοποι—
present a usage of διάκονος that contrasts the one cited
above. The pairing of ἐπίσκοποι and διάκονοι in both
passages and the inclusion of qualifications in the 1 Timothy
text suggest a more technical usage.

Within which one of these two groupings does Rom.
16:1 belong? It must be observed that Phoebe's recommendation as διάκονος has neither unambiguous terms for
church offices in its semantic field nor qualifications. Even
if Phoebe is the letter-carrier, the use of διάκονος to
commend Phoebe to the readers does not require a technical
meaning. In Eph. 6:21, Tychikos, the apparent letter-
carrier, is commended to the readers as a "beloved brother
and faithful διάκονος in the Lord," but translation of
διάκονος as "deacon" is not warranted. Neither does the
description of Phoebe as a προστάτις demand that διάκονος
be taken as an office. In fact, the meaning "servant" for
διάκονος could refer merely to Phoebe's work as a patron.

However, the modifying clause "of the church in
Cenchrea" separates the Phoebe text from the general usages
of διάκονος.[41] In all early Christian literature, we find in
Rom. 16:1 the formulation "διάκονος of the church in".[42]
If Paul only wished to convey that Phoebe had acted as a
servant in the church, it is probable that he would have used
διακονέω or διακονία as in Rom. 15:25 and 1 Cor. 16:15.[43]
If his appeal was to the tirelessness of her labor in behalf of
others in the church, likely he would have used κοπιάω as in
16:6, 12 (see also 1 Cor. 16:16; 1 Thess. 5:12). The
occurrence of διάκονος after the participle οὖσα and its
relation to the limiting phrase "the church in Cenchrea"

---

[41] Kazimierz Romaniuk, "Was Phoebe in Romans 16,1 a
Deaconess?" *ZNW* 81 (1990): 133.

[42] Richardson, *From Apostles to Virgins*, 259, n. 18.

[43] See Dunn, *Romans* 2.886.

suggest a recognized ministry or position of responsibility, if not an office.[44]

Unfortunately, even if agreement is reached that Paul used διάκονος here as a quasi-technical term, we would not be in a much better position to ascertain Phoebe's activities in the early church. Our knowledge of what it meant to be a deacon in early Christianity is very limited because it is based primarily on hypotheses that stem from the meaning of the word.[45]   Beyer argues that the primary task of deacons was one of administration and practical service. However, he is forced to deduce his conclusion from the following:

a) from the use of the term for table waiters and more generally for servants; b) from the qualities demanded of them; c) from their relationship to the bishop; and d) from what we read elsewhere in the NT concerning the gift and task of διακονία.[46]

---

[44]So Käsemann, *Romans*, 411, "Insofar as Phoebe has a permanent and recognized ministry, as is emphasized by the participle and the place name, one may at least see an early stage of what later became the ecclesiastical office." C. E. B. Cranfield, *The Epistle to the Romans* (ICC; Edinburgh: T. & T. Clark, 1979): 2:781, sees a "definite office," as do Otto Michel, *Der Brief an die Römer* (12th ed.; Göttingen: Vandenhoeck and Ruprecht, 1963): 377, and Hans Lietzmann, *An die Römer* (5th ed.; Tübingen: J. C. B. Mohr, 1971): 124. Dunn, *Romans* 2.887, on the other hand, favors "recognized ministry" or "position of responsibility."

[45]Hermann Beyer, "διάκονος," *TDNT* 2:90, notes "The task of the διάκονοι can in fact be deduced only from the actual name of their office and from their later function." E. Best, *The Letter of Paul to the Romans* (Cambridge: Cambridge Univ. Press, 1967): 174, suggests "the word Paul uses to describe her activity is from the same root as 'administration' in 12:7," but in view of the serious problems inherent in "root usage" addressed by J. Barr, *The Semantics of Biblical Language* (Oxford: Oxford Univ. Press, 1961) and F. Sawyer, *Semantics in Biblical Research* (SBT, 24; London: SCM, 1972) it is best not to read "administration" into the word in Rom. 16:1.

[46]*Ibid.*

We have no text from early Christianity that details the responsibilities or activities of the deacons.[47]

Earlier comments regarding the problem of anachronistic interpretations of terms used for evolving offices in earliest Christianity are relevant here as well. The later *office* of deaconess is irrelevant to a study of Rom. 16:1 since no such office is known to have existed in earliest Christianity.[48] Rare references to deaconesses (διακόνισσα) in Christian literature occur in the second and third centuries. For instance, the Syrian Didascalia of the late third-century details their activities as assisting the baptisms of women and caring for sick women; however, to read Rom. 16:1 in light of this description would involve gross anachronism.[49] There is no evidence that Phoebe was called διάκονος because of her service to women. On the contrary, Rom. 16:2 suggests that she served the church at Cenchrea as a

---

[47]1 Tim. 3:8ff. presents a list of qualifications but no description of what these individuals do. Appeals to the appointment of the Seven in Acts 6 are not persuasive because the term διάκονος is not used and because the contrast between "ministry of the word" and "serving tables" does not hold in the passage.

[48]W. Sanday and A. C. Headlam, *The Epistle to the Romans* (ICC; Edinburgh: T. & T. Clark, 1895): 417, postulate that since women would have had special needs in Christian communities, there must have been an office of deaconess in the early church. A similar projection is R. Haldane, *Exposition of The Epistle to the Romans* (London: Banner of Truth, 1963 reprint): 633, "As deacons were appointed to attend to the poor, so deaconesses were specially set apart in the churches in order to attend to the wants of their own sex." 1 Tim. 3:11 is not helpful because even if the qualifications are for female deacons, there is no suggestion of what their activities were nor whether they were limited to serving women. Neither does Pliny's report to Trajan (AD 112) that he had tortured two Christian slaves who were called *ministrae* further our understanding of Phoebe. Whether the Latin *ministrae* is equivalent to deacon is unclear and even if it is, their activities are not detailed. If the terms are equivalent, this text would prove only that women deacons existed in Bithynia by AD 112 (Pliny, *Epist.* 10.96.8).

[49]See M. H. Shepherd, "Deaconess," *IDB* 1.786.

whole, not the women only,[50] and that she also served Paul. To translate διάκονος as "deacon(ess)" is, as Arichea[51] notes, "to make a distinction which the text does not make, namely, between men and women who performed 'deacon' functions."

In view of continuing debate regarding the evolution of offices in earliest Christianity, Käsemann is correct in forcing the reader to place Paul's description of Phoebe as διάκονος next to his teaching on *charismata* in Rom. 12. He warns that debate over whether διάκονος already means an ecclesiastical office "masks the Pauline view that each Christian is officially brought into the service of the Lord, entrusted with a particular ministry, and must exercise it, as no one else can, in and toward the community."[52]

Even if all the ambiguities regarding Phoebe's role in the church at Cenchrea cannot be clarified, the readers of English Bibles must be made more aware of the dilemma that translators face in rendering Paul's language in Rom. 16:1-2.[53] If διάκονος is translated "deacon," the reader is likely to assume that Phoebe held an ecclesiastical office that she probably did not hold. However, to translate generically as "servant" surely communicates less to the modern reader than Paul intended to say.

Because Phoebe's description as *diakonos* is followed by elaboration of her activities as a "patron," it is reasonable to conclude that she was a Christian woman who had the gift that belonged to a προιστάμενος (Rom. 12:8). Because of

---

[50]See M. Black, *Romans* (London: Oliphants, 1973): 178-79.

[51]Daniel Arichea, "Who was Phoebe," *BT* 39 (1988): 406. The assumption that Paul would have used the feminine form of the noun if it had been available in current usage cannot be pressed too far. The lexical choice is between "deacon" and "servant." See also C. K. Barrett, *The Epistle to the Romans* (New York: Harper & Bros., 1957): 282, and F. F. Bruce, *The Letter of Paul to the Romans* (2nd ed.; Grand Rapids: Eerdmans, 1985): 252.

[52]Käsemann, *Romans*, 411.

[53]See Arichrea, *BT* (1988): 406.

Phoebe's continual efforts on behalf of those who were socially vulnerable, she came to be regarded as having a special responsibility in this particular area of service. Although Clement knows of women who minister fundamentally to other women or children, Phoebe's activities are not gender specific. Undoubtedly, Phoebe would have been viewed as a leader in the church at Cenchrea because of her status and labor in behalf of the community. However, to infer that she had a "position of great authority" in the church presses Paul's descriptive terms into hierarchical categories that are not justified in view of Pauline usage. Although a developing organization may be discernible already in Pauline letters, "offices" in the later patristic sense are not. Hence, Dodd[54] nuanced it appropriately, when he wrote, "Whatever the 'deacons' were at Philippi, that Phoebe was at Cenchrea."

2. Junia(s)

One of the three earliest surviving comments on Rom. 16:7 is that of John Chrysostom[55] (d. 407), who writes:

> To be an apostle is something great. But to be outstanding among the apostles—just think what a wonderful song of praise that is! They were outstanding on the basis of their works and virtuous actions. Indeed, how great the wisdom of this woman must have been that she was even deemed worthy of the title of apostle.

What stands out in this brief statement is that one of the apostles mentioned in Rom. 16:7 may have been a woman. Early Christian writers unanimously took the name to be feminine, the accusative singular of the feminine name Junia

---

[54]C. H. Dodd, *The Letter of Paul to the Romans* (New York: Harper and Bros., 1932): 235.

[55]Chrysostom, *Epistolam ad Romanos, Homilia* 31.2 in J.-P. Migne, *Patrologia Graece* 60.669f.

or Julia.[56] Philologists have no difficulty explaining the consistency with which ancient writers took the name to be feminine. Researchers have been unable to locate a single example of the male name *Junias* in ancient literature or inscriptions, either Latin or Greek. Lampe,[57] however, has found over 250 examples of the feminine name Junia!

Nevertheless, the relatively modern tradition of reading *Junias* resists correction. By accentuating 'Ιουνιᾶν with a circumflex accent over the alpha, the Nestle-Aland text interprets the name as the accusative singular of the masculine *Junias*.[58] Certainly, 'Ιουνίαν should have an acute accent over the iota to indicate that the name is feminine. The argument in Aland's textual apparatus that the feminine "Junia" does not appear in the manuscript tradition is both misleading and incorrect. It is misleading because the distinction based on accentuation noted above cannot be observed in the uncials, but we know that the earlier patristic writers read the name as feminine. It is incorrect because at least one minuscule (the ninth-century ms. 33) has the feminine reading.[59]

Modern commentators and translators who persist in reading *Junias* regularly explain the lack of evidence for the

---

[56]*Julian*, a variant reading supported by one Greek manuscript (𝔓[46]), may have entered the manuscript tradition because of the name's occurrence in Rom. 16:15, but it does not affect the issue at hand since Julia is also feminine. Origen, the earliest commentator on Rom. 16:7, took the name to be feminine, as did later writers such as Hatto of Vercelli, Theophylact, and Abelard. Aegidius of Rome (AD 1245-1316) appears to be the first extant writer to take the name as masculine. See Bernadette Brooten, "'Junia . . . Outstanding among the Apostles' (Romans 16:7)," *Women Priests* (ed. L. Swidler and A. Swidler; New York: Paulist Press, 1977): 141-42.

[57]Peter Lampe, *Die Stadtrömischen Christen in den ersten beiden Jahrhunderten* (Tübingen: J. C. B. Mohr, 1989): 147.

[58]See O. Bardenhewer, *Der Römerbrief des heiligen Paulus* (Freiburg: Herder, 1926): 213, and Leitzmann, *An die Römer*, 125.

[59]For discussion of the text-critical issues, see Lampe, *Die Stadtrömischen Christen*, 223.

masculine name by suggesting that it is a contraction of a longer form, *Junianus, Junianius, Junilius,* or *Junius*.[60] Although these names are common enough in antiquity, there is absolutely no evidence that any man named *Junianus, Junianius, Junilius,* or *Junius* was ever called *Junias*.[61] In other words, there is no more evidence for reversing the gender of this name by positing a contraction than for reversing the gender of any other name by the same means. The only reason for doing so would be a starting premise that a woman could not have been an apostle. The contraction hypothesis is rendered even less likely by the fact that the patristic writers did not resort to it and by the fact that Latin hypocoristica are usually formed by lengthening rather than shortening names.[62]

Also debated in Rom. 16:7 is whether ἐπίσημοι ἐν τοῖς ἀποστόλοις should be translated "outstanding 'among' the apostles" or "outstanding 'in the eyes of' the apostles." Both renderings are grammatically possible (see 1 Cor. 15:12 and 14:11). However, as Cranfield[63] notes, "It is much more probable—we might well say, virtually certain—that the words mean 'outstanding among the apostles'." This is the way the phrase was understood by all of the patristic writers, by most all modern commentators, and by virtually all English translations.[64] It is highly unlikely that Paul would have recommended this pair to the Roman Christians by saying they were "outstanding in the eyes of the apostles." Would Paul be including himself in this grouping of apostles? With regard to Paul's apostolic status, it is one thing to say that these two compare favorably with

---

[60]See among others, H. W. Schmidt, *Der Brief des Paulus an die Römer* (THKNT; Berlin: Evangelische Verlagsanstalt, 1963): 253, and T. Zahn, *Der Brief des Paulus an die Römer* (KNT; Leipzig: A. Deichert, 1910): 607, n. 58.

[61]Valentin Fabrega, "War Junia(s), der hervorragende Apostel (Rom. 16,7), eine Frau?" *JAC* 27/28 (1984-85): 49.

[62]So Brooten, "Junia . . .,"*Women Priests,* 142.

[63]Cranfield, *Romans,* 2.789.

[64]The other reading has been defended by Cornely and Zahn. For discussion of this position, see Fabrega, *JAC* (1984-85): 52.

their apostolic colleagues and quite another to appeal to the opinions of "the apostles" to bolster the Roman Christians' opinions of Andronicus and Junia. This type of recommendation seems less than probable, given the view Paul communicated in Gal. 2:6-9.

Although there is agreement that Paul intended to say that these two were "outstanding among the group called 'apostles'," debate persists over what Paul intended by the term. Fiorenza[65] notes, "Non-specialists may feel certain who the apostles were, (but) the numerous exegetical studies of the last twenty-five years demonstrate that the case is not at all clear." "Apostle" was used in four distinct ways in the NT: 1) the Twelve original followers of Jesus, 2) persons who had seen the risen Lord and been commissioned by Him (1 Cor. 9:1; 15:1-11); 3) a missionary successful in church planting, labor and suffering (which underlie Paul's arguments in 2 Cor.); and 4) an emissary or missionary sent out by a particular church to perform specific tasks (2 Cor. 8:23 and Phil. 2:25).

The first and fourth usages can be ruled out easily, as Andronicus and Junia were not among the "twelve" nor was their apostleship specifically associated with a particular church or specific task. Deciding between the second and third is more difficult. Dunn[66] thinks that the straight-forward description "the apostles," coupled with the phrase "who were also in Christ before I was," suggests that Andronicus and Junia belonged to the larger group who saw the risen Christ (1 Cor. 15:7) and were appointed apostles by the Lord. Schnackenburg,[67] on the other hand, holds that they "belonged to a group of 'apostles' who were early and recognized heralds of the gospel, without being able to

---

[65]Elisabeth Schüssler Fiorenza, "The Apostleship of Women in Early Christianity," *Women Priests*, 135.

[66]Dunn, *Romans*, 2:894. See also Best, *Romans*, 174, and Bruce, *Romans*, 258.

[67]R. Schnackenburg, "Apostles before and during Paul's Time," *Apostolic History and the Gospel—Essays in Honor of F. F. Bruce* (ed. W. Gasque and R. Martin; Exeter: Paternoster, 1970): 294.

lay claim to an appearance of the risen Lord." Available data is insufficient to place Andronicus and Junia in either group with any confidence. A decision is not vital unless one wishes to interpret the Christophany as an ordination, resulting in a more official status or more authority than those who were merely successful church planters. One should be careful not to read more into this distinction than early Christians did.[68] Collins[69] rightly warns modern interpreters that "the category 'ordination' is problematic for the Pauline letters. The question should thus be rephrased in terms of the participation of women in what Paul considered the primary forms of ministry."

Although details of Andronicus and Junia's apostolic calling are unclear, Paul's comments concerning the pair indicate clearly what distinguished their apostolic careers in his eyes: they are Jewish Christians ($\sigma\upsilon\gamma\gamma\epsilon\nu\epsilon\hat{\iota}\varsigma$; see Rom 9:3; 16:11, 21);[70] they have a record of apostolic sufferings (fellow-prisoners = $\sigma\upsilon\nu\alpha\iota\chi\mu\alpha\lambda\sigma\tau\sigma\dot{\upsilon}\varsigma$; see 1 Cor. 4:9ff.; 2 Cor. 11;16ff.);[71] they have been in Christ even longer than Paul (thus among the early Palestinian Christians).[72] If Andronicus and Junia were a missionary couple,[73] i.e., husband and wife rather than a brother and sister, they reflect what is already known from 1 Cor. 9:5. Clement of Alexandria[74] reflects at least one advantage, noting

---

[68]Although Paul mentions the Christophany in 1 Cor. 9:1 and 15:8, it does not form the basis of his apostolic defense in 2 Cor.

[69]Adela Yarbro Collins, "The Ministry of Women in the Apostolic Generation," *Women Priests* (ed. L. Swidler and A. Swidler; New York: Paulist Press, 1977): 163.

[70]See James Walters, *Ethnic Issues in Paul's Letter to the Romans* (Philadelphia: Trinity Press International, 1993), on why their Jewish identity recommends them to Paul.

[71]See Fabrega, *JAC* (1984-85): 50-51.

[72]See P. Lampe, "Iunia/Iunias: Sklavenherkunft im Kreise der vorpaulinischen Apostel (Röm. 16,7)," *ZNW* 76 (1985): 133.

[73]Best, *Romans*, 174-75. See also the discussion in M.-J. Lagrange, *Épître aux Romains* (Paris: J. Gabalda, 1950): 366.

[74]Clement of Alexandria, *Stromateis* 3.6.53.3f.

... (they) took their wives with them ... that they might be their co-ministers (συνδικόνους) in dealing with housewives. It was through them that the Lord's teaching penetrated also the women's quarters without any scandal being aroused.

However, no gender-specific roles are attached to Paul's greeting of Andronicus and Junia and nothing in Paul's language here or elsewhere indicates that women missionaries were limited to same-gender settings.

So, Andronicus and Junia were "outstanding among the apostles" by virtue of their Jewish background, their apostolic sufferings, and the years they had been in Christ.

Conclusion

Marshall's (see n. 24) criticism—that estimates of women's influence in Roman antiquity focus too much on whether they were able to hold civic office—is appropriate for the study of women in early Christianity. To investigate the role of women in early churches via their access to positions of power artificially limits the inquiry and tends to introduce later clericalism into an earlier period when participation in ministry was not regulated by ordination but by spiritual endowment.[75] The brevity of the commendation of Phoebe and the greetings in Rom. 16 nevertheless leaves the impression that women filled a variety of roles within missionary communities of early Christianity. It is doubtful that Phoebe or Junia (or Andronicus, for that matter) served in "positions of great rank or power," but they did minister powerfully in the expansion of nascent Christianity, serving in a variety of ways, in behalf of a variety of people—not only women.

---

[75]See R. Reuther, "Ordination: What is the Problem?" *Women Priests* (ed. L. Swidler and A. Swidler; New York: Paulist Press, 1977): 33f., regarding ordination and the early church.

Chapter Seven

1 COR. 11:2-16—A RE-INVESTIGATION

Mark C. Black

1 Cor. 11:2-16 figures prominently in discussion of women in the church, though it is beset by a variety of interpretations.[1] While Paul approved women praying and prophesying at Corinth, on the other hand, he required women to cover their heads. Most understand this text to refer to public worship, but some hold that only "unofficial" worship is addressed. Some believe Paul advocates egalitarianism here, while others think Paul did not allow women speaking roles at all in public worship. Details regarding the situation which might lend clarity to the modern reader apparently were sufficiently understood by the ancient readers as to need no comment. Exegetical work on this text can only attempt to reconstruct the situation Paul addressed.

This section of 1 Cor. is probably a response to information Paul has received from one of two sources:

---

[1]The literature occasioned by this text in recent decades is enormous. See the bibliography in Linda Mercadante, *From Hierarchy to Equality: A Comparison of Past and Present Interpretations of 1 Cor. 11:2-16 in Relation to the Changing Status of Women in Society* (Vancouver: G-M-H Books for Regent College, 1978), and D. R. MacDonald, *There Is No Male and Female: The Fate of a Dominical Saying in Paul and Gnosticism* (HDR 20; Philadelphia: Fortress, 1987): 72-111; Gordon D. Fee, *The First Epistle to the Corinthians* (NICNT; Grand Rapids: Eerdmans, 1987): 491-530; and Joël Delobel, "1 Cor. 11, 2-16: Towards a Coherent Interpretation," *L'Apôtre Paul: Personnalité, Style et Conception du Ministère* (BETL 73; Leuven: Leuven Univ. Press, 1986): 369-89; and Craig S. Keener, *Paul, Women, and Wives: Marriage and Women's Ministry in the Letters of Paul* (Peabody, MA: Hendrickson, 1992).

either from an "official" letter written by the Corinthians requesting information on various issues (7:1)[2] or from a private report from the household of Chloe (1:11). Apparently, the head-covering problem was reported by Chloe's people, since that topic is not introduced with the recurrent περὶ δέ (now concerning),[3] a phrase which seems to indicate his responses to their written inquiries.[4] Paul probably deals with the matter of head-coverings at this point in the letter because he wants to treat several problems relating to worship in a single unit (chaps. 11-14). Thus, he follows this discussion with instructions regarding abuses at the Lord's Supper (11:17-34) and advice on practice of spiritual gifts in worship (12:1-14:40).[5]

Although there are no significant variants in the manuscript tradition, numerous attempts have been made to remove these verses as an embarassing text. Walker,[6] for instance, contends that these verses are an interpolation, but there is no manuscript support and very little scholarly support for his theory.[7] Similarly creative is the view of

---

[2]Likely delivered by Stephanas, Fortunatus, and Achaicus (16:17), this letter at least asked for information regarding sexual relations (chap. 7), eating food offered to idols (8-10), spiritual gifts (12-14), and the collection for Jerusalem (16:1-4).

[3]7:1; 8:1; 12:1; 16:1. See Charles Talbert, *Reading Corinthians: A Literary and Theological Commentary on 1 and 2 Corinthians* (New York: Crossroad, 1989): 66.

[4]Fee, *The First Epistle to the Corinthians*, 491, argues that Paul only deals with the issue because of their inquiry and that he did not feel strongly about it. However, the tone of vv. 6 and 16 seem to reveal a very real concern.

[5]It may be that the discussion of eating food offered to idols (10:14-22) is also to be seen as a discussion of worship that leads into the following topics.

[6]William Walker, Jr., "1 Corinthians 11:2-16 and Paul's Views Regarding Women," *JBL* (1975): 94-110. See also Lamar Cope, "1 Cor. 11:2-16: One Step Further," *JBL* 97 (1978): 435-36; and G. W. Trompf, "On Attitudes Toward Women in Paul and Paulinist Literature: 1 Corinthians 11:3-16 and Its Context," *CBQ* 42 (1980): 196-215.

[7]See among others J. Murphy-O'Connor, "The Non-Pauline Character of 1 Corinthians 11:2-16?" *JBL* 95 (1976): 615-21.

Padgett and Shoemaker[8] that vv. 3-7 are Paul's quotation of a Corinthian position that he then proceeds to refute. But such theoretical suggestions reflect more the stance of the interpreters than that of Paul.

Others, on the basis of 1 Cor. 14:33-36 and 1 Tim. 2:8-15, deny that Paul condoned women speaking in the worship assembly. Some reason that the women were simply praying and prophesying along with the men who were leading these activities.[9] However, it may be asked why Paul is so adamant about their head-coverings if theirs is only a passive role, and even more why he restricts his discussion to the activities of praying and prophesying. Did they not need to remain covered during other worship activities? Further, while we might easily imagine women praying along with the men, we are hard-pressed to determine what it might mean to prophesy in a passive sense.

Others acknowledge the speaking role of women, but argue that reference here is not to the worship assembly, but to an informal gathering or a separate assembly for women only.[10] But it must be asked why Paul would be so concerned with head-coverings in such informal settings that he would pen this response. As he addresses both men and

---

[8]Alan Padgett, "Paul on Women in the Church: Contradictions of Coiffure in 1 Corinthians 11:2-16," *JSNT* 20 (1984): 69-86; and Thomas P. Shoemaker, "Unveiling of Equality: 1 Corinthians 11:2-16," *BTB* 17 (1987): 60-63. Admittedly, in 6:12; 7:1; and 8:1, Paul does seem to quote those he is countering, but those texts are short, usually followed by sustained qualification and unambiguous Pauline response. See D. A. Carson, *Showing the Spirit: A Theological Exposition of 1 Corinthians 12-14* (Grand Rapids: Baker, 1987): 55.

[9]E.g., F. C. Synge, "Studies in Texts—1 Cor. 11:2-16," *Theology* 56 (1953): 143.

[10]Philipp Bachmann, *Der erste Brief des Paulus an die Korinther* (3rd ed.; Leipzig: A. Deichert, 1921): 350-51; Gordon Clark, "The Ordination of Women," *Trinity Review* 17 (1981): 3-4; E. Earle Ellis, *Prophecy and Hermeneutic in Early Christianity: New Testament Essays* (Grand Rapids: Eerdmans, 1978): 27, suggest the occasion is other than a worship assembly. Cf. F. W. Grosheide, *The First Epistle to the Corinthians* (NICNT; Grand Rapids: Eerdmans, 1953): 251-52.

women, what reason is there to think that Paul is concerned with separate gatherings for women? The clear link with vv. 17-34 (esp. 2, 17) and chaps. 12-14 argues strongly for a worship setting. As will be seen, the two activities of 11:2-16 (praying [in tongues] and prophesying) are precisely the primary worship activities discussed in 12-14.

Finally, some think Paul forbids women to pray and prophesy but does not issue a prohibition until chap. 14. So here Paul simply states that women must wear the covering, showing submission to men,[11] i.e., the sign that they may *not* speak. However, there is no disapproval of women praying and prophesying here. In view of Peter's words at Pentecost, "Your sons *and your daughters* shall prophesy" (Acts 2:17; cf. 21:9), any disapproval of women praying and prophesying would require substantial exegetical basis.

This text does not concern women exclusively. Just as the women are to keep their heads covered, the men's heads were to be uncovered (4, 7, 14). Most have assumed Paul's real concern to be with the women and that the men are mentioned only in that connection.[12] However, in Roman culture (Corinth was a Roman colony),[13] both men and

---

[11]Noel Weeks, "Of Silence and Head Coverings," *WTJ* 35 (1972): 21-27, and apparently Neil Lightfoot, *The Role of Women: New Testament Perspectives* (Memphis: Student Assn. Press, 1978): 34-35. The argument states that Paul does the same thing in chaps. 8-10, condoning in chap. 8 what he condemns in chap. 10. However, not only are the two issues very different, but this interpretation of of chaps. 8-10 is not without major problems.

[12]See among others Fee, *The First Epistle to the Corinthians*, 495, 505-07. However, cf. Richard Oster, "When Men Wore Veils to Worship: The Historical Context of 1 Corinthians 11:4," *NTS* 34 (1988): 481-505. Cynthia Thompson, "Hairstyles, Head-coverings, and St. Paul: Portraits from Roman Corinth," *BA* 51 (1988): 99-115, offers helpful photographs in her discussion of statues, statuettes, and coins. See also David W. J. Gill, "The Importance of Roman Portraiture for Head-Coverings in 1 Corinthians 11:2-16," *TynBul* 41 (1990): 245-60.

[13]See Gerd Theissen, *The Social Setting of Pauline Christianity: Essays on Corinth* (Edinburgh: T. & T. Clark, 1982): 75-76, on Latin influence in Corinth at this period.

women covered their heads in some religious settings. While no evidence exists of Jewish or Greek men doing so,[14] there is evidence from first-century Corinth that Roman men did wear head-coverings in worship, e.g., when offering sacrifices, praying and prophesying.[15] Gill suggests that head-covering on Roman men was a sign of social status and thus Paul disallowed it.[16] Thompson[17] argues that Paul takes this stance because male head-coverings were associated with idol worship. For whatever reason, it may well be that men were wearing head-coverings in the Corinthian church.

On the other hand, there are good reasons to believe that this is not Paul's great concern in 1 Cor. 11. First, Paul gives much more attention to the attire of the women than the men. Within those verses which discuss either men's or women's head-coverings (4-10, 13-15), he uses 103 words to discuss the women and only 39 regarding the men. Second, the one section regarding the head-dress of one sex for which there is no parallel statement regarding the other (13) may well express the point of the whole: "Judge for yourselves: is it proper for a woman to pray to God uncovered?"[18] Third, it is not difficult to imagine why Paul would mention the head-covering practices of men even in the absence of the practice in the church. In each case, the reference to the men is easily construed as part of the argument for women being covered. The women's failure to wear head-coverings was inappropriate because it violated the distinction between men and women, which is the heart of the passage.

---

[14]There is no reason to view the male covering as the *tallith* or *yarmulke*. See Oster, *NTS* (1988): 487-88.

[15]See Oster, *NTS* (1988): 504-05; Thompson, *BA* (1988): 101-05; and Gill, *TynBul* (1990): 246-51.

[16]Gill, *TynBul* (1990): 246-51. Within 1 Cor., divisions exist along socio-economic lines. It is reasonable to suppose that Paul would disallow such distinctions as dishonoring man's head, who is Christ (11:4).

[17]Thompson, *BA* (1988): 104.

[18]Delobel, "1 Cor. 11, 2-16," *L' Apôtre Paul*, 379-80.

1 Cor. 11:2-16, then, requires re-investigation if its ancient meaning is to impact current thought accurately.

1. *1 Cor. 11:2*

Paul begins by praising the Corinthians for "holding to" his teachings (2), a somewhat odd introduction since vv. 3-16 contain only criticism for their practices. V. 2 cannot mean that as a group they have adhered faithfully to his teaching regarding head-coverings. Most take v. 2 as a *captatio benevolentiae* (praise before scolding), indicating general acceptance of Paul's teaching.[19] Vv. 3-16, then, are seen as an exception to their normal willingness to accept his teaching (3; *but* I want you to know) or a new or expanded teaching which he is urging upon them (3; *and* I want you to know).[20] It is possible, however, that Paul does intend to praise the majority for holding to his teachings on this subject and that the following criticism is directed toward a small group of contentious members (see 16). This may be supported by the parallel v. 17, which introduces the next topic (Lord's Supper) for which he has no praise for them.

2. *1 Cor. 11:3-6*

A. *The Meaning of* κεφαλή. Vv. 3-6 cohere by virtue of Paul's play on the word κεφαλή (head). A man who prays or prophesies with his (literal) κεφαλή *covered* dishonors his (metaphorical) κεφαλή, i.e., Christ. The woman who prays or prophesies with her (literal) κεφαλή *uncovered* dishonors her (metaphorical) κεφαλή, i.e., man.

---

[19]See Fee, *The First Epistle to the Corinthians*, 500. Troels Engberg-Pedersen, "1 Corinthians 11:16 and the Character of Paul's Exhortation," *JBL* 110 (1991): 681, suggests that the Corinthians women *believe* that they are following his traditions by not wearing head-coverings, so that he is here actually clarifying his earlier teachings.

[20]The particle δέ may be either adversative or conjunctive. See Antoinette Clark Wire, *The Corinthian Women Prophets: A Reconstruction through Paul's Rhetoric* (Minneapolis: Fortress, 1990): 116.

It is not accidental that Paul has chosen the term κεφαλή to describe the relationship between God and Christ, Christ and man, and man and woman.[21] The metaphorical meaning of κεφαλή, however, raises an important problem. The traditional understanding (one having authority over another, chief, ruler) has been strongly challenged. Scroggs[22] and others opt for the translation "source" or "origin," which takes away the hierarchical structure that places women under the authority of men. Fee comments,[23]

> Paul's concern is not hierarchical (who has authority over whom), but relational (the unique relationships that are predicated on one's being the source of the other's existence). Indeed, he says nothing about the man's authority; his concern is with the woman's being man's *glory*, the one without whom he is not complete (vv. 7c-9).

Thus, Paul is only advocating distinction between the sexes.

Which view is correct? The classical Greek lexicon[24] offers "source" (of a river) or "origin" (of muscles), but not

---

[21]Several have noted the unusual order of v. 3. God is at the highest level and woman at the lowest; however, while the series ends with God, it does not start with woman but with man. See Delobel, "1 Cor. 11, 2-16," *L'Apôtre Paul*, 379.

[22]Robin Scroggs, "Paul and the Eschatological Woman," *JAAR* 40 (1972): 283-303; and "Paul and the Eschatological Woman: Revisited," *JAAR* 42 (1974): 532-37, follows the lead of Stephen Bedale, "The Meaning of κεφαλή in the Pauline Epistles," *JTS* n.s. 5 (1954): 211-15. Among those who have followed Bedale and Scroggs are Fee, *The First Epistle to the Corinthians*, 502-04; Jerome Murphy-O'Connor, "Sex and Logic in 1 Corinthians 11:2-16," *CBQ* 42 (1980): 491-93; Morna D. Hooker, "Authority on Her Head: An Examination of 1 Cor. 11:10," *NTS* 10 (1964): 410-11; C. K. Barrett, *The First Epistle to the Corinthians* (New York: Harper & Row, 1968): 248; and F. F. Bruce, *1 and 2 Corinthians* (NCB; London: Marshall Morgan & Scott, 1971): 103.

[23]Fee, *The First Epistle to the Corinthians*, 503-04.

[24]H. G. Liddell and R. Scott, *A Greek-English Lexicon* (9th ed., rev. H. S. Jones and R. McKenzie; Oxford: Clarendon, 1973): 945.

"ruler" or the like, as possible translations for κεφαλή, while
the standard lexicon for early Christian literature[25] does the
opposite. Fitzmyer[26] and Grudem,[27] although approaching
the problem from very different perspectives, conclude that
the meaning "authority over" is very well attested, whereas
its occurrences meaning "source" are very rare.[28] Writers
contemporary with the NT, such as Philo and Plutarch, used
κεφαλή in the sense of "authority," as is often the case in the
LXX. Further, Grudem[29] argues that the few ancient texts
often cited in support of the meaning "source" actually fail to
substantiate unambiguously that meaning. In fact, the text
which most clearly supports the meaning of "source"
(Herodotus, 5th cent. BC) uses the term in the plural
(κεφαλαί) rather than the singular, as in 1 Cor. 11. If Paul
meant "source" in this instance, he was using κεφαλή in an
unusual sense, not an impossible usage but certainly an
unlikely one. The lexical evidence thus forces us to give
first consideration to the more usual metaphorical usage,
"one having authority over," unless the context strongly
urges the other rendering.[30]

---

[25]Walter Bauer, *A Greek-English Lexicon of the New Testament
and Other Early Christian Literature* (2nd ed., rev. F. W. Gingrich and
F. W. Danker; Chicago: Univ. of Chicago Press, 1979): 430.

[26]Joseph A. Fitzmyer, "Another Look at ΚΕΦΑΛΗ in 1
Corinthians 11:3," *NTS* 35 (1989): 503-11.

[27]Wayne Grudem, "Does ΚΕΦΑΛΗ ('Head') Mean 'Source' or
'Authority Over' in Greek Literature? A Survey of 2,336 Examples,"
Trinity Journal 6 (1985): 38-59. For a good treatment of the lexical
data favoring "source," see Philip Barton Payne, "Response," *Women,
Authority & the Bible* (ed. Alvera Mickelsen; Downers Grove, IL:
InterVarsity Press, 1986): 118-32.

[28]See also Peter Cotterell and Max Turner, *Linguistics and
Biblical Interpretation* (Downers Grove: InterVarsity, 1989): 141-45.

[29]Grudem, *Trinity Journal* (1985): 43-44.

[30]Even the meaning "source" would not preclude the possibility
that Paul was advocating female subordination. In fact, Bedale, *JTS*
(1954): 214-15, argues in the oft-cited article which spawned the more
recent interpretation that Paul grounds woman's subordination to man
in her being created from man. See also Delobel, "1 Cor. 11, 2-16,"
L' Apôtre Paul, 378-79.

Contextual indications that Paul is speaking of sub-ordination occur in vv. 7 and 9, where "woman is the glory of man" and "woman was created for man." As we will argue below, Paul introduces in v. 11 (note the adversative πλήν [but]) the interdependence of man and woman in order to qualify the sense in which woman is subordinate to man, lest his idea of *submission* be confused with *inferiority*.[31] A further contextual argument for κεφαλή meaning subordination is that Paul argues that the "head" relationshp between men and women is somehow like that between God and Christ. Not only is it difficult to account for God as "source" of Christ in Pauline theology,[32] but Paul writes later (1 Cor. 15:28) of the subordination of the Son to the Father (see also Phil. 2:8).[33]

B. *"Man and woman" or "husband and wife"?* Many have argued that this text demands the more restricted meaning of ἀνήρ and γυνή, i.e., that husbands and wives are the focus rather than males and females. It is true that 1 Cor. 14:33 refers to husbands and wives in a similar context involving public worship ("let them ask their own husbands at home"). However, the more general reference to "men and women" is the better reading here, as is seen when the attempt is made to substitute consistently "husband and wife" for ἀνήρ and γυνή.[34] Otherwise, v. 3 envisions Christ as head of every *husband*, and only husbands dishonor Christ by

---

[31]Cotterell and Turner, *Linguistics and Biblical Interpretation*, 317; and Delobel, "1 Cor. 11, 2-16," *L'Apôtre Paul*, 381.

[32]Cf. Murphy-O'Connor, *CBQ* (1980): 494; Delobel, "1 Cor. 11, 2-16," *L'Apôtre Paul*, 378; and Payne, "Response," *Women, Authority & the Bible*, 126-27.

[33]For the view taken here ("ontological equality" with "economic subordination"), see James B. Hurley, *Man and Woman in Biblical Perspective: A Study in Role Relationships and Authority* (Leicester, Eng.: InterVarsity Press, 1981): 166-67.

[34]It is possible that Paul moved back and forth between the two meanings, as suggested by Thomas R. Schreiner, "Head Coverings, Prophecies and the Trinity: 1 Corinthians 11:2-16," *Recovering Biblical Manhood and Womanhood* (ed. John Piper and Wayne Grudem; Wheaton, IL: Crossway, 1991): 124-39, 485-87.

wearing head-coverings (4). Similarly, vv. 11-12 would suggest that "the wife came from the husband" and "the husband is born of the wife," an impossible understanding.

C. *Hair or head-covering?* Another difficulty concerns the nature of the head-covering. The phrase translated "with his head covered" (v. 4) is κατὰ κεφαλῆς ἔχων (having down the head). The corresponding phrase relating to the women is ἀκατακαλύπτῳ τῇ κεφαλῇ (with the head uncovered). One popular view postulates that Paul is discussing hairstyles rather than head-coverings.[35] Paul, according to one variation of this view, is not demanding that women wear veils but that they not let their hair down—it is to be kept on the top of the head.[36] It is argued that Paul would not have used κατά (down) with the genitive to refer to something "resting upon" the head, that he nowhere uses the term for veil (κάλυμμα), and that, in fact, v. 14 informs us what is hanging down the head, namely, hair. The issue therefore would have little to do with subordination but rather with sexual distinctions—women were not to be adorned in an unfeminine way nor were men to look unmasculine. Murphy-O'Connor believes that Paul's (unstated) concern is actually homosexuality.[37] Others argue that the unusual hairstyles were like those of the

---

[35]The view seems to have been introduced by Abel Isaksson, *Marriage and Ministry in the New Temple: A Study with Special Reference to Mt 19.3-12 and 1 Cor. 11.3-16* (ASNU 24; Lund: C. W. K. Gleerup, 1963). See also William J. Martin, "1 Corinthians 11:2-16: An Interpretation," *Apostolic History and the Gospel: Biblical and Historical Essays Presented to F. F. Bruce on His 60th Birthday* (ed. W. Gasque & R. P. Martin; Exeter: Paternoster, 1970): 231-41; James B. Hurley, "Did Paul Require Veils or the Silence of Women? A Consideration of 1 Cor. 11:2-16 and 1 Cor. 14:33b-36," *WTJ* 35 (1973): 190-220; Murphy-O'Connor, *CBQ* (1980): 484-91; and Padgett, *JSNT* (1984): 70-71.

[36]Hurley, *Man and Woman in Biblical Perspective*, 169-71. See also Murphy-O'Connor, *CBQ* (1980): 481.

[37]Murphy-O'Connor, *CBQ* (1980): 487, writes, "The real issue was the way the hair was dressed. The slightest exaggeration was interpreted as a sign of effeminacy; it hinted at sexual ambiguity."

prostitutes,[38] while still others think that by letting down their hair in ecstatic worship the Corinthian women were imitating the pagan worship of the mystery cults.[39]

There are numerous reasons for rejecting the hairstyle hypothesis.[40] First, to translate the word associated with the women's hair, ἀκατακάλυπτος (uncovered), as "unbound" is highly unusual.[41]   Second, though Paul does discuss hairstyles in verse 14-15, his argument is that a woman's long hair is given her "as" a (natural) covering,[42] while a man's (naturally) short hair is evidence that he should not wear the head-covering. Third, while it is true that Paul's phrase κατὰ κεφαλῆς ἔχων may seem an unusual one for a head-covering,[43] it is no less unusual for "long hair."[44] Most significantly, the context of vv. 3-10 simply will not allow for the meaning "long (or tended) hair." That Paul is speaking of something worn on the head seems obvious, especially from v. 7 ("a man ought not to *cover the head*")[45] and from v. 10 (see below).

It should be mentioned that the "veil" in question is neither the oriental veil which covered the head and face

---

[38]See Hurley, *WTJ* (1973): 202.

[39]Elisabeth Schüssler Fiorenza, *In Memory of Her: A Feminist Theological Reconstruction of Christian Origins* (New York: Crossroad, 1983): 227-30; Stefan Lösch, "Christliche Frauen in Corinth (1 Cor. 11:2-16)," *Theological Quarterly* 111 (1947): 216-61.

[40]See esp. Delobel, "1 Cor. 11, 2-16," *L'Apôtre Paul*, 372-76, for an excellent response to the technical details of the theory.

[41]Delobel, "1 Cor. 11, 2-16," *L'Apôtre Paul*, 375.

[42]The preposition ἀντί can mean "instead of," but here means "as" or "like." See MacDonald, *There Is No Male and Female*, 87.

[43]However, see Plutarch, *Regum et imperatorum apophthegmata* 200F; *Aetia Romana et Graeca* 267C; *Vitae decem oratorum* 824B; *Pyrrhus* 399B; *Caesar* 739D.

[44]Oster, *NTS* (1988): 486, examining the usage in Plutarch (who also uses the phrase κατὰ κεφαλῆς with reference to head-coverings), criticizes Murphy-O'Connor's thesis that κατά without the genitive can scarcely refer to something "resting upon" the head.

[45]Delobel, "1 Cor. 11,2-16," *L'Apôtre Paul*, 372.

except for the eyes nor the separate head-dress of religious functionaries. It is rather the outer garment simply pulled up from the back and across the head approximately to the ears.[46] The common Latin term for this arrangement was *capite velato*. The phrase "having down the head," therefore, may not be at all unusual, since this covering did proceed down the sides of the head. That this is the head-covering in question seems to be confirmed by Paul's use of the term περιβολαῖον in 11:15 (a mantle, cloak, gown, or the like). This also explains why Paul is able later in the argument to compare it to a woman's long hair (which hangs down from the sides of the head, not across the face).[47]

D. *The meaning of head-coverings.* While it is certain that Paul wanted the Corinthian women to cover their heads, the meaning attached to female head-coverings is less certain. Even more difficult is the question of the reason some of the Christian women in Corinth chose to go uncovered. The problem is complicated by the presence of three cultures in ancient Corinth. There was the Jewish element, in which the church had its roots and which represented Paul's training. There was also the Greek culture, Corinth being the leading city of Achaia. Finally, there were the Romans, who had colonized Corinth in 44 BC. To compound the problem, people behaved differently at home, in public, and in religious and other special settings.[48] Sufficient information for mid-first century Corinth is simply unavailable. Nonetheless, we are not without helpful information.[49]

---

[46]Oster, *NTS* (1988): 496; Ben Witherington III, *Women in the Earliest Churches* (SNTSMS 59; Cambridge: Univ. Press, 1988): 83.

[47]Witherington, *Women in the Earliest Churches*, 82-83. Additionally, it would seem odd to have Paul requiring a veil to cover the face of women who are speaking in the assembly.

[48]We are not sure what evidence is most relevant: the domestic customs (after all, Christians met in houses), customs at religious settings, or more general customs.

[49]See esp. Keener, *Paul, Women, and Wives*, 22-31. For helpful though limited citations of ancinet texts, see Hans Conzelmann, *1 Corinthians* (Hermeneia; Philadelphia: Fortress, 1975): 185, n. 40. For a fuller discussion of the evidence dating back to the 5th century

On the one hand, evidence from ancient coins, statues, and statuettes leaves little doubt that it was acceptable for women to go bareheaded in public in Corinth.[50] There is little reason to think, for example, that a woman in the market without a head-covering would be thought a prostitute.[51] Klaus Thräde is representative of many scholars who look primarily at this evidence and conclude that Paul is trying to force Jewish customs on the Corinthians.[52]

On the other hand, there is evidence which suggests that *Roman* women (just as Roman men) quite often and for various reasons wore head coverings. For example, female priests apparently wore head-coverings.[53] Plautus writes of a woman who put on the veil during labor pains in order to pray to the immortal gods.[54] Also, there are marble carvings showing husbands uncovered and wives covered at wedding ceremonies, perhaps exhibiting "the republican ideal of dutiful womanhood."[55] There is also some evidence that head-coverings functioned to identify a woman's place in society, and that a woman who removed her veil would

---

BC in Greece, see C. M. Galt, "Veiled Ladies," *American Journal of Archaeology* 35 (1931): 373-93.

[50]See especially Thompson, *BA* 51 (1988): 107-113.

[51]Gill, *TynBul* 41 (1990): 251.

[52]Klaus Thräde, "Ärger mit der Freiheit. Die Bedeutung von Frauen in Theorie und Praxis der alten Kirche," *"Friende in Christus werden . . ." Die Beziehung von Mann und Frau als Frage an Theologie und Kirche* (ed. G. Scharffenorth and K. Thräde; Gellhausen/ Berlin: Burckhardthaus, 1977): 104-16.

[53]Gill, *TynBul* 41 (1990): 251-56, notes that the Vestal Virgins in a frieze of the Ara Pacis are shown *capite velato*, whereas the other women pictured are not.

[54]Oster, *NTS* (1988): 501. See his quotation of Juvenal 6.390-92 on 503: "There she stood before the altar, thinking it no shame to veil her head on behalf of a harper" in the context of a sacrificial offering.

[55]Gill, *TynBul* 41 (1990): 253. Quote from D. Strong, *Roman Art* (London: Pelican, 1988): 46.

reflect poorly on her husband.[56] Oster notes that among the Romans, "apparel more often indicated the social rank of the individual."[57] Plutarch writes that among the Romans, it is more usual for women in public to have their heads covered (ἐγκεκαλυμμέναις) and men with their heads uncovered (ἀκατακαλύπτοις)."[58] He goes on to state that at religious festivals Romans (men and women) wear head-coverings.

As was normal among oriental cultures, *Jewish* women were expected to wear head-coverings.[59] This is important inasmuch as the church began among Jews and no doubt had a fair Jewish representation (Acts 18). It is also of interest that head-coverings were the norm for females in Tarsus, Paul's early home.[60]

There is also evidence that it was not abnormal for *Greek* women to wear head coverings at religious activities. Apuleius, writing about the Isis festival in Corinth, writes, "The women had their hair anointed, and their heads covered with light linen, but the men had their crowns shaven and shining bright."[61] There also is ample evidence that in the Hellenistic age it was customary for adult women in Greece to wear head-coverings in ritual contexts.[62] Tertullian notes that even as late as his day, the Corinthian woman was known for covering her head.[63] Many scholars have

---

[56]Gill, *TynBul* 41 (1990): 251-55, cites inscriptional evidence to the effect that women who wished to honor their husbands appeared with heads covered. The evidence, however, is capable of other interpretations.

[57]Oster, *NTS* (1988): 493.

[58]*Roman Questions* 267a (LCL 4:27).

[59]The evidence is offered and summarized by many interpreters. See Conzelmann, *1 Corinthians*, 185, n. 39; MacDonald, *There Is No Male and Female*, 82-83; Talbert, *Reading Corinthians*, 67.

[60]Dio Chrysostom, *Discourses* 33.48-49. See the discussion by Albrecht Oepke, "καλύπτω," TDNT 3.562. Oepke writes that the custom becomes "stricter as one moves east."

[61]*The Golden Ass (Metamorphoses)* 11.10 LCL (1915), 555.

[62]Galt, *American Journal of Archaeology* 35 (1931): 373-93.

[63]*Virg.* 8.8, *Corin.* 4.

therefore argued that head-coverings were a universal sign of the subordinate status of women.[64]

Though we cannot be sure, the evidence seems to favor the position that in Corinth, women in the marketplace would often be covered, and in religious contexts they would usually be covered. All that can be stated with assurance, however, is that "the wearing of a head-covering by an adult woman (especially in a ritual context) was a traditional practice known to Jews, Greeks, and Romans."[65] We hope that future discoveries and study will heighten our understanding of this issue. However, at present we must rely at least as much on the *context* of 1 Cor. 11 as on the other ancient evidence in order to reconstruct the historical circumstances.

Paul does not insist on head-coverings for women solely on the basis of the situation at Corinth, no matter what they may have signified there. In v. 16 Paul insists that the Corinthians abide by the practice of the churches everywhere. This means that either 1) they are to abide by the universal practice no matter what the meaning of head-coverings in Corinth or, more likely, 2) the meaning of veils had such a universal significance that Paul's mandate would not be seen as totally unreasonable. Whatever different individuals thought about head-coverings, Paul believed that for a woman to be bareheaded when she prayed and prophesied was a violation of the female's relationship with her (metaphorical) "head." So it is reasonable to think that the Corinthian women were expected to have understood (even if they might not have agreed with) the position that head-coverings in some sense denied the authority of the male.

---

[64]MacDonald, *There Is No Male and Female*, 89, writes, "But in spite of the wide diversity of actual veiling practices, the veil consistently represented a woman's inferiority and subordination and was used by Jews, Greeks, Romans, and Christians as an effective form of social control."

[65]Witherington, *Women in the Earliest Churches*, 82.

E. *"As if her hair were shaven."* Paul's statement that, "it is just as though her head were shaved," is less difficult, since the evidence clearly associates a shaven head with shame or mourning.[66] Dio Chrysostom associates shaving of the head with humiliation and, citing a law given by Demonassa of Cyprus, says, "a woman guilty of adultery shall have her hair cut off and be a harlot."[67] Aristotle and Tacitus also write of the shame inherent in a shaven female head.[68] This analogy also helps to clarify that, in Paul's thinking, the bareheaded woman in worship was a source of shame.

F. *Praying and prophesying.* The interpreter must give attention to the fact that it is apparently only during the activities of praying and prophesying that head-coverings were at issue. We cannot here examine all the various aspects of these activities in the letters of Paul, but several observations should be noted. First, both of these activities were probably Spirit-inspired gifts. As many interpreters have noted, the activity of "prayer" in 1 Cor. 11-14 is virtually synonymous with speaking in tongues. In 1 Cor. 14:2 Paul states that tongues-speaking is addressed "not to men but to God." In 14:14-16, as he argues for the superiority of prophecy over tongues, he asks, "For is I pray in a tongue, my spirit prays but my mind is unfruitful. . . . Otherwise, if you bless with the spirit, how can anyone in the position of an outsider say the 'Amen' to your thanksgiving when he does not know what you are saying?"[69]

---

[66]See esp. Keener, *Paul, Women, and Wives*, 25-27; also Hurley, *Man and Woman in Biblical Perspective*, 169; see Deut. 21:12.

[67]Gill, *TynBul* 41 (1990): 256. It is also worthy of note that Lucian and other Greek writers criticized the practice of some (especially Spartan women) for their closely cropped hair, making them look masculine, according to Witherington, *Women in the Earliest Churches*, 255, n. 43.

[68]Aristotle, *Thes.* 837; Tacitus, *Germ.* 19. See Fee, *The First Epistle to the Corinthians*, 510, esp. n. 79.

[69]See MacDonald, *There Is No Male and Female*, 86. For the recent discussion of prophecy in this text and elsewhere in the first century, see the works of Wayne Grudem, "Prophecy—Yes, but

Second, a few scholars have noticed that covering the head during these activities seems to have been common in (Greco-)Roman worship. From the archeological evidence, it appears that women depicted *capite velato* in worship are often performing sacrifice, praying, or prophesying.[70] Thus the Corinthian Christians could have been imitating Roman and perhaps Greek ways of worship, perhaps for status or related reasons. However, while this would account for the activity of the men (if they were indeed wearing head-coverings), it scarcely speaks to the reasons for women participating uncovered; for women (especially the Romans) also regularly wore head-coverings in such settings.

3. 1 Cor. 11: 7-10

In vv. 7-10 Paul argues from Gen. 1-2 that woman should wear a head-covering and man should not because 1) man is God's image and glory, whereas woman is man's glory, and 2) woman was made for the sake of man, not vice versa.[71] Again, the idea of the subordination of female to male is difficult to miss.

It is also argued that vv. 7-8 imply that man and not woman is the image of God and that Paul arrived at this stance by his (mis)reading of Gen. 1:27.[72] While this reading is understandable, it fails to notice that Paul's

---

Teaching—No: Paul's Consistent Advocacy of Women's Participation Without Governing Authority," *JETS* 30 (1987): 11-23; and *The Gift of Prophecy in 1 Corinthians* (Washington, D.C.: University Press of America, 1982). See also David Aune, *Prophecy in Early Christianity and the Mediterranean World* (Grand Rapids: Eerdmans, 1983); and David Hill, *New Testament Prophecy* (New Foundations Theological Library; Atlanta: John Knox, 1979).

[70]Oster, *NTS* (1988): 503-4; Gill, *TynBul* 41 (1990): 247-50.

[71]Witherington, *Women in the Earliest Churches*, 169, correctly remarks that there is a "presumed connection between the first man, Adam, and all ensuing men who are likewise the image and glory of God."

[72]Wire, *The Corinthian Women Prophets*, 119-22.

emphasis is on δόξα, not εἰκών. Paul's point is that (because
of his interpretation of Gen. 1:26-27 and 2:21-23) man is the
glory of God and woman the *glory* of man.[73] Woman is
never denied to be the image of God.

A. *"Authority on her head."* V. 10 presents the most
difficult interpretive problems of all. The term ἐξουσία
(authority) in the phrase, "the woman ought to have
authority on her head," has traditionally been understood to
refer to the head-covering (note RSV "veil"), which implies
the *husband's* authority allowing her to speak. Recently this
interpretation has been challenged.

One intriguing reading of v. 10 suggests that in worship
Paul wants to ensure that it is God's glory and not man's
glory that is on display. Hooker thinks that Paul means that
just as a man's uncovered head reflects the glory of his
"head" who is God, the uncovered head of a woman reflects
the glory of her "head" who is man.[74] Consequently, the
woman who prays and prophesies must wear a head-
covering so that she will not reflect man's glory. When in v.
10 Paul writes, "the woman ought to have authority
(ἐξουσία) on her head," he refers not to her husband's
authority (evidenced by the head-covering) but rather to the
authority which has now been given to woman, allowing her
to pray and prophesy. The primary support for this reading
is the fact that the term "authority" in 1 Cor. always refers to
someone's "active" right to decide rather than to some
"passive" authority which comes from another.[75]

Though this interpretation has gained many adherents,[76]
it is difficult to see how Paul could speak in this way of the

---

[73] See Morna D. Hooker, "Authority on Her Head: An
Examination of 1 Cor. 11:10," *NTS* 10 (1964): 415; also
Witherington, *Women in the Earliest Churches*, 87.

[74] Hooker, *NTS* 10 (1964): 410-16.

[75] Hurley, *Man and Woman in Biblical Perspective*, 176.

[76] For example, Barrett, *The First Epistle to the Corinthians*, 253-
4; Bruce, *1 and 2 Corinthians*, 106; Wire, *The Corinthian Women
Prophets*, 121-22.

significance of head-coverings. Whereas in v. 5 woman is said to *dishonor* man by praying and prophesying without the head-covering, Hooker's reading demands that the woman's failure to wear the covering actually reflects the *glory* of the man.[77] Paul does not suggest this. It is a *non sequitur* that a woman's uncovered head reflects the glory of her head since a man's uncovered head reflects the glory of his head. It was the semantic significance of head-coverings in culture rather than a concern for consistency of meaning between male and female head-coverings which led Paul to his conclusions.

It may be best therefore to understand the "authority on her head" in v. 10 to be that of the man (husband), an authority which allows her to pray and prophesy. In other words, she is allowed to engage in these activities as long as it is evident that she is under the authority of man.[78] Whatever position is taken, the interpreter should not overlook the fact that the term ἐξουσία is used where we would expect a reference to the head-covering. Notice the chiasm which structures vv. 7-10:

a   (7) For a man ought (ὀφείλει) not to cover his head,
  b   since he is the image and glory of God;
  b´   but woman is the glory of man.
                  (8) For woman was not made from
                  woman, but woman from man.
                  (9) Neither was man created for
                  woman, but woman for man.
a´ (10) For this reason a woman ought to (ὀφείλει) have authority on her head, because of the angels.

---

[77]This reading seems to correlate best with the view that the κεφαλή relationship does not imply the authority of man over woman. Cf. Cotterell and Turner, *Linguistics and Biblical Interpretation*, 317-25.

[78]It may be argued that the metonymic use of the term ἐξουσία allows for a "passive" sense of the term. It is a very complex issue, for which there is no happy solution.

This structure suggests that the phrase in v. 10, "for this reason" (διὰ τοῦτο), looks back to v. 7 (woman is the glory of man) and that Paul has intentionally substituted the metonym "authority" for the expected reference to a head-covering. Vv. 8-9 are explanatory, offering the reasons for woman being the glory of man: the creation order and purpose.[79]

B. *"Because of the angels."* Of the many interpretations of the "angels" reference, we must limit our discussion to three. First, some understand the reference to evil angels who look lustfully at women with uncovered heads (a reading supposedly supported by Gen. 6:3).[80] Second, the angels may be playing the role of God's guardians of the created order and enforcers of his law.[81] This interpretation is based on 1 Cor. 4:9 (angels as observers of human activity), Gal. 3:19 (angels' involvement in giving the law), and various Jewish texts, especially several from Qumran.[82] There it was believed that the angels were present in worship, so that worshipers must watch their behavior. If

---

[79]Another possible reading would translate "the woman has to exercise control (ἐξουσία) over her head," and therefore does not directly refer to the head-covering at all. Because of the creation principles (8-9) and because of the angels (10), she must behave correctly with regard to her head (which of course means wearing the covering). This is a case on which we dare not be dogmatic—the text is simply too obscure. In any case, a particular understanding of this verse (including the reference to the angels, to be discussed below) should not become the key to the whole passage.

[80]See Gail Patterson Corrington, "The 'Headless Woman': Paul and the Language of the Body in 1 Cor. 11:2-16," *Perspectives in Religious Studies* 18 (1991): 230.

[81]Murphy-O'Connor, *1 Corinthians* (New Testament Message 10; Wilmington, DE: Michael Glazier, 1979): 108-9, believes that the head-coverings signalled to the angels, God's guardians, that a new order has dawned which allows women such rights. One wonders, however, why angels would need to be told by human worshipers of such a significant event.

[82]Henry J. Cadbury, "A Qumran Parallel to Paul," *HTR* 51 (1958): 1-2, and Joseph Fitzmyer, "A Feature of Qumran Angelology and the Angels of 1 Cor. 11:10," *NTS* 4 (1957): 48-58.

this view of angels was behind his thinking, Paul was encouraging the Corinthians to abide by God's created order so that they would not offend the angels, who were concerned with such matters.

A third interpretation is said to be supported by 1 Cor. 6:3, in which Paul writes, "we will judge angels," implying the (future) subordination of angels to humanity. This view draws attention to an ancient Jewish belief that the angels were God's worshipers, who, nonetheless, began to worship Adam when he was created. While some "Adam legends" envision God commanding this worship of man, certain rabbis contended that God put Adam to sleep to stop this misdirected worship.[83] If this is the background, Paul would be counseling the women to keep their heads covered to keep the angels from worshiping man whose glory the uncovered woman reflects.[84] This interpretation is the favorite of those (cited above) who think woman's uncovered head reflects man's glory, and thus is suspect.

Whereas most contend that the reference to the angels in v. 10 either does little to advance the argument or is impossible to interpret, a few interpreters have made this obscure phrase the key to the whole discussion,[85] e.g., that the women at Corinth were removing their head-covering to show their momentary denial of mortal contingencies during ecstatic worship. This "more perfect ontology" placed them in a position of authority over the angels, a belief they held because of their reading of Gen. 1-3. That reading understood the first man as a sexually unified *Urmensch* who enjoyed hegemony over the spirit world. Although a fascinating theory, it is based on an unlikely hypothetical

---

[83]Cotterell and Turner, *Linguistics and Biblical Interpretation*, 325.

[84]Wire, *The Corinthian Women Prophets*, 280, cites *Life of Adam and Eve* 13-17; *Gen R* 8, 10; *Eccles R* 6, 9, 1. See also Jervell, *Imago Dei: Gen 1, 26f im Spätjudentum, in der Gnosis und in den paulinischen Briefen* (Göttingen: Vandenhoeck & Ruprecht, 1960), 38-39, 100; and Hooker, *NTS* 10 (1964): 415.

[85]MacDonald, *There Is No Male and Female*, 91-98.

reconstruction. We are asked to believe that we can discover the Corinthians' exegesis of Gen. 1-2 by reading between the lines in this text. In actuality there is no reason to believe that the women were thinking along these lines. Such thinking was later influential among Gnostics, but there is no evidence for such thought in first-century Corinth. This writer prefers the "angels as guardians of the created order."

4. *1 Cor. 11:11-12*

Precisely because Paul has written of female subordination, he takes an ameliorating stance in vv. 11-12. That he is qualifying what he has just written is clear from his use of the adversative "nevertheless" (πλήν) at the beginning of v. 11.[86] In these verses Paul declares that man is no more independent of woman than woman is of man—males are, after all, born to females. The crucial question is, What does he mean by the phrase, "In the Lord"? He cannot mean that the male/female relationship described up to this point (3-10) has been corrected now that the "order of redemption" has superseded the "order of creation."[87] V. 3 also deals with the "order of redemption," as it specifically explains the relationship between Christ, man, and woman. Vv. 11-12, therefore, qualify but do not reverse what Paul has already said. Most likely the phrase "in the Lord" implies that Christ is the basis of the creation order (see 1 Cor. 8:6). This seems confirmed by the parallel reference to God at the end of v. 12.[88]

Another popular reading holds that Paul here addresses the eschatological equality of man and woman "in Christ" in

---

[86]Engberg-Pederson, *JBL* 110 (1991): 683, rightly criticizes those such as Shoemaker and Scroggs who translate πλήν as "the point is," thereby reversing Paul's argument in order to arrive at an egalitarian interpretation.

[87]This is the position of Else Kähler, *Die Frau in den paulinischen Briefen: unter Besonderer Berücksichtigung des Begriffes der Unterordnung* (Zürich: Gotthelf, 1960): 50-51.

[88]Delobel, "1 Cor. 11, 2-16," *L'Apôtre Paul*, 381-84.

the same sense as Gal. 3:28.[89]   However, we are then
surprised that he argues not from some aspect of Christian
existence but from the order of creation. Paul's concern is
that no one misunderstand what he has said. Neither male
nor female may claim spiritual superiority. Man and woman
have equal *value*.[90]   But this aspect of the creation order
does not invalidate the other aspect (female subordination).
Male and female are therefore mutually interdependent, but
this does not nullify vv. 3-10, as is seen in the following
verses (13-16), which return to the theme of shame/glory.

5. *1 Cor. 11:13-15*

Vv. 13-15 present a further argument for women and
not men to have their heads covered in worship: they are to
keep their behavior in line with nature.[91] A woman's long
hair is already like a covering; therefore she is following the
lead of nature in wearing the head-covering. The man
should also do what nature suggests: nature has given him
no natural covering, and thus he must not wear one. Paul is
able to make such an argument because the accepted custom
of Paul's day was for men to have short hair and women to
have long hair.[92]

There is no reason to think, with Murphy-O'Connor,
that Paul's hidden agenda here is to combat male
homosexuality, evidenced by long hair on males.[93] If that
were the problem, Paul would have had no hesitation to deal

---

[89]F. F. Bruce, *1 and 2 Corinthians*, 107, writes, for example,
"The covering or uncovering of the head is neither here nor there *in the
Lord*, but Christians, living in the period when the two ages overlap,
should as far as possible respect the ordinances of both, 'giving no
offence' (cf. 10:32)."

[90]See Madeleine Boucher, "Some Unexplored Parallels to 1
Corinthians 11:11-12 and Galatians 3:28," *CBQ* 31 (1969): 50-58.

[91]Delobel, "1 Cor. 11, 2-16," *L'Apôtre Paul*, 373.

[92]Thompson, *BA* (1988): 104. This is in spite the fact that
many of the Greek men before Paul's time had long hair, a fact that
would be constantly in front of Paul's eyes on public statues.

[93]Murphy-O'Connor, *CBQ* (1980): 484-87.

with the situation in a direct way, as he did, for example, in chap. 5 in the case of the incestuous man.[94]

6. *1 Cor. 11:16*

Knowing that his arguments thus far would not be accepted by all, Paul finally appealed to the practice of all the churches and the unacceptability of contentiousness.[95] The phrase, "the churches of God," likely refers not just to Paul's other churches but to all the churches, including those of Jerusalem, Judea, and other locales where Jewish (and other) sensibilities were predominant. Although Paul is often criticized for this "feeble appeal to conventions in other communities"[96] he is in this verse helping his readers to understand his concern over what may have seemed a minor matter. Although Paul is the great champion of liberty in Christ, he is no less the champion of unity and "becoming all things to all men" (1 Cor. 9:22).

7. *Conclusion*

Clearly, no two interpreters agree on the details of 1 Cor. 11:2-16. There are simply too many exegetical choices to make in each subsection of this passage to hope for a consensus. In the final analysis, however, the most important division between interpreters occurs over whether or not Paul is arguing for the subordination of women to men. The majority of interpreters argue that for women not to wear head-coverings either signifies failure to honor the man's authority or it signifies failure to honor sexual distinctions.

---

[94]See Cotterell and Turner, *Linguistics and Biblical Interpretation*, 321.

[95]The "custom" is that of women prophesying and praying bareheaded, not the "custom" of contentiousness. See Barrett, *The First Epistle to the Corinthians*, 258.

[96]MacDonald, *There Is No Male and Female*, 80. Cf. also Luke T. Johnson, *The Writings of the New Testament: An Interpretation* (Philadelphia: Fortress, 1986): 205.

I would argue that the interpretation of Fee and others who maintain that the problem concerns women who disregard sexual distinctions is that Paul is left saying very little at all of importance. Fee recognizes this and writes very frankly,[97]

> Even though Paul has now spent considerable effort on this issue, the very nature of his argumentation reveals that it is not something over which he has great passion. Indeed, there is nothing quite like this in his letters, where he argues for maintaining a custom, let alone predicating a large part of the argument on shame, propriety, and custom.

> What they were doing with the Supper [in 11:17-34] cut at the heart of both the gospel and the church; therefore, much is at stake. But here it is not quite so. The distinction between the sexes is to be maintained; the covering is to go back on; but for Paul it does not seem to be a life-and-death matter.

However, we are left to wonder what sexual distinctions mattered in the assembly, if not that related to the issue of authority. Why does Paul care what they wear on their heads? And why is it an issue during the activities of prayer and prophecy? "It is difficult to maintain that all these elements only wish to express the *distinction* between man and woman without any nuance of *priority*."[98]

Why were the women so adamant about praying and prophesying bareheaded? It is in many ways hard to resist the assumption that these women were attempting to exercise their new-found freedom in Christ, perhaps even on the basis of (their misunderstanding of) Paul's teaching that "there is neither male nor female in Christ."[99] There is slight

---

[97]Fee, *The First Epistle to the Corinthians*, 530.

[98]Delobel, "1 Cor. 11, 2-16," *L'Apôtre Paul*, 379.

[99]However, there is no reason to think that Paul is arguing in the opposite direction from his earlier remark in Gal. 3:28., contra Hans

evidence that a few at Corinth may have had an "overrealized" eschatology. They may have believed that they had achieved the resurrection existence (see 4:8: "Already you are filled! Already you have become rich!" and 15:12: "How can some of you say that there is no resurrection of the dead?" and those in chap. 7 who may have advocated celibacy on the basis of its greater spiritual value). Perhaps some of the women at Corinth were going bareheaded to make a statement that in Christ all are equal.

This is surely the best guess, but it is little more than a guess. The fact is that we simply cannot know why they were so insistent about praying and prophesying uncovered. Their reasons may have been theological, socio-economic, or based on other (unknown to us) concerns of their subcultures. They may have been following the example of women in some of the mystery religions, who worshiped with uncovered heads.[100] Their reasons may have corresponded to those of their male counterparts, if there were such who insisted on wearing the coverings. It does seem, however, that Paul saw in their behavior a theological issue having to do with the relationship between men and women. His analysis was that they, intentionally or not, were shaming the men by effectively denying their authority.

Thus Paul argues for the subordinate role of women (4-6) based on 1) creation (3, 7-9), 2) angels (10), 3) nature (13-15), and 4) the custom of the churches (16). Yet he makes it clear that subordination does not imply inferiority. For Paul, "it is not a shame to have a κεφαλή."[101]

Dieter Betz, *Galatians: A Commentary on Paul's Letter to the Churches in Galatia* (Philadelphia: Fortress, 1979): 181-85, 199-201; Wayne A. Meeks, "Image of the Androgyne: Some Uses of a Symbol in Earliest Christianity," HR 13 (1973-74): 201-6; MacDonald, *There Is No Male and Female*, 87-111; and Elaine Pagels, "Paul and Women: A Response to a Recent Discussion," JAAR 42 (1974): 538-49.

[100]Among many, see Fiorenza, "Women in the Pre-Pauline and Pauline Churches," *USQR* 33 (1978): 159-60.

[101]Delobel, "1 Cor. 11, 2-16," *L'Apôtre Paul*, 379.

I suggest three possibilities regarding Paul's view of women speaking in the assembly. First, it could be that in Paul's churches women were allowed to do whatever men were allowed to do, so long as they wore the head-coverings symbolizing their subordination. Of course, one must examine the other relevant Pauline texts, but there is *no necessary reason from this text alone* that this could not be the case. This is, however, the only text in the NT in which women are shown clearly in speaking roles in worship.

Second, it may be that praying and prophesying are mentioned simply because those are the primary activities in which women were actively involved. That is, the nature of the activities may be somewhat incidental to the real problem of women participating in worship in any role without wearing head-coverings. Several contend that women were not allowed the more authoritative roles such as teaching, and thus the discussion focuses on prophesying and praying.[102] In this case it is not their Spirit-inspired nature but their non-authoritative nature that makes these activities allowable for women. Again, the argument is based on silence: Paul mentions only these two activities.

The third possibility stresses that the activities of praying and prophesying were Spirit-inspired gifts. If so, it may be that the women were allowed to exercise these functions simply because they were inspired by God to do so.[103]

There is insufficient evidence upon which to base a firm conclusion. The other relevant Pauline texts must be compared, and even then there are gaps in our knowledge. I presently favor the third alternative because it best accounts for all the evidence, though not without difficulties.

In conclusion, this text must not be used to encourage the overbearing domination of women by men of an earlier

---

[102]Grudem, *JETS* 30 (1987): 11-15, argues that the term "prophet" in the NT did not imply divine authority as it did in the OT.

[103]Johnson, *Writings of the NT*, 285.

day. However, as much as previous generations read this
text with their own ideas of male domination, the present
generation is tremendously influenced by the feminist
agenda. The attempt to rescue Paul from male chauvinism
has led to several ingenious proposals: the interpolation
theory, the theory that Paul is quoting the Corinthians,
theories based on κεφαλή meaning "source," and a host of
others. It is no accident that only recently has this text been
used to prove that Paul placed no restrictions on women.
Despite our inability to stand outside of space and time as we
read this passage, we must do everything possible to let Paul
be the first-century Jewish Christian he consistently shows
himself to be.

Chapter Eight

THE INTERPRETATION OF 1 COR. 14:34-35

Carroll D. Osburn

In 1 Cor. 14:34-35, Paul admonishes women to be silent in the assembly. At first glance, the meaning appears obvious. Yet over the centuries this text has acquired a variety of meanings and has become a virtual battleground in discussions concerning women in the church. This is not surprising in view of at least a dozen questions that arise from the text.

Do vv. 34-35 occur after v. 33, as in most ancient mss and modern editions, or after v. 40, as in only a few mss? Does v. 33b, "as in all the churches," go with vv. 34-35, as is the case in most modern editions, or with v. 33a as in all ancient mss? What are vv. 34-35 doing in a context of tongues and prophecy? What is the actual problem behind vv. 34-35? Does γυναῖκες (v. 34) mean "wives" or "women"? What is meant by "silence"? What is meant by "to speak"? To whom are the women to be in submission? What is meant by "as the law says"? How do vv. 34-35 relate to v. 36, which some see directed only to males? How is one to understand the possible contradiction with 11:2-16, where Paul approves women praying and prophesying? Is the message of vv. 34-35 consistent with Pauline theology?

Though only two verses, they have had, and still have, great influence in Christian churches. However, these significant questions of the text require clarification if appropriate use is to be made of this admonition in current practice.

1. *Quotation, Interpolation, or Transposition?*

It has been argued that vv. 34-35 represent a quotation from the letter which Paul is answering (see 7:1) and that, as such, they express not Paul's view, but the thinking of *the men* whom Paul chides in v. 36.[1] This view posits that, due to competition for ministries, arrogant males had devised a plan to eliminate women from competition.[2] The argument suggests 1) that the disjunctive force of the particle ἤ (or) at the beginning of v. 36 means "What!" and 2) the shift from the third-person pronoun ("they," females in vv. 34-35) to the second-person masculine pronoun μόνους (only) are crucial.[3] Thus, following this "citation" of these Corinthian males, Paul responds, "What! Did the word of God originate with you *men* only?" However, it is difficult to understand how this view of vv. 33b-36 could function within the unit of discourse developing from v. 26,[4] all of which is expressed in terms of the gender-inclusive masculine. There is nothing unique or surprising about the generic masculine μόνους (you only) in v. 36 referring to the entire congregation.[5] Further, the disjunctive particle ἤ

---

[1] See Katherine Bushnell, *God's Word to Women* (Oakland, CA: K. Bushnell, 1930): para. 189-215; Neal Flanagan and Edwina Snyder, "Did Paul Put Down Women in First Corinthians 14:34-36?" *Foundations* 24 (1981): 216-220; and Charles Talbert, *Reading Corinthians* (New York: Crossroad, 1987): 91, 93.

[2] Gilbert Bilezikian, *Beyond Sex Roles* (2nd ed.; Grand Rapids: Baker, 1985): 146-47.

[3] David Odell-Scott, "Let the Women Speak in Church. An Egalitarian Interpretation of 1 Cor. 14:33b-36," *BTB* 13 (1983): 90-93; Bilezikian, *Beyond Sex Roles*, 286-88.

[4] Bilezikian's, *Beyond Sex Roles*, 146-47, proposal that the prohibition is framed by two sets of parallel statements (vv. 31 and 39; vv. 33 and 40) misunderstands the literary structure of vv. 26-36, as well as the relation of that unit to chaps. 12-14, and fails to grasp vv. 37-40 as the conclusion not only of vv. 26-36, but the larger unit of chaps. 12-14.

[5] See Charles Talbert, "Paul's Understanding of the Holy Spirit: The Evidence of 1 Corinthians 12-14," *Perspectives on the New Testament* (ed. C. Talbert; Macon, GA: Mercer, 1985): 106.

(or) does not necessarily contradict and dismiss a preceding clause, but often introduces a direct question or statement in support of that clause.[6] Liefeld[7] observes correctly that, "what Paul negates by his use of the adversative Greek particle ἤ is *not* the *command* in verses 34-35 but the assumed *disobedience* of it."

More common is the argument that the verses are not original with Paul, but added into the text at a later period by another writer.[8] Conzelmann's[9] rejection of the verses purely on internal grounds is inexcusable. Including text-critical matters, Fee[10] follows Bengel's rule that the reading is preferred which explains the origin of the other readings. He argues that here the shortest reading is likely the original

---

[6]D. A. Carson, "'Silent in the Churches': On the Role of Women in 1 Cor. 14:33b-36." *Recovering Biblical Manhood & Womanhood: A Response to Evangelical Feminism* (ed. J. Piper and W. Grudem; Wheaton: Crossway, 1991): 149-51, forcefully denounces Bilezikian's, *Beyond Sex Roles*, 286-88, forced misunderstanding of ἤ.

[7]Walter Liefeld, "Women, Submission, and Ministry in 1 Corinthians," *Women, Authority and the Bible* (ed. A. Mickelsen; Downers Grove, IL: InterVarsity Press, 1986): 149, who also notes the structurally similar passage 6:18-19.

[8]Only vv. 34-35: H. Lietzmann, *An die Korinther I/II* (Tübingen: Mohr, 1931): 75; Jerome Murphy-O'Connor, "Interpolations in 1 Corinthians," *CBQ* 48 (1986): 90-92; and with caution, C. K. Barrett, *The First Epistle to the Corinthians* (London: A. & C. Black, 1971): 330-32.

Vv. 33b-35: John Reuf, *Paul's First Letter to Corinth* (Philadelphia: Westminster, 1977): 154-55.

Vv. 33b-36: Johannes Weiss, *Der erste Korintherbrief* (Göttingen: Vandenhoeck & Ruprecht, 1910): 342-43; James Moffatt, *The First Epistle of Paul to the Corinthians* (London: Hodder & Stoughton, 1938): 233-34; Hans Conzelmann, *Der erste Brief an die Korinther* (Göttingen: Vandenhoeck & Ruprecht, 1969): 289-90; Robin Scroggs, "Paul and the Eschatological Woman," *JAAR* 40 (1972): 284; and Robert Jewett, *Christian Tolerance: Paul's Message to the Modern Church* (Philadelphia: Westminster, 1982): 17.

[9]Conzelmann, *Der erste Brief an die Korinther*, 246.

[10]Gordon Fee, *The First Epistle to the Corinthians* (Grand Rapids: Eerdmans, 1987): 699-702.

and makes four principal arguments in favor of this view.
1) The manuscript support for placing the text after v. 40
represents "the entire Western tradition."[11] 2) Since transpositions of this sort do not occur elsewhere in the NT,
except in the "inauthentic adulterous woman pericope" in
John's gospel, one would need particularly strong reasons
for arguing a transposition in this one instance. 3) Vv. 34-
35 impede the flow of the argument. 4) Some of the words
used are not Pauline.[12] Thus, he concludes, in vv. 34-35
there is an absolute rule for "all churches" that stands in
conflict with 11:2-16. It was, he says, inserted into the text
at the end of the first century either to reconcile the text with
1 Tim. 2 or to thwart a rising feminist movement.

However, such an addition must have been made *very*
early as it occurs in virtually all mss. As 1 Cor. had been in
circulation for several decades, it is difficult to explain why
no copies exist of the original short text if the words were
added at the end of the first century. As glosses tend to
explain or clarify the text, not to introduce major problems
into the flow of the text, why would a gloss be introduced
that creates an apparent conflict with chap. 11? Such
transpositions do occur in classical Greek,[13] Septuagint,[14]
and intertestamental Jewish literature,[15] as well as in John
7:53-8:11, which occurs in at least five different places.
Too, textual data, being "local" rather than "Western,"
militates against Fee's view. The evidence for the Western
text is not so widespread as Fee suggests, for mss having

---

[11]Manuscripts D F G 88* it[ar.d.e.f.g] plus Sedulius-Scotas and
Ambrosiaster.

[12]See also Gunther Zuntz, *The Text of the Epistles* (London:
British Academy, 1953): 17.

[13]See W. Clausen, "Silva Coniecturarum," *AJP* 76 (1955): 47-
49; and R. Renehan, *Greek Textual Criticism* (Cambridge: Harvard
Univ. Press, 1969): 35-37. E.g., Euripides, *Helen* 255-60, and *Hecuba*
243-52.

[14]See W. Headlam, "Transpositions of Words in Mss," *CR* 16
(1902): 243-56; and H. S. Gehman, "Some types of errors of
transmission in the LXX," *VT* 3 (1953): 397-400.

[15]E.g., 1 Enoch 5:1 to the opening of chap. 3.

vv. 34-35 after v. 40 are limited to northern Italy and Irish monastics.[16] All it would take would be one lone scribe, making what was thought to be an improvement, whose text was picked up in a few places elsewhere. Also, the significant terms in vv. 34-35 occur both before and after it ("submission," vv. 32, 34; "speak," vv. 27-30, 34-35, 39; "silent," vv. 28, 30, 34; "in the assembly," vv. 28, 35).[17] Therefore, there is no compelling reason to view vv. 34-35 as a post-Pauline interpolation, especially if the text can be demonstrated to make sense in its context.[18] All theories of interpolation look suspiciously like attempts to liberate Paul in terms of modern agendas.

All ancient mss have vv. 34-35, most after v. 33. Certainly, a transposition has occurred. Three observations are pertinent just here. 1) Never was v. 36 included with vv. 34-35 after v. 40; only vv. 34-35. 2) Never was v. 33b taken with vv. 34-35 to a position after v. 40. 3) Vv. 34-35 occur after v. 40 only in limited circles in the Latin tradition. But someone in antiquity was bothered by the text after v. 33.[19] It is likely that vv. 34-35 were thought to be intrusive in a context dealing with "prophecy" (vv. 29-33, 37), possibly contradictory with 11:2-16, and that vv. 33b and 36-37 naturally belonged together. Thus it was transposed to after v. 40 as a secondary matter in a few mss, where it

---

[16] I am indebted to Curt Niccum for this observation. On the Latin text of vv. 34-35, see Antoinette Clark Wire, *The Corinthian Women Prophets* (Minneapolis: Fortress, 1990): 149-52, 283-85.

[17] Ben Witherington, III, *Women in the Earliest Churches* (Cambridge: Cambridge Univ. Press, 1988): 91.

[18] There is no reason to omit 1 Cor. 14:34-35 in studies of women in the NT, as does Denise L. Carmody, *Biblical Woman: Contemporary Reflections on Scriptural Texts* (New York: Crossroad, 1992).

[19] E. Earle Ellis, "The Silenced Wives of Corinth (1 Cor. 14:34-35)," *New Testament Textual Criticism: Essays in Honour of Bruce M. Metzger* (ed. E. Epp & G. Fee; Oxford: Clarendon, 1981): 219, conjectures that vv. 34-35 may have originated with a careless scribe correcting his omission in the margin or even that Paul himself added it as a marginal note.

could conceivably make sense as an application of v. 40. Fee is correct in asserting that the flow of thought in the passage is important to the resolution of the problem and the text does make sense if vv. 34-35 are removed from the context. However, external evidence certainly favors placing vv. 34-35 after v. 33 and taking it as an integral part of the letter.[20] Fee is also correct in following Bengel's rule that the reading is to be preferred which best explains the origin of the other readings, but his application of that rule is not convincing. It remains to be asked if vv. 34-35 make sense in the context if placed after v. 33 and if that view coheres with 11:2-16, with each passage understood in its own context.

2. *1 Cor. 14:34-35 in its Context*

It must be observed at the outset that Paul's remarks concerning the wives in vv. 34-35 are part of the larger context of chapters 11-14. Following the initial sermon on "wisdom," which advocates a strong christological basis for resolving conflict among the Corinthian Christians, Paul addresses interpersonal and marital propriety in chaps. 5-7 and the implications of eating food offered to idols in chaps. 8-11:1. Chapters 11:2-14:40, then, address matters of corporate worship. Chap. 11 specifically treats women's "covering" for worship (vv. 2-16) and abuses at the Lord's Supper (vv. 17-34). Chaps. 12-14 are devoted to abuses of "spiritual manifestations," i.e., "tongues" and "prophecy."

Continuing his argument that tongues, while not to be disdained, are minimally useful and certainly not the ultimate expression of Christian spirituality, Paul stresses in chap. 14 that prophecy is more useful. In 14:16, Paul points out that if a stranger[21] enters the place where Christian worship is

---

[20]See Bruce Metzger, *A Textual Commentary on the Greek New Testament* (corr. ed.; New York: UBS, 1975): 565.

[21]The "stranger" here is not a Christian who does not speak in tongues, but (in view of 14:23-25) a non-Christian. See H. Schlier, "ἰδιότης," *TDNT* 3:215-17, for uses of the term in pagan religion for "non-members" at the sacrifices.

being conducted and hears a "spiritual" prayer (i.e., in a tongue), he will not understand what is happening. The prayer may have been a good one, he says in v. 17, but the stranger will have no insight into the Christian experience. So in v. 19 Paul appeals not to the experiential, but to the cognitive.[22]

In v. 21, then, Paul paraphrases from Isa. 28:11-12,[23] evidently not treating the historical meaning of Isa. 28 here,[24] but setting out the idea of "not listening to tongues." Paul then says in v. 22 that tongues are a sign not to the believers, but to the unbelievers, and conversely that prophecy is not for the unbelievers, but for the believers. Now, this seems to contradict what has just been said in vv. 16-20 and what will be said in vv. 23-25,[25] leading Phillips to conclude that "we have here either a slip of the pen on the part of Paul, or, more probably, a copyist's error."[26] V. 22

---

[22]Although Rudolf Bultmann, *Theology of the New Testament* (trans. K. Grobel; New York: Scribner, 1951): 1.156, takes πνευμα- τικόν and χάρισμα synonymously, E. Earle Ellis, *Prophecy and Hermeneutic in Early Christianity* (Grand Rapids: Eerdmans, 1978): 24, rightly notes that while χάρισμα is used of any or all of the spiritual endowments (Rom. 12:6; 1 Cor. 1:7; 7:7; 12:4, 28-31), πνευματικόν appears restricted to "inspired perception, verbal proclamation and/or its interpretation." Cf. Siegfried Schatzmann, *A Pauline Theology of Charismata* (Peabody, MA: Hendricksen, 1989): 14, 34. See also D. W. B. Robinson, "Charismata versus Pneumatika: Paul's Method of Discussion," *Reformed Theological Review* 31 (1972): 49-55.

[23]A. Robertson and A. Plummer, *The First Epistle of St. Paul to the Corinthians* (Edinburgh: T. & T. Clark, 1914): 317, are incorrect in viewing the context here as one in which tongues are used judgmentally rather than for salvation. The context of vv. 16-20 and vv. 23-25 is, indeed, salvation.

[24]John Bright, *The Kingdom of God* (New York: Abingdon, 1953): 84, notes "If they will not hear the lesson spelled out in plain Hebrew, then God will be forced to teach it to them in Assyrian!"

[25]There is nothing to support the suggestion of R. St. John Parry, *The First Epistle of Paul the Apostle to the Corinthians* (2nd ed.; Cambridge: Cambridge Univ. Press, 1926): 205, that v. 22 is an interpolation.

[26]J. B. Phillips' translation, note on 1 Cor. 14:22.

is quite understandable, however, if it is not understood as
the proper way to use tongues and prophecy, but
unfortunately how the Corinthians have come to use them![27]
If this is true, then vv. 23-25 set out the proper use of
prophecy, which is cognitive, rather than tongues (not
cognitive, v. 14) on the stranger.

Similarly, in v. 26 Paul sets out a list of things done in
worship. While many would view this verse as setting out a
proper agenda for Christian worship, v. 26 is rather to be
understood as indicating Paul's frustration with what the
Corinthians are actually doing in worship. The Greek
question τί οὖν ἐστιν ἀδελφοί is best rendered, "How
stands the case, brothers?"[28] In this context of misuse and
abuse of tongues and prophecy in Christian gatherings, Paul
specifies that when they assemble, each[29] has a psalm, a
teaching, a revelation, a tongue, or an interpretation. These
should be for the purpose of edification,[30] but in the
following discussion he specifically states how they are not
conducting their worship for edification. Although good to
do in Christian worship, the items mentioned in v. 26 are
being abused by the Corinthians. Pandemonium is the
problem. Paul's admonition in v. 26, "All things must be

---

[27]See Charles Isbell, "Glossolalia and Propheteialalia: A Study of
1 Corinthians 14," *Wesleyan Theological Journal* 10 (1975): 18; and
Bruce C. Johanson, "Tongues, a Sign for Unbelievers?" *NTS* 25
(1979): 180-203.

[28]G. G. Findlay, *St. Paul's First Epistle to the Corinthians*
(Expositors Greek NT; London: Hodder & Stoughton, 1917): 911.

[29]Bilezikian, *Beyond Sex Roles*, 146, erroneously concludes that
Paul wants each member to come prepared to make some presentation
for the edification of the group. Hans Lietzmann, *Der erste Brief an die
Korinther* [Göttingen: Vandenhoeck & Ruprecht, 1969]: 291, and Leon
Morris, *1 Corinthians* (2nd ed.; Grand Rapids: InterVarsity Press,
1985): 194, correctly observe that we need not press "each" to mean
that every member was expected to participate. Jean Héring, *The First
Epistle of Saint Paul to the Corinthians* (trans. A. Heathcote & P.
Allcock; London: Epworth, 1962): 154, notes that "there is hardly any
need to stress the point that all 'inspired' movements have encountered
similar difficulties."

[30]Reuf, *Paul's First Letter to Corinth*, 153.

for edification!", is the point of the overall context in chap. 14 and sets the stage for addressing the three following examples, each of which involves verbal misconduct and chaos. It is the "guiding rule" for the three following topics.

Each of the three topics is addressed at the beginning boldly with the term "tongues" (v. 27), "prophecy" (v. 29), and "women" (v. 34). Regarding tongues,[31] "only one may speak at a time," ἀνὰ μέρος indicating that more than one speaking in tongues simultaneously creates confusion. No more than two or three at the most should speak in any one assembly, and then only if there is an interpreter[32] to render matters cognitive. There is no room for giving free rein to "irresistible impulse" to speak in a tongue. If there is no interpreter, there is to be no speaking in tongues in the assembly and the Greek σιγάτω means, "Be silent!" "Speak to yourself and to God," otherwise there is disorder and lack of cognition.[33] While speaking in tongues in worship is approved, it must contribute to edification (v. 26). It is with this problem of disorderliness that Paul is concerned in his directive that "tongue-speakers" *defer* to the assembly, respecting decorum and cognitive edification.

---

[31]See Schatzmann, *A Pauline Theology of Charismata*, 42-43; and J. Behm, "γλῶσσα," *TDNT* 1:719-27. Note Ira J. Martin, "Glossolalia in the Apostolic Church," *JBL* 63 (1944): 123-130 [ecstatic speech]; Frank Pack, *Tongues and the Holy Spirit* (Abilene, TX: Biblical Research Press, 1972): 63-70 [known languages]; H.-D. Wendland, *Der Brief an die Korinther* (8th ed; Göttingen: Vandenhoeck & Ruprecht, 1962): 119 [angelic speech].

[32]Robertson and Plummer, *First Epistle to the Corinthians*, 321, note, "One, and one only (εἷς not τις), was to interpret; there was to be no interpreting in turn, which might lead to profitless discussion." See also A. Thiselton, "The 'interpretation' of tongues: a new suggestion in the light of Greek usage in Philo and Josephus," *JTS* 30 (1979): 15-36.

[33]There is no way to determine whether those causing the problem belonged to the educated elite (with Richard Oudersluys, "Charismatic Theology and the New Testament," *Reformed Review* 28 [1974]: 54) or were illiterate converts (with Gerd Theissen, *The Social Setting of Pauline Christianity: Essays on Corinth* [trans. J. Schütz; Philadelphia: Fortress, 1982]: 69-102).

Regarding prophecy,[34] Paul stipulates in v. 29 two or three[35] at the most in an assembly, one at a time, while the others[36] discern.[37] If another wants to prophesy, the first must "Be silent!" (σιγάτω) before the second person begins.[38] "The spirits of prophets are subject to prophets" (v. 32) is axiomatic: a prophet can refrain from speaking. Unlike tongue-speaking, prophecy is viewed by Paul as intelligible.[39] As with speaking in tongues, it is the verbal

[34]See David Aune, *Prophecy in Early Christianity and the Ancient Mediterranean World* (Grand Rapids: Eerdmans, 1983); Terrance Callan, "Prophecy and Ecstasy in Greco-Roman Religion and in 1 Corinthians," *NT* 27 (1985): 125-40; and Christopher Forbes, "Early Christian Inspired Speech and Hellenistic Popular Religion," *NT* 28 (1986): 257-70.

[35]Héring, *The First Epistle of Saint Paul to the Corinthians*, 153-54, observes that as each message in tongues had to be interpreted and each prophecy discussed, that alone involved eight to twelve speakers, and additional time would be taken with biblical readings and discussions, singing, prayers, etc.

[36]While in 14:5 and 14:31 Paul indicates that "all" can prophesy, Paul probably means here that all who do prophesy must do so one by one "so that all may learn." Those who "discern" are possibly other prophets (Reuf, *Paul's First Letter to Corinth*, 154) or the congregation (Barrett, *First Epistle to the Corinthians*, 328). Hans Conzelmann, *1 Corinthians* (Philadelphia: Fortress, 1975): 245, views v. 31 as an argument in favor of taking "the others" as the rest of the prophets and notes, "the emphasis naturally does not lie on πάντες, 'all,' but on 'singly,' i.e., that you may be understood." See Heinrich Greeven, "Propheten, Lehrer, Vorsteher bei Paulus. Zur Frage der 'Ämter' im Urchristentum," *ZNW* 44 (1952): 1-43.

[37]See Gérard Thérrien, *Le Discernment dans les Écrits Pauliniens* (Paris: J. Gabalda, 1973): 76. G. Dautzenberg, "Zum religions-geschichtlichen Hintergrund der διάκρισις πνευμάτων (I Kor. 12:10)," *BZ* 15 (1971): 104, incorrectly suggests a charismatic interpretation of spiritual revelations. Prophecy did not require a supplemental "gift," as did tongues. See W. Grudem, "Response to Gerhard Dautzenburg on 1 Cor. 12:10," *BZ* 22 (1978): 253-70.

[38]Cf. H. L. Goudge, *The First Epistle to the Corinthians* (5th ed.; London: Methuen, 1926): 130, who prefers that the speaker give way. Either way, "deference" is mandated.

[39]Isbell, *Wesleyan Theological Journal* (1975): 15-22. Wayne Grudem, *The Gift of Prophecy in 1 Corinthians* (New York: Univ.

chaos generated by too many people prophesying at once
that Paul rebukes, because there must be orderliness in the
assembly and an emphasis upon edification (v. 26).[40] That
is why Paul states that one prophet must *defer* to the next.
Again, there is no room for giving free rein to "irresistible
impulse" to prophesy. Instead, self-control is urged. Paul
says that this is the case "in all the churches."

While "as in all the churches of the saints" is taken with
vv. 34-35 in many modern editions and translations,[41] it
appears with v. 33a in many others.[42] However, taking 33b
with what follows does produce an awkward repetition of
"in the churches." "As in all the churches of the saints" does
not introduce a new thought, but goes with the previous
thought (vv. 27-32) as its fitting conclusion. It is difficult to
understand the objection[43] that "as in all the churches of the
saints," does not give a pertinent sense if connected with v.

Press of America, 1982): 222-23, argues that prophecy at Corinth was
far removed from the frenzied, unintelligible utterances such as those of
the Pythia at Delphi; however, cf. Aune, *Prophecy in Early
Christianity*, 33-34. See also Margaret Thrall, *The First and Second
Letters of Paul to the Corinthians* (Cambridge: Cambridge Univ. Press,
1965): 97-98, for discussion of "tongues" as meaning "foreign
languages" in Acts 2, but "ecstatic speech" in 1 Cor. 12-14.

[40]U. Müller, *Prophetie und Predigt im Neuen Testament: Form-
geschichtliche Untersuchungen zur urchristlichen Prophetie* (Gütersloh:
G. Mohn, 1975): see index, defines prophecy as hortatory proclamation,
esp. of judgment and salvation, but neglects the element of spontaneity.
Rather than a sermon, prophecy seems to have been a spontaneous
utterance in a specific situation for the upbuilding of the body. R. P.
Brown, "Gifts of the Holy Spirit," *Reformed Review* 28 (1975): 176,
defines prophecy as "the ability to see clearly into a subject and discern
the right and wrong of it."

[41]Griesbach (1809), Nestle-Aland[26], UBS Greek NT[3]; RV, ASV,
RSV, JerB, NEB, NIV, RSV.

[42]C. B. Williams, LBP, Phillips, Knox, C. K. Williams,
Goodspeed, NASB; as well as most earlier editions and translations.

[43]Among others, Charles Hodge, *First Epistle to the Corinthians*
(Grand Rapids: Eerdmans, 1953): 304; Carson, "Silent in the
Churches," *Recovering Biblical Manhood & Womanhood*, 140-41.

33.   The major problem in chaps. 12-14 is verbal misconduct by tongue-speakers and prophets. It is widely held that the unit of text in vv. 26-32, appealing for the cessation of this verbal misconduct, ends appropriately with 33a, "God is not the author of confusion but of peace," a thought directly related to "all things must be done for edification" (v. 26). In this connection, an appeal is made at the conclusion of the section in v. 33b for those involved to conduct themselves in terms of customary Christian practice elsewhere.[44]   This appeal to common practice is similar to that of women wearing veils while praying or prophesying in 11:16, where "if anyone is disposed to be contentious, we have no other practice, nor do the churches of God" closes the section of 11:2-16. So, with reference to abuse of tongues and prophecy in worship, v. 33b states that "God is not a God of confusion but of peace, as in all the churches of the saints," stressing self-control and mutual deference.

However, a third item addressing the admonition to orderliness and edification from v. 26 begins in v. 34, as with the two above, simply admonishing γυναῖκες (females) to "silence" in the assembly. It is important to remember that women are not the only ones on whom this silence is imposed, but that σιγάω was also employed for disruptive tongue-speakers and prophets in vv. 27-33.

Initially, just what is meant by these women "speaking" is variously understood. While some suggest speaking of any sort in worship,[45] chattering,[46] "sacred cries" common

---

[44]Barrett, *First Epistle to the Corinthians*, 329; Bruce, *1 and 2 Corinthians*, 135; William Barclay, *The Letters to the Corinthians* (2nd ed.; Philadelphia: Westminster, 1956): 149.

[45]Ernest Evans, *The Epistles of Paul the Apostle to the Corinthians* (Oxford: Clarendon, 1930): 136; F. W. Grosheide, *The First Epistle of Paul to the Corinthians* (Grand Rapids: Eerdmans, 1953): 343; Neil Lightfoot, "The Role of Women in Religious Services," *RQ* 19 (1976): 134.

[46]Moffatt, *First Epistle of Paul to the Corinthians*, 232; and John Bristow, *What Paul Really Said About Women* (San Francisco: Harper, 1991): 63.

to women in pagan worship, [47] or teaching men,[48] most view "speaking" to be limited by this context.   Thus, while some see special spiritual manifestations (e.g., speaking in tongues)[49] being prohibited, others think women judging the prophecies mentioned in vv. 29-33[50] is meant.

Now "in gatherings for worship the ancient synagogue did not on principle forbid women to speak in public, but did so in practice."[51] In the Greco-Roman world also, negative views were being expressed on women speaking in public. For example, Plutarch, *Conjugal Precepts* 31, says, "Not only the arm but the voice of a modest woman ought to be kept from the public, and she should feel shame at being heard, as at being stripped." In the next paragraph, Plutarch continues, "She should speak either to, or through, her husband."   And Valerius Maximus (8:3) notes "those women whom their sex and the modesty of their dress could not cause to refrain from speaking in the market-place and public law-courts." In accord with ancient custom, then, is Paul here stating a general rule of silence for all women in worship?

---

[47]Richard and Catherine Kroeger, *Women Elders . . . Saints or Sinners?* (New York: Council on Women and the Church of the United Presbyterian Church in the U.S.A., 1981): 13.

[48]Knight, *Role Relationship of Men and Women* (Chicago: Moody, 1985): 24-25; and Werner Neuer, *Man & Woman in Christian Perspective* (trans. G. Wenham; Wheaton: Crossway, 1991): 117, based upon 1 Tim. 2:11-14!

[49]Frederick D. Bruner, *A Theology of the Holy Spirit* (Grand Rapids: Eerdmans, 1970): 301; Burton Coffman, *Commentary on 1 and 2 Corinthians* (Austin, TX: Firm Foundation, 1977): 240-41.

[50]Thrall, *First and Second Letters of Paul to the Corinthians*, 102; Héring, *First Epistle of St. Paul to the Corinthians*, 154; Howard Loewen, "The Pauline View of Women," *Direction* 6 (1977): 9; James Hurley, *Man and Woman in Biblical Perspective* (Grand Rapids: Zondervan, 1981): 193; Witherington, *Women in the Earliest Churches*, 100-102; Ellis, "Silenced Wives of Corinth," *New Testament Textual Criticism*, 218; and J. N. Sevenster, *Paul and Seneca* (Leiden: Brill, 1961): 198.

[51]H. L. Strack and Paul Billerbeck, *Kommentar zum Neuen Testament aus Talmud und Midrasch* (Munich: Beck, 1926): 3.467.

It is taken for granted by Paul in 1 Cor. 11 that women
prayed and prophesied in the early church, thus presenting
an apparent contradiction with the prohibition in 14:34-35.
Some are willing to accept a contradiction.[52] Others see two
different situations involved.[53] Still others, however, argue
that 11:2-16 involves only praying or prophesying at home
or in small groups of females, thus making 14:34-35 an
absolute rule for public assemblies.[54] However, this view
overlooks the unmistakable connection of vv. 2 and 17 with
vv. 17-34, which obviously treats worship, as does the
whole of 11:17-14:40. In 11:2-16, Paul addresses both men
and women and nowhere suggests that his concern is with
informal gatherings or private practice.[55] If vv. 34-35 are
intended as a universal rule for all women in all churches,[56]
it is difficult to understand the purpose of such a universal

---

[52]J. W. MacGorman, *The Gifts of the Spirit: An Exposition of
1 Corinthians 12-14* (Nashville: Broadman, 1974): 113. John L.
McKenzie, "St. Paul's Attitude Toward Women," *Women Priests: A
Catholic Commentary on the Vatican Declaration* (ed. L. Swidler and
A. Swidler; New York: Paulist, 1977): 214, suggests that Paul "seems
to have forgotten in 14:33-36 what he said in 11:5."

[53]There is no evidence in the text to support the view of W.
Schmithals, *Gnosticism in Corinth* (Nashville: Abingdon, 1971): 90-
96, that 1 Cor. 11 and 14 belong to two separate Pauline letters, nor
that of Constance Parvey, "The Theology and Leadership of Women in
the NT," *Religion and Sexism* (ed. R. Reuther; New York: Simon and
Schuster, 1974): 128, that much of what Paul says in 1 Cor. 11 and 14
is directed against Gnostic excesses. Nor is Wayne Meeks, "The Image
of the Androgyne: Some Uses of a Symbol in Earliest Christianity,"
HR 13 (1974): 202f, convincing in suggesting gnostic androgyny as
central to the Corinthian problem. See R. McL. Wilson, "How
Gnostic Were The Corinthians?" *NTS* 19 (1972): 65-74.

[54]Philip Bachmann, *Der erste Brief des Paulus an die Korinther*
(3rd ed.; Leipzig: A. Deichert, 1921): 345-62; and Adolf Schlatter,
Paulus der Bote Jesu (Stuttgart: Calwer, 1969): 390.

[55]As Carl Holladay, *The First Letter of Paul to the Corinthians*
(Austin, TX: Sweet, 1979): 189, observes, "It is difficult to imagine
why wearing or not wearing a head covering would even pose a problem
'at home'."

[56]See Hodge, *First Epistle to the Corinthians*, 305; and
Grosheide, *First Epistle to the Corinthians*, 342.

rule in the present context treating disorder in the Corinthian worship and in direct contradiction with 1 Cor. 11:2-16.[57]

It seems rather that the terse admonition in 14:34-35 is directed to a particular problem in Corinth. The only information offered in the text is that the women involved should ask questions of their husbands at home if they wish to learn (v. 35). Since "tongues" and "discern" are used for specific types of speaking in this context, it is difficult to argue that the general verb λαλεῖν (to speak) refers here only to one of these particular forms of speech.[58] From the emphatic ἀλλά (but) about the need for women to be submissive (v. 34), it does seem that some form of seriously disruptive speech is involved among these particular women.[59]

It may be suggested that the present infinitive λαλεῖν (to be speaking), which occurs twice in vv. 34-35, provides the crucial insight into the "speaking" which so annoys Paul. This verb λαλέω always takes its precise meaning from the context. In v. 28, it refers to "silent meditation." In vv. 23 and 27, it refers to "speaking in tongues." In v. 19 it refers to "cognitive prayer." Here in vv. 34-35, however, there is no clear contextual indication of what is meant, but there is a

---

[57]The argument of John Rice, *Bobbed Hair, Bossy Wives and Women Preachers* (Wheaton: Sword of the Lord, 1941): 45, that 14:34-35 must be a rule for all Christians since 1:2 reads, "all that in every place call upon the name of Christ," is blatant "proof-texting." C. C. Ryrie, *The Place of Women in the Church* (New York: Macmillan, 1958): 76, suggests that 14:33-35 presents the general rule and 11:2-16 is a Corinthian exception, but fails to explain why Paul does not condemn a woman praying or prophesying as long as she is properly veiled. The praying and prophesying of women in 11:2-16 is not presented as a concession.

[58]Ellis, "Silenced Wives of Corinth," *New Testament Textual Criticism*, 218, unconvincingly relates λαλεῖν to "pneumatic gifts" in the preceding verses.

[59]See Barrett, *First Epistle to the Corinthians*, 332; William Baird, *The Corinthian Church—A Biblical Approach to Urban Culture* (Nashville: Abingdon, 1964): 127.

significant grammatical indication. In moods *other than the indicative*, the present does not necessarily refer to the present, nor does the aorist necessarily refer to past time, the distinction being rather in the *manner* in which the action is viewed. Thus, the aorist infinitive refers to the action without indicating anything about its continuance or repetition; the present infinitive, on the other hand, specifically refers to the action as continuing or being repeated in some way.[60] Indeed, Robertson[61] says in this regard, "the force of the pres. inf. is so normal as to call for little comment."[62] Here, the two present infinitives make it clear that the "ongoingness" of the "speaking" is in focus. It seems improbable that they were merely "chatting," paying no attention to the speaker and thus disturbing the learners,[63] for Paul's admonition concerns their interest in learning. There is nothing in the text prohibiting normal pursuit of learning by women in the assembly, including asking appropriate questions. Rather, λαλεῖν should be taken here to mean that they were "piping up," giving free rein to "irresistible impulses" to ask question after question either of the speaker or of their husbands, creating chaos in the assembly by interfering with communication.[64]

---

[60]F. Blass and A. Debrunner, *A Greek Grammar of the New Testament* (trans. & ed. R. Funk; Chicago: Univ. of Chicago Press, 1961): 174.

[61]A. T. Robertson, *A Grammar of the Greek New Testament in the Light of Historical Research* (Nashville: Broadman, 1934): 890, who also illustrates the difference between the aorist and present infinitive with Matt. 14:22.

[62]On the Greek infinitive, see E. Schwyzer, *Griechische Grammatik* (2nd ed.; Munich: Beck, 1959): 2.1, pp. 357-84.

[63]Cf. J. K. Howard, "Neither Male nor Female: An Examination of the Status of Women in the New Testament," *EvQ* 55 (1983): 31-42. Likewise, there is nothing to support the notion of Stephen Clark, *Man and Woman in Christ* (Ann Arbor: Servant, 1980): 185-86, that these women were silenced due to being uneducated.

[64]Goudge, *First Epistle to the Corinthians*, 131; F. F. Bruce, *1 and 2 Corinthians* (Grand Rapids: Eerdmans, 1971): 135; Krister Stendahl, *The Bible and the Role of Women* (Philadelphia: Fortress, 1966): 30.

Is this disruptive speech, though, by wives or women in general? To whom are these women to submit themselves? It is improbable that this submission refers to v. 32 (i.e., that their "spirit of prophecy" should be in submission[65]), for the grammar points to submission on the part of the women themselves, not to their having control over their own "prophetic spirit."[66] There is no indication that Paul is telling women to be in submission to church officials since he does not mention them in this context.[67] But are wives told here to be submissive to their husbands or are women to be submissive to the church as a whole in worship? Arguing that females are to be subject to males, Lenski[68] says that since the OT Law subjects woman to man by the creation both before and after the fall, Paul means that "what is recorded concerning woman in Genesis is not a temporary arrangement but a permanent one that endures as such for the Christian church." On the other hand, most view γυναῖκες in this context to refer not to all women, but to certain Corinthian wives.[69] This latter view is preferred, since in the text the demand for silence is tied directly to the request for the wives involved to direct their questions to their husbands outside the assembly.

But what is meant by "silence"? Of course, those wrongly reading "women," rather than "wives," argue the "silence" to be total.[70] However, Liefeld argues correctly

---

[65]Ralph Martin, *The Spirit and the Congregation: Studies in 1 Corinthians 12-15* (Grand Rapids: Eerdmans, 1984): 87.

[66]Fee, *First Epistle to the Corinthians*, 707.

[67]Witherington, *Women in the Earliest Churches*, 101.

[68]R. C. H. Lenski, *The Interpretation of St. Paul's First and Second Epistle to the Corinthians* (Columbus, OH: Wartburg, 1946): 615-16. See also Knight, *Role Relationships of Men and Women*, 25.

[69]See William Orr and James Walther, *I Corinthians* (Garden City, NY: Doubleday, 312; J. Massingbyrde Ford, "Biblical Material Relevant to the Ordination of Women," *JES* (10 (1973): 681.

[70]Neuer, *Man & Woman in Christian Perspective*, 117; F. LaGard Smith, *Men of Strength for Women of God* (Eugene, OR: Harvest House, 1989): 250-53; David Lipscomb, *First Corinthians* (ed. J. Shepherd; Nashville: Gospel Advocate, 1935): 216.

that since the verb σιγάω is used in vv. 28 and 30 with
regard to tongue-speakers and prophets, its meaning in v. 34
is not a universal silence, but one dictated by circumstances.[71] This understanding is illustrated by other uses of
this verb where not creating a disturbance is the meaning,
not total silence (Acts 12:17; 21:40). As with the tongue-
speakers and prophets, where self-control and mutual
deferment is the emphasis, so in vv. 34-35 an appeal is made
to Corinthian wives to "pipe down" and, in accord with v.
26, let everything be done with decorum and edification.

In what way, then, is Paul's appeal to "the law" to be
understood? In view of his appeal to "the law" in 1 Cor.
9:8-9, there is no reason to accept the view that this text
could not be Pauline.[72] Once accepted as authentic,
however, the possibilities of interpretation are several. The
view that "law" refers to Paul's own ruling in v. 29,[73]
broken by these women "taking the lead," is unacceptable
because "law" is capable of a better understanding in this
context and nothing supports the notion that these women
were "taking the lead." Seeing "female submission" as the
point, some view the entire OT as the focus of the appeal,[74]
but many tend to see a particular text in view, such as Gen.
3:16[75] or Gen. 2:21-24.[76] Yet if appeal is made to the OT,
it is curious that no such text is quoted and that virtually no
argumentation is presented.[77] Alternatively, some take "the
law" here to refer to "female silence," either in Rabbinic

---

[71]Liefeld, "Women, Submission, and Ministry in 1 Cor.,"
Women, Authority and the Bible, 150.

[72]Fee, *First Epistle to the Corinthians*, 707. Cf. Reuf, *Paul's
First Letter to Corinth*, 155.

[73]Martin, *The Spirit and the Congregation: Studies in 1
Corinthians 12-15*, 87.

[74]E.g., Hodge, *First Epistle to the Corinthians*, 305.

[75]See Evans, *Epistles of Paul the Apostle to the Corinthians*,
136; Barrett, *First Epistle to the Corinthians*, 330; Orr and Walther, *1
Corinthians*, 312; Lipscomb, *First Corinthians*, 216.

[76]See Bruce, *1 and 2 Corinthians*, 136.

[77]In fact, this is one of Fee's, *First Epistle to the Corinthians*,
707, arguments for the inauthenticity of the passage. See 9:8; 14:21.

tradition of women's silence in worship settings[78] or Greco-Roman expectations of women not speaking publicly.[79] However, taking "the law" here to refer to women's silence is grammatically incorrect, for "as the law says" is related not to λαλεῖν (speaking), but to "being in submission"!

So, what is meant by "submission, as the law says"? If appeal is made to Gen. 3:16, "he shall rule over you," emphasis is placed upon the "post-fall" patriarchal model of husband/wife relationship, whereas if Gen. 2:21-24 (1:26) is in mind, then emphasis may be upon the "pre-fall" ideal of mutuality.[80] But, Paul does not say "be in submission *to your own husbands*," but "submit yourselves."[81] The reason for the admonition to silence is caused by disorder in the worship service, not disorder in family relations. Women are not being commanded to "submit" to their husbands in this text, but to orderliness in public worship, to silence and respect when another is speaking.[82]

Delling[83] notes that the verb ὑποτάσσω (submit) "does not immediately carry with it the thought of obedience." When it occurs in the active voice, always in the NT with God or Christ as subject, forceful subjugation with

---

[78]Paul Jewett, *Man as Male and Female* (Grand Rapids: Eerdmans, 1975): 114. Note Josephus, *Against Apion* 24, and see S. Aalen, "A Rabbinic Formula in I Cor. 14.34," *Studia Evangelica* 2 (TU 87; Berlin: Akademie, 1964): 513-25. Although correctly understanding vv. 34-35 not to pertain to all women but only to certain wives, Elisabeth Schüssler Fiorenza, "Women in the Pre-Pauline and Pauline Churches," *USQR* 33 (1978): 161, incorrectly views Paul as deriving his argument from Jewish-Hellenistic propaganda that roots subordination of wives in the Law.

[79]Liefeld, "Women, Submission and Ministry in 1 Cor." *Women, Authority & the Bible*, 149.

[80]Though Neuer, *Man & Woman*, 115, suggests that with Gen. 2 male primacy is not the result of a fall, but part of the order of creation.

[81] Ὑποτασσέσθωσαν (ℵAB) is preferred to ὑποτάσσεσθαι (DFGKL).

[82]Witherington, *Women in the Earliest Churches*, 102-03.

[83]Gerhard Delling, "ὑποτάσσω," *TDNT* 8.41-42.

resistance or antagonism is in focus (e.g., 15:27-28). Never in the NT does ὑποτάσσω suggest the propriety of a human being forcefully subjugating another for any reason. The middle and passive forms of the verb are identical.[84] Only the context can determine whether the meaning is middle or passive.[85]　Regarding ὑποτάσσομαι in the NT, Delling (p. 45) notes, "the general rule demands readiness to renounce one's own will for the sake of others, i.e., ἀγάπη [love], and to give precedence to others." ʹΥποτάσσομαι as middle invariably involves willing submission, as is obvious in the conclusion of 1 Cor. at 16:16, "submit yourselves to one another." In 14:32, voluntary submission is obvious in the directive that a prophet willingly control the prophetic spirit.[86] Since the entire context of chaps. 11-14 evidences Paul's appeal for voluntary submission in the Corinthian congregation and is specifically the point in 14:26-40, "submit yourselves" in v. 34 should be taken to refer to the same sort of *deferential* behavior to the congregation demanded of the clamorous tongue-speakers and prophets, who are castigated for emphasizing freedom at the expense of Christian mutuality.

---

[84]The middle form of this verb is described in A. T. Robertson, *A Grammar of the Greek New Testament in the Light of Historical Research* (Nashville: Broadman, 1934): 807, 809, and J. H. Moulton, *A Grammar of New Testament Greek* (3rd ed.; Edinburgh: T. & T Clark, 1967): 161-63. J. H. Thayer, *A Greek-English Lexicon of the New Testament* (4th ed.; Edinburgh: T. & T. Clark, 1901): 645, lists 1 Cor. 14:34 as an example of the middle use. See also Erwin Preuschen, *Griechisch-Deutsches Handwörterbuch zu den Schriften des Neuen Testaments* (Gießen: Töpelmann, 1910): col. 1120-1121. Walter Bauer, *A Greek-English Lexicon of the New Testament and Other Early Christian Literature* (2nd ed. rev. by F. W. Gingrich and F. Danker; Chicago: Univ. of Chicago Press, 1979): 848, unfortunately omits discussion of the middle form. The best discussion of the middle of ὑποτάσσω is Delling, *TDNT* 8:42-45.

[85]This verb in James 4:7 is correctly rendered as middle (submit yourselves to God) in KJV NIV NRSV, rather than as passive (be submissive) in NEB Phillips. Also, in 1 Pet. 2:13, "submit your-selves to every human authority" in KJV NIV NEB NASB is preferable to "be subject" in RSV.

[86]See Greeven, *ZNW* 44 (1952): 13.

The two rhetorical questions in v. 36,[87] then, are a direct confrontation, not with the Corinthian wives, but with the congregation as a whole: "Did the word of God originate with you? Or are you the only people it has reached?" Fee[88] correctly notes that "in both style and content these questions are so thoroughly Pauline" that one is puzzled that some would view them as part of an interpolation involving vv. 34-35, especially since no textual evidence supports moving v. 36 along with vv. 34-35 to a position after v. 40.[89] Admittedly, v. 36 makes excellent sense following v. 33, but Fee is quite wrong in suggesting that v. 36 makes no sense following v. 35. Dautzenburg[90] observes that vv. 34-35 are similar to the previous regulations of tongue-speakers and prophets in that three structural elements occur in each: 1) a third person imperative instruction, an explanatory sentence, and an example in conditional form telling what to do in a given case. Words recur: "speak" (λαλέω) vv. 27, 28, 29, 34, 35; "submission" (ὑποτάσσω) vv. 32, 34; "learn" (μανθάνω) vv. 31, 35; "be silent" (σιγάω) vv. 28, 30, 34. From v. 36, it appears that the disruptive behavior Paul disdains in vv. 34-35 is related closely to v. 33: 1) God is not a God is disorder, and 2) this is true in all the churches of the saints. Vv. 34-36, then, do function at the same level of discourse as vv. 27-33, adding yet another significant dimension to regulation of verbal misconduct to those of tongue-speaking and prophecy.[91] The Corinthians have no right to be "marching to their own drum" with regard to verbal misconduct by tongue-speakers or prophets, or by certain questioning wives.

---

[87]NIV curiously omits the conjunction ἤ that relates v. 36 to what precedes.

[88]Fee, *First Epistle to the Corinthians*, 710.

[89]Ford, *JES* (1973): 681.

[90]Gerhard Dautzenburg, *Urchristliche Prophetie: Ihre Erforschung, ihre Voraussetzung im Judentum und ihre Struktur im ersten Korintherbrief* (Stuttgart: Kohlhammer, 1975): 254-55.

[91]Wire, *Corinthian Women Prophets*, 155, goes much too far in viewing vv. 34-35 as "the turning point in his argument." It seems rather to be "attendant to" his argument.

Vv. 37-40, far from being "an aside,"[92] are the conclusion, not only to this sub-section of 26-36, but the entire unit of chapters 11-14, all of which treats matters pertinent to Corinthian public worship. Here, Paul sums up in that while various spiritual manifestations are to be encouraged, it is mandatory that orderliness be maintained in the proceedings. So, v. 37, "if anyone seems to be a prophet or 'spiritual',"[93] does not continue v. 32,[94] but appeals to all involved in disruptive behavior to recognize Paul's directive[95] as "from the Lord." This does not mean that here Paul is referring to some specific teaching of Jesus that has been handed down (as in 7:10). Though complicated by a textual problem,[96] fortunately the main thrust of the

---

[92]Cf. Fee, *First Epistle to the Corinthians*, 712.

[93]Note "if anyone seems to be . . ." in 3:18 and 8:12.

[94]S. Aalen, "A rabbinic formula in 1 Cor. 14.34," *Studia Evangelica* (ed. F. Cross; Berlin: Akademie, 1964): 2.514, is certainly incorrect in linking v. 37 with v. 34. Erik Sjöberg, "Herrens bud 1 Kor. 14:37," *SEÅ* 22/23 (1957/58): 168-71, incorrectly links v. 37 with v. 33a.

[95]The singular (collective, referring to all that is written in this section) is attested solidly in the earlier mss, but several later mss altered the reading to the plural. Barrett, *First Epistle to the Corinthians*, 333, correctly notes that, "it is much more likely that the short text was made more explicit by the addition of *command(s)* than *vice versa*."

[96] Ἀγνοείτω, read by most mss, is rendered in KJV "if any man be ignorant, let him be ignorant." However, ἀγνοεῖται in *UBS Greek NT*[3] is rendered variously as "he is not recognized" (RSV; NASB; Barrett, *First Epistle to the Corinthians*, 334); "you should not recognize him" (JerB); "God does not acknowledge him" (NEB; Lietzmann, *Der erste Brief an die Korinther*, 291); and "anyone who disregards this will be himself disregarded" (Moffatt). I am inclined to follow Zuntz, *The Text of the Epistle*, 107-08, in reading the third person imperative as "a natural and effective *praeteritio*: according to it, Paul suppresses all invective by a brief *habeat sibi*." As Paul had said in 12:1 that he did not want them to be "ignorant" concerning the abuse of "spiritual manifestations," it is not unexpected that he would conclude a section dominated by those concerns with a strong appeal not to be "ignorant." The third person imperative is not the most difficult reading. Cf. Fee, *First Epistle to the Corinthians*, 709, n. 4.

strong statement in v. 28 is clear: all are to recognize the voice of God in what Paul says and will ignore his directive at their peril.[97] So, in v. 29, Paul summarizes his extended discussion from chap. 12, mentioning only two topics: prophesying and tongues, and emphasizing the priority of the former. There is no mention of the silence of women. We may infer from this that the third of the topics in vv. 27-36 was not major to his discussion, but significantly attendant to it since it involved serious disruption of decorum. V. 40, then, summarizes not vv. 26-33,[98] but the entirety of the unit beginning in 11:2 which treats conduct in Corinthian worship. Everything should be done decently (12:23f) and orderly (33a). This certainly accords with the theme in 1 Cor. that respect for others is greater than any uncontrolled expression of personal rights.

3. Conclusion

There is no convincing reason to view vv. 34-35 as a Corinthian quote that Paul refutes in v. 36 or as an interpolation from a later period. There is no evidence that Paul contradicts what he had taught earlier in 11:2-16, that 11 represents a reluctant concession, or that he changed his mind between chapter 11 and 14. Two different matters are involved: the praying and prophesying by the women in chap. 11 in the assembly differs markedly from some wives continually "piping up" in the assembly in chap. 14. The patent insubordination which these wives had in common with that of the tongue-speakers and prophets called for Paul's inclusion of this firm directive at this point in the text.

---

[97]Note 12:28, where Paul had stressed, "first apostles, second prophets." However, Karl Kertelge, *Gemeinde und Amt im NT* (Munich: Kösel, 1972): 119-21, overstates prophecy as an established order in the early church second only to the apostles. Gotthold Hasenhüttl, *Charisma: Ordnungsprinzip der Kirche* (Freiburg: Herder, 1969): 193, also overstates matters by attributing to the prophets an "independence which does not permit their subjection to any other group." Barrett, *First Epistle to the Corinthians*, 334, observes correctly that there is nothing here to suggest excommunication.

[98]Cf. Fee, *First Epistle to the Corinthians*, 713.

Since 1 Cor. 14:34-35 cannot be excluded on text-critical grounds, it is exegetically sound to conclude with Héring[99] that, "14:33b-36 are in their right place and quite authentic," and that Paul is dealing with a particular problem in Corinth. The problem is not one of disdain for creation order or family order, but one of church order. Far from being intolerant, Paul neither teaches nor suggests in this text anything regarding patriarchalism or female subjection. The real issue is not the *extent*[100] to which a woman may participate in the work and worship of the church, but the *manner*. Paul's corrective does not ban women from speaking in public,[101] but stops the disruptive verbal misconduct of certain wives who are giving free rein to "irresistible impulses" to "pipe up" at will with questions in the assembly by redirecting these questions to another setting where they can gain access to information without causing chaos.

Referring, as it does, to a very specific problem of disruptive questions by these women, 1 Cor. 14:34-35 teaches that these particular wives, like the uncontrolled tongue-speakers and prophets at Corinth, must *defer* to the assembly by voluntarily yielding to orderliness. The general principle that is to be applied to contemporary church life is that decorum is mandatory for all in the public assembly without regard for gender.

---

[99]Héring, *First Epistle of Saint Paul to the Corinthians*, 155. See also Bruce, *1 and 2 Corinthians*, 137, "Much of the teaching in this chapter is relevant only to such exceptional circumstances as prevailed in the church of Corinth."

[100]Smith, *Men of Strength for Women of God*, 250, wrongly concludes, "The real issue is the extent to which a woman may *participate* in the work and worship of the church."

[101]Grosheide, *First Epistle to the Corinthians*, 343, has missed the point of the text in arguing that "everybody will agree that it is unbecoming for a woman to speak in a public meeting of the church." Neither in this nor in any other biblical text is there a prohibition against women speaking in public, *on the ground that it is public.*

Chapter Nine

"SUBMISSION" IN EPH. 5:21-33

Kenneth V. Neller

Some three and one-half centuries before Paul, Aristotle reflected a typically negative attitude toward women.

> For that some should rule and others be ruled is a thing not only necessary, but expedient; from the hour of their birth, some are marked out for subjection, others for rule. . . . The male is by nature superior, and the female inferior; and the one rules, and the other is ruled.[1]

Even toward the end of the first century AD, Josephus[2] could say, "'The woman,' says the Law, 'is inferior to her husband in all things.' Let her, therefore, be obedient to him." For many centuries, even among Christians, a deprecatory and restrictive view of women was maintained. Eph. 5:21-33 was viewed often as endorsing the authoritative, dominating role of the husband and the subjected, servile role of the wife. Aquinas,[3] for instance, translates Eph. 5:22, "Let women be subject to their husbands as to a lord," and comments, ". . . *as to a lord* since the relation of a husband to his wife is, in a certain way, like that of a master to his servant, insofar as the latter ought to be governed by

---

[1]Aristotle, *Politics* 1254.

[2]Josephus, *Against Apion* 2.24. The translation of H. St. John Thackeray, *Josephus* (New York: G. P. Putnam's Sons, 1926): 373, unacceptably softens the force of ὑπακουέτω (let her be obedient) by rendering "let her be submissive."

[3]Thomas Aquinas, *St. Paul's Epistle to the Ephesians* (trans. M. Lamb; Albany, NY: Magi, 1966): 2.216f. See also p. 218 that "the wife must be obedient to her husband."

the commands of his master." Similarly, Calvin[4] says of wives that "it is also for their benefit to be under their husbands and to yield them obedience."

Even in recent scholarship, terms such as "authority," "govern," "rule," "superior," "inferior," and "obey," are used in explanation of Eph. 5:21-33. E.g., Robinson,[5] asserts that subordination is "the recognition of the sacred principles of authority and obedience." Clark[6] notes, "obeying commands is part of subordination." Park[7] views the husband as "governing authority," as does Bruce.[8] Such emotionally volatile language has promoted no little misunderstanding, such as Shaw's[9] remark that Paul was a "rash and not very deep man, as his contempt for women shows."

It may be suggested, however, that never is "obedience" of wives to husbands found in the NT and, further, that nowhere in the NT is there basis for male superiority. A fresh examination of Eph. 5:21-33 is fully warranted.

---

[4]John Calvin, *Sermons on the Epistle to the Ephesians* (Rev. trans.; London: Banner of Truth, 1973): 572.

[5]J. Armitage Robinson, *St. Paul's Epistle to the Ephesians* (2nd ed.; London: Macmillan, 1904): 123.

[6]Stephen B. Clark, *Man and Woman in Christ* (Ann Arbor: Servant, 1980): 82.

[7]D. M. Park, "The Structure of Authority in Marriage: An Examination of *Hupotasso* and *Kephale* in Eph. 5:21-33," *EvQ* 59 (1987): 118f.

[8]F. F. Bruce, *The Epistles to the Colossians, to Philemon, and to the Ephesians* (NIC; Grand Rapids: Eerdmans, 1984): 384. See also p. 386, n. 89, that a wife give "obedience to her husband."

[9]G. B. Shaw, *The Intelligent Woman's Guide to Socialism and Capitalism* (New York: Brentano's, 1928): 3. Vern and Bonnie Bullough, *The Subordinate Sex. A History of Attitudes toward Women* (Chicago: Univ. of Illinois Press, 1973): 101f, cite Eph. 5:22-25, along with Col. 3:18-19 and 1 Pet. 3:1, as examples of "continuous admonitions for women to obey their husbands" in the NT. They conclude (p. 119) that "Christianity was a male-centered, sex-negative religion with a strong mysoginistic tendency."

1. *The Literary Context of Eph. 5:21-33*

Paul's injunction that wives should submit themselves to their own husbands (Eph. 5:22, 24) and that husbands, as head of their wives, should love them (5:23, 25) can be understood properly only when these verses are viewed in their literary context. In this respect, it is crucial to understand Paul's meaning in light of Eph. 5:21, for that verse governs the entire following passage of 5:22-6:9.[10]

Grammatically, 5:21 belongs with 5:19-20, where it contains the fifth of five imperatival participles: speaking, singing, making melody, giving thanks, and submitting, all of which are part of the Christian walk. Thematically, and grammatically, however, 5:21 is linked even more closely with 5:22-6:9, where the concept of mutual submission is elaborated. The omission of a verb in 5:22 indicates clearly that the verbal thought of v. 22 is to be supplied by the verb in the immediately preceding statement. In fact, many Greek mss added some form of "submit" in v. 22.

The connection of 5:21 to 5:22-6:9 is suggested also by the thematic unity. Following the admonition in 5:21 to "submit yourselves to one another," 5:22ff. specifies how this mutual submission should be applied in the common household[11] among husbands and wives, parents and

---

[10]M. Barth, *Ephesians* (Garden City, NY: Doubleday, 1974): 609, observes correctly, "The single imperative of v. 21 ('subordinate yourselves to one another') anticipates all that Paul is to say not only to wives, children, and slaves, but also to husbands, fathers, and masters." See also Else Kähler, *Die Frau in den paulinischen Briefen* (Zürich: Gotthelf-Verlag, 1960): 99f, 138; and J. Paul Sampley, *And The Two Shall Become One Flesh. A Study of Traditions in Ephesians 5:21-33* (SNTSMS, 16; Cambridge: Cambridge Univ. Press, 1971): 10, 27, 117.

[11]*Haustafel* (house table) refers to an organized list of injunctions having to do with various household duties and relationships. For a survey of literature, see, J. E. Crouch, *The Origin and Intention of the Colossian Haustafel* (Göttingen: Vandenhoeck & Ruprecht, 1972): 9-31; W. Schrage, "Zur Ethik der neutestamentlichen Haustafeln," *NTS* 21 (1975): 1-22; R. P. Martin, "Haustafeln," *New International*

children, masters and slaves,[12] always pointing each partner in the relationship to Christ. It must be observed as well that 5:21 is linked to 5:22ff thematically with φόβος (fear, respect),[13] which occurs only in 5:21, 33, and 6:5 in Ephesians.

Failing to maintain the connection between 5:21 and the following material, some have arrived at the erroneous conclusion that Paul was merely maintaining the subjected and servile position of wives, as well as children and slaves, common in that day by "Christianizing" a commonly used "household code."[14] Consequently, some reject Eph. 5:22-6:9 as irrelevant to contemporary Christian living.[15] Others have countered that Paul is not *endorsing* prevailing customs and attitudes, but *revolutionizing* customs and attitudes within the Christian family by reminding his readers that every relationship is sanctified when one understands the will of God, remembers the example of Christ, and is filled with the Spirit.[16]

Dictionary of New Testament Theology (Grand Rapids: Zondervan, 1975): 3.928-32. See also 1 Clem. 21:6-9; Ignatius, *Polycarp* 4:1-6:1; Didache 4:9-11.

[12]Heinrich Schlier, *Der Brief an die Epheser* (3rd ed.; Düsseldorf: Patmos-Verlag, 1962): 250; and Barth, *Ephesians*, 603f.

[13]See Sampley, *One Flesh*, 147.

[14]Among others, Martin Dibelius, *An die Kolosser, Epheser, an Philemon* (Tübingen: J. C. B. Mohr, 1953): 48-50, 93-95.

[15]J. T. Sanders, *Ethics in the New Testament. Change and Development* (Philadelphia: Fortress, 1975): 75, concludes that "the *Haustafeln* must therefore be seen as completely worthless for Christian ethics . . . since the regulations are by and large derived from non-Christian sources."

[16]See K. H. Rengstorf, "Die neutestamentlichen Mahnungen an die Frau, sich dem Manne underzuorden," *Verbum Dei manet in aeternum* (ed. W. Foerster; Witten: Luther, 1953): 131-45, esp. 133-36, 139-40; and G. F. Wessels, "Ephesians 5:21-33. 'Wives, Be Subject to Your Husbands . . . Husbands, Love Your Wives . . .'" *JThSoAfrica* 67 (1989): 67-76, esp. 69-70.

2. *Wifely Submission*

The verb ὑποτάσσω, when used in the active voice in the NT, means "to subject," "to subordinate." With the lone exception of Phil. 3:21, where Christ is the subjugator, God is the subject of the verb in the NT.[17] In every context where the active voice is used, except Heb. 2:5, antagonism or resistance between the subjugator and the subjugated is involved. Similarly, the subjection of antagonistic forces is meant when the passive form of the verb is used.[18] Nowhere in the NT is authority or power given to a human to subjugate anyone against his or her will with this verb.

There are, however, instances where clearly passive forms of ὑποτάσσω carry a middle sense, i.e., to submit one's self.[19] This middle reflexive understanding of the passive occurs when the ones subjugated are humans who are willingly submissive. For instance, in James 4:7, it is preferable to read the aorist passive imperative as "submit yourselves therefore to God" (KJV; NIV; NRSV), rather than "be submissive" (NEB; Phillips). Similarly, in 1 Pet. 2:13 should read "submit yourselves to every human authority" (KJV; NIV; NEB; NASB), rather than "be subject" (RSV). Likewise, in Heb. 12:9, the readers are

---

[17]Rom. 8:20; 1 Cor. 15:27 [bis], 28; Eph. 1:22; Heb. 2:5, 8 [bis]. See G. Delling, "ὑποτάσσω," *TDNT*, 8:41f.

[18]See Lk. 10: 17, 20; Rom. 8:20; 1 Cor. 15:27-28; Heb. 2:8.

[19]For discussion of this common phenomenon in Greek, see J. H. Moulton, *A Grammar of New Testament Greek* (3rd ed.; Edinburgh: T. & T. Clark, 1908): 1.161-63; and A. T. Robertson, *A Grammar of the Greek New Testament in the Light of Historical Research* (Nashville: Broadman, 1934): 333f. Although noted by J. H. Thayer, *A Greek-English Lexicon of the New Testament* (4th ed.; Edinburgh: T. & T. Clark, 1901): 645, most major lexicons do not note middle uses of ὑποτάσσω. See H. G. Liddell and R. Scott, *A Greek-English Lexicon* (rev. H. Jones & R. McKenzie; Oxford: Clarendon, 1968): 1897; and W. Bauer, *A Greek-English Lexicon of the New Testament and Other Early Christian Literature* (trans. W. F. Arndt & F. W. Gingrich; 2nd ed. rev. F. W. Gingrich & F. W. Danker; Chicago: Univ. of Chicago Press, 1979): 847f. In light of this, it is astounding that Delling, *TDNT*, 8.41-45, makes no mention of the passive uses.

exhorted "submit ourselves (ὑποταγησόμεθα) to our
spiritual Father" (JB), rather than "be subject" (KJV; NASB;
NRSV).

Whether the passive form of ὑποτάσσω carries a
middle reflexive sense must be determined by the context.[20]
As mentioned, in the NT only God and Christ have power
and authority to subjugate and they do so only when the
object is antagonistic. When an individual is urged to
submit, such submission involves a voluntary act of the
subject's will. For instance, Christians are urged to "submit
themselves to governing powers" (Rom. 13:1; Tit. 3:1), to
each other (1 Cor. 16:16; Eph. 5:21), and to Christ (Eph.
5:24). Wives are to "submit themselves" to their husbands
(Eph. 5:22; Col. 3:18; Tit. 2:5; 1 Pet. 3:1, 5) and slaves to
their masters (Tit. 2:9; 1 Pet. 2:18). In each of these
instances, ὑποτάσσομαι refers to the *voluntary* surrender of
one's own rights or will.[21]

In some instances, submission includes the obligation
of obedience, as in Christians submitting to the government
or slaves submitting to their masters. Nevertheless,
submission and obedience in the NT are not synonymous
concepts.[22] It is significant that children are often

---

[20]Moulton, *A Grammar of New Testament Greek*, 163, and
Robertson, *A Grammar of the Greek New Testament*, 817, disagree on
whether in Rom. 10:3 Paul laments that the Israelites "were not
subjected" by God or "did not submit themselves" to God.

[21]See Delling, *TDNT*, 8.40; Barth, *Ephesians*, 710; and Kähler,
Die Frau in den paulinischen Briefen, 122ff, 138-40. For refusal to
submit voluntarily, see Rom. 8:7.

[22]Delling, *TDNT*, 8.40-41, notes that if the subjugation is
forced, obedience is mandatory. If the submission is voluntary,
however, ὑποτάσσω does not necessitate the idea of obedience. For
instance, in 1 Pet. 3:1, 5, wives are admonished to "submit themselves" to their husbands and Sarah is given in v. 6 as an example of
one who "obeyed." Sarah is cited as a model apparently because of her
spirit of submissive self-surrender. She *chose* to submit. In this text,
Peter could have commanded obedience, but chose instead to use the
more liberating "submit yourselves." See also Kähler, *Die Frau in den*

commanded to obey (ὑπακούω) their parents, yet the relationship of Jesus to his parents in Lk. 2:51 is rather one of submission (ὑποτάσσομαι). Similarly, in Eph. 5:21ff. (and Col. 3:18ff.), under the general rubric of "submitting yourselves to one another," children and slaves are urged "to obey" (ὑπακούω), but wives are to "submit themselves" (ὑποτάσσομαι). So, a distinction between submission and obedience must be made and one must determine from each context whether submission necessitates obedience.

The primary focus of "submit yourselves" must be on attitude. One can be forced to obey the government or a slave can be made to obey a master, but Christian submission is a voluntary surrender of one's own rights, a placing of oneself at the disposal of, or in the service of, someone else. Submission is a willing deference.[23]

The ultimate Christian model of willful submission is Jesus, who voluntarily surrendered his rights and humbly submitted himself to God (Phil. 2:5-11) and to man (1 Pet. 2:21ff.) in loving service (John 13:1ff.). The voluntary nature of Jesus' submission, in contrast to the forced subjugation of his enemies, is clearly stated in 1 Cor. 15:24-28. In light of Jesus' submission, then, Christians are called upon to surrender their own rights voluntarily.

---

paulinischen Briefen, 109f. Cf. A. T. Lincoln, *Ephesians* (Dallas: Word, 1990): 367f.

[23]Submission, in the sense of willing deference for the sake of a worthy goal, is viewed in extra-biblical literature as a commendable virtue. For example, in Pseudo Callisthenes 1.22.4, Alexander urges his mother, who was wrongly treated by her husband Philip, to "submit herself" and be reconciled to him. See Delling, *TDNT*, 8:40. Willfully "submitting oneself" in a spirit of humility in order to gain the favor of strangers is commended in Epist. Arist. 257. See M. Hadas, ed., *Aristeas to Philocrates* (New York: Harper & Bros., 1951). "Submission of oneself" and humility are also closely linked in 1 Pet. 5:5. From a Christian viewpoint, then, the "worthy goal" which motivates self-submission is the imitation of Christ and the pleasing of God.

In Eph. 5:22, 24, wives are admonished to submit themselves to their own husbands. While the emphasis may be on "their *own*,"[24] it is more likely that mutual submission is meant, as in 5:21. The submission of wives to husbands was considered a virtue and socially proper by contemporary writers.[25] Unfortunately, what often goes unnoticed is that Paul elevates and develops the concept of wifely submission by placing it in a christological and ecclesiological context.

Wives are to submit themselves to their husbands "as (in the same way) they submit to the Lord" (5:22). Sampley's[26] leaving the phrase ambiguous is unsatisfactory, as the translation "as to a lord" opens the door to the horrendous misunderstanding shared by Aquinas (see n. 3 above) that the husband-wife relationship is analogous to a master-slave relationship. On the other hand, some[27] interpret "as to the Lord" to mean that because they fear the Lord, they should submit to their husbands, but the context seems to call for a comparative understanding. In the same way that the church voluntarily submits itself to Christ (5:24), a wife voluntarily submits herself to her husband. She is not subjugated unwillingly. A Christian husband no more subjugates his wife to his will through intimidation or force than Christ forcibly subjugates the church to his will. Christ subjugates his enemies, but not his disciples. By placing wifely submission in the context of Jesus and his church, Paul clearly teaches that the husband-wife relationship should not be one of animosity, antagonism, servitude, or oppression, but one of love and respect.

---

[24]However, Moulton, *A Grammar of New Testament Greek*, 1.87-90, and Bruce, *Epistles to the Colossians, to Philemon, and to the Ephesians*, 384, conclude that the force of ἴδιος (own) should not be pressed too far.

[25]E.g., Plutarch, *Moralia* 142E, states, "If [women] submit themselves (ὑποτάττουσαι ἑαυτάς) to their husbands, they are commended; but if they want to have control, they cut a sorrier figure than the subjects of their control."

[26]Sampley, *And The Two Shall Become One Flesh*, 112.

[27]See Bruce, *Epistles to the Colossians, to Philemon, and to the Ephesians*, 384.

But does the relationship of a wife to her husband as described in Eph. 5:21ff. also include obedience? Much hinges on the difficult phrase ἐν παντί in 5:24: "wives should submit themselves to their husbands *in everything*." Taken out of context, this could be understood as saying that wives must submit to everything their husbands say and do whether or not they like it or agree with it. To be sure, the submission advocated in 5:24 is a complete self-surrender,[28] yet Paul certainly never intended to infer a master/slave relationship between husband and wife.[29] As Lincoln[30] observes, "As the following verses will make explicit, full and complete commitment of the husband to his particular role of loving is also required." Miletic[31] is on firm ground in noting that wifely submission "is to selfless love— expressed through the husband's headship—and not to the whims of the husband." Certainly Paul and other NT writers had every opportunity to command wives to obey their husbands, but never is such an injunction given, thus acknowledging a degree of freedom and self-determination on the part of the wives. If any obedience is involved, it is a voluntary acquiescence on the part of the wife. Any attempt of the husband to enforce obedience is beyond the Christian perspective. Christian wives willingly submit to responsible headship on the part of loving husbands.

3. *Husbandly Headship*

The husband's role in marriage as "head of the wife" (Eph. 5:23) is vitally related to the wife's voluntary submission. Unfortunately, what Paul meant by "head" is the topic of a raging debate which has polarized most scholars into one of two major camps.

---

[28]Lincoln, *Ephesians*, 373, stresses subordination, noting that "Ephesians calls for complete submission of wives to husbands. . . . There is no limit to the submission expected of wives."

[29]See Barth, *Ephesians*, 620f.

[30]Lincoln, *Ephesians*, 373. See also Schlier, *Der Brief an die Epheser*, 254.

[31]S. F. Miletic, *"One Flesh": Eph. 5.22-24, 5.31. Marriage and the New Creation* (Rome: Pontifical Biblical Institute, 1988): 105.

On the one hand, some such as Berkeley and Alvera Mickelsen,[32] Bilezikian,[33] Kroeger,[34] and Fee[35] claim that "head" in the Greek NT rarely[36] or never[37] designates a leader or anyone with some type of authority. Instead, they see "head" in the Pauline epistles as referring to "source" or "beginning."[38]   Consequently, men/husbands are the "source" of women/wives, but have no "authority" over them. While Christ does have authority over the church, that authority is not in focus here, but the oneness of Christ and the church. Discussing what it means to "be filled with the spirit," Paul stresses "submitting yourselves to one another." This mutual submission is addressed to all Christians, including husbands and wives. On the basis of the context, the imagery of the head/body metaphor in Eph. 5:23 is taken to refer to the mutual dependence and unity that, as Christ enabled the church to be what it was meant to be, enables a husband to help a wife to be all she was meant to be.

---

[32]Berkeley and Alvera Mickelsen, "The 'Head' of the Epistles," *Christianity Today* 25 (1981): 264-67; *idem*, "What Does *Kephale* Mean in the New Testament?" *Women, Authority & the Bible* (ed. A. Mickelsen; Downer's Grove, IL: InterVarsity, 1986): 97-117; A. Mickelsen, "There is Neither Male nor Female in Christ," *Women in Ministry* (ed. B. and R. G. Clouse; Downer's Grove, IL: InterVarsity, 1989): 173-206.

[33]Gilbert Bilezikian, "A Critical Examination of Wayne Grudem's Treatment of *Kephale* in Ancient Greek Texts," *Beyond Sex Roles* (2nd ed.; Grand Rapids: Baker, 1985): 215-52.

[34]Catherine Kroeger, "The Classical Concept of Head as 'Source'," *Equal to Serve: Women and Men in the Church and Home* (ed. G. G. Hull; Old Tappan, NJ: F. H. Revell, 1987): 267-83.

[35]Gordon D. Fee, *The First Epistle to the Corinthians* (Grand Rapids: Eerdmans, 1987): 502f.

[36]Kroeger, "The Classical Concept of Head as 'Source'," *Equal to Serve*, 277.

[37]B. and A. Mickelsen, "What Does *Kephale* Mean in the NT?" *Women, Authority & the Bible*, 110.

[38]The impetus for this view seems to be the work of S. Bedale, "The Meaning of κεφαλή in the Pauline Epistles," *JTS* 5 (1954): 211-15. For typical expression of this view, see Aida Besançon Spencer, *Beyond the Curse: Women Called to Ministry* (Nashville: Thomas Nelson, 1985): 104, n. 14.

Alternatively, Grudem,[39] Fitzmyer,[40] and others argue that "head," when used metaphorically by Greek writers (including Paul), may signify some type of leadership role with varying degrees of authority.[41] According to them, "head" rarely[42] or never[43] means "source." Thus, "head" here denotes some sort of leadership/authority over the wife.

Such polarization of scholarship may lead some to despair of ever understanding the phrase, "the husband is head of the wife." Nevertheless, a fairly clear picture of the concept is possible when one looks carefully at the evidence and interprets Eph. 5:23 in its literary context.

In extra-biblical Greek literature, κεφαλή (head) refers primarily to what is first or supreme, or to an extremity, end, or point. As such, the term was used to designate not only the head of a person or animal, but also the prow of a ship, head of a pillar, top of a wall, source or mouth of a river, or start of a period of time. The word could also signify what was prominent, outstanding, or determinative.[44] While

---

[39]Wayne Grudem, "Does *Kephale* Mean 'Source' or 'Authority Over' in Greek Literature? A Survey of 2,336 Examples," *Trinity Journal* 6 (1985): 38-59; *idem*, "The Meaning of *Kephale* (Head): A Response to Recent Studies," *Recovering Biblical Manhood and Womanhood* (ed. J. Piper & W. Grudem; Wheaton: Crossway, 1991): 425-68.

[40]Joseph Fitzmyer, "Another Look at κεφαλή in 1 Corinthians 11:3," *NTS* 35 (1989): 503-11.

[41]In this regard, it should be noted that "leadership" should not be equated with "rulership" or "having authority over," as Grudem, "The Meaning of *Kephale*," *Recovering Biblical Manhood and Womanhood*, 425ff., observes. The concepts of leadership and rulership are not synonymous. D. M. Park, "The Structure of Authority in Marriage," *EvQ* 59 (1987): 118, overstates the case and inflames the controversy by suggesting that "head" in Eph. 5 should be understood as "one entrusted with superior rank, authority, or power."

[42]Fitzmyer, *NTS* (1989): 509.

[43]Grudem, "The Meaning of *Kephale*," *Recovering Biblical Manhood and Womanhood*, 467-68.

[44]H. Schlier, "Κεφαλή," *TDNT*, 3.673-74.

Liddell-Scott[45] give no indication that "head" includes the idea of leadership, Schlier[46] notes that in the NT period Greek writers such as Philo and the Stoics associated "head" with τὸ ἡγεμονικόν (leadership). Nevertheless, there is no example of "head" being used figuratively for a *person* as "leader" or "chief" before the Septuagint.

In the Septuagint, the word κεφαλή almost always translates the Hebrew ראשׁ (*ro'sh*, head), approximating the use of the word "head" in secular Greek. When *ro'sh* refers to a leader, chief, or ruler, the Septuagint prefers the use of the familiar words ἀρχηγός (leader) or ἄρχων (ruler). Yet there are a few instances where the Septuagint departs from previous Greek usage and maintains the Hebrew use of "head" to refer to a leader.[47] Fitzmyer[48] demonstrates convincingly that not only in the Septuagint, but also in Philo and Josephus, "head" can connote one who leads. Writers such as the Mickelsens ignore the connection of "head" with the concept of leadership as expressed in writings contemporary with the NT, and devalue the uses of "head" for leaders in the Septuagint as statistically insignificant. While it is true that "head" is not used often to refer to a leader, this meaning for "head" cannot be dismissed simply because it is used infrequently. That κεφαλή was used to mean "head" in Greek literature prior to and contemporary with the NT cannot be doubted.

However, "head" could also signify "source" or beginning" in Greek literature. Fitzmyer[49] notes one instance in Philo (*De cong. erud. causa* 12 #61) and a few

---

[45]Liddell and Scott, *A Greek-English Lexicon*, 945.

[46]Schlier, *TDNT*, 3.674.

[47]See the references in Schlier, *TDNT*, 3.675; Fitzmyer, *NTS* (1989): 506-09; and Grudem, "The Meaning of *Kephale*," *Recovering Biblical Manhood and Womanhood*, 451-52. It seems significant that in Isa. 9:13f. κεφαλή and ἀρχή are used synonymously and that in Judg. 11:11 κεφαλή is used in conjunction with ἡγέομαι (to lead).

[48]Fitzmyer, *NTS* (1989): 509-10.

[49]*Ibid.*

others are noted by Fee.[50] But the evidence for the use of "head" to mean "source" is scant, if not more scant, than for the meaning "leader." It is certainly overstating the case, as the Mickelsens[51] and Fee[52] do, that a Greek Christian who read Paul's "head" metaphor would have understood it naturally to mean "source" or "source of life."

Having said this, it must be recognized that the previous usage of a word does not alone determine its meaning. Significance is given to a word as it is used *in its context*.[53] Along these lines, three things should be noted. 1) While Paul was heavily influenced in his thinking by his rabbinic training in the OT and by the Greek culture of which he was a part, it was not beyond Paul or any other of the NT writers to redefine words or concepts in light of their Christian experience.[54] 2) The "head" metaphor in Eph. 5:23 is actually part of a head/body metaphor: "the husband is the head of the wife just as Christ is the head of the church, his body." When the word "head" is used metaphorically in the OT to refer to a person, it never refers to the people associated with the person as a "body."[55] Therefore, Paul's metaphor of Christ as head of the body, his church (Eph. 1:22-23; 4:15-16; 5:23; Col. 1:18), is unique in biblical literature. Although it remains unclear what led Paul to use

---

[50]Fee, *The First Epistle to the Corinthians*, 503. Orphic Frag. 21a, cited so often in support of the meaning "source" for the word "head" in the NT, seems irrelevant, since the fragment dates five centuries before the NT.

[51]B. and A. Mickelsen, *Christianity Today* (1981): 265; idem, "There is Neither Male nor Female in Christ," *Women in Ministry*, 193ff. Ironically, the Mickelsens reject "leader" as a common Greek usage for "head" and insist that a definition for "head" in Paul's epistles be chosen from the "common Greek meanings of head." They seem unaware that the meaning "source" is anything but common in Greek literature of the period!

[52]Fee, *The First Epistle to the Corinthians*, 503.

[53]See M. Silva, *Biblical Words and Their Meaning* (Grand Rapids: Zondervan, 1983): 138ff.

[54]*Ibid.*, 75ff.

[55]Barth, *Ephesians*, 184f.; Schlier, *TDNT*, 3.675.

the head/body metaphor, it does seem clear that Paul is not alluding to the Gnostic concept of Christ as the source or originator of the church, nor is he teaching the pantheistic idea of the body of Christ as "all things" in the universe.[56] Conveyed in "head of his body, the church," rather, is the idea of Christ as preeminent, first (firstborn from the dead), leader, and guide of the purpose and growth of the church.[57] The husband's headship of the wife must be understood in the context of this head/body metaphor. 3) The discussion of "head" regarding the relationship of men and women has focused primarily around 1 Cor. 11:3, with the conclusions from that passage being applied directly to Eph. 5:23. This is exegetically irresponsible. Just as the church/body metaphor has changed from 1 Cor. to Eph., so the significance of the head metaphor may be different in each epistle.

---

[56]See Barth, *Ephesians*, 185f. Against H. Schlier, *Christus an die Kirche im Epheserbrief* (Tübingen: J. C. B. Mohr, 1930) 37-50; Rudolf Bultmann, *Theology of the New Testament* (trans. K. Grobel; New York: C. Scribner's Sons, 1951): 1.178f; and Eduard Schweizer, "Die Kirche als Leib Christi in den paulinischen Antilegomena," *TLZ* 86 (1961): 241-56; *idem*, "The Church as the Missionary Body of Christ," *NTS* 8 (1961): 1-11. Edgar J. Goodspeed, *The Meaning of Ephesians* (Chicago: Univ. of Chicago Press, 1933): 61-62, incorrectly notes that Paul writes this text, "not so much because of his interest in the marriage relation as because he sees in it a glorious parable of the mystic union between Christ and the Church."

[57]Misunderstanding of Col. 1:15-20 has contributed greatly to confusion over the leadership of the church which has been given to Christ. The concept of "head" is wrongly connected with Christ being the source of all creation, thus rendering him source of the church. Properly understood, however, Col. 1:18a ("he is the head of the body, the church") should be interpreted as a transitional line introducing the second strophe of the hymn, vv. 18b-20. Therefore, Christ as head of the church is to be understood in light of his work in reconciliation rather than in terms of being the agent through whom the world was created (first strophe, vv. 15-16; summed up by the first part of the transition in v. 17). See P. Benoit, "L'hymne christologique de Col. 1, 15-20," *Christianity, Judaism and Other Greco-Roman Cults* (ed. J. Neusner; Leiden: Brill, 1975): 1.229; and Paul Beasley-Murray, "Colossians 1:15-20: An Early Christian Hymn Celebrating the Lordship of Christ," *Pauline Studies* (ed. D. Hagner & M. J. Harris; Grand Rapids: Eerdmans, 1980): 170.

So, what does Paul mean in 5:23 when he says that "the husband is head of the wife just as Christ is head of the church"? Kähler[58] rightly cautions that analogies must not be pressed too far. For instance, Paul goes on to say that Christ is the "savior of the body," but would it not be saying too much to say that the husband is savior of his wife?[59] The strong adversative ἀλλά (but) at the beginning of v. 24 would seem to indicate that the part of the analogy Paul wishes to emphasize is the leadership/submissiveness aspect, not the savior relationship.[60] Christ is "head" in some cases because of who he *is*: eternal, preeminent, firstborn, Savior, etc, but a husband could not possibly imitate these traits. On the other hand, Christ is "head" in some cases because of what he *did* through his incarnation and death, and it is along this line that Paul exhorts husbands to be head of their wives. Like Christ, husbands are to become servants (Phil. 2:5-7; Mk. 10:45), be patient, kind, and compassionate (Matt. 11:19; Rom. 5:6-8), lead by example (Jn. 13:15; 1 Jn. 3:16), love their wives as their own bodies (Eph. 5:28, 33), nurture and care for their wives (Eph. 5:29-31), and give their lives (Eph. 5:25; Acts 20:28; Tit. 2:14; Mk. 8:34-35).

The "headship" of the husband derives not so much from who he *is* (male), but by what he *does* (serve),[61] i.e., his leadership in loving self-denial and sacrificial service.

---

[58]Kähler, *Die Frau in den paulinischen Briefen*, 138.

[59]Indeed, R. W. Wall, "Wifely Submission in the Context of Ephesians," *ChrSchR* 17 (1988): 281-82, claims that the husband *is*, in some respects, savior of the wife. Cf. Sampley, *And the Two Shall Become One Flesh*, 124f.

[60]See Robinson, *Ephesians*, 124; and Lincoln, *Ephesians*, 370.

[61]Bedale, *JTS* (1954): 213-15, is influenced by 1 Cor. 11:3, "The head of every man is Christ, and the head of the woman is man, and the head of Christ is God." Taking man as the *source* of the woman (Gen. 2:21-23; 1 Tim. 2:13), it is concluded that the husband has authority over the wife. Transferring this idea to Eph., he understands "husband as head of the wife" in 5:23 as a statement recognizing the authority of males over females, based upon Gen. 2. However, there is no

John Chrysostom[62] (5th cent. AD) put it well:

Take then thyself the same provident care for her as
Christ takes for the Church. Yea, even if it shall be
needful for thee to give thy life for her, yea, and to
be cut to pieces ten thousand times, yea, and endure
and undergo any suffering whatever, refuse it not.
Though thou shouldst undergo all this, yet wilt thou
not, no, not even then, have done anything like
Christ. . . . In the same way then as He laid at His
feet her who turned her back on Him, who hated,
and spurned, and disdained Him, not by menaces,
nor by violence, nor by terror, nor by anything else
of the kind, but by His unwearied affection; so also
do thou behave thyself towards thy wife. Yea,
though thou see her looking down upon thee, and
disdaining and scorning thee, yet by thy great
thoughtfulness for her, by affection, by kindness,
thou wilt be able to lay her beneath thy feet. For
there is nothing more absolute than these chains, and
especially for husband and wife. A servant, indeed,
one will be able, perhaps, to bind down by fear; nay
not even him, for he will soon start away and be
gone. But the partner of one's life, the mother of
one's children, the foundation of all one's joy, one
ought never to chain down by fear and menaces, but
by love and good temper. For what sort of union is
that, where the wife trembles at her husband? And
what sort of pleasure will the husband himself enjoy,
if he dwells with his wife as with a slave, and not as
a free-woman? Yea, though thou shouldst suffer
anything on her account, do not upbraid her; for
neither did Christ do this.

---

indication here that Paul bases his idea of the headship of the husband
upon the man's priority in creation. See Barth, *Ephesians*, 618.

[62]John Chrysostom, *Commentary on the Epistle to the Galatians
and Homilies on the Epistle to the Ephesians* (rev. ed.; London: Walter
Smith, 1884): 317-18.

Conclusion

The heading found in Eph. 5:21, "Submit yourselves to one another in reverence to Christ," controls and influences everything Paul says in the following *Haustafel* (5:22-6:9). The ideal relationship between a husband and wife is defined by the concept of a mutual submission patterned after and in deference to the example modeled by Christ.

Wives should submit themselves to their husbands (5:22, 24). This submission is not a forced subjection which implies weakness, nor does it imply inferiority. If Christ could submit himself to humans to become like them, to save them, and to be killed by them, a woman can follow his example, submitting herself to her husband without being inferior in the least.

Christian submission, like Christ's submission, is a voluntary surrendering of one's own rights. This is clarified and emphasized by the use of the middle voice of the verb "submit" (ὑποτάσσομαι) and by the qualifying phrases "as to the Lord" (5:22) and "as the church submits to Christ" (5:24). Christ does not forcibly subject the individual Christian nor the church, but his followers voluntarily give up their lives and submit to him (see Mk. 8:34). In the same way, when a woman marries, she chooses to submit herself to her husband.

When describing the husband's role in marriage, it must be remembered that the context is one of mutual submission (5:21).[63] The husband is "head of the wife just as Christ is head of the church" (5:23). Taken out of context, this analogy has been misinterpreted in terms of power, authority, and superiority. Yet, the context is submission. Carefully, Paul describes the husband's headship in terms of

---

[63]B. F. Westcott, *St. Paul's Epistle to the Ephesians* (London: Macmillan, 1906): 84, notes, "The Church offers to Christ the devotion of subjection, as the wife to the husband. Christ offers to the Church the devotion of love, as the husband to the wife. Both are equal in self-surrender."

Christ's headship of the church (5:23, 25-33). Perhaps more space is allotted to discussion of the husband's role than the wife's in order to preclude misunderstanding and abuse. Here the relationship of the husband to the wife is redefined radically in comparison with the contemporary understanding of that day. Christ is head of the church due to who he *is* (Son of God, firstborn, etc.) and what he *did* (gave himself, loved, sacrificed, etc.), but Paul defines the husband's headship in terms of what Christ *did*, not because the husband is male. Consequently, the emphasis in "headship" is not on gender superiority, but on role.

The husband's role as "head" is likened to Christ's love for the church—a sacrificial "giving up" of oneself for the sake of another (5:25). It is a tender, nurturing, caring type of love (5:28-29) which will reap its own delightful rewards (5:26-27). Certainly, any abuse of the wife by the husband in his role as "head" of the wife would indicate misunderstanding of this passage, an ignorance of Christ and his relationship with the church, or both.

In the mutually submissive relationship which Paul is describing, there is no stipulation for "commanding" and "obeying," but a commonality of focus and purpose. Rather than having a husband commanding and a wife obeying, both are urged to submit themselves to one another in Christian deference.

Chapter Ten

WOMEN IN THE EARLIER PHILIPPIAN CHURCH (ACTS 16:13-15; PHIL. 4:2-3) IN RECENT SCHOLARSHIP

J. Paul Pollard

Although not much is known of women in the earlier Philippian church, estimates vary in recent scholarship. For instance, Portefaix[1] notes Lydia to be a "prestigious model" who as, "A woman dealer in purple needed to be well-dressed herself in order to advertise her goods as her appearance would place her high in the estimation of other women." However, Oster[2] observes that this depiction of Lydia as a "Christian Avon Lady of the first century" depends more on fertile imagination than fact. Similarly, Spencer,[3] holds that Paul allowed Lydia "to take a leadership role in the Philippian church," but Rackham[4] mentions only her hospitality and good works, noting her to be one of the "nursing mothers of the infant church." In this vein, Euodia and Syntyche are viewed often as prominent women leaders in the Philippian church,[5] but they are regarded only as

---

[1]Lilian Portefaix, *Sisters Rejoice: Paul's Letter to the Philippians and Luke-Acts as Seen by First-Century Philippian Women* (Stockholm: Almquist and Wiksell, 1988): 170.

[2]Richard E. Oster, Jr., "Women, Diaspora Synagogues (προσ-ευχή) and Acts 16:13 (Philippi)," *Faith in Practice, Studies in the Book of Acts* (forthcoming): 25.

[3]A. B. Spencer, *Beyond the Curse: Women Called to Ministry* (Nashville: T. Nelson, 1985): 112.

[4]R. B. Rackham, *The Acts of the Apostles* (WC; 3rd ed.; London: Methuen, 1906): 283.

[5]Shirley Stephens, *A New Testament View of Women* (Nashville: Broadman, 1980): 125; J. T. Bristow, *What Paul Really Said About Women* (San Francisco: Harper, 1991): 56.

strong-willed women who had quarrelled by Martin.[6] Such diverse understandings call for a fresh investigation of the biblical texts pertaining to these women.

1. *Lydia*

A. *The "place of prayer" as "synagogue."* Following the "Macedonian call" (Acts 16:9-10), Paul and his fellow missionaries went, on the Sabbath, outside the gates of Philippi supposing a προσευχή (place of prayer) to be located alongside the river. Here they encountered a group of women, including Lydia. While some have understood this "place of prayer" to be a synagogue,[7] others disagree.[8] Banks,[9] for instance, states, "At Philippi, a Roman colony where apparently there was no synagogue, Paul and his colleagues sought out Jews and Gentile 'god-fearers' who might be gathered for prayer by the river." Thomas[10] argues

> There does not seem to have been a synagogue at Philippi which was a Roman colony and there were probably few Jews in the place. . . . The absence of a synagogue is suggested by a careful reading of the account of Paul's first visit to the town. . . . Generally, upon entering a new town Paul would find the synagogue and use his privilege to address the Jewish congregation. This he did not do at

---

[6]R. P. Martin, *Philippians* (NCBC; Grand Rapids: Eerdmans, 1980: 152.

[7]See among others, K. Lake and H. Cadbury, *Beginnings of Christianity* (London: Macmillan, 1933): 1.4: 191.

[8]See F. F. Bruce, *Commentary on the Book of the Acts* (NIC; Grand Rapids: Eerdmans, 1977): 331; W. Neil, *The Acts of the Apostles* (NCB; Greenwood: Attic, 1973): 181; W. M. Ramsay, *St. Paul the Traveler and the Roman Citizen* (London: Hodder and Stoughton, 1895): 214.

[9]Robert Banks, *Paul's Idea of Community: The Early House Churches in their Historical Setting* (Grand Rapids: Eerdmans, 1980): 156.

[10]W. Derek Thomas, "The Place of Women in the Church at Philippi,"*ExpTim* 73 (1972): 117.

Philippi, presumably because there was no synagogue in the town. Had there been ten male Jews
permanently resident there, the quorum required by
Jewish law, it would have been enough to constitute
a synagogue. It was left to a number of women,
probably Jewesses and proselytes, to maintain a
limited form of worship and prayer.

Denial of an actual synagogue service at Acts 16:13 is based
upon three reasons: 1) the verb νομίζω "suppose" in v. 13,
2) the use of προσευχή (place of prayer) rather than
συναγωγή (synagogue), and 3) the fact that no men are
present. Each of these items presents difficulties.

First, ἐνομίζομεν (we supposed) is taken to mean that
Paul and his company were strangers and did not know their
way around.[11] Filson,[12] however, argues that the meeting
place of these women was not a synagogue because νομίζω
refers to a view falsely held in Luke. Thus, in v. 13 Paul
seeks a synagogue, but finds only women, and only later in
v. 16 does he find the synagogue where the place of prayer
(προσευχή) actually was. While νομίζω does often have to
do with erroneous thinking, this context does not demand
such a meaning. The term "come together" (συνέρχομαι)
used here does refer in Acts 1:6; 10:27; 19:32; 22:30; and
28:17 to gatherings for special purposes and there is no
reason to preclude these women gathering for synagogue
worship. Why would these women gather for worship if
there was another "place of prayer" or "synagogue" in town?
Filson's reading of this text is unnecessary. The reference to
"place of prayer" in v. 16 is best understood as a reference to
the same "place of prayer" in v. 13.[13]

---

[11]See Bernadette J. Brooten, *Women Leaders in the Ancient
Synagogue: Inscriptional Evidence and Background Issues* (BJS, 36;
Chico: Scholars Press, 1982): 139.

[12]F. V. Filson, "Ancient Greek Synagogue Inscriptions," *BA* 32
(1969): 43.

[13]See Lake and Cadbury, *Beginnings of Christianity*, 1.4: 192,
for several options on the connection of v. 13 with v. 16. Probably,

Second, some have suggested that the use of "place of prayer" rather than "synagogue" may be due to Luke's use of sources[14] or terminological variation.[15] However, several inscriptions and papyri from this period use "place of prayer" for "synagogue."[16] For instance, an inscription from Alexandria dating from the reign of Ptolemy III (246-221 BCE)[17] reads, "In honour of King Ptolemy and Queen Berenike his sister and wife and their children, the Jews built the προσευχή." Similarly, a synagogue inscription from Alexandria in 37 BCE[18] reads, "For the queen and the king, to the great God who hears (prayers) Alypos made the προσευχή." When such archaeological evidence is combined with the literary testimony of Josephus and others who regularly used "place of prayer" for "synagogue,"[19] the "place of prayer" where Lydia and the other women assembled seems to have been a synagogue.[20]

---

while they were searching for the "place of prayer," a girl with a spirit followed them. After the group had encountered the women at the "place of prayer" and taught them, the casting out of the spirit from the possessed girl occurred later and is thus put after the Lydia narrative.

[14]E. Hänchen, *The Acts of the Apostles* (trans. B. Noble and G. Shinn; rev. R. McL. Wilson; Philadelphia: Westminster, 1979): 494.

[15]Brooten, *Women Leaders*, 139.

[16]G. H. R. Horsley, *New Documents Illustrating Early Christianity* (AHDC; Sydney: Macquarie Univ. Press, 1983): 3.121.

[17]A. Tcherikover, ed., *Corpus Papyrorum Judaicarum* (Cambridge: Harvard Univ. Press, 1964): 3.1440.

[18]Horsley, *New Documents Illustrating Early Christianity*, 3.121.

[19]Josephus, *Against Apion* 2.10; *Antiquities* 14.258; Philo, *Life of Moses* 2.216. See W. Bauer, *A Greek-English Lexicon of the New Testament* (trans. W. F. Arndt and F. W. Gingrich; 2nd ed. rev. F. W. Danker; Chicago: Univ. Of Chicago Press, 1979): 713, where the statement is made that among Jews προσευχή is "nearly always equivalent to συναγωγή."

[20]See Richard Oster, Jr., "Women, Diaspora Synagogues . . .," (unpublished manuscript), 6-7, and Martin Hengel, "Proseuche und Synagoge: Jüdische Gemeinde, Gotteshaus und Gottesdienst in der Diaspora und in Palästina," *The Synagogue: Studies in Origins, Archaeology and Architecture* (ed. J. Gutman; New York: KTAV, 1975): 157-83.

Third, the relationship of women to the synagogue requires clarification. Women were exempted from the study of Torah and were not required to attend the synagogue.[21] Clearly, however, the NT mentions women in attendance at the synagogue (Acts 17:4 and 18:26). Brooten[22] argues that women served as leaders in various synagogues during the Roman and Byzantine periods since Greek and Latin inscriptions describe women with such titles as "president of the synagogue," "leader," "elder," and "mother of the synagogue." The traditional view is that such titles are honorific and given only because their husbands held such positions. However, this claim can be maintained only if rabbinic laws were the norm for Diaspora Judaism and there is no evidence that the Diaspora looked to the rabbis of Palestine for leadership or that the "Palestinian rabbinate attempted to impose its leadership on the diaspora."[23] The notion that in ancient synagogues women sat in a gallery or side room has no literary or archaeological support.[24] Good reason exists, then, for the view that women served as leaders in various synagogues in antiquity.

---

[21]See Léonie J. Archer, "The Role of Jewish Women in the Religion, Ritual and Cult of Graeco-Roman Palestine," *Images of Women in Antiquity* (ed. A. Cameron and A. Kuhrt; Detroit: Wayne State Univ. Press, 1983): 280.

[22]B. J. Brooten, "Inscriptional Evidence for Women as Leaders in the Ancient Synagogue," (*SBLSP*; Chico: Scholars Press, 1981): 1, citing inscriptions from 27 BCE to about the sixth-century CE and range from Italy to Asia Minor, Egypt, and Palestine. See also R. S. Kraemer, *Maenads, Martyrs, Matrons, Monastics: A Source-book on Women's Religions in the Greco-Roman World* (Philadelphia: Fortress, 1988); Dorothy Irvin, "The Ministry of Women in the Early Church: The Archaeological Evidence," *Duke Divinity School Review* 45 (1980): 76-86; Harry J. Leon, *The Jews of Ancient Rome* (Philadelphia: Jewish Publication Society of America, 1960): 187ff.; and R. A. Kearsley, "Asiarchs, Archiereis, and the Archiereiai of Asia," *Greek, Roman, and Byzantine Studies* 27 (1986): 190.

[23]S. J. D. Cohen, "Women in the Synagogues of Antiquity," *Conservative Judaism* 34 (1980): 24, 27.

[24]Brooten, "Inscriptional evidence for Women as Leaders in the Ancient Synagogue," *SBLSP* (1981): 10-12, and Brooten, *Women Leaders in the Ancient Synagogue*, 122-30. See also A. R. Seager,

A question remains about the *minyan* (quorum of ten males, age thirteen or over, necessary for official synagogue services or other religious ceremonies).[25] Among others, Bruce observes that there was no synagogue in Philippi and very few Jewish males, since if ten men had been found there could have been a synagogue. Citing Mishnaic texts, he observes, "No number of women could compensate for the absence of even one man necessary to complete the quorum of ten."[26] Oster,[27] however, has argued that 1) care must be taken in using such texts to establish a homogenous pattern of Jewish practice in antiquity, 2) it is dangerous to imagine that only one text on a subject represented the beliefs and practices of all Jews, and 3) since the Mishna and Talmud did not receive their final form until well after the first century, one must not impose these later views on first-century Judaism. Thus, the argument that no synagogue existed in Philippi because there was no *minyan* is flawed.

B. *Lydia and her household.*   Lydia is mentioned at the beginning of the section in Acts 16:11 and at the end in v. 40. More than a mere travel narrative, [28] it is of theological importance that Lydia extends hospitality, in contrast to the exploitative conduct of the owners of the possessed slave girl.[29] Clues to the function of 16:11-15 and Lydia's conversion exist in the previous section (vv. 6-10) where Paul received the "Macedonian call." As the first convert in Macedonia, Lydia marks the beginning of an important stage in evangelization and continues the Lukan emphasis upon

---

"Ancient Synagogue Architecture: An Overview," *Ancient Synagogues: The State of Research* (ed. J. Gutman; Chico: Scholars Press, 1981): 46, n. 13.

[25]See *Encyclopaedia Judaica* 12: 67; and *The Universal Jewish Encyclopedia* 7:577-78.

[26]Bruce, *The Book of the Acts*, 331.

[27]Oster, "Women, Diaspora Synagogues . . . ," *Faith in Practice: Studies in the Book of Acts*, 11.

[28]Hänchen, *Acts of the Apostles*, 502.

[29]See J. A. Crampsey, *The Conversion of Cornelius (Acts 10:1-11:18): Societal Apologetic and Ecclesial Tension* (Unpublished Ph.D. dissertation, Vanderbilt Univ., 1982): 94-106.

prominent women (see 13:50; 17:4, 12, 34)[30] and the Pauline practice of looking initially in local synagogues for those who might be interested in his message.

Evidently, Lydia was a well-known name.[31] To conjecture that she was called "the Lydian" to distinguish her from other sellers of purple and that her name actually was either Euodia or Syntyche is fanciful.[32] It has been observed that "Lydia" was frequently used as a slave name, indicating that this Lydia of Acts was a freedwoman.[33] Inscriptions do mention purple dealers[34] and several in that business are designated specifically as ex-slaves.[35] However, women with the name Lydia were also of the highest rank, such as Julia Lydia of Sardis and Julia Lydia Laterane of Ephesus, high priestess and daughter of Asia.[36]

---

[30]See R. Allen Black, *The Conversion Stories in the Acts of the Apostles: A Study of Their Forms and Functions* (Unpublished Ph.D. dissertation, Emory Univ., 1985): 166-70.

[31]H. Conzelmann, *Acts of the Apostles* (trans. J. Limburg, et al., Hermeneia; Philadelphia: Fortress, 1987): 130.

[32]Hänchen, *Acts of the Apostles*, 494, n. 8, discusses this conjecture of Theodor Zahn, as well as Renan's notion that the phrase "true yoke-fellow" in 4:3 means that Paul married Lydia! The addition of ὀνόματι (name) in Acts 16:14 indicates that Lydia was a proper name. See J. H. Moulton and G. Milligan, *The Vocabulary of the Greek Testament* (London: Hodder and Stoughton, 1929): 381.

[33]J. Leipoldt, *Die Frau in der antiken Welt und im Urchristentum* (Gütersloh: G. Mohn, 1962): 109.

[34]See Rosalie Ryan, "Lydia: A Dealer in Purple Goods," *TBT* 22 (1984): 287; I. I. Ziderman, "Seashells and Ancient Purple Dyeing," *BA* 53 (1990): 98-101; and Horsley, *New Documents Illustrating Early Christianity*, 3.54.

[35]Horsley, *New Documents Illustrating Early Christianity*, 2.27, suggests that the latinized form of her name may be a clue that her former master was a Roman, especially since Philippi was a Roman colony. He also notes that a fragmentary inscription from Miletos indicates that the imperial monopoly in purple dates as far back as Nero and speculates that "those involved in the purple trade—who appear to be of freed status, as noted above—are members of the *familia Caesaris*" (28), but this must not be pressed too far.

[36]Horsley, *New Documents Illustrating Early Christianity*, 3.54.

More importantly, Lydia is described in Acts 16:14 by the much-debated phrase σεβομένη τὸν θεόν. At issue is whether reference is to Lydia as a "god-fearer," i.e., a Gentile favorably impressed with Judaism but who had not yet become a proselyte.[37] However, Kraabel[38] has denied that anything like the "god-fearers" existed and that Luke himself created the term for his own theological purpose of explaining why Gentiles responded to the Gospel and not the Jews, and to show that Gentiles replaced Jews as the people of God.[39] Alternatively, Feldman,[40] among others,[41] pre-

---

[37]*Encyclopedia Judaica* 10:55, states, "In the Diaspora there was an increasing number, perhaps millions by the first century of *sebomenoi* (*metuentes, yereim*—God-fearers), gentiles who had not gone the whole way towards conversion."

[38]R. S. MacLennan and A. T. Kraabel, "The God-Fearers—A Literary and Theological Invention," *BAR* 12 (1986): 52, note, "Luke uses the device to show how Christianity had legitimately become a gentile religion, without losing its roots in the traditions of Israel."

[39]See A. T. Kraabel, "Synagoga Caeca: Systematic Distortion in Gentile Interpretations of Evidence for Judaism in the Early Christian Period," *"To See Ourselves as Others See Us": Christians, Jews, "Others" in Late Antiquity* (ed J. Neusner and E. Frerichs: Chico: Scholars Press, 1985): 228.

[40]L. H. Feldman, "The Omnipresence of the God-Fearers," *BAR* 12 (1986): 59-68.

[41]Note extensive debate in Lake and Cadbury, "Proselytes and God Fearers," *Beginnings of Christianity*, 1,5: 74-96; L. Feldman, "'Jewish Sympathizers' in Classical Literature and Inscriptions," *Transactions of the American Philological Association* 81 (1950): 200-08; R. Markus, "The *Sebomenoi* in Josephus," *Journal of Semitic Studies* 14 (1952): 247-50; M. Wilcox, "The God Fearers in Acts: A Reconsideration," *JSNT* 13 (1981): 102-22; T. M. Finn, "The God Fearers Reconsidered," *CBQ* 47 (1985): 75-84; A. T. Kraabel, "The Diaspora Synagogue: Archaeological and Epigraphic Evidence Since Sukenik," *ANRW* 2.19.1 (Berlin: de Gruyter, 1979): 477-510; Kraabel, "The Disappearance of the God-Fearers," *Numen* 28 (1981): 113-26; Kraabel, "The Roman Diaspora: Six Questionable Assumptions," *JJS* 33 (1982): 445-64; R. F. Tannenbaum, "Jews and God-Fearers in the Holy City of Aphrodite," *BAR* 12 (1986): 55-57; J. G. Gager, "Jews, Gentiles, and Synagogues in the Book of Acts," *HTR* 79 (1986): 91-99; Kraabel, "Greeks, Jews, and Lutherans in the Middle

sents impressive circumstantial evidence from references in pagan, Christian and Jewish literature, as well as literary and epigraphic evidence to show that there was a substantial group of "sympathizers" or "semi-Jews." The famous statement of Josephus, that no one should be surprised at the wealth of the temple because Jews through-out the inhabited world and the ones σεβόμενον τὸν θεόν had contributed to it for a long time,[42] clearly contrasts two groups, the Jews and the "god-fearers." There is no convincing reason why Lydia should not be viewed as a "god-fearer" in the traditional sense, a Gentile impressed with Judaism but not yet a convert.

The baptism of the "god-fearer" Lydia "and her household" in v. 15 is consistent with the pattern seen throughout Acts. In addition, the household of the jailer is baptized (16:33) and probably that of Crispus, the ruler of the synagogue at Corinth (18:8), and Cornelius (10:47-48).[43] Vogler[44] has shown that at each of the major phases in the development of the early church, the conversion of whole households and the house churches played a major role.[45] Outside of the synagogue, the private home was the most important locale for Paul's preaching in Acts. Preaching in the synagogue often led to conflict and could not serve as a permanent base for evangelization. Access to

---

Half of Acts," *HTR* 79 (1986): 147-57; and J. A. Overman, "The God-Fearers: Some Neglected Features," *JSNT* 32 (1988): 17-26.

[42]Josephus, *Antiquities*, 14.110.

[43]Although J. Jeremias, *Infant Baptism in the First Four Centuries* (London: SCM, 1960), and *The Origins of Infant Baptism: A Further Reply to Kurt Aland* (London: SCM, 1963), detects infant baptism in these texts, K. Aland, *Did the Early Church Baptize Infants?* (London: SCM, 1963), argues convincingly that such was not the case.

[44]Werner Vogler, "Die Bedeutung der urchristlichen Hausgemeinden für die Ausbreitung des Evangeliums," *TL* 107 (1982): 790, 794.

[45]Due to the importance of her conversion for evangelization, R. L. Pervo, *Luke's Story of Paul* (Minneapolis: Fortress, 1990): 56, describes Lydia as the "Cornelius" of this new missionary phase. See F. V. Filson, "The Significance of the Early House Churches," *JBL* 58 (1939): 112.

theaters, schools, or other public facilities was not a viable option. Such a house-church posed no threat to existing political institutions and actually highlighted those values of social life held by society in general.[46] It gave a sense of belonging. The private home, therefore, provided an audience and social legitimation not available elsewhere.[47]

Hospitality was a central service provided by the house church.[48] In this connection, it is interesting that after her conversion Lydia strongly asserts that Paul and his company stay at "her house" (v. 15), an invitation Paul was reluctant to accept.[49]

---

[46]See David C. Verner, "The Household in the Hellenistic-Roman World," *The Household of God: The Social World of the Pastoral Epistles* (Chico: Scholars Press, 1983): 27-81. See also Hans-Josef Klauck, *Hausgemeinde und Hauskirche im frühen Christentum* (Stüttgart: Katholisches Bibelwirk, 1981). E. Earle Ellis, *Pauline Theology: Ministry and Society* (Grand Rapids: Eerdmans, 1989): 144-45, suggests that pagans likely viewed house-churches as religious associations (*collegium*) and for this reason local authorities were unlikely to intrude into their affairs.

[47]Following the pattern of Hellenistic teachers, speakers, and philosophers who often used the homes of private citizens, Paul and other Christian teachers used them to maximum effect. See A. Malherbe, *Social Aspects of Early Christianity* (2nd ed.; Philadelphia: Fortress, 1983): 95-96; and R. F. Hock, *The Social Context of Paul's Ministry: Tentmaking and Apostleship* (Philadelphia: Fortress, 1980): 29-30. S. Stowers, "Social Status, Public Speaking and Private Teaching: The Circumstances of Paul's Preaching Activity," *NovT* (1984): 65, 81, makes a strong case that "the widespread picture of Paul the public orator, sophist, or street-corner preacher is a false one."

[48]J. Koenig, *New Testament Hospitality* (Philadelphia: Fortress, 1985): 87, 116-17.

[49]It is not surprising that some have read modern feminist issues into the situation. R. J. Cassidy, *Society and Politics in the Acts of the Apostles* (Maryknoll: Orbis, 1988): 58, for instance, states, "Significantly, Luke portrays Paul accepting Lydia's invitation and, by implication, her challenge to a relationship involving mutuality." In another vein, Sabine Baring-Gould, *A Study of St. Paul* (London: Ibister, 1897): 213, fancied that Paul became more than a guest of Lydia and that she and Paul were either married at Philippi or would have "but for untoward circumstances" (!).

Many women in Macedonia from the Hellenistic period onward had a great amount of freedom, influence, and status. Numerous inscriptions dating from the first to the third centuries CE attest the prominent roles played by wealthy Greek women, some of whom held Roman citizenship.[50] Whether Lydia herself was wealthy or merely well-to-do is debated,[51] but apparently she had a sizeable house[52] and was involved in business.[53] It is not certain whether Lydia was married,[54] unmarried,[55] widowed,[56] or divorced.[57]

No doubt, female heads of house where the church met had some leadership role, but the nature of that leadership remains unclear. Banks[58] speculates without evidence that if

---

[50]See A. J. Marshall, "Roman Women and the Provinces," *Ancient Society* 6 (1975): 123, and further R. Van Bremen, "Women and Wealth," *Images of Women in Antiquity*, 227.

[51]W. Meeks, *The First Urban Christians: The Social World of the Apostle Paul* (New Haven: Yale Univ. Press, 1983): 62, opts for wealth.

[52]Horsley, *New Documents Illustrating Early Christianity*, 4.89-93, examined some 124 census returns from Egypt and determined that 32% of the houses were owned or partially owned by females and of these 63% are owned by a woman with no spouse.

[53]See Jane F. Gardner, "Women at Work," *Women in Roman Law and Society* (Indianapolis: Indiana Univ. Press, 1986): 228, and Eva Cantarella, *Pandora's Daughters: The Role and Status of Women in Greek and Roman Antiquity* (trans. M. Fant; Baltimore: Johns Hopkins Univ. Press, 1987): 24-34.

[54]Horsley, *New Documents Illustrating Early Christianity*, 2.28.

[55]Bruce, *Acts*, 314, but also noting the possibility of her being a widow.

[56]R. B. Rackham, *The Acts of the Apostles*, 282; Portefaix, *Sisters Rejoice*, 159. G. Stählin, *TDNT*, 9:451, n. 107, conjectures that Lydia was a widow along with others such as Tabitha, Mary, Phoebe, and Chloe, who are to be regarded as fore-runners of the congregational widows of 1 Tim. 5:3ff.

[57]Horsley, *New Documents Illustrating Early Christianity*, 4.89-93.

[58]Banks, *Paul's Idea of Community*, 127. Elizabeth Shüssler Fiorenza, "The Biblical Roots for the Discipleship of Equals," *Duke*

a wealthy or influential woman who was divorced or widowed hosted a group of believers, it is unlikely that one who managed her family, slaves, and perhaps the family business would take an insignificant role in the services in favor of socially inferior males. Instead, in the absence of a husband, the female host would behave in home and church as her husband would have done if present. It is known from Phil. 1:1 that there were elders and deacons in the church at Philippi, but it is not known from what date nor how much authority they had nor how they functioned.[59] Women in Acts have diaconal tasks, teach (18:26), and prophesy (21:9), but nowhere else in Acts do women have leading functions. Fiorenza[60] speculates that the household codes found in the NT (Eph. 5:22-6:4; Col. 3:18-25; 1 Pet. 2:18ff.; etc.) are a later patriarchal reaction to the leadership of women within the early house churches, but cannot reflect the original situation in the church where women exercised authority in worship. 1 Tim. 2:11-14, where women in the context of regulations for worship are told to be submissive and not to teach, is claimed as support, yet this text does not

---

Divinity School Review 45 (1980): 96, says no good reason exists to assume that women did not lead in worship and preside at house church meetings in their homes. See her "Women, Spirit and Power: Women in Early Christian Communities," *Women of the Spirit: Female Leadership in the Jewish and Christian Traditions* (ed. R. Reuther and E. McLaughlin; New York: Simon and Schuster, 1979): 32, and *In Memory of Her: A Feminist Theological Reconstruction of Christian Origins* (New York: Crossroad: 1983): 160-204. See also Stuart Love, "Women's Roles in Certain Second Testament Passages: A Macro-sociological View," *BTB* 17 (1987): 53.

[59]See G. F. Hawthorne, *Philippians* (WBD, 43; Waco: Word, 1983): 7-10; and R. P. Martin, *Philippians*, 61-62.

[60]E. Schüssler Fiorenza, "Women in the Pre-Pauline Churches," *USQR* 33 (1978): 156. The same line of argumentation occurs in W. Meeks, "The Image of the Androgyne: Some Uses of a Symbol in Earliest Christianity," *History of Religions* 13 (1974): 165-208; and L. Swidler, "Greco-Roman Feminism and the Reception of the Gospel," *Traditio-Krisis-Renovatio aus theologischer Sicht* (ed. B. Jaspert and R. Mohr; Marburg: Elwert, 1976): 41, i.e., early in the Pauline churches women are liberated and have equality with men but reactions set in against them later on.

contain a household code and is misapplied by Fiorenza.[61] The role of women in house churches remains speculation.

In a sense, the host of a private home acted as a patron to others such as Paul.[62] It was in the context of patron-client relations that Christianity emerged and flourished, as its leaders utilized social networks providing protection, material support, legal aid, hospitality, opportunities for employment and trade, and places for assembly.[63] Such relations were personal and "asymmetrical, in the sense that the two parties are of unequal status and offer different kinds of goods and services in the exchange."[64] The patron assisted the client who in turn enhanced the prestige, reputation, and honor of the patron.[65] While it is not known if Lydia was the force behind the generous material assistance the Philippian church rendered time and again to Paul (Phil. 4:15-18), he protected Lydia from the authorities after his arrest and release by refusing to sneak out of town, and deliberately met with the believers in her house (Acts 16:35-40).[66] It must be remembered that the patronage system "is

---

[61]See Verner, "The Household in the Hellenistic-Roman World," *The Household of God*, 92.

[62]L. M. White, "Social Authority in the House Setting and Ephesians 4:1-16," *RQ* 29 (1987): 218, is correct in observing, "The house church patrons must be looked upon as local church leaders," yet their roles in this connection remain unclear.

[63]John H. Elliott, *A Home for the Homeless: A Sociological Exegesis of 1 Peter* (Philadelphia: Fortress, 1981): 46. See also Derek Tidball, *"The Social Context of the New Testament: A Sociological Analysis* (Grand Rapids: Zondervan, 1984): 88.

[64]Richard Saller, "Patronage and Friendship in Early Imperial Rome: Drawing the Distinction," *Patronage in Ancient Society* (ed. A. Wallace-Hadrill; London: Routledge, 1989): 49.

[65]John H. Elliott, "Patronage and Clientism in Early Christian Society," *Forum* 3 (1987): 42-43. See also, Halvor Moxnes, "Patron-Client Relations and the New Community in Luke-Acts," *The Social World of Luke-Acts* (ed. J. Neyrey; Peabody, MA: Hendrickson, 1991): 241-68.

[66]See Kenneth E. Bailey, "Women in Ben Sirach and in the New Testament," *For Me To Live: Essays in Honor of James Leon Kelso* (ed. R. Coughenour; Cleveland: Dillon, 1972): 62.

characterized by an essential fluidity, ambiguity and flexibility."[67]   Although the term "patron" is not used here,[68] Paul had a genuinely personal relationship with the Philippian church. It was not legal sanctions that bound them together,[69] but the new reality of their being "in Christ."[70] So, while Paul and Lydia (and/or the Philippian church) may not have verbalized their association as a formal patron-client relationship, the patronage system was flexible enough to meet the needs of both.[71] It is strange that Lydia is not mentioned in Philippians.

2. *Euodia and Syntyche*

Euodia and Syntyche were fairly common names, as numerous inscriptions attest.[72] Undoubtedly, these two women were very important in the Philippian church and their relationship to each other and to the body of Christ concerned Paul greatly.

---

[67]Johnson and Dandeker, "Patronage: Relation and System," *Patronage in Ancient Society*, 240. See also Pheme Perkins, "Christology, Friendship and Status: The Rhetoric of Philippians," (*SBLSP*; Atlanta: Scholars Press, 1987): 515. A useful summary is Andrew Wallace-Hadrill, "Patronage in Roman Society: From Republic to Empire," *Patronage in Ancient Society*, 63-87.

[68]See T. Johnson and C. Dandeker, "Patronage: Relation and System," *Patronage in Ancient Society*, 226.

[69]*Ibid.*, 231. See also H. Montgomery, "Women and Status in the Greco-Roman World," *ST* 43 (1989): 116.

[70]White, *RQ* (1987): 221.

[71]Illustration of this flexibility is provided by Fronto, who in 163 CE wrote a recommendation to his former student, the emperor Lucius Verus, for senator Gavius Clarus, a close personal associate. Fronto indicated that Clarus, although not his client, performed duties that a client would be expected to do normally. See Saller, "Patronage and Friendship in Early Imperial Rome," *Patronage in Ancient Society*, 59, and further F. W. Danker, *Benefactor: Epigraphic Study of a Graeco-Roman and New Testament Semantic Field* (St. Louis: Clayton, 1982).

[72]See Horsley, *New Documents Illustrating Early Christianity*, 4. 178-79; and C. H. van Rhijn, "Euodia en Syntyche," *TS* 21 (1903): 300-09.

Paul notes in 4:3 that they "*fought* at my side in (spreading) the gospel." In 1:27, the term συναθλέω[73] was used to describe Paul's struggle for the gospel against opponents.[74] Acts 16 demonstrates clearly the perilous situation in which the gospel was first preached in Philippi, and Paul says that no one stood any braver than did Euodia and Syntyche in planting the church there. Now, Malinowski[75] says that while Paul calls these two women "brave Christians, unafraid of being humiliated, injured, or killed in witnessing to the Gospel," they were not ministers of the word in the way Paul and other males were at Philippi and that their help must have been in the form of rendering material support. The reference to their contending side-by-side with Paul for the gospel, however, seems to indicate full participation in the missionary effort.

While in some passages the term "gospel" focuses upon the content of what is preached (as Phil. 1:7, 12, 16; 1 Cor. 15:1), in others the activity of preaching itself is emphasized. The dative case with the noun "gospel" in 4:3 occurs elsewhere in the NT. In Rom. 1:9, the context of Paul's serving in the gospel involves his preaching the gospel in Rome. In 1 Thess. 3:2, where the noun συνεργός is used in the dative construction with ἐν, Timothy is described as God's fellow-worker in the gospel. Regarding the use in 1

---

[73]See Bauer, *Greek-English Lexicon of the NT*, 323, 783. This intensive form of ἀθλέω indicates competition or conflict, sometimes athletic or gladitorial, but here indicating hard work under pressure.

[74]Raymond Brewer, "The Meaning of Politeuesthe in Philippians 1:27," *JBL* 73 (1954): 76-83, argues that these opponents were non-Christians pressuring the Christians to participate in the imperial cult. For other views, see G. B. Caird, *Paul's Letters from Prison* (NCB; Oxford: Oxford Univ. Press, 1976): 116; J. L. Houlden, *Paul's Letters from Prison* (WC; Philadelphia: Westminster Press, 1977): 65; Hawthorne, *Philippians*, 58; J.-F. Collange, *The Epistle of Saint Paul to the Philippians* (trans. A. W. Heathcote; London; Epworth, 1979): 55-56; and E. C. Miller, "*Politeuesthe* in Philippians 1:27: Some Philological and Thematic Observations," *JSNT* 15 (1982): 86-96.

[75]Francis X. Malinowski, "The Brave Women of Philippi," *BTB* 15 (1985): 62-63.

Cor. 9:18, Friedrich[76] observes that the substantive use of
the term *gospel* is a *nomen actionis* that "describes the act of
proclamation" and notes further that "Phil. 4:3, [is] a
reference to those who help the apostle in the work of
evangelization." No doubt, Euodia and Syntyche
participated fully with Paul and the other men in evangelizing
and in so doing had the same esteem and respect as their
male counterparts.[77] As Harper[78] pointedly states, "We
should beware of the idea that when men labour in the
Gospel, they preach, but when women labour in the Gospel,
they provide refreshments and accommodation for the man."

This equality of Euodia and Syntyche in the earliest
evangelization of Philippi is indicated further by their linkage
with Clement and the rest of Paul's "fellow workers." It is
not at all clear how Fiorenza[79] arrives at the wishful
conclusion that, "Without question they were equal and
sometimes even superior to Paul in their work for the
gospel." Bertram[80] rather has the correct idea that one is not
to see in all this an unconditional equality with the apostle;
only that they had the same function in ministry as did Paul
(μοι; with me) and the rest of the male workers. References
in Paul's various epistles to "fellow workers" are several,
including that in Rom. 16:3 to Prisca. Far from being one
who only provided provisions or was limited to teaching
women, in Acts 18:26 she and her husband taught Apollos.
According to Acts 18:2, 1 Cor. 16:19, and 2 Tim. 4:19, their
home was a virtual center of evangelistic activity in several
cities. Apparently, both Euodia and Syntyche functioned in

---

[76]Gerhard Friedrich, "εὐαγγέλιον," *TDNT*, 2:729.

[77]See Darrell J. Doughty, "Women and Liberation in the
Churches of Paul and the Pauline Tradition," *The Drew Gateway* 50
(1979): 4.

[78]See J. Harper, *Women and the Gospel* (CBRF Occasional
Paper, 5 [1974]): 22, cited by R. Fung, "Ministry in the New
Testament," *The Church in the Bible and the World* (ed. D. A. Carson;
Grand Rapids: Baker, 1987): 181.

[79]Fiorenza, *In Memory of Her*, 161.

[80]Georg Bertram, "συνεργός," *TDNT*, 7:875.

much the same way as did Prisca, teaching the gospel to both men and women.[81]

Paul, however, does not describe the exact nature and circumstances of this activity. Overlooking the role of Euodia and Syntyche as "fellow workers," Stuart Love[82] rejects any public role for Christian women in spreading the gospel due to the "agrarian model" which relegated women mostly to household duties. Similarly, Sigountos and Shank[83] argue that cultural norms and not theological reflection determined what was appropriate for women, making praying and prophesying acceptable since they were controlled by the Spirit, but teaching unacceptable. However, such studies unacceptably force onto the text twentieth century conceptions of women preaching sermons in a church building to other Christians, rather than seeing public and private ministry activities by women to non-believers, as in the case of Euodia and Syntyche.[84] Problematic also is the forcing of the text into ill-fitting

---

[81]See V. Paul Furnish, "Fellow Workers in God's Service," *JBL* 80 (1961): 366; and Ellis, "Paul and His Co-Workers," *NTS* 17 (1971): 437-52. R. Scroggs, "Paul and the Eschatological Woman," *JAAR* 40 (1972): 294, argues that Euodia and Syntyche worked on an equal basis with men and reflect Paul's egalitarian attitude. However, Elaine Pagels, "Paul and Women: A Response to Recent Discussion," *JAAR* 42 (1974): 538-49, is sharply critical of Scrogg's view that Paul was a champion of women's liberation and equality. Elisabeth Shüssler-Fiorenza, "The Study of Women in Early Christianity: Some Method-ological Considerations," *Critical History and Biblical: New Testament Perspectives* (ed. T. J. Ryan; Villanova: Horizons, 1979): 50, argues that in the early church women shared fully in all aspects of ministry, but that later the church changed into a "patriarchal institution" that now perpetuates the inequality of women.

[82]Love, *BTB* (1987): 56-57.

[83]J. G. Sigountos and M. Shank, "Public Roles for Women in the Pauline Church: A Reappraisal of the Evidence," *JETS* 26 (1983): 293-95.

[84]See Alfons Weiser, "Die Rolle der Frau in der Ur-christlichen Mission," *Der Frau im Ur-christentum* (Basel: Herder, 1983): 179; and Peter Richardson, "From Apostle to Virgins: Romans 16 and the Roles of Women in the Early Church," *TJT* 2 (1986): 247.

twentieth century models of ministry. For instance, Cerling[85] argues that "fellow worker" used in reference to Euodia and Syntyche was also applied to Prisca, Aquila, and Philemon, "none of whom was a minister." This modern division of ministry into "clergy and laity," however, is unknown in the NT, where *every Christian* had a ministry of some sort.[86] As such, Euodia and Syntyche had as much a ministry as any of the males at Philippi.[87]

In 4:2-3, Paul appeals to these two women to settle their differences.[88] To each is addressed a strong appeal (παρακαλέω) for reconciliation,[89] making it unlikely that the two sided together against the remainder of the church on some matter.[90] The conflict is clearly between the two

---

[85]C. E. Cerling, "Women Ministers in the New Testament Church?" *JETS* 19 (1976): 209.

[86]See Ellis, *Pauline Theology*, 45ff.

[87]The suggestion of Portefaix, *Sisters Rejoice*, 137, that Euodia and Syntyche may have been deaconesses, is based upon no evidence.

[88]See J. A. Beet, "Did Euodia and Syntyche Quarrel?" *ET* 5 (1893-94): 179-80; and J. C. Watts, "The Alleged Quarrel of Euodia and Syntyche," *ET* 5 (1893-94): 286-87, who argues that there was no quarrel.

[89]The appeal in 4:3 for the "true yokefellow" to assist in this reconciliation strengthens the appeal. See Milan Hájek, "Comments on Philippians 4:3—Who was 'Genésios Syzygos'?" *Communio Vietorum* 7 (1964): 261-62, for the various suggestions as to the identity of this individual.

[90]Schmithals, *Paul and the Gnostics* (trans. J. Steely; Nashville: Abingdon, 1972): 76, n. 47, suggests that the two had opened their doors to heretical false-teachers. See further, R. Jewett, "Conflicting Movements in the Early Church as Reflected in Philippians," *NovT* 12 (1970): 366-90; A. F. J. Klijn, "Paul's Opponents in Philippians III," *NovT* 7 (1964): 279ff; Helmut Koester, "The Purpose of the Polemic of a Pauline Fragment," *NTS* 8 (1962): 318ff.; Chris Mearns, "The Identity of Paul's Opponents at Philippi," *NTS* 33 (1987): 201ff.; and J. Gnilka, "Die antipaulinischen Mission in Philippoi," *BZ* 9 (1965): 258-76. However, G. D. Kilpatrick, "ΒΛΕΠΕΤΕ: Philippians 3:2," *In Memoriam Paul Kahle* (ed. M. Black and G. Föhrer; Berlin: Töpelmann, 1968): 146-68, argues forcefully that there were no external opponents at Philippi.

women,[91] but the matter has come to involve the entire church.[92] Thus, Paul urged not only the two women (4:2), but the congregation in Philippi to have unity of thought and will and a uniform direction (1:27-30; 2:2, 5; 3:15) with a strong christological basis.[93] Against the background of external hostility (1:28; 3:2) certainly enhanced by this internal conflict, the appeal to unity which forms the literary thrust of the epistle culminates in the admonition to the two women in 4:2.[94] There is good reason for accepting Garland's[95] opinion that all the argumentation in the epistle was intended to shine like a laser on Paul's pastoral confrontation of these two women. He observes,

> Perhaps because Euodia and Syntyche were women, it has been tacitly assumed by many interpreters that they could be only minor players in the plot of Philippians. It is my contention that Paul carefully and covertly wove his argument to lead up to the impassioned summons in 4:2. He wrote primarily to defuse the dispute between these two women that was having disastrous repercussions for the unity of the church (173).

---

[91]Note the observation of Bernadette Brooten, "Women and the Churches in Early Christianity," *Ecumenical Trends* 14 (1985): 53, that the tendency is to trivialize conflicts between women, calling them "cat-fights," but to see disagreements between men as historic struggles over important issues.

[92]See Elizabeth Barnes, "Women in Ministry: A Matter of Discipleship," *Faith and Mission* 4 (1987): 66.

[93]Note J. Paul Sampley's, *Pauline Partnership in Christ* (Philadlephia: Fortress, 1980): 63, suggestion that the Philippians were familiar with the phrase "to think the same thing," understanding it to mean a *societas Christi*. They are to have the same love and concern for each other as Christ has in 2:5-11 (68).

[94]On the literary unity of Philippians, see D. F. Watson, "A Rhetorical Analysis of Philippians and Its Implications for the Unity Question," *NovT* 30 (1988): 57-88; and David E. Garland, "The Composition and Unity of Philippians: Some Neglected Literary Factors," *NovT* 27 (1985): 141-73.

[95]Garland, *NT* 1985): 171.

Conclusion

Women certainly brought to the evangelization of the Roman colony of Philippi essential assets which helped Christianity gain a foothold. Lydia, as a representative of the merchant class, had economic resources and the status that went with it. Her house became the center of teaching and evangelism in that city. She was a patroness to Paul. It is possible that through her influence the Philippian church supplied Paul with financial assistance over the course of several years as he took the gospel throughout the Greco-Roman world. Like Lydia, the distinguished ministries of Euodia and Syntyche were very important to the Philippian church. As fellow workers with Paul, they had shared in the evangelization of the pagan community. Their unfortunate dispute had a chilling effect on the church and its perception in the community, and the Philippian epistle was directed to the resolution of that conflict.

It is fair to conclude that women in the earlier Philippian church had equal status with the males in spreading the gospel. No barrier prevented them from teaching and evangelizing the pagan population of Philippi, both male and female. Suggestions that they were prominent leaders in the Philippian church are without foundation. The modern question of whether these women "preached" in the Christian assembly is not addressed by Paul. To focus only on that narrow aspect of ministry, as most modern studies tend to do, is to miss the point of the valuable ministerial tasks, both public and private, accomplished so well by these women.

Chapter Eleven

ADMONITIONS TO WOMEN IN 1 TIM. 2:8-15

Thomas C. Geer, Jr.

1 Timothy 2:8-15 illustrates for modern Christians as well as anything else in the NT the "strange world of the Bible." Things are said here that appear quite insensitive, and even offensive, in our present settings and arguments are used that employ reasoning foreign to the Western way of thought. Why are women not permitted to teach? What is meant by "She will be saved through childbirth?" What is the significance of grounding an argument in creation? How do we in the modern church deal responsibly with a two-thousand year old text in a setting very different from the one in which it was written? These questions must be dealt with in any serious examination of this text that has been so very influential in church order through the centuries. This text has been so influential, in fact, that a recent volume dedicated to its exposition stated in the introduction: "Many evangelicals view all biblical passages about the role and ministry of women through the lens of 1 Tim. 2:12. It becomes the key verse on women, the one on which all others turn."[1]

1. *The Literary and Historical Context*

Everything in 1 Timothy centers around how things should be done "in the house of God" (3:15). Paul[2] left

---

[1]Richard C. Kroeger and Catherine C. Kroeger, *I Suffer Not A Woman; Rethinking I Timothy 2:11-15 in Light of Ancient Evidence* (Grand Rapids: Baker, 1992): 12.

[2]The question of the authorship of the Pastoral letters in general is a continuing problem. E. Earle Ellis, *Paul and His Recent Interpreters*, (Grand Rapids: Eerdmans, 1961): 57, concluded his chapter on the

Timothy in Ephesus hoping to return there soon (3:14), and in his absence sent instructions to him.[3]   Any attempt to understand 1 Tim. 2:8-15 must recognize that it is an integral part of a letter, and that it is necessary first to delineate the larger context of the entire letter[4] before turning to this specific section within it.[5]

Pastoral epistles: "Among those favouring their genuineness are scholars representing a considerable variety of theological viewpoints: Zahn (1906), Torm (1932), Thoernell (1933), Schlatter (1936), Michaelis (1946), Spicq (1947), Behm (1948), de Zwaan (1948), Jeremias (1953), Simpson (1954), and Guthrie (1957). For a minority report, this roster is not unimpressive and, if conjecture is to be made, it may be that the future trend will lie in their direction."   Ellis' conjecture has proven true, as increasing numbers of well-respected scholars find too little evidence to conclude against possible Pauline authorship.   See Luke T. Johnson, *The Writings of the New Testament: An Interpretation* (Philadelphia: Fortress, 1986): 255-57.

[3]See John L. White, "New Testament Epistolary Literature in the Framework of Ancient Epistolography," *Aufstieg und Niedergang der römischen Welt* II. 25.2 (ed. H. Temporini and W. Haase; New York: Walter de Gruyter, 1984): 1731, and "Ancient Greek Letters," *Greco-Roman Literature and the New Testament* (ed. David E. Aune: Atlanta: Scholars Press, 1988): 86.

[4]Because little is known with precision about the status of women in ancient Ephesus and conflicting conclusions have been drawn from the sources, analysis of the larger historical context is beyond the purview of this essay.   For the purposes of this study, the context as detected within the document itself, with the limitations included, serves as the primary historical context.   For extensive bibliography on different aspects of life in Ephesus, see Richard E. Oster, *A Bibliography of Ancient Ephesus* (ATLA Bib. Ser., 19; Metuchen, NJ: The Scarecrow Press, 1987).   See also Richard E. Oster, "Ephesus as a Religious Center under the Principate, I. Paganism before Constantine," *Aufstieg und Niedergang der römischen Welt*, II 18.3 (ed. H. Temporini and W. Haasa; New York: de Gruyter, 1990): 1661-1728, and "The Ephesian Artemis as an Opponent of Early Christianity," *Jahrbuch für Antike und Christentum* 19 (Münster: Aschendorff, 1976): 24-44.

[5]This is generally recognized as appropriate exegetical procedure. See Gordon D. Fee, *New Testament Exegesis* (Philadelphia: Westminster, 1983);   John H. Hayes and Carl Holladay, *Biblical Exegesis: A Beginner's Handbook* (Atlanta: John Knox, 1982); and

Paul began with his typical greeting (1:1,2), followed by a thanksgiving (beginning in 1:3).[6] Though the thanksgiving in 1 Tim. is longer than most Pauline thanksgivings, it is clearly marked by χάριν in 1:12.[7] Since the beginning of the body of the letter is marked in 2:1[8] by παρακαλῶ (I urge), the thanksgiving extends from 1:3 through 1:20.[9]

I. H. Marshall, ed., *New Testament Interpretation: Essays on Principles and Methods* (Grand Rapids: Eerdmans, 1977).

[6]See Romans 1:8-15; 1 Cor. 1:4-9; 2 Cor. 1:3-7; Eph. 1:3-14; Phil. 1:3-11; Col. 1:3-8; 1 Thess. 1:2-10; 2 Thess. 1:3-12; 2 Tim. 1:3-5; Phlm. 4-7. For the role of the thanksgiving in the ancient letter, see Peter T. O'Brien, *Introductory Thanksgivings in the Letters of Paul*, (Göttingen: Vandenhoeck & Ruprecht, 1967): 4-15; and *idem*, "Thanksgiving Within the Structure of Pauline Theology," *Pauline Studies* (ed. D. A. Hagner and M. J. Harris; Grand Rapids: Eerdmans, 1980): 50-66, as well as P. Schubert, *Form and Function of the Pauline Thanksgivings* (Berlin: A. Töpelmann, 1939): 145-46.

[7]Χάριν also marks the thanksgiving section in 2 Tim. 1:3.

[8]John L. White, "Introductory Formulae in the Body of the Pauline Letter," *JBL* 90 (1970):93; and *idem, Aufstieg und Niedergang der römischen Welt* (II. 25.2): 1744. See 1 Cor. 1:10 and Phlm. 9-10.

[9]For discussion of the literary structure and outline, see P. Bush, "A Note on the Structure of I Timothy," *NTS* 36 (1990): 152-56:

    I. Greeting (1:1, 2)
   II. Introductory background (1:3-11)
  III. The body of the letter (1:12-6:21a)
      A. Inclusio - Passing on the Gospel under Paul's supervision (1:12-20)
      B. How to conduct oneself in the house of God (2:1-3:15)
        -Practical instructions
           (concluding marker: 3:14,15)
      C. The sound doctrine of godliness (3:16-4:11)
        - Attack on apostasy   (concluding marker: 4:11)
      D. Instructions to Timothy about leadership (4:12-6:2)
        - Practical Instructions (concluding marker: 6:2b)
      E. Dealing with the apostate (6:3-10)
        - Attack on apostasy
        - 6:17-19 belong here   (concluding marker: 6:17)
      F. Inclusio - Passing on the Gospel under God's supervision (6:11-16, 20,21a)
  IV. Greeting (6:21b)

The thanksgiving in ancient letters, consisting of much more than an expression of thanks from the author to the recipient, also introduces the body of the letter.[10]

It is clear from 1:3-7 that Paul is very concerned with false teachers and false teaching. He reminds Timothy that he left him in Ephesus to instruct certain people (τισίν[11]) not to teach different teachings. Included in those "different teachings" were myths (v. 4), endless genealogies (1:4), some sort of teaching about "law"[12] or "the Law"[13] (1:7), and meaningless talk (1:7). Though some of the false teaching involved the Law,[14] the Law itself was not the

---

I disagree with Bush only in that I see the inclusio sections as part of the thanksgiving and conclusion, respectively, rather than as the beginning and end of the body. For the signal of the end of the thanksgiving, see Terence Y. Mullins, "Disclosure: A Literary Form in the New Testament," *NovT* 7 (1964): 44-50.

[10]Terence Y. Mullins, *NovT* (1964): 44-50. See also Jack T. Sanders, "The Transition From Opening Epistolary Thanksgiving to Body in the Letters of the Pauline Corpus," *JBL* 81 (1962): 361.

[11]Though sometimes translated "certain *men*" (NIV), the indefinite pronoun may refer to either women or men (see RSV, JB, NRSV—"certain people").

[12]Some have suggested that Paul's reference to "law" here may not be a reference to the Mosaic traditions, but to standards in general. See J. N. D. Kelly, *A Commentary on the Pastoral Epistles* (New York: Harper and Row, 1963): 49; C. Spicq, *Les Épîtres pastorales* (Paris: J. Gabalda et Cie, 1969): 331.

[13]Others think that Paul is actually speaking of the Mosaic Law at this point. See Ronald A. Ward, *Commentary on 1 & 2 Timothy & Titus* (Waco: Word, 1974): 32, 33; Homer A. Kent, *The Pastoral Epistles* (Chicago: Moody, 1958): 84-89; M. Dibelius and H. Conzelmann, *The Pastoral Epistles* (Philadelphia: Fortress, 1972): 22; Donald Guthrie, *The Pastoral Epistles* (Grand Rapids: Eerdmans, 1957): 60, 61; Walter Lock, *A Critical And Exegetical Commentary on the Pastoral Epistles* (Edinburgh: T. & T. Clark, 1924): 33.

[14]The presence of the article at the first mention of the law in v. 7 indicates the law of Moses is intended. Also, one might wonder why Paul would be thinking of anything else with νόμος (law); the Law of Moses was the focus of so much attention in his ministry among Gentiles, some of whom had been greatly influenced by the Law. It is quite clear that in general Paul thought standards were very important

problem, for "We know that the Law is good, if one uses it legitimately" (1:8). Although Paul refers to the misuse of the Law, there is no indication that these are "Judaizers."[15] Paul's frustration is with a much wider syncretism among these teachers. Such misinformation clearly leads to serious life-style problems (vv. 8-11).[16] Paul illustrates from his own past in verses 12-17 the woeful results of such misinformation in his own life.[17]

Verses 18-20 conclude the thanksgiving-introduction. They remind Timothy of his mission in Ephesus and encourage him to maintain his faith and good conscience. The latter is particulary important for Paul, for he mentions two, Hymenaeus and Alexander,[18] who suffered shipwreck in the faith because they rejected their consciences. More than a derogatory reference to false teachers, vv. 18-20 are actually the focus of the introduction and point decisively to the conclusion in 6:3-20. While Paul's earlier emphasis in the thanksgiving was on the false teachers, his conclusion of this section makes it clear that he is primarily concerned with Timothy's own conduct in the current situation, particularly with regard to those false teachers.

Moving into the body of the letter (2:1), Paul introduces items concerning appropriate Christian behavior (2:1-15),

---

for the Christian lifestyle; it was the misuse of the Law of Moses that he protested so greatly. Thus it is unwise to see Paul concerned with legalism in Lutherian terms when he refers to "law." Supporting this is the list of sins in vv. 9-10 that have been recognized to reflect some of the major aspects of the Decalogue. See E. K. Simpson, *The Pastoral Epistles* (Grand Rapids: Eerdmans, 1954): 29-30.

[15]Against Neil McEleney, "The Vice Lists of the Pastoral Epistles," *CBQ* 36 (1974): 204-10.

[16]Against R. J. Karris, "The Function and Significance of the Polemic of the Pastoral Epistles," *JBL* 92 (1973): 549-64.

[17]With Kelly, *The Pastoral Epistles*, 52, who accurately understands vv. 12-17 to point back to vv. 3-11, against Simpson, *The Pastoral Epistles*, 32-37, who detects no such development.

[18]The mention of these two, also appearing separately in 2 Tim. 2:17 and 4:14, makes it obvious that Paul would not permit male false teachers to teach in Ephesus.

and then includes details concerning the leadership of the local congregation (3:1-13). That these two chapters deal primarily with community matters is affirmed at 3:14,15:

> I wrote these things to you, hoping to come to you soon; but since I am delayed, I wrote so that you may know how we must behave *in the house of God, which is the church of the living God*, the pillar and ground of the truth.

Paul follows this with a brief christological statement (3:15) in which the behavior called for in the first three chapters is grounded. In 4:1-6:2, Paul addresses Timothy directly about some of the specific problems in the Ephesian house churches, including the false-teaching, and how he is to deal with the situation with integrity. 1 Tim. 6:3-20, then, concludes the brief letter by reminding Timothy of the misguided desires of the false teachers and how he is to conduct himself and approach his task.

Despite all this emphasis on false teaching, there is very little direct information concerning the identity of the false teachers themselves. Judging from Paul's conclusion (6:17-20), many of the false teachers may have seen their false teaching as a means of accumulating wealth but still the identity of the false teachers is simply not specified clearly enough to know for certain—we cannot even be sure whether they were Jews or Gentiles.

Also, we can ascertain the content of the false teaching only from what is in the text.[19] This presents problems to

---

[19]M. Dibelius and Hans Conzelmann, *The Pastoral Epistles*, 66, suggest that the kind of problem indicated in 1 Tim. may be "attributed to a kind of Gnosticisim. However, it is impossible to identify the particular heresy attacked here with one of the Gnostic sects known to us." Kelly, *The Pastoral Epistles*, 11, adds, "The most obvious characteristic of the heresy is its combination of Jewish and Gnostic ingredients." And later (12), "It is perhaps best defined as a Gnosticizing form of Jewish Christianity." Obviously, specifics are unattainable.

the modern interpreter because Paul and Timothy might have conversed on an earlier occasion about some things which Paul does not, then, include in this letter. However, it is clear that the false teaching was, in some way, connected with the OT (1:6-10). This accounts for the details of asceticism (4:3; 5:23) along with the endless myths and genealogies (1:4; 4:7). The brief descriptions of the teachers in 1:3-7 and 6:3-10, coupled with the instructions for appropriate leaders in 3:1-13, indicate that there were both theological and ethical deviations.

Reflected in the letter is, at minimum, a blending of Christianity with certain aspects of Hellenistic Judaism very similar to what had happened earlier in Corinth and Colossae. 1 Tim. 6:20 refers to what is falsely called "knowledge" and there were those in Corinth and Colossae who had become infatuated with knowledge and considered themselves the "spiritual ones" (see 1 Cor. and Col. 2:3-8). In Ephesus, some had begun to deny sexual relations within marriage (1 Tim. 4:3) and a future bodily resurrection (see 2 Tim. 2:18 which is connected to 1 Tim. by the mention of Hymenaeus). Both items are reflected in 1 Cor. (see 1 Cor. 7:1-7 for the call to celibacy and see 1 Cor. 15:12 for the denial of a bodily resurrection) and the denial of marriage is probably reflected in the ascetic tendencies among the Colossians (see Col. 2:16-23).

The similarities in the situations in Corinth, Colossae, and Ephesus are not just coincidental. As the church progressed westward from Jerusalem, syncretism became an increasingly serious problem.[20] Paul realized that the mixture he was observing was just as dangerous to "the truth of the Gospel" as the Judaizers he had to combat in other places. This early syncretism no doubt gave rise to all sorts of problems, but it is best to see in Paul's own lifetime the

---

[20]For insights into how prevalent syncretism was in religious circles just prior to and within the first century, see Everett Ferguson, *Backgrounds of Early Christianity* (Grand Rapids: Eerdmans, 1987): esp. 180, 252, 307.

early syncretism that later led to the more fully developed heresies and not the heresies themselves.[21]

2. *1 Timothy 2:8-15 Within the Letter*

Important concerns of the overall letter surface within this paragraph, particularly in regard to teaching and women. All of 2:1-15 deals with appropriate Christian behavior in Ephesus, and the ἐν παντὶ τόπῳ of v. 8 makes it clear that verses 8-15[22] deal primarily, though not perhaps exclusively, with the Christian assembly.[23]

The paragraph begins with βούλομαι οὖν (therefore, I wish). Although παρακαλέω (I exhort) is the typical word Paul uses to express strong directives in his letters, it has

---

[21]It must be noted that the situation in both Colossae and Corinth can be described without resorting to Gnosticism. See R. McL. Wilson, "How Gnostic were the Corinthians?" *NTS* 19 (1972-72): 65-74, and M. D. Hooker, "Were There False Teachers in Colossae?" *Christ and Spirit in the New Testament* (ed. B. Lindars and S. Smalley; Cambridge: Cambridge Univ. Press, 1973): 315-32.

[22]There is some debate about where the paragraph should begin. Both the NA[26] and the UBS[3] begin the paragraph with v. 8. English translations that start a new paragraph with v. 8 include RSV, NRSV, NIV. The Jerusalem Bible presents v. 8 has an additional paragraph within vv. 1-8 and begins a new section at v. 9.

The question revolves specifically around whether οὖν (therefore) or ὡσαύτως (likewise) is the discourse marker for a new paragraph. Both Greek conjunctions build on a previous statement. Some have suggested the paragraphs should be divided 1-8 and 9-15, since the first eight verses deal with men and the next seven deal with women. I have chosen to recognize a new paragraph at v. 8 because of the οὖν and because vv. 8-15 all seem to deal with more of a worship setting within the larger framework of appropriate Christian behavior.

[23]See Everett Ferguson, "'τόπος' in I Timothy 2:8," *RQ* 33 (1991): 65-73; Lock, *The Pastoral Epistles*, 30. Jerome Murphy-O'Connor, "Community and Apostolate," *TBT* 67 (1973): 1260-1266, has suggested that Paul's primary concern in 2:1-7 has to do with Christian behavior and not just on what happens within a worship setting. It seems to me that for the verses following that point is continued, but with special emphasis on Christian behavior in the assembly and the impact that may make on the community of Ephesus.

been suggested that in the Pastoral epistles Paul employs βούλομαι to indicate an apostolic command.[24] The οὖν indicates that his directives of this paragraph are based on 2:1-7, particularly 2:7, in which he recalls his appointment as a herald, apostle, and teacher of the Gentiles, backed up with his solemn, "I speak the truth, I do not lie."[25] Based on his authority as "herald, apostle, and teacher of Gentiles," he expresses his desire for what should take place in the worship of the predominantly Gentile churches of Ephesus.

A major ambiguity in the text is whether ἀνήρ is to be taken as "man" or "husband," and whether γυνή should be translated as "woman" or "wife." There is no way to know for certain which Paul meant. However, in this immediate context, in which Paul mentions Adam and Eve and the possibility of child bearing, Paul probably means for his readers to understand his terms as "husband" and "wife."[26]

Paul desires that prayers should be made in every assembly without anger and arguments. The phrase "raising holy hands," which has received the most attention from this verse, is in fact a circumstantial participial phrase. Paul

---

[24]1 Tim. 5:14; Titus 3:8. See Dietrich Müller, "βούλομαι," *The New International Dictionary of New Testament Theology* (ed. Colin Brown; Grand Rapids: Zondervan, 1978): 3.1017.

[25]See Paul's use of this solemn phrase in Rom. 9:1; 2 Cor. 1:23; 11:31; 1 Thess. 2:5; and Gal. 1:20. For discussion, see J. Paul Sampley, "'Before God, I Do Not Lie' (Gal.1.20) Paul's Self-Defence in the Light of Roman Legal Praxis," *NTS* 23 (1977): 477-82.

[26]The following think Paul means women in general here, though of course applicable to the marriage relationship: Dibelius and Conzelmann, *The Pastoral Epistles*, 44-49; Lock, *The Pastoral Epistles*, 31; C. K. Barrett, *The Pastoral Epistles* (Oxford: Clarendon, 1963): 53-54; Simpson, *The Pastoral Epistles*, 45-46; and Guthrie, *The Pastoral Epistles*, 73-79.

The following think Paul means wife here: N. J. Hommes, "Let Women Be Silent in Church . . .," *Calvin Theological Review* 4 (1969): 5-22; Douglas J. Moo, "I Timothy 2:11-15: Meaning and Significance," *Trinity Journal* 1 (1980): 63-64. In the rest of this essay "women" and "men" will be used, with the realization that the terms may be more specific than those words indicate.

typically assumed that hands would be lifted in prayer.[27] He is not wishing for that; he assumes it. He wishes that prayer could take place in the assemblies without interruption from arguments. This anticipates the situation Paul describes in 6:3-5, where he says that quarreling, wrath, disputing, and controversy resulted from those who taught false doctrine.

It is sometimes assumed that since Paul used ἀνήρ (male) here he therefore disqualified women from praying in the Ephesian assemblies.[28] It is true that Paul addresses this particular concern to men, but may he not have done so because the problem with arguments at prayer times in the assembly was one among the men, not the women? Paul's use of ἀνήρ by itself does not automatically indicate that women were excluded from this activity. In fact the ὡσαύτως of v. 9 *may* relate back to the concept of praying in v. 8. Just as he wants men to pray without arguments, Paul wants women to pray "in modest clothing" (ἐν καταστολῇ/ κοσμίῳ).[29] His concern for that is apparently strong, for he takes several lines to explain in some detail what he means:

---

[27]See Barrett, *The Pastoral Epistles*, 54. For gestures accompanying prayer in antiquity, see Ludwig von Sybel, *Christliche Antike* (Marburg: Elwert, 1906): 256-58.

[28]Apparently, this general conclusion is drawn from passages such as Matt. 14:21. But there it is explicitly stated that women and children are not included. In several other places, where that distinction is not made, it would seem unwise to make it. For example, Acts 1:16; 2:5, 14, 22; James 1:8, 12, 20, 23; 3:2. Paul's use of ἀνήρ in 1 Tim., wherever distinguishable (2:12; 3:2, 12; 5:9), refers to husbands. But the general question remains. Even if Paul instructs husbands here specifically to pray without arguments, does that necessarily exclude women from praying at all?

[29]This possibility provides, of course, a nice corollary to 1 Cor. 11, where Paul admits that women are prophesying; he just wants them to be dressed appropriately when they do. See Dibelius and Conzelmann, *The Pastoral Epistles*, 45, and Spicq, *Les Épîtres pastorales*, 374-75. Καταστολή is an ambiguous term denoting both life-style and clothing. See K. H. Rengstorf, "στέλλω," *TDNT*, 2: 595-96. That Paul intentionally used a word with this ambiguity is suggested by the following discussion in which he speaks of both aspects.

". . . the women should adorn themselves modestly[30] and sensibly,[31] not with braided hair, with gold pearls, or expensive clothes,[32] but with good works."[33]

The first imperative of the paragraph occurs in v. 11, μανθανέτω: a woman "must learn" in quietness and complete submission. Paul's emphasis on a woman's learning is important; he obviously assumes that women are learning as part of the assemblies. But while he wants women to learn,

---

[30]Like καταστολή, αἰδώς is ambiguous. It can refer either to modesty or reverence–again, the distinction between dress and behavior. See Walter Bauer, *A Greek-English Lexicon of the New Testament and Other Early Christian Literature* (trans. W. F. Arndt and F. W. Gingrich, 2nd ed. rev. and aug. by F. W. Gingrich and F. W. Danker: Chicago: Univ. of Chicago Press, 1979): 22. See also J. P. Louw and E. A. Nida, ed., *Greek-English Lexicon of the New Testament Based on Semantic Domains* (2 vols.; New York: United Bible Societies, 1988): 748, who suggest "the quality of modesty with the implication of resulting respect."

[31]Σωφροσύνη seems to be limited to behavior, including "reasonableness, rationality, mental soundness, good judgment, moderation, and self control." See W. Bauer, *A Greek-English Lexicon of the New Testament and Other Early Christian Literature*, 802. Louw and Nida, *A Greek–English Lexicon of the New Testament Based on Semantic Domains*, 753, suggest, "to behave in a sensible manner, with the implication of thoughtful awareness of what is best."

[32]Alan Padgett, "Wealthy Women at Ephesus; I Timothy 2:8-15 in Social Context," *Int* 41 (1987): 19-31, says "This concern for modesty in dress was also a standard Greco-Roman virtue for women." Yet the selection of what not to wear indicates that these women were wealthy. See also the parallel in Juvenal *Satire* 6.457-60: "There is nothing that a woman will not permit herself to do, nothing that she deems shameful, when she encircles her neck with green emeralds, and fastens huge pearls to her elongated ears: there is nothing more intolerable than a wealthy woman." Although Paul lists what the women are not to wear, the point is probably still about behavior rather than appearance, though here their behavior is grounded in their appearance. By wearing such things the women would be arrogant and elite, attitudes not conducive to a strong sense of community at worship.

[33]This last phrase confirms that Paul's main concern is with behavior and not appearance.

he is again concerned with the manner in which they learn—
he demands that they learn ἡσυχίᾳ (in quietness). Ἡσυχία
(quietness) deals with demeanor, that is, a quiet spirit; it
does not demand total silence.[34] To whom is the learning
woman to be in subjection? Elsewhere, Paul sees
"submission" as a dynamic within a community (Eph. 5:21),
and also in the marriage relationship (Eph. 5:22; Col. 3:18).
The following verses, in which the argument is built on
Adam and Eve and on child bearing, suggest that Paul would
be thinking primarily of the marriage relationship, though
that he would require submission to the leaders of the church
cannot be excluded.[35]

Paul does not simply say how he wants women to learn;
he proceeds to add a negative aspect: "I am not permitting
(ἐπιτρέπω[36]) a woman to teach (διδάσκειν) or to be
domineering (αὐθεντεῖν[37]) over a man, but to conduct

---

[34]M. J. Harris, "Quiet, Rest, Silence, Sound, Voice, Noise," *The New International Dictionary of New Testament Theology* (ed. C. Brown; Grand Rapids: Zondervan, 1978): 3. 111, 12. See also 1 Tim. 2:2. When Paul wished to specify silence he usually used σιγάω (1 Cor. 14:28, 30, 34). In 2 Thess. 3:12, it is clear that Paul does not imply silence with this word, but intends "a quiet/gentle manner."

[35]For the suggestion that Paul intends "the officials and regulations of the church," see Lock, *The Pastoral Epistles*, 32.

[36]There is a certain ambiguity in Paul's use of the present tense. According to H. W. Smyth, *Greek Grammar* (Cambridge: Harvard Univ. Press, 1920): 421, the Greek present tense may be used to indicate "customary action" or a "general truth," but "the present stem may denote the simple action of the verb in the present time without regard to its continuance" (414). Since Paul uses no modifiers to indicate a wider audience or larger time frame, the simple action is implied, meaning that it is unwise to export this statement out of 1 Tim. into other contexts and other times.

[37]This term has been the subject of much attention. Among others, see George W. Knight III, "'ΑΥΘΕΝΤΕΩ' in Reference to Women in I Timothy 2.12," *NTS* 30 (1984): 143-57; Armin J. Panning, "ΑΥΘΕΝΤΕΙΝ—A Word Study," *Wisconsin Lutheran Quarterly* 78 (1981): 185-91; Carroll D. Osburn, "ΑΥΘΕΝΤΕΩ (I Timothy 2:12)," *RQ* (1982): 1-11; L. Wilshire, "The TLG Computer and Further Reference to ΑΥΘΕΝΤΕΩ in I Timothy 2.12," *NTS* 34 (1988): 120-34. Much of the discussion has centered around the nature

herself (literally, "to be") in a quiet spirit or demeanor (ἡυχία)."   The concern about a "domineering" woman may reflect the general attitude in antiquity about women assuming the role of teacher.[38] Because of the authority inherent in the role of a teacher in antiquity, it is possible that any woman teacher may well have been regarded as domi-

---

of the word, that is, whether it involves a negative or neutral concept. As helpful as historical studies of words are, the final decision must be based on the word's context in its paragraph. Here Paul does seem to use it in a rather negative way.

[38]James G. Sigountos and Myron Shank, "Public Roles for Women in the Pauline Church: A Reappraisal of the Evidence [I Cor.11:2-16; I Cor. 14:33-36; I Tim. 2:15]," *JETS* 26 (1983): 289, observe:

> The Greek view of teachers prevented 'respectable' women from occupying that role. Greek education was centered around a master who had a deep, personal, extended relationship with his pupils. Originally this relationship included pederasty. While the sexual element receded, reverence for the teacher never did. By definition he was an authority figure. The paucity of women teachers, then, is not surprising. Because of the authority inherent in the Greek conception of the role, women teachers would have been unacceptably domineering. They could not have been teachers and still have appeared to be the submissive figures society demanded them to be.

This state of affairs can be acknowledged without concluding as Catherine C. Kroeger does that the women teachers typically afforded sexual favors. For her view see "Ancient Heresies and a Strange Greek Verb," *The Reformed Journal* 29 (1979): 60-63. For her more recent, modified view, see Catherine C. Kroeger, "Women in the Church: A Classicist's View of I Tim 2:11-15," *Journal of Biblical Equality* 1 (1989): 3-31. In response to this latter article, see Elodie Ballantine Emig, "Response to Catherine Kroeger on I Timothy 2," *Journal of Biblical Equality* 1 (1989): 32-38; Robert L. Hubbard, Jr., "Response to Catherine Kroeger on I Timothy 2," *Journal of Biblical Equality* 1 (1989): 39-43; and Craig Blomberg, "Response to Catherine Kroeger on I Timothy 2," *Journal of Biblical Equality* 1 (1989): 44-49. In her most recent contribution to the discussion, C. Kroeger argues for the translation, "I do not permit a woman to teach nor to represent herself as originator of man . . . ." See Richard Clark Kroeger and Catherine Clark Kroeger, *I Suffer Not a Woman*, 79-104, esp. 103.

neering. While that may well be part of the dynamic of this situation, Paul seems to be more concerned throughout this letter about women teaching incorrect things than merely to their presence as possible teachers.[39] In fact, Paul probably intends to communicate the idea of women "domineering in their teaching,"[40] a "domineering" which is made worse by the deficient and/or erroneous content of their instruction.

The γάρ [for] of v. 13 indicates that Paul's statements in verses 9-12 are grounded in what he adds in vv. 13 -15.[41]

---

[39]There is, in fact, no indication that Paul is concerned with women overstepping someone else's "authority." For years, the discussion has centered around that issue and it is simply not a part of Paul's argument. Paul is just as against men domineering as he is women (e.g., Eph. 5:21; 1 Cor. 11:11,12). In Ephesus, he is facing the issue of domineering women. In a more general sense, it is inappropriate, in a church in which Jesus has been given all authority (Matt. 28:19-20), for individuals to be overly concerned with power/authority issues.

[40]Both infinitives διδάσκειν and αὐθεντεῖν have ἀνδρός as a direct object. The object is in the genitive case because αὐθεντέω takes the genitive for its direct object and "the case of an object common to two verbs is generally that demanded by the nearer," Smyth, *Greek Grammar*, 364. Smyth also suggests (365) that "the farther verb may contain the main idea." This suggests that the "domineering" is understood as something that is accomplished by teaching; implying, then, not two distinct prohibitions, but one. In a paper delivered at a recent Society of Biblical Literature meeting, Andreas J. Köstenberger analyzed syntactical parallels to this verse in extrabiblical Greek literature. In forty-eight citations that are syntactically parallel to the structure of this phrase, Köstenberger found that all of them express some type of parallelism between the first infinitive and the second. He found six kinds of parallels: 1) Synonymous (14 instances), 2) Conceptual (18 instances), 3) Complementary (2 instances), 4) Sequential (5 instances), 5) Ascensive (7 instances), and 6) Specific to general (1) or general to specific (1).

[41]Richard Clark Kroeger and Catherine Clark Kroeger, *I Suffer Not a Woman*, 105-113, argue that the γάρ is quite appropriate since Paul is arguing against those who, based on the worship of the mother goddess, were teaching that the female is the originator of the male. While that certainly may be part of the matrix of the Ephesian

Unfortunately, these three verses are among the most difficult for modern interpreters of any Paul wrote. I am indebted to a conversation with Carroll Osburn for the suggestion that v. 13, "for Adam was formed first, then Eve,"[42] comments upon the earlier statement, "I am not permitting a woman to domineer over a man," and that v. 14, "and Adam was not deceived, but the woman was deceived and became a transgressor," comments on the other earlier statement, "I am not permitting a woman to teach." Paul bases his arguments on the creation stories in Genesis.

I am inclined to agree with Osburn[43] that the reference in v. 13 to Adam's being formed first, then Eve, has nothing to do with the "order of creation" argument in which man is seen as superior to woman, but with the nature and purpose of her creation, i.e., as man was incomplete, woman was created as a complement. When, in this instance, the intended complementary relationship between man and woman is destroyed due to the domineering attitude of the women, Paul's appeal to remember that woman was created after man is not an appeal for a return to male dominance and female subjection, but to return to a complementary role.

It is my view that something about Eve being deceived is the basis for his appeal in v. 14. What makes this reference appropriate is that, apparently, the false teachers of the Ephesian house-churches had found fertile ground among the women; from Paul's point of view, they have been deceived, much as was Eve in Genesis 3. Although it is clear from Genesis 3 that Adam was perhaps more culpable since he was deceived only second hand, that is not the issue in this text. Though the false teachers have been

---

situation, it does not seem to answer all the questions of Paul's comments in these three verses.

[42] See Sirach 25:24: "From a woman sin had its beginning, and because of her we all die." For other Jewish writings that attribute the origin of sin to Eve, see Bruce J. Malina, "Origin of Sin in Judaism and St. Paul," *CBQ* 31 (1969): 24.

[43] See Carroll D. Osburn, *Women in the Church: Refocusing the Discussion* (Abilene, TX: Restoration Perspectives, 1993).

deceived, the issue facing Timothy is their deception of the women. Because these particular women have been deceived as Eve was deceived, Paul does not permit them to teach.[44] Certainly, Paul would not want Timothy to allow the male false teachers to teach either, but that is an obvious point and not the concern here. In chiastic style,[45] Paul bases his arguments for behavior among the Ephesian women on the Genesis material,[46] not with reference to some inherent hierarchical structure as such, but on the events and how they correspond to the situation in Ephesus.

It is generally agreed that v. 15 qualifies vv. 13, 14, but the nature of that qualification is widely debated. V. 15 is set up by the last phrase of v. 14, "But the woman was deceived and became a transgressor." Again, there is no mention of male culpability, for that is not the point of concern at Ephesus. The woman, being deceived, has become a transgressor. However, Paul does not leave the

---

[44]Paul was vague about the identity of those "teaching other doctrines" in 1:3; here it becomes clear that at least among those Paul was targeting were some deceived women.

[45]Thus, Osburn suggests the following chiastic structure:

    a   I am not permitting a woman to teach
     b nor domineer over a man
     b′ for Adam was formed first, then Eve
    a′   the woman, when she was deceived, became a
              transgressor

[46]Many conclude that Paul's statements in this passage have no situational basis in Ephesus because his response is based on the creation account. This view reflects lack of awareness of how Paul worked among his churches and how his letters originally functioned. Paul is not writing a theological treatise, but is responding to a situation with arguments, not because they are the only arguments that might be brought to bear on a particular situation, but ones he thought would modify behavior. Note 1 Cor. 11:2-16, where Paul includes an argument from creation, but obviously was not convinced that it was the end of the matter since he went on to introduce other arguments into the discussion. Those who argue that Paul's statements do not reflect situations because they are grounded in creation must explain why Paul speaks of a "new creation" in Christ and has already said that "in Christ there is . . . neither male nor female," yet here builds on the original creation story to make his point.

deceived women in that position, noting, "*She* shall be saved through [the] childbirth if *they* remain in faith and love and holiness with reverence." At least four views exist of what Paul means, none of which is free from difficulties:

1) Christian women are not saved through teaching and domineering, but by attention to their traditional role, represented by bearing children.[47]
2) Despite Eve's transgression, Christian women will be saved through *the* childbirth, namely the coming of the messiah.[48]
3) Despite the curse (Gen. 3:16), Christian women are brought safely through the birth experience.[49]
4) In their proper role, Christian women disdain teaching and domineering over men.[50]

---

[47]At present, this seems to be the majority view. See Robert Falconer, "I Timothy 2 14,15. Interpretive Notes," *JBL* 60 (1941): 375-79. Kelly, *The Pastoral Epistles*, 69; Spicq, *Les Épîtres pastorales*, 382-83; Paul W. Barnett, "Wives and Women's Ministry (I Tim. 2:11-15)," *EvQ* 61 (1989): 225-38; Douglas Moo, *Trinity Journal* (1980): 71-73; Krijn A. Van der Jagt, "Women are Saved Through Bearing Children (I Timothy 2.11-15)," *BT* 39 (1988): 201-08.

[48]This was the prevalent interpretation among the Western Church Fathers, though it never found much support in the East.   For more recent advocates of this view, see C. J. Ellicott, *Commentary on the Pastoral Epistles* (2nd ed.; Andover: Draper, 1897): 54; Lock, *The Pastoral Epistles*, 33; Philip B. Payne, "Libertarian Women in Ephesus: A Reponse to Douglas J. Moo's Article, 'I Timothy 2.11-15: Meaning and Significance,'" *Trinity Journal* 1 (1981): 169-97; Thomas C. Oden, *First and Second Timothy and Titus* (Louisville: John Knox Press, 1989): 100-02; Kent, *The Pastoral Epistles*, 118, 119; Mark D. Roberts, "So Men Shall Be Saved: A Closer Look at I Timothy 2:15," *TSF Bulletin* (1981): 4-7, and "Woman Shall Be Saved; a closer look at I Timothy 2:15," *The Reformed Journal* (1983): 18-22.

[49]See the translation by James Moffatt, and C. F. D. Moule, *An Idiom-Book of New Testament Greek* (Cambridge: Cambridge Univ. Press, 1971): 56. For a view closely connected with this one, that Christian women will be saved even though they must bear children, see E. F. Scott, *The Pastoral Epistles* (London: Harper, 1936): 28.

[50]See S. Jebb, "A Suggested Interpretation of I Tim 2^{15}," *Expository Times* 81 (1969-70): 221.

These four views are easily reduced to two. The third possibility demands an unnatural meaning for διά, and places too much emphasis on the curse, which involved the pain of childbirth, not the act of childbirth. It has two other difficulties: (1 it is simply not true to experience since many Christian women have died while giving birth and (2 Paul uses σώζω (save) to refer to redemption from sin, not to being "kept safe" in a dangerous situation.[51] The fourth view includes the same problems as the third with the additional unlikelihood that Paul would speak of being saved from the errors of vv. 11-12 without saying so explicitly.

While it is is easy to reduce the discussion to the first two alternatives, it is difficult to decide between them. As mentioned earlier, the first view appears to be the predominant one presently (see n. 46). It has in its support Paul's concern elsewhere in the letter that women maintain their proper roles in their families (see especially 5:14). Paul mentions childbirth as a symbol of a typically well-run family. Though the women have been deceived, they will be saved through maintaining their role in the family structure.

While there is a certain plausibility in seeing the statements in this way, interpreting the phrase along these makes the last part of the verse redundant. Is not the woman's proper role indicated even better by "If they remain in faith and love and holiness with modesty," than by "Through (the) childbirth"? Why the mention of bearing children at all, especially since it leaves out of consideration any unmarried woman or married woman who was unable to give birth?

Paul is probably referring primarily to "the birth," viz., Mary's birth of Jesus. This makes good sense of the Greek article preceding "child bearing," which would be strange in a discussion about childbearing in general,[52] and of the

---

[51]In the Pastorals, Paul uses ῥύομαι for the concept of being rescued or being kept safe. See 2 Tim. 3:11 and 2:4.

[52]Even if this is considered a "generic article" as some have argued, its presence still more appropriately refers to a particular birth.

change from singular (she) to plural (if they remain). If Paul had one particular, history-changing birth in mind, the article is appropriate and the shift in number would be expected. This also fits the context better than the other suggestions. Paul arrived at this conclusion after referring to Adam and Eve and particularly Eve's deception, which set in motion a series of events that put all of humanity in a fallen state. What better way to address that ultimate transgression than by God's answer in Jesus?

If there is any plausibility to this suggestion, then Paul is very near Romans 5:12-20, where, responding to a completely different set of circumstances, he mentions Adam's sin and the result it had on the rest of humanity. But through Jesus Christ, that was corrected. In 1 Tim., where the women are the focus, Paul uses the same concepts, but from a different direction. Now Eve is on center stage instead of Adam and woman is the focus instead of man. But unlike the man, the woman was both part of the problem (Eve) *and* part of the solution (Mary).

Thus, Paul is not making a radically strange statement that may be taken to mean that a woman earns salvation through giving birth or even by performing usual household duties. Rather, like men, women are saved through Jesus Christ. However, women have an intricate connection to God's saving activity, since he chose for his son to enter the world by birth to a woman. The women at Ephesus (just like the men) will be saved through that childbirth, *if* they continue in the things Paul lists at the end of the verse: faithfulness, love, and holiness with reverence.

This brief look at 1 Tim. 2:8-15 allows the following conclusions. In Ephesus, false teachers had found an accepting audience among some of the women(probably wives) in the house churches, resulting in these women not only teaching erroneous information, but doing so in a

---

Smyth, *Greek Grammar*, 288, says about the generic article: "In the singular the generic article makes a single object the representative of the entire class."

domineering manner. Thus Timothy is told that the women there should learn (the correct things) in a spirit of quietness and submission and should not domineer over men (probably, their husbands) in their teaching. To buttress his advice, he draws from the early chapters of Genesis in a typically Jewish way,[53] using arguments with which we may not be familiar or even comfortable. But clearly, Paul wants the women in Ephesus not to cause problems in the assembly, either by speech or action. Nor does he want the men to cause problems with prayers.

3. 1 Tim. 2:8-15 in Contemporary Perspective

One important aspect of the exegesis of any NT passage is an awareness of the shortcomings of the method. All an exegesis can even attempt to do is reveal what Paul said; the larger question of how Paul's statements should function in the modern church has been left to one side. However, it is an inevitable question. It is most important to maintain the distinction between what a text meant and what it means (or may mean).[54] We are not living in Ephesus, nor are we first-century people. We are living in our own time and place and must find ways of interpreting Paul's concerns across the centuries. Just because Paul wanted the wives in Ephesus not to teach, it does not necessarily follow that he wanted all women in all places and in all times to behave in exactly the same way.[55]

---

[53]For examples of first-century Jewish exegesis, see Richard Longenecker, *Biblical Exegesis in the Apostolic Period* (Grand Rapids: Eerdmans, 1975).

[54]Among many others, see Krister Stendahl, "Biblical Theology, Contemporary," *Interpreter's Dictionary of the Bible* (ed. K. Crim; Nashville: Abingdon, 1962): 1. 418-32.

[55]To argue as has H. Wayne House, *The Role of Women in Ministry Today* (Nashville: Thomas Nelson, 1990): 48, that "Paul's instruction regarding women teaching men was not prompted by a specific problem in the church at Ephesus, but rather emerged from his understanding of Genesis 1-3," is to show a total misunderstanding of how Paul worked. Paul does not bring up topics in his letters just to take up space in the letter; he addresses problems about which he has

In this text, Paul does not speak in universal (or non-specific) language, but addresses the men concerning the problems he has heard in their regard and the women about the difficulties he has heard concerning them. It is unwise to argue that because Paul said something to men in this context it could never be applied to women if they became involved in similar situations. The opposite is also true. Things said to women in 1 Tim. may, in other situations, be said to men. Paul addresses each situation as he knows it.[56]

In Paul's time, women generally were not public figures. While Paul certainly recognized freedom for women in Christ, he was as much a child of his own time as we all are, but he simply had no concept of a world order in which women would be accepted in leadership positions equal, or almost equal, to men. Any attempt to see in Paul the modern attitudes toward women in society are misdirected.[57]

However, the world has changed radically since Paul's time. Women have achieved a measure of equality with men in our society. How, then, do we read this text, written in

---

been informed in an attempt to correct behavior he views as inappropriate (see footnote 40).

[56]This can be illustrated by the way Paul deals with many subjects in his letters. For instance, when writing to a group of newly-converted Gentiles in Galatia who had become infatuated with the Law of Moses, Paul says, "For freedom Christ set you free." Paul says almost nothing positive about the law in the entire letter and he utilized every rhetorical device possible to dissuade them from subjecting themselves to the Law of Moses. However, when writing to a group of (mostly) Gentile Christians in Corinth who had become infatuated with freedom, he writes, "Wives, be in submission to your husbands *as the law says*." This kind of thing does not occur in Paul's letters because he cannot remember how he thinks Gentile Christians should view the law, but because different situations called for different responses.

[57]A glance at any bibliography on this topic reveals numerous articles and books in which it is argued that Paul is an egalitarian, and that he has simply been misunderstood by the church. This expects too much of any first-century man.

and to a much different world? Paul's statements certainly
are not irrelevant, but since the specifics are not exactly the
same, it is the principle that has continuing validity. Why
does Paul want the women in Ephesus to maintain decorum
in dress and at least some silence? Paul was concerned that
Christians not do things that would bring the reproach of the
community upon them and that the Christians within those
communities get along.   In Ephesus, there was danger of
Christians drawing disfavor from the community by
inappropriate social behavior and the very real possibility of
disagreement between Jewish and Gentile women over the
extent of their freedom in Christ. These concerns, coupled
with the inroads that false teachers had made among these
particular women and the domineering attitude they adopted,
caused Paul to disallow women in Ephesus from assuming
teaching roles. In Ephesus, as in other cities of the empire,
Paul battled syncretistic tendencies of recently converted
Gentiles and Hellenistic Jewish Christians, who sometimes
failed to see the uniqueness of Christianity. Part of that
uniqueness no doubt involved freedom for women, but not
of the same sort as in the better known mystery religions.
Freedom here, as in Corinth, could not be exercised at the
expense of the welfare and reputation of the church.
Apparently because teachers in the house churches were
promoting unlicensed freedoms and syncretistic theology,
Paul wanted only those teachers that either he or Timothy
had taught to do the teaching.

If we find ourselves in a similar situation in which
women of a particular congregation are being influenced too
greatly by false teachers and/or are doing their teaching in a
domineering manner, those women should not be permitted
to teach. However, it is also implied in 1 Tim. that no man
teaching false doctrine or influenced by false teachers should
be allowed to teach either. It is clear that Paul was concerned
that the assemblies be conducted responsibly. However,
when freedoms do not disrupt the worship and health of the
congregation, Paul supports those freedoms.

Chapter Twelve

THE IDENTITY OF THE "WOMEN" IN 1 TIM. 3:11

Barry L. Blackburn

Does 1 Tim. 3:11 bear witness to the existence of female deacons[1] in at least some first- or second-century churches? Though this question was debated at least as early as the fourth century,[2] the rise of Christian feminism in recent decades has provoked a re-examination of all early Christian texts which pertain to the ministry of women. In 3:1-13, the author describes the sorts of persons who should serve as bishops (vv. 1-7) and deacons (vv. 8-10, 12-13). In v. 11 he says, "Women (γυναῖκας) likewise must be serious, not slanderers, but temperate, faithful in all things."[3] Are these 1) Christian women in general, 2) wives of bishops and deacons, 3) wives of deacons, or 4) female deacons?

---

[1]With respect to the first and second centuries, "female deacons" is employed rather than "deaconesses" for two reasons. First, prior to canon nineteen of the Council of Nicea (AD 325), there are no certain examples of the Greek feminine διακόνισσα. In this earlier period, the masculine διάκονος was used for female as well as male deacons, e.g., διάκονον γυναῖκον in Clement of Alexandria, *Stromateis* 3.53.3. See also C. H. Turner, "Ministries of Women in the Primitive Church," *Catholic and Apostolic* (ed. H. N. Bate; London: A. R. Mowbray, 1933): 328f. Second, the office of deaconess as it has developed in several denominations does not enjoy some of the prerogatives of the office of deacon. Thus "deaconess" might seem erroneously to imply *from the outset* that if such existed in the NT period, her work likewise would have been more restricted than that of her male counterparts.

[2]Ambrosiaster, *Commentarium in Epistolam B. Pauli ad Timotheum Primam*, in J.-P. Migne, *Patrologia Latina* 17.496.

[3]For the sake of convenience, biblical citations are from NRSV.

1. *All Christian Women*

A reference in 1 Tim. 3:11 to Christian women in general was found by Ambrosiaster[4] in the fourth century and more recently by Davies.[5] However, it must be asked why the author would address suddenly all female Christians in the midst of a unit devoted to deacons. Davies correctly notes that the author of 1 Timothy is capable of abrupt transitions. However, in each example adduced by Davies[6] there is some point of connection. He can offer no reason why the author in 3:8-13 would have shifted from deacons to women in general, then back to deacons. The view that the reference to "women" in 1 Tim. 3:11 is to Christian women in general has nothing to commend it and can be rejected safely.

2. *The Wives of Bishops and Deacons*

The understanding of the term with reference to wives of both bishops and deacons[7] likewise fails to carry conviction. While one could conceive of some attention being given to the character of bishops' and deacons' wives

---

[4]Ambrosiaster, *Commentarium in Epistolam B. Pauli ad Timotheum Primam*, in *PL* 17:496, specifically denied that Paul in 1 Tim. 3:11 was speaking of female deacons; rather the apostle was urging that all Christians, including women, *quae inferiores unidentur*, possess the same virtues demanded for male leaders.

[5]J. G. Davies, "Deacons, Deaconesses, and the Minor Orders of the Patristic Period," *JEH* 14 (1963): 1f. In addition, ASV, NASB, and NRSV translate γυναῖκας (without a definite article) as "women," which *could* be taken as a reference to Christian women in general.

[6]Davies, *JEH* 14 (1963): 2, calls attention to 2:3-7 [vv. 1f., 8]; 2:9 [vv. 1f., 8]; 5:23 [vv. 22, 24]; 6:11-16 [vv. 6-10, 17-19].

[7]B. Coffman, *1 & 2 Thessalonians, 1 & 2 Timothy, Titus, & Philemon* (Austin, TX: Firm Foundation, 1978): 182f., knew this to be one of the three options mentioned by A. C. Hervey, *I. Timothy* (Pulpit Comm.; New York: Funk & Wagnalls, n.d.): 53, who, however, rejected the view. It is also noted and rejected by G. Wohlenberg, *Die Pastoralbriefe* (3rd ed.; KzNT 13; Leipzig: A. Deichert, 1923): 134, and J. Hurley, *Man and Woman in Biblical Perspective* (Grand Rapids: Zondervan, 1981): 230.

in a unit *following* vv. 1-13, there is no discernible reason why such qualifications should appear *within* a paragraph concerned with deacons. Weighing against this view is also the fact, examined in more detail below (309-10), that the four qualifications of the women in v. 11 closely correspond to the four given for deacons in v. 8. This suggests strongly that these women sustain a peculiar relationship to the deacons in vv. 8ff.

In light of these cogent objections against the first two options, most scholars have argued that there are only two tenable options, "wives of deacons"[8] or "female deacons."[9]

3. *The Wives of Deacons*

Those advocating that the author is speaking of the deacons' wives adduce two principal considerations. First, it is argued, had the author been introducing new office-bearers in v. 11 (female deacons as such are not mentioned otherwise in the Pastorals), surely he would not have used such a general term as γυναῖκας.[10] Second, if γυναῖκας of v. 11 is introducing the female counterparts of the male deacons of vv. 8-10, then why in v. 12 does the talk revert to male deacons?[11]

---

[8]"Their wives" is read by Geneva Bible, KJV, NEB, GNB, NIV, Phillips, NKJB and The Living Bible Paraphrased.

[9]The recently published Revised English Bible clearly opts for female deacons: "The women in this office." "The women," read by Rheims-Douai, RSV, NAB, JB, and NRSV is amenable to this interpretation, though ultimately ambiguous.

[10]See B. S. Easton, *The Pastoral Epistles* (New York: Charles Scribner's Sons, 1947): 134, and P. Lippert, *Leben als Zeugnis: Die werbende Kraft christlicher Lebensführung nach dem Kirchenverständnis neutestamentlicher Briefe* (SBM, 4; Stuttgart: Katholisches Bibelwerk, 1968): 34.

[11]See Martin Dibelius and Hans Conzelmann, *The Pastoral Epistles* (trans. P. Buttolph and A. Yarbro; Hermeneia; Philadelphia: Fortress, 1972): 58 (on the condition that vv. 8-10 are not dealing with deacons of both genders); Lippert, *Leben als Zeugnis*, 34. That vv. 12f. are addressed to male deacons is clear from "husband of one wife."

The first consideration, however, is rendered innocuous when one observes that in the first and subsequent centuries the masculine διάκονος was applied to women as well as men. Phoebe, for instance, is said to be διάκονος of the church in Cenchreae (Rom. 16:1). C. H. Turner[12] and Roger Gryson[13] have shown the probability that this linguistic practice also characterized the Greek original of the third-century, Syriac *Didascalia Apostolorum*. The feminine διακόνισσα is not attested until AD 325.[14] Thus, in the absence of a specific technical term to denote female deacons, it is hardly surprising that the author of 1 Timothy should employ γυναῖκας when dealing with virtues that specifically should characterize female deacons.[15]

If the γυναῖκας of v. 11 are female deacons, it does seem strange, admittedly, that the author should direct his attention again to male deacons in v. 12. It is not what might be expected, but it hardly eliminates a reference to female deacons. Fee,[16] for example, observes correctly that vv. 12f. could very well be "something of an afterthought." Certainly Paul was capable of such (see 1 Cor. 1:16). Moreover, the reference to females in v. 11 might have

---

[12]C. H. Turner, "Ministries of Women in the Primitive Church: Widow, Deaconess, and Virgin in the First Four Centuries,"*Catholic and Apostolic*, 329, n. 1.

[13]Roger Gryson, *The Ministry of Women in the Early Church* (trans. J. LaPorte and M. Hall; Collegeville, MN: Liturgical Press, 1976): 42.

[14]See n. 1.

[15]See, among others, Ceslaus Spicq, *Saint Paul: Les épîtres pastorales* (Ebib; Paris: J. Gabalda, 1947): 101; J. N. D. Kelly, *A Commentary on the Pastoral Epistles* (HNTC; San Francisco: Harper and Row, 1960): 83f; C. K. Barrett, *The Pastoral Epistles* (Oxford: Clarendon, 1963): 61; Gordon Fee, *1 and 2 Timothy, Titus* (Good News Commentaries; San Francisco: Harper & Row, 1984): 50; Jürgen Roloff, *Der erste Brief an Timotheus* (EKK, 15; Zurich: Benziger, 1988): 165; Philip Towner, *The Goal of Our Instruction: The Structure of Theology and Ethics in the Pastoral Epistles* (JSNTSup., 34; Sheffield: JSOT Press, 1989): 228.

[16]Fee, *1 and 2 Timothy, Titus*, 51.

reminded the author to address himself to the marriage and family life of the male deacons (v.12). At any rate, Roloff[17] has observed astutely that the position of v. 11 can be used *against* the notion that deacons' wives are under consideration. Had they been, would not such a reference be more natural *after* v. 12, with its requirement concerning the deacon's marriage?[18]

Though the identification of the γυναῖκας of v. 11 as deacons' wives continues to claim support from some English Bible translations and some scholars,[19] the two arguments commonly used to substantiate it are not compelling. This becomes increasingly evident as one examines the case for adopting the only viable alternative to this exegetical tradition.

4. Female Deacons

One should not reject dogmatically the possibility that v. 11 contains a reference to deacons' wives, but there are several reasons for favoring the probability that the verse speaks of female deacons. First, no one has explained convincingly why the author would have given attention to

---

[17]Roloff, *Der erste Brief an Timotheus*, 164f.

[18]Dibelius and Conzelmann, *The Pastoral Epistles*, 58, suggest the possibility that vv. 8-10 apply to deacons of both genders, v. 11 specifically to females and vv. 12-13 to males. If sustainable, this hypothesis would resolve the problem of the position of v. 11. However, "γυναῖκας (women) likewise must be σεμνάς (sensible)" clearly implies that these women are not included among the deacons in vv. 8-10. Moreover, ὡσαύτως (likewise), which introduces v. 11, functions elsewhere in the Pastorals to introduce a new group of persons (as in Tim. 2:9; 3:8; Tit. 2:3, 6).

[19]NEB, TEV, NIV. See Gerhard Delling, *Paulus' Stellung zu Frau und Ehe* (BWANT, 56; Stuttgart: W. Kohlhammer, 1931): 136; Easton, *The Pastoral Epistles*, 133f; Joachim Jeremias, *Die Briefe an Timotheus und Titus* (NTD, 9; Göttingen: Vandenhoeck & Ruprecht, 1953): 21; Lippert, *Leben als Zeugnis*, 34; James Barnett, *The Diaconate: A Full and Equal Order* (New York: Seabury, 1981): 37; and A. T. Hanson, *The Pastoral Epistles* (NCB; Grand Rapids: Eerdmans, 1982): 80f.

the wives of the deacons, but not those of the bishops (2:1-
7; see also Tit. 1:5-9). A. T. Hanson[20] suggests that a
deacon's marriage probably would be more recent than a
bishop's and that, therefore, the former's wife would be
lesser known to the church "and perhaps more inclined to
unsuitable behavior." Perhaps, but such reasoning hardly
explains why the author gives so much more attention to
bishops than to deacons (see vv. 1-7 with 8-10, 12-13; also
Tit. 1:5-9, where no mention of deacons appears). Furthermore, one might argue cogently that "unsuitable behavior"
by a bishop's wife (no mere theoretical possibility!) has even
more potential for undermining the church's life and work
than the misbehavior of a deacon's spouse.

Second, had the author of v. 11 meant to refer to
deacon's wives, NT linguistic usage strongly suggests that
he would have written τὰς γυναῖκας αὐτῶν (their wives)
rather than just γυναῖκας.[21] Of some forty-six instances in
which γυνή/γυναῖκες occurs after a reference to the
husband(s), there are only four cases, all singular, where
γυνή has no article or personal or reflexive pronoun (Mk.
10:2; 12:19 (par. Lk. 20:28); Lk. 18:29; 1 Cor. 7:11.[22]
Moreover, in each of these cases, unlike the situation in 1
Tim. 3:11, γυνή is very closely related to the prior reference
to the husband, either by the use of the correlatives ἀνήρ/
γυνή[23] or by wording that makes it absolutely certain that
the γυνή is the wife of the man just mentioned.[24] By

---

[20]Hanson, *The Pastoral Epistles*, 81. See also Lippert, *Leben als
Zeugnis*, 34.

[21]This point is routinely made by scholars, though without sub-
stantiation.

[22]In light of 1) the prohibition of sexual immorality in 1 Cor.
6:12-20, 2) the use of ἄνθρωπος rather than ἀνήρ in 7:1, and 3) Paul's
use of the modifiers ἑαυτοῦ and ἴδιον in 7:2, γυνή in 1 Cor. 7:1
probably means "woman" rather than "wife."

[23]Mk. 10:2; 1 Cor. 7:11.

[24]Mk. 12:19; Lk. 18:29. On the anarthrous γυνή, see A. T.
Robertson, *A Grammar of the Greek New Testament in the Light of
Historical Research* (Nashville: Broadman, 1934): 794, and F. Blass and

xcontrast, in twenty-four of the remaining occurrences, γυνή is accompanied by both definite article and genitive personal (or reflexive) pronoun.[25] The article without the pronoun appears in sixteen instances, but careful examination reveals that in almost every one of these occurrences γυνή is correlative with ἀνήρ (or designations for other family members, e.g., children, father, mother) or refers to a prior occurrence of γυνή *with* article and pronoun.[26] Such data make it improbable that the γυναῖκας of 3:11, accompanied by neither article nor personal pronoun, refers to wives of deacons.

In the third place, viewing γυναῖκας of 3:11 as female deacons, a recognized category not dissimilar to bishops (3:1-7) and (male) deacons (vv. 8-10, 12-13), makes better sense of two features.   1) The introductory ὡσαύτως ("likewise") of v. 11 picks up on the same word appearing in the transition from bishops to deacons (v. 8), and both are syntactically dependent on the δεῖ [τὸν ἐπίσκοπον]. . . εἶναι ([the bishop] must be . . .) of v. 2.[27] In addition, there is an undeniable parallelism between the qualifications of the διακόνους of v. 8 and the γυναῖκας of v. 11.[28]

A. Debrunner, *A Greek Grammar of the New Testament* (trans. R. W. Funk; Chicago: Univ. of Chicago Press, 1961): 134 (sect. 257 [3]).

[25]Matt. 1:20, 24;   5:31, 32; 19:3, 5 (par. Mk. 10:7), 8, 9 (par. Mk. 10:11: Lk. 16:18);   22:24, 25;   27:19;   Lk. 1:13, 18, 24;   Acts 5:7;   1 Cor. 7:2;   Eph. 5:28 (2x), 31, 33;   Rev. 19:7.

[26]Matt. 18:25;   19:10;   Mk. 12:19 (par. Lk. 20:28);   Lk. 14:26; Acts 5:2;   1 Cor. 7:3, 4, 14, 16, 33; Eph. 5:23, 25; Col. 3:19;   1 Tim. 2:14; 1 Pet. 3:1.   In Lk. 1:5 and Acts 18:2, γυνή appears with a personal pronoun, but without an article.

[27]Wohlenberg, *Die Pastoralbriefe*, 134; Spicq, *Les épîtres pastorales*, 101; Kelly, *The Pastoral Epistles*, 83; Barrett, *The Pastoral Epistles*, 61; Norbert Brox, *Die Pastoralbriefe* (RNT; Regensburg: F. Pustet, 1969): 154; Hurley, *Man and Woman in Biblical Perspective*, 230; Fee, *1 and 2 Timothy, Titus*, 50; Roloff, *Der erste Brief an Timotheus*, 164; Towner, *The Goal of Our Instruction*, 228.

[28]Wohlenberg, *Die Pastoralbriefe*, 134; Walter Lock, *A Critical and Exegetical Commentary on the Pastoral Epistles* (ICC; Edinburgh: T. & T. Clark, 1924): 40; Spicq, *Les épîtres pastorales*, 101; Kelly,

Σεμνούς ("serious") becomes the feminine σεμνάς. It is possible that both μὴ διλόγους (not double-tongued, v. 8) and μὴ διαβόλους (not slanderers, v. 11) forbid gossip/slander.[29] At the very least, Roloff argues,[30] "in both cases, it is a matter of the veracity of one's speech and thus the lack of ambiguity and the clarity with which one expresses his or her view to others." Μὴ οἴνῳ πολλῷ προσέχοντας (not indulging in much wine) becomes the positive νηφαλίους (temperate). And μὴ αἰσχροκερδεῖς (not greedy for money) has its counterpart in πιστὰς ἐν πᾶσιν (faithful in all things), even if the latter phrase bears a broader meaning.

Exegetical considerations based upon 1 Tim. 3 point to the probability that, at least in some churches of the NT era, women functioned as and were called διάκονοι (deacons).[31]

The Pastoral Epistles, 83; Brox, Die Pastoralbriefe, 154; Roland Schwarz, Bürgerliches Christentum im Neuen Testament? Eine Studie zu Ethik, Amt und Recht in den Pastoralbriefen (OBS, 4; Kosterneuburg: Osterreichisches Katholisches Bibelwerk, 1983): 44; Fee, 1 and 2 Timothy, Titus, 50; and Roloff, Der erste Brief an Timotheus, 164.

[29]Although διλόγους (v. 8, occurring here for the first time in Greek literature, according to Hanson, The Pastoral Epistles, 79) is generally understood to mean "double-tongued" (KJV) or "insincere" (NIV), it is tempting to give it the meaning "given to gossip." Διλογέω means "to say again, repeat," and the noun διλογία "repetition." Moreover, Polycarp, Phil. 5.2, in discussing the deacon's behavior, juxtaposes "not slanderers, not double-tongued."

[30]Roloff, Der erste Brief an Timotheus, 165 (my translation).

[31]With Wohlenberg, Die Pastoralbriefe, 134; Lock, The Pastoral Epistles, 40; Turner, Catholic and Apostolic, 331-333; E. F. Scott, The Pastoral Epistles (MNTC; London: Hodder and Stoughton, 1936): 36f; Spicq, Les épîtres pastorales, 101; A. Kalsbach, "Diakonisse," RAC 3.917; Barrett, The Pastoral Epistles, 62; Kelly, The Pastoral Epistles, 83f; Brox, Die Pastoralbriefe, 154; Jean Daniélou, The Ministry of Women in the Early Church (trans. G. Simon; London: Faith Press, 1961): 14; Gryson, The Ministry of Women in the Early Church, 8; Carl Spain, The Letters of Paul to Timothy and Titus (Austin, TX: R. B. Sweet, 1970): 66f; Hurley, Man and Woman in Biblical Perspective, 229-33; Schwarz, Bürgerliches Christentum im

5. *Other Texts Bearing On "Female Deacons"*

There are two other probable references to female deacons in literature of the first and early second centuries.

The earliest, emanating from the mid-fifties of the first century, appears in Rom. 16:1, in which Paul says, "I commend to you our sister Phoebe, a διάκονον (deacon) of the church at Cenchreae, . . . a benefactor of many and of myself as well." Some scholars[32] in agreement with earlier English translations (KJV and ASV), deny that διάκονον in this verse denominates an office or a distinctive function. Paul does, in fact, use διάκονος of himself and other workers in the Christian mission who were hardly equivalent to the "deacons of local churches" of 1 Tim. 3:8 and Phil. 1:1.[33] On this basis, it is argued, the proper translation would be "servant," understood in a general and unofficial sense.

Martimort has offered two additional reasons for following this second line of interpretation. 1) It is anachronistic to render διάκονον in Rom. 16:1 as "deacon(ess)," since uncontested references to female deacons emanate from a much later date—after AD 200.

Neuen Testament? 44; Gerhard Lofink, "Weibliche Diakone im Neuen Testament," *Die Frau im Urchristentum* (ed. G. Dautzenberg, et al.; QD, 95; Freiburg: Herder, 1983): 332-34; Fee, *1 and 2 Timothy, Titus*, 50f; Roloff, *Der erste Brief an Timotheus*, 164; Towner, *The Goal of Our Instruction*, 228; and Susanne Heine, *Women in Early Christianity: A Reappraisal* (trans. J. Bowden; Minneapolis: Augsburg, 1988): 136. While R. M. Lewis, "The 'Women' of 1 Timothy 3:11," *BS* 136 (1979): 167-75, does not find full-fledged female deacons in 3:11, he does regard them as (unmarried) assistants to (male) deacons.

[32]E.g., Delling, *Paulus' Stellung zu Frau und Ehe*, 136; Kalsbach, *RAC*, 917; Daniélou, *Ministry of Women in the Early Church*, 7f.; Davies, *JEH* (1963): 1; Aimé Martimort, *Deaconesses: An Historical Study* (trans. K. Whitehead; San Francisco: Ignatius, 1986): 18-20.

[33]Paul alone (2 Cor. 11:23; Eph. 3:7; Col. 1:23, 25); Paul and his missionary associates (1 Cor. 3:5 [Apollos]; 2 Cor. 3:6); Tychicus (Eph. 6:21; Col. 4:7); Epaphras (Col. 1:7); Timothy (1 Thess. 3:2).

312 Barry L. Blackburn

2) Also, the word προστάτις, used in v. 2 to describe Phoebe, suggests that she served by providing hospitality and assistance to travellers. Apparently Martimort sees a discrepancy between such work and the charitable work which apparently looms large in the ministry of deacons.[34]

However, two observations have convinced most recent scholarly students of Romans that Paul designates Phoebe a διάκονος, not simply because she serves Christ in just any way, but because she (and probably certain others in the Cenchreaen church) was engaged in a rather specific type of ministry.[35]

In the first place, the construction οὖσαν [καὶ] διάκονον (being [also] a "deacon"), especially if the καί is judged original,[36] suggests that διάκονος says something much more precise about Phoebe than that she is an ἀδελφή (sister). Secondly, she is specifically διάκονον τῆς ἐκκλησίας τῆς ἐν Κεγχρεαῖς ("deacon of the church in Cenchreae). Just as ἀπόστολοι (emissaries, representatives) of particular congregations are to be distinguished from "apostles of the Lord," so one should not confuse διάκονοι of particular churches with missionaries or their

---

[34]Martimort, *Deaconesses*, 18-20.

[35]Otto Michel, *Der Brief an die Römer* (MeyerK, 4; 14th ed.; Göttingen: Vandenhoeck & Ruprecht, 1978): 473; Ernst Käsemann, *Commentary on Romans* (trans. and ed. G. Bromiley; Grand Rapids: Eerdmans, 1980): 342; C. E. B. Cranfield, *A Critical and Exegetical Commentary on the Epistle to the Romans* (ICC; Edinburgh: T. & T. Clark, 1979): 2.781; Heinrich Schlier, *Der Römerbrief* (HTKNT, 6; Freiburg: Herder, 1977): 441; Ulrich Wilckens, *Der Brief an die Römer* (EKK, 6; Zurich: Benziger, 1982): 3.131. See also, Georg Blum, "Das Amt der Frau im Neuen Testament," *NovT* 7 (1964): 145, and Lofink, *Die Frau im Urchristentum*, 325f.

[36]Καί is read by 𝔓[46] B C* 81 cop[bo] and judged probably original by Michel, *Der Brief an die Römer*, 473; Cranfield, *Epistle to the Romans*, 2.781, n.1; Schlier, *Der Römerbrief*, 441; and Wilckens, *Der Brief an die Römer*, 3.131. NA[26] and UBS[3] use brackets.

helpers.[37] If διάκονοι in Phil. 1:1 refers to a select group within the Philippian church, and if Pauline churches were generally so arranged, then surely Paul's reference to a person who was a διάκονος "of the church at Cenchreae" would have been interpreted accordingly.

Martimort's two additional reasons for rejecting this interpretation are weak. Deacons of at least one gender are attested by Paul himself as early as the composition of Phil. 1:1. Moreover, as this essay demonstrates, one can make a good case that apart from Rom 16:1 female deacons are mentioned twice in literature earlier than AD 115.[38] To build a case on προστάτις (v. 2) is likewise precarious since it very well may bear the general sense of "helper."[39]

Whether Phoebe was formally appointed to her particular ministry is unknown.[40] It does appear probable, however, that she and perhaps others in the Cenchreaen church were linguistically singled out as διάκονοι in virtue of a ministry (διακονία) which was distinguishable from other activities. One can probably deduce something of the nature of Phoebe's work as deacon from the fact that the verb διακονέω and the noun διακονία are used often in a

---

[37]The use of ἀπόστολος (apostle) in 2 Cor. 8:23 and Phil. 2:25 clearly does not mean the same as when attached to the twelve and to Paul (and possibly a few others). Not correctly judging the force of the modifying phrase τῆς ἐκκλησίας τῆς ἐν Κεγχρεαῖς has led Elisabeth Fiorenza, *In Memory of Her: A Feminist Theological Reconstruction of Christian Origins* (New York: Crossroad, 1983): 171, to posit that Phoebe was "an official teacher and missionary in the church of Cenchreae."

[38]Besides 1 Tim. 3:11, Pliny *Epist.* 10.96.8.

[39]See W. Bauer, *A Greek-English Lexicon of the New Testament and Other Early Christian Literature* (2nd ed.; Chicago: Univ. of Chicago Press, 1979): 885. See also Käsemann, *Romans*, 411.

[40]The origin of the later practice of ordination of deaconesses is uncertain. See *Acts of Matthew* 28, *Apostolic Constitutions* 8.19.2 and 8.20, and the Council of Nicea (canon 19) and Council of Chalcedon (canon 15).

restricted sense for serving a meal or tending to the poor.[41]
Cranfield,[42] in fact, makes a convincing case that διακονία
in Rom. 12:7 should be taken in this narrower sense.
Διακονία in its broad sense, encompassing all Christian
activity (see 1 Pet. 4:10), would hardly be appropriate in a
list illustrating the diversity of gifts (vv. 4-6).[43]

The second text which probably refers to female
deacons is found in Pliny's letter to Trajan (*Ep.* 10.96.8),
written from Bithynia c. AD 112. In order to learn the truth
about Christian activities, Pliny interrogated by torture "two
female slaves, who were styled *deaconesses* [*quae ministrae
dicebantur*]."[44] *Ministrae* most likely translates the Greek
διάκονοι,[45] and *dicebantur* strongly suggests that *ministrae*
(διάκονοι) is the term by which the women described
themselves rather than one arbitrarily chosen by Pliny.
Since in the NT διάκονοι does not function as a general

---

[41]Verb: Matt. 8:15 par.; 25:44; Lk. 8:3; 10:40; 12:37; 17:8;
22:27; Jn. 12:2; Acts 6:2; Rom. 15:25; 2 Cor. 8:19f. Noun: Lk.
10:40; Acts 6:1; 2 Cor. 8:4; 9:1, 12f.

[42]Cranfield, *Romans*, 2.622. Käsemann, *Romans*, 342, who
advocated the same exegesis prior to Cranfield's commentary,
commented on the social state that gave rise to the διακονία of 12:7:
". . . the composition of communities like those at Rome and Corinth,
with many neglected widows and orphans, with the proletariat of the
world harbor and a constant flow of newcomers, not to speak of the
poor and the sick, demands laborers who can completely devote
themselves to the tasks which grow therewith and in them recognize
something like a calling."

[43]A helpful survey of the usage of διακονεῖν, διακονία, and
διάκονος from the classical period through the early fourth-century
church appears in Lawrence Hennessey, "*Diakonia* and *Diakonoi* in the
Pre-Nicene Church," *Diakonia: Studies in Honor of Robert T. Meyer*
(ed. T. Halton and J. P. Williman; Washington, D.C.; Catholic Univ.
of America Press, 1986): 60-86.

[44]*Pliny* (LCL: Cambridge, MA: Harvard Univ. Press, 1915):
2.405.

[45]See among others, A. N. Sherwin-White, *The Letters of Pliny*
(Oxford: Clarendon, 1966): 708. Davies, *JEH* (1963): 2, notes the
obvious: we do not know for a fact that *ministrae* = διάκονοι.

designation for Christians,[46] it is probable that by the term *ministrae* these women were claiming a function, or office, which distinguished them from other Christians.

On the basis of the foregoing evidence, it is justified to view the "women" of 1 Tim. 3:11 as "female deacons," i.e., women who were appointed to serve in specific ways and who consequently wore the appellation διάκονοι (deacon). Undoubtedly, however, the most serious objection to this understanding is based on the evidence of the second and third centuries. The first completely unambiguous reference to female deacons appears in the third-century *Didascalia Apostolorum* 16, a witness to the practice of (probably) Syrian churches, and even here some believe that the author is promoting and defending a recent innovation.[47] Moreover, an order of female deacons did not exist in the churches of the West in the third through the fifth centuries (and earlier, as far as we know).[48] That female deacons

---

[46]This is true in spite of such texts as Matt. 20:26 [par.]; 23:11; Mk. 9:35; and Jn. 12:26. Note general designations for Christians, such as "disciples," "saints," "Christians," etc.

[47]See Gryson, *The Ministry of Women in the Early Church*, 42f., 109; Jean LaPorte, *The Role of Women in Early Christianity* (Studies in Women and Religion, 7; New York: Edwin Mellen, 1982): 114. The crucial texts in English are in Arthur Vööbus, *The Didascalia Apostolorum in Syriac* (CSCO 401-02, 407-08; 4 vols.; Louvain: CSCO, 1979): 4: 156, lines 8-11, and esp. 157, lines 9-12 and 158, lines 1-6 which read: "On this account, we say that the ministry of a woman deacon is especially required and urgent. For our Lord and Savior also was ministered unto by deaconesses who were 'Mary Magdalene, and Mary the daughter of James and mother of Jose, and the mother of the sons of Zebedee,' with other women as well. Also for you the ministry of a deaconess [sic] is necessary for many things. Indeed, a deaconness [sic] is required for the houses of the pagans where there are believing women . . . ." Though this can be read as the defense of a recent innovation, the use of similar language (159, lines 3-17; 160, lines 1-10) explaining the work "required" of (male) deacons, as well as a grounding of their office in the Lord's earthly ministry, cautions against a hasty decision.

[48]Not mentioned in Tertullian or the *Apostolic Tradition* of Hippolytus, and are positively rejected by Ambrosiaster (n. 4 above).

existed in third-century Egyptian churches is possible, but not certain.[49]   Second-century sources, excepting the reference in Pliny's letter, sometimes mention deacons, but never specifically female deacons. In fact, a few texts seem to assume that the deacons are exclusively male.[50]

This state of affairs, of course, can be explained easily if none of the three texts examined above—1 Tim. 3:11; Rom. 16:1; Pliny, *Ep*. 10.96—really refers to the existence of female deacons. It is noteworthy that those who argue that female deacons *were* known in the first or early second century often deal almost exclusively with these three texts, failing to integrate their conclusion with subsequent development of the female diaconate in the early church.

On the other hand, the strength of the exegetical arguments for viewing the women of 1 Tim. 3:11; Rom. 16:1; Pliny, *Ep*. 10.96 as deacons necessitates asking whether the evidence of the second and third centuries is compatible with this position. The answer is "yes."

There are two possibilities. One is that the order of female deacons attested, e.g., in the *Didascalia*, was no innovation, but represents a practice that had characterized some sectors of Christianity since the first century. Relevant second-century sources are meagre, and those texts that seem to presuppose that all deacons are male, especially

---

[49]Both Clement of Alexandria, *Strom.* 3.53.3f., and Origen, *Comm. Romans* 10.17, refer to female deacons, but Gryson, *The Ministry of Women in the Early Church*, 30-32, argues that they knew only the female diaconate as an institution of an earlier time, not a ministry current among Egyptian churches. This view is advocated also by Peter Hünermann, "Conclusions Regarding the Female Diaconate," *TS* 36 (1975): 326, and Martimort, *Deaconesses*, 76-83. In this connection, note also that the *Apostolic Church Order*, apparently composed in Egypt c. AD 300, dictates that churches appoint three widows, of which one will assume the task of nursing sick women, the other two giving themselves to prayer and revelations. Female deacons are not mentioned.

[50]Ignatius, *Smyrn.* 8.1 and *Pol.* 6.1; Polycarp, *Phil.* 5:2f; esp. see *Didache* 15.1.

Didache 15.1 (in which deacons are described as ἄνδρες, males), might possibly include women on the principle that the females are subsumed under their male counterparts.

At any rate, the absence of female deacons in the (probably Syrian) churches whose practices are reflected in the *Didache* does not necessarily rule out their presence elsewhere. The putative existence of female deacons in Asia (1 Tim.), Bithynia (Pliny), and Achaia (Rom.) and their corresponding absence in the West (and possibly Egypt[51]) could be explained if female deacons were more or less peculiar to the Pauline mission. It might be countered that Paul also spent time in Rome. So he did, but under the circumstances of his imprisonment it is conceivable that he did not have a significant impact upon forms of ministry that had developed prior to his association with this church.

One can also envision the possibility that at some point after the composition of 1 Tim. the order of female deacons effectively disappeared, at least in the sense that an appointment or ordination to the diaconate became an exclusively male prerogative. It may be possible that this disappearance of the order of female deacons was, at least in part, a reaction to the prominent role of women in heterodox movements, such as Gnosticism and Montanism.[52] At any

---

[51]Gryson, *Ministry of Women in the Early Church*, 30-32, and Martimort, *Deaconesses*, 76-83, may be correct that Clement and Origen cannot be used as evidence for the presence of female deacons in Egypt in the third century, but one may be excused for wondering whether both would have commented on a ministry sanctioned by Paul, employed by the early church, and yet unknown in their own churches, without offering any comment or explanation as to why female deacons were no longer to be found.

[52]See Daniélou, *Ministry of Women in the Early Church*, 16; Gryson, *Ministry of Women in the Early Church*, 15f.; and Bonnie B. Thurston, *The Widows: A Women's Ministry in the Early Church* (Philadelphia: Fortress, 1989): 58f. In particular, the continuation of the female diaconate in the church catholic vis-à-vis these heterodox groups may have proved increasingly problematic as deacons came to have a limited share in the liturgical and sacramental tasks of the bishop (see Turner, *Catholic and Apostolic*, 333).

rate, it is conceivable that the ministry of female deacons coalesced with the order of "enrolled" widows (first attested in 1 Tim. 5), so that while female ministries continued, they did so under the name "widows."[53] Given the qualifications for enrollment in 1 Tim. 5:10, one would expect that those widows who were physically able would continue to show mercy to the "afflicted."[54] Once this practice of enrolling widows became firmly and widely ensconced, it may have proved difficult to distinguish sharply between "female deacons" and "widows," particularly if most or at least many of the female deacons had been widows.[55] This would explain the fact that while there is only one possible reference to female deacons in the second century (Pliny), "the widows" figure prominently, existing in the West as well as in the East.[56]

Aside from 1 Tim. 5:10, there is evidence that these widows not only were recipients of the church's charity, but also engaged in service. Well into the second century, Lucian describes how widows and orphans supported the Christian (but later apostate) Peregrinus, imprisoned for his faith, by standing all day out-side of the jail.[57] Tertullian held that enrolled widows should have experienced mother-hood so that they would be able to "counsel and comfort" others with a wisdom borne of experience.[58] Other third and fourth-century documents associate widows with making clothing for the poor and pastoral visits to the sick.[59]

---

[53]See esp. Kalsbach, *RAC*, 917-919, apparently followed recently by Thurston, *The Widows*, 52, 114.

[54]Kalsbach, *RAC*, 918, and Thurston, *The Widows*, 50-53, *pace* Turner, *Catholic and Apostolic*, 320-22.

[55]For evidence that some deaconesses of the third and fourth centuries were widows, see Davies, *JEH* (1963): 5f.

[56]See, among others, Kalsbach, *RAC*, 917f.; Turner, *Catholic and Apostolic*, 317-28; Daniélou, *Ministry of Women in the Early Church*, 16-20; Davies, *JEH* (1963): 4f.

[57]Lucian, *Peregrinus* 12.

[58]Tertullian, *De virginibus velandis* 9.2f.

[59]*Didascalia Apostolorum* 14f.; *Apostolic Church Order* 20f. In this latter text, the widow is required to be εὐδιάκονος, and two other

If the existence of female deacons had been, as it were, swallowed up by the order of widows, then for reasons concerning which one can only speculate,[60] an office of female deacons was revived in the East at least as early as the third century. A trajectory from the *Didascalia Apostolorum* to the *Apostolic Constitutions* (fourth century), *inter alia*, suggests that the institution of female deacons, or deaconesses as they came to be called, came to eclipse the dominance of the order of widows.[61]

Conclusion

The evidence presented and interpreted in this study makes it probable that 1 Tim. 3:11, nestled among verses addressed to male deacons (vv. 8-10, 12-13), contains qualifications for those women who would share in the work of their male counterparts. In other words, here we probably encounter female deacons who served their community—especially its poor, sick, and aged. Of course, we could wish that the second and third-century literature provided a clearer picture of the development or permutations of the female diaconate. On the other hand, our study has demonstrated that the data of this literature cohere with the understanding of "women" in 1 Tim. 3:11 as female deacons.

---

requirements—absence of greed, moderation in drink—parallel qualifications for deacons in 1 Timothy.

[60]Kalsbach, *RAC*, 918f., suggests growing asceticism, accompanied by cloistering, among the order of widows. Daniélou, *Ministry of Women in the Early Church*, 20, theorizes "the rise of the ideal of Virginity with which it [office of deaconess] was associated," the growing importance of the functions of deaconesses, and the increasing desire of the clergy to exert more control over female ministry. Davies, *JEH* (1963): 4, conjectures the growth of the church to be sufficient basis. Thurston, *The Widows*, 105, 116f., surmises the clergy's desire to transfer women's ministry from widows, whose work was based upon possession of a *charism*, to deaconesses, who worked closely with and were definitely subordinated to the bishops.

[61]See Turner, *Catholic and Apostolic*, 336f.; Kalsbach, *RAC*, 219f; Thurston, *The Widows*, 96-105.

Chapter Thirteen

THE "WIDOWS" IN 1 TIM. 5:3-16

Marcia D. Moore

The vulnerability of widows is a problem dating back to ancient times. Various attempts to protect widows are found in codes of ancient civilizations,[1] as well as in the OT,[2] intertestamental literature,[3] and in the NT.[4] 1 Tim. 5:3-16, the most extensive NT textdiscussing the care and financial support of widows, has been variously interpreted. (1) Some maintain that the entire passage treats only the issue of enrolling the widows who are to receive aid from the church.[5] (2) Others argue that the "enrollment" denotes those appointed to serve the church as paid workers, and that the entire passage deals with qualifications for this position.[6] (3) Alternatively, it has been advanced that two separate issues are being dealt with, viz., widows who need aid (5:3-8, 16) and other widows to be enrolled as special servants (5:9-15).[7] The principal question posed by the text, then, is

---

[1] F. Charles Fensham, "Widow, Orphan and the Poor in Ancient Near Eastern Legal and Wisdom Literature," *JNES* 21 (1962): 129-39.

[2] E.g., Deut. 10:18, 24:17-22; Psa. 68:5; Isa. 1:17; Zech. 7:9-10.

[3] E.g., Wis. Sol. 2:10-11; Sirach 35:4-15; Baruch 4:15-16. See also S. Safrai, "Home and Family," *The Jewish People in the First Century* (Philadelphia: Fortress, 1976): 2.787-91.

[4] E.g., Matt. 23:13; Lk. 7:12; Acts 6:1ff; James 1:27.

[5] J. G. Davies, "Deacons, Deaconesses and the Minor Orders in the Patristic Period," *JEH* 14 (1963): 5; and C. H. Turner, "Ministries of Women in the Primitive Church," *Catholic and Apostolic* (ed. H. N. Bate; London: A. R. Mowbray, 1931): 317-320.

[6] M. Dibelius and H. Conzelmann, *A Commentary on the Pastoral Epistles* (trans. P. Buttolph & A. Yarbro; Philadelphia: Fortress, 1972): 73-76; and Bonnie B. Thurston, *The Widows: A Woman's Ministry in the Early Church* (Minneapolis: Fortress, 1989).

whether the entire passage addresses the issue of enrollment, and if not, is there some other aspect of these church widows which serves as the unifying theme? Thus, the purpose of the enrollment as well as the interconnections both within the passage and between the passage and its larger literary context require clarification.

1. *Assumptions in Critical Scholarship*

Extensive literature on the question of the authorship of the Pastoral Epistles has channeled contemporary scholarship into two unfortunate assumptions. First, it is assumed that by locating parallels between the Pastoral Epistles and some other body of literature it will be possible to determine the date of the letters and their level of "Paulineness." This results in the Pastorals ceasing to be the primary object of exegetical inquiry as increasing attention is placed upon the non-Pastoral parallels. Second, it is assumed that the epistles to Timothy and Titus are to be treated as a single block of material rather than as three separate letters.[8] In this regard, Bush notes,[9] "This leads to the logical conclusion that there is no real structure to any of these letters, or at least not a structure that matters."

Traditionally, 1 Tim 2:1-6:2 has been viewed in critical scholarship as paraenesis discussing church order and as Haustafeln (traditional household codes based on social ethics).[10] Dibelius observes that paraenetic material is

---

[7]Joachim Jeremias, *Die Briefe an Timotheus und Titus* (12th ed.; NTD, 9; Göttingen: Vandenhoeck & Ruprecht, 1981): 36-40.

[8]A. T. Hanson, *The Pastoral Epistles* (Grand Rapids: Eerdmans, 1982): 42, notes, "The Pastorals are made up of a miscellaneous collection of material. They have no unifying theme; there is no development of thought."

[9]Peter G. Bush, "A Note on the Structure of 1 Timothy," *NTS* 36 (1990): 152.

[10]See David C. Verner, *The Household of God: The Social World of the Pastoral Epistles* (SBLDS, 71; Chico, CA: Scholars Press, 1983): 16-23.

often in the form of proverbs either loosely strung together or simply following one another without any connection . . . they lack an immediate relation with the circumstances of the letter . . . [they] are not formulated for special churches and concrete cases, but for the general requirements of earliest Christendom.[11]

Verner,[12] however, notes that such traditional paraenetic material can be freely adapted and modified in addressing concrete problems in the church. In fact, he argues (180-86) that the Haustafel in 1 Tim. does address a specific situation for a specific purpose. Yet, with most commentators, he does not detect a logical, coherent sequence of thought from paragraph to paragraph in 2:1-6:2. Rather, he says, ". . . it is not easy to decide whether certain material should be viewed as . . . developing the schema or simply intruding upon it."[13] So, it remains a question whether 1 Tim. is, in fact, a separate epistle from 2 Tim. and Tit., and if so, in what way its contents are related to form the document and in what way the document is intended to relate to an historical situation.

2. *The Importance of Literary and Historical Analysis*

In spite of abuses, there exists no viable alternative to proper literary and historical exegesis of the text of 1 Tim. if we are to ascertain the meaning of 5:3-16.[14] Still useful in determining an ancient writer's intention is the work of

---

[11]M. Dibelius, *From Tradition to Gospel* (New York: C. Scribner's Sons, 1976): 238.

[12]Verner, *The Household of God*, 102-106, esp.106.

[13]*Ibid.*, 95. See also Dibelius & Conzelmann, *The Pastoral Epistles*, 5-6.

[14]See Peter Stuhlmacher, *Historical Criticism and Theological Interpretation of Scripture* (trans. R. Harrisville; Philadelphia: Fortress, 1977), for discussion of methodological verifiability, effective historical consciousness, and the principle of consent. For a practical implementation of these principles, see Victor Paul Furnish, "Some Practical Guidelines for New Testatment Exegesis," *PSTJ* 26 (1973): 1-16.

Hirsch.[15] Much is now known about letters in antiquity that provides useful background for studying NT letters. The literary procedure called "discourse analysis" is most useful in detecting the intent of an ancient writer.[16] Analysis of the semantic structure of a larger document requires that one go beyond the usual reliance upon grammars, lexicons, and commentaries, and treat the relationship of various semantic units as they cohere to form the larger document. In this procedure, then, the "function" of a text within the developing whole is the principal task of literary analysis.

But literary analysis is only the first component of the procedure. Historical analysis is controlled by the literary analysis. Perhaps the best practical discussion of historical controls is that of Dahl,[17] who suggests: (1) the historical situation envisaged in the document must be sought in the writer's own perspective, (2) any reconstruction of that situation must be based upon information contained within the document itself, (3) the integrity of the document may be assumed if the unit of text under consideration can be explained in terms of its function within the document, (4) materials from other sources should not be introduced until the epistolary situation has been clarified as far as possible on the basis of information contained within the epistle itself, and (5) any reconstruction of the historical background will be, at best, a reasonable hypothesis, which is commended to the extent that it is able to account for the material in the document with minimal dependence upon hypothetical inferences derived from outside sources.

---

[15]E. D. Hirsch, *Validity in Interpretation* (New Haven: Yale Univ. Press, 1967).

[16]See Peter Cotterell and Max Turner, *Linguistics and Biblical Interpretation* (Downers Grove, IL: InterVarsity, 1989). John Beekman and John Callow, *Translating the Word of God* (Grand Rapids: Zondervan, 1974 [reissued by Summer Institute of Linguistics, Duncanville, TX]): 267-367, remains the best practical introduction.

[17]Nils Dahl, "Paul and the Church at Corinth According to 1 Corinthians 1:10-4:21," *Christian History and Interpretation: Studies Presented to John Knox* (ed. W. Farmer, et al.; Cambridge: Cambridge Univ. Press, 1967): 317-18.

3. *Literary and Historical Analysis of 1 Timothy*

A. *Literary Analysis.* Discourse analysis of 1 Tim. results in a well-defined literary structure.

Section 1:1-2—The salutation, which affirms Paul's apostleship and Timothy's authority as Paul's representative.

Section 1:3-20 —This section presents both the occasion and the purpose of the letter, as Paul sets forth the reason for Timothy's presence in Ephesus (1:3-7), and urges Timothy to persevere in his task (1:18-20).

Section 2:1-4:5 —The word οὖν (therefore) at the beginning of this section indicates that the section is closely connected with the purpose set forth in chapter 1. The main petition verb παρακαλῶ (I urge) indicates that the actions urged in this section are crucial to the success of Timothy's mission in Ephesus.[18] The purpose statement made toward the end of the section (3:14-16) and the closely connected[19] section about the false teachers[20] (4:1-5) function together as a transition passage. They look back over section 2:1-3:13, emphasizing the importance and significance of the instructions given up to this point. They also look forward, underscoring the need for Timothy to persevere, which begins the next section.

Section 4:6-6:2—In 1:3-4:6, Paul sets the task before Timothy. Now, in 4:6-6:2, he explains how to accomplish it. First, in 4:6-16, Paul focuses on Timothy's role both as a minister/teacher and as an example. Then, in 5:1-6:2, Paul

---

[18]See Terence Y. Mullins, "Petition as a Literary Form," *NovT* 5 (1962), and Dahl, "Paul and the Church at Corinth," *Christian History and Interpretation*, 319, for the significance of the use of this verb.

[19]Though most translations indicate a major break here, note the connective δέ (but).

[20]The literal description (in 1:3) is "certain ones (who) teach something different." Because of strong contextual clues (see 1:10-11; 4:1-2; 6:3-5, 20-21) that it was deceitful and opposed to the true gospel, this will hereafter be designated "false" teaching/teachers.

discusses specific groups to whom Timothy must give special attention. Paul indicates the best ways to encourage them, to honor those who are doing well, and to deal with those who are causing problems or having problems in living lives of godly ministry and service.

Section 6:3-21—In this closing section, Paul summarizes the problems Timothy faces (6:3-10), giving some new information about the false teachers. This section also reiterates the charge to Timothy to deal with these problems by focusing on a godly life of faithful relationship with God and loving ministry to others (6:11-16). Vv. 17-19 appear almost as a postscript, to clarify Paul's comments about money (6:9-10). Then Paul's concluding statement (6:20-21) brings the letter full circle, appealing again for Timothy to carry out the commission with which the letter begins.

B.   *Historical Analysis.* With this literary structure in mind, let us consider the historical situation, using the categories of information suggested by Dahl:

> Relatively clear and objective statements concerning the situation . . . must serve as a basis. Evaluations, polemical and ironical allusions, warnings and exhortations may next be used to fill out the picture. Only when these possibilities have been exhaused, and with great caution, Paul's own teaching should be used as a source of information . . . .[21]

Relatively clear and objective statements will be considered first. The reason for Timothy's presence in Ephesus is the need to deal with the false teachers (1:3-4). Only one passage (4:1-5) gives specific information about the content of this false teaching: marriage was forbidden, and abstinence from (unspecified) foods enjoined. Otherwise, only vague descriptions are given: myths and endless genealogies (1:4), fruitless discussion (1:4,6), godless and old-women's myths (4:7), controversy and word-battles

---

[21]Dahl, "Paul and the Church at Corinth," *Christian History and Interpretation*, 317.

Paul's primaryconcern, one would expect such concepts to be specifically refuted, but this occurs only once (4:3-5). Instead, the concern which Paul repeatedly expresses is the *effect* of such constant controversy on the life of the church: their obsession with debating these matters has resulted in the rejection or neglect of what is *really* important—faith, moral integrity, and especially, love (1:5,6 and 19; 4:1; 6:21)). The false teaching also brings about endless speculation rather than the οἰκονομίαν of God (1:4).[23] If the meaning is "stewardship,"[24] the Ephesian church[25] is

Backgrounds, Leicten: E. J. Brill, 1973). One explanation for such "vague" descriptions is given by Robert J. Karris, "The Background and Significance of the Polemic of the Pastoral Epistles," *JBL* 92 (1973): 549-564, who argues that one of the main weapons of the Pastorals' author was "name-calling polemic,"based on a traditional schema used by philosophers to criticize sophists, and that all such "stock" charges should not be understood as reflecting the actual situation, "unless there is a clear indication in other sections of the Pastorals to the contrary." However, if 1 Tim. was actually written by Paul to a specific colleague in a specific location about the conduct and teaching of specific individuals (two of whom he names), the usage of a traditional schema which did not reflect the actual situation would surely backfire and discredit Paul instead of the false teachers.

[23]Though many translate οἰκονομίαν as the "training" of God or "God's plan of salvation," it can also mean "stewardship, commission, administration." See Walter Bauer, *A Greek-English Lexicon of the New Testament and Other Early Christian Literature* (trans. by W. F. Arndt and F. W. Gingrich; 2nd ed. rev. F. W. Gingrich and F. Danker; Chicago: Univ. of Chicago Press, 1979): 559-60. This word is used in 1 Cor. 9:17, Eph. 3:2, 9, and Col. 1:25, and a similar word (οἰκονόμος; steward) is used in 1 Cor. 4:1 and Tit. 1:7, in each instance referring to a person being entrusted with sharing the message of God's grace.

[24]See Markus Barth, *Ephesians* (AB, 34; Garden City, NY: Doubleday, 1974): 86-88, 358-359; Walter Lock, *A Critical and Exegetical Commentary on the Pastoral Epistles* (ICC; Edinburgh: T. & T. Clark, 1924): 9-10; and Ronald A. Ward, *Commentary on 1 and 2 Timothy and Titus* (Waco: Word, 1974): 30.

[25]Gordon D. Fee, *1 and 2 Timothy, Titus* (Peabody, MA: Hendrickson, 1988): 7-8, suggests that the false teachers were part of the elders, and the reference in Tit. 1:7 is to the overseer as God's steward, thus only the false teachers are neglectful of stewardship.

too distracted by pointless discussions concerning the false teaching to exert themselves to share the gospel, as faithful stewards. The final "clear statement" is that the false teaching fosters destructive greed (6:9-10).

A consideration of evaluations, warnings, and exhortations suggests additional problems caused by this false teaching. These endless discussions generate conceit, envy, constant strife and quarreling (6:4-10). The repeated encouragement of good works (2:10; 5:10; 6:18) suggests that ministry and service, especially to those in need, were being neglected. If the situation in the Ephesian church was one of controversy, greed, and a refusal to focus on love, such neglect is not surprising. The repeated juxtaposition of the false teaching and godliness (3:16-4:1-5; 4:7; 6:3, 5-8, 11) suggests that godliness was misunderstood by the false teachers. It is possible that the false teaching was creating problems especially for those groups singled out for exhortation: women (2:9-15), widows and their families (5:3-16), the elders and deacons (3:1-13; 5:17-25), and slaves (6:1-2).[26]

The false teaching seems also to have had a effect on prayer—both in manner (without quarreling; 2:8) and its objects (for all people; 2:1). Evidently these teachers were fostering an attitude of exclusivism,[27] a possibility supported by Paul's repeated and emphatic affirmations that Jesus is the Savior of all (1:12-17; 2:4-7; 4:10). Such exclusivism would certainly contribute to friction between

---

[25]Gordon D. Fee, *1 and 2 Timothy, Titus* (Peabody, MA: Hendrickson, 1988): 7-8, suggests that the false teachers were part of the elders, and the reference in Tit. 1:7 is to the overseer as God's steward, thus only the false teachers are neglectful of stewardship. However, there is indication in 1 Tim. that the false teaching affected the whole congregation, resulting in wider neglect of stewardship.

[26]See Fee, *1 and 2 Timothy, Titus*, xiv, 7-8, 70, 76, 114, 127-128, 136-137.

[27]See Jerome Murphy O'Connor, "Community and Apostolate," *TBT* 67 (1973): 1261.

the church and outsiders, hinted at repeatedly (2:2; 3:2, 7; 5:7, 14; 6:1).

To summarize the situation, then, false teaching has caused three major problems. (1) Endless debates have caused the Ephesian Christians to lose sight of their task of sharing the message of God's grace to all people. (2) By turning from love to speculation and controversy, Christian lifestyle has been degraded from godliness and loving service to envy, quarreling and greed, evoking pagan ridicule, disbelief, and even hostility. (3) The number and severity of these problems have not only created difficulties in the lifestyle and witness of the church, but several passages which encourage Timothy to persevere (1:18-19; 4:6-16; 6:11-16, 20) suggest that he is having difficulty dealing with these problems, even to the point of giving up on his mission in Ephesus.

So how does Paul advise Timothy to proceed? While the basic task is to eradicate the influence of the false teachers in the congregation, this cannot be accomplished by adopting their tactics of constant debate. Timothy is to avoid this (4:7; 6:11) by focusing on God's concern for sinners and his ability to redeem even the most sinful (1:12-17). Various metaphors (1:8; 4:8; 6:12) indicate that Timothy's task will not be easily or quickly accomplished, but will require determination and genuine faithfulness (4:6-16).

Finally, Timothy is to help the Ephesian Christians present a clear witness affirmed by a godly lifestyle. This strategy is delineated in 2:1-7, affirmed in 3:14-15, and the means for its implementation are outlined in 4:6-16. In 2:1-7, prayers must be made for all, especially rulers, so that hostility against Christians can be reduced.[28] Godliness and respect must overcome pagan prejudice and hostility.[29]

---

[28]See Murphy O'Connor, *TBT* (1973): 1261-1262.

[29]In the Hellenistic world, εὐσέβεια (godliness) denotes a proper attitude of respect for the gods, expressed in cultic acts of worship. See Werner Foerster, "σέβομαι," *TDNT*, 7.168-196. For Paul, godliness is a deeper, stronger force: a reverence for God that compels the shaping of

1 Tim. 3:14-15 affirms this as the reason for the behavioral prescriptions in 2:8-3:13. While focusing on the behavior of the church, Paul refers to the church as the "support" and "mainstay" of the truth. Thus 3:14-15 might be rephrased: "I am writing to you so that you might know the way God's household must behave in order to support and establish the truth of its message."

Finally, Paul indicates that it is vital for Timothy himself to model such behavior. Devotion to studying and teaching the truth (4:6, 13-16) is important, but not enough. He must also set an example of a lifestyle marked by godliness, righteousness, love and faithfulness in ministry (4:12-16; 6:11). His perseverance and progress in this life of service and outreach should serve to motivate the Ephesian congregation to faithful ministry and godly lifestyle as well, especially the "problem" groups mentioned in 5:1-6:2.

This literary and historical analysis of 1 Tim. indicates that 2:1-6:2 plays an integral part in addressing the specific occasion for this letter, and that there is a logical, coherent sequence of thought from paragraph to paragraph. These sections (including 5:3-16), then, are not disconnected paraenesis, nor even just parts of a Haustafel, but specific teachings intended to remedy specific problems.

4. *1 Tim. 5:3-16 in its Literary Context*

There are three principal views of this passage. (1) Some note Paul's emphasis on financial concerns at the beginning and end of this passage, and argue that the

---

lives and actions to reflect God's will. (See 1 Tim. 4:7-12; 2 Tim. 3:5; Tit. 2:11-14.) Such reverence is expressed in caring for one's family (5:4) as well as in service to others (2:10). Σεμνότητι (respectfulness) and καλόν (good) are also used to describe the Christian lifestyle, but the usual ET do not convey the full meanings. Each word signifies that which evokes profound respect: the former by its grandeur, the latter by its excellence and beauty. See Murphy-O'Connor, *TBT* (1973): 1261-1263.

enrollment is simply a listing of those in need of financial aid. Though not overtly concerned with the unity of the text, these scholars do unify the text in practice by using criteria from the entire passage to determine which widows qualify for financial aid from the church. (2) Others focus on the verses about enrollment and argue that the enrollment is a list of those personifying the ideal godly widow who were appointed as paid servants of the church. Unity of the text is a primary concern for such scholars, and is accomplished by equating enrolled widows and "true" widows and seeking to determine which widows meet the qualifications posed in 5: 5, 9, 10 to be enrolled as paid servants and which do not qualify for this position. (3) Still others, noting the different topics in vss. 3-8, 9-15, and 16, and the lack of connectives between these sections, do not try to unify the passage, but argue that it deals with two separate topics: financial care of widows, and enrollment of widows.

Such diversity of interpretation is due in large part to the ambiguity of many phrases in this passage, and by our historical distance from the concerns it addresses. However, with responsible literary analysis and firm historical controls, it is possible to sift through the various options and move beyond the impasse posed by these different views.

Based on a detailed discourse analysis of 5:3-16, the following literary structure of this passage is proposed. Section 5:3-8 deals with the "true widows" and Timothy's instructions concerning them. Section 5:9-13 deals with those widows who should and should not be enrolled. Section 5:14-16, as indicated by the inferential particle οὖν (therefore), states Paul's conclusions. It serves as a chiastic summary, offering solutions to the problems raised in the first two sections:

a	5:3-8	Widows who need to serve/be served
b	5:9-13	Widows who should/shouldn't be enrolled
b'	5:14-15	Solution for widows not enrolled
a'	5:16	Solution for those not serving/being served

A.   *1 Timothy 5:3-8, 16—The true widow.* Paul instructs
Timothy to "honor widows—those who are true widows,"
but three problems arise concerning 1) the identity of these
widows, 2) what is meant by "honor," and 3) why Paul
limits those to be helped/ honored.

1) *Who are these "true widows?"* The phrase "true
widow" is understood by some[30] to indicate one who
personifies the ideal qualities and behavior expected of a
godly woman. Most taking this position also equate the true
widow of vv. 3, 5 and 16 with the enrolled widows of vv. 9
and 10. Indeed, this equation may be largely responsible for
this interpretation of "true widow," since it automatically
includes the criteria of vv. 9 and 10 (marital fidelity, child-
raising, hospitality, devoted to good works) in defining a
"true widow."[31] A methodologically sound approach is to
consider those verses which discuss explicitly the true
widows, before including information from verses which
may or may not do so (see discussion at beginning of section
4. B.). Χήρα (widow) is a feminine form of the masculine
adjective χῆρος which means "bereft".[32] The adverb ὄντως
(true) comes from the participle of the verb "to be" and
emphasizes the *true* nature of the word it modifies. Thus,
the literal meaning of "a widow who is a true widow" would
be "a widow who is *truly* bereft." This meaning of "true
widow" is supported by one explanatory statement in v. 5,

---

[30]See e.g., Fee, *1 and 2 Timothy and Titus*, 114-115; C. K.
Barrett, *The Pastoral Epistles in the New English Bible* (Oxford:
Clarendon, 1963): 74-75; and Ward, *1 and 2 Timothy and Titus*, 81-83.

[31]Many points in Fee's discussion of this passage (*1 and 2
Timothy and Titus*, 114-126) are based on this equation (true widow =
enrolled widow = ideal widow), for which he gives no rationale. It is
simply an undiscussed assumption by Fee.

[32]Against James Hurley, *Man and Woman in Biblical Perspective*
(Grand Rapids: Zondervan, 1981): 137, that "the Greek language has no
word for 'widower'," see H. G. Liddell and R. Scott, *A Greek-English
Lexicon* (9th ed. rev. H. Jones & R. McKenzie; Oxford: Clarendon
Press, 1973): 1990, who state that this masculine adjective was also
used substantively to mean "widower." See also Gustav Stählin,
"χήρα" *TDNT* 9. 440.

and by three sets of contrasts: v. 3 to v. 4; v.16a,b to v.16c,d; and v. 5 to v. 6. In v. 5, the phrase "true widow" is followed by the explanatory phrase "that is, one who has been left alone."[33]

The first contrast to the true widow is in v. 4: one who has children or descendants. One should conclude that a true widow, then, has no children or descendants. This poses a serious obstacle to defining a true widow as an "ideal widow." Since v. 10 (and 5:14 and 2:15) views child-rearing in a positive way, a widow with children would be *identified with* an ideal widow, not placed in contrast to her.

The contrast found in v. 16 is similar, but more exclusive. The Greek text of v. 16 begins, " If any believing woman has widows, let her help them." The NIV has added the interpretive phrase "in her family" (not found in the Greek text) after the word "widow." The verb ἔχω (I have) sometimes refers to family relationships (1 Tim. 5:4; 1 Cor. 7:2), but can also refer more generally to relationships which involve various types of connection or responsibility.[34] Thus the "believing woman" referred to in 16a could be connected to a widow by ties of family, friendship, or employment/slavery.

Verse 16 concludes "and let not the church be burdened, so that it might help the true widows." According to the contrast, a true widow can be further defined as one who has no close personal connection in the church—whether of family, friendship, or mistress/employer.

The third contrast, between the true widow who has been left all alone and the widow who lives luxuriously and

---

[33]The phrase begins with an explicative καί (that is). Beekman and Callow, *Translating the Word of God*, 30-31, cite this as an example of using explicit information (v. 5) to understand implicit information (v. 3).

[34]See Verner, *The Household of God*, 162-163. Cf. B. W. Winter, "Providentia for the Widows of 1 Tim. 5:3-16," *TynBul* 39 (1988): 94.

self-indulgently, is found in vv. 5-6.[35] Any widow able to
live luxuriously obviously has personal financial
resources,[36] while the word μεμονωμένη (having been left
alone) emphasizes the bereft condition of the "true widow."
Such complete bereavement has both practical and spiritual
consequences. The practical result is that she has no means
of support. The spiritual result is reflected in the latter part
of v. 5 and in v. 6. In this extremity of grief and desolation,
she must choose how to respond. She can turn to God for
healing and renewal, or she can seek comfort and
forgetfulness in worldly activities and relationships. This
latter course is the one chosen by the widow in v. 6, but the
true widow reaffirms her faith in God, pouring out her heart
to him in prayer, and drawing on his love for strength and
endurance.

---

[35] Burton S. Easton, *The Pastoral Epistles* (New York: Charles
Scribner's Sons, 1947): 152, argues that ἡ σπαταλῶσα (one living
indulgently) refers instead to prostitution. Hanson, *Pastoral Epistles*,
97, similarly argues that this "must refer to something worse than mere
self-indulgence," but this misses Paul's point that focusing on wealth
can only result in spiritual ruin. Cf. Walter K. Lacey, *The Family in
Classical Greece* (Ithaca: Cornell Univ. Press, 1968): 171-172; Sarah B.
Pomeroy, *Goddesses, Whores, Wives and Slaves: Women in Classical
Antiquity* (New York: Schocken, 1975): 73, 198-202, and J. P. V. D.
Balsdon, *Roman Women: Their History and Habits* (New York: John
Day, 1963): 276-277, for other ways a woman could have supported
herself. A different interpretation of "one living indulgently" is given
by Fee, *1 and 2 Timothy and Titus*, 117, who says v. 6 "seems to fit
the further description of the young widows in 11-13" and "the widows
given to self indulgence are exposed in detail (vv. 11-13)," apparently
taking the younger widows to be the same group as the self indulgent
widows, i.e., all the younger widows are self-indulgent. But if this is
true, why would one need the criterion of godliness in vv. 9-10? The
ungodly younger widow could be disqualified simply by age. If one
answers that the criterion must be there to disqualify *older* ungodly
widows, then one cannot argue that the widow described in v. 6 refers
only to the younger widows. Also, if v. 6 and vv. 11-13 describe the
same group, one wonders why Paul does not use the verb στρηνιάω
(running wild) from which the verb in v. 11 is formed.

[36]That there were wealthy women in the Ephesian congregation
seems clear from 2:9-10. See Alan Padgett, "Wealthy Women at
Ephesus: I Timothy 2:8-15 in Social Context," *Int* 41 (1987): 23.

2) *What does Paul mean by "honor"?*   Both the practical predicament and the spiritual condition of these true widows should call forth a response from the church. Because she has come through this extreme test of her faith[37] with a deeper trust in God, she should be respected (v. 3). If only the spiritual condition of these widows was being considered, one could—and should—limit the meaning of Paul's command in v. 3 (honor) to "showing respect."[38] However, the passage repeatedly calls attention to her predicament (completely bereft) as well, and finally (v. 16) urges that the church respond with very practical assistance. In light of the context, then, the commandment to honor should be understood to include elements of respect, considerate treatment, and financial assistance.[39]

3) *Why does Paul find it necessary to give these instructions and to limit those who are helped by the church?* Though the text does not provide any "clear and objective statements" about the situation to answer this question directly, an answer is suggested by the "evaluations, warnings and exhortations" found in vv. 4, 6-8, and 16. In v. 4, the children/descendants[40] of a widow are commanded to "pay back" their ancestors by practicing godliness to their own household. The widow who copes with her loss by focusing on her wealth and a self-indulgent lifestyle (v. 6), incurs Paul's judgment that she is spiritually dead.[41]

---

[37]Which the widows in v. 4 have not experienced to the same degree, and to which the widows in v. 6 have responded inappropriately.

[38]If true, this would support the argument that "true widow" refers to one who is an "ideal" widow, worthy of such respect.

[39]See Bauer, *A Greek-English Lexicon*, 817-18, and Verner, *The Household of God*, 162-63.

[40]In view of the context (esp. v. 8), "children" as the subject of "learn" seems most likely. Cf. J. N. D. Kelly, *A Commentary on the Pastoral Epistles* (New York: Harper and Row, 1963): 113; Scott, *The Pastoral Epistles*, 58; and Lock, *The Pastoral Epistles*, 56, that "let them learn" refers to the widows.

[41]This contrast seems to foreshadow the instruction to the rich in chapter 6 to put their hope, not on their wealth, but on God. There is a close similarity in the Greek wording between 5:5 and 6:17.

Timothy is to command "these things" (v. 7), so that
they might be irreproachable (see also 3:2; 6:14). Fee[42]
argues that "these things" refers only to the desired behavior
for widows discussed in vv. 5 and 6. While his orderly
chiasm is certainly appealing, there is nothing in v. 7 to limit
"these things" to vv. 5 and 6.[43] In fact, to exclude vv. 3 and
4, one would need to support at least one of the following
three assumptions. (1) There is a major break between vv.
3-4 and vv. 5-6. However, δέ (but) which begins each
verse (4, 5, and 6) in this section indicates a tightly woven
argument. (2) The ideas expressed in vv. 3-4 should not be
commanded. However, the imperatives in this section are
found in vv. 3 and 4 ("honor" and "let them learn to practice
godliness"), not in vv. 5 and 6, which are only a description
of widows' behavior. (3) The behavior commanded in vv. 3
and 4 would not affect the church's reputation. However, v.
8 militates against this by strongly condemning anyone who
does not care for his family and his household as worse than
an unbeliever, and obviously because even unbelievers care
for their parents.[44] A less obvious interpretation is that a

---

[42]Fee, *1 and 2 Tim., Tit.*, 117-118, suggests on 5:4-8,

a	words to the relatives (v. 4)
b	words to the widows (v. 5)
b'	judgment on disobedient widows (vv. 6-7)
a'	judgment on disobedient relatives (v. 8)

Another reason Fee limits "these things" to vv. 5-6 is his belief that
the strongest locus of concern in the passage is the behavior of the
young widows, which he sees described in v. 6 as well as vv. 11-13.
However, while Paul is very concerned about the young widows'
behavior, discourse analysis of the passage leads me to believe that this
is *not* the concern being addressed in vv. 3-8.

[43]Ward, *1 and 2 Timothy and Titus*, 83, and Kelly, *Pastoral
Epistles*, 114, view this verse with reference only to the widows'
behavior (vv. 5-6), because they see it as a reference to the need to
"screen" the widow to be enrolled, just as the bishop must be screened.
However, this assumes incorrectly that the widows of v. 5 are in fact
the widows who are to be considered for enrollment.

[44]See Lacey, *The Family in Classical Greece*, 109-110, 116-117;
Pomeroy, *Goddesses, Whores, Wives and Slaves*, 62-63, 91, 163; and
Balsdon, *Roman Women*, 186-188, 222.

Christian who willfully refuses to care for his own family is in a worse position than one who never made such a commitment to a life-style of concern for others. This interpretation of verse 8 reflects Paul's concern throughout this epistle that Christian lifestyle should match its message.[45] So, vv. 7 and 8 are not separate summary statements of vv. 5 and 4, respectively. Instead, v. 8—by portraying blameworthy behavior which forms a contrast to the praiseworthy behavior depicted in v. 4, and commanded in v. 7—reinforces the thoughts of v. 7, and seems to indicate that the main concern in 5:3-8 is that widows be cared for properly.

V. 16 repeats this concern.[46] Careful attention to grammar yields the following translation of this verse: "If any believing woman has widows, let her help them from now on[47] and let not the church continue[48] to be burdened, so that it might help the true widows." If indeed these verses reflect the actual historical situation, then the Ephesian church was actually caring for widows who did have other sources of support, thus making it difficult to support those widows who did not have other resources. This problem was likely caused by two factors. First, there might have been some confusion about who should support widows. Second, the influence of the false teachers resulted in some Christians' failure to care for their widows—either willfully (through greed) or inattentively (through speculations and debates which detract from loving service).[49]

---

[45]Fee, *1 and 2 Tim., Tit.*, 118, and Barrett, *Pastoral Epistles*, 75.

[46]Karris, *JBL* (1973): 560, and Verner, *The Household of God*, 137, affirm that a concern which is elaborated is more likely to be a genuine part of the historical setting.

[47]Usually the present imperative indicates an action which is to begin now and be continued—"do this from now on." See A. T. Robertson, *A Grammar of the Greek New Testament in the Light of Historical Research* (Nashville: Broadman Press, 1934): 855-856.

[48]μή with the present imperative usually expresses prohibition of an action already in progress. See Robertson, *Grammar*, 851-854, 890.

[49]See Simpson, *Pastoral Epistles*, 73; and Winter, *TynBul* (1988): 88, 90, 93 for further discussion.

Paul's advice is summarized in v. 16: "If any believing woman has widows, let her help them" (16 a,b). The choice of a feminine adjective here[50] serves two purposes. First, it refers back to vv. 4 and 8, and acknowledges that the actual care of the widows will probably fall on the women of these households.[51] Second, Paul also encourages *any* Christian woman who has the position or resources to help widows to do so. I am indebted to Carroll Osburn for the suggestion that Paul specifically has in mind the self-indulgent widow of v. 6. Instead of wasting her resources on self-indulgent luxuries, she should help other widows with whom she has ties of friendship, kinship, or employment.[52] Finally, any widow with no family, no personal wealth, and no friend/employer who might help her, is truly bereft. If she remains firm in her faith, she is a "true" widow, and should be honored and cared for by the church (16c,d).

B.   *1 Tim. 5:9-15 —The enrolled widows*

1) *Possible grounds for equating the true widows and the enrolled widows.* Some, both those who argue that the whole passage deals with financial aid and those who argue that it deals with paid church servants, equate the "true widows" of vv. 3, 5, and 16 with the "enrolled widows" of vv. 9 and 10. Such an equation is vital for the former view, since the only verses which explicitly (v. 16) or implicitly (v. 3) command church support of widows indicate that such support is only to be given to true widows. The verses which explicitly discuss enrollment (vv. 9-13) do not say anything about either financial need or financial support. Therefore, unless the true widow is equated with the enrolled widow, there is no basis for saying that the purpose of enrollment is financial aid. Such an equation is also important for the latter view, since this equation forms the

---

[50]"Believing woman" (RSV NIV) is better attested than the textual variant "believing man or woman" (KJV NEB). See Bruce M. Metzger, *A Textual Commentary on the Greek New Testament* (corr. ed.; London: United Bible Societies, 1975): 642.

[51]See Kelly, *Pastoral Epistles*, 120-121.

[52]See Dibelius & Conzelmann, *The Pastoral Epistles*, 76.

basis for the unity of the passage which is of such concern to these scholars. Yet most scholars make this equation automatically, without offering any rationale for doing so.[53]

Now the true widow might be equated with the widow to be enrolled: a) if there were some grammatical connection between v. 9 and vv. 3-8, b) if "widow," without a qualifying adjective, was used throughout this section as a technical term to denote "an official church widow," c) if "widow" was used throughout this section without any qualifying words or phrases to differentiate one group of widows from another, d) if the phrase "true widow" was used at any point in the verses which explicitly discuss enrollment (vv. 9-13), e) if the criteria for identifying the "true widow" and the "widow to enroll" were identical, or f) if "to honor" and "to enroll" had the same lexical meaning.

a) *If there were some grammatical connection between v. 9 and vv. 3-8.* However, no such connection exists, e.g., a conjunction, or a pronoun whose antecedent could only be found in vv. 3-8, or if v. 9 read "*such* widows should be enrolled." In fact, discourse analysis reveals a distinct pattern of imperatives which divides this passage into subsections: (in the Greek word order)

v.3	widows *honor*
v.7	*and* these things *command*
v.9	a widow should *be enrolled*
v.11	*but* younger widows *refuse.*

Notice that v. 7 has a conjunction which ties it to vv. 3-6, and v. 11 has a conjunction which ties it to vv. 9-10, but there is no such conjunction in v. 9 to tie it to the preceding section. Lacking a grammatical connection, the next three options consider the possibility of a semantic connection.

---

[53]See e.g., N. J. D. White, *The First and Second Epistles to Timothy and the Epistle to Titus* (London: Hodder and Stoughton, 1910): 130, and Jean Daniélou, *The Ministry of Women in the Early Church* (trans. G. Simon; London: Faith, 1961): 13. Scott, *Pastoral Epistles*, 57, raises the question but provides no answer.

b) *If the word "widow" was used throughout this section as a technical term to denote "an official church widow" or "a widow to be helped by the church" each time the word "widow" occurred without a qualifying adjective.* Dibelius and Conzelmann, as well as Scott,[54] suggest that χήρα (widow) is sometimes used as a technical term in this passage, but they do not offer either definite conclusions about which verses so use this word or criteria by which such a distinction could be made. In fact, in v. 16a the word "widow" occurs without a qualifying adjective, and the context clearly indicates that this does *not* refer to an "official" or "true" widow, by contrasting this widow in 16a with a "true widow" in 16d.

c) *If the word "widow" was used throughout this section without any qualifying words or phrases to differentiate one group of widows from another, so that it was clear that the same group of widows was being discussed throughout the passage.* Bassler states:

> The primary problem here is the apparent lack of unity in this passage, though it seems to deal with a single issue. Verses 3-16 are all concerned with widows, and apart from an insistence that the church seek out real widows (ἡ ὄντως χήρα) there is no evidence in the text to suggest that the term shifts in meaning. Thus a clear word pattern is established that points to the unity of the passage.[55]

Bassler suggests that because the word "widow" is used throughout the passage, only a single issue is being dealt with. She argues that the unity of the passage depends on the word "widow(s)" referring to the same person or group each time it is used. It is true that the word "widow" does not shift in meaning in this passage, i.e., it always means a woman whose husband has died. However, "widow" is

---

[54]Dibelius & Conzelmann, *The Pastoral Epistles*, 74, and Scott, *Pastoral Epistles*, 57.

[55]See Jouette Bassler, "The Widows' Tale: A Fresh Look at 1 Tim. 5:3-16," *JBL* 103 (1948): 33.

used repeatedly in this passage with qualifying words or phrases which *do* cause a "shift" in meaning: "true" widow(s) (vv. 3, 5, 16), "younger" widows (v. 11), and a widow who has children/descendants (v. 4). Since the passage clearly does discuss different groups or types of widows,[56] one cannot merely assume that vv. 9-10 and vv. 3-8 refer to the same people, simply because both sections discuss "widows."

d) *If the phrase "true widow" was used at any point in the verses which explicitly discuss enrollment (vv. 9-13).* Even a cursory study of the text disproves this option.

e) *If the criteria for identifying the "true widow" and the "widow to enroll" were identical (or even similar).* In fact, the two sets of criteria have nothing in common, except that both are applied to widows. The first set (vv. 3-6, 16) addresses financial/relational resources and the locus of one's trust/well-being: a true widow is one completely bereft of resources for sustenance, and in this complete bereavement she commits herself to God through prayer. The second set (vv. 9-10) addresses age, virtue, and observable behavior: a widow who qualifies for enrollment is not younger than 60, a "one-man woman," and well-known for devotion to good works, e.g., raising children, hospitality, washing the feet of the saints, and helping the afflicted.[57]

f) *If "to honor" and "to enroll" had the same lexical meaning.* Since "to honor" and "to enroll" are not *ipso facto* synonyms,[58] the equation of these two activities should be

---

[56]Cf. F. C. Synge, "I Timothy 5:3-16," *Theology* 68 (1965): 200-201, who concludes curiously that χήρα surely doesn't mean "widow," since so many types of widows are mentioned.

[57]This criterion (and that of "hospitality") imply some financial resources, either personally, or some provided by the church to finance such benevolence. Hanson, *Pastoral Epistles*, 96, suggests that this refers to actions performed while the woman's husband was still alive.

[58]A point which seems lost on Barrett, *Pastoral Epistles*, 75. He seems to think that if the meaning of the word "widow" doesn't change

made only if clearly demanded by the context, i.e., if equating "honor" and "enroll" is the only possible interpretation of this passage, or if it is clearly the best interpretation of this passage. Therefore, the truth or falsity of this option depends on a better understanding of the significance and purpose of enrollment.

This discussion of six possible grounds for equating the true widows and the enrolled widows reveals no reasonable semantic or grammatical basis for such an equation. It is possible that some *contextual* basis for this equation might be found, by considering further the criteria and the purpose of enrollment. The text does not *explicitly* state the purpose of enrollment. Two[59] possibilities for the purpose of enrollment have been proposed from the context: (1) financial assistance and (2) appointment to serve the church.

The view that enrollment is for financial assistance is suspect because it rests squarely on the incorrect equation of the true widows with the enrolled widows. The view that enrollment is for church service is challenged by three arguments. (1) Some[60] argue that this passage does not indicate such an "order" of widows, because it does not

---

between vv. 3 and 9, then the two verses can automatically be interpreted as addressing the same subject.

Liddell and Scott, *Greek Lexicon*, 897, give the following meanings for καταλέγω: 1) recount; 2) reckon up, count; 3) to enumerate, draw up a list, enroll; 4) select. 1 Tim. 5:9 is the only occurrence of this word in the NT. If there were any instances of widows being enrolled for a specific purpose in Hellenistic society, such parallels might prove helpful in understanding the meaning of enrollment here. However, a complex search through the *Thesaurus Linguae Graecae* computer database using all the case endings for "widow" and the various tense stems for "enroll" revealed that all other uses of this verb with "widow" occur only later in Patristic literature.

[59]Cf. C. J. Ellicott, *The Pastoral Epistles* (2nd ed.; Andover: Draper, 1897): 86, who subdivides the purpose of service into an active role of physical care and service ("deaconesses") and a more sedentary role of teaching/counseling ("female elders").

[60]See Fee, *1 and 2 Timothy and Titus*, 119.

specify duties. However, as Verner[61] points out, neither are the duties of deacons specified, yet none would deny that such a position existed. (2) Fee argues that the greatest locus of concern in 5:3-16 is the behavior of the younger widow.[62] However, he adds the *non sequitur* that, because there is not as much urgency about the older widows in vv. 9-10, such an "order" of widows is not indicated in this passage. (3) Some question the idea of enrollment for service on the basis of age, arguing that women older than 60 would be too decrepit to perform much service. While this was probably true for some, health and vitality have never been determined solely by age. Also, since widows' duties are not explicitly delineated, conclusions about how much strength and energy would be required of widows seem premature at best.

Since neither purpose receives unequivocal support from the text, a sensible approach is to see which of the two proposed purposes makes the best sense of the criteria for inclusion (vv. 9-10), the reasons for exclusion (vv. 11-13, 15), and the solution for those excluded (vv. 14-15).

2) *1 Tim. 5:9-10—Criteria for inclusion.* If the true widows and the widows-to-be-enrolled are the same, then a widow would have to meet all of the criteria in vv. 3-6, 9-10, and 16 to receive support from the church. It would also be true that all the enrolled widows would be supported by the church (v. 16). This creates two problems.

a) *Misogynistic limitation of the enrolled widows?* This view could lead to the hypothesis suggested by Bassler:[63]

---

[61]Verner, *The Household of God*, 164-165.

[62]Fee, *1 and 2 Timothy and Titus*, 114 and 119.

[63]Bassler, *JBL* (1948): 34. This view is the launching pad for the rest of Bassler's article, in which she asks why the circle of widows had grown so large. Her answering suggestion is twofold. First, she argues for a broader understanding of "widow." Based on Stählin's "χήρα," *TDNT*, 9.440, statement that this term can mean "a woman living without a husband," Bassler contends that "widows" in 1 Tim. 5 included divorcees, recently converted Christians who left their

Many of the difficulties presented by the text stem
from the fact that the author is not initiating a new
benevolence, . . . but is seeking to limit an existing
one. Indeed, this goal unites the content of the two
otherwise somewhat disparate halves of the passage,
since both seek to exclude various categories and
reduce the circle of widows to a minimum. . . . it
seems clear that the circle of widows had grown to
an unacceptable size, unacceptable both because of
the financial strain this placed on the church (v. 16)
and because of potential and real abuse of the office.

However, the passage contains only one phrase which
indicates concern about the *number* of widows under
discussion, viz., "Let not the church be burdened" (v. 16).
This concern about size is directed toward the widows being
supported, not necessarily the widows being enrolled. Even
this is not simply a complaint that too many widows are
requesting support. Rather, it is one more reason (in
addition to vv. 4, 7, and 8) why families and wealthy
women should support their widows, i.e., so that the church
will have resources to help those truly bereft.

---

husbands, and especially virgins. Yet a close reading of Stählin
indicates that while the Latin equivalent of χήρα often referred to "one
who had never married," the Greek term usually refers to one who had
been married, but—through separation, divorce, or death—was not
living currently with her husband. In the whole of Scripture, including
1 Tim. 5, there is no instance where the context necessitates understanding "widow" to mean "virgin." There are numerous instances in
which "widow" clearly does *not* refer to a virgin, e.g., Gen. 38:11; Lev.
21:14; 2 Sam. 14:5; 1 Cor. 7:39, and 1 Tim. 5:9. Thus, I do not find
Bassler convincing that "the widows' circle had evolved to the point that
chastity, not widowhood, was the determinative feature," and that therefore, the widows' circle had grown unacceptably large. Second, Bassler
argues that the widows' circle offered freedom from "the hierarchical
dominance of either father or husband, . . . from the demands of
childbearing and rearing, [as well as] economic concerns." (p. 36). See
my discussion on pp. 344-45.

In vv. 9-13 Paul sets stringent requirements on who can be enrolled. However, this need not be understood as a patriarchal attempt to "reduce the circle of widows to a minimum"[64] or as a misogynistic desire to "minimize . . . the involvement of widows in the official structure of the church."[65] No such motives are specified in the text, which simply states that Timothy should be careful to enroll only older widows well-known for service and to refrain from enrolling younger widows who might harm the church's reputation. So, if vv. 9-13 are read apart from v. 16, it is not the *number* of enrolled widows that concerns Paul, but simply their *behavior* (and their age—which seems related to behavior—vv. 11-13).

b) Stringent criteria for financial assistance. A second, and more troublesome, problem is that one who holds this view must admit the possibility that some destitute widows might have been denied support. A widow could have been truly bereft and devoted to God in prayer, yet still have been disqualified by any of the criteria in vv. 9-10: age, marital history,[66] or because, though a faithful Christian, she did not have a reputation for good works.[67]

One might argue that Paul intended for those disqualified by the age criterion to be supported by a second husband. This argument might have more validity if 16c-d came immediately after v. 14 and the text thus read:

I wish the younger widows to marry, bear children, manage their houses, and give no opportunity for abuse to the enemy, and let not the church be burdened, so that it might help the true widows.

---

[64] *Ibid.*, 34.

[65] See Verner, *The Household of God*, 166.

[66] E.g., scandalous sexual behavior prior to her conversion, of which outsiders could create scandal, not recognizing the change.

[67] E.g., a recent convert, or because her health might prevent the activities mentioned in v. 10.

However, the reason for such re-marriage is not the financial difficulty of supporting the younger widows, but the behavioral problems among the younger widows (v. 15). And if no one wanted to marry the younger widow, would the church still refuse to help her?

The phrase ἑνὸς ἀνδρὸς γυνή (one-man woman) is the feminine counterpart of the requirement for bishop and deacons (3:2, 12; μιᾶς γυναικὸς ἄνδρα; one-woman man). Five interpretations of this phrase have been offered: (1) marriage is demanded of all in this category, (2) polygamy is prohibited, (3) re-marriage after divorce is prohibited, (4) re-marriage after death of one's spouse is prohibited, (5) marital fidelity is demanded of all in this category. For a widow, the first option cannot be the issue,[68] nor is the third as pertinent to widows.[69] Since polyandry was no real problem in Jewish and Greco-Roman culture, the second option can also be discarded.[70]

In arguing against the fifth option, Kelly states that it "squeeze[s] more out of the Greek than it will bear."[71] Any one of the last three options could have been stated more clearly: μὴ ἀπολελύμενον (one who has not been divorced), ἔσχων μιᾶς γυναικὸς μονῆς (having *only* one wife), or μὴ μοιχός (not an adulterer).[72]

However, two reasons exist for accepting the fifth option. First, the problem of "ambiguity" is considerably lessened by realizing that instead of prohibiting a certain state (re-marriage, polygamy, adultery), Paul is urging a positive

---

[68]See Ed Glasscock, "'The Husband of One Wife' Requirement in I Timothy 3:2," *BSac* 140 (1983): 245; Kelly, *Pastoral Epistles*, 75; Lock, *Pastoral Epistles*, 36; and Fee, *1 and 2 Timothy and Titus*, 80, for discussion in relation to men.

[69]Robert L. Saucy, "The Husband of One Wife," *BSac* 131 (1974): 230-239; and Verner, *The Household of God*, 129-130.

[70]Glasscock, *BSac* (1983): 254.

[71]Kelly, *Pastoral Epistles*, 75.

[72]See Glasscock, *BSac* (1983): 247, 251, and Verner, *The Household of God*, 129-130, for these suggestions.

characteristic: just as a bishop should be a "one-woman type of man," a widow should have been[73] a "one-man type of woman," i.e., faithful and devoted to their spouse alone.[74]

Secondly, concern that bishops (3:2, 7) and widows (5:12, 14) not evoke criticism or bring reproach upon the church is crucial.[75] Therefore, the option most likely to evoke respect and least likely to bring reproach should be accepted. Marital fidelity would obviously evoke respect. Among Romans, the woman who was only married once (*univira*) was respected and played a special role in religious ceremonies.[76] However, Lightman and Zeisel[77] indicate that *univira* originally referred to living women with living husbands, then came to be used as a laudatory epithet for a woman, married only once, who predeceased her husband. Not until the Christian era was it commonly used to refer to widows who did not remarry. Among Greeks, widows were expected to re-marry; the concept of only one marriage was not idealized.[78] The OT emphasizes the lowly position of a widow who does not remarry.[79] Later, only Judith 16:22 and Luke 2:36 hint at Jewish respect for a widow who does not re-marry.

What about the converse? Did re-marriage provoke contempt or censure? On the contrary, re-marriage was

---

[73]For discussion of the participle γεγονυῖα (having become), and whether it should be taken with 9b or 9c, see Glasscock, *BSac* (1983): 255-256, and Ellicott, *The Pastoral Epistles*, 86.

[74]Glasscock, *BSac* (1983): 249-252; and Saucy, *BSac* (1974): 238-239.

[75]E.g., Lock, *Pastoral Epistles*, 36-38; and Fee, *1 and 2 Timothy and Titus*, 83.

[76]Balsdon, *Roman Women*, 185, 208.

[77]Marjorie Lightman and William Zeisel, "*Univira*: An Example of Continuity and Change in Roman Society," *CH* 46 (1977): 19-32.

[78]Pomeroy, *Goddesses, Whores, Wives, and Slaves*, 161.

[79]E.g., Psa. 109:9; Isa. 1:23, 10:2; Ezek. 22:7, 25. God will protect her (Psa. 68:5; 146:9), not because she represents an ideal, but because of concern for the defenseless.

considered appropriate behavior among Romans,[80] Greeks,[81] and Jews.[82] Paul himself urges re-marriage for the younger widow in 1 Tim. 5:14,[83] and sanctions it in Rom. 7:2-3 and 1 Cor. 7:8-9, 39-40.[84] Prohibition of marriage is in fact one of the few false teachings which Paul specifically mentions (1 Tim. 4:3) in his condemnation of the false teachers.

It was not until the second century AD that Christian writers began to idealize celibacy, both by virgins and by widows/widowers who did not re-marry. Any attempt to understand the phrases "one-woman man" and "one-man woman" as a prohibition of re-marriage, reads second-century ideals back into these NT texts and interprets Paul's clear teachings (1 Tim. 5:14; Rom. 7; 1 Cor. 7) by these more ambiguous statements. So, the best interpretion is the idea of marital faithfulness. To use this as a criterion for present financial support seems unreasonable, because failure to meet this criterion would (for a widow) automatically refer to *past* sin, of which she might have repented. Is she then to be left destitute for a problem she is totally unable to remedy?

Little attention has been paid to the "good works" criterion. Is Paul really saying the church should only help those widows who are "well attested" in good works, no

---

[80]Pomeroy, *Goddesses, Whores, Wives, and Slaves*, 164. In fact, Augustus passed legislation penalizing widows for *not* remarrying. See Balsdon, *Roman Women*, 75-77 and 221-222.

[81]Lacey, *The Family in Classical Greece*, 108.

[82]See Lev. 21:14; Ruth. See also Stählin, "χήρα," *TDNT*, 9.442 and 457. Thurston, *The Widows*, 13, references Stählin in support of her statement that the Jews frowned on remarriage, but he actually says that only Roman Judaism idealized the *univira*.

[83]Note that understanding "one-man woman" as "married only once" means that any widow who follows Paul's advice will automatically be excluded from enrollment if she is widowed again.

[84]Note that Paul also sanctions remaining unmarried. But this is not because such a state is more "ideal" or virtuous, or less evocative of censure, but because it allows greater devotion to the Lord.

matter how desperate their financial need? What about those who have done good works, but in secret? Just how many good works must one have done to qualify?

The whole notion of having criteria for financial assistance based on age, marital fidelity, and devotion to good works is contrary to the rest of Scripture. Numerous passages urge the care of widows.[85] Not one of them mandates criteria, other than the fact of widowhood and need.

The only other option (for those who erroneously equate true widows and enrolled widows) is to argue that Paul does intend to help all the destitute widows, and knows that they would not be disqualified by the other criteria— i.e., he knows that all of the destitute widows in the Ephesian church are both older and devoted to good works. But if this is true, why have so many criteria? Why insist on a criterion that does not exclude anyone? If Paul knows that all the widows under 60 in the Ephesian church either have other resources, or are not devoted to good works, why include the age criterion at all? Further, what would happen if a destitute widow, younger and devoted to good works, became a Christian? This view makes Paul's advice seem remarkably short-sighted, while the first option makes it seem unbiblically hard-hearted.

c) *The criteria for inclusion if two problems are involved.* So far this discussion of criteria for inclusion raises serious problems for the other views: (1) the impression that Paul was trying to limit the number of enrolled widows, and (2) the possibility that some destitute widows might be refused support. Does the third view fare any better? The view that a true widow is one who is truly bereft, i.e., no resources on which to depend except God and his people, agrees with the view that the purpose of enrollment was for service to the church, but disagrees with

---

[85]E.g., Exod. 22:22-24; Deut. 10:18; 14:29; 16:14; 24:17-21; 26:12-13; Zech. 7:9-10; Isa. 1:17; Jer. 7:6, 22:3; Acts 6:1ff.; James 1:27. However, see 1 Tim. 5:5; note that 5:9 gives no criteria for financial aid, but treats those who should be enrolled for service.

the other views by asserting that an *enrolled* widow is not necessarily the same as a *true* widow.[86]

If the purpose of enrollment is for service to the church, each of the three criteria listed in vv. 9-10[87] has immediate relevance, and also a comparative relevance when contrasted with the reasons for excluding young widows. Note also the marked similarities between the criteria for enrolled widows and for those appointed to public roles of service or leadership in the church (3:1-13):[88] marital fidelity, hospitality, proper care of children, a good reputation, and (by inference from the negative example of the younger widow—v. 13) exemplary speech.

The importance of the age criterion is twofold: (1) older widows would be more free of domestic/child-raising[89] responsibilities, and (2) in Hellenistic society older women had more freedom to go about outside their homes,[90] thus house to house visitation by an older widow would be less likely to cause scandal. The criterion of marital fidelity

---

[86]A true widow might also be enrolled as a church servant, but such an equation is not automatic. Other types of widows, e.g., the wealthy in v. 6, might conceivably be enrolled to serve the church, if they met the criteria in vv. 9-10.

[87]The specific deeds listed in v. 10 are not additional criteria, but examples of the "noble deeds" mentioned as the verse begins. Note the different Greek adjective (ἀγαθός; good) used at the end of the verse. See Lock, *Pastoral Epistles*, 22-23 for a useful comparison.

[88]Verner, *The Household of God*, 163-164.

[89]Possibly this reflects concern for societal opinion. In 18 BC, Augustus passed a law that all widows under 50 should re-marry or face penalties. It is true that there is a discrepancy of 10 years between the age stipulated in the law and in 1 Tim. 5:9. However, since the purpose of the law was to increase the number of births, it is possible that only by age sixty would a widow be free of child-raising responsibilities and able to devote her energies to the church full-time.

[90]Lacey, *The Family in Classical Greece*, 158-62, 175. Balsdon, *Roman Women*, 45, 277, notes that Roman matrons of all ages had more freedom to go about in public than did their Greek counterparts, who spent much of their time in seclusion in their homes. See Pomeroy, *Goddesses, Whores, Wives, and Slaves*, 72-87.

would enrich the widows' ability to counsel and aid Christian wives. Timothy could also be certain that such women would not bring reproach on the church from past scandal.

The discussion of good works in the third criterion suggests the type of services which the enrolled widows would perform, without necessarily limiting her services to those listed. Many[91] have correctly noted that v. 10 lists qualifications, not duties. Yet surely these good works are not "merit badges" which earn the reward of an honorary position, nor simply laurels on which to rest, but practical experiences which prepared and qualified them to render service beyond the sphere of their homes. Just as it is logical to postulate that the reason a bishop should be skillful in teaching (3:2) is so that he can effectively serve as a teacher (5:17), it is reasonable to suggest that these widows would serve according to their past experience.[92]

So, it is more convincing to suppose that the criteria of vv. 9-10 are designed to select experienced and trustworthy servants, than to select appropriate recipients of aid.

3) *1 Tim. 5:11-13,15—Reasons for exclusion.* Two reasons are given for the exclusion of younger widows from enrollment: a) sexual problems (vv. 11-12), and b) inappropriate conduct (v. 13). Verse 14 offers an alternative for these younger widows. The reason for this alternative, as well as for the exclusion in v. 11, is given in v. 15. Though Paul does not explicitly state the connection which he perceives between enrollment and the younger widows' behavior (described in vv. 11-13), two options are possible: either (1) this behavior is typical of young widows and therefore they should not be enrolled or (2) this has happened before with enrolled young widows, therefore, they should not be enrolled.

---

[91]E.g., Mary J. Evans, *Woman in the Bible* (Downer's Grove, IL: InterVarsity, 1983): 112; and Fee, *1 and 2 Tim., Tit.*, 119.

[92]See Kelly, *Pastoral Epistles*, 116-117.

In support of the second option, v. 15 plainly states that
problems with the young widows have already occurred.[93]
While it is possible that Paul is bringing up a completely new
and different type of problem in v. 15, the location of this
verse in the concluding remarks and its brevity militate
against such a view. It is better to view v. 15 as referring to
the problems discussed in this earlier section. It is also
possible that vv. 11-13 and 15 refer to problems among
young widows who were not enrolled. However, the
position of these verses immediately after the discussion of
enrolled widows in vv. 9 and 10 and Paul's use of the
present deponent imperative (5:11)[94] seem to indicate that
these problems had been exhibited by young widows who
were enrolled. An additional argument is Paul's use of the
verb "learn" in v. 13, i.e., he does not say that young
widows *are* idle, but that they *learn* to be idle.[95]

Therefore, vv. 11-13 are to be taken as a description of
the actual experiences of some younger widows while they
were enrolled, not a description of behavior generally
exhibited by young widows which should preclude their
enrollment. If this is true, two conclusions can be drawn.
(1) These verses reflect specific, historical events. The
young widows actually wanted to marry because of sensual
urges,[96] and because of this they were being criticized for
rejecting a faith or a pledge, they were going from house to
house,[97] and they were acquiring some bad habits, e.g.,

---

[93]In 5:3-16, this is the only "clear and objective statement"
(Dahls' primary historical category), and as such should be taken very
seriously in determining the historical background of this section.

[94]This supports the view that young widows had been enrolled in
the past, and that they are to be refused enrollment from now on.

[95]See Scott, *Pastoral Epistles*, 62; and Ward, *1 and 2 Tim. and
Titus*, 85.

[96]This phrase makes it difficult to accept Bassler's, *JBL* (1948):
35-36, 39-40, thesis that the reason a "disturbing" number of women
were eagerly embracing the celibate lifestyle of the widows' group is
that it offered freedom from patriarchal domination of a male.

[97]Thus suggesting that this was one of the expected duties of the
enrolled widows. The argument that this cannot be true, because Paul

laziness, inappropriate inquisitiveness, and talking about things which they should not. (2) Enrollment, in some way, *caused* these problems for the young widows.[98] This has significant implications for the understanding of vv. 11-12.

a) *The first reason for the exclusion of the younger widows* is given in vv. 11 and 12: " For whenever they feel sensual urges against Christ, they want to marry, coming under condemnation because they set aside their first faith/pledge."

The crucial question in v. 11 is: does the phrase "want to marry" function (1) as a *clarification* of the verb κατα-στρηνιάω,[99] equating sensual urges and the desire to marry or (2) as the *result* of "feeling sensual urges against Christ"? The first option seems unlikely due to the grammatical structure and the context. The syntax of this sentence (ὅταν followed by an aorist subjunctive) normally indicates that "the action of the subordinate clause precedes that of the main clause."[100] So, the grammar seems to support the second option: i.e., because sensual urges alienate young

---

condemns this activity (Bassler, "Widows' Tale," 40, n. 61) is only one view. An equally plausible view is that Paul is condemning the young widows' *misuse* of one of their duties. See Dibelius and Conzelmann, *Pastoral Epistles*, 75; Kelly, *Pastoral Epistles*, 118; and H. Wayne House, "A Biblical View of Women in the Ministry (Part 5 of 5 parts): Distinctive Roles for Women in the Second and Third Centuries," *BSac* 146 (1989):45.

[98]Since Paul does not discuss the older widows having these problems, either he does not think that enrollment automatically causes these problems for all widows or he doesn't care if the older widows exhibit such problems. This is contradicted by his repeated concern that the behavior of all the Ephesian Christians (2:2, 3:14-15, 4:12), including the older widows (5:9-10), be exemplary. Therefore, it must be some combination of widowhood, youth, and enrollment that precipitates these problems. This is similar to the comments about the potential problems of new converts being appointed as elders (3:6).

[99]Bauer, *Greek Lexicon*, 420, "become wanton against . . . feel sensuous impulses that alienate."

[100]Bauer, *Greek Lexicon*, 592.

widows from Christ,[101] they desire to marry, so that their needs might be met in a manner consistent with their profession of Christianity.

Contextually, if sensual urges equals a desire to marry, then this verse says that the desire to marry puts one at odds with Christ. This would be true only if the church taught that widows should not re-marry, or if a widow wanted to marry a non-believer. Since 5:14 clearly teaches that widows may re-marry,[102] this view leads to the conclusion that Paul's concern about the young widows in vv. 11-15 was that they wanted to marry non-believers.[103] However, such a concern is not specified either in Paul's statement of the problem (vv. 11-12) or in the solution he proposes (v. 14), but must be read into the text. Each verse uses the same verb (γαμεῖν; to marry), without any qualifying comment about the type of husband recommended. Yet this activity provokes condemnation in vv. 11-12 and is encouraged in v. 14. What reason does the context give for this apparent discrepancy? V. 12 says that they are condemned because "they set aside the first faith/pledge." There are five options for understanding this phrase: (1) re-marriage means rejecting the Christian faith or breaking their pledge to be a Christian,[104] (2) re-marriage means breaking the pledge to

---

[101]Either by leading to sexual immorality or by preoccupying their minds to the neglect of Christian thoughts and responsibilities. See Ward, *1 and 2 Timothy and Titus*, 85.

[102]Since 5:14 ("Therefore I wish the younger to marry") has no explicit mention of widows or re-marriage, the KJV translates this as a reference to young women, not young widows. However, the position of this verse in the middle of the discussion about widows, and the continuation from vv. 11-13 implied by "therefore" argue overwhelmingly that 5:14 is speaking of widows, not women in general. See Easton, *Pastoral Epistles*, 151. And if this verse does address widows, there is no need to specify *re*-marriage, for when a widow marries it is, by definition, a "re-marriage" (1 Cor.7:39 uses the same verb as 1 Tim. 5:14 in a clear reference to widows marrying a second time).

[103]See Fee, *1 and 2 Timothy, Titus*, 120-122.

[104]See 1 Cor. 7:8-9, 25-40. Also, in all of the passages in 1 Tim. where Paul is clearly discussing those who have rejected the

one's first husband, and Paul believes that this results in spiritual condemnation, (3) re-marriage means breaking the pledge to one's first husband, and this results in censure from society for not upholding the highest ideal of only one marriage, (4) re-marriage to a non-believer means rejecting the Christian faith, (5) re-marriage would cause a widow to break an earlier vow.[105]

The first two options are contradicted by Paul's recommendation that young widows should marry in 5:14. The third option depends on interpreting "one-man woman" (5:9) to mean "married only once," an unlikely interpretation. Previous discussion of this phrase pointed out that this ideal was not uniformly held by all segments of the culture, yet remarriage was uniformly considered appropriate behavior.

The fourth option requires considerable eisegesis. If the concern in vv. 11-12 is fear that young widows will marry unbelievers, the choice of words is ambiguous. Certainly in 1 Cor. 7:39, Paul had no difficulty expressing this concern plainly.[106] Surely, if indeed this is the *crux* of the problem in 1 Timothy 5, Paul could have been similarly articulate here. If Paul's obscurity is problematic in vv. 11-12, his failure to clearly state his concern when he proposes a solution (v. 14) is incomprehensible. This option simply strains too hard against the historical controls proposed by Dahl.

The objections to these first four options demand serious consideration of the last option, in which vv. 11 and

---

Christian faith (1:5-6,19; 4:1; 5:8; 6:10, 21), he never calls it the "first" faith, nor does he use there the verb used here in 5:12.

[105]Fee, *1 and 2 Timothy, Titus*, 121, mentions this option, but gives no reason for rejecting it. One assumes he rejects it because such a vow strongly indicates that there was an order of widows who served the church, and Fee rejects such an idea.

[106]Nor in 2 Cor. 6:14-16 (if this indeed deals with marriage, rather than other types of relationships). See Victor Paul Furnish, *II Corinthians* (AB, 32A; Garden City, NY: Doubleday, 1984):372.

12 would read: "Refuse (to enroll) the younger widows, for whenever they feel sensual urges against Christ, they want to marry. This brings them under judgment, because (by wanting to marry) they break their earlier pledge." If one accepts this view, the widows made some type of vow or pledge when they were enrolled.[107] The type of pledge is not specified in this passage. However, since wanting to marry means breaking the vow, a reasonable hypothesis is that it was either a pledge[108] of celibacy[109] and/or a vow to devote one's life to serving the church. This interpretation does the best job of using only the ideas presented in the passage to offer an explanation that is clear, consistent with the surrounding verses, and clears up textual ambiguities.

If an enrolled widow did take such a vow, this would explain Paul's insistence that enrolled widows be experienced in service, his distress over the younger widows' behavior in v. 13, and the significance of the criteria of old age and marital fidelity. Older widows would be more free of overwhelming sexual urges and yearnings to marry[110] which so distract younger widows (v. 11). They would also have had experience in disciplining their sexual urges while practicing faithfulness in their marriage.

Finally, this last option is the only one which is consistent with the thesis that enrollment in some way caused these problems for the young widows. It is difficult to see how enrollment for support or church service would cause a widow to wish to marry an unbeliever, or how it would be the basis for condemning such a wish. However, a pledge of celibacy, combined with normal sexual urges and temptations, would place the young widow in an unenviable position. If she stayed celibate, these urges would continue to distract her and might tempt her into sexual immorality. If

---

[107]Cf. Alexander Sand, "Witwenstand und Ämterstrukturen in den urchristlichen Gemeinden," *BibLeb* 12 (1971): 196.

[108]See Rudolph Bultmann, "πιστεύω," *TDNT*, 6.177.

[109]There is no reason to assume that this was an actual vow of "betrothal" to Christ, as does Stählin, "χήρα," *TDNT*, 9.454-456.

[110]Ward, *1 and 2 Timothy and Titus*, 83-84.

she decided to avoid such immorality by marriage, she would incur censure for breaking her pledge.

This interpretation of vv. 11-12 strongly supports, and is supported by, the view that enrollment is for church service. How does the view that enrollment is only for financial aid fit with this interpretation that a vow of celibacy[111] was taken upon enrollment? In this section, Paul repeatedly urges any widow who has other resources to be supported by such resources, so that the church would not be burdened. If this is true, and if enrollment is only for financial aid, why would any widow, regardless of age, be asked to promise never to re-marry, when such re-marriage would remove the burden of her support from the church?

b) *The second reason for the exclusion of the younger widows* is in v. 13: Paul states that the younger widows go around from house to house,[112] they learn to be idle, and not only idle,[113] but babblers, meddlesome, and talking

---

[111]If one insists that these widows were *not* church servants, a vow of dedication to church service would not be a viable option.

[112]If the participle is used in this verse as a circumstantial or adverbial participle (see Robertson, *Grammar of the Greek New Testament*, 1040, 1103, 1121), it indicates an activity that is simultaneous with (not a result of) the learning, and possibly even causal or instrumental: "while going about, they learn . . ." or "by going about, they learn . . . ."

[113]The charge of idleness has significance for the question "Did the church support the enrolled widows?" A definite affirmative to this question can only be given by equating the enrolled widow with the "true" widow of vv. 3 and 16. But if such an equation cannot be assumed, there are no conclusive arguments which prove that enrolled widows were supported by the church. However, if they had had to do secular work to support themselves, the charge of idleness surely would not have been appropriate. Therefore, it seems likely that the enrolled widows had some form of support. Does this reasoning lead inevitably to the idea that enrollment was simply for financial aid and did not entail any church duties, hence the charge of idleness? No, for Paul does not seem to view the problem of idleness as an automatic result of *any* widow being enrolled, but only as a potential problem for the younger widows. The enrolled widows theoretically could have received

about unnecessary things. The Greek words here could be translated to indicate a simple tendency to gossip,[114] or could be understood in a more serious light: these young widows were discussing and investigating things which were foolish, unnecessary, and wrong. The significance of this second option is illuminated by a consideration of v. 15, which states the reason for the exclusion urged in v. 11 and the corrective actions urged in verse 14: "for some have already turned away after Satan." This "clear and objective statement" affirms that Paul has not been discussing a hypothetical situation, but is dealing with actual problems facing the Ephesian church.[115] Since it is part of Paul's conclusions about the problems in vv. 11-13, it is best to understand "turned away after Satan" as an additional description of the problems portrayed in 11-13.

There are four possible meanings for this phrase. (1) It could mean the young widows have rejected Christianity altogether.[116] This seems unlikely, since it is difficult to see how being enrolled would precipitate such apostasy, or how marriage and child-bearing would prevent or solve it. Also, if one accepts the preceding interpretation of vv. 11-13, there is no hint that such an irrevocable break has been made.

(2) "Turned away after Satan" could be a general reference to any number of unspecified sinful behaviors.[117] However, if one accepts the previous suggestion that v. 15 is part of the conclusions about the problems in vv. 11-13,

---

support from a variety of sources, e,g., family, friends, personal wealth, or the church. The passage does not deal with this question explicitly.

[114]See Winter, *TynBul* (1988): 97, who suggests that the young widows are using this means to find another husband. The conjunction here (ἄμα) does not automatically imply any causal relationship between the two actions, but simply a "coincidence in time of two actions together" (see Bauer, *Greek Lexicon*, 41).

[115]See Kelly, *Pastoral Epistles*, 119-120; and Fee, *1 and 2 Timothy, Titus*, 123.

[116]See e.g., Ward, *1 and 2 Timothy and Titus*, 86.

[117]See e.g., Scott, *Pastoral Epistles*, 62.

this option can be rejected as well. (3) Some of the young widows were indulging in sexual immorality.[118] This understanding certainly fits the context better, especially the concerns in 5:11-12.

(4) It is possible that the young widows were caught up in the false teaching.[119] An instructive, though inconclusive, point is that all other substantive uses of the plural form of τις (a certain person) in 1 Tim. refer to the false teachers.[120] Also, four out of the five NT occurrences of the verb ἐκτρέπω (turn away) are found in the Pastorals. Whether one is turning away from the false teaching (6:20) or away from the truth to false teaching (1:6, 2 Tim. 4:4) is determined by the words associated with the verb in the particular context.[121] In 1 Tim. 5:15 the words "after Satan" clearly indicate turning from the truth to heresy.[122] Understanding v. 15 as a reference to involvement in the false teaching certainly illuminates Paul's concern about the young widows' speech in v. 13.[123] The problem is not that they were gossiping, but that they were promoting the false teaching and wasting their time in useless controversy.

This discussion suggests two interpretations of v. 15. (1) V. 15 could be a general summary which uses the

---

[118]See e.g., Hanson, *Pastoral Epistles*, 99.

[119]See Fee, *1 and 2 Timothy, Titus*, 122-123; and David M. Scholer, "I Timothy 2:9-15 and the Place of Women in the Church's Ministry," *Women, Authority & the Bible* (ed. A. Mickelsen; Downer's Grove, IL: InterVarsity, 1986): 197-200.

[120]1:3, 6, 19; 4:1; 5:24; 6:10,21. See Johannes Müller-Bardoff, "Zur Exegese von I. Timotheus 5,3-16," *Gott und die Götter: Festgabe für Erich Fascher* (Berlin: Evangelische Verlagsanstalt, 1958): 132.

[121]See Hans-Werner Bartsch, *Die Anfänge urchristlicher Rechtsbildungen: Studien zur Pastoralbriefen* (Hamburg: H. Reich, 1965): 134.

[122]Cf. Norbert Brox, *Die Pastoralbriefe* (Regensburg: F. Pustet, 1969): 197.

[123]As well as his harsh comments forbidding women to teach in 2:11-12. See Fee, *1 and 2 Timothy, Titus*, 122; and Scholer, "I Timothy 2:9-15," *Women, Authority & the Bible*, 203.

somewhat ambiguous phrase "turning away after Satan" to refer to two different problems, i.e., fornication resulting from the struggle described in vv. 11-12 and involvement with the false teaching as described in v. 13. (2) "Turning away after Satan" could refer only to involvement with the false teaching, in which case both problems (vv. 11-12 and 13) would somehow be precipitated by such involvement. The only real difference is that the second view is more difficult to reconcile with young widows' desire to marry.

It is impossible to say if the young widows adhered to the false teaching *before* being enrolled and were attracted to enrollment because of the vow of celibacy (see 4:3). It is also possible that they sincerely desired to serve when they were first enrolled and only later were attracted to the false teaching. In either case, they soon found their minds distracted from their devotion to service by strong sexual urges. Visiting from house to house, it would have been easy to neglect the true task (service) and become enmeshed in discussions about their struggles with celibacy (and by association, other topics being discussed by the false teachers). The result is the same as that described in 1 Timothy 1:3-6. The heart of the Christian message (godliness and loving service) is neglected for unproductive discussions.

If this scenario is accurate, the reason for the criteria of proven devotion to good works and marital faithfulness in vv. 9 and 10 becomes clearer. Such women have demonstrated their understanding that true godliness consists of righteousness, love and service, not proficiency in controversial discussion. Because their lives are concomitant with their understanding of truth, they should not be as susceptible to the false teachers.

Once again, if enrollment is for a recognized role as a servant to the church, it is clear that the detrimental behaviors in v. 13 ought to disqualify the younger widows who display such behaviors. It is harder to reconcile the view that enrollment is only for financial aid with the concerns in v. 13. If enrollment is simply for financial aid, why should the younger widows be refused enrollment because of their behavior? Surely a better solution than refusing support would be either to disfellowship them if their behavior is that ungodly, or to assist them in changing their behavior.

4) *1 Tim. 5:14-15—Solution for those excluded from enrollment* . The inferential particle οὖν (therefore) in verse 14 signals the conclusions with which Paul will finish the passage.[124] In light of the problems in vv. 11-13, an alternative is offered to enrollment for the younger widows in vv. 14-15. Rather than criticizing, ridiculing, or punishing the younger widows in vv. 11-13, he acknowledges that enrollment has created difficulties and precipitated unchristian behavior. An arrangement which was intended to enable service has actually hindered the service of some. For *this* reason,[125] Paul advocates a situation for the younger widows which he believes will be more conducive to Christian behavior.

The preferred alternative is expressed in four present active infinitives: to marry,[126] to bear children, to rule their households,[127] and to give no opportunity for abuse to the enemy.[128] Some argue that the widows were bringing

---

[124]The immediate reference of "therefore" is to vv. 11-13, as it gives an alternative for the young widows. However, in the literary structure of this section, it also functions to initiate the entire concluding section (vv. 14-16).

[125]Not in an effort to thrust them into a "subordinate lifestyle," as Bassler, *JBL* (1948): 38-39, conjectures.

[126]This refutes the false teaching in 4:3. Paul's concern here is not so much the opinion of outsiders (contra Fee, *1 and 2 Timothy, Titus*, 123) as the problems which this false teaching is causing for the Christians.

[127]Note the similarity between 5:14 and 3:4, 12. In both Greek and Roman culture, it was the wife's duty to manage the household slaves (Balsdon, *Roman Women*, 282; and Pomeroy, *Goddesses, Whores, Wives, and Slaves*, 71-73, 169, who also discusses on 79, 160, 169, and 194, the situation of a household including male slaves).

[128]The "enemy" is understood either as hostile pagan neighbors (e.g., Lock, *Pastoral Epistles*, 61) or as Satan, working through human

reproach on the church by flouting the traditional role of wife and mother which society affirmed.[129] They may have flouted such roles, but this is not Paul's point in this verse. If it were, then the first three exhortations to marry, to bear children and to rule households would be conditions which would result in the fourth phrase "to give no opportunity for abuse." If this fourth phrase did function as a result clause, one would expect it to employ a telic participle or to be introduced by a conjunction such as ἵνα (in order that). Instead, the fourth verb is identical in form to the first three, suggesting that it too functions as a concluding alternative to the problematic behaviors of vv. 11-13.

In other words, Paul does not urge marriage, child-bearing and household management in order to avoid reproach, but as a means of dealing with the problems of sensual urges (get married), of idleness (bear children, manage household), and of inappropriate speaking/involvement with the false teachers (be obliged to focus on service instead).[130] "Give no opportunity for abuse" provides an additional (more general) means of dealing with these problems: since their behavior has been causing problems, their behavior must now be above reproach in every way.

So, if the purpose of enrollment is solely for financial aid, one would expect this to be the reason offered in v. 15 for the exclusion of younger widows and the encouragement to remarry. But, this is not the case. However, if the purpose of enrollment is for service, these verses offer a productive solution for those whose behavior disqualifies them from enrollment for church service.

---

agents (Kelly, *Pastoral Epistles*, 119; Fee, *1 and 2 Timothy, Titus*, 123).

[129]E.g., Bassler, *JBL* (1948): 31-32, 36-39; and Scholer, "I Timothy 2:9-15," *Women, Authority and the Bible*, 198.

[130]See E. K. Simpson, *The Pastoral Epistles: The Greek Text with Introduction and Commentary* (Grand Rapids: Eerdmans, 1954): 76; Ward, *1 and 2 Timothy and Titus*, 86; Kelly, *Pastoral Epistles*, 119, and Winter, *TynBul* (1988): 97.

C. Summary and analysis of the three views

1) *Conclusions about equating true widows and enrolled widows, and about the purpose of enrollment* . The discussion of the possible grounds for equating true and enrolled widows concluded that there is no valid grammatical or sematic basis for this equation and proposed that contextual basis be sought by further examination of the criteria for and purpose of enrollment of widows.

Further consideration of the criteria, instead of providing contextual grounds for equating the true widows and the enrolled widows, revealed at least two additional difficulties with such an equation. a) When v. 16 is understood to refer to enrolled widows, it is tempting to conclude that Paul was a misogynist, trying to minimize both the size and influence of the group of enrolled widows. b) If the criteria in vv. 9-10 must have been met in order to receive financial aid, this marks a clear departure from biblical precedent and might have resulted in some destitute widows not receiving aid from the church.

Investigation of the two proposed purposes for enrollment (financial aid or church service) revealed that the purpose of church service is a tenable option, often clarifying ambiguities better than the purpose of financial aid. Therefore, the context does not demand that "enroll" and "honor" be understood as synonyms.

In light of the difficulties facing each of the six options discussed, true widows should not automatically be equated with enrolled widows. As noted, if the true widows are not the same as the enrolled widows, there is nothing in this passage to indicate that the purpose of enrollment was for financial aid. Thus, the views that the true widows are to be equated with the enrolled widows and that enrollment was for financial assistance do not withstand rigorous analysis.

2) *Final analysis of the view that two problems are involved.* This view is attractive because it automatically avoids the problems raised by the other views, by not

forcing every verse to address the same issue. Apparent difficulties involve textual unity and the fact that the text does not explicitly state that the purpose of enrollment is church service. This latter difficulty was addressed above; the first difficulty will be dealt with below. According to this view, the section (5:3-16) deals with two problems: support of widows and enrolling widows.

a) *Support of Widows (5:3-8, 16).* The church (both collectively and individually) seems confused about how to care for Christian widows financially. Vv. 3-8 and 16 clarify matters. Any widow who still has family should be cared for by that family. Any widow who has personal financial resources is able to care for herself as well as other widows with whom she has either friendship or kinship. Widows not enrolled are free to remarry and would then no longer belong in this category. Any widow who has no family, personal wealth, or opportunity for remarriage, is truly bereft. If she remains firm in her faith, she is a "true" widow and should be honored and cared for by the church.

b) *Enrollment of Widows (5:9-15).* Second, there are problems concerning widows who had been enrolled. These widows made a pledge, either of celibacy (to free her time and attention to focus on church service) or simply of devotion to full time service to the church. Such a pledge proved too difficult for some of the younger widows to keep, and they are torn between wanting to keep the vow and wanting to marry to avoid sexual temptations. Perhaps because of this celibacy issue, some of the younger widows are also getting embroiled in the false teaching, indulging in controversial speculations. Thus, 5:13 offers the same portrait of these young widows involved with the false teaching as is found in 1:3-6, i.e., Christians whose preoccupation with false doctrine is causing them to neglect the loving service which should be the goal and the ultimate expression of their Christian faith. The suggestion that these young widows marry (v. 14) does not penalize them. Rather, Paul advocates a way for them to lead useful lives of service and at the same time meet their sexual needs in a godly fashion.

c) *Unity of the passage.* This interpretation of vv. 3-8, 16 and 9-15 best fits the discourse analysis of 1 Tim. 5:3-16. Unity of the passage is an important matter. Most seem to think that the passage can only be unified by insisting that all the verses deal with either the issue of financial aid, or the issue of enrolling widows as paid church workers. Verner astutely suggests an alternate basis for unity:

> When one views the whole of 5:3-16 together, one finds that to a certain extent it does reflect a unified perspective after all. Throughout the author views widows, official or otherwise, as a problem with which the church is forced to deal. . . It thus appears that he wants to minimize both the involvement of the church in the lives of widows and the involvement of widows in the official structure of the church.[131]

Thus Verner finds unity not in an analysis of the particulars of the passage, but in a meta-analysis of the underlying themes of the passage as a whole. However, Verner states that the problem is the widows, and that Paul's solution is to minimize their involvement with the church. I rather suggest that the problem is how the widows are to be both subject and object of service in the church.[132] Paul's solution is to try to *maximize* both the service received by the widows and the service performed by the widows. Verses 3-8 deal mainly with service received by the widows. Verses 9-13 deal with certain widows who are appointed to serve the church, and try to sort out the problems caused by appointing widows of all ages to perform such services. Verses 14-16, then, function beautifully as a chiastic summary of the *problems* discussed in verses 3-13.

---

[131]Verner, *The Household of God*, 166.

[132]Roger Gryson, *The Ministry of Women in the Early Church* (trans. J. Laporte and M. L. Hall; Collegeville, MN: Liturgical Press, 1976): 9, uses similar language, but fails to see this as the unifying theme. Similarly, Inger Marie Lindboe, "Recent Literature: Development and Perspectives in New Testament Research on Women," *ST* 43 (1989): 159, recognizes that "the widows both gave and received help," but draws no conclusions.

This interpretation, that service is the central idea which unifies 1 Tim. 5:3-16, is based on a literary analysis of the larger section, 4:6-6:2, in which this passage is imbedded. The focus of 4:6-6:2 is Timothy's twofold task: (1) to set an example of ministry and (2) to assist specific groups who are having problems living godly lives of service. The principles of godliness and service which are urged in this text must not be lost on the church today. According to 1 Tim. 5:3-8, 16, Christian widows with no other resources must be honored and supported financially by Christians. Although in this text Paul addresses the support of Christian widows, the principle certainly would include others, as far as resources permit. The "widows" in 1 Tim. 5:9-10 were a specially appointed group who met certain criteria and were designated to perform specific tasks of service in the church. Nothing is said of their being "ordained" or paid. For the edification of both the church and its widows, all Christian widows should be encouraged to serve as their circumstances and abilities allow, whether in prayer, in serving their families, or the church, or supporting other widows.

Chapter Fourteen

TITUS 2:5—MUST WOMEN STAY AT HOME?

Stanley N. Helton

Claiming that women who work away from home are partially responsible for America's moral laxness, Malone[1] advocates that Titus 2:5 unequivocally orders women to "stay at home." Malone (328) begins his argument with, "The actual Greek word in Titus 2:5 for the three English words 'keepers at home' is made up of two words: 'house' and 'work' or 'worker.'"[2] After concluding from Proverbs 31 that God praises "the woman who keeps the home," he

---

[1]Joe Malone, "Difficult Texts from 1 & 2 Timothy and Titus: Consideration of Titus 2:5: 'Keepers at Home'," *Difficult Texts of the New Testament Explained* (ed. W. Winkler; Hurst, TX: Winkler Pub., 1981): 328-31. Note this view in Hallie Kellog, *The Woman of God* (Austin, TX: Firm Foundation, 1962): 105, who writes, "The wife who willfully neglects the duties she owes her children and home for the public life *for which man was created* leaves her work, her character, and her mission" (italics mine). Similarly, A. C. Hervey, *Titus* (Pulpit Comm., 21; Grand Rapids: Eerdmans, 1950 reprint): 31, suggests, "The wife's business is in her household, not in the great world of society. Gadding abroad . . . tends to the spreading of evil."

[2]Apparently he is unaware that the renderings "keepers at home" in KJV and "workers at home" in ASV reflect Greek textual variants. Note the similar confusion in J. Burton Coffman, *1 and 2 Thessalonians, 1 and 2 Timothy, Titus and Philemon* (Austin: Firm Foundation, 1978): 333, who further misunderstands the problem when he asserts that questions over the word are contrived to cast doubt on Pauline authorship of Titus. See also Rachel Howard, *In the Hands of a Woman* (Kendallville, IN: Sacred Selections, 1969): 117, who defines "keeper" as "stayer at home" or "good housekeeper," and Lucibel Van Atta, *Women Encouraging Women* (Portland: Multnomah, 1987): 95.

appeals to surveys that show well over one-third of all women aged 14 and over in the labor force.[3] He then states (329),

> Many do not know the teaching of God's word. Should they attend church services, they might never hear the truth on the subject because preachers and teachers are afraid, in many instances, to deal with the matter. Sometimes their own families are guilty. Worse still, there are those who know the teaching of God's word but who do not want that teaching. They want a career outside the home. They want to fatten their purse. They want whatever materialism can afford. They want to avoid what to them is the drudgery of home responsibilities. Finally, there are some who, through economic necessity, are compelled to work outside the home. For them, there is genuine sympathy. As soon as conditions permit, they will return to that niche God would have them occupy.

Malone, however, fails to satisfy the very title of his essay. For him, apparently the only "difficulty" in this text is in not obeying it.[4] Malone makes no attempt to understand this text in its first-century literary and historical contexts, but unfortunately seems content to follow the "proof texting" procedure. Thus, the question of whether Titus 2:5 teaches that women must stay at home warrants clarification.

---

[3]Malone conveniently avoids mentioning that the wife in Proverbs 31 is in charge of virtually every aspect of family life, including business activity outside the home, and not at all like the stereotypical American homemaker, e.g., June Cleaver. Note also the out-dated paranoia reflected in Howard, *In the Hands of a Woman*, 119, who states, "According to a recent survey, twenty percent of all children have employed mothers. It is perhaps not generally known that this condition is not incidental, but is the central plan of the Communist ideology."

[4]On the increase of women into the American work force, see Lois W. Banner, *Women in Modern America: A Brief History* (2nd ed.; New York: Harcourt, Brace, Jovanovich, 1984): 218-224 and 236-243.

1. *Textual Variants in Tit. 2:5*

A. Οἰκουρός. The KJV rendering, "keepers at home," translates the term οἰκουρούς, supported by manuscripts אᶜ Dᶜ H L P 𝔐 and, according to Metzger,[5] most of the Fathers. Part of the confusion evident in the view of which Malone is typical is over the connotation of the English word "keeper." The *Oxford English Dictionary* has as one of its meanings "one who continues or remains at a place," even citing Titus 2:5 (KJV) as such a case.[6] Trapp,[7] a seventeenth-century commentator, understood the term in this way, commenting, "The Aegyptian women ware no shoes, that they might better keep home." The Geneva Bible (1560) has "keping at home," with the amusing footnote, "not running to & fro without necessarie occasions." The KJV, then, reads the text as an apostolic command for older women to teach younger women to stay at home.

But, is the KJV rendering of οἰκουρούς adequate? According to Arndt and Gingrich,[8] the term can denote either

---

[5]Bruce Metzger, *A Textual Commentary on the Greek New Testament* (New York: UBS, 1975): 654. C. Tischendorf, *Novum Testamentum Graece* (8th ed.; Leipzig: Giesecke and Devrient, 1872): 2. 887, lists Clement of Alexandria (II cent.), Basel (IV), Chrysostom (IV), Euthalius (IV), Theodoret (V), and John of Damascus (VII). By "most of the Fathers," Metzger must refer to *later* Fathers. In the extant literature of the first five centuries, there are only five citations or allusions to Tit. 2:5. Twice Origen refers to the passage, but the one text that survives in Greek is an allusion, lacking the word in question, and the other text survives in Latin, thus concealing Origen's Greek text. Clement of Alexandria does cite the passage with the reading οἰκουρούς, while Clement of Rome alludes to the passage using the alternate verb οἰκουργεῖν. Basil later quotes the passage in a catena in his *Regulae Moralae* (69,2), reading οἰκουρούς.

[6]*The Oxford English Dictionary*, (2nd ed.; Oxford: Clarendon, 1989): VIII, 376, § 7, and 373, § 33.

[7]John Trapp, *Annotations upon the Old and New Testaments* (London: Bellamy, 1647): V, 343.

[8]W. Bauer, *A Greek-English Lexicon of the New Testament and Other Early Christian Literature* (W. F. Arndt & F. W. Gingrich; 2nd ed., F. Gingrich & F. Danker; Chicago: Univ. of Chicago, 1979): 561.

"domestic" or "staying at home." With reference to women, the term carries the idea of "keeping at home," and as a substantive it means "housekeeper," according to Liddell.[9] Illustrative of the former usage is Ceasar's taunt, "Then why don't you . . . keep at home (δεδιὼς οἰκουρεῖς)?" (Plutarch, *Life of Caesar* 15). Illustrative of the latter is the description of Fulvia as one who takes no interest in spinning or managing the household (ταλασίαν οὐδ ' οἰκουρίας) (Plutarch, *Life of Anthony* 10). The Vulgate favors the latter of these connotations, reading *domus curam habentes*, as do several Old Latin manuscripts with *domus custodientes*.[10] It is also this latter reading that one finds in the later church Fathers.[11] In fact, several writers use the word οἰκουρός to mean "management of the household," yet qualify the term with another phrase when "staying at home" is specified.[12]

The KJV rendering of Titus 2:5 as "keepers at home" is too specific for the semantic range of the Greek term. Had the KJV translators rendered the term correctly as "manages [well] the home," Malone certainly could not have made his point.

---

[9]See G. H. Liddell, Robert Scott, and H. S. Jones, *A Greek-English Lexicon* (Oxford: Clarendon, 1989): 1205, and G. W. H. Lampe, *A Patristic Greek Lexicon* (Oxford: Clarendon, 1961): 945.

[10]See Johannes Wordsworth, H. J. White, et al., *Novum Testamentum Domini Nostri Iesu Christi Latine* (Oxford: Clarendon, 1913-41): 659.

[11]Both Oecumenius, *Comm. in Titus* (J.-P. Migne, *Patrologia Graeca* 119: cols. 252-53), and Theophylact, *Comm. in Titus* (Migne, *PG* 125: cols. 157D1-160A2), explain the meaning as οἰκονομικός, "management of a household or family."

[12]Frederick Field, *Notes on the Translation of the New Testament* (Cambridge: Cambridge Univ. Press, 1899): 3.221, cites Stobaeus, *Flor. T.* 74, 61, "but his wife cares for him (οἰκουρέν), remaining inside (καὶ ἔνδον μένεν) to receive and nurture her husband." See also Basil, *Sermon* 13 (Migne, *PG* 31: col. 880 C 1-4), καὶ πρὸς οἷς ἂν συμφέρῃ τὸ οἰκουρεῖν, καὶ ἐντὸς τοῦ οἴκου μένειν. For other citations, see J. J. Wettstein, *Novum Testamentum Graecum* (Graz: Akademische Druck, 1962 reprint of 1725 ed.): 2.372-73.

B. Οἰκουργός. The alternative reading in the Greek manuscripts, οἰκουργός, differs from the previous reading only in the presence of the gamma. With manuscript support in ℵ* A C D* F G I Ψ 33 81 177 330 623 Clement of Rome, it is certainly the better attested of the two readings.[13] Other than Tit. 2:5, this adjective appears only in Soranus, a second-century AD gynecologist from Ephesus.[14] Although later editors of the critical texts of Soranus emended his text to read the classical οἰκουρός,[15] there is no doubt of the original reading of his text. However, since there exists a paucity of data concerning οἰκουργός, an etymological analysis must serve as the last resort. In this connection, Bauer suggests "workers at home," or "domestic."[16] The

---

[13]Unfortunately, the third-century 𝔓[32] contains a lacuna here. Only the final sigma of our word remains. See A. S. Hunt, ed., *Catalogue of the Greek Papyri in the John Rylands Library* (Manchester: Univ. of Manchester Press, 1911): 1.10-11.

[14]Note the error in Thayer, *Greek-English Lexicon of the New Testament* (Grand Rapids: Zondervan, 1962 reprint of 1885 ed): 442, who stated that the word is not found elsewhere. This is also the case in N. Brox, *Die Pastoral Briefe* (Regensburg: Pustet, 1969): 293.

[15]Soranus, *Gynaeciorum* 1.27. Two editions of Soranus are available to me: Joannes Ilberg's edition in *Corpus Medicorum Graecorum* (Leipzig: Teubner, 1927): 4.18 and 244 (index, where the textual emendation is noted), and that of Valentino Rose, *Sorani Gynaeciorum Vetus Translatio Latina nunc primum edita* (Leipzig: Teubner, 1882): 190. Both were working from a single fifteenth-century manuscript (P), which reads οἰκουργόν, but instead of following this text, they emended the reading to the classical form, following Franciscus Z. Ermerins in his 1869 edition.

J. K. Elliott, *The Greek Text of the Epistles to Timothy and Titus* (St.Doc., 36; Salt Lake City: Univ. of Utah Press, 1968): 181-82, labels οἰκουργούς "Hellenistic," in contrast to the classical οἰκουρούς. Since the former only occurs in the two texts mentioned above and, as a verb, in 1 Clement, one wonders if this is sufficient data to label a word "Hellenistic." Elliott attributes this to Bauer, but Bauer only stated that the latter word was classical; nothing was said by Bauer about the former term being "Hellenistic."

[16]See Bauer, *A Greek-English Lexicon*, 561; J. H. Moulton and G. Milligan, *The Vocabulary of the Greek New Testament* (Grand Rapids: Eerdmans, 1949): 443; and W. F. Howard, *A Grammar of New*

verbal form of the word, however, occurs in 1 Clement 1:3 in an allusion to Titus 2:5 where Clement writes, "and you taught them to keep in the rule of obedience, and to manage the affairs of their household (τὰ κατὰ τὸν οἶκον σεμνῶς οἰκουργεῖν; in seemliness) with all discretion."[17] In terms of external textual evidence, this term οἰκουργός has claim to originality and is rendered "domestic" or "manages well the home," but without any suggestion that she be homebound.

2. The Context of Titus 2:5

Thiselton[18] emphasizes accurately the way in which the larger context limits a word's relationship to other words in a sentence, and that sentences themselves depend on larger thought-units, which in turn depend upon the total discourse. Titus 2:5, though, presents a problem in this regard. Not only does the word in question occur only once outside the NT (excluding the verb in 1 Clem.) and only here in the NT, but here it also occurs in a list that weakens the semantic interaction. Semantic relationships are not absent, however, and may be examined at three levels: 1) the immediate context, 2) the literary context of Titus, and 3) the larger literary context of the Pastoral Epistles.

Testament Greek (Edinburgh: T. & T. Clark, 1929): 2.274. M. R. Vincent, *Word Studies in the New Testament* (Grand Rapids: Eerdmans, 1887): IV, 342, correctly observes, "The meaning is not *stayers* at home, but *keepers* or *guardians* of the household."

The observation of Adam Clarke, *The New Testament: A Commentary and Critical Notes* (new ed.; Nashville: Abingdon, nd): 2. 652, "not only *staying in the house*, . . . but *working* in the *house*," has no lexical basis, nor does the comment of G. Barlow, "Titus,"*A Homiletic Commentary on the Epistles of Paul* (New York: Funk and Wagnalls, nd): IX, 93, that "The term in the RV comprehends and adds to that in the AV."

[17]See J. B. Lightfoot, *The Apostolic Fathers* (London: Macmillan, 1891): vol. 2, part 1, 11-13, and Karl Bihlmeyer, *Die Apostolischen Väter* (Tübingen: J. C. B. Mohr, 1956): 35-36.

[18]A. C. Thiselton, "Semantics and New Testament Interpretation," *New Testament Interpretation: Essays on Principles and Methods* (ed. I. H. Marshall; Grand Rapids: Eerdmans, 1977): 75-104.

A. *The Immediate Context*. Initially, the relationship of our term to the following ἀγαθάς, "good," must be examined. "Good" could stand as a separate quality[19] that older women are to teach younger women,[20] resulting in a list of seven items. Quinn,[21] taking "good" as a distinct quality, argues that it cannot modify the previous item because that would alter the formal structure of the list, which is adjectival to "young women," and "good" preserves the "septuple" arrangement.[22] However, if "good" modifies "domestic," as he translates the term, the combined phrase still modifies "young women." Also, Titus shows no predisposition for grouping items into sets of seven. In 2:2, six items apply to old men, only one to young men in 2:6, and five to slaves in 2:9-10. Even Quinn himself notes (122) that, "only here in the PE [pastoral epistles] does *agathos* directly qualify a person . . . . In thirty-seven other Pauline uses it never describes a person."   As if this was not enough to encourage another line of reasoning, Quinn also notes incorrectly (122) that "good" modifies "domestic" from the

---

[19]This is the view taken in G. Fee, *1 and 2 Timothy, Titus* (NIC; Peabody, MA: Hendrickson, 1988): 187; J. N. D. Kelly, *The Pastoral Epistles* (London: A. & C. Black, 1963): 241; Brox, *Die Pastoral Briefe*, 293-94; H. von Soden, *Die Pastoralbriefe* (HKNT, 3; Leipzig: J. C. B. Mohr, 1893): 213; E. K. Simpson, *The Pastoral Epistles* (Grand Rapids: Eerdmans, 1954): 103; Ceslas Spicq, *Saint Paul: Les épîtres pastorales* (Paris: J. Gabalda, 1969): 2.620-21; R. Ward, *1 and 2 Timothy and Titus* (Waco: Word, 1974): 253; and J. W. Roberts, *Titus, Philemon, and James* (Austin, TX: Sweet, 1962): 24-25.

[20]The Vulgate (*domus curam habentes, benignas*) favors this reading, as does Chrysostom, *Hom. in Epist. ad Titum* (PG 62, col. 683), "They are 'good' and 'household managers' (ἀγαθαὶ καὶ οἰκουροί) from love to their husband."

[21]Jerome Quinn, *The Letter to Titus* (AB, 35; New York: Doubleday, 1990): 121-22, and 137. Note also that on p. 121 Quinn is incorrect in stating that there is a variant in Soranus' text. Critical texts since Ermerins (1869) have followed the emendation to οἰκουρόν. See n. 15 above.

[22]Among others, Kelly, *The Pastoral Epistles*, 241, argues that to take ἀγαθάς as adjectival to οἰκουργός "destroys the rhythm of the sentence." This argument is traceable as early as von Soden, *Die Pastoralbriefe*, 213.

time of the Syriac Peshitta to Theophylact (XI cent.) through UBS[3 corr] and N-A[26].[23] Actually, the UBS[3 corr] and N-A[26] drop the commas of the previous editions.[24]

"Good," then, could modify "domestic," resulting in only six qualities.[25] As Quinn[26] observed, "good" is not elsewhere a personal characteristic in the epistles to Timothy and Titus, and the Peshitta and Theophylact both take "good" with "domestic." Dibelius and Conzelmann[27] appropriately suggest the translation, "fulfill their household duties well," which fits the larger context of Titus.

B. *The Literary Context of the Epistle to Titus.* Titus has every appearance of being a genuine epistle.[28] The stated purpose of the letter is in 1:5, where two tasks are reassigned to Titus: 1) set certain things in order and 2) appoint leaders city by city. Tit. 1:6-16 explains the latter. The seriousness of intruders in Cretan congregations who are "teaching things that are not necessary for a profit" underscores the necessity for strong leadership. Titus 2 addresses the earlier of the two tasks. The emphasis upon "healthy doctrine" in 2:1 is addressed specifically to older men on Crete in 2:2 and to older women in 2:3, who in turn are to train the younger women in 2:4-5. Titus also has responsibilities toward young men (vv. 6-8) and slaves (vv.

---

[23]Quinn, *The Letter to Titus* , 122. Theophylact, *ad Titum* (PG 123, col. 157, line D3+).

[24]See Metzger, *Textual Commentary*, 654.

[25]This view is favored, among others, by A. T. Hanson, *The Pastoral Letters* (NCBC; London: Marshall, Morgan, and Scott, 1982): 180-81; M. Dibelius and H. Conzelmann, *The Pastoral Epistles* (Hermeneia; trans. P. Buttolph and A. Yarbro; Philadelphia: Fortress, 1972): 140-41; and B. Weiss, *Der Briefe Pauli an Timotheus und Titus* (Göttingen: Vandenhoeck und Ruprecht, 1902): 354-55.

[26]See also Hanson, *The Pastoral Letters*, 113.

[27]Dibelius and Conzelmann, *The Pastoral Epistles*, 141.

[28]See W. G. Kümmel, *Introduction to the New Testament* (rev. and trans. H. C. Kee; Nashville: Abingdon, 1975): 370-87, and D. Guthrie, *New Testament Introduction* (Downers' Grove, IL: IVP, 1970): 584-624, for discussion of various views.

9,10). The ethical behavior sought among these people is not only for itself, but for public image and reputation.[29] At 3:1, the ethical paraenesis shifts from relationships within churches to those of churches to society.

"Domestic," then, occurs in a series of observations designed to inform Cretan Christians, because of the current situation caused by insidious teachers,[30] how better to live so as not to bring the Gospel and Christian fellowship into disgrace. Women neglecting their household duties would further contribute to general chaos on Crete and undermine the Christian mission by generating negative comment.

C. *The Context of the Pastoral Epistles.* While it is inappropriate to read Titus "through the glasses of" the epistles to Timothy,[31] one passage, 1 Tim. 5:14, is instructive regarding the admonition in Titus 2:5. In counseling Timothy how to deal with younger widows, the apostle encourages them "to marry, to have children, and to manage their homes and to give the enemy no opportunity for slander" (NIV). Though the situations behind each epistle differ, the similarity of instructions to women regarding domestic matters is significant. The phrase, "to manage their homes," renders the compound οἰκοδεσπο- τεῖν.[32] Not as scarce as οἰκουργός, the substantive

---

[29]See Alan Padgett, "The Pauline Rationale for Submission: Biblical Feminism and the *hina* Clauses of Titus 2:1-10," *EvQ* 59 (1987): 39-52.

[30]See further, Luke T. Johnson, *The Writings of the New Testament* (Philadelphia: Fortress, 1986): 402-06.

[31]See David C. Verner, *The Household of God: The Social World of the Pastoral Epistles* (SBLDS, 71; Chico: Scholars Press, 1983).

[32]As with Tit. 2:5 and οἰκουργεῖν, 1 Tim. 5:14 suffers from changes in the English language. KJV rendered "guid the house," following Coverdale's (1535) "gyde the house," while Geneva Bible (1560) translated "governe the house." The *Oxford English Dictionary* (VI, 931) gives as one of the possible meanings of "guide," "to conduct the affairs of (a household, state, etc.)" Although "guide" denotes a lesser degree of authority than "rule" in current English, this was certainly not the case in 1611.

(οἰκοδεσπότης) occurs twelve times, all in the Synoptic gospels, each time referring to the master or steward of a household, or as a metaphor for Jesus himself. In extra-biblical literature the word describes God's relationship to the universe, as in Philo *On Dreams* 1.149, "and you will have house-rule (οἰκοδεσπότην), caring for your own house," and Epictetus *Frag.* 3.22.4, "the master of the house (οἰκοδεσπότης) who orders everything."[33] The word denotes, then, a position of some authority and responsibility.[34] In neither 1 Tim. 5:14 nor Tit. 2:5 are women urged to stay at home, but to supervise their households with discretion and industry, thus avoiding slander.

Conclusion

"A woman's place is in the home," so the proverb goes, but the proverb itself is not a biblical proverb. Some would deny that contemporary culture shapes us. Unwittingly equating cultural expectations for the will of God, these would suppress others with their cultural expectations. In Titus 2:5, however, there is no enjoinder for women to stay at home, but to conduct domestic life well, an exhortation of considerable value today.

---

[33]For other occurrences, see W. H. P. Hatch, "Some Illustration of New Testament Usage from Greek Inscriptions of Asia Minor," *JBL* 27 (1908): 142, who finds the earliest occurrence of οἰκοδεσπότης in Alexis (mid-fourth century BC). However, Phrynichus, the Atticist, finds the form distasteful, commenting, "Say 'master of the house,' not 'housemaster' as Alexis does," thus revealing the formation of this compound. See W. G. Rutherford, ed. *The New Phrynichus* (Hildesheim: G. Olms, 1968): 470-71.

[34]Bauer (Gingrich and Danker), *A Greek-English Lexicon*, 558, suggests "keep house," which in current English usage does not denote leadership as does the Greek term. Two factors militate against this possibility. 1) The lexical evidence for both the verb and the noun is more accurately carried by the phrase, "rule the house." 2) The German edition of Bauer from which the Gingrich-Danker edition derive (*Griechisch-Deutches Wörterbuch* [3rd rev. ed.; Berlin: A. Töpelmann, 1937]: 924) does not contain the connotation of Gingrich and Danker.

Chapter Fifteen

THE SUBMISSION OF WIVES IN 1 PETER

James W. Thompson

For centuries, bridegrooms have promised in the wedding ceremony to "provide for and protect" their brides, and brides have promised to "love, honor, and obey" their husbands. Marriage vows were given a symmetry of duties which were commonly believed to be a necessary part of the structure of the marriage relationship. This symmetry of protection and obedience, which was largely unquestioned by society, was influenced by the instructions to wives in the New Testament. These instructions are given in the NT in almost identical language in Ephesians, Colossians, and 1 Peter. According to the King James Version, the translation which influenced the practice of churches for centuries, wives are instructed, "be in subjection to your own husbands" (1 Pet. 3:1; see Eph. 5:21f., Col. 3:18). The language of the modern translations is not significantly different from the KJV.

Until the modern era, this call for obedience presented little problem for the common understanding of marriage. Moreover, this symmetry presented no problem in traditional societies where, in marriage, women passed from the authority of their fathers to the authority of their husbands. Today, however, the instructions present an enormous problem in western society, as they run counter to modern expectations. The vow to "love, honor, and obey" has quietly dropped from the marriage ceremony as a relic of a past era when women were not the equals of men in education and professional qualifications. To "love, honor, and obey" presents difficulties within a culture which gives equal rights in society to the women.

This new situation presents both an exegetical and a hermeneutical problem for Christians. On the one hand, the exegetical question requires that we ask once more what the call for submission actually meant in NT times. On the other hand, one must ask the hermeneutical question: how do commandments that were given within a specific social ethos function in a changed society? If the call for submission of women in the marriage relationship in the NT was actually a challenge to fit in with the expectations of popular culture of that time, how does the Christian appropriate this commandment in the modern world? Schillebeeckx[1] has raised the question in an appropriate way:

> Are we confronted here with a Christian confirmation of existing forms which are thus presented in the New Testament as an unchangeable norm? Or is this just a call to experience "in the Lord" and from Christian motives the ethical values and social structures already present in society? And, if this latter is the case, is it not also the case that the New Testament, by not rejecting the contemporary situation but simply giving it a Christian motivation, has in effect put it forward as a principle that the actual, existing social structures of this world should be preserved?

Two quite different solutions have been offered as means for solving this hermeneutical problem. On the one hand, a popular view is that such commandments are simply transferred to the modern world. Larry Christianson,[2] for instance, offers one approach to the hermeneutical problem. In a chapter entitled "God's Order for Wives," he argues that the subordination of women belongs to the order of creation, and that they therefore need the protection of their husbands for many of the demanding tasks of life. On the other hand, an alternative approach is to view the instructions to wives in

---

[1]E. Schillebeeckx, *Marriage: Sacred Reality and Saving Mystery* (London: Sheed and Ward, 1965): 246.

[2]Larry Christianson, *The Christian Family* (Minneapolis: Bethany Fellowship, 1970): 41.

the NT as a call for early Christians to adopt a standard of conduct which was appropriate under the conditions of ancient life, but not for all time. Under this view, in a social ethos where women are regarded as equals, this commandment cannot simply be transferred and understood as an imperative for the women in the changed social situation.

In this essay, I shall examine one of the passages on the role of women in the home in order to address the exegetical and hermeneutical issues. By placing the epistle of 1 Peter within its own context, I shall see how the instructions for wives function in the epistle. An understanding of the author's intent will clarify the hermeneutical problem of the passage.

1. *The Setting in 1 Peter*

The instructions on domestic relationships in 1 Pet. 3:1-7 belong to a wider context of specific instructions that involve Christian conduct in relation to the governmental authorities (2:13-17) and the conduct of Christian slaves in relation to their masters (2:18-25). In each of these instances, the instruction is initiated by a verb form of ὑποτάσσω (submit).

The similarity between these instructions to ethical advice elsewhere in the NT has suggested that ancient writers relied on a common storehouse of ethical advice which was given to new converts. According to this view, the ancient catechism for new converts contained instructions for Christians in their various relationships, and individual writers often used them in providing ethical instruction. The pattern for these lists of duties, which Christian writers employed, was provided first by Greek philosophers and then adapted by Hellenistic Jewish authors before they came into the Christian tradition.[3]

---

[3]See David L. Balch, *Let Wives Be Submissive: The Domestic Code of 1 Peter* (SBL, 26; Chico, CA: Scholars Press, 1981): 1-61.

While the household codes may have a long history in Greek and Jewish sources, the various forms in which they appear suggest that the codes were highly adaptable for various purposes. In 1 Peter, for example, the household code does not have the reciprocal relationships of husband-wife, parent-child, and slave-master that one finds in Ephesians and Colossians. Nor does the sequence of the domestic instructions in 1 Peter follow that of the other household codes. In 1 Peter, except for the brief instruction to husbands (3:7), the entire code is addressed to those who were in a subordinate position. In the instruction to "submit" to those in superior positions, Christians in subordinate positions are called upon to do precisely what non-Christian moralists would have expected of those who were in subordinate positions. In each instance, those who are in positions of power are non-Christians.

The distinctive features of the domestic code of 1 Peter correspond to the particular issues which dominate the epistle. It is addressed to "the exiles of the dispersion in Pontus, Galatia, Cappadocia, Asia, and Bithynia." Despite the descriptive term "dispersion," which was commonly used for the scattering of the Jews throughout the ancient world, the readers are Gentile converts who have "been liberated from the futile ways inherited from the fathers" (1:18). Because they have left behind the ancestral customs, they are now exiles (1:17; see 2:11) who experience the social alienation that is common for the minority groups of all cultures. While organized persecution has not been initiated by the government, the community faces the hostility of neighbors, who have noticed their rejection of civic life (4:4) and who now slander them, calling them "evildoers" (see 2:12; 3:16).[4]

The pagan charges against the Christians probably reflect the suspicion that Christians represented a threat to the established order. Tacitus' criticism of the Jews may suggest the kinds of charges that were being made against

---

[4]See John K. Elliott, *Home for the Homeless* (Philadelphia: Fortress, 1981): 80.

Christians. The first lesson the Jews teach new converts, according to Tacitus,[5] is "to despise the gods, to disown the country, and to regard their parents, children, and brothers of little account." One may compare a charge made against Christians by the pagan author Celsus, who noted that Christianity was a religion of the slaves and lower classes, and who asked why Christians encouraged slaves to run away from their masters.[6] Other ancient writers criticized Christians for neglecting their civic duty.[7] Thus Christians were suspected of undermining public order and civic life.

The situation of the readers, who are apparently new Christians (see 1:3, 23; 2:1-3) living in a hostile world, is the background of the epistle, which is written to encourage exiles to "stand fast" in the grace of God (5:12).[8] Thus, the strategy of 1 Peter is to encourage those who may now live in fear by providing the strength to meet the challenges before them.[9]

In the first segment of the epistle (1:1-2:10), the readers are reassured that, while they may be exiles in society, they are "a chosen race, a royal priesthood, a holy nation, God's own people" (2:9). Even if their Christian faith has made them exiles in their own land, they are to recall that Christ himself was the "rejected one" (2:7). Despite the social costs of their new Christian commitment, they find strength to be nonconformists (1:14f) and a "holy people" (1:15-16) through the hope that is now theirs (1:13, 21) and the knowledge that they have been ransomed by the precious blood of Christ (1:19).

---

[5]Tacitus, *Hist.* 5.5.

[6]Origen, *Against Celsus* 3.44 and 6.63.

[7]See Robert L. Wilken, *The Christians as the Romans Saw Them* (New Haven: Yale, 1984): 118.

[8]N. Brox, *Der erste Petrusbrief* (EKK; Neukirchen: Vluyn, 1979): 18.

[9]See John K. Elliott, " I Peter: Its Situation and Strategy: A Discussion with David Balch," *Perspectives on First Peter* (NABPR Special Studies; Macon, GA: Mercer, 1986): 65-66.

2. The Specific Instructions of 1 Peter

The specific instructions which follow describe the instances of Christian interaction with pagans. Unlike the household codes of Ephesians and Colossians, the situation reflected here presupposes Christian conduct in relation to non-Christians who hold power. The specific instructions are introduced in 2:11-12, providing the framework for understanding the instructions which follow. Christians are "aliens and exiles" who are summoned to "have good conduct among the Gentiles." The focus of this central section is conduct of Christians in this situation, as the repetition of ἀναστροφή (conduct) indicates (1:17-18; 2:12; 3:1-2, 16). Having been liberated from the futile "conduct" of the fathers (1:18), Christians are now summoned to practice good "conduct" among the Gentiles. The instructions in the household code of 2:13-17 describe the specific nature of this "good conduct." Having been slandered for undermining public order, Christians respond by living responsibly within the institutions of society.[10]

The result of this good conduct, according to 2:12, is that Gentiles will observe the good works of Christians and "glorify God on the day of visitation."[11] The impact of Christian conduct on Gentile observers is a theme in this parenetic section. According to 2:15, Christian conduct will silence the ignorance of foolish people. According to 3:16, Christian conduct ultimately will put the pagan slanderers to shame.[12]

---

[10]L. Goppelt, *Theology of the New Testament* (Grand Rapids: Eerdmans, 1982): 2.167.

[11]See J. Ramsey Michaels, *I Peter* (Waco: Word, 1988): 118, who notes, "'Glorifying God' is an act of worship performed specifically by Christian believers (cf. 4:14b, 16f.), and the use of the term here evidently signals repentance or religious conversion at or before the last day."

[12]See W. C. Van Unnik, "Die Rücksicht auf die Reaktion der Nicht-Christen als Motiv in der altchristlichen Paränese," *Judentum, Urchristentum, Kirche—Festschrift für Joachim Jeremias* (ed. W. Eltester; BZNW, 26; Berlin: Töpelmann, 1964): 230.

This Christian conduct which pagan slanderers will observe is described concretely in the three successive paragraphs which begin with ὑποτάσσειν (be in submission). The general heading to these instructions is given in the words, "Be submissive to every human creation." As the context suggests, the unusual term κτίσις, "creation," is not to be understood as "institution," but as a reference to individuals who are in authority.[13] Except for one reference in this context (3:6), ὑποτάσσειν is used in all of these relationships rather than the narrower word ὑπακούειν, "obey." Whereas one finds ὑπακούειν in the instructions to slaves (and children) in the household codes of Eph. 6:1,5 and Col. 3:20; 4:1, 1 Peter prefers ὑποτάσσειν in describing all of the relationships where Christians find themselves in subordinate positions in relation to pagans. Ὑπακούειν is used elsewhere in 1 Peter for one's obedience to Christ (1:2, 14, 20; see 2:8; 3:1, 20; 4:17).

The terms ὑποτάσσειν and ὑπακούειν may overlap at points, but they are scarcely interchangeable, for ὑποτάσσειν has a broader meaning.[14] The root verb τάσσειν means "order," "position," and "determine."[15] With the prepositional prefix, the word means literally to "subordinate," with the accent on placing oneself in an orderly arrangement.[16] Thus, the word can mean "defer to" or "acquiesce."[17]

The verb ὑποτάσσειν has a significant place in the ethical teaching of the NT. Prior to 1 Peter, it had already

---

[13]G. Petzke, "κτίσις," *TDNT*, 2.326.

[14]See W. Bauer, *A Greek-English Lexicon of the New Testament and Other Early Christian Literature* (trans. W. F. Arndt & F. W. Gingrich; 2nd. ed., rev. F. W. Gingrich & F. W. Danker; Chicago: Univ. of Chicago, 1979): 847-48.

[15]Bauer, *Greek-English Lexicon*, 855.

[16]See Elliott, *Home for the Homeless*, 139, and Goppelt, *Theology of the New Testament*, 2.168.

[17]Brox, *Der erste Petrusbrief*, 118.

been used for one's submission to government authorities (Rom. 13:1,2,5), for the submission of family members to each other (Eph. 5:21), for wives specifically in relation to their husbands (Eph. 5:22; Col. 3:18), for women in the public assembly (1 Cor. 14:34), and for the submission of the church to those who are called the "first fruits of Achaia and to every fellow worker" (1 Cor. 16:16). The accent of this verb, therefore, is on the orderly arrangement that results from deference to another.

Although ὑποτάσσειν was a term already in use before 1 Peter was written, the verb takes on its own significance in this epistle. In the first of the instructions on submission, the call for submission is placed within the context of the pagan charge that Christians are "evildoers" who upset public order. In 1 Pet. 2:16, submission involves the Christians' refusal to use their freedom as a "pretext for evil." Those who have been liberated from the "way of life" inherited from their fathers (1:18) are instructed not to misuse this liberation. In a context where Christians could have concluded that the exilic existence allows them to be free from established relationships, they are called upon not to misunderstand Christian freedom. Christians will silence the slanderers if they will "do right" (2:14-15).

The emphasis upon ἀγαθοποιεῖν (doing right) is pervasive throughout these instructions as a way of clarifying the meaning of submission. Against the charge that Christians are κακοποιεῖν (evildoers), they are consistently challenged to "do right," ἀγαθοποιεῖν (2:14, 15, 20; 3:6; see. 3:13, 16). To "do right" in this context involves not offending public order.[18] It is assumed that the pagan neighbors will recognize and appreciate this behavior. It is to live in such a way that one's behavior is "blameless from the viewpoint of society."[19] In the wider context of

---

[18]W. C. Van Unnik, "The Teaching of Good Works in I Peter," *NTS* 1 (1954/55): 99.

[19]B. Reicke, *The Epistles of James, Peter, and Jude* (AB; Garden City: Doubleday, 1964): 211f.

this passage, "doing right" is the equivalent of submission. It involves accepting one's place within the institutions of society in a way that fits with the expectation with the populace. Thus, citizens, slaves, and wives all "do right" (2:14-15, 20; 3:6).

While the instruction to "be submissive" involves adapting to the expectations of the populace, it takes on a deeper meaning in 1 Peter. The instruction to Christian slaves who live under cruel masters is followed, for example, by a hymnic recitation of the Christian story. The hymnic statement indicates that those who are submissive under difficult circumstances actually walk in the steps of Jesus, who was the model for submissive endurance. Moreover, the household code ends with a summary that is reminiscent of the hymnic statement of 1 Pet. 2:21-25. All Christians are called upon to have "unity of spirit, sympathy, love of the brethren, and a humble mind" (3:8). All Christians are to bless those who curse them and to return good for evil (3:9-12). In the concluding section, younger people are instructed to "be submissive" to their elders (5:5). This passage also is placed within the context of humility, inasmuch as it is followed by the instructions for all: "Clothe yourselves, all of you, with humility toward one another, for 'God opposes the proud, but gives grace to the humble'."

The call for submission, therefore, involves a life in conformity with the Christian story in which everyone walks in the steps of the one who did not resist the evil done to him by others. While submission involves a life in conformity with the expectations of others, it takes on a new dimension as Christians walk "in the steps" of the crucified one.

3. Instructions for Wives

The instructions for wives, "be submissive to your own husbands," must be placed within the larger context of the strategy of 1 Peter. Here also the command is not to "obey," but to "defer to" or "subordinate" oneself in an orderly arrangement. As with the other instructions on submission, this instruction involves adapting to the expectations of that

society. Ancient literature has numerous examples of this
commandment. Plutarch,[20] for example, affirms:

> So it is with women also; if they subordinate
> themselves to their husbands, they are commended,
> but if they want to control, they cut a sorrier figure
> than the subjects of their control.

Similarly, Josephus[21] defends Jewish morality, indicating
that the law required that wives be submissive to their
husbands:

> Let her accordingly be submissive, not for her
> humiliation, but that she may be directed, for the
> authority has been given by God to man.

While the call for submission would have been understood in antiquity as an example of "doing right," the fact
that husbands are "disobedient to the word" is a reminder
that Christian wives are already violating one of the principles of ancient moralists.[22] Ancient authors indicate that
the duty of the wife is to follow the religion of her
husband.[23] Thus, the submission of Christian wives has
limits, for in being Christians they have already challenged a
common expectation of ancient society. A tense situation
existed for Christian wives, for, in a society that was divided
between the "disobedient" (2:8) and God's people, husbands
were among those who "disobeyed the word." One can
assume also that husbands were among those who slandered
the Christians.[24]

This hostility in the home is to be overcome by the
conduct of the wives, who will have an impact on their

---

[20]Plutarch, *Advice to Bride and Groom*, 142E.

[21]Josephus, *Against Apion*, 2.10.

[22]See Balch, *Let Wives Be Submissive*, 99.

[23]Plutarch, *Advice to Bride and Groom*, 140D. See Michaels,
I Peter, 157.

[24]Balch, *Let Wives Be Submissive*, 99.

husbands. Like the populace in general, husbands will "gaze" at Christian conduct and may well be "won" by this nonverbal behavior. Paradoxically, while Christians have been saved by the "word" (1:23-25), husbands will be won "without a word." The Christian wife, like the citizen and the slave, demonstrates that she is not upsetting the order of an institution. Her behavior has a definite evangelistic impact upon her husband.[25]

The prohibition in 3:3-4, like the prohibitions following earlier commands for submission (2:16; see 2:20), clarifies the nature of the submission. The outward adornment, with the braiding of hair and wearing of gold and expensive clothing, is thus to be understood as the expression of freedom and a challenge to the authority of the husband. One may note that similar instructions for modest adornment appear in 1 Tim. 2:9, which also occurs in the context of the submission of women. In each instance, submission is demonstrated by the absence of extravagant outward adornment.

The prohibition of expensive adornment is to be seen against the background of both Jewish and Greek traditions. A prophetic denunciation of excessive adornment by the women is found as far back as Isa. 3:18-26, where the prophet portrays a day of judgment as a time when

> the Lord will take away the finery of the anklets, the headbands, and the crescents; the pendants, the bracelets, and the scarves; the headdresses, the armlets, the sashes, the perfume boxes, and the amulets; the signet rings and nose rings; the festal robes, the mantles, the cloaks, and the handbags; the garments of gauze, the turbans and the veils.

The portrayal of the great harlot in Rev. 17:4 may reflect later Jewish values regarding the adornment of women. There the harlot "was arrayed in purple and scarlet, and bedecked with gold and jewels and pearls."

---

[25]See Van Unnik, *Judentum, Urchristentum, Kirche*, 222-225.

However, Selwyn[26] observes correctly that here Peter
makes no explicit reference to the Isaiah passage, for similar
teaching was commonplace among poets and moralists in
antiquity. In both Hellenistic and Jewish texts, "dressing
up" on the part of women was associated with sexual
wantonness and wifely insubordination.[27] To wear
expensive clothing and jewelry was tantamount to
unfaithfulness by the wife. For instance, Diodorus, *History*
12.21[28] mentions the wearing of gold jewelry or a garment
with a purple border as signifying a "courtesan," and
Epictetus, *Encheiridion* 40[29] laments that from an early age
girls tend to beautify themselves with outward adornments.
One finds the maxim in the *Sentences of Sextus*,[30] "A wife
who likes adornment is not faithful." One may compare the
extensive treatment by Ps.-Lucian,[31] who describes the
husband's "horrible experiences" of living with a woman
who spends her day before the mirror attempting to beautify
herself. The writer describes the woman who occupies
herself first with various facial creams and powders before
she turns to the treatment of her hair with various dyes.
Finally, she adorns herself with various jewels—earrings,
bracelets, necklaces—which are very expensive. When she
is arrayed in this way, she visits the various gods[32] and
returns home after being unfaithful to her husband. Such a
woman is unbearable for her husband, for her attention to
her attire was accompanied by her disobedience to her
husband's authority.

---

[26]E. G. Selwyn, *The First Epistle of St. Peter* (London:
Macmillan, 1958): 183.

[27]Gordon D. Fee, *1 and 2 Timothy, Titus* (GNC; San Francisco:
Harper, 1984): 71.

[28]*Diodorus of Sicily* (LCL; Cambridge: Harvard Univ. Press,
1956): 4.416-17.

[29]*Epictetus* (LCL; Cambridge: Harvard Univ. Press, 1985):
2.525.

[30]*Sentences of Sextus*, 513.

[31]Ps.-Lucian, *Affairs of the Heart*, 38-43.

[32]See also Philo, *On the Virtues*, 39-40.

The Christian wives of 1 Peter are instructed not to wear expensive clothing, but to adopt the pattern of conduct that is πολυτελής (precious) to God, viz., a meek and quiet spirit. The focus on behavior that is πολυτελής, "precious," to God is intended as a contrast to clothing that is πολυτελής "expensive" (1 Tim. 2:9).[33]

The "meek and quiet spirit," which is recommended as the contrasting behavior to the expensive clothing in 3:4, would have been appreciated in the ancient world. The Neo-pythagorean Phintys,[34] for example, insisted that a woman should not adorn herself with expensive garments which reflect arrogance and pride. She should adorn herself through modesty rather than through art. However, the "meek and quiet spirit" that is recommended is more than an accommodation to ancient attitudes. Meekness has an important place in early Christian moral instruction. Indeed, in 1 Peter, it fits well with the challenge for all Christians to respond to their pagan inquirers with "gentleness and respect" (3:16). "A meek and quiet spirit" is the distingish-ing feature of all those who suffer unjustly (3:16-17) as Christians in a hostile environment. It is to be equated with submission as the characteristic of Christians who do not challenge the social order. Thus, the "meek and quiet spirit" demanded of wives is the demeanor that is expected of all Christians in their relations with their neighbors.

The imperatives of 3:1, 3 are followed by the indicative stating the basis for the behavior of wives. Whereas the instructions to slaves appealed to the example of Christ (2:21-25), the instructions to wives appeal to the example of Sarah as the model of submission.[35] The community has been reminded earlier in the epistle that it is the heir of ancient Israel (2:4-10). Thus, Christian women now regard

---

[33]On πολυτελής, see Bauer, *Greek-English Lexicon*, 696. The word was used most frequently in Greek literature for expensive clothing or precious stones. See also Michaels, *I Peter*, 162.

[34]Phintys, *On the Temperance of a Woman*.

[35]F. Schröger, *Gemeinde im 1. Petrusbrief* (Passau: Passavia Universitätsverlag, 1981): 154.

themselves as the heirs of Sarah,[36] just as all Christians are the heirs of the "elect race" and "royal priesthood" of the past.

Because Christians are heirs of ancient Israel, they are challenged to conduct themselves in a way that is appropriate for the holy people of God. The specific instructions of 1 Peter thus describe a pattern of conduct that is both rooted in the cross and supportive of the institutions of that society.

4. *Hermeneutical Considerations*

The call for the submission of women in 1 Peter derives its meaning from the setting of the instruction in 1 Peter. Christian women are commanded to demonstrate deference to their disobedient husbands by avoiding behavior that would offend them or appear rebellious, e.g., the braiding of hair and the wearing of jewelry. In the ancient cultural setting, the braiding of hair and the wearing of jewelry were understood as acts of defiance toward the husband. Thus under conditions when Christians were being accused of undermining the basic institutions of society, Christian wives are challenged to silence these rumors with their submissive behavior.

This demand on Christian wives belongs to a situation very different from our own. The command to submit, we have noted, belongs within the context of the call for submission to governmental authorities and the submission

---

[36]The OT reference is to Gen. 18:12. In Jewish literature, which emphasized the obedience of wives, the relationship between Abraham and Sarah created an embarrassment, for Sarah is not presented as the obedient wife. In the only reference to obedience, it is Abraham who "hearkened" (ὑπέκουσε) to the voice of Sarah. In Gen. 18:12, Sarah's words are actually spoken in *derision*. In presenting Sarah as the model of the submissive wife, the author of 1 Peter reflects the problems of Hellenistic Jewish authors, particularly Josephus and Philo, as they interpreted the story of Sarah. See Mark Kiley, "Like Sarah: The Tale of Terror Behind 1 Peter 3:6," *JBL* 106 (1987): 689-92. Cf. Dorothy I. Sly, "1 Peter 3:6b in the Light of Philo and Josephus," *JBL* 110 (1991): 126-29.

of slaves to their masters. These calls for submission in 1 Peter are not grounded in the order of creation, as if they are to be transferred into every cultural situation. The call for submission reflects the structure of ancient institutions, where one accepted a predetermined "place" in society. Therefore, one cannot simply transfer these instructions directly into the modern situation. No one seriously attempts to transfer the instructions to slaves to our own time. Moreover, the challenge to submit to governmental magistrates (2:13-17) is more functional within autocratic societies than in democratic societies, where one has the opportunity for various forms of participation. In autocratic societies, one's options may be limited to the choice between submission and rebellion, while in democratic societies the options are considerably greater.

Instructions addressed to the Christian wives of non-Christian husbands in the first century cannot simply be transferred into the modern situation. The difficulty of making this transference is suggested by the presence of instructions on adornment, which are given to illustrate the meaning of submission. Although many of our predecessors (and a few of our contemporaries) have attempted to treat the instruction on jewelry and braided hair as commandments for all time, few today take that hermeneutical step. The apparel referred to in 1 Peter (and 1 Tim. 2:9) was worn as a deliberate attempt at defiance. Thus the ancient words to citizens, slaves, and wives cannot be transferred to our own time without considerable reflection.

The hermeneutical appropriation of the instructions to wives must reflect the deeper intent of the entire list of duties in 1 Peter. One can neither dismiss the ancient instructions as relics of cultural values of the past nor uncritically adopt them as commandments for our own time. While submission is not rooted in the order of nature, it is far more than an ancient cultural norm to be cast aside. As the instructions to slaves indicate, submission is rooted in the cross. According to 1 Pet. 2:21-25, Christian slaves, who are abused by non-Christian masters, are told that they have been "called" to "walk in his steps" by refusing to return evil for evil.

The deeper intention of 1 Peter becomes apparent when one compares the words addressed to slaves in 2:21-25 with those addressed as "all" in 3:8-12. "All" are expected to be humble and to avoid returning evil for evil (3:8-9). As with the slaves in 2:21, the entire Christian community is "called" (3:9) to a specific conduct rooted in the way of the cross.

This deeper intention of 1 Peter is to be seen also in the instructions to those who hold the dominant role in the ancient institutions. Christian husbands are encouraged to "live considerately" with one who is a "joint heir of the grace of life" (3:7). Similarly, those who hold authority in the church are challenged not to abuse power (5:1-4). The entire church is expected to know the value of humility (5:5). Thus the order of the ancient society is assumed in 1 Peter, but the ancient order is transformed by the story of the cross. Even those who hold authority are challenged to show consideration toward those who are in subordinate roles. Within the Christian community, where people are "joint heirs of the grace of life" (3:7), the understanding of authority is transformed by the story of the cross.

If the deeper intention of 1 Peter is to call on Christians to follow in the steps of Jesus within the institutional expectations of their own time, the challenge to the contemporary church is to follow "in his steps," not by transferring the ancient views of authority to our time, but by recognizing that those who follow "in his steps" reject the pursuit of power and the will to dominate. Thus in subordinating themselves to their husbands, Christian wives continue to walk in the steps of the crucified one. However, since the call for submission is rooted in the story of the cross, the Christian husband is also "called" (3:9) in the modern situation to share with his wife in reciprocal submission.

Chapter Sixteen

MARKAN CHARACTERIZATION OF WOMEN

Frederick D. Aquino and A. Brian McLemore

Current studies reflect diverse understandings of the role of women in Mark's gospel. Munro,[1] contending that Mark depreciates the prominent place of women, says the question of women among Jesus' following "is not only beside the point for Mark, but even something which he perhaps seeks to avoid." Alternatively, Fiorenza,[2] asserting that Mark views women as superior role models compared to male followers, observes, "Mark's portrayal of the leading male disciples is rather critical and almost negative. . . . The circle of women disciples exemplifies true discipleship."[3]

---

[1]Winsome Munro,"Women Disciples in Mark?" *CBQ* 44 (1982): 228, 237ff.

[2]For Elisabeth Schüssler Fiorenza, *In Memory of Her: A Feminist Theological Reconstruction of Christian Origins* (New York: Crossroad, 1983), 32ff., the locus of authority and revelation is not in texts but in community experience. Her "socio-pragmatic" hermeneutic endows the community of women with the authority to choose and reject biblical texts. "Only those traditions and texts that critically break through patriarchal culture and 'plausibility structures' have the theological authority of revelation." Cf. Anthony C. Thiselton, *New Horizons in Hermeneutics: The Theory and Practice of Transforming Biblical Reading* (Grand Rapids: Zondervan, 1992); and Susan Heine, *Matriarchs, Goddesses and Images of God: A Critique of Feminist Theology* (trans. John Bowden; Minneapolis: Augsburg, 1988).

[3]Fiorenza, *In Memory of Her*, 319. Mary Ann Tolbert, *Sowing the Gospel: Mark's World in Literary-Historical Perspective* (Philadelphia: Fortress, 1989): 291f., considers female characters not as "surrogates but superiors." See also Marla Selvidge, *Woman, Cult, and Miracle Renewal: A Redactional Critical Investigation on Mark 5:24-34* (Lewisburg: Bucknell Univ. Press, 1990): 98f., 107; Alice Buchanan Lane, "The Significance of The Thirteen Women in the Gospel of

Taking an intermediate position, Malbon[4] argues that all disciples, including women, are presented by Mark as "fallible followers of Jesus." She maintains that discipleship in Mark is not a question of gender, but women and other characters demonstrate that "followership is neither exclusive nor easy."

Given the variety of viewpoints about Markan character-ization of women, it is necessary to *hear* again Mark's narrative. This study focuses on the theological intent, literary structure, and aural impact of Mark's gospel.[5] Using compositional, narrative, and reader-response criticism, we explore whether Mark obscures women, or women represent "paradigms of true discipleship," or they illustrate certain aspects of "the kingdom of God" announced by "Jesus Christ, Son of God" (1:1,15).[6]

Mark," *The Unitarian Universalist Christian* 38 (1983): 18-27; and Athol Gill, "Women Ministers in the Gospel of Mark," *AusBR* 35 (1987): 14-21.

[4]Elizabeth Struthers Malbon, "Fallible Followers: Women and Men in the Gospel of Mark," *Semeia* 28 (1983): 32, 46. See also C. Clifton Black, *The Disciples According to Mark: Markan Redaction in Current Debate. JSNT Sup 27* (Sheffield, Eng.: JSOT Press, 1989): 278, n. 37.; Grant R. Osborne, "Women in Jesus' Ministry," *WTJ* 51 (1990): 266-270; and Mary Ann Beavis, "Women as Models of Faith in Mark," *BTB* 18 (1988): 3-15.

[5]Tolbert, *Sowing the Gospel,* 44, points out that "all ancient dis-course has a *speaking voice* behind it, even if the speaking voice was the reader's own. The Gospel of Mark, then, like its counterparts up and down the aesthetic scale of Hellenistic literature, was an *aural text*, a spoken writing, a performed story."

[6]On the textual problem of "Son of God," see Bruce M. Metzger, *A Textual Commentary on the Greek New Testament* (corr. ed.; New York: UBS, 1975): 73; Bart D. Ehrman, "The Text of Mark in the Hands of the Orthodox," *Biblical Hermeneutics in Historical Perspective, Studies in Honor of Karlfried Froelich on His Sixtieth Birthday* (ed. Mark S. Burrows and Paul Rorem; Grand Rapids: Eerdmans, 1991): 26-31; and M. Eugene Boring, "Mark 1:1-15 and the Beginning of the Gospel," *Semeia* 52 (1990): 47, 70, n. 8.

1. On Reading Mark

Although our concern is Mark's narrative world, the "extratext"—the language, culture, literary devices, and history—helps the reader fill the gaps in the story.[7] To disregard the "extratextual repertoire" assumes a naive reading of Mark. As Boring[8] observes, "historical and literary considerations are not mutually exclusive," but are "most often helpful in determining the meaning of a text." Therefore, we see a dynamic interaction between reader, narrative, and extratext.

Surely Mark wrote with a theological intention.[9] In noting theological intention, however, we are not attempting to reconstruct a psyche of the author of Mark's story. We concede that any exact understanding of an author's intent is problematic.[10] Still, the "coherence" of Mark's story reveals

---

[7]John A. Darr, *On Character Building: The Reader and the Rhetoric of Characterization in Luke-Acts* (Louisville, KY: John Knox/Westminster Press, 1992): 22. See also, Susan R. Garrett, *The Demise of the Devil: Magic and the Demonic in Luke's Writings* (Minneapolis: Fortress, 1989): 6.

[8]Boring, *Semeia* (1990): 62. Tolbert, *Sowing the Gospel*, 12, points out, that "by its own insistence on the absolute autonomy of a literary work, New Criticism itself eventually provoked reaction, for literature clearly is related in important ways to the historical and cultural milieu out of which it comes." See also Mary Ann Beavis, *Mark's Audience: The Literary and Social Setting of Mark 4.11-12* (JSNT Sup 33; Sheffield: JSOT Press, 1989): 7-58; J. Andrew Overman, *Matthew's Gospel and Formative Judaism: The Social World of the Matthean Community* (Minneapolis: Fortress, 1990): 2; Sean Freyne, *Galilee, Jesus and the Gospel: Literary Approaches and Historical Investigations* (Philadelphia: Fortress, 1988): 25-30; and Black, *The Disciples According to Mark*, 222-256.

[9]Amos N. Wilder, *The Bible and the Literary Critic* (Minneapolis: Fortress, 1991): 29, the narrative is "intentional and suasive, undercut[ting] any strict view of the autonomy of the text."

[10]Johannes P. Louw, *Semantics of New Testament Greek* (Atlanta: Scholars Press, 1982): 48, states that interpreters "can only analyze the text at hand and try to establish what the text says—and then hope that the text is a fair representation of the author's intent."

intentionality. Mark is a theological document written as a relatively unified story, clothed in a first century worldview.

Markan characterization of women involves story and discourse levels. At the story level, characters serve as a medium to advance what happens in Mark's story. They are inseparably connected by the plot of the story. Through both reliable and unreliable characters, Mark's narrator[11] establishes his story. Sometimes, they are predictable (flat characters—the religious leaders), complex (round characters—the disciples), or illustrative of a certain quality (stock characters—the widow in the temple).[12] At the discourse

---

For post-modern skepticism regarding intentionality and history in Mark's narrative, see Stephen D. Moore, *Mark and Luke in Poststructuralist Perspectives: Jesus Begins to Write* (New Haven: Yale Univ. Press, 1992); and Frank Kermode, *The Genesis of Secrecy: On the Interpretation of Narrative* (Cambridge, MA: Harvard Univ. Press, 1979). Cf. Wilder, *The Bible and the Literary Critic*, 14-36; and Black, *The Disciples According to Mark*, 233-241.

[11]Mark's narrator (third person singular) is not the author (first person singular) of his gospel, but a rhetorical device that the author uses to tell a story in a certain way and guide the reader. Mark's narrator knows the whole story, has access to thoughts and feelings of characters, clarifies the meanings of certain customs and words, and clues the reader in on significant events in the story (e.g., 1:11, 27; 2:8; 3:19; 5:41; 6:52; 7:3f., 19; 11:13; 13:14). In these ways, Mark's narrator provides reliable commentary, making the reader aware of things the participants themselves may not know. See Seymore Chatman, *Story and Discourse: Narrative Structure in Fiction and Film* (Ithaca: Cornell Univ. Press, 1978): 146-162. Tolbert, *Sowing the Gospel*, 92-98; Fowler, *Let the Reader Understand*, 31-36, 64-73, and David Rhoads and Donald Michie, *Mark As Story* (Philadelphia: Fortress, 1982): 35-44.

[12]"Flat" characters have a consistent, ideological perspective throughout the narrative. The scribe in 12:34 and Joseph in 15:43 prevent the interpreter from categorizing all religious leaders in Mark as enemies of Jesus. "Round" characters display "changing and conflicting traits." "Stock" characters are "completely flat, having only one trait" (see Rhoads and Michie, *Mark as Story*, 102f.). Markan characters lack the introspective psychologizing of characters in the modern novel, tending rather to be more flat and static—perhaps because they reflect

level, Mark's narrator uses characters to move his readers to consider the demanding implications of following Jesus.[13] Through characterization, the reader is led to evaluate his/her own situation. Decisions must be made. For example, the reader has the privilege of accepting or rejecting the perspectives of different characters (the disciples, the leaders, or the crowd). Will Mark's readers learn from these characters or repeat their mistakes? So, we approach Mark's gospel "as a consciously constructed narrative in which the author uses various literary devices (e.g., characters) for theological purposes."[14]

2. Women and Mark's Kingdom Point of View

From beginning to end, the kingdom of God, as a "tensive symbol," rules the entire Markan narrative.[15] As the narrator unfolds the story,[16] Jesus reveals his kingdom

---

"sociological" stereotyping of people typical to dyadic societies (e.g., the first-century Mediterranean world). See Bruce J. Malina, *The New Testament Word: Insights from Cultural Anthropology* (Atlanta: John Knox, 1981), esp. chapter three, "The First Century Personality: The Individual and the Group."

[13]For discussions on the function of characterization in a narrative, see Chatman, *Story and Discourse*, 107-138; Rhoads and Michie, *Mark as Story*, 4, 101-136; Jack Dean Kingsbury, *Conflict in Mark: Jesus, Authorities, Disciples* (Minneapolis: Fortress, 1989): 4-27; Malbon, "Disciples/Crowds/ Whoever: Markan Characters and Readers," *NovT* 28 (1986): 104-130; and Mark Allan Powell, *What is Narrative Criticism?* (Minneapolis: Fortress, 1990): 51-67.

[14]Ronald F. Thiemann, *Revelation and Theology: The Gospel as Narrated Promise* (Indiana: Univ. of Notre Dame Press, 1985), 113.

[15]M. Eugene Boring, "The Kingdom of God in Mark," *The Kingdom of God in 20th-Century Interpretation* (ed. Wendell Willis; Peabody, MA: Hendrickson, 1987): 131-145. See also Freyne, *Galilee, Jesus and the Gospels*, 51; and Fiorenza, *In Memory of Her*, 118-130.

[16]See Joel Marcus, "The Time has been Fulfilled," *Apocalyptic and New Testament, Essays in Honor of J. L. Martyn* (ed. Joel Marcus and Marion L. Soards; JSNT Sup 24; Sheffield, Eng.: JSOT Press, 1989): 52.

vision to the disciples (4:10ff.; 9:1).[17] Ironically, they apprehend the message of the kingdom with some difficulty, more like outsiders (4:40f.; 6:52; 7:18; 8:14-21). Their incomprehension perplexes both Jesus and the reader of Mark's gospel. Alternatively, unexpected characters in the story contribute meaningfully to the reader's perception of what it truly means to be a disciple in God's kingdom. In this way, Mark's characterization of women reflects Jesus' apocalyptic proclamation about the proleptic reality of the kingdom of God.

A. *Mk. 1:29-31: A Paradigm of Suffering Discipleship or True Christian Leadership?*

Mark's narrator discloses reliable commentary,[18] to persuade the reader to accept his evaluation of the protagonist Jesus.[19] As the "beloved Son of God," Jesus calls disciples, heals the impaired, restores the possessed, and teaches with authority unlike the theologians of his day.[20] Jesus has already announced the nearness of the

---

[17]Helmut Koester, *Ancient Christian Gospels: Their History and Development* (Philadelphia: Trinity International Press, 1990): 13, correctly points out that εὐαγγέλιον (gospel; 1:1, 15) "form[s] an inclusio which indicates that the Baptist's message of repentance belongs together with Jesus' announcement of the nearness of the kingdom of God which resumes the call for repentance." See also Robert A. Guelich, "'The Beginning of the Gospel': Mark 1:1-15," *Papers of the Chicago Society Biblical Research* 27 (1982): 5-15 and Boring, *Semeia* (1990): 43-81.

[18]See Wayne C. Booth, *A Rhetoric of Fiction*, 2nd. ed. (Chicago: Univ. of Chicago Press, 1983): 169-209; Robert Fowler, *Let the Reader Understand: Reader-Response Criticism and the Gospel of Mark* (Minneapolis: Augsburg/Fortress, 1991): 61-64; and Beavis, *Mark's Audience*, 177-180.

[19]See Chatman, *Story and Discourse*, 227.

[20]On 1:16-3:6, see Tolbert, *Sowing the Gospel*, 132f. Vernon K. Robbins, *Jesus the Teacher: A Socio-Rhetorical Interpretation of Mark* (Philadelphia: Fortress, 1984): 198f., points out that the pattern of Jesus' preaching, teaching, summoning, casting out demons, and healing is "a familiar pattern of expectation and fulfillment throughout the narrative."

kingdom of God. Now, specific praxes follow his declaration of God's rule (see 1:15, 24, 39).

Simon's mother-in-law serves as one example of Jesus' victory over Satan. Departing from the synagogue, Jesus enters Simon's house (1:29). After the disciples inform Jesus about Simon's ill mother-in-law, he responds compassionately, restoring her health. She replies with a διακόνει (servant) disposition (1:31).

While the story of Simon's mother-in-law may foreshadow the theme of sacrificial service in Mark's narrative (e.g., 9:35; 10:43-45; 12:41-44; 14:1-9; 15:41), the immediate context of 1:29-34 functions as an example of Jesus' power. Previously the angels served him (1:13),[21] and now a person does. Fiorenza argues that Simon's mother-in-law and other women have "understood and practiced true Christian leadership." For Fiorenza, διακόνειν (to serve) cannot be restricted to menial tasks; but signifies an alternative attitude to the prevalent idea of tyrannical Greco-Roman lordship. Servitude reflects the proper conduct of anyone who would lead in Jesus' community. Therefore, women supplant the male disciples and "emerge as examples of suffering discipleship and true leadership."[22]

---

[21]Marcus, *Apocalyptic and the New Testament*, 56, cites *Testament of Naphtali* 8:3-4, arguing that "if Mark's readers knew this tradition, then even before reading the rest of ch. 1, they would have interpreted 1:13 as a description of the dethronement of Satan." Howard Clark Kee, "Testaments of the Twelve Patriarchs," *Old Testament Pseudepigrapha: Apocalyptic Literature & Testaments* (ed. James H. Charlesworth; New York: Doubleday & Co., 1983): 1.813, n. 8b, notes that "the link between the devil and the wild animals recalls the account of Jesus' temptation in the synoptic gospel tradition (*T. Naph.* 8:4; Mk. 1:13)."

[22]Fiorenza, *In Memory of Her*, 320ff. Monika Fander, *Die Stellung der Frau im Markusevangelium: Unter besonderer Berucksichtigung kultur- und religionsgeschichtlicher Hintergrunde* (Altenberg: Telos, 1989): 32ff., sees 1:29-31 as an insertion in the

But, it must be asked what role the story of Simon's mother-in-law plays in Mark's narrative? Although διακόνει ("she serves") tips the reader off to a prominent Markan theme, elevating Peter's mother-in-law to a paradigmatic status of discipleship and Christian leadership is problematic. Christian leadership is not the focus of 1:29-34. The story of Simon's mother-in-law reflects Jesus' message of the kingdom of God (1:15). Jesus dethrones Satan's dynasty. He is the hero of the story, acting out the narrator's regal point of view by actualizing the imminent presence of God's reign. To extrapolate the presence of women leaders in the Markan community from this text stretches the narrative beyond the textual evidence. So, "it cannot be inferred from these passages [1:31; 15:41] that women occupied the leading offices in the community of Mark, but rather that the menial tasks they performed were regarded as praiseworthy and as fully compatible with God's purpose for his people."[23]   Most likely, Simon's mother-in-law illustrates the narrator's view of discipleship; Jesus' new society exemplifies sacrificial service.

B. *The House (Οἰκία, Οἶκος): A Place of Hiding (1:29)?*

In Mark's story, how does the house (οἰκία/οἶκος) relate to the identity of women? Munro maintains that "Mark is aware of a female presence in Jesus' following . . . but for him women do not seem properly to belong in the public ministry of Jesus." She argues that "the anonymity and relative invisibility of women in Mark [prior to 15:40] is due in part to the androcentric bias of his culture that viewed women only in terms of their relations to men . . . women are further obscured by the androcentric nature of the language which uses masculine forms for common gender," (crowd). Munro maintains that the "house" is the new locus for Jesus' healing ministry and encounters with women (e.g., 1:29ff.; 5:35-43; 7:24-30; 14:1-9).   Mark excludes

---

Markan understanding of discipleship. Simon's mother-in-law realizes the demands of Jesus and demonstrates true discipleship.

[23]Kee, *Community of the New Age,* 91.

them from missionary endeavors, and vaguely mentions their activity in Jesus' healing and teaching ministry among the crowds. He does not depict women following Jesus in public places, but situates them in private places, i.e., "houses."[24]

Does Mark use "the house" to exclude women from Jesus' public ministry? To conclude that "house" serves as an androcentric tool for removing women from the public scene is dubious.[25] Munro oversimplifies the complex nature of language in antiquity. Undoubtedly, Mark shaped his story through androcentric lenses. Although ancient languages employed gender distinctions, grammatical gender should not be confused with sexism. First, the diminutives τὸ παιδίον (little child; 5:39-41; 7:28; 9:24, 36-37; 10:13-15), τὸ θυγάτριον (little daughter; 5:23; 7:25; the only two references in the NT), and τὸ τέκνον (child; 7:27; 10:24, 29-30; 12:19; 13:12) negate Munro's conclusion. Sometimes a diminutive referring to a person "can [even] be resumed by" a personal pronoun of another gender. Mark 5:23 serves as an example. Αὐτῇ (she) refers to τὸ θυγατρίον (little daughter). See also 5:41; 6:46.[26] Οἰκία (feminine) and οἶκος (masculine), the place where women and men are restored, taught, and called, does not fit Munro's androcentric argument.

---

[24]Munro CBQ (1982): 226f. Although Malbon, *Semeia* (1983): 34, 36, accuses Munro of "underestimat[ing] the importance of women characters prior to 15:40," she agrees with her critique of Mark's androcentric bias.

[25]Marla J. Selvidge, "And Those Who Followed Feared (Mark 10:32)," *CBQ* 45 (1983): 400, accurately retorts that "the primary problem is not the androcentric culture of Mark. The problem lies with a 1900-year-old androcentric approach to the text."

[26]F. Blass and A. Debrunner, *A Greek Grammar of the New Testament and Other Early Christian Literature* (trans. and rev. Robert W. Funk; Chicago: Univ. of Chicago Press, 1961): 111.1, comment that "Mark "exhibits the greatest frequency" of diminutives (note also 134.1, 282.4). See also A. T. Robertson, *A Grammar of the Greek New Testament in the Light of Historical Research* (Nashville: Broadman, 1934): 252-254, 404-411, 683f.

Second, a word can only be defined within its specific context. Louw shows that "meaning, is not understood from the meaning of a word, but from its reference." For example, ἄνθρωποι in Luke 12:36 "means 'people', but refers to 'servants'."[27] Third, the *constructio ad sensum* ὄχλος violates grammatical rules. It "embrace[s] a plurality of persons in a singular noun." It "is construed as if the subject were plural" (e.g., ὄχλος [crowd], λάος [people], στρατιά [army], οἰκία [house], πλῆθος [multitude], σπέρμα [seed]).[28]

Typically, Jesus teaches and heals in the synagogue (1:21, 23, 39; 3:1; 6:2) and "in the house" (οἰκία: 1:29; 2:15; 7:24; 9:33; 10:10; 14:3; οἶκος: 2:1,11; 3:20; 5:19, 38; 7:17,30; 8:3,26; 9:28). Eventually, the synagogue becomes a place of conflict during Jesus' ministry (e.g., 3:6; 6:1-6). After 6:6, "never again is a synagogue the setting of the teaching or healing or even the presence of the Markan Jesus."[29] For Mark the house becomes, not the place of "female space,"[30] but a training ground for the disciples. Ironically, the house, not the synagogue or the temple is the place where Jesus is anointed. It replaces synagogue and temple, and dominates the Markan narrative as the locus for

---

[27]Louw, *Semantics of New Testament Greek*, 50f. He correctly observes that "a word does not have a meaning without a context, it only has possibilities of meaning" (40).

[28]Blass and Debrunner, *A Greek Grammar of the New Testament*, 134.1, explain that the *constructio ad sensum* was "very widespread in Greek from early times and is found in the NT and in the papyri." As Robertson, *A Grammar of the Greek New Testament in the Light of Historical Research*, 410, observes, substantives "have two sorts of gender, natural and grammatical. The two do not always agree. The apparent violations of the rules of gender can generally be explained by the conflict in these points of view with the additional observation that the grammatical gender of some words changed or was never firmly settled. All constructions according to sense are due to analogy."

[29]Malbon, "TH ΟΙΚΙΑ ΑΥΤΟΥ: Mark 2.15 in Context," *NTS* 31 (1985): 286.

[30]Malina, *The New Testament World*, 43.

instruction.[31]   Perhaps, the house became a place for Markan readers to make sense out their present circumstances (e.g., 13:2).

Jesus' teaching in the house produces conflict with supposed authorities and family (2:1-17; 3:20-35). Unlike the scribes, he comes with a new and authoritative teaching (1:22,27) that ruptures Satan's domain and commands allegiance. For the first time, Mark's narrator illumines his reader about the plan of the religiously elite to destroy this Galilean (3:6).   Jesus includes his disciples in the "reordering of power" that he initiated.[32] They now have authority and power to drive out demons (3:15). The scribes, however, come from Jerusalem and attack the very source of Jesus' power. They accuse him of casting out demons by the authority of Satan (3:22). Curiously, Jesus' "relatives"[33] forcefully seize him and declare him "mad" (3:21; cf., 6:51).

Mark sandwiches Jesus' conflict with the scribes (3:20-35). In 3:13-19, Jesus commissions his disciples.   Framed by two references to Jesus' family (vv. 20-21; 31-35), Mark's narrator informs the reader of his theological

---

[31]Munro's interpretation misses the "architectural space" and the "significant connotation"of the house in Mark's story. "In the house," followers receive kingdom instruction as opposed to the synagogue and temple," Malbon, *Semeia* (1983): 40; and *NTS* (1985): 285-9. See also Ernest Best, *Following Jesus: Discipleship in the Gospel of Mark* (JSNT Sup 4; Sheffield, Eng.: JSOT Press, 1981): 226-9; Ched Myers, *Binding the Strong Man: A Political Reading of Mark's Story of Jesus* (Maryknoll: Orbis, 188): 150-152; and Herman C. Waetjen, *A Reordering of Power: A Socio-Political Reading of Mark's Gospel* (Minneapolis: Fortress, 1989): 483.

[32]Waetjen, *A Reordering of Power*, 86-100.

[33]We assume that οἱ παρ' αὐτοῦ refers to "his relatives" not merely townspeople. See C. F. D. Moule, *An Idiom Book of New Testament Greek* (Cambridge: Cambridge Univ. Press, 1959): 52; and Blass and Debrunner, *A Greek Grammar of the New Testament and Other Early Christian Literature*, 237.2. Cf. Tolbert, *Sowing the Gospel*, 99, n. 19.

intention (vv. 22-30).[34] The scribes label Jesus a deviant character ("he has Beelzebub") who breaks purity boundaries—incorporating the impure and the marginal into the fellowship of the righteous (e.g., 1:21-24; 40-45; 2:1-12; 13-17; 3:1-6; 11).[35] This text (3:23b-27) invokes the reader to remember that the kingdom of God has dealt a fatal blow to Satan's domain. "Satan's hold on the present order is being successfully challenged by the exorcisms which Jesus is performing."[36] The logic of Jesus' argument stands; the scribal attack against his authority fails.

Similarly, Jesus' mother and brothers "stand outside" of God's rule, expecting royal treatment. They, like the scribes, challenge his authority, and attempt to "restrain Jesus from his mission or redirect him to another course [3:21]."[37] Here, Mark discloses his "theme of rejection."[38] He contrasts Jesus' physical family with Jesus' true family. Jesus' physical family should respond favorably to his teaching. Instead, they do their will and not the will of God. Mark's narrator informs the reader that faith, not flesh, marks a disciple. In the kingdom of God, "the response of faith breaks across all the traditional social, cultural, and religious boundaries."[39] Jesus' new family comprises men

---

[34]See James R. Edwards, "Markan Sandwiches: The Significance of Interpolations in Markan Narratives," *NovT* 31 (1989): 196. Fowler, *Let the reader Understand,* 143, points out that "the intercalated episodes are sharply opposed to each other, but at the same time they frequently contain so many verbal echoes of each other that the reader can scarcely fail to take up the implicit invitation to read the framed episode [e.g., 3:22-30] in light of the frame episode [e.g., 3:21, 31-35] and vice versa."

[35]See Bruce J. Malina and Jerome H. Neyrey, "Conflict in Luke-Acts: Labelling and Deviance Theory," *The Social World of Luke-Acts: Models for Interpretation* (ed. Jerome H. Neyrey; Peabody, MA: Hendrickson, 1991): 97-122.

[36]Kee, *Community of the New Age,* 37.

[37]Edwards, *NovT* (1989): 210.

[38]Mary R. Thompson, *The Role of Disbelief in Mark: A New Approach to the Second Gospel* (New York: Paulist, 1989), 121-135.

[39]Tolbert, *Sowing the Gospel,* 174.

and women who do God's will, inheriting the familial benefits of the kingdom of God. (3:35; 9:29-31).[40] But those who declare him unclean stand outside opaquely looking inside (3:29, 31f.; 4:10ff.).[41]

C. Mk. 5:24b-34: A Symbol of Suffering?

Mark's narrator sandwiches the story of the hemorrhaging woman (5:24b-34) between the story of Jairus' daughter (5:21-24a, 35-43).[42] Previously, Jesus invited would-be followers to hear and respond to his parabolic presentation of the kingdom (4:1-34). The following four episodes (4:35-5:43) illustrate a fear versus faith motif. After Jesus calms the storm, he questions his disciples about their cowardly disposition and lack of faith (4:40). Fear reveals a lack of faith, whereas faith demonstrates a courageous

---

[40]Mark portrays Mary (3:21, 31-35; 6:4), Herodias, and her mother (6:14-29) in a negative light. Selvidge, *CBQ* (1983): 399, incorrectly assumes that "the only negative tradition about women preserved by Mark is the story of Herodias (6:14-29)." Munro, *CBQ* (1982): 238, sees Mark's negative portrayal of Jesus' family "alongside the rejection of the Twelve [i.e., anti-Jerusalem church hierarchy polemic]." Malbon, *Semeia* (1983): 35, contends that "Jesus' mother is no more central to the action than Jesus' brothers, and no more—or less—fleshed out as a character." For good discussions on Mark's negative portrayal of Jesus' family, see Ernest Best, *Disciples and Discipleship: Studies in the Gospel According to Mark* (Edinburgh: T&T Clark, 1985): 49-63; and Thompson, *The Role of Disbelief in Mark*. Cf. David M. May, "Mark 3:20-35 From the Perspective of Shame/Honor," *BTB* 17 (1987): 83-87.

[41]The ἔξω (without) theme pervades Mark's story (e.g., 3:31f.; 4:11ff.; 7:15ff.; 8:17-22). See James D. G. Dunn, *Jesus, Paul, and the Law: Studies in Mark and Galatians* (Louisville: Westminster/ John Knox, 1990): 41. Malbon, *Semeia* (1983): 42, playing on the insider/ outsider theme, remarks that "being family (expected insider status) does not necessarily make one a follower (true insider status; see 3:31-35)."

[42]See J. Lee Magness, *Sense and Absence: Structure and Suspension in the Ending of Mark's Gospel* (Atlanta: Scholars Press, 1986): 91-102, for a discussion on the five common functions that characterize Mark's miracle stories.

response that drives out fear.[43] The disciples hear only the roar of the chaotic sea, but they do not recognize the sea's master. Nor have they truly appropriated the perspective of insiders, who have been given "the mystery of the kingdom of God" (4:11-12).[44]

Mark's verbal irony perplexes the reader. The reader knows that prior to the first boat scene, Jesus explained everything to the disciples (4:33f.; see 35-41). Their incomprehension counters expectations of success. The disciples should see, hear, and understand. Yet they misunderstand the nature of the kingdom of God, seeing and hearing like outsiders (4:13; see 8:14-21). The "least expect[ed] to turn around and be forgiven do turn around and are forgiven" (5:1-20).[45] The disciples' inability to understand Jesus' message introduces the reader to Mark's ironic motif of blindness versus sight (8:22-10:52).

---

[43]Tolbert, *Sowing the Gospel,* 165, sees these four episodes "contrasting the disciples to three people seeking healing, distinguish[ing] the rocky ground from the good earth and the human response of fear from the healing one of faith [cf. 4:3-8, 13-20]." She labels the disciples as "rocky ground," asking the question, "if Jesus' disciples do not constitute the good earth, who does?" Cf. Fowler, *Let the Reader Understand,* 183.

[44]Kermode, *The Genesis of Secrecy,* 23-47, especially 45, maintains that in Mark's parables "the divine author made his stories obscure in order to prevent the reprobate from understanding them." However, Wilder, *The Bible and the Literary Critic,* 27, arguing against Kermode, insists that "the incomprehension [e.g., the disciples, authorities] was due to the hardness of heart and not to obscurity in the parables." For a thorough discussion on the literary, social, and oral elements of 4:11-12, see Beavis, *Mark's Audience,* 87-173.

[45]Fowler, *Let the Reader Understand,* 169. He shows convincingly that 8:22-26 and 10:46-52 (matched pairs of episodic narrative) form an ironic tension (144ff.). "The ironic tension is not between the two frame episodes themselves, but between the blind men in the frame stories and the stubborn, persistent blindness of the disciples in chapters in between." See also Best, *Following Jesus,* 134-145; *Disciples and Discipleship,* 185ff.; Michie and Rhoads, *Mark as Story,* 126f.; and Tolbert, *Sowing the Gospel,* 179f.

What part does the story of the hemorrhaging woman play in Mark's fear versus faith schema? How are we to understand this story in light of the disciples' incomprehension? Selvidge views the hemorrhaging woman as "an example of faith to everyone." The entire Markan community is to view her "work of faith" as "an example of a faithful follower."[46] Selvidge presupposes a Markan polemic against the disciples, which Mark's readers endorse. They "therefore are open to leadership possibilities found within the women of the community."[47] For Selvidge, the hemorrhaging woman "qualifies as model and leader of the emerging community." She "is characterized as 'suffering' under the hands of many physicians (5:26)." She knows "what it means to suffer, and thus can identify best with Jesus who suffered to the point of death [e.g., 8:31-32; 9:12]." Thus, the story of the hemorrhaging woman becomes "a symbol for the suffering Jesus and all suffering peoples."[48]

Selvidge's analysis of the story of the hemorrhaging woman is questionable. First, her identification of the twelve as the opponents of Mark's church is tenuous. A close reading of Mark's story does not lead the reader to see it as a polemical document.[49] Selvidge's reconstruction of Mark's

---

[46]Selvidge, *Woman, Cult, and Miracle Recital*, 100. Fander, *Die Stellung der Frau im Markusevangelium*, 54, says that this healing story summons the reader to imitate it.

[47]Selvidge, *Woman, Cult, and Miracle Recital*, 31 (see also 32-46).

[48]*Ibid.*, 106, and "Mark and Women: Reflections on Suffering," *Explorations: Journal for Adventurous Thought* 1 (1982): 28, where she argues that πάσχω and πολλά "are only used of Jesus and women. "In no instance is the word 'suffering' linked with the twelve." She also proposes the philological argument that αἷμα (blood) "is only used of Jesus' own blood, the blood of the new covenant, and the woman with the flow of blood." See also, Susan Lochie Graham, "Silent Voices: Women in the Gospel of Mark," *Semeia* 54 (1992): 148f.

[49]Best, *Disciples and Discipleship*, correctly argues, 128f., 177f., that Mark was not polemicizing against the "reputation of the historical disciples," nor "against a definite heresy," . . . "but seeking to preserve and deepen the Christian faith of his readers" . . . his main aim was to

community stretches the narrative beyond its intentionality.[50] Second, Selvidge's elevation of the hemorrhaging woman to a symbol of suffering is unlikely. Although Mark uses πάσχω (suffer) and πολλά (many things) only to describe the hemorrhaging woman and Jesus, perhaps anticipating the passion predictions (e.g., 8:31; 9:12), Selvidge unnecessarily restricts suffering to Jesus and women. True, Mark never uses πάσχω and πολλά to describe the Twelve, but he mentions their destiny: they will be delivered over to the Sanhedrin, hated, beaten in synagogues, and stand before governors because of Jesus (13:10-13). The story of the hemorrhaging woman does not inform the reader that she understands "the pain and social outrage that Jesus experiences before his death."[51]

The hemorrhaging woman and Jairus illustrate fear versus faith. These two stories share common features. Both involve healing stories of women sharing identical numerology. Jairus' daughter is twelve years old and a twelve year illness plagues the hemorrhaging woman.[52] The

---

show his readers what God could do for them through Jesus and tell them what their response ought to be." See also Beavis, *Mark's Audience*, 180.

[50]For discussions on the weaknesses of the polemical position, see Malbon, *Semeia* (1983), 47; Powell, *What Is Narrative Criticism?*, 87; Best, *Disciples and Discipleship*, 98-130, Black, *The Disciples According To Mark*, 151-153; and Thomas E. Boomershine, "Peter's Denial as Polemic or Confession: The Implications of Media Criticism for Biblical Hermeneutics," *Semeia* 39 (1987): 47-68.

[51]Selvidge, *CBQ* (1983): 399. See also Graham, *Semeia* (1992): 149.

[52]Waetjen, *A Reordering of Power*, 122, maintains that the story of Jairus' daughter and the story of the hemorrhaging woman "constitute a world building myth." The hemorrhaging woman "represents "tradition-bound Judaism. Unclean, isolated from the world and oppressed by the law, her life is restored by mak[ing] contact with the new human being." Jairus' daughter "embodies the new Israel . . . who is on the verge of bearing children and bringing new life to the world." Tolbert, *Sowing the Gospel*, 168, argues that Mark's use of twelve [contrasting the Twelve] could be "a subtle clue to the identity of Jesus'

story of Jairus' daughter opens Mark's sandwich. Jairus, a synagogue leader, falls before Jesus asking him to restore his daughter. She is near the point of death. Jesus agrees to go with Jairus to his house. At this point, Jairus' actions show significant faith. Mark views the synagogue as a place of controversy for Jesus and his followers (e.g., 3:6). Jairus is an exception to the rule. He, unlike his fellow synagogue comrades, believes that Jesus' can restore life (5:23).

As Jesus walks with Jairus, a crowd follows and presses on him (5:25). From within the crowd emerges a woman with a twelve-year illness. Mark's narrator describes her condition. Suffering under many physicians and "spending all that she had,"[53] her condition grew worse (5:26). Hearing about Jesus, she reaches out and touches his garment. Mark's narrator discloses the private speech of the woman and Jesus to his readers. The woman believes that if she touches Jesus, she will be restored (5:28). Jesus knows someone has tapped his healing power (5:30). Mark's interior disclosure of the characters aids the reader to assess the behavior of Jesus, the woman, and the disciples.[54] Jesus wants to know who touched him (5:30)? The disciples, however, respond with a sarcastic and uninformed question: "you see the crowd pressing around you, yet you say 'who touched me' (5:31)?" Hearing Jesus' question, the woman, with fear and trembling, falls before Jesus and tells him everything (5:33).[55] Contrary to Jewish purity laws, Jesus does not rebuke the woman for violating

---

true family." Edwards, *Nov Test* (1989): 205, says that "twelve may signify Israel to Mark's readers, indeed, Israel coming to faith in Jesus." Myers, *Binding the Strong Man,* 203, posits an egalitarian position. "If Judaism wishes to 'be saved and live' (5:23), it must embrace the 'faith' of the kingdom: a new social order with equal status for all."

[53]See Moule, *An Idiom Book of New Testament Greek,* 51.

[54]Fowler, *Let the Reader Understand,* 125-126.

[55]Jacob Neusner, *The Idea of Purity in Ancient Judaism* (Leiden: E.J. Brill, 1973), 60, says that the woman feared, "perhaps because she had made [Jesus] unclean by her touch."

them. He himself violates restrictive purity laws (e.g., 1:41; 2:14-17; 5:41; see Lev. 12, 15). Noting the woman's action, Jesus pronounces a blessing: "your faith has restored you; go in peace and be healed of your disease" (5:34).

The hemorrhaging woman's faith in Jesus' power enabled her to be healed.[56] She saw more in a touch than the disciples. The expected insiders should know more about Jesus' power, already experiencing his control over nature (4:35-41). Yet their question resembles the speech of uninformed outsiders. After the interruption of the story of the hemorrhaging woman, Mark's narrator shifts back to the story of Jairus' daughter. While Jesus is speaking, some people come from Jairus' house and tell him that his daughter is dead. Under this hopeless situation, they add: "why bother the teacher any further?" (5:35f.). Overhearing their words, Jesus commands Jairus to "stop fearing, only believe" (5:36). Fear hinders Jairus from witnessing the powerful works of Jesus. Jairus listens and goes with Jesus to his house. When they arrive, the mourners laugh at Jesus because he says the child is not dead, just sleeping. Jesus takes Jairus and his wife into the room and brings their little girl back to life (5:41f.).

What is the relationship between the story of Jairus' daughter and the story of the hemorrhaging woman? Are these stories juxtaposed? Both characters face extreme situations. The story of the hemorrhaging woman functions as the theological center of Mark's intercalation. Her interruption is not a coincidence. Mark places her in between the story of Jairus to show his readers a faithful act. Jesus did not have to command the woman to believe, but acknowledged her great demonstration of faith. Though she approached him fearfully, her fear transformed to faith. Unclean, isolated, and rejected, the woman moved through the crowd, around the disciples, believing that if she touched Jesus, she would be restored. She had reason to fear. Her

---

[56]Tolbert, *Sowing the Gospel,* 169, correctly points out that at first "the woman is not courageous; when she must confess, she does so 'in fear and trembling.' Faith can drive out fear."

condition rendered her unfit for community life. According to Jewish purity laws, she lived "on the margins of the covenant map."[57]

Mark's readers expect Jairus, a ruler of the synagogue, to display superior faith. He holds a prominent position in the community. Typical Markan irony shows that the least important do what is expected of the religious elite. "Jesus reverses their roles, for it is the woman who displays the greater faith."[58] Jairus, like the disciples, had to be challenged by Jesus to stop fearing, and believe. He should have exhibited the faith of the hemorrhaging woman. She provides instruction for Mark's readers. Faith, like the woman displays in 5:24b-34, overcomes social, ritual, and political boundaries. The kingdom reverses roles. Sometimes the least expected become great testimonies of faith.

D. *Mk. 7:24-31: A Bested Jesus?*

Mark's narrator inserts the story of the Syrophoenician woman directly after the controversy section over ritual purity (7:1-23). From 6:45 to 8:10, Jesus' ministry occurs predominantly in Gentile territory. He has healed, fed, and extended his regal message to those beyond the borders of the righteous. For the narrator, purity is not the real issue. Purity rituals were simply a way of drawing lines of fellowship. The unclean were purged from the community of holiness.[59] The real issue is the inclusion of the Gentiles.

---

[57]Jerome H. Neyrey, "Idea of Purity in Mark's Gospel, *Semeia* 35 (1986): 98. Marla J. Selvidge, "Mark 5:25-34 and Leviticus 15:19-20: A Reaction to Restrictive Purity Regulations," *JBL* 103 (1984): 622-623, contends that the story of the hemorrhaging woman "subtly shatters the legal purity system and its restrictive social conditioning. . . . The portrait of the woman 'with the flow of blood' is in direct contrast to the portrait of women preserved by the androcentric Levitical writers."

[58]Edwards, *NovT* (1989): 204.

[59]L. William Countryman, *Dirt, Greed and Sex: Sexual Ethics in the New Testament and Their Implications for Today* (Philadelphia:

Is this story about a feminist triumph, or a lesson about the unlimited nature of the kingdom? Some respond: "We do need another hero!" A woman puts Jesus in his place. In no other place does Jesus grant a petitioner his/her request. An argument, not faith, is the justification for healing. This Gentile woman's quick-witted response (7:28) confounds Jesus' own rebuke: "for it is not good to take the children's bread and throw it to the dogs" (7:29). In this view, she cures Jesus of his ethnocentrism—Jewish nationalism. [60]

However, Beavis observes correctly that the woman's saying does not refer to gender but "the question of the relationship between Jews and Gentiles."[61] Previously, Jesus instructed the crowd and his disciples about the ethical values of the kingdom. An impure heart, not unclean foods, defiles a person, thus excluding them (7:21ff.). To interpret Jesus' statement literally is to ignore the ironic and rhetorical nature of text. Is it proper to snatch the children's bread and throw it to dogs?

Jesus parodies the disciples' ideology. After his parabolic discourse on purity, the disciples remain baffled (7:17). The story of the Syrophoenician woman discloses

---

Fortress, 1988): 56f., argues that purity law in first-century CE Palestinian Judaism "was also important in the way it could draw boundaries between Jew and Jew." Anyone outside the boundaries of the early Jewish sects [e.g., the Pharisees] were considered unclean, and "removed from holiness."

[60]For proponents of this view, see Fiorenza, *In Memory of Her*, 137; John J. Schmitt, "Women in Mark's Gospel,"*The Bible Today* 19 (1981): 230; Sharon H. Ringe, "A Gentile Woman's Story," *Feminist Interpretation of the Bible* (ed. Letty Russell; Philadelphia: Westminster; 1985): 65-72; and Lane, *The Unitarian Universalist Christian* (1983): 21.

[61]Beavis, *BTB* 18 (1984): 6. See also, Gerd Theissen, "Lokal- und Sozialkolorit in der Geschichte von der syrophonikischen Frau (Mk 7 24-30)," *ZNW* 75 (1984): 202-225. Malbon, *Semeia* (1983): 37; and Osborne, *WTJ* (1989): 267, identify the universal nature of 7:24-30; however, their assumption that the woman convinces Jesus to change his mind, ignores Mark's play on the disciples' mindset.

the disciples' restrictive membership (no Gentiles allowed!) and Jesus' attempt to broaden their vision.[62] She invades their table fellowship through a rhetorical question and a clever response. Jesus rewards her insight with a blessing of wholeness for her daughter. Her bold faith, not cultic status, gives her and the readers the right to participate in the new age.[63] She functions as a living parable to reinforce Jesus' earlier teaching (7:14-23). To assume that Jesus endorses the position in 7:27 is improbable. Earlier, Jesus exorcised the Gerasene demoniac, and commanded him to proclaim to his Gentile family what the Lord had done (5:19). Yet, this former demoniac extends Jesus' instruction throughout Decapolis, thus providing Jesus with a warm reception (7:31-37).

E. *Mk. 12:41-44: A Poor Widow's Story—Praise or Lament?*

The story of the poor widow, which concludes Jesus' conflicts in the temple, parallels the scribal exploitation of God's people (12:38-40). Jesus' "non-triumphal triumphal entry" prompts the reader to consider his or her own messianic, kingdom, and discipleship presuppositions (11:1-25).[64] His temple activities anger the scribes and chief priests who seek to destroy him (11:18). With the elders, they question his authority (11:27f.), but Jesus confounds them with questions that they fearfully refuse to answer.

How does the poor widow's story relate to Jesus' denouncement of the Scribes?[65] "Widow" in 12:42 points

---

[62]We are indebted to Carroll D. Osburn for his observation on the rhetorical aspects of this pericope.

[63]See Kee, *Community of the New Age*, 92.

[64]Paul B. Duff, "The March of the Divine Warrior and the Advent of the Greco-Roman King: Mark's Account of Jesus' Entry into Jerusalem," *JBL* 111 (1992): 55f.

[65]Mark's narrator extends Jesus' conflict through parabolic language, indicting his opponents (12:12). Next, as Stephen H. Smith, "The Literary Structure of Mark 11:1-12:20," *NovT* 31 (1989): 119ff., shows that Mark's narrator chiastically arranges 12:13-12:40.

the reader to Jesus' condemnation of the scribes, who "devour widows' houses" (12:40). Instead of protecting widows, they rob them of their livelihood.   Desiring communal respect, they forfeit true Torah religion (12:38-39). They wish to be "endowed with special status and privileges," that express the "most important commodities in the attainment of social power in the Mediterranean honor culture" of the first century CE.[66] Jesus, however, praises the widow's sacrificial act in order to instruct his disciples.[67] It is to be understood that following Jesus involves a life of self denial, not exploitation (12:40). Mark's narrator uses the poor widow as a stock character to depict this quality of discipleship. She, unlike the scribes who take all, gives all that she has (12:44).   Mark's narrator possibly uses this story to foreshadow Jesus' death.   He prepares the reader for the passion narrative, challenging him/her to identify with the suffering servant.[68]

Jesus' opponents attempt to condemn (a=12:13-17) and ridicule (b=12:18-27) him through political and theological sophistry. A scribe's critique of the temple system (c=12:28-34), Jesus' Davidic query (b´=12:35-37), and condemnation of scribal impropriety (a´=12:38-40) set the agenda for the poor widow's story (12:41-44).

[66]Myers, *Binding the Strong Man*, 320.

[67]Addison G. Wright, "The Widow's Mites: Praise or Lament? " *CBQ* 44 (1982): 262f., argues that "Jesus' attitude to the widow's gift as a downright disapproval and not as an approbation. The story does not provide a pious contrast to the conduct of the scribes in the preceding section (as is the customary view); rather it provides a further illustration of the ills of official devotion . . . . Her contribution was totally misguided, thanks to the encouragement of official religion, but the final irony of it all was that it was a waste." Harry Fleddermann, "A Warning about the Scribes (Mark 12:37b-40)," *CBQ* 44 (1982): 67, says that "although Jesus praises her generosity (12:43), the tragedy of her desperate situation remains. Her house [is] completely destroyed [13:2]."

[68]Joseph A. Grassi, *The Hidden Heroes of the Gospels: Female Counterparts of Jesus* (Collegeville, MN: Liturgical Press, 1989), 22, suggests that "the widow's offering is meant to be a model for the ideal disciple in Jesus' last discourse; such a disciple is willing to give even his or her life in imitation of the Master."

How does this story relate to Mark's negative picture of the temple in chapter thirteen? Mark's narrator extends his kingdom vision through this episode. He frames the eschatological discourse in chapter thirteen with two stories of stock characters who introduce important aspects of discipleship (12:41-44; 14:3-9).[69] Dewy notes correctly that both stories "are joined by the hook word 'poor'" (12:42; 14:5,6), and each "forms a contrast with its immediate setting."[70] Thus the poor widow's story condemns scribal injustice, and the Bethany woman's story contrasts with the treacherous behavior of Jesus' opponents.

F. *Mk. 14: 3-9: Another Paradigm for True Discipleship?*

Mark's narrator introduces the passion narrative by inserting the story of the anointing of Jesus between the religious leaders' plot to kill Jesus (14:1-2) and Judas' decision to betray his king (14:10-11).[71] On two other occasions, the scribes and chief priests attempted to destroy Jesus, but feared the crowd's response (11:18; 12:12). Finally, through their accomplice Judas, they crystallize their schemes (14:10f.). Therefore, they hurry to slaughter the

---

[69]Elizabeth Struthers Malbon, "The Poor Widow in Mark and Her Poor Rich Readers," *CBQ* 53 (1991): 598, cogently argues (against Wright) that the poor widow story extends beyond "its immediate juxtaposition with the scribes." Mark 13 "is framed by two stories about exemplary women [12:41-44; 14:3-9] in contrast to villainous men." Kermode, *The Genesis of Secrecy*, 127-128, 134, sees this discourse as a model of Mark's whole narrative and "the largest of [Mark's] intercalations." For some rhetorical dimensions of Mark 13, see C. Clifton Black, "An Oration at Olivet: Some Rhetorical Dimensions of Mark 13," *Persuasive Artistry: Studies in New Testament Rhetoric in Honor of George A. Kennedy*, ed. Duane F. Watson (Sheffield: JSOT Press, 1992), 66-92.

[70]Joanna Dewey, "Mark as Interwoven Tapestry: Forecasts and Echoes for a Listening Audience," *CBQ* 53 (1991): 233.

[71]John Paul Heil, "Mark 14:1-52: Narrative Structure and Reader-Response," *Bib* 71 (1990): 306, notes that the verb "seek" (ἐζήτουν, ἐζήτει) and the temporary notices of "passover," "festival," and "right time" (πάσχα, ἑορτῆ, εὐκαίρως) in 14:1f.,11 clues the reader to this literary device. See also Edwards, *NovT* (1989): 209.

lamb of God before the Passover and the feast of Unleavened Bread. They must now use deceitful tactics to avoid a disturbance among the people during the festival (14:1-2). Jesus jeopardizes the leaders' status in the Jewish community. The reader already knows, because of Jesus' passion predictions, that the scribes and chief priests will trap him and put him to death (10:33). The scribes and chief priests prepare to celebrate the salvific deeds of God even as they plan the death of God's most precious gift (12:6-8).

As the scribes and chief priests prepare their ritual sacrifice, Jesus reclines in the house of Simon the leper. Again, his location (house) and fellowship with the unclean signals to the reader a change in religious space.[72] The woman's anointing of God's Son in a leper's house reverses sacred expectations. This setting would annoy Jewish leadership "since [they] banned anyone with leprosy from worship in the temple and full participation in the community."[73] Beyond the sacred place, a woman from Bethany anoints Jesus with precious ointment worth a year's wages.

Indignant disciples criticize her extravagance, observing that with the funds this ointment would bring she could have helped the poor (14:5). Jesus, however, praises her act of devotion as a "good work." He interprets it as a preparation for his burial (14:6, 8), and says "wherever the gospel is preached *throughout the whole world*, even what she has done will be spoken in memory of her" (14:9).[74] By these words, the reader recognizes that Jesus' message extends beyond the borders of Israel; God's rule has universal implications (e.g., 5:1-20; 7:24-31; 11:17; 14:9). Clearly, Jesus deconstructs religious parochialism.

---

[72]See Stephen C. Barton, "Mark as Narrative: The Story of Anointing Woman (Mk 14:3-9)," *ExpTim* (1989): 232.

[73]Heil, *Bib* (1990): 310. See also Neyrey, *Semeia* (1986).

[74]Tolbert, *Sowing the Gospel*, 274, argues that with Markan irony "this memory will not bring name and fame to a special individual but will instead serve to memorialize the anonymity of loving kindness."

Is the Bethany woman another paradigm for true discipleship?[75] What role does she play in Mark's passion narrative? Unlike the story of the hemorrhaging woman, Mark's narrator never reveals this particular woman's private thoughts or intentions for anointing Jesus (see 5:28). Jesus himself, however, interprets her charitable act specifically as a preparation for his forthcoming burial (14:8). Mark's narrator also displays dramatic irony in that the woman spends money to anoint Jesus, whereas Judas takes money to sell out his master. She enters the house to perform this act, while he departs from the house to betray Jesus (14:3, 11).[76]

As a stock character, then, the woman at Bethany illustrates a quality of discipleship. In the developing story, her act of devotion introduces the passion narrative and foreshadows Jesus' death on the cross. Her sacrificial faith certainly critiques the disciples' incomprehension (14:4f.), while at the same time showing the reader a contrast between a woman's charitable act and the treacherous deeds of Judas and the Jewish leaders (14:1-2,10f.).[77] Judas, unlike the woman, "refuse[s] to remain in fellowship with Jesus on his way to [the cross]."[78] So, with this story Mark's narrator prepares the reader for Jesus' impending journey to the cross.

---

[75]Fiorenza, *In Memory of Her*, xiv, contends that this unnamed woman "who names Jesus with a prophetic sign-action in Mark's gospel is the paradigm for true discipleship." She maintains that Peter confessed Jesus as the "anointed one" but did not understand (8:29-33). The Bethany woman "recognize[d] clearly that Jesus' messiahship mean[t] suffering and death." Grassi, *The Hidden Heroes of the Gospels*, 36-38, agreeing with Fiorenza, says that the Bethany woman "anointed Jesus' head as king but understood his messianic kingship in terms of his coming death." She "presents a full view of the ideal disciple: one who recognizes a suffering and dying Messiah, and one who gives her life in imitation."

[76]Malbon, *Semeia* 28 (1983): 40.

[77]Tolbert, *Sowing the Gospel*, 274, maintains that the story of the Bethany woman contrasts good earth with rocky ground (Judas and the chief priests; see 4:1-20).

[78]Heil, *Bib* (1990): 312.

G. *Mk. 15:40-16:8—Fear or Faith?*

Mark's narrator makes an important shift. Jesus told his disciples that they would desert him; still he promised to "go before them to Galilee" (14:27-28). After seeing their master's fate, the disciples flee, and Peter denies even knowing Jesus (14:50, 66-72). In 15:40-41, Mark's narrator analeptically comments about women disciples of Jesus: they followed and served him in Galilee and traveled with him to Jerusalem. The delayed appearance of these followers is an example of Mark's rhetoric of indirection.[79] The narrative's intensity increases. The male disciples have abandoned Jesus. The women take center stage as the only ones left to tell the story. The reader wonders, "will they bravely continue in the ministry of Jesus, or will they follow the path of the male disciples? Mary Magdalene, Mary, mother of James and Joses, and Salome view Jesus on the cross "from a distance" (15:40). This reminds the reader of Peter, who followed Jesus at his arrest "from a distance" (14:54).[80] The women are on their way to the tomb to anoint Jesus' body (16:1).

Between the crucifixion story and the resurrection story, Mark's narrator inserts a story about Joseph of Arimathea, a respected member of the Sanhedrin, who is "waiting for the kingdom of God" (15:43). Mary Magdalene and Mary look for the place "where Jesus was laid" (15:47). Of all people, a Sanhedrist buries Jesus (cf. 14:55; 15:1). The women stand by and watch, but Joseph courageously requests the body of Jesus from Pilate (15:43ff.).[81] Joseph's heroic performance "casts additional shame on

---

[79]Fowler, *Let the Reader Understand*, 111. For additional discussions on the function of analepsis in narrative, see Gerard Genette, *Narrative Discourse: An Essay in Method* (Ithaca: Cornell Univ. Press, 1980): 51-54; and Malbon, *Semeia* (1983): 41.

[80] Malbon, *Semeia* (1983): 43, sees this phrase as "a mark of fallibility—for Peter and for the women."

[81]Edwards, *NovT* 31 (1989): 213, notes that Joseph "is the first individual since the woman at Bethany who acts from courage and conviction."

[Jesus'] absent male disciples . . . and perhaps even impugns the women followers who see what happens but again take no active role (15:47)."[82] The reader expects Jesus' family or his disciples to bury him. Yet Joseph "musters the courage to emulate what John the Baptist's disciples earlier did for their master [see 6:29]."[83] As a stock character, *he* displays a quality of discipleship— courageous service.

When the women arrive at the tomb, their actions puzzle the reader. Previously, Jesus interpreted the Bethany woman's act of devotion as a preparation for his burial (14:8). Nevertheless the women buy spices to anoint Jesus (16:1). Does 16:1 parallel 14:3-9? If so, this would add an ironic twist to the narrative. The nameless woman has already anointed Jesus. Is a second anointing necessary? Although the women's intentions seem proper, the reader questions them. "Ambiguity stalks the characterization of these women much as it earlier did the portrait of the Twelve."[84]

Discovering that the stone had been rolled away from Jesus' tomb, the women enter (16:3ff.). To their surprise, they find a young man clothed in bright garments (16:5), who commands them to "stop being alarmed!" Jesus of Nazareth whom they seek is not here; he is risen (16:6). The reader recalls the promise that Jesus has gone before them to

---

[82]Tolbert, *Sowing the Gospel*, 293. She sees Joseph "among Jesus' former opponents who rejected his claim to be 'the Son of the Blessed' (14:61-62). Yet he, like Jesus, longs for the coming of God's rule and shows compassion for the body or corpse (πτῶμα; 15:45) of his former enemy. However, Raymond E. Brown, "The Burial of Jesus (Mark 15:42-47)," *CBQ* 50 (1988): 244, argues that Joseph of Arimathea was "a Sanhedrist responsible for sentencing Jesus to death but active in burying him out of fidelity to the Jewish law." See also Myers, *Binding the Strong Man*, 394ff. The nature of Markan irony seems to escape Brown and Myers.

[83]Kingsbury, *Conflict in Mark*, 27. See also Elizabeth Struthers Malbon, "The Jewish Leaders in the Gospel of Mark: A Literary Study of Marcan Characterization," *JBL* 108 (1989): 259-281.

[84]Tolbert, *Sowing the Gospel*, 293.

Galilee (14:28). There they shall see him, just as he told the disciples (16:7). After hearing the young man's message, the women flee from the tomb, "for terror and amazement possessed them; and they said nothing to anyone; for they were *afraid* " (16:8).

The two oldest Greek manuscripts (‭א‬ and B) do not have the last twelve verses of Mark 16.[85] Accordingly, NIV notes that "The most reliable early manuscripts omit Mark 16:9-20" before presenting those verses, and NRSV notes that "Some of the most ancient authorities bring the book to a close at the end of verse 8," and presents both the shorter ending which occurs in four Greek manuscripts (L Ψ 099 0112) and the longer reading of 9-20.[86] The longer reading occurs in most manuscripts and in KJV.[87] Nevertheless, vv. 9-20 are not considered original in current Greek texts[88] or most English translations. Reasons given are 1) these verses do not occur in codices Sinaiticus and Vaticanus,[89] 2) there is an awkward connection between vv. 8 and 9,[90] 3) several terms in vv. 9-20 are non-Marcan,[91] and 4) it seems strange that no mention is made of post-resurrection appearances in Galilee.[92]

---

[85]For a text-critical discussion of the ending of Mark 16, see Metzger, *A Textual commentary on the Greek New Testament*, 122-28.

[86]See John Christopher Thomas, "A Reconsideration of the Ending of Mark," *JETS* 26 (1983): 407-19.

[87]Note the strong defense in John W. Burgon, *The Last Twelve Verses of the Gospel according to S. Mark* (London: J. Parker, 1871).

[88]Kurt Aland, Matthew Black, Carlo Martini, Bruce Metzger, and Allen Wikgren, ed., *The Greek New Testament* (3rd ed.; New York: UBS, 1983), and *idem*, *Novum Testamentum Graece* (26th ed.; Stuttgart: Deutsche Bibelstiftung, 1979).

[89]Neil R. Lightfoot, *How We Got the Bible* (2nd ed.; Grand Rapids: Baker, 1988): 74-75.

[90]William R. Farmer, *The Last Twelve Verses of Mark* (SNTS MS, 25; Cambridge: Cambridge Univ. Press, 1974): 103.

[91]Metzger, *Textual Commentary of the Greek New Testament*, 125.

[92]Harvie Branscomb, *The Gospel of Mark* (London: Hodder and Stoughton, 1937): 314.

Although many readers assume closure in a narrative,[93] recent studies show that open and suspended endings existed in ancient literature.[94] Some ancient writers deliberately suspended their endings, thereby encouraging their readers to supply an ending and to enter the narrative world. In other words, the narrator intentionally leaves "unfinished business for the reader to complete, thoughtfully and imaginatively, not textually."[95] Very likely, Mark's narrative ends with "for they were afraid" (ἐφοβουντο γάρ). Is this typical of Markan narrative technique? In Mark, the particle γάρ provides parenthetical comments, or answers questions generated by the narrative. It equips the reader with insider information, explaining and clarifying unclear events (e.g., 3:21; 5:28, 42; 11:13; 16:4, 8). Γάρ also ends stories in Mark. For example, Mark's narrator concludes the second boat scene with the ambivalent comment "for they did not understand about the loaves" (οὐ γὰρ συνῆκαν ἐπὶ τοῖς ἄρτοις; 6:52; see also 14:2). Since a Greek sentence, story, or even a book can end with γάρ, it is indeed possible that the narrative ends with "for they were afraid." This would certainly cohere with Mark's narrative technique.[96]

How should readers interpret Mark's abrupt ending? We must remember that ancient writers intended for their literature to be heard publicly, not privately. In the Greco-Roman world, texts "were prepared to be 'performed' before

---

[93]Norman R. Petersen, "When is the End not the End? Literary Reflections on the Ending of Mark's Narrative," *Int* 34 (1980): 152.

[94]See J. Lee Magness, *Sense and Absence: Structure and Suspension in the Ending of Mark's Gospel* (Atlanta: Scholars Press, 1986).

[95]Petersen, *Int* 34 (1980): 153.

[96]E.g., Plotinus' thirty-second treatise (*Ennead*; τελειότερον γάρ); Plato, *Protagoras* 328c (νέοι γάρ); Musonius Rufus, *12th Tractate* (γνώριον γάρ). See P. W. van der Horst, "Can a Book End with ΓΑΡ? A Note on Mark XVI. 8," *JTS* 23 (1972): 121-124; Andrew T. Lincoln, The Promise and the Failure: Mark 16:7, 8," *JBL* 108 (1989): 284; and Thomas E. Boomershine and Gilbert L. Bartholomew, "The Narrative Technique of Mark 16:8," *JBL* 100 (1981): 213-223.

a group, read aloud, with all the techniques of oral communication available to the reader."[97] Mark's narrative, rhetorically structured, concentrates on "the needs of a listening audience" (e.g., 13:14)."[98] The narrative does not resolve the question: do the women eventually go and tell the disciples? It confronts the reader at the discourse level. The "burden of response-ability lies on those of us standing outside the story."[99] The narrator compels the reader to fill the gaps, even to insert a personal conclusion.

In 16:8, "for" (γάρ) resolves questions generated by the previous statements. The first γάρ addresses the question: why did the women flee from the tomb? "For" (γάρ) terror and amazement possessed them. "They fled" (ἔφυγον) registers a negative picture for the reader. The male disciples and the young man fled (ἔφυγον) at Jesus' arrest (14:50-52). Like them, the women's flight suggests a shameful situation. The reader wonders if the women will abandon Jesus. The second γάρ answers the question: why did the women say nothing to anyone? "For" (γάρ) they were afraid. Their silence signifies a cowardly response, not an epiphanic reaction.[100] Unlike the story of the hemorrhaging woman, their fear does not lead to faith.

---

[97]L. W. Hurtado, "The Gospel of Mark: Evolutionary or Revolutionary Document," *JSNT* 40 (1990): 17. See Mary Ann Beavis, "The Trial before the Sanhedrin (Mark 14:53-65): Reader Response Criticism and the Greco-Roman Readers," *CBQ* 49 (1987): 581-596; *Mark's Audience*; George A. Kennedy, *New Testament Interpretation Through Rhetorical Criticism* (Chapel Hill: Univ. of North Carolina Press, 1984); and Joanna Dewey, "Mark as Interwoven Tapestry: Forecasts and Echoes for a Listening Audience," *CBQ* 53 (1991): 221-237 on the importance of oral communication in the first century.

[98]Dewey, "Oral Methods of Structuring Narrative in Mark," *Int* 43 (1989): 33.

[99]Fowler, *Let the Reader Understand*, 250.

[100]Cf. David Catchpole, "The Fearful Silence of the Women at the Tomb: A Study in Marcan Theology," *Journal of Theology of South Africa* 18 (1977): 3-10; Graham, *Semeia* (1992): 154f., and Malbon, *Semeia* (1983): 44. Gerald O'Collins, "The Fearful Silence

Mark's ending challenges the reader. Like the Twelve, the women flee as cowards (14:50), but Jesus keeps his promise. He has gone before the disciples to Galilee, just as he told them (14:28; 16:7). Frightened, the women leave the tomb in silence (16:8). They do not share the Galilean story with anyone. Jesus' post-resurrection permission to speak about him falls on terrified ears (e.g., 9:9). Earlier in the narrative, Jesus prohibited people from speaking about him. Still they went out and spoke about him openly (1:44-45; 7:36). Now through the young man, Jesus lifts the restriction and commands the women to announce his presence in Galilee. Ironically, the women who served and followed Jesus refuse to tell the disciples that Jesus waits for them.

The reader faces reversed expectations. Observing the inadequacies of the women characters in 16:8, one feels tension between proclamation and fear. Mark's narrator prods his readers "to reflect on [their] own response to the dilemma which the women faced."[101] Although the readers identify with the women's "situation," they must incorporate the "values" of the true disciple of God, Jesus Christ the Son of God (1:1,11; 9:7).[102] Accepting the narrator's reliable commentary, the protagonist Jesus emerges as the true hero of the story. But tension remains, threatening the reader's presuppositions about the kingdom and discipleship. Will

---

of Three Women (Mark 16:8c)," *Greg* 69 (1988): 491, argues that "the conventions of narrative suggest that the women's silence should be understood as temporary." O'Collins argument ignores Mark's orality. Mark's narrative concentrates more on the reader than the temporal nature of the women's silence. Unfortunately, our familiarity with the story of Christianity compels us to read other grids into Mark's story (Matthew and Luke). See Fowler, *Let the Reader Understand*, 228-266, for his invaluable insights on the history of reading Mark.

[101]Thomas E. Boomershine, "Mark 16 and the Apostolic Commission," *JBL* 100 (1981): 237.

[102]Joanna Dewey, "Point of View and the Disciples in Mark," (SBLSP 1982: ed. K. H. Richards; Chico, CA: Scholars Press, 1982): 104. See also Robert C. Tannehill, "The Disciples in Mark: The Function of a Narrative Role," *JR* 57 (1977): 386-405.

the readers tell others that Jesus waits for them in Galilee, or will they flee from the empty tomb frightened and silent? Mark's story leaves this question open for a reader's response.

Conclusion

Mark's open-ended narrative transforms an affected reader. At the discourse level, the reader must understand (hear) the narrator's summons to seek the kingdom, not plot resolution. She/he submits to Jesus the Son of God, because he faithfully proclaims and practices the new order. No other character models true discipleship.

Markan characterization remains an open-ended dialogue, subject to new understandings. Yet to satisfy some expectations of our readers, we offer a perspective on the role of women in Mark. Women, like other characters, develop the plot of Mark's story and reveal his kingdom point of view. Women are not devalued (e.g., Munro), neither do they *represent* true, ideal, or perfect disciples (e.g, Fiorenza), but they *illustrate* certain characteristics of discipleship, essential for Jesus' followers in any age (e.g, Malbon). In God's domain, neither status, wealth, gender, purity, or race determine one's position. What one does, not who one is, initiates one into the kingdom of God.

Mark wrote his story for a community; but his message about the kingdom is not captive to any one situation. Neither can any contemporary theology, whether fundamentalist or feminist, impose its agenda on Mark's story or characters. Mark's narrative calls all to accept God's vision and resist the temptation to rule his story.

Chapter Seventeen

WOMEN IN MATTHEW'S GOSPEL: A METHODOLOGICAL STUDY

Larry Chouinard

An important contribution associated with recent literary-critical studies is the increased attention given the Gospels as unified narratives.[1] Instead of focusing on the origin, growth, and the making of Gospel materials, recent trends reflect an interest in the narrative aspects of Gospel literature.[2] Within this approach, the Gospels are studied in terms of their plot, characterization, and the repertoire of rhetorical and literary skills exhibited within the story-form. The insights of literary critics into the nature of narrative and how stories are told have provided an agenda for research that has introduced not only new questions but also new tools for analysis.[3]

---

[1]However, Stephen D. Moore, *Literary Criticism and the Gospels: The Theoretical Challenge* (New Haven: Yale Univ. Press, 1989), has challenged the notion that the text possesses an inner structure or inherent unity. [Ed.—See now Stephen D. Moore, *Mark and Luke in Post-structuralist Perspectives: Jesus Begins to Write* (New Haven: Yale Univ. Press, 1992).]

[2]Standard works in narrative criticism include David Rhoads and Donald Michie, *Mark as Story* (Philadelphia: Fortress, 1985); R. Alan Culpepper, *Anatomy of the Fourth Gospel: A Study of Literary Design* (Philadelphia: Fortress, 1983); Jack D. Kingsbury, *Matthew as Story*, (2nd ed.; Philadelphia: Fortress, 1988). See more recently, Mark A. Powell, *What Is Narrative Criticism?* (Philadelphia: Fortress, 1990).

[3]Stephen Neill and Tom Wright, *The Interpretation of the New Testament: 1861-1986* (2nd ed.; New York: Oxford Univ. Press, 1988):

One area in which biblical literary critics have contributed significant insights is in the study of characters portrayed in biblical narratives. The story-world of the Gospel
narratives is populated by diverse characters who contribute
in varying degrees to the story's plot. The nature and motivation of characters can be revealed in a number of ways.
Before we attempt to ascertain how Matthew intended his
readers to understand the role of women in his story, an
overview of the methods and purpose of characterization will
clarify how characters are portrayed in ancient texts.

1. A Methodological Study of Characterization

Recent literary studies of character in Gospel narratives
are not concerned with establishing a character's historicity
in the real world, but to demonstrate how the various
characters function or what role they play in a Gospel story.
The precision of historical correspondence between a
character's portrayal in a story and the actual historical
person is a question not immediately addressed by literary
studies.   Now, this is not to deny the importance of
historical investigations or that historical data can be drawn
from Gospel narratives. It is simply an attempt to take
seriously the narrative character of the Gospels and to
determine meanings and significance from within the
framework of the story. The interpretive agenda of a literary
study of character is amply illustrated by noting three recent
literary-critical studies of the Jewish leadership in the
synoptic tradition.[4]

402-403, observe that source, form, and redaction-criticism play no
more than an ancillary role in Gospel interpretation. Literary studies of
the Gospels have been preoccupied with questions of unity, cohesion,
and a holistic reading of the text.

   [4]Jack D. Kingsbury, "The Religious Authorities in the Gospel of
Mark," NTS 36 (1990): 42-65; Elizabeth Struthers Malbon, "The
Jewish Leaders in the Gospel of Mark: A Literary Study of Marcan
Characterization," JBL 108 (1989): 259-281; Mark Allan Powell, "The
Religious Leaders in Luke: A Literary-Critical Study," JBL 109 (1990):
93-110.

Kingsbury's treatment of the religious authorities in Mark is contrasted with two earlier studies which were either concerned to determine how familiar Mark was with the Jewish leadership groups active in the time of Jesus, or to use Mark's descriptions of conflict between Jesus and the Jewish leadership as a means of reconstructing the controversy between Mark's own community and contemporary Jewish groups. Both proposals ultimately derive the significance of the Jewish leaders in Mark from factors outside the Markan story. In contrast, Kingsbury proposes to study the religious authorities from a literary or narrative critical appraisal. This method entails an examination of "the story-line of the religious authorities in Mark's Gospel to gain insight into Mark's presentation of them."[5]

Powell insists that to interpret "literary elements in terms of supposed antecedents in the real world" is to commit the "referential fallacy." His study of the religious leaders in Luke "is not [concerned] to answer the historical questions posited by others, but rather to determine the intended literary effect of Luke's portrayal on the implied reader of his narrative."[6] Accordingly, characters are assigned function according to the writer's outlook and theological purpose.

Malbon observes that the danger of explaining a text solely by reference to hypothetical sources is that "one might substitute a theory of genesis for an interpretation of significance." In contrast with the quest for hypothetical sources or historical reconstructions, she proposes that the Jewish religious establishment be studied in terms of "their significance in and to the Gospel as a whole."[7] Culpepper's observation concerning characters in John is helpful here:

> Even if one is disposed to see real historical persons behind every character in John and actual events in every episode, the question of how the author chose

---

[5]Kingsbury, *NTS* (1990): 42-43.
[6]Powell, *JBL* (1990): 93.
[7]Malbon, *JBL* (1989): 263.

to portray the person still arises. With what
techniques or devices has he made a living person
live on paper, and how is this 'person' related to the
rest of the narrative? . . . The writer has a distinct
understanding of a person and his or her role in a
significant sequence of events.[8]

Whereas formerly studies of figures narrated in the Gospels
were concerned with historical questions, recent investigations pay more attention to a character's assigned role.

Characters in a textual narrative are not viewed,
therefore, as carbon copies of their real life counterparts, but
re-creations exhibiting the author's selectivity and specific
emphases. Unlike fiction, however, characters in the
Gospel narratives are not merely fabricated creatures with no
referential significance. Because the characters portrayed
have real-life counterparts, their function within the story is
not open to limitless possibilities. As Bal points out,
"referential characters are more strongly determined than
other characters."[9] In Gospel literature, the tradition has
established the boundaries of character development. Within
a textual expression, the image we receive of a character is
determined by various intertextual features. Too, a critical
perspective of characterization must reflect a sensitivity to a
text's cultural context. As modern readers are far removed
from the cultural context of the first century world, any
intertextual conclusions must reflect a knowledge of relevant
cultural conventions and patterns of communication.[10]
Thus, there will be "gaps" between the "givens" of a text and
the total personality of a character portrayed.

In literary terms, "characterization" involves the way in
which an author brings a character to life in a narrative,

---

[8]Culpepper, *Anatomy of the Fourth Gospel*, 105.

[9]Mieke Bal, *Narratology: Introduction to the Theory of Narrative*
(Toronto: University of Toronto Press, 1985): 83.

[10]See Mary Ann Tolbert, *Sowing the Gospel: Mark's World in
Literary—Historical Perspective* (Philadelphia: Fortress, 1989): 35-79.

either by "showing" the reader the speech or actions of the character, or by "telling" the reader directly about the character.[11] Modern novelistic and fictional literature abound in providing detailed specificity about its characters. A character's physical appearance and social status are often itemized solely out of a concern for "realistic fullness."[12] The minute analysis of motives or the detailed rendering of a character's thought processes are distinctive of modern characterization. Compared to characters in modern literature, characters in ancient literature may appear to lack depth and individuality. However, while the portrayal of persons in ancient literature differs from what one might expect in a modern short story, it should not be concluded that all characters in ancient literature are static or one-dimensional.[13] As noted by Korfmacher,[14] the depth of characterization largely depended on the genre in which the character happened to appear. Thus it was possible for a "type characterization" in one genre to become "an almost modern, individualized and highly personalized portrayal" in another genre. Nevertheless, it does appear that character-ization in classical literature was not primarily depicted by providing a psychological profile. As Stanton has pointed out, "direct analysis of the subject's character was rare in Peripatetic biography; the ethos of a person was portrayed

---

[11]See M. H. Abrams, *A Glossary of Literary Terms* (3rd ed.; New York: Holt, Rinehart, and Winston, 1971): 21-22; also Rhoads and Michie, *Mark As Story*, 101-103.

[12]See discussion in Meir Sternberg, *The Poetics of Biblical Narrative: Ideological Literature and the Drama of Reading* (Bloomington, IN: Indiana University Press, 1985): 329.

[13]Contra Robert Scholes and Robert Kellogg, *The Nature of Narrative* (New York: Oxford Univ. Press, 1966): 164. Recent studies of OT figures have found Scholes' and Kellogg's assessment too sweeping. See Meir Steinberg, *Expositional Modes and Temporal Ordering in Fiction* (Baltimore: Johns Hopkins Univ. Press, 1978): 92; Adele Berlin, *Poetics and Interpretation as Biblical Narrative* (Sheffield: Almond, 1983): 23ff; Robert Alter, *The Art of Biblical Narrative* (New York: Basic Books, 1981): 115-130.

[14]William C. Korfmacher, "Three Phases of Classical Type Characterization," *Classical Weekly* 27 (1934): 86.

through his praxeis."[15] Gill's analysis of character portrayal in Plutarch and Tacitus confirms Stanton's observation:

> These writers . . . talk as if their job was to pass judgements on the qualities of great men of history, and to see how they measure up to certain preconceived norms of excellence, as statesman and as men. They do not suggest that their job is to understand these people as interesting individuals or personalities, to give a sympathetic or "empathetic" picture of them, to "get inside their skin" psychologically, as a modern biographer might.[16]

It appears that the reading conventions of the ancient world assumed that the burden of understanding a character falls first and foremost on indirect means, such as speeches and actions. It follows that the modern reader must be attentive to all aspects of a text that may be disclosive of character—e.g., gestures, actions, words, social status and physical features. These elements are fundamental for creating the reader's impression of a character. Indeed, the image that the reader develops concerning women in Matthew's story comes largely from observing what they do and say. However, on occasion the author will speak directly about a character, or Jesus will give his own assessment of a character's actions. Characterization is thus a very complex matter that demands a reader's critical involvement with the text.

2. Matthew's Story and the Role of Women

It is generally recognized that there are five principal character groups in Matthew's story: Jesus, the disciples, the religious leaders, the crowds, and the minor characters.[17]

---

[15]G. N. Stanton, *Jesus of Nazareth in New Testament Preaching* (London: Cambridge Univ. Press, 1974): 122.

[16]Christopher Gill, "The Question of Character-Development: Plutarch and Tacitus," *Classical Quarterly* 33 (1983): 473.

[17]Kingsbury, *Matthew as Story*, 10; Janice C. Anderson, "Matthew: Gender and Reading," *Semeia* 28 (1983): 10, identifies the

Jesus is no doubt the central character around whom all action revolves and by whom all the other characters are evaluated. The story lines involving the disciples and Jewish leaders are essential to move the plot forward as Jesus interacts with each group. Even the crowds in the story take on certain traits as they respond to Jesus, and he to them.[18] Minor characters are those who appear sparingly throughout the story and are depicted with varying degrees of insight into their person. Although in some scenes they seem merely to function as "props" to establish a setting, on certain other occasions they serve as positive "foils" against which to view the deficiencies of major characters. Thus minor characters often exemplify values endorsed and commended by Jesus and the narrator. Although they usually remain nameless and appear in only one scene, their importance for the overall story is not to be slighted because of the brevity of their appearances.

It is important to remember that the casting of characters to convey commendable traits and values owes its origin to the storyteller. It is Matthew, as narrator, who selectively highlights certain actions and statements of his characters in order to emphasize what is acceptable or unacceptable practice or ideology. When the Gospel narrator consistently uses the socially marginal and religious outcasts as models of virtue and insight, the evangelist may be countering conventional stereotyping and cultural assumptions. A reader sharing the conventions and cultural framework of first-century Judaism would not expect tax collectors and foreigners to be exemplary. In this way, elements within the textual-world of Matthew's Gospel are intended to influence and transform the reader's perception of the real world.

---

five major character groups as the Jewish leaders, the disciples, the crowds, the supplicants, and the Gentiles.

[18]In Matthew the "crowds" function as a collective chorus (see 7:28; 8:1; 9:8, 25, 33; 12:23; 15:29-31; 21:9-11; 22:33), providing an assessment of Jesus, many times, in contrast to the Jewish leaders. Their reactions and questions function to stimulate the reader to address the same issues.

Women constitute a representative segment of first century Jewish society which was considered religiously "marginal."[19] The portrayal of women as positive models of religious virtue was rare in the ancient world.[20] While the Gospels assume the patriarchal structure of Jewish culture, they do portray women in a remarkably positive and exemplary role. Most studies concerned with women in the NT have treated Gospel materials in terms of the broader subject of Jesus' attitude toward women, and thus have tended to put the Gospels together and treat them thematically. Some studies have focused on the portrayal of women in a single Gospel story, usually highlighting their significance in Mark or Luke. Only a few studies have discussed Matthew's portrayal of women.[21] It may seem that Matthew has little interest in women since most of the episodes involving women appear to be only shortened versions of the Markan account. Furthermore, with only a few notable exceptions, women remain nameless and are not assigned any speaking roles. However, the significance of women in Matthew's story is not determined by the frequency of their appearance, but by the positive exemplary qualities exhibited by their actions: commendable virtues that, in Anderson's words "strain the boundaries of the Gospel's patriarchal world view."[22] In fact, with only a few exceptions, women are used consistently in Matthew's story to educate the reader in fundamental values and insights that are to govern a life of discipleship.[23] Certainly, they are not "characterized as deficient in faith, understanding, or

---

[19]See J. Jeremias, *Jerusalem in the Time of Jesus* (Philadelphia: Fortress, 1969): 359ff.

[20]Mary Ann Beavis, "Women as Models of Faith in Mark," *BTB* 18 (1988): 3-9.

[21]See Anderson, *Semeia* (1983); Jane Kopas, "Jesus and Women in Matthew," *Today* 47 (1990): 13-21; Grant R. Osborne, "Women in Jesus' Ministry," *WTJ* 51 (1989): 271-77; E. M. Tetlow, *Women and Ministry in the New Testament* (New York: Paulist Press, 1980): 98-101.

[22]Anderson, *Semeia* (1983): 26-27.

[23]For a listing of all references to women in Matthew, see Anderson, *Semeia* (1983): 26-27.

morality due to gender."[24] As a matter of fact, not only do Matthew's major female characters exhibit commendable character traits, Jesus' teaching and direct narratorial comments challenge a world view based upon patriarchal assumptions.

A. *Women in the Genealogy 1:1-17*

It is well known that the opening scenes of a narrative are fundamental for orienting the reader into the unfamiliar world of the story. Studies of Gospel prologues have demonstrated that the beginning of Gospel stories enables the writer to influence a reader's first impressions by molding the proper response to various characters, creating certain moods and expectations, establishing thematic concerns, and foreshadowing the course of subsequent events.[25] The genealogy in Matt. 1:1-17 constitutes the narrator's explicit commentary on the identity and significance of Jesus. For the most part, the genealogy is concerned to uphold Jesus' continuity with Israel's history and messianic expectations.

By means of the symmetrical structure of the genealogy, the narrator highlights the age inaugurated by the birth of Jesus. Israelite history is compressed to accentuate various phases and to show its culmination in Jesus. In the pre-monarchical period from Abraham to David (1:2-6), the reader is reminded of the divine selective process that culminated in the Davidic monarchy. In the second period (1:7-11) Matthew reminds his readers of both the glory of

---

[24]*Ibid.*, 21.

[25]J. M. Gibbs, "Mark 1:1-15; Matthew 1:1-4, 16; Luke 1:1-4, 30; John 1:1-51: The Gospel Prologues and Their Function," *StEv* VI (TU 102, Berlin: Akademie, 1973): 154; see also O. J. F. Seitz, "Gospel Prologues: A Common Pattern," *JBL* 83 (1964): 262-268; W. D. Davies, *The Setting of the Sermon on the Mount* (Cambridge: Cambridge Univ. Press, 1961): 61; U. Luz, *Das Evangelism nach Matthaus* (Zürich: Beniziger, 1985): 23-24; cf. Brian Nolan, *The Royal Son of God: The Christology of Matthew 1-2 in the Setting of the Gospel* (Göttingen: Vandenhoeck and Ruprecht, 1979): 103.

the Davidic reign and the steady decline of Israel's fortunes, ultimately resulting in Israel's darkest period, the Babylonian exile. By initiating the third period (1:12-16), with the Babylonian exile and portraying Israel without a king, subject to foreign powers, the narrator rekindles in the reader basic hopes and expectations characteristic of God's people during this period. As has been observed, "at each break the reader is confronted with a well-known Israelite, a pious foreigner, and with a significant act of God which leads Israel beyond a threat to the promise and finally to the age of the Messiah."[26]

The most striking breaks in the patriarchal symmetry of the genealogy occur with the inclusion of four women (1:3, 5, 6; i.e., Tamar, Rahab, Ruth, and Uriah's wife). The significance and ramifications of their appearance has been the subject of much debate.[27] Essentially, scholarly appraisals have sought to answer the question, "What did the four women have in common that prompted Matthew's choice?" It seems that any adequate interpretation must give due consideration both to their foreignness[28] and their gender. While Jewish sources spoke favorably of all four women, the presence of these particular women, rather than more exemplary female ancestresses, reminds the reader of the ways in which the royal line of Israel has been maintained. In spite of their alien and marginal status "they

---

[26]Charles T. Davis, "The Fulfillment of Creation: A Study of Matthew's Genealogy," *JAAR* 41 (1973): 523. See also Rodney T. Hood, "The Genealogies of Jesus," in *Early Christian Origins* (Chicago: Quadrangle, 1961) on characterization in a genealogy (5), and his development of the historical significance of Matthew's genealogy (10).

[27]For discussion of the major proposals see Raymond E. Brown, *The Birth of the Messiah: A Commentary on the Infancy Narratives in Matthew and Luke* (New York: Doubleday, 1979): 71-74; M. T. Johnson, *The Purpose of the Biblical Genealogies* (SNTSMS 8; Cambridge: Cambridge Univ. Press, 1969): 159-179.

[28]Although the OT accounts do not state explicitly that Tamar and Bathsheba were Gentiles, the evidence weighs heavily in favor of their Gentile status. See discussion in Johnson, *Purpose of the Biblical Genealogies*, 159-179.

are uniquely used by God in furthering the course of salvation history toward its climax in Christ."[29]

It should also be observed that each of these women take initiative to overcome their powerless state and questionable circumstances to participate in the plan of God. Through divine intervention, neither their Gentile status, gender limitations, nor questionable behavior proved to be an obstacle to their becoming instrumental in the divine plan.[30] As such, they foreshadow an important story-line in Matthew's Gospel wherein Jesus' teachings and messianic deeds are calculated to remove barriers that prohibited full participation based upon race, sex, or conduct.

B. *Women in the Teachings of Jesus.* In Matthew, the teaching of Jesus involving references to women does not reflect negatively upon women due to gender considerations or patriarchal norms. As a matter of fact, there is a definite egalitarian strain throughout Jesus' teaching that runs counter to Jewish cultural conventions and practice. Unlike some Jewish thinking, Jesus does not regard women as the sole or primary causal factor of male involvement in sexual sins.[31] According to certain rabbis, men do not initiate a lustful look or an adulterous act but are merely enticed by the alluring look of a woman.[32] Rather than demanding the

---

[29]David A. Bauer, "The Literary Function of the Genealogy in Matthew's Gospel," *SBLSP* (Atlanta: Scholars Press, 1990): 463.

[30]See the discussion on these four women in Kopas, *Today* (1990):14-15; Thomas H. Graves, "Matthew 1:1-17," *RevExp* 86 (1989): 599; and Edwin T. Freed, "The Women in Matthew's Genealogy," *JSNT* 29 (1987): 2-19.

[31]See T. Reub. 5:1-6:2; T. Jud. 15:5f; T. Issa. 4:4; ben Sirach 25:23-26; 26:10-12. It appears that some tendencies toward sequestering women in the home (Philo, Spec. Leg. 169) and rabbinic attempts to reduce contact between the sexes (b. Kidd. 70a; b. Erub. 53b; b. Ber. 61a; b. Ned. 20a) were motivated by the prevailing notion of female seductiveness.

[32]As noted by Eduard Schweizer, *The Good News According to Matthew* (trans. David E. Green; Atlanta: John Knox Press, 1975): 121, ". . . it is always the woman who is considered a danger to the

seclusion of women, Jesus places the responsibility upon the male to exercise sexual restraint (5:28). Both male and female are responsible for eliminating every source of stumbling, no matter how drastic the cost (5:29-30).

In the narrative on divorce (5:31-32; see 19:1-9), Jesus implicitly challenges the male prerogative of initiating a divorce. In a world where only the husband initiates a divorce, Jesus' "illustrations of adultery transform the concept of prerogative into a demand for responsibility."[33] Men will be held accountable for subsequent adulterous unions if women are discarded and forced to seek another relationship because of a husband's frivolous displeasure. Later Jesus will affirm that such actions are wrong because from the beginning God intended that marriage result in male and female being no longer two, but one (19:6). These intimations of male responsibility and female equality within the family pave the way for an even more pervasive emphasis on male-female equality.

Both women and men are challenged to the same rigors of discipleship. It is clear that no distinction based upon gender can be discerned with respect to the demand of one's allegiance to Jesus:

> For I have come to turn a man against his father, a daughter against her mother, a daughter-in-law against her mother-in-law. A man's enemies will be the members of his own household. Anyone who loves father or mother more than me is not worthy of me; anyone who loves his son or daughter more than me is not worthy of me (10:35-37).

---

man—such a danger the devout man will shut his eyes when a woman approaches, preferring to stumble rather than sin, neither speaking to her nor even extending his hand."

[33]Jack Levison, "A Better Righteousness: The Character and Purpose of Matthew 5:21-48," *Studia Biblia et Theologica* 12 (1982): 184-5.

Even Jesus' own family is distinguished from those who "do the will of God" (12:46-50). Conventional privileges associated with kinship are not in effect with the new state of affairs inaugurated by Jesus. Status before God is not conditioned upon race, kinship, or sex, but upon acceptance and practice of the norms of the Kingdom.

It should be observed as well that on occasion the narrator chose activities conducted by women as illustrative of certain features of discipleship and life in the Kingdom. In 13:31-33, the man who sows the mustard seed is paired with a baker-woman whose actions modeled the actions of God in the Kingdom. The women who are caught unaware while "grinding with a hand mill" (24:14) are paired with men who suffer the same plight. As symbols of preparedness, the wise and foolish virgins represent both positive and negative responses to the coming King (25:1-13).

Jesus' teaching has the effect of undermining oppressive values and social norms that reduced women to victims in relationship to men and "outsiders" in their social status. This emphasis is reinforced by the positive qualities exhibited by female characters encountered in Matthew's story.

C. *Women Characters in Matthew's Story.* Although the various scenes in Matthew's story detailing Jesus' encounters with women are usually shorter than Mark, women characters play a significant role in modeling commendable qualities and furthering distinctive themes and values developed throughout the story. Female characters usually remain anonymous, and unlike the Jewish leaders, the disciples, and the crowds, they have no continual narrative role. Nevertheless, their appearance and requests of Jesus often constitute a challenge to conventional androcentric bias, as well as the boundaries of Jewish cultic legislation. Although the connotative value of women in the story is not determined solely by sexual distinctions, it is true that their female gender "renders the exemplary behavior of women as more of an achievement and heightens contrasts with male characters."[34] In short, the women characters in Matthew's story receive a positive evaluation because they exemplify values that are endorsed by the protagonist (Jesus) and the reliable narrator of the story.

Following the Sermon on the Mount, the narrator temporarily retards the linear progression of the story by recording a series of episodes. Similar in form, they are calculated to give specificity to the programmatic summaries (4:23-25; 9:35; 11:3-6) by underscoring Jesus' therapeutic involvement with the people (8:1-9:34). Jesus' proclamation of God's reign (chaps. 5-7) is accompanied by "mighty deeds" that verify that in Jesus God has drawn near to his people. Of the ten episodes detailing Jesus' authoritative power, three involve his response to the needs of women (8:14-15; 9:18-26). It is important to remember that in Matthew's narrative-world there is no sharp distinction between one's socio-physical state and one's spiritual condition (see 8:17; 9:5). Sickness represented a disordered state having serious social and religious implications. Therefore, Jesus' therapeutic ministry is calculated to produce visible signs of the removal of barriers and boundaries that prohibited full participation in community and cultic ceremony.[35]

The first female character encountered in Matthew's story is Peter's mother-in-law (8:14-15). She is portrayed as in a helpless condition, "lying in a bed with a fever" (8:14). With Jesus' "touch" the fever leaves and the woman is made fit for service. Unlike Mark (cf. Mk. 1:31), Matthew focuses the reader's attention on her special relationship with Jesus. Her rendering of service to Jesus foreshadows the ministry of other women manifested only later (27:55), as well as highlights a fundamental element of those who will be called "great" in the Kingdom (20:21-28).

---

[34]Anderson, *Semeia* (1983): 21.

[35]This theme is developed extensively by Marcus Borg, *Conflict, Holiness and Politics in the Teachings of Jesus* (New York: Edwin Mellen Press, 1984).

The scene involving the woman with the hemorrhage is inserted between two halves of the raising of the ruler's daughter (9:18-26). The placement of the story encourages the reader to read each episode in the light of the other and to compare the supplicant's approach and petitions of Jesus. While the socially acceptable "ruler" publicly approaches, does obeisance to Jesus, and makes his request, the ritually unclean woman approaches Jesus from behind, hoping only to touch the fringe of his garment.[36] Although the two are not equal in social or religious status (Mk. 5:21-43), they are equal in the exhibition of exemplary faith and trust in Jesus' power to resolve their situation. The narrator provides the reader with an insightful glimpse of the woman's thought processes that motivated her act of faith. She "thought to herself" that a mere touch of the "edge of his cloak" would result in her healing (9:21).[37] Jesus commends her faith by acknowledging that her healing was the result of her faith (9:21). Jesus' positive assessment establishes her as a role model alongside other notable examples of active faith (see 8:10; 9:2). Moreover, the woman's impediment, or lack of wholeness, that rendered her ritually unclean (see Lev. 15:19-20) has been removed, thus liberating her from cultic and social restrictions.[38] By exhibiting bold faith and taking the initiative, this woman's faith resulted not in further defilement but in her salvation. It should also be observed that Jesus overcomes cultic defilement by giving life to the ruler's daughter (9:25). These episodes highlight the fact that no barrier can preclude his redemptive powers to overcome and dramatically transform.

In the scene depicting an encounter of Jesus with a Canaanite woman (15:21-28), Matthew once again casts a

---

[36]Anderson, *Semeia* (1983): 21.

[37]H. J. Held, "Matthew as Interpreter of the Miracle Stories," in *Tradition and Interpretation in Matthew* (Philadelphia: Westminster, 1963): 217, notes, "In Matthew's arrangement it is the saying which brings the healing about . . . ." (see Mk. 5:34; Lk. 8:48).

[38]See the discussion of Marla J. Selvidge, "Mark 5:25-34 and Leviticus 15:19-20," *JBL 103* (1984): 619-23, who argues that Jesus' healing had cultic significance as well as physical benefits.

woman as an outsider, alienated by social and cultic boundaries. Jesus leaves the land and people who are clean in order to enter "unclean" Gentile territory (15:21). The mention of "Tyre and Sidon" is not merely to document Jesus' geographical location, but to conjure up images of Israel's most hated enemies (e.g., Isa. 23; Ezek. 26-28; Joel 3:4).[39] Matthew further accentuates the religious and national distance between Jesus and the woman who approaches him by calling her a "Canaanite" (see Mk. 7:26). Nevertheless, the woman's petition, "Lord, Son of David, have mercy on me" (15:22), indicates an acknowledgement of Jesus' messianic authority. Such an insight in the context of Matthew 15 is clearly intended as a foil against which are heightened the "blindness of Israel's leaders" (15:14, 24; see 2:1-4), and the lack of perception among the disciples (15:16ff). This Gentile woman not only exhibits a reverent regard for Jesus (she calls him "Lord" three times and worships him), her persistent and undaunted faith over-comes all obstacles and culminates in a bold request that the blessings of Jesus' messianic mission be extended to include a small portion for those not of the immediate household (15:27). It is her "great faith" that sees the possibilities beyond what others see that enables Jesus to use her insight to stretch the disciple's perspective concerning the dimensions of his messianic mission (see 15:23; 15:29-39). Although the unnamed woman never reappears in the story or becomes part of the inner circle of disciples, "Matthew asks that we, like Jesus himself, listen to her and be transformed through a faith like hers: persistent, vigorous, and confident in God's faithfulness to God's promises."[40]

It has been observed that in Matthew's passion narrative women play a decisive role in modeling the elements of true discipleship. At Bethany, an unnamed woman takes the initiative to display openly her devotion to Jesus, anointing

---

[39]On the symbolic value of Tyre in the OT, see Carol Newsom, "A Maker of Metaphors—Ezekiel's Oracle Against Tyre," *Int* 38 (1984): 151-164.

[40]Gail R. O'Day, "Surprised by Faith: Jesus and the Canaanite Woman," *Listening* 24 (1989): 300.

his head with "very expensive perfume" (26:6-7). However, conflicting assessments follow. The disciples interpret
the act as wasteful and lacking in discretion concerning the
proper use of resources (vv. 8-9). However, Jesus defends
the woman by interpreting her deed as an insightful response
to the reality of his approaching death (v. 12). Furthermore,
the woman is to be memorialized "wherever this gospel is
preached throughout the world" (v. 13).

Once again, a woman is contrasted with the disciples to
point to deeper dimensions of Jesus' messianic task.[41] Her
act is called a "beautiful thing" (26:10) because it benefited
Jesus by affording him an opportunity to reinforce the
contours of his messianic mission. While the disciples
struggle with the reality of Jesus' imminent passion, this
woman is portrayed as understanding the necessity of the
passion and responding accordingly. By her "prophetic
anointing" and Jesus' positive appraisal of her deed the
reader is led to see that genuine devotion must also embrace
the reality of Jesus' death. Consequently, the proclamation
of "this gospel throughout the world" will necessarily entail
a proper integration of Jesus' majestic person alongside his
role as one who gives up his life in accord with the Father's
will. It is an unnamed woman at Bethany who first exhibits
a devotion that accepts the reality of Jesus' approaching
passion. As such, she inaugurates Jesus' passion by
illustrating an integral element of genuine discipleship.

In the concluding scenes of Matthew's story, women
assume a role that the selected disciples (i.e., the twelve)
should have played (27:55, 61; 28:1-10). In the hour of
Jesus' death, "many women" were present "watching from a
distance" (27:55), in marked contrast to the disciples who
had forsaken and fled (26:56). For the first time the reader
learns that Jesus' entourage from Galilee included "many
women" followers who were devoted to "serving him"
(27:55-56). While in Matthew's story women usually

---

[41]See the helpful article by Ronald F. Thiemann, "The Unnamed
Woman at Bethany," *Today* 44 (1987): 179-188.

remain nameless or are hidden in the anonymity of the crowds (see 14:21; 15:38), of the many who travel with Jesus, three are identified: "Mary Magdalene, Mary the mother of James and Joses, and the mother of Zebedee's sons" (27:56; see 20:21-28).

Two of these women are present during Jesus' burial and are the first to learn of Jesus' resurrection (27:61; 28:1-7). The reader observes that women, not the disciples are "last at the cross and first at the tomb."[42] Certainly, the prior actions of the women ("follow" and "serve him") and their presence at such critical junctures in the story (i.e., crucifixion, burial, and resurrection) establishes that these women should be viewed as authentic disciples, though they were not counted among the twelve.[43]

The details of the resurrection appearances also underscore the role of the women as foils, contrasting with both the soldiers (28:2-5, 11) and the disciples (28:7-10, 17). The story of the women at the tomb is interlocked with that of the soldiers by the common motif of "fear" (see 4, 5, 10). Matthew intended to contrast their responses with the appearance of the angel. Although both the women and the soldiers are gripped with "fear," the women are addressed directly and told not to be afraid (5), while the soldiers' fear leaves them as "dead men" (4). Not only does the angel interpret events for the women, he also demands of them certain actions: "come and see . . . go quickly and tell his disciples. . . ." (6-7). Instead of being incapacitated like the soldiers, the authoritative character of the event, coupled with its divine interpretation, moves the women to action. Although the soldiers eventually report all that happened (11), they are ultimately reduced to silence by a bribe (15).

---

[42]Anderson, *Semeia* (1983): 18.

[43]Contra Kingsbury, "The Verb Akolouthein as an Index of Matthew's View of His Community," *JBL* 97 (1978): 58; and Anderson, *Semeia* (1983): 20, who contends that "although the women play an important part in the narrative, gender seems to prevent their identification as disciples. They are an auxiliary group which can conveniently stand in for the disciples."

As the women hurry from the tomb, "afraid yet filled
with joy," they encounter the risen Jesus whom they
approach with reverence (see 8:2; 9:18; 20:20),[44] resulting
in "worship."[45]   Their response stands in contrast to the
disciples who later respond to the risen Jesus with
"worship" but, unlike the women, it is a devotion mixed
with "confusion" (28:17; see 14:31).[46] Their commission to
tell the disciples is reaffirmed by Jesus as he also seeks to
calm their "fear" (28:10).

Clearly, the women followers of Jesus function as post-
resurrection models of discipleship.[47] Exemplary devotion
enables them to be present as witnesses of both the crucifixion and the resurrection. Discipleship, as defined by the
action of these women, consists of recognizing and worship-
ping Jesus as the crucified and risen Christ, and being
obedient to a commission to bear witness to others. The
charge to the women to announce that Jesus is risen leads
directly to the reassembling of the disciples and the ultimate
world-wide commission (28:18-20).

---

[44]On the importance of προσέρχομαι (I come, go) in Matthew,
see James R. Edwards, "The Use of προσέρχεσθαι in the Gospel of
Matthew," *JBL* 106 (1987): 65-74.

[45]On the use of προσκυνέω (I worship) in Matthew, see
Anderson, *Semeia* (1983): 16, n. 35.

[46]See the discussion involving K. Grayston, "The Translation of
Matthew 28:17," *JSNT* 21 (1984): 105-109; K. L. McKay, "The Use
of *hoi de* in Matthew 28:17," *JSNT* 24 (1985) 71-72; P. W. van der
Horst, "Once More: The Translation of οἱ δὲ in Matthew 28:17,"
JSNT 27 (1986): 27-30. R. T. France, *Matthew: Evangelist and
Teacher* (Grand Rapids: Zondervan, 1989): 314, observes that
"διστάζω, often translated 'doubt' in 28:17, refers not to intellectual
uncertainty but to the disorientation produced by an unfamiliar and
overwhelming situation."

[47]See Elisabeth Schüssler Fiorenza, *In Memory of Her: A Feminist
Theological Reconstruction of Christian Origins* (New York:
Crossroad, 1983): 32ff.

Conclusion

Gospel writers were not driven by a documentary impulse simply to record the historical facts. Thus, the Matthean narrator casts women as one group of social outcasts who exhibit commendable qualities commensurate with discipleship. Their lower social and cultic status heightens the impact of their exemplary behavior. They do not allow their powerless state or foreign status to inhibit their exhibition of faith and desire to participate in the blessings of God's reign. Furthermore, it is their "great faith" and sacrificial devotion that often provide Jesus the occasion to stretch the disciples' perspective concerning the contours of his mission. Jesus' redemptive purpose will not be stymied by ethnic boundaries or contemporary standards.

The narrator's casting of women as exemplary in service (8:14-15; 27:55), active in faith (9:22; 15:28), insightful (both of the person and purpose of Jesus; see 15:22; 26:6-13), and as the first to give a witness to the resurrected Lord (28:5-7), certainly attests to a new order of relationships and participation inaugurated by the inbreaking kingdom. Read against the cultural milieu of first-century Judaism, Matthew's characterization of women functions as a challenge to special stereotyping based upon patriarchal assumptions. In Matthew's story, neither gender nor social status are categories that explicitly define discipleship or ministerial participation. Readers of this Gospel are led to evaluate female characters in a positive way because of their faith and acts of service, not because they are aligned with contemporary standards or limitations associated with gender. It appears that this emphasis on the paradigmatic function of women as exemplary of Christian discipleship and service is reflective also of the early churches' struggle to work out the kingship of God in a world divided according to socio-economic, racial, and sexual distinctions.

Chapter Eighteen

WOMEN IN THE GOSPEL OF LUKE

Allen Black

The numerous references to women in Luke and the corresponding references to women in Acts have been noticed many times before.[1] However, as in the case of all biblical references to women, Luke's statements about women have come under increasing scrutiny during the last two decades.[2] The result of this research has not been

---

[1]James Hastings, "Notes of Recent Exposition," *ExpTim* 4 [1892-93]: 434, observes, "Every reader notices it [the importance of women in Acts], every expositor comments on it." See, for example, Adolf Harnack, *Luke the Physician* (2nd ed.; London: Williams and Norgate, 1909): 153-55; Alfred Plummer, *The Gospel according to S. Luke*, (ICC, 4th ed.; Edinburgh: T. & T. Clark, 1910): xlii-xliii.

[2]See especially Constance F. Parvey, "The Theology and Leadership of Women in the New Testament," in *Religion and Sexism* (ed. Rosemary R. Ruether; New York: Simon and Schuster, 1974): 138-46; Neal M. Flanagan, "The Position of Women in the Writings of St. Luke," *Marianum* 40 (1978): 288-304; Leonard Swidler, *Biblical Affirmations of Women* (Philadelphia: Westminster, 1979): 163-216, 254-81; Elizabeth Tetlow, *Women and Ministry* (New York: Paulist, 1980): 101-108; Jacob Jervell, "The Daughters of Abraham: Women in Acts," *The Unknown Paul: Essays on Luke-Acts and Early Christian History* (Minneapolis: Augsburg, 1984): 146-57; Elizabeth Schüssler Fiorenza, "A Feminist Critical Interpretation for Liberation. Martha and Mary. Luke 10:38-42," *Religion and Intellectual Life* 3 (1986): 21-36; *idem*, "Theological Criteria and Historical Reconstruction. Martha and Mary. Luke 10:38-42," *Center for Hermeneutical Studies Protocol Series* 53 (1987): 1-12; E. Jane Via, "Women in the Gospel of Luke,"*Women in the World's Religions* (ed. Ursala King; New York: Paragon House, 1987): 38-55; Ben Witherington III, *Women in the Ministry of Jesus* (*SNTSMS* 51; Cambridge: Univ. Press, 1984); *idem*,

uniformity of viewpoint, but rather widely differing analyses—both in terms of methodology and conclusions. At one extreme, Luke has been portrayed as an early feminist and at the other, as one who sought to curtail the activities of women in early Christianity.

1. *Luke's References to Women*

The references to women in Luke's Gospel may be tabulated as follows. The second column notes occasions where men are paired with women.[3] The references with an asterisk occur only in Luke.

*1. Elizabeth (1:5-25, 36, 39-60)   Zechariah (husband)
*2. Mary (1:26-56; 2:1-52)   Zechariah (parallel)
*3. Anna (2:36-38)   Simeon
 4. Herodias (3:19)   Herod (husband)
*5. Widow of Zerephath (4:25-26)   Naaman
 6. Peter's Mother-in-Law (4:38-39) Possessed Man

Women in the Earliest Churches (*SNTSMS* 58; Cambridge: Cambridge Univ. Press, 1988): 128-57; *idem*, *Women and the Genesis of Christianity* (Cambridge: Cambridge Univ. Press, 1990): 201-24; Grant Osborne, "Women in Jesus' Ministry," *WTJ* 51 (1989): 277-81; Mary Rose D'Angelo, "Women in Luke-Acts: A Redactional View," *JBL* 109 (1990): 441-61; Wayne V. Whitney, "Women in Luke: An Application of a Reader-Response Hermeneutic" (Ph.D. diss., Southern Baptist Theological Seminary, 1990); Stuart Love, "Women in Luke's Gospel: A Macrosociological Analysis of Gender Specific Behavior," paper read at the SBL Annual Meeting, November 1990; and Stevan Davies, "Women in the Third Gospel and the New Testament Apocrypha," *'Women Like This': New Perspectives on Jewish Women in the Greco-Roman World* (ed. A.-J. Levine; SBL Early Judaism and Its Literature 1; Atlanta: Scholars Press, 1991): 185-97. Ingar Marie Lindboe, provides a brief overview of research on women in all of the New Testament from 1970-87 ("Recent Literature: Development and Perspectives in New Testament Research on Women," *ST* 43 [1989]: 153-63).

[3]H. J. Cadbury, *The Making of Luke-Acts* (London: SPCK, 1968): 234, observes that these pairings are part of a larger phenomenon of parallel pairings in Luke-Acts.

*7. Widow of Nain's Son (7:11-17) Centurion's Servant
 8. Those Born of Women (7:28)
*9. Sinful Woman (7:36-50)   Simon the Pharisee
*10. Women With Jesus(8:1-3)   The Twelve
 11. Jesus' Mother and Bros. (8:19-21)
 12. Jairus' Daughter and   Gerasene Demoniac(?)
     Woman with Hemmorhage
         (8:40-56)
*13. Mary and Martha (10:38-42)
*14. Woman Praises Jesus' Mother
         (11:27-28)
 15. Queen of the South (11:31)   Ninevites
 16. Mother vs. Daughter (12:53)   Father vs. Son
*17. Crippled Woman (13:10-17)   Man with Dropsy
 18. The Leaven (13:20-21)   The Mustard Seed
 19. Discipleship and Family (14:26) Father and Brothers
*20. The Lost Coin (15:8-10)   The Lost Sheep
 21. The Divorce Saying (16:18)
*22. Lot's Wife (17:32)   Lot (husband)
 23. Women Grinding (17:35)   Men (?) Sleeping
*24. Widow and the Judge (18:1-8)   Pharisee and the
                                        Tax Collector
 25. Leaving House, Wife, Etc. (18:29)
 26. Woman with 7 Husbands (20:27-40)
 27. Devouring Widows' Houses (20:47)
 28. Widow's Offering (21:1-4)   Scribes (see 20:47)
 29. "Those with child" (21:23)
 30. Maid Accuses Peter (22:56)   Man Accuses Peter
*31. Women Who Wail (23:27-31)
 32. Women at Crucifixion (23:49)   Other Acquaintances
 33. Women Witnesses (24:1-11,   2 on Road to Emmaus
         22-24).

These references to women are impressive both in the number of instances and in the number of pairings. Luke contains an emphasis on women and women paired with men that calls for explanation. To a large extent, redaction critical analysis based on the two source hypothesis supports the notion of a special Lukan emphasis on women. Roughly half of the tabulated instances are distinctive to Luke.

Presumably, Luke has taken over twelve references to women from Mark.[4] Minor evidence against a Lukan emphasis on women may be found in the few cases of Luke's omission of Markan references to women. The most important of these are his omission of the Salome incident found in Mark 6:17-29 (which, of course, would not contribute to a positive emphasis), the Syro-Phoenician woman and her daughter found in Mark 7:24-30 (which is part of Luke's enigmatic "great omission" of Mark 6:45-8:26 and which Luke may have omitted because of its geographical location),[5] and the anointing at Bethany found in Mark 14:39 (Luke has a similar incident in 7:36-50).[6] As indicated in the parentheses, these three instances may be explained in ways that do not raise serious objections to the overall impression of Luke's interest in women.

Seven of Luke's references to women have parallels in Matthew alone.[7] Five of these involve male-female pairings, showing that such pairings (which also appear in Mark) are not unique to Luke. In fact, although male-female pairings are more prevalent in Luke, in the case of Luke 17:34-35 Luke's pairing is less clear than the parallel in Matt. 24:40-41. Nevertheless, it deserves repeating that redaction critical analysis generally upholds the notion of Luke's emphasis on women and male-female pairings.

An examination of Luke's second volume also supports this emphasis. The book of Acts contains quite a few references to women, frequently paired with men. Luke mentions four married couples (Acts 5:1-11; 16:1; 18:2-3, 26; 24:24) and a pair of siblings (25:13). More significantly, on several occasions he specifies that both men and women became believers (5:14; 8:12; 17:4, 12, 34; cf.

---

[4]Numbers 4, 6, 11, 12, 25, 26, 27, 28, 29, 30, 32, and 33.

[5]Joseph A Fitzmyer, *The Gospel according to Luke (I-IX)* (AB; Garden City, NY: Doubleday, 1981): 94.

[6]Also compare Luke to Mark 3:35; 7:12; 10:1-12 and 10:30.

[7]Numbers 8, 15, 16, 18, 19, 21, and 23.

1:14). He cites Joel's prophecy that both men and women are to receive the Spirit and prophesy (2:17-18). He observes that both were persecuted by Saul (8:3; 9:2; 22:4) and (demonstrating that all parallels do not elevate women) that both persecuted Paul (13:50).

Beyond these pairings, Acts contains several other references to women. The early church is concerned about widows (6:1-6). Peter raised from the dead the beloved Tabitha, a woman commended for her great service to widows (9:36-42). Mary, mother of John Mark, hosts the saints at her house (12:12-17). Paul converts Lydia and her household as the first converts in Macedonia (16:11-15). Priscilla, along with her husband, teaches Apollos (18:26), and Philip's daughters prophesy (21:9).

Although women are not as prominent in Acts as in Luke's Gospel, they appear often enough to confirm a Lukan emphasis.[8]

The emphasis on women in Luke's Gospel is clear. It is evident in the frequency of references to women and in Luke's practice of pairing men and women. It is confirmed by source critical comparisons of Luke with Mark and Matthew and by the prevalence of references to women in

---

[8]D'Angelo, *JBL* (1990): 445, correctly notes that compared to Luke, there are significantly fewer appearances of women in Acts and that "the pairs in the two works differ significantly. In Luke the pairs consist of a variety of paired stories forming a single unit or a sequence and architectural pairs of stories, while in Acts most (though not all) of the references consist not of paired stories but either the names of couples or the *merismus* 'both men and women'." Tetlow, *Women and Ministry*, 101-108, seeks to relate this to Conzelmann's rigid periodization of salvation history in Luke-Acts. Thus, for Luke women were active in proclaiming the word during the period of Israel, but not in the period of the church. This sort of explanation depends both on Conzelmann's overstated schema and on minimizing the import of Luke's references to Priscilla and to Philip's daughters. Though the differences may be hard to explain, Luke's concern for women is present in both volumes.

Luke's second volume. However, as D'Angelo observes, "If it is easy to see that Luke's redactional techniques are at work in the deliberate inclusion of women, it is much less easy to see exactly what purposes they serve."[9]

2. *Rationales for Luke's Frequent References to Women*

What purposes do Luke's frequent references to women and pairings of men and women serve? Most of the suggested rationales are questionable. Before examining the major suggestions, it is important to note that there are two factors that every hypothesis should reckon with, but which do not provide comprehensive explanations by themselves.

Every attempt at a comprehensive explanation of Luke's interest in women needs to take into account the special influences that may affect individual cases. For example, Peter's mother-in-law may be linked with the possessed man in the first pair of healings (Luke 4:31-39) because that is how these miracles appeared in Mark (1:21-31). The raising of the widow of Nain's son (Luke 7:11-17) may have caught Luke's eye partially because of the similarity with the miracles of Elijah and Elisha (cf. Luke 4:25-26).[10] The brief description of the women who follow Jesus in 8:1-3 may be presented partially in anticipation of their role as witnesses to the empty tomb and the words of the angels in 24:1-11.[11]

These and similar explanations of other individual references to women and man-woman pairings in Luke-Acts should not be overlooked in our attempts to explain the phenomenon as a unit. However, it seems unlikely that most of Luke's references to women can be explained in a piecemeal fashion without any theory to account for the cumulative evidence of the whole.

---

[9]D'Angelo, *JBL* (1990): 447.

[10]Fitzmyer, *The Gospel according to Luke (I-IX)*, 213-15, 656.

[11]John Nolland, *Luke 1-9:20* (WBC 35A; Dallas: Word, 1989): 364.

Another factor that every explanation needs to take into account is the simple likelihood that women were heavily involved in the story Luke tells and in the church of his day. This likelihood is commonly recognized by advocates of all positions, usually with the complementary idea that Luke envisioned many women as part of his readership.[12] Davies[13] seems to regard this explanation as sufficient in itself:

There is a simple solution to the problem of why Luke's gospel contains more stories about women than the others: Luke was writing for an audience wherein women were numerous. . . . The evangelist seeks to capture the attention of the female portion of the audience.

The participation of many women in the story of Jesus and the church and the presence of women in Luke's audience would seem to be something we could assume a priori. And yet this does not provide a full explanation of why Luke does what he does. Other men in antiquity wrote about events that included many women participants without pointing that out as often as Luke does. Other men wrote for audiences that included women without saying as much about women. The other Gospel writers wrote the story of Jesus with fewer references to women. Ancient Graeco-Roman culture was, after all, a generally patriarchal system.

In addition to piecemeal explanations with respect to individual selections and to the likelihood that many women were involved in Luke's story and in his audience, there is still a need for a comprehensive explanation of Luke's interest in women.

---

[12]See especially Parvey, "The Theology and Leadership of Women," *Religion and Sexism*, 138-39; Jervell, "Daughters of Abraham," *The Unknown Paul*, 148; and D'Angelo, *JBL* (1990): 448.

[13]Davies, "Women in the Third Gospel," *'Women Like This'*, 190.

A. *The Thoroughgoing Feminist Interpretation*

One explanation, represented most thoroughly and extremely by Swidler, is that both Jesus and Luke were concerned to liberate women from the system of patriarchy and create a new egalitarian religious and social system.[14] According to Swidler, "Jesus himself was a vigorous feminist" and Luke followed the same path.[15] Swidler repeatedly contrasts Lukan references to women with a reconstruction of Jewish patriarchy and then asserts that Luke wants to liberate women from that system. For example, he sees sharp contrasts with Judaism in Jesus using a woman (searching for a lost coin) to symbolize God (Luke 15:8-10), his speaking to women in public (e.g., Luke 7:11-17), and the presence of women travelling among his followers (Luke 8:1-3).[16]

In this interpretation, virtually every reference to women is viewed in connection with the feminist agenda. For example, Luke supposedly puts the reference to the Queen of the South before the Ninevites (Luke 11:31-32; contrast Matt. 12:41-42) because he is "pro-feminist."[17] Swidler argues that the story of Mary and Martha (Luke 10:38-42) shows that women can step out of the role of housekeeper and live the intellectual life[18] and that the woman who praised Jesus' mother in Luke 11:27 had a "baby machine

---

[14]Swidler, *Biblical Affirmations of Women*, 163-216, 254-81. See also Parvey, "Leadership of Women," *Religion and Sexism*, 138-46; Via, "Women in the Gospel of Luke," *Women in the World's Religions*, 40-50 (Via modifies this position slightly); Frederick W. Danker, *Jesus and the New Age: A Commentary on St. Luke's Gospel* (rev. and expanded; Philadelphia: Fortress, 1988): 9, 172-73, 225.

[15]Swidler, *Biblical Affirmations of Women*, 280.

[16]*Ibid.*, 170-71, 182, 194.

[17]*Ibid.*, 168.

[18]*Ibid.*, 192. See Parvey, "Leadership of Women," *Religion and Sexism*, 141. Both view the Mary and Martha incident as a key text advocating a new liberated role for women.

image" of women which Jesus then rejected.[19]

In its worst forms, the thoroughgoing feminist interpretation becomes highly allegorical. For Via, Jairus's daughter (Luke 8:40-56) represents all Jewish women who were dying of patriarchy; the woman with the hemorrhage (Luke 8:43-48) represents the perpetual bleeding of Jewish women wounded by patriarchy; and the bent over woman (Luke 13:10-17) represents all women bent over by patriarchy.[20]

This line of interpretation has even led to the suggestion that "proto-Luke" or even Luke-Acts itself was written by a woman.[21]

Even without the fanciful allegorical details, the feminist interpretation falters on two grounds. One, which I will discuss in connection with the next line of interpretation, is the weakness of the prevalent reconstructions of Jewish attitudes towards women in first century Palestine. The other is a blindness to the evidence that Jesus and Luke implicitly endorse at least some elements of patriarchy. Jesus chose twelve *men* to be the core group of his disciples. *Men* (like Peter and Paul) dominate the story Luke tells in Acts. Even if Jesus and Luke deliberately sought to expand women's religious and social roles, there is clear evidence they were working within, and not in total opposition to, the prevailing patriarchal framework.[22]

---

[19]Swidler, *Biblical Affirmations of Women*, 193.

[20]Via, "Women in the Gospel of Luke," *Women in the World's Religions*, 42-44.

[21]Swidler, *Biblical Affirmations of Women*, 261-62, suggests a woman wrote proto-Luke and/or women were responsible for the oral tradition found in L. Via, "Women in the Gospel of Luke," *Women in the World's Religions*, 49-50, goes further to suggest a woman author for Luke-Acts. D'Angelo, *JBL* (1990): 443, clearly undercuts Via's theory by pointing out the use of a masculine participle for the author in Luke 1:3.

[22]See Janice Capel Anderson, "Mary's Difference: Gender and Patriarchy in the Birth Narratives," *JR* 67 (1987): 200-201;

B. The "Ministry to the Oppressed" Interpretation

A more convincing line of interpretation, best represented by Witherington's three volumes, is that both Jesus and Luke sought to improve women's religious and social position *within* the overall system of patriarchy.[23] The difference between this interpretation and the former one is comparable to the difference between advocating women's right to vote or better treatment for women in the work place and advocating thoroughgoing egalitarianism in all social structures. This softer line of interpretation pays due attention to the overall patriarchal framework of Luke-Acts and generally refrains from extremely allegorical interpretations of the references to women. Nevertheless, it sees the references to women as indicating Jesus' and Luke's desire to improve women's position in contrast to their commonly accepted status and roles in the first century.

According to this view the attention given to women in Luke is part of the theme "Jesus' Ministry to the Oppressed and Excluded,"[24] which includes the poor, tax collectors, sinners, Samaritans, Gentiles, and women. This is unquestionably a major Lukan theme, highlighted especially

---

Witherington, *Women in the Ministry of Jesus*, 126. Love, "Women in Luke's Gospel," 1-27, using a sociological methodology that compares the treatment of women in Luke with a model of women's roles in advanced agrarian societies, concludes that "The gospel simultaneously assumes a rigid, hierarchical, authority centered social structure which informs and constrains the treatment of its women characters all the while laying stress to their inclusion."

[23]Witherington, *Women in the Ministry of Jesus*, 125-6; *Women in the Earliest Churches*, 128-57; *Women and the Genesis of Christianity*, 88-120, 210-24. See also Osborne, *WJT* (1989):280; Whitney, "Women in Luke," 98-324; Fitzmyer, *The Gospel according to Luke (I-IX)*, 191-92, 696-97; Charles H. Talbert, *Reading Luke* (New York: Crossroad, 1982): 90-93; Robert C. Tannehill, *The Narrative Unity of Luke-Acts, A Literary Interpretation*, vol. 1: *The Gospel according to Luke* (Philadelphia: Fortress, 1986): 132-39; Nolland, *Luke 1-9:20*, 365-67.

[24]The title of a chapter in Tannehill, *The Narrative Unity of Luke-Acts*, 103-39.

in the programmatic passage from Isa. 61 that Jesus reads in the synagogue at Nazareth (Luke 4:18-19) and detectable throughout Luke-Acts. Probably most contemporary scholars would agree with including Jesus' concern for women within the scope of this theme.[25] But this interpretation overlooks the fact that, in contrast to the other groups (the poor, tax collectors, sinners, Samaritans, and Gentiles), women are not explicitly or implicitly described as oppressed or excluded within Luke-Acts.[26]

Widows are portrayed as in need of help (e.g., Acts 6:1; 9:39), but women in general are not portrayed in a way that would cause us to see them as oppressed or excluded. Modern interpreters see them as such partly because of modern views of the history of men and women; and partly because of a prevalent, but problematic, historical reconstruction of Jewish attitudes concerning women during the time of Jesus. In the absence of a direct Lukan statement or at least an implication that women were an oppressed group, we can only attribute this understanding to Luke if 1) we *assume* he held modern egalitarian perspectives (surely a mistake) or if 2) he portrays Jesus as conflicting with the prevailing cultural norms in such a way that his readers would see Jesus' teaching and actions as liberating women from well-known cultural restrictions.[27]

---

[25]See, e.g., most of the sources in note 23.

[26]Davies, "Women in the Third Gospel," *'Women Like This'*, 185-86, notes, "If an author advocated the elevation of a particular class from subjugation, then one would expect to find in the literary product evidence of both the subjugation and the liberation. . . . In the case of women no subjugation is stated or implied [in Luke]. . . . Although some assert 'that Luke will stress again and again that women are among the oppressed that Jesus came to liberate,' this assumption, unsupported by the evangelist's specific mention of women's oppression and liberation, must be termed erroneous." (The citation by Davies is to Witherington, *Women in the Earliest Churches*, 128).

[27]*Ibid.*

Witherington examines a variety of instances in Luke-Acts in which he believes approved behavior by women or Jesus' reactions to women stand in contrast to the prevailing customs of first century Palestine. His primary instances are: 1) The Queen of the South's testimony (Luke 11:31) was striking because it would probably have been thrown out of court by the rabbis.[28] 2) Jesus going to a woman's house and teaching a woman personally (Luke 10:38-42) was unheard of and even scandalous.[29] 3) The presence of women among Jesus' travelling companions (Luke 8:1-3) was also unprecedented.[30] 4) The story of Lydia (Acts 16:11-15, 40) indicates that in contrast to Judaism, the Lukan Paul believed women could form a church.[31]

In addition to such contrasts, Witherington argues that a concern to elevate women's status is seen in the instances, especially man-woman pairings, in which women are praised, but men are criticized. These include: 1) Mary, who exemplifies belief as opposed to Zechariah's example of unbelief (Luke 1:26-56; 2:1-52); 2) the sinful woman who is forgiven rather than Simon the Pharisee (Luke 7:36-50); 3) the bent over woman, healed on the sabbath over the objections of men (Luke 13:10-17); and 4) the widow who was finally vindicated by the unjust judge (Luke 18:1-8).[32]

But the *gender* significance of each of these examples of women praised at the expense of men is dubious. Mary, the sinful woman, the bent over woman, and the persistent widow are not favored in Luke because of their gender, but because they are respectively faithful, thankful, crippled, and persistent. Gender also has little to do with the criticism of the men in these stories.

---

[28]Witherington, *Women in the Ministry of Jesus*, 45.
[29]*Ibid.*, 101, 114.
[30]*Ibid.*, 117.
[31]Witherington, *Women in the Earliest Churches*, 148.
[32]*Ibid.*, 130-43.

The crucial element in Witherington's case for Jesus' and Luke's concerns to elevate women's position is the contrast with contemporary Judaism. However, this contrast depends on a reconstruction of the roles of women in first century Judaism which is currently undergoing a major overhaul. Until recently, all scholarly portraits of women's positions and roles in first century Judaism have depended primarily on the rabbinic literature, Philo, and Josephus.[33] A bleak picture has been constructed. For example, Jeremias concludes:

> We have therefore the impression that Judaism in Jesus' time also had a very low opinion of women, which is usual in the Orient where she is chiefly valued for her fecundity, kept as far as possible shut away from the outer world, submissive to the power of her father or her husband, and where she is inferior to men from a religious point of view.[34]

Against this background Jesus and Luke, we are told, stand out as liberators.

---

[33]See Johannes Leipoldt, *Die Frau in der antiken Welt und im Urchristentum* (Leipzig: Koehler & Amelang, 1954): 74-114; J. Jeremias, *Jerusalem in the Time of Jesus* (Philadelphia: Fortress, 1969): 359-76; L. Swidler, *Women in Judaism: The Status of Women in Formative Judaism* (Metuchen, N.J.: Scarecrow, 1976); Leonie Archer, "The Role of Women in the Religion, Ritual, and Cult of Graeco-Roman Palestine," in *Images of Women in Antiquity* (ed. A. Cameroun and A. Kuhrt; Detroit: Wayne State Univ. Press, 1983): 273-87; and Whitney, "Women in Luke," 60-67.

Numerous texts express negative attitudes towards women, e.g., *t. Ber.* 7.18, 16, "Blessed (be God) that hath not made me a woman"; *b. Kidd.* 82b "Woe to him whose children are daughters"; *y. Sota* 19a.7 "Better to burn the Torah than to teach it to women"; Philo *De Spec. leg.* 3.169 "All public life with its discussions and deeds . . . are proper for men. It is suitable for women to stay indoors"; and Josephus *Ag. Ap.* 2.201 "The woman, says the Law, is in all things inferior to a man."

[34]Jeremias, *Jerusalem in the Time of Jesus*, 375.

The recent work of Brooten, Kraemer, and others has raised a question mark over all previous portrayals.[35] As in every other area of study with regard to pre-AD 70 Judaism, the rabbinic statements about women must be used with great caution due to the problems of dating the ideas found there and determining how representative they are for Judaism before 70.[36] Furthermore, such rabbinic statements are more prescriptive than descriptive. They reflect how certain male leaders wanted things to be, not necessarily how things actually were.[37] The statements of Philo and Josephus are more pertinent, but we must use caution in extrapolating their views to all first century Jewish culture.

Inscriptional, papyrological, and some literary materials provide a counter portrait of some Jewish women—in Palestine as well as the Diaspora—who were heads of

---

[35]Bernadette Brooten, *Women Leaders in the Ancient Synagogue: Inscriptional Evidence and Background Issues* (BJS 36; Atlanta: Scholars Press, 1982); *idem*, "Early Christian Women and Their Cultural Context: Issues of Method in Historical Reconstruction," in *Feminist Perspectives on Biblical Scholarship* (SBLBSNA 10; ed. A. Y. Collins; Chico, CA: Scholars Press, 1985): 65-91; *idem*, "Jewish Women's History in the Roman Period: A Task for Christian Theology," in *Christians among Jews and Gentiles* (ed. G. W. E. Nickelsburg and G. W. MacRae; Philadelphia: Fortress, 1986): 22-30; Ross Kraemer, "Hellenistic Jewish Women: The Epigraphical Evidence," (SBLSP, 1986; ed. K. H. Richards; Atlanta: Scholars Press, 1986): 183-200; *idem*, "Non-Literary Evidence for Jewish Women in Rome and Egypt," in *Rescuing Creusa: New Methodological Approaches to Women in Antiquity* (= *Helios* 13), (ed. Marilyn B. Skinner; Lubbock, TX: Texas Tech University Press, 1986): 85-101; *idem*, *Maenads, Martyrs, Matrons, Monastics: A Sourcebook on Women's Religions in the Greco-Roman World* (Philadelphia: Fortress, 1988); Shaye J. D. Cohen, "Women in the Synagogues of Antiquity," *Conservative Judaism* 34 (1980): 23-29; Levine, ed., *'Women Like This', passim.*

[36]Kraemer, "Hellenistic Jewish Women," SBLSP, 183-84.

[37]Jacob Neusner, *Method and Meaning in Ancient Judaism* (BJS 10; Missoula: Scholars Press, 1979): 95.

synagogues, elders, and priests.[38] Recent scholarship has challenged such time honored notions as that women sat in synagogue galleries separated from the men,[39] or that Jewish women did not have the right to divorce their husbands.[40]

In the climate created by such far reaching reevaluations of Jewish practices and attitudes, it is precarious to compare the treatment of women in Luke-Acts with earlier reconstructions of women's roles in first century Judaism which now appear to be overstated and anachronistic. To be sure, the new studies do not overturn the concept of a

---

[38]See especially Brooten, *Women Leaders in the Ancient Synagogue*. Some pertinent texts are: "O Marin, priest, good and a friend to all . . . farewell!" (CII 1514, an inscription from Leontopolis dated 28 BC); "Rufina, a Jewess, head of the synagogue, built this tomb for her freed slaves and the slaves raised in her house" (CII 741; a probably 2nd century AD funerary inscription from Smyrna, Ionia) ; "Sophia of Gortyn, elder and head of the synagogue of Kisamos (lies) here" (CII 731c; a 4th or 5th century AD sepulchral inscription from Crete); and "Sara, daughter of Naimia, mother of the priest, Lady Maria, lies here" (CII 1007; a catacomb inscription from Beth She'arim, probably dating to the fourth century).

Brooten, *Women Leaders in the Ancient Synagogue*, 149, correctly concludes that "There is no reason not to take the titles as functional, nor to assume that women heads or elders of synagogues had radically different functions than men heads or elders of synagogues." Although the later inscriptions are chronologically problematic as backgrounds for Luke-Acts, they are contemporary with much of the rabbinic material frequently used to paint a monolithically negative picture of Jewish viewpoints.

In addition to the inscriptions identified by Brooten, D'Angelo, *JBL* (1990): 459-60, cites evidence of Jewish women prophets and interpreters of the law from Juvenal: "A palsied Jewess . . . She knows and can interpret / The Laws of Jerusalem: a high priestess under the trees, / A faithful mediator of heaven on earth. She too / Fills her palm, but more sparingly: Jews will sell you / Whatever dreams you like for a few small coppers" (*Satire* 6.541-48).

[39]Brooten, *Women Leaders in the Ancient Synagogue*, 103-38.

[40]Brooten, "Early Christian Women," *Feminist Perspectives on Biblical Scholarship*, 73-74.

general patriarchal framework for ancient Judaism, but they do provide counterpoints to monolithically negative portraits. It is no longer clear that the Queen of the South's testimony would be discounted by Jesus' audience or Luke's, or that it was scandalous for Jesus to teach a woman[41] or for women to travel with him.[42] Correctly understood, Acts 16:13-14 indicates that Lydia and the other women at Philippi were part of a synagogue before they formed the beginnings of a church.[43]

In this connection it is important to emphasize that Luke does not portray Jesus' teachings or actions with respect to women as something which disturbed his contemporaries.[44] In Luke Jesus is faulted for keeping company with tax collectors and sinners (Luke 15:1-2), but not for keeping company with or for teaching women. This silence would be surprising if Jesus' behavior in this regard was revolutionary.

It may be that additional evidence and more thorough investigation of existing materials will eventually demonstrate that some aspects of Luke's portrayal of Jesus' teachings or behavior with respect to women were out of line

---

[41]Davies, "Women in the Third Gospel," *'Women Like This'*, 186, rightly observes that to argue that Jesus teaching Mary (in Luke 10:38-42) constitutes a liberation of women "One must dismiss from serious consideration the fact that it is another woman who objects to Mary's listening role; one must overlook the fact that listening to a man is far from an unusual or liberated role for a woman; and one must regard as irrelevant the fact that in each of the gospels Jesus speaks publicly to crowds of male *and female* listeners."

[42]Cf. David C. Sim, "The Women Followers of Jesus: the Implications of Luke 8:1-3," *HeyJ* 30 (1989): 61, n. 3.

[43]Brooten, *Women Leaders in the Ancient Synagogue*, 139-40. My understanding of Acts 16:13 has been significantly affected by an unpublished manuscript by Richard Oster entitled, "Women, Diaspora Synagogues (*proseuche*) and Acts 16:13 (Philippi)."

[44]Davies, "Women in the Third Gospel," *'Women Like This'*, 185, 188.

with cultural norms, but that is not clear at the present time. As Brooten observes, "before meaningful comparisons can be drawn, many more detailed historical studies of Jewish and Christian women's lives and of cultural understandings of the female in this period need to be written."[45] This problem undercuts both the thoroughgoing feminist interpretation and the softer position that Jesus and Luke wanted to better women's social position within a patriarchal framework.

C. *The Anti-Feminist Interpretation*

A third position, best represented by Fiorenza and Tetlow, maintains that although Jesus and some segments of the early church moved in the direction of improving women's social status over that of contemporary Judaism, Luke went the other direction and sought to suppress the activities of women in the church of his day.[46] Fiorenza uses the Mary and Martha incident (Luke 10:38-42) as an illustration of Luke's suppression of women. She suggests that for Luke's time Martha represents a woman providing leadership in her house church. According to Luke, the woman (Mary) who is silent is praised and the woman (Martha) who defends her case is silenced. Thus Luke seeks to suppress women like Martha.[47] This interpretation

---

[45]Brooten, "Jewish Women's History," *Christians among Jews and Gentiles*, 25.

[46]Fiorenza, *Religion and Intellectual Life* (1986): 21-36; *idem*, "Theological Criteria," *Center for Hermeneutical Studies*, 1-12; Tetlow, *Women and Ministry*, 101-109. D'Angelo, *JBL* (1990): 457, presents a similar position, and argues that Luke's rationale for distancing Christian women from prophecy and similar ministries was "to distinguish Christianity from threatening oriental cults." See also Jane Schaberg, *The Illegitimacy of Jesus: A Feminist Theological Interpretation of the Infancy Narratives* (San Francisco: Harper & Row, 1987): 142-44.

[47]Fiorenza, "Theological Criteria," *Center for Hermeneutical Studies*, 7-9. See D'Angelo, *JBL* (1990): 454-55.

contrasts strikingly with that of Swidler, who describes the
Mary and Martha incident as a "Magna Charta for
women."[48] Both readings erroneously place importance on
the role of women in the story. As Reinhardtz correctly
observes, ". . . Jesus' words to Martha convey the
evangelist's attitudes toward discipleship in general, not his
views on women's discipleship specifically."[49]

Tetlow and Fiorenza also argue their position with
respect to other Lukan texts which those like Swidler and
Witherington have cited as representing elevations of
women's position. Accordingly, the women who follow
Jesus (Luke 8:1-3) are said to be *restricted* to providing
financial support, and it is suggested that although Luke
mentions the work of Priscilla (Acts 18:26) and of Philip's
daughters (Acts 21:9), he deliberately does not elaborate on
their activities.[50] These interpretations, however, depend
both on an ability to reconstruct what Luke knew but did not
say concerning these women's activities (only a little of
which can be done through other NT documents) and, even
more problematically, on the assumption that Luke's failure
to describe their activities more fully constitutes an attempt to
suppress that knowledge.

The feminist methodology used by Fiorenza and Tetlow
involves a highly subjective effort to find women's activities
between the lines of New Testament books authored by men
and thus assumed to be biased toward covering up the truth
regarding any active roles women may have played in
earliest Christianity. In his "Response" to Fiorenza's
"Theological Criteria," Anderson is justly "troubled about

---

[48]Swidler, *Biblical Affirmations of Women*, 273.

[49]Adele Reinhardtz, "From Narrative to History: The Resurrection
of Mary and Martha," in *'Women Like This'*, 170; so also William S.
Anderson, "Response" (to Fiorenza's "Theological Criteria"), *Center for
Hermeneutical Studies Protocol Series* 53 (1987): 18-19.

[50]Tetlow, *Women and Ministry*, 103, 108; Fiorenza,
"Theological Criteria," *Center for Hermeneutical Studies*, 8. See
D'Angelo, *JBL* (1990): 453.

the divisiveness and tendentiousness of a hermeneutics that operates from gynocentric suspicion and feels compelled to brand large tracts of the NT [sic] as androcentric."[51]

3. A Proposal

If Luke is not seeking to enhance or to suppress the social position of women, then what is the purpose of his inclusion of so many references to women and women paired with men?

The best explanation is found in connection with Luke's pervasive interest in the fulfillment of OT prophecies concerning the restoration of the people of God. Luke's heavy emphasis on this theme can be seen throughout both volumes of his work, from the opening reference to "the events that have been fulfilled among us" (Luke 1:1)[52] to the closing quotation from Isa. 6:9-10 (Acts 28:26-27). Especially significant in this regard are the two opening chapters of Luke (which provide a montage of OT portraits of the restoration of Israel and prepare the reader for the story to come in both volumes), the closing chapter of Luke (in which Jesus opens the disciples' eyes to understand the prophecies concerning himself and the coming events in Acts), and the opening chapters of Acts (which are replete with references to and fulfillments of prophecies concerning restoring the kingdom to Israel). But, of course, Luke's emphasis on this theme is scattered throughout both volumes, as can easily be seen by perusing the Lukan quotations, allusions, and verbal parallels to prophetic texts in the UBSGNT indices.[53] That Luke is immersed in the prophetic texts concerning the restoration of Israel is widely recognized in contemporary scholarship.[54]

---

[51]Anderson, "Response," *Center for Hermeneutical Studies*, 19-20.

[52]All biblical citations are from the NRSV.

[53]UBSGNT[3] 897-911.

[54]For recent explications of this theme see Jacob Jervell, *Luke*

Jervell looks in this direction for an explanation of
Luke's references to women in his article on "The Daughters
of Abraham." According to Jervell, Luke's interest in
women is not in women in general, but in the "daughters of
Abraham," Jewish women in particular.[55] Luke knows that
many Jewish women played a decisive role in the
development of the church and he seeks to explain this
theologically. In this respect, Luke 13:16 is especially
important. Jesus can heal this woman because she is a
"Daughter of Abraham." According to Jervell, nearly all the
women mentioned in Luke-Acts are daughters of Abraham.
Luke emphasizes not their social role—they maintain a role
of subordination to the men—but their Jewishness. For
Luke, "women are simply daughters of Abraham, devout
Jewesses, who have found their proper place in the
church."[56] Thus for Luke the emphasis on women is part of
the theme of the restoration of Israel.

There are two flaws in Jervell's interpretation. First, it
depends on labeling virtually every woman mentioned in
Luke-Acts as Jewish.[57] He downplays evidence to the
contrary (e.g., Acts 8:12; 11:21, 24; 18:8) and even

---

and the People of God (Minneapolis: Augsburg, 1972); *idem, The
Unknown Paul*; Eric Franklin, *Christ the Lord: A Study in the Purpose
and Theology of Luke-Acts* (Philadelphia: Westminster, 1975): 95-99;
Nils Dahl, "The Purpose of Luke-Acts," in *Jesus in the Memory of the
Early Church* (Minneapolis: Augsburg, 1976): 87-98; David L. Tiede,
Prophecy and History in Luke-Acts (Philadelphia: Fortress, 1980): 1-7,
50; James Parker, *The Concept of Apokatastasi in Acts: A Study in
Primitive Christian Theology* (Austin: Schola, 1978): 62-63; Donald
Juel, *Luke-Acts: The Promise of History* (Atlanta: John Knox, 1983);
Allen Black, "The Conversion Stories in the Acts of the Apostles: A
Study of Their Forms and Functions," (Ph.D. diss., Emory University,
1985): 109-208; Luke T. Johnson, *The Writings of the New
Testament: An Interpretation* (Philadelphia: Fortress, 1986): 197-243;
and Robert L. Brawley, *Luke-Acts and the Jews: Conflict, Apology,
and Conciliation* (SBLMS 33; Atlanta: Scholars Press, 1987).

[55]Jervell, "Daughters of Abraham," *The Unknown Paul*, 146-57.
[56]*Ibid.*, 157.
[57]*Ibid.*, 148-150.

relegates Damaris (Acts 17:34) to a footnote.[58]

Second, and more significantly, he does not thoroughly investigate the prophetic connection. He briefly discusses the significance of the Joel 2 text (cited by Peter in Acts 2:16-18)[59] for women prophets in Acts, but for Jervell the fundamental text is Luke 13:16 with its brief reference to the term "daughter of Abraham."

There are two prophetic texts that provide the key to Luke's interest in women. The first of these is the Joel quotation in Peter's Pentecost sermon. This quotation is particularly important because of the widely recognized programmatic nature of Acts 2[60] with its heavy emphasis on the restoration theme.[61] The Pentecost story is permeated with features of the hope of the restoration of Israel, including the restoration of the Davidic dynasty, the outpouring of the Spirit, the proclamation of forgiveness and repentance, the acceptance of this message by thousands of devout Jews gathered in Jerusalem from all the nations of the world, the inclusion of the nations in the mission of the restored Israel, and the idyllic communal existence of the restored community.[62]

Acts 2:16-18, 21 reads:

No, this is what was spoken through the prophet Joel: "In the last days it will be, God declares, that I will pour out my Spirit upon all flesh, and *your sons and your daughters* will prophesy, and your young

---

[58]*Ibid.*, 149, 188 n. 30.

[59]*Ibid.*, 154-55.

[60]Richard F. Zehnle, *Peter's Pentecost Discourse* (SBLMS 15; Nashville: Abingdon, 1971): 61-70, correctly describes Acts 2 as "An Epitome of Lukan Theology."

[61]See the sources in note 55 and David L. Tiede, "Acts 2:1-47," *Int* 33 (1979): 62-67; Richard Oster, "The Significance of Pentecost in Acts," *The Exegete* 3 (1984): 1-2, 10-11.

[62]Black, "Conversion Stories," 109-16.

men shall see visions, and your old men shall dream
dreams.   Even upon my slaves, *both men and
women*, in those days I will pour out my Spirit; and
they shall prophesy. . . . Then everyone who calls
on the name of the Lord shall be saved."

This quotation from Joel 2 is more than an explanation of the
speaking in tongues of Acts 2:1-15: it is an announcement
that "the last days" have begun. In particular, it interprets
the outpouring of the Spirit as a prophetic fulfillment and
announces the availability of salvation to all who call on the
name of the Lord.

In this context the prophecy uses men-women pairings
twice ("your sons and your daughters" and "slaves, both
men and women").   Jervell and others rightly draw
connections between these pairings and the prophesying of
Philip's daughters in Acts 21:9 and even of Mary, Elizabeth,
and Anna in Luke 1-2.[63] But the Joel prophecy is not only
about both men and women prophesying, but also about
both men and women participating in the pouring out of the
Spirit and in the salvation of everyone who calls on the name
of the Lord. It is not only the women prophets in Luke-Acts
who fulfill this prophecy, it is all the women who receive the
Spirit and the promised salvation. Joel's prophecy highlights the participation of both men and women in the events
of the last days, the events that are the focus of Luke-Acts.

The validity of this understanding is supported by the
similar use of men-women pairings in the prophecies of Isa.
40-66, clearly a foundational prophetic text for Luke.[64] The
function of Isa. 40-66 as a substructure for Luke's thinking
is apparent from both citations and allusions in Luke-Acts.[65]

---

[63]Jervell, "Daughters of Abraham," *The Unknown Paul*, 154-55.

[64]Richard Oster alerted me to these texts in Isaiah and their
importance for the role of women in Luke-Acts.

[65]Luke cites Isa. 40:3-5 (Luke 3:4-6), Isa. 62:1-2 (Luke 4:18-19),
Isa. 53:12 (Luke 22:37), Isa. 53:7-8 (Acts 8:32-33), and Isa. 49:6 (Acts
13:47). In each of these cases he demonstrates how the story of Jesus

Since Isa. 40-66 is foundational for Luke's view of what would happen in the prophesied restoration of God's people, it is important to see what Isaiah says about women.

I will say to the north, "Give them up," and to the south, "Do not withhold; bring *my sons* from far away *and my daughters* from the end of the earth—everyone who is called by my name, whom I created for my glory, whom I formed and made" (Isa. 43:6-7).

I will soon lift up my hand to the nations, and raise my signal to the peoples; and they shall bring *your sons* in their bosom, *and your daughters* shall be carried on their shoulders (Isa. 49:22).

Lift up your eyes and look around; they all gather together, they come to you; *your sons* shall come from far away, *and your daughters* shall be carried on their nurses' arms (Isa. 60:4).

In Isaiah these "sons and daughters" texts are not limited to a context involving the prophesying of the sons and daughters, a limitation some erroneously place on the prophecy from Joel 2. They are general restoration texts which refer to the ingathering of Israel in the prophesied restoration. They indicate that both sons and daughters will

---

and the early church fulfills the prophetic expectation. Beyond these citations, the "Index of Allusions and Verbal Parallels" in UBSGNT[3] identifies 44 passages in Luke-Acts that allude to Isa. 40-66. A few of the many items in Luke-Acts which have clear connections to the prophecies in Isa. 40-66 include : the salvation of the Gentiles (Isa. 49:6; Luke 2:32; Acts 13:47; 26:23), the redemption of Jerusalem (Isa. 52:9; Luke 2:38), the suffering of the Messiah (Isa. 53; Luke 22:37; 24:46; Acts 8:32-33), Israel grieving the Spirit of God (Isa. 63:10; Acts 7:51), the trampling of Jerusalem (Isa. 63:18; Luke 21:24), and a place for eunuchs in the people of God (Isa. 56:3-5; Acts 8:26-40). Cf. James A. Sanders, "Isaiah in Luke," *Int* 36 (1982): 144-55; Darrell L. Bock, *Proclamation from Prophecy and Pattern: Lucan Old Testament Christology* (JSNTSup 12; Sheffield: JSOT Press, 1987): *passim.*

be involved. It is likely that these texts, along with Joel 2, are the matrix for Luke's emphasis on women and men-women pairings in Luke-Acts.

Counter to Jervell's interpretation, it is not necessary to downplay the participation of Gentile women in this plan. As is clear in Acts 15:13-18 and elsewhere in Luke-Acts, the inclusion of Gentiles in the restored people of God was also a matter of prophecy.[66]

Luke's interest in the fulfillment of the prophecies concerning the restored people of God provides a theological explanation for his inclusion of many women and men-women parallels in Luke-Acts. Through both volumes of his work, Luke demonstrates that men and women are healed, hear Jesus' teaching, become disciples, bear witness, receive the Spirit, prophesy, and receive salvation. For Luke, this is not a matter of being pro- or anti-feminist, or of seeking to relieve women from oppression within a patriarchal framework, but rather a matter of demonstrating how God has kept his promises to Israel and to the nations.

---

[66]On the inclusion of the Gentiles see Jervell, "The Divided People of God: The Restoration of Israel and Salvation for the Gentiles," in *Luke and the People of God*, 41-74; and Fitzmyer, *The Gospel according to Luke (I-IX)*, 187-92.

Chapter Nineteen

"ANTI-FEMINIST" TENDENCY
IN THE "WESTERN" TEXT OF ACTS?

Jeffrey Childers and Curt Niccum

Recent attempts to locate an "anti-feminist" tendency in the "Western" text of Acts belong to a sub-discipline of textual criticism which has developed a life of its own, the search for theological tendencies.[1] Initially, questions about the history of textual transmission motivated investigations into theological tendencies.[2] When such investigations serve that interest and are subject to its methodological concerns, they are most welcome. Unfortunately, several recent studies of "tendency," especially "anti-feminist" tendency, have lost sight of this text-critical aim and neglected the importance of controlled methodology.[3]

---

[1]The following exemplify works in the field: Matthew Black, "The Holy Spirit in the Western Text of Acts," *New Testament Textual Criticism: Essays in Honour of Bruce M. Metzger* (ed. Eldon J. Epp and Gordon D. Fee; Oxford: University Press, 1981): 159-170; Eldon J. Epp, "The Ascension in the Textual Tradition of Luke-Acts," *New Testament Textual Criticism: Essays in Honour of Bruce M. Metzger*, 131-145; Carlo Martini, "La tradition textuelle des Actes et les tendances de l'Eglise ancienne," *Les Actes des Apôtres* (ed. J. Kremer; *BETL,* 48; Leuven: Univ. Press, 1979): 21-35; Mikeal C. Parsons, "A Christological Tendency in P[75]," *JBL* 105 (1986): 463-479.

[2]See A. F. J. Klijn, *A Survey of the Researches into the Western Text of the Gospels and Acts, Part Two: 1949-1969* (Leiden: Brill, 1969): 59-61; Eldon J. Epp, *The Theological Tendency of Codex Bezae Cantabrigiensis in Acts* (Cambridge: Cambridge Univ. Press, 1966): 5; Merrill M. Parvis, "The Nature and Tasks of New Testament Textual Criticism: An Appraisal," *JR* 32 (1952): 173.

[3]Richard I. Pervo, "Social and Religious Aspects of the 'Western' Text," *The Living Text: Essays in Honor of Ernest W. Saunders* (ed.

1. A Critique of Methodology Used in Establishing "Theological Tendencies"

The earliest attempts at identifying theological tendencies had no clear method.[4] Methodology began with Epp's important work on the "anti-Judaic tendency" of the "Western" text of Acts. Epp proposed to determine theological motivation by an inductive analysis of the variants in Codex Bezae. Only variations, he decided, have any significance since agreements with the text to which it is compared (which may be inconsistent with the supposed tendency) may be due to the conservative nature of textual transmission.[5] When examining these variations, he found the theological motivation for some variants ambiguous. He argued, however, that these readings still could be used to build a case for a tendency, if handled carefully.[6]

Dennis E. Groh and Robert Jewett; New York: Univ. Press of America, 1985): 229-241; J. Philip Schaelling, "The Western Text of the Book of Acts: A Mirror of Doctrinal Struggles in the Early Christian Church," *Apocryphal Writings and the Latter-Day Saints* (ed. C. Wilfred Griggs; Provo: Brigham Young Univ., 1986): 155-172; and Ben Witherington, "The Anti-Feminist Tendencies of the 'Western' Text in Acts," *JBL* 103 (1984): 82-4.

[4]See J. H. Ropes, *The Beginnings of Christianity* (London: Macmillan, 1926): 1.3: ccxxxiv; Adolph von Harnack, "Über die beiden Rezensionen der Geschichte der Prisca und Aquila in Act. Apost. 18:1-27," *Studien zur Geschichte des Neuen Testaments und der alte Kirche 1: Zur neutestamentlichen Textkritik* (Berlin: de Gruyter, 1931): 48-61; W. M. Ramsay, *The Church in the Roman Empire before A.D. 170* (London: Hodder and Stoughton, 1893): 161-2.

[5]Epp, *Theological Tendency*, 35, notes that "Agreements with the main-line text tell us very little." See also 38. P. H. Menoud, "The Western Text and the Theology of Acts," *Bulletin of the Studiorum Novi Testamenti Societas* 2 (1951): 32, characterizes D as "both conservative and innovating."

[6]Epp, *Theological Tendency*, 24, acknowledges that such variants may be due to non-theological factors. It must be noted that Epp's work has received just criticism. Bezae could simply be explaining, emphasizing, and exaggerating what is already in the text. This hardly qualifies as a conscious, anti-Judaic theological tendency. See C. K. Barrett, "Is there a Theological Tendency in Codex Bezae?" *Text and*

By allowing the use of these variants of uncertain origin, Epp was able to expand his database. Unfortunately, this left room for abuse. Others elevated these readings to a level of importance equal to that of variants clearly motivated by theological concerns. Any variant into which a particular theological tendency could be read became primary evidence for that tendency. For example, Pervo finds an anti-feminist tendency in the accidental omission of the article at Acts 2:17![7]

Terminological problems continue to plague investigations into theological tendency. Scholars know well the problems of defining the "Western" text. The "Western" text is more a scattered textual phenomenon which appears in certain loosely related witnesses than an identifiable text-type.[8] In order to prove that an homogeneous "Western" text existed, many scholars look for a consistent viewpoint or theological frame of reference which gives coherence to the "Western" evidence. Consequently, the scholar in search of a theological tendency necessarily assumes what the establishment of the tendency is trying to prove, viz., a definite "Western" text, supposed to derive from a systematic recension, or at least an homogeneous *Urtext*. Scholars who attempt this precarious exercise must employ careful controls or risk prejudicing their research.

Because of ill-defined parameters of the "Western" text, incautious scholars can treat the evidence erroneously. Conclusions about the homogeneity of the "Western" text can be based on very scant evidence indeed. In the anti-

---

Interpretation (ed. E. Best and R. McL. Wilson; Cambridge: University Press, 1979): 25. Reginald H. Fuller speaks of a "Procrustean bed of theological *Tendenz*" in his review of Epp's *Theological Tendency* in *CBQ* 30 (1968): 448.

[7]Pervo, "Social and Religious Aspects of the 'Western' Text," *The Living Text*, 237.

[8]See Kurt Aland and Barbara Aland, *The Text of the New Testament* (2nd rev. ed., trans. E. F. Rhodes; Grand Rapids: Eerdmans, 1989): 53-55; and Bruce M. Metzger, *The Text of the New Testament* (3rd ed.; Oxford: Oxford Univ. Press, 1992): 213.

feminist studies, the majority of the variations used are *singular readings* (1:14; 2:17; 16:14-15; 17:12, 34) of a fifth century manuscript!

Scholars who find a tendency in the text have as yet to define "tendency" clearly. Its typical use indicates a conscious, thoroughgoing theological agenda on the part of one or more early redactors.[9]   J. H. Ropes and W. M. Ramsay stretch this definition to the breaking point when they identify an "anti-feminist" tendency in the "Western" text of Acts based on two examples.[10] We do not doubt the possibility that two variants could reflect a theological tendency, especially since extant witnesses may present "corrected" versions of previously existent theological variations.   Scholarship needs, however, a quantitative definition of "tendency" that states on what basis two variants in fact do constitute a "tendency."

The proponents of an anti-feminist tendency in Bezae also fail to define "anti-feminism" historically.[11]   Their

---

[9]See Klijn, *Survey*, 60-62; Epp, *Theological Tendency*, 22-24; Pervo, "Social and Religious Aspects of the 'Western' Text," *The Living Text*, 240; Witherington, *JBL* (1984): 83.

[10]J. H. Ropes, *The Beginnings of Christianity*, 1.3: ccxxxiv, cites 17:12 and chapter 18. Of the latter, he says, "The desire to reduce the prominence of Priscilla seems to have been at work in a number of places" (178 n.). William M. Ramsay points to 17:12 and 17:34 in *The Church in the Roman Empire Before A.D. 170*, 162, but expands his list to include 17:4 and 18:26 in *St. Paul the Traveller and the Roman Citizen* (London: Hodder and Stoughton, 1925): 268. See Schaelling, "The Western Text of the Book of Acts . . .," *Apocryphal Writings and the Latter-Day Saints*, 165-7; and Witherington, *JBL* (1984): 82-4. Schaelling uses only six examples and Witherington only nine. Any attempt to locate theological *tendency* with so few examples is highly suspect.

[11]Ramsay, *The Church in the Roman Empire Before A.D. 170*, 161-2, associates the variants in 17:12, 34 with a "Universal and Catholic type of Christianity [which] became confirmed in its dislike of the prominence and public ministration of women" that was typical in Asia Minor. He does not argue this point, and it depends on his thesis that the "Western" text is based on a revision done in Asia Minor.

language reveals their bias. For example, they say that the text tends to "tone down" or "eliminate" references to women, to "elevate men," and to "remove any impression that early Christianity held special attraction for women."[12] These characterizations suggest the modern category of "feminism" rather than some archaic issue.

The parameters of the anti-feminist issues of the past must be defined to establish a "theological tendency" in an ancient text. Doubtless, by modern standards, Greco-Roman society "undervalued" women, but no proof has been presented that this ancient standard was an *issue* in the second century church. Without establishing the existence of feminism and anti-feminism as issues in the early church, proponents of an anti-feminist tendency merely read modern categories back into antiquity on the basis of what they find in the "Western" text of Acts.[13]

Witherington, *JBL* (1984): 83, speaks only of a "concerted effort" in the late first or early second century, citing Ramsay. Pervo, "Social and Religious Aspects of the 'Western' Text," *The Living Text*, 239-240, attempts to find an historical background for the "Western" variations by connecting the revision with an ill-defined emerging catholicism he detects in other NT documents by an unexplained comparison with Marcion and a connection with "right-wing Deutero-Paulinism of second-century C.E. Asia Minor" (241). He does not substantiate these various connections.

[12]See Witherington, *JBL* (1984): 82-4; and Schaelling, "The Western Text of the Book of Acts. . . ," *Apocryphal Writings and the Latter-Day Saints*, 165. See also G. W. H. Lampe, "Acts," *Peake's Commentary on the Bible* (ed. Matthew Black; London: Nelson, 1967): 885. Pervo, "Social and Religious Aspects of the 'Western' Text," *The Living Text*, 236-9, provides a contemporary example which illustrates this problem. He regards the "Western" variant in Acts 1:14 to evidence anti-feminism "because of such expressions as 'the pioneers moved West, taking their wives and children with them,'" (237, n.18). This language may express anti-feminism in modern times, but it could not prove that anti-feminism was an issue at the time the statement was originally made—even if contemporary statements were found which placed women on a more equal footing.

[13]See the chapter by Everett Ferguson. Discussions in the first three Christian centuries do not contain issues compatible with the

The historical problem transcends terminology. Pervo[14] reveals a common abuse which many of these studies share when he expresses his intent "to use textual variants to help write church history." This appears to be the particular aim of the "anti-feminist" studies. Colwell, however, has made it clear that this is unsound methodologically.[15] Using textual variation to reconstruct the history of the manuscript

---

modern connotations of "feminism" or "anti-feminism." See *infra* pp. 488-92.

Scholars bring other feminist assumptions to the text. By claiming that *later* centuries saw women reduced "to the status of a possession," Schaelling, "The Western Text of the Book of Acts. . . ," *Apocryphal Writings and Latter-Day Saints*, 168, assumes a certain high regard for women in the earlier "standard" text. See also Harnack, "Über die beiden Rezensionen der Geschichte der Prisca und Aquila in Act. Apost. 18:1-27," *Studien zur Geschichte des Neuen Testaments und der alte Kirche 1 . . .* , 56. Pervo, "Social and Religious Aspects of the 'Western' Text," *The Living Text*, 235, believes that Luke has consciously glorified women as early disciples in Luke-Acts. See Witherington, *Women in the Earliest Churches* (Cambridge: Univ. Press, 1988): 128-157. Such assumptions make virtually any change in the text glaringly "anti-feminist."

Witherington, *JBL* (1984): 82-84, could be accused of circular reasoning in this regard. The "Western" text is anti-feminist because the "standard" text underlines the importance of women and their roles in the early church. On the other hand, Witherington, *Women in the Ministry of Jesus* (Cambridge: University Press, 1985): 129-130, cites the "Western" text's anti-feminism as "all too clear" evidence for Luke's pro-feminist stance.

It is interesting that others view Luke as decidedly anti-feminist. See, for instance, the discussion by Mary Rose D'Angelo, "Women in Luke-Acts: A Redactional View," *JBL* 109 (1990): 441-61. For a fair assessment of Luke's view, see Jacob Jervell, "The Daughters of Abraham: Women in Acts," in *The Unknown Paul, Essays in Luke-Acts and Early Christian History* (trans. Roy A. Harrisville; Minneapolis: Augsburg, 1984): 146-157, 186-190.

[14]Pervo, "Social and Religious Aspects of the 'Western' Text," *The Living Text*, 230.

[15]E. C. Colwell, "Hort Redivivus: A Plea and a Program," *Studies in Methodology in Textual Criticism of the New Testament* (*New Testament Tools and Studies*, 9; ed. Bruce M. Metzger; Leiden: E. J. Brill, 1969): 150-151.

tradition is one thing. Using variation to reconstruct history itself, including the history of theology, is quite another. Colwell wisely suggests reversing the process. Instead of using textual variants to write history and trace theological developments, scholars should approach textual study with independent historical and theological knowledge well in hand. History controls textual criticism. A reasonable, historical setting for a theological tendency makes the identification of that tendency more sure. Although a theological tendency may exist which history cannot yet corroborate, a theological tendency cannot be positively identified without that history.[16] The mere possibility of an historically uncorroborated tendency does not negate the importance of having as a control an objective history which is unaffected by our estimation of the "Western" text or by a theological bias.

Our appeal for a controlled methodology in "tendency" research is not new,[17] but bears repeating. Discussions on the anti-feminist tendency in the "Western" text of Acts clearly suffer when they lack text-critical and historical controls, and the terms "anti-feminist," "tendency," and "Western text" remain undefined. Scholars must concern

---

[16]"Thus I deny," Colwell writes, "that those have salvaged historical value who point out that every variant may tell us something about the history of the church. The current enthusiasm for manuscript variations as contributions to the history of theology has no solid foundation. Granted that a number of readings have been theologically motivated, would any serious student of the history of theology turn to these as a major source? Is it not true on the contrary that we can be sure of theological motivation for a variant reading only when the history of theology in that manuscript's time and place is already well known?" (*Ibid.*, 150).

[17]See Epp, *Theological Tendency*, 21-40; Mark Dunn, "Toward the Clarification of Theological Tendency as a Task of Textual Criticism," unpublished paper presented at the Annual Meeting of the Society of Biblical Literature, Anaheim, Ca., 20 November 1989; Colwell, "Hort Redivivus. . .," *Studies in Methodology in Textual Criticism of the New Testament*, 149-151; Larry W. Hurtado, *Text-Critical Methodology and the Pre-Caesarean Text: Codex W in the Gospel of Mark* (Grand Rapids: Eerdmans, 1981): 68.

themselves with such questions as these if they wish their research to further our understanding of the history of the NT text.

2. The Search for an "Anti-feminist Tendency" in Codex Bezae

The search must begin with establishing the texts to be collated, since one identifies theological tendency in textual variation.[18] As has already been discussed, establishing a "Western" text proves particularly difficult. All attempts at establishing a "Western" text have failed.[19] Therefore, it seems best to begin with a single textual witness. This serves as a control by providing a known, textual quantity instead of an hypothetical text.

For the purpose of this study, we shall use Bezae. Although Bezae's value as a "Western" witness has recently been challenged,[20] it may still be considered a fair representation of the "Western" phenomenon. Since it has

---

[18]It should be clear that theological bias can only be detected where there is textual variation. See B. F. Westcott and F. J. A. Hort, *Introduction to the New Testament in the Original Greek* (New York: Harper and Brothers, 1882): 283.

[19]The earlier attempts by such scholars as Blass and Hilgenfeld are merely conglomerations of readings (even singular ones!) found in any witness remotely considered "Western." The recent attempt by M.-E. Boismard and A. Lamouille, *Le texte occidental des Apôtres*, Vol. 2, *Apparat critique: Index des caractéristiques stylistiques, Index des citations patristiques* (Synthese 17; Paris: Éditions Recherche sur les Civilisations, 1984), is more responsible (at least with regard to singular readings), but has not fared much better. See the critiques of Robert Hull, Jr., "'Lucanisms' in the Western Text of Acts? A Reappraisal," *JBL* 107 (1988): 695-707, and Thomas C. Geer, Jr., "The Presence and Significance of Lucanisms in the 'Western' Text of Acts," *JSNT* 39 (1990): 59-76.

[20]Barbara Aland, "Entstehung, Charakter, und Herkunft des sogenannten westlichen Textes untersucht an der Apostelgeschichte," *ETL* 62 (1986): 5-65. See also, Epp, "Coptic Manuscript G67 and the Role of Codex Bezae as a Western Witness in Acts," *JBL* 85 (1966): 197-212.

served as the main witness for the most recent discussions on anti-feminist tendencies in the "Western" text, it proves especially useful for our study. Unfortunately, this limits our results to Bezae. Being ultimately interested in the theology of the "Western" text and not just Bezae, additional studies on all of the so-called "Western" witnesses will be needed to determine any underlying tendencies attributable to the supposed second-century text-type.

Determining the theological bias responsible for a change in textual character requires comparing the "Western" witness to the type of text from which the "Western" text emerged. This, of course, presents its own problems. Since no workable theory of the early history of the text exists,[21] we shall follow the previously set pattern by comparing Bezae with the B-ℵ texts.

After a full collation of the manuscript with these comparison texts, *all* of the variant readings should be analyzed.[22] This, however, exceeds the scope of this paper. For this study, only those variations which previously have been labeled "anti-feminist" will be examined. The textual analysis consists of two levels. The first level distinguishes between intentional and unintentional variations. The second level examines the intentional variations and distinguishes between theologically motivated readings, readings of questionable motivation, and non-theologically motivated

---

[21]For discussion, see Epp, "The Twentieth Century Interlude in New Testament Textual Criticism," *JBL* 93 (1974): 390-401; Kurt Aland, "The Twentieth Century Interlude in New Testament Textual Criticism," *Text and Interpretation: Studies in the New Testament Presented to Matthew Black* (ed. E. Best and R. McL. Wilson; Cambridge: Cambridge Univ. Press, 1979): 1-14; Epp, "A Continuing Interlude in New Testament Textual Criticism?" *HTR* 73 (1980): 138-151; and "New Testament Textual Criticism—Past, Present, and Future: Reflections on the Alands' *Text of the New Testament*," *HTR* 82 (1989): 221-223.

[22]Dunn, "Toward the Clarification of Theological Tendency," 12-13.

readings.[23] This second level of investigation does not determine a passage's theological bias. It merely determines the most likely motive behind each variation. Discussions about theological tendency too often overlook this subtle distinction. A variation may *result* in a reading into which anti-feminist interests may be read when its actual *purpose* was not anti-feminist at all. One bases a theological tendency not upon the *result* of a variation, but on the *original motivation* behind it. Both the unintentional variations and the non-theologically motivated variations contribute nothing towards finding a theological tendency.

There should be no need for an analysis at the first level in this paper, since unintentional variations by definition cannot be part of a tendency. Pervo, however, mentions Acts 2:17 as a variant which supports the supposed anti-feminist tendency. At Acts 2:17, Bezae omits the article αἱ before θυγατέρες (daughters). Since this is a singular reading and the article immediately follows καί in the comparison text, obviously the article dropped out accidentally due to haplography. Pervo's suggestion that Bezae "appears to imply that only *some* of their daughters will prophesy, as opposed to *all* their sons" is tendentious in itself and a poor, if not impossible, reading of Bezae's text.[24] Therefore, of the nine passages labeled "anti-feminist," eight (possibly) contain intentional variation: 1:14; 16:14-15; 17:4, 12, 34; 18:2, 26, 27f. These will be examined individually in order to determine the original motivation behind each variation, where possible.[25]

---

[23]There is no doubt that some variants are doctrinally motivated. Since Westcott and Hort, there has been an abundance of material on this subject. See K. W. Clark, "The Theological Relevance of Textual Variation in Current Criticism of the Greek New Testament," *JBL* 85 (1966): 1-16; and Epp, *Theological Tendency*, 17.

[24]Pervo, "Social and Religious Aspects of the 'Western' Text," *The Living Text*, 237.

[25]We are grateful to Carroll D. Osburn and Thomas C. Geer, Jr., for access to the collations of the *International Project on the Text of Acts* at Abilene Christian University.

Acts 1:14. Codex Bezae is the only known witness for the addition of "and children" after γυναιξίν. According to Witherington, this addition reduces the women to being "simply the wives of the apostles."[26] The reading in the comparison text is ambiguous, for γυναιξίν could refer to the "wives" of the apostles or to the "women" (usually identified as the special group of disciples mentioned in Luke 8:2). The absence of the definite article with γυναιξίν favors making the referents the apostles' wives.[27] Therefore, if the scribe naturally understood γυναιξίν as "the (apostles') wives," the addition of "and children" did not alter the meaning of the text, and could not be interpreted as anti-feminist.

Even if one could prove that the scribe went against the contemporary interpretation of γυναιξίν, one should doubt that καὶ τέκνοις was added in order to lower the status of women. The addition merely solves an inconsistency, a common trait of Bezae.[28] It solves the mathematical

---

[26]Witherington, *JBL* (1984): 82. See also Ernst Hänchen, *The Acts of the Apostles* (trans. R. McL. Wilson; Philadelphia: Westminster, 1979): 154, n. 3.

[27]Both the Bezan and B-ℵ texts focus on Jesus' family. This supports the suggestion that the original meaning of γυναιξίν was "wives." Thus the author presents the royal families--that of the Messiah and those of the (soon to be Twelve) Princes. Bezae certainly clarifies this focus by adding "and children" and substituting "disciples" for "brothers" in 1:15. That Bezae adds the article before γυναιξίν is not surprising. Ropes, *Beginnings of Christianity*, 1.3: lxx, lists the arbitrary placement of articles, usually by addition, as an "eccentricity" of Bezae. See also James D. Yoder, "The Language of the Greek Variants of Codex Bezae," *NovT* 3 (1959): 245. The article's presence, though, makes it less likely that it is an abbreviation of the Attic phrase μετὰ γυναικῶν καὶ τέκνων (with women and children) or that it has been assimilated to 21:5. See Lake and Cadbury, *Beginnings of Christianity*, 1.4: 11.

[28]Ropes, *Beginnings of Christianity*, 1.3: ccxxxi-ii. The following passages exemplify this tendency. Acts 3:11 in Bezae reads "when Peter and John went out, holding on to them, he (the man who was healed) went out with them," which brings the party out of the temple where the portico was actually located. Assuming the Gaius of

problem posed by 1:14-15. The church, according to 1:15, numbered about 120. The immediate context explicitly identifies 29.[29] That leaves about 91 unaccounted people! The inclusion of the apostles' children helps solve the problem. A number of Vulgate manuscripts solve the mathematical problem similarly.[30] The chapter heading for this particular pericope in these manuscripts lists the apostles and "the nursing mothers their wives" as part of the group assembled on the day of Pentecost. Whereas Bezae placed the explanation in the text itself, these Latin manuscripts merely relegated it to the chapter heading, which then, as today, could serve as a short commentary.

We find, then, no anti-feminist tendency in Acts 1:14-15 in codex Bezae.

Acts 16:14-15. Bezae alone reads that Lydia was a worshiper of the "Lord" (v. 14) and considered herself faithful to "God." Witherington[31] uses the *tentative* conclusions of Epp to suggest a contrast between Gentiles and God-fearers. Witherington holds that since God-fearers are, "on the whole," presented "in a positive light," Lydia's status is being lowered by making her a Gentile with no connection to the synagogue.[32] Such an argument derives

---

20:4 to be the Macedonian Gaius of 19:29, Bezae "corrects" Δερβαῖος(Derbe in Asia Minor) to Δουβέριος (Doberus in Macedonia). Perceiving that "the voices" of the prophets were not read every Sabbath (13:27), Bezae substitutes "the Scriptures."

[29]There are eleven apostles (1:13), two additional disciples (1:23), eleven wives, Jesus' mother and (four) brothers (1:14; see also Matt. 13:55).

[30]Walter Thiele, "Eine Bemerkung zu Act 1,14," *ZNW* 53 (1962): 110-111, considers these chapter headings to be witnesses of an Old Latin text. If correct, Bezae's reading is no longer singular. However, since the headings witness to a completely different reading (*altricibus*) than the Old Latin, we question Thiele's conclusions.

[31]Witherington, *JBL* (1984): 83.

[32]Acts generally presents God-fearers in a positive light. 13:50, however, highlights god-fearing women as Paul's opponents in Pisidian Antioch. Interestingly, Bezae evidences no offense at this! Bezae's text

from Witherington's concern for what he believes to be Luke's message that "women could constitute the embryonic church, but not the embryonic synagogue."[33] Only by presuming this to be Luke's theological program at this point is Witherington able to read Bezae's variants as anti-feminist. That Luke intends to contrast Christian and traditional Jewish views of women here is farfetched. Epp states that it is by no means certain that Bezae is disassociating Lydia from the synagogue. In fact, Epp argues, this may be "the exception that proves the rule," pointing out that the difficult combination of readings in 16:14-15 makes a final decision impossible.[34]

Whatever the origin of these readings, they are not anti-feminist. Witherington's use of this passage as evidence supporting an anti-feminist tendency is incomprehensible.

Acts 17:4. The B-ℵ texts contain an ambiguous reading (γυναικῶν τε τῶν πρώτων). The phrase refers either to a group of "leading women" or to the "wives of leading men." Bezae's καὶ γυναῖκες τῶν πρώτων (and the wives of the leading men) removes this ambiguity, a tendency long recognized in this codex.[35] It must be remembered that all

---

merely heightens the intensity of the persecution by adding "a great affliction."

[33]See Witherington, *Women in the Earliest Churches*, 148.

[34]Epp, *Theological Tendency*, 90.

[35]Bezae often attempts to remove ambiguities. In 1:15 Bezae reads "disciples" instead of "brothers" in order to make it clear that the referents are not Jesus' immediate family. See n. 27. In 5:35, Bezae replaces "them" with "the rulers and the Sanhedrin." Bezae defines "those who received the word" in 2:41 as "those who believed." The enigmatic release of Paul and Silas in 16:35 is explained by Bezae as resulting from the impression which the earthquake had on the magistrates. The ambiguous reference to the growth of "the Lord's word" in 19:20 is clarified by the substitution "the faith of God." For other examples, see the Bezan text at 4:15; 5:34; and 7:1.

It appears that Bezae's readings τῇ διδαχῇ (the teaching) and γυναῖκες (wives) at 17:4 clarify the text while πολλοί (many) and καί (and) serve to make the mission more successful: "*Many* God-possible interpretations of an ambiguous reading are not all equally plausible. For the clarification to be tendentious, it must either oppose the cultural norm or contradict contemporary interpretations of the passage. Bezae does not oppose the former,[36] and apparently Bezae does not go against the interpretation of the day.[37] Therefore, far from reflecting anti-feminist tendency, we see no reason to suggest anything here beyond the already well established Bezan tendency of removing ambiguity as a motivation for this variant.

Acts 17:12. Among a number of different variations in this verse, Bezae reads καὶ τῶν εὐσχημόνων ἄνδρες καὶ γυναῖκες (prominent men and women) instead of γυναικῶν τῶν εὐσχημόνων καὶ ἀνδρῶν (prominent women and men). Metzger states that, "Besides being better Greek the readjusted order has the effect of lessening any importance given to women."[38] The women's status, however, remains unaltered. Characterizing the elevation of men as "anti-feminist" sounds distinctly modern. A number of more probable explanations for Bezae's reading follow: 1) The variation resulted from the impulse to improve the Greek

---

fearers *and* a large crowd of Greeks *and* not a few *wives* of leading men followed *the teaching* of Paul and Silas."

[36]See Ferguson's article in this volume.

[37]In four volumes of J. Allenbach, et al., ed., *Biblia Patristica*, vol. 1: *Des origines à Clément d'Alexandrie et Tertullien*; vol. 2: *Le troisième siècle*; vol. 3: *Origène*; vol. 4: *Eusèbe de Césarée, Cyrille de Jerusalem, Epiphane de Salamine* (Paris: Centre National de la Recherche Scientifique, 1975-1987), there are only three references to this passage. None of these patristic references shed light on the contemporary interpretation of this verse, but the paucity of allusions may suggest that these verses played no part in contemporary theological discussions about women. See Irenaeus, *Against Heresies*, 3.14.1; D. de Bruyne, "Prologues bibliques d'origine marcionite," *RBén* 24 (1907): 10; and Cyril of Jerusalem, *Catecheses* 17.30.

[38]Metzger, *A Textual Commentary on the Greek New Testament*, (3rd corr. ed.; New York: UBS, 1975): 454; Hänchen, *Acts*, 508, n. 5, states that by including the men, "the emphasis on the noble women is here effaced."

style.[39] Τῶν εὐσχημόνων does not necessarily refer only to women, even in the comparison text.[40] Bezae, therefore, does not interpret the text, but merely smooths out the rough grammar and conforms the language to what may be considered a Lucan formula.[41] 2) By making both men and women prominent the mission becomes more successful (see 17:4).[42] 3) Making the Greek men also prominent

---

[39]Bezae often exhibits a smoother and more polished Greek style than the comparison text. For example, the double omission of καί (and) in 1:13 in Bezae results in a more symmetric grouping of names. Bezae reads "they rested upon" instead of "it rested upon" in 2:3 so as to agree with the plural "tongues." Bezae's omission of "lame" in 14:8 alleviates a redundancy. Bezae removes another redundancy in 20:1 by reading "he left" instead of "he left to go." Additional examples exist.

[40]K. Lake and H. Cadbury, *Beginnings of Christianity: The Acts of the Apostles* (London: Macmillan, 1933): 1.4: 207, write, "The Western text reads 'and of the Greeks and of those of good position many women and men,' which gives the same meaning as the B-text, but is preferable grammar."

[41]See 5:14; 8:3, 12; [9:2]; and 22:4. This is especially true if Bezae's Latin reading *et uiri et mulieris* reflects an earlier ἄνδρες τε καί γυναῖκες. Codex Bezae has a tendency to reproduce formulaic language. In 3:17 the address ἀδελφοί is expanded to ἄνδρες ἀδελφοί (1:16; 2:29, 37; 7:2, 26; 13:15, 26, 28; 14:15; 15:7, 13; 19:25; 22:1; 23:1, 6; 27:10, 21, 25; and 28:17). Bezae's additions at 6:10 and 16:4 include "with great boldness," a concept frequent in Acts (2:29; 4:29, 31; 18:31). At 14:10 Bezae adds "I say to you in the name of the Lord Jesus Christ," and at 18:8 "through the name of our Lord Jesus Christ." 19:5 reads "they were baptized into the name of the Lord Jesus Christ for the forgiveness of sins." At 20:24 Bezae reads "Jews and Greeks" (14:1; 18:4; 19:10, 17; 20:21), and at 22:23 changes "into the air" to "into the sky (heaven)."

[42]A number of Bezan variations appear to highlight the success of the Christian mission and the Lord's word. The words "is more apparent" appear at 4:16 in reference to the witness of Peter's miraculous sign, rather than "apparent." The effect of Stephen's speaking in 6:10 is underscored in Bezae with the addition of the words "because he corrected those who were against him with all boldness." The conclusion of Paul's speech at 13:41 is punctuated by Bezae's description of the response: "and they were silent." Bezae tells us in 13:43 that "the word of God went through the whole city." While the comparison text narrates that Paul and Barnabas taught the gospel in the

strengthens the contrast between the more noble Berean Gentiles and the Jews of Thessalonica and Berea (some believed but some disbelieved).[43]

Acts 17:34. The omission of "and a woman named Damaris" has long troubled textual critics,[44] and it appears to have been the first Bezan variation labeled "anti-feminist."[45] The presence of εὐσχήμων (prominent) presents problems for viewing the omission as "anti-feminist." If "and a woman named Damaris" was accidentally omitted,[46] εὐσχήμων would have been added intentionally after "Dionysius the Areopagite," creating a redundancy. However, since εὐσχήμων refers to men earlier, the possibility exists that a scribe conformed this verse to 17:12. Neither the omission nor addition could be considered anti-feminist.

---

region around Lycaonia (14:6-7), Bezae adds in v. 7 that "the whole multitude was moved at the teaching."

[43]Boismard and Lamouille, *Le Texte Occidental: des Actes des Apôtres*, 2.120, suggest that 17:12 may have been lacking in Bezae's Greek exemplar and the lacuna was filled by translating the Latin back into Greek. In this scenario the "anti-feminist" effect of the reading was caused by the "*licence de traduction*" and not an anti-feminist tendency.

[44]Bezae reads:

ΤΙΝΕΣΔΕΑΝΔΡΕΣΕΚΟΛΛΗΘΗΣΑΝ
ΑΥΤΩΕΠΙΣΤΕΥΣΑΝ
ΕΝΟΙΣΚΑΙΔΙΟΝΥΣΙΟΣΤΙΣΑΡΕΟΠΑΓΕΙΤΗΣ
ΕΥΣΧΗΜΩΝΚΑΙΕΤΕΡΟΙΣΥΝΑΥΤΟΙΣ

But some men joined
him (and) believed
among whom was also Dionysius the Areopagite
who was prominent and another with them.

[45]J. Hastings, "Women in the Acts of the Apostles," *Exp. Times* 4 (1892-3): 434-6, attributes this omission to anti-heretical editing on account of the prominence of women in Asia Minor.

[46]Theodor Zahn, *Die Apostelgeschichte des Lucas*, (2nd ed., *Kommentar zum Neuen Testament*; Leipzig: A. Deichert, 1921): 2.629, n. 5, suggests that a line accidentally dropped out in transmission. He was followed here by Albert C. Clark, *The Acts of the Apostles* (Oxford: Oxford Univ. Press, 1933): 367; and Metzger, *A Textual Commentary on the Greek New Testament*, 459.

If a scribe intentionally omitted καὶ γυνὴ (εὐσχήμων) ὀνόματι Δάμαρις (and a [prominent] woman named Damaris),[47] as most assume, then εὐσχήμων probably referred to Damaris in an ancestor of Bezae, and the scribe retained εὐσχήμων to refer to Dionysius, even though redundant. The use of εὐσχήμων with women (13:50 and 17:12 in the comparison text), the use of τίμια (*honesta*, esteemed) for Damaris in codex Laudianus, and the beginning of a new sense line with εὐσχήμων in Bezae, support this. If so, the earlier "Western" reading elevated Damaris' status!

Omission characterizes neither the textual character of Bezae nor the supposed anti-feminist tendency. If motivated by an "anti-feminist tendency," why did the scribe not make Damaris a wife as in 1:14 or 17:4?[48] At 18:26 Bezae does not even omit Priscilla, a more likely candidate. We find it improbable that anti-feminism motivated Bezae's reading. The awkwardness of Damaris being one of "some men" may have brought about the omission.[49]

Acts 18:2. Bezae changes "he came to them" to "Paul came to him." The variations here and in the following verses appear to be for the purpose of improving the Greek or making the implicit explicit.[50] The construction of v. 2 is

---

[47]We assume here that if εὐσχήμων (prominent) appeared in an exemplar which contained the reference to Damaris, that although it might have followed καὶ γυνὴ ὀνόματι Δάμαρις (and a woman named Damaris), the line actually read καὶ γυνὴ εὐσχήμων ὀνόματι Δάμαρις (and a prominent woman named Damaris), as one would expect. Codex Laudianus' καὶ γυνὴ τίμια ὀνόματι Δάμαρις (and an esteemed woman named Damaris) supports this.

[48]This was done by others. See the Georgian version of Acts, as well as Chrysostom, *On the Priesthood*, 4.7.

[49]Boismard and Lamouille, *Le Texte Occidental des Apôtres*, 2.125.

[50]In any case, Bezae typically makes explicit what is implicit in the comparison text. There are three clear examples in chapter two alone: While the comparison text holds simply that the people in 2:12 "were perplexed," Bezae reads that they "were perplexed about what had

more natural if Paul approaches "him" (a certain Jew) and then stays with "them." This and other variations in chapter 18 do not consciously distance Priscilla from Aquila.

Acts 18:26. Instead of reading "Priscilla and Aquila," Bezae names Aquila first. It is striking that the comparison text often mentions Priscilla first in references to this duo (Rom. 16:3; 2 Tim. 4:19; Acts 18:18, 26). The significance of this is unclear. While it may be true that convention called for the husband to be named first (see Acts 18:18), it is unsound to assume that the order of the comparison text results from a deliberate emphasis on explicit female roles. Even worse is the assumption that the reversal (the naming of Aquila first) could have been motivated only by conscious anti-feminism.[51] The references in Acts 18:2 and 1 Cor. 16:19, which mention Aquila first, underscore this point.[52]

Probably, the variant in Bezae did not arise from the convention of mentioning the husband's name first since Bezae mentions Priscilla first in 18:18.[53] A simple accidental transposition may have produced the variant, but

---

happened." In 2:37 Bezae draws out the implication of the crowd's question, "what shall we do?" by adding, "show us." A variant in 2:42 specifies the obvious locale for the activities described in 2:42-47 by adding "in Jerusalem."

In 5:18, Bezae openly expresses the implication of the comparison text that "each [of the Jewish leaders] went to his own home" at the end of the day. It is obvious in 5:22 that the attendants must open the prison before checking its contents, but Bezae explicitly describes their doing so anyway. Bezae provides the obvious subject "Paul" in 19:8, and explains that the centurion reported to the chiliarch about Paul, because "he (Paul) says he is a Roman" (22:26). There are many other examples of this phenomenon in codex Bezae (see 4:18, 24; 5:12, 15; 6:10; 12:3; 13:44; 16:10; 17:31; 18:4, 11).

[51]Cf. Witherington, *Women in the Earliest Churches*, 153-4.

[52]The amount of importance given to the order of these names is questionable. See Menoud, "The Western Text and the Theology of Acts," *Bulletin of the Studiorum Novi Testamenti Societas* (1951): 30.

[53]It is tendentious to assume that Bezae retains the comparison text's order here only because of Aquila's (highly questionable) connection with the vow.

Bezae's flawless presentation of other named pairs (e.g., Paul and Barnabas, Barnabas and Paul, and Paul and Silas) in agreement with the comparison text of Acts tells against this. Theological motivation may indeed underlie this variation. There may have been concern over what was perceived to be Priscilla's leading role in teaching Apollos.[54] The order in 18:18 carries no theological baggage, while in 18:26 we see orthodox doctrine being conveyed to an important teacher. While Bezae does not remove Priscilla from participating in these activities (which it might easily have done), it affirms that Aquila initiated them. At this point, we can only acknowledge the possibility of theological motivation in this variant.

Acts 18:27f. Harnack[55] regards Bezae's rather lengthy addition here[56] to be an attempt to prevent Priscilla from exercising church authority. According to him, since there had been no time for a church to have been established in Ephesus, Aquila and Priscilla (the "brothers") wrote the letter of recommendation for Apollos. Codex Bezae completely removes her from this ecclesial correspondence. Despite the clever argumentation, Apollos' reason for leaving poses a greater problem than Priscilla's supposed role in composing this letter. Bezae's addition explains

---

[54]See Ramsay, *St. Paul the Traveller*, 268; Ropes, *Beginnings of Christianity* 1,3: ccxxxiv, 178 n.; Harnack, *Studien zur Geschichte des Neuen Testaments und der Alte Kirche*, 55-7; Witherington, *JBL* (1984): 82; but also Menoud, "The Western Text and the Theology of Acts," *Bulletin of the Studiorum Novi Testamenti Societas* (1951): 30-31.

[55]Harnack, *Studien zur Geschichte des Neuen Testaments und der Alte Kirche*, 55-57.

[56]The addition reads, "And some Corinthians staying in Ephesus who heard him, asked him to cross with them to their own country. And when he consented the Ephesians wrote to the disciples in Corinth to receive him, and while he stayed in Achaia he was very helpful in the churches. . . ." (Translation of Lake and Cadbury, *Beginnings of Christianity*, 1,4: 234).

Apollos' sudden departure for Corinth,[57] and is merely another attempt to remove an apparent inconsistency (see n. 28). This avoids the "desperate expedient" of equating Priscilla and Aquila with "the brothers" as Harnack does.[58]

These eight variations fall into the following groupings. First, 1:14; 17:4, 12; 18:2 and 27 are "non-theologically motivated variants." These non-theologically motivated variants evidence neither an "anti-feminist" tendency, nor any theological tendency.[59] Second, variants whose origin can be attributed to a number of equally plausible causes, one of which is theological, are placed in a separate category. One draws these "readings of questionable motivation" into the picture only after definite contours of a tendency have emerged. The omission at 17:34 fits this category. "Theologically motivated readings" comprise the third and most important category. Here lies the basis for any construction of a theological tendency.[60] Of all the readings adduced as "anti-feminist," only 18:26 belongs here.[61] We still question whether historically the theological problem behind 18:26 can be labeled anti-feminism (see discussion below), but for the sake of argument, we will

---

[57]Ropes, *Beginnings of Christianity* 1, 3:179-180; Hänchen, *Acts*, 551. W. Ernst is the only one of whom we know who accepts Harnack's theory, "Die Blaß'sche Hypothese und die Textgeschichte," *ZNW* 4 (1903): 310-20.

[58]See Hänchen, *Acts*, 551, n. 8.

[59]Barrett, "Is There a Theological Tendency in Codex Bezae?" *Text and Interpretation*, 19.

[60]In this category all singular readings should be noted. Singular readings are especially useful for defining tendencies within a single manuscript (see Hurtado, *Text-Critical Methodology*, 69-80). They are less valuable for tendencies within a text-type since they may be of a later origin. In the past, any singular reading from any "Western" manuscript was considered a witness to the ancient "Western" text (Ropes, *Beginnings of Christianity*, 1,3: ccxlvii). Fortunately, this view is becoming less common.

[61]16:14-15 may also be theologically motivated, but since it is not motivated by anti-feminist concerns, it can be removed from the immediate discussion.

grant 18:26 as Bezae's lone "anti-feminist" *reading* in Acts. Since "tendency" implies a recurring phenomenon, no "anti-feminist *tendency*" exists in Bezae. This in turn suggests, though does not prove, that the motivation behind the omission of Damaris in 17:34 was not anti-feminism.

Those scholars who wish to identify an anti-feminist tendency in the "Western" text have, as Pervo describes his own work, been "poaching in the forests and preserves of textual criticism."[62] They have trespassed and used the discipline of textual criticism to serve their own purposes, manipulating basic tenets in order to manufacture support for pre-existing agendas. By following general text-critical principles, however, we have ruled out the possibility of an anti-feminist tendency in Bezae.

3. *The Role of History in Establishing Theological Motive*

If enough textual evidence were found to suggest the probability of an anti-feminist tendency, a genuine historical context would have to be located for that tendency. Any study of tendency is incomplete without this independent historical investigation to determine if the theologically motivated variations can be attributed to a particular historical context.[63] This is important for two reasons: 1) History provides a control for one's identification of a theological tendency, and 2) The historical context may provide a specific period or situation in which the variants (or possibly a whole textual tradition) originated.[64] Without an historical context, though, scholars can only speculate. Such speculations contribute nothing towards identifying the character of the "Western" text. Certainly, they cannot be used to make historical conclusions.

---

[62]Pervo, "Social and Religious Aspects of the 'Western' Text," *The Living Text*, 229-30.

[63]On this, Colwell, "Hort Redivivus. . .," *Studies in Methodology in Textual Criticism of the New Testament*, 150, is outspoken.

[64]Ernest W. Saunders, "Studies in Doctrinal Influences on the Byzantine Text of the Gospels," *JBL* 71 (1952): 92.

An historical study can also identify those passages which figured in a particular theological debate. If, for instance, a theological debate on anti-feminism occurred in the second century, the documented history of that debate would provide a number of passages used by people on both sides of the debate. These passages, when collected, would comprise a database against which supposed theologically motivated variations could be compared. Variations which match readings within this pool would strongly indicate the existence of a theological tendency. This provides another important control since historically not all passages which could be considered theologically offensive by either side in a theological debate were altered. For example, Osburn has shown that a theological debate on the pre-existence of Christ resulted in the change from "Christ" to "Lord" in 1 Cor. 10:9. 1 Cor. 10:4, however, places Christ at the wilderness wanderings of the Jews, yet this text was not altered! Osburn demonstrates that, since this verse did not figure in the debate, change was unnecessary.[65]

The variation at Acts 18:26 may now be taken up again as an example. A survey of the occurrences of Acts 18:26 in patristic literature listed in the first four volumes of *Biblia Patristica* uncovered no instances in which a Church Father used this verse to discuss the roles of women in the church. This fact in itself does not eliminate the possibility of such a theological motivation behind the variant. Nevertheless, the lack of direct evidence of theological interest and activity surrounding this verse must be taken into account by anyone who wants to relate early church history to the textual tradition in a responsible way. It would be irresponsible to compose a portrait of the early church based on the possible cause of this one reading.

Although 18:26 plays no part in early patristic discussion, one can still detect an historical situation which would affirm the possibility that the variation was

---

[65]Carroll D. Osburn, "The Text of 1 Corinthians 10:9," *New Testament Textual Criticism: Essays in Honour of Bruce M. Metzger*, 201-212.

theologically motivated. It is well known, for example, that early heresiologists wrote against heretical women, particularly in their arguments against Montanism. However, it is of the utmost importance to note that in most of these discussions they speak ill only of the women's association with heresy, and in no way reflect on their femininity nor on female roles.[66] Yet in many other instances ecclesiastical writers complain that some Montanist women exercise authority in ways that violate their views on the proper and scriptural place for women in the church.[67] Therefore, the role of women in the church was certainly a topic of discussion in the first few centuries, and not only in polemical connections.[68] However, this does not presuppose a background of "anti-feminism," unless that term is redefined apart from modern categories and with reference only to second and third-century ecclesiological discussions about women. Still, the absence of 18:26 from the larger discussion of women's roles suggests that those who questioned or condemned the prominent roles sometimes given to women did not find the comparison text's order at 18:26 offensive.

---

[66]See Eusebius, *Eccl. Hist.*, 5.16.9 and 5.14; Epiphanius, *Pan.* 48.2.12-13; 51.33; 79.1; Hippolytus, *Refut. Her.*, 8.19; 10.25-6; Cyprian, *Epist.*, 75.7; Theodore of Heraclea, *On the Gospel of John* 14.15; Cyril of Jerusalem, *Catechetical Lectures* 16.8; Pseudo-Athanasius, *Sermon Against all Heresies* 10; Ambrosiaster, *On the Second Epistle to the Thessalonians* 5; Basil of Caesarea, *Epist.* 188.1; Pacian of Barcelona, *Epistle 1 to Symphronus* 2; Filastrius, *Book of Heresies* 49; Didymus of Alexandria, *Fragments from the Exposition of Didymus on the Acts of the Apostles* 10.10. For other examples from beyond the fourth century, see Ronald E. Heine, *The Montanist Oracles and Testimonia* (Macon: Mercer Univ. Press, 1989).

[67]Origen, *Catenae on Paul's Epistle to the Corinthians* 14.36; Cyprian, Epistle 75.10; *Debate of a Montanist and an Orthodox Christian*; Ambrosiaster, *Commentary on the First Epistle to Timothy* 3.11; Epiphanius, *Pan.* 42.3 and 49.1-3; Didymus of Alexandria, *On the Trinity* 3.41.3; *Praedestinatus* 1.26-7; Augustine, *On Heresies* 26-7.

[68]E.g., Tertullian, *On the Soul* 9.4, in which a (Montanist) prophetess was asked to relate her visionary experience after the worship service ended.

In any case, the verse did not enter the debate, which raises the question of who would be motivated theologically to alter 18:26 and why. History provides no clear answer. It merely affirms the possibility. The patristic texts provide a reasonable, albeit indirect, backdrop for the editing which occurs at 18:26. However, we cannot go beyond *possibility* in our quest for theological motive underlying this variant. In the light of responsible historical construction, probability is out of reach. To speak of certainty regarding the origin of the "Western" variant in 18:26 is altogether unreasonable.

Clearly, then, there is no "anti-feminist tendency" in Codex Bezae.[69] This casts doubt upon the presence of an "anti-feminist tendency" in the "Western" text as a whole, especially since most of the evidence adduced for such a tendency consists of readings found only in Bezae. To speak of an "anti-feminist" tendency in the "Western" text of Acts is to speak of a phantom.[70]

---

[69]The paucity of evidence for an anti-feminist tendency in Bezae precludes establishing a more accurate delineation of terminology in this area of study. However, we suggest the following procedure. Once a database of relevant readings has been established, if a small percentage of those passages contain variation motivated by a particular theology, then there is "theological *variation*." One can speak of a "theological *tendency*" only when a majority of those passages have variations motivated by contemporary theological debate. When an overwhelming majority of the relevant passages have been theologically motivated, there exists "theological *revision*."

[70]Considering the influence of Metzger's handbook on NT textual criticism, his uncritical adoption of Pervo's and Witherington's work in his third edition is unfortunate. Metzger, *The Text of the New Testament*, 295-96, suggests erroneously that "anti-feminist tendency" has been found in the Western text and can be applied as a text-critical criterion in evaluating readings beyond the Western text.

Chapter Twenty

WOMEN IN THE POST-APOSTOLIC CHURCH

Everett Ferguson

Women wrote very little of early Christian literature. And not much more was written about them. In these respects, early church history reflects the circumstances of the time. Consequently, women are known mainly as types and not often as individuals in the second and third centuries. Only in the fuller light of the fourth century are many known as individuals. Enough is recorded, however, to provide a glimpse of the significant place women had in the success of early Christianity.

1. *Women as Mothers and Wives*

The place of women as wives and mothers was taken for granted and hence called forth less comment than their appearance in other roles. Two early non-canonical writings contain instructions about duties of various classes of persons comparable to the "household codes" in the New Testament. *First Clement* in commending the "good past" of the Corinthians includes the following praiseworthy conduct:

> And to the women you gave instruction that they should do all things with a blameless and seemly and pure conscience, yielding a dutiful affection to their husbands. And you taught them to remain in the rule of obedience and to manage their households with seemliness, in all circumspection (1.3).[1]

---

[1] Translation by K. Lake, *Apostolic Fathers* (LCL; Cambridge, MA: Harvard Univ. Press, 1952): 11.

This statement reflects the Hellenistic ideal of the wife as obedient to her husband and working at home, conducting its affairs under his instructions.

Polycarp's letter "on Righteousness" to the *Philippians* combines duties of members of the household with duties of leaders of the church. Concerning women, he says:

> Next teach our wives to remain in the faith given to them, and in love and purity, tenderly loving their husbands in all truth, and loving all others equally in all chastity, and to educate their children in the fear of God (4.2).[2]

Here the role of the wife is extended to her responsibility to educate (train and discipline) the children.

Clement of Alexandria (late second century) and Tertullian (early third century) were quite different in personality and in approach to the relation of Christianity to pagan culture, yet they exhibit a remarkable similarity in their views on social morality. Both take the same positions on, among other things, the role of women, what constitutes modesty, and the understanding of marriage.[3] The usually irrascible Tertullian, who could use some very negative words about women,[4] writes To His Wife (between 198 and 203) a sensitive and very appealing picture of Christian marriage:

> How beautiful, then, the marriage of two Christians, two who are one in hope, one in desire, one in the way of life they follow, one in the religion they practice. They are as brother and sister, both servants of the same Master. Nothing divides them, either in flesh or in spirit. They are, in very truth, *two in one flesh*; and where there is but one flesh there is also but one spirit.

---

[2]*Ibid.*, 287-289.

[3]See Clement of Alexandria, *Miscellanies* 4.20; *Instructor* 3.11; Tertullian, *Against Marcion* 1.29; *On the Veiling of Virgins* 9.

[4]*On the Apparel of Women* 1.1.

They pray together, they fast together; instructing one
another, encouraging one another, strengthening one
another. Side by side they visit God's church and
partake of God's banquet; side by side they face
difficulties and persecution, share their consolations.
They have no secrets from one another; they never
shun each other's company; they never bring sorrow to
each other's hearts. Unembarrassed they visit the sick
and assist the needy. They give alms without anxiety;
they attend the sacrifice without difficulty; they
perform their daily exercises of piety without hindrance
. . . . Psalms and hymns they sing to one another, . . .
Hearing and seeing this, Christ rejoices. To such as
these he gives peace: *Where there are two together*,
there also he is present; and where he is, there evil is
not (2.8).[5]

From the fourth-century we know the names and something of the character of some outstanding mothers—Nonna,
the mother of Gregory of Nazianzus, Anthusa, the mother of
John Chrysostom, and Emmelia, the mother of Macrina the
Younger, Basil the Great, and Gregory of Nyssa. I select
the last for comment here, as less well-known but not less
worthy.[6] The measure of Emmelia as a mother was her
children. She had ten in all, and they included three bishops
and a woman who was a model of ascetic piety. Gregory of
Nazianzus in the eulogy on his friend Basil, her eldest son,
paid her this tribute:

The union of [Basil's] parents, cemented as it was by a
community of virtue, no less than by cohabitation, was
notable for many reasons, especially for generosity to
the poor, for hospitality, for purity of soul as the result
of self-discipline . . . . [I]n my opinion, however,
their greatest claim to distinction is the excellence of
their children. For the attainment of distinction by one

---

[5]Translation by W. P. Le Saint, *Tertullian: Treatises on Marriage
and Remarriage* (ACW, 13; Westminster, MD: Newman, 1951): 35-36.

[6]On Nonna and Anthusa, see Everett Ferguson, *Early Christians
Speak* (Abilene: ACU Press, 1987): 229-230, 232-234.

or two of their offspring might be ascribed to their
nature; but when all are eminent, the honor is clearly
due to those who brought them up. This is proved by
the blessed roll of priests and virgins, and of those
who, when married, have allowed nothing in their
union to hinder them from attaining an equal repute.
[After describing her husband, Basil the elder,
Gregory continues:] Who has not known Emmelia,
whose name [harmoniousness, gracefulness] was a
forecast of what she became, or else whose life was an
exemplification of her name? For she had a right to the
name which implies gracefulness, and occupied, to
speak concisely, the same place among women, as her
husband among men (*Oration* 43.9-10).[7]

Few women had such distinguished children, and not all
Christian women possessed Emmelia's virtues, but
descriptions of mothers like her and others show what
qualities were admired in Christian motherhood.

Women as wives and mothers gave the Christian home
the strength that made it such a powerful influence in the
spread of Christianity in the Roman world.

2. *Women as Martyrs*

Justin Martyr tells of a wife converted from a wanton
life to the teachings of Christ.[8] Her husband did not
approve of her efforts to reform him and continued in his
immoralities. Feeling that maintaining the marriage made her
a partaker in her husband's vices, she divorced him. The
husband then brought charges before the authorities against
her and her teacher, Ptolemy, as being Christians. Imperial

---

[7]Translation by C. G. Browne and J. E. Swallow in NPNF,
Second Series (ed. P. Schaff and H. Wace; Grand Rapids: Eerdmans,
1955 reprint): 7.398. Gregory refers to Emmelia also in his *Epistle* 5
(a "great supporter of the poor") and he wrote her epitaph.

[8]Robert M. Grant has studied the episode and ascribed the name of
"Flora" to the woman—"A Woman of Rome: The Matron in Justin,
2 Apology 2.1-9," *CH* 54 (1985): 461-472.

intervention delayed proceedings against the woman, but Ptolemy and two other Christians were executed (2 *Apology* 2). Justin has not given us the name of the woman, nor the outcome of her case. The experience of one spouse converted and the other not was probably common, so this case was unusual only for its extremes; it is a reminder that domestic differences in matters of religion were often a factor in persecution.

Persecution was an equal opportunity experience, shared by women and men. Some of the most famous martyrs of the early church were women. I select two of these heroic figures from the days of persecution for consideration. Unlike Justin's matron in Rome their names are known: the slave Blandina and the noble woman Perpetua.[9]

In 177 a severe persecution against Christians broke out in Lyons and Vienne in the Rhone River valley of Gaul. When the persecution subsided, the survivors wrote to their fellow believers in Asia and Phrygia a letter preserved in Eusebius, *Church History* 5.1-5. Although a woman, a slave, and supposedly weak physically, Blandina's courage and endurance made her the heroine of the account. I quote from the sections of the letter devoted to her.

> [The wrath of the mob fell, among others, on] Blandina, through whom Christ showed that the things that to men appear mean and deformed and contemptible, are with God deemed worthy of great glory, on account of love to him. . . . For while we were all afraid, and especially her mistress in the flesh, who was herself one of the combatants among witnesses, that she would not be able to make a bold confession on account of the weakness of her body,

---

[9]They are studied by W. H. C. Frend, "Blandina and Perpetua: Two Early Christian Martyrs," *Les Martyrs de Lyon (177)* (Paris: Centre National de la Recherche Scientifique, 1987): 167-177. For women martyrs in general see Francine Cardman, "Acts of the Women Martyrs," *ATR* 70 (1988): 144-150.

Blandina was filled with such power, that those who tortured her one after the other in every way from morning till evening were wearied and tired, confessing that they had been baffled, for they had no other torture they could apply to her; and they were astonished at Blandina bearing her testimony, for one kind of torture was sufficient to have killed her. But the blessed woman, like a noble athlete, recovered her strength in the midst of the confession; and her declaration, "I am a Christian, and there is no evil done amongst us," brought her refreshment, and rest, and insensibility to all the sufferings afflicted on her. . . . [Later she was exposed to the wild beasts.] Blandina was hung up fastened to a stake, and exposed, as food to the wild beasts that were let loose against her; and through her presenting the spectacle of one suspended on something like a cross, and through her earnest prayers, she inspired the combatants with great eagerness: for in the combat they saw, by means of their sister, with their bodily eyes, him who was crucified for them. . . . When none of the wild beasts at that time touched her, she was taken down from the stake and conveyed back to prison. She was thus reserved for another contest. . . . For though she was an insignificant, weak, and despised woman, yet she was clothed with the great and invincible athlete Christ. On many occasions she had overpowered the adversary, and in the course of the contest had woven for herself the crown of incorruption. . . . On the last day of the gladiatorial shows, Blandina was again brought in. . . . [The] blessed Blandina, last of all, after having like a noble mother encouraged her children and sent them on before her victorious to the King, trod the same path of conflict which her children had trod, hastening on to them with joy and exultation at her departure, not as one thrown to the wild beasts, but as one invited to a marriage supper. And after she had been scourged and exposed to the wild beasts, and roasted in the iron chair, she was at last enclosed in a net and cast before a bull. And after having been well tossed by the bull, though without having any feeling of what was happening to her, through her hope and firm hold of what had been entrusted to her and her converse with Christ, she also was sacrificed, the heathen themselves acknowledging that never among them did woman endure so many and such fearful tortures.[10]

A French writer remarked with Gallic flair, "It was not Spartacus who eliminated slavery; it was rather Blandina."[11] The element of truth in that exaggeration is that martyrdom created a new spiritual aristocracy. Christ was present with the martyrs and was seen in their sufferings, so there was a close identification of the martyr with the Lord. The heroic performance of women believers brought them a status equal to and higher than that of men, as devotion to the martyrs led to the cult of the saints.

Twenty-five years later (AD 203), a young woman about twenty-two years old, walked, singing a psalm, into a Roman arena in Carthage in North Africa to face a martyr's death. Her name was Vibia Perpetua and the contemporary account of her martyrdom describes her as "respectably born, well educated, a married matron, having a father and mother and two brothers, one of whom, like herself, a catechumen, and an infant son at the breast" (1.1).[12] She left a diary giving an account of her ordeal up to the day of her martyrdom; another person completed the story of that last day. Thus we not only know Perpetua's name but also have one of the rare documents from the early church written by a woman and one of our earliest documents of Latin Christianity.[13]

---

[10]Translation by B. P. Pratten (but at one place adopting his alternative in a footnote) in ANF, 8.779-783.

[11]Quoted in *ibid.*, 784.

[12]The translations from this work follow, with slight modification, R. E. Wallis in ANF, 3. In the Musurillo edition, the reference is section 2, and other references also differ.

[13]Rosemary Rader, "*The Martyrdom of Perpetua*: A Protest Account of Third Century Christianity," *A Lost Tradition: Women Writers of the Early Church* (ed. Patricia Wilson-Kastner, et al.;

Perpetua was marked out for punishment along with other catechumens, including two slaves, one of whom, Felicitas, later gave birth prematurely in prison. The catechumens received baptism before being led away to prison. On four separate occasions, while she awaited martyrdom, Perpetua's father pled with her to reject her faith and offer sacrifice to the gods, giving demonstration of Jesus' words that "One's foes will be those of his [her] own household"; but she insisted, "I cannot call myself anything else than what I am, a Christian" (1.2). Much of Perpetua's diary is occupied with accounts of visions she had while in prison. In one of these she saw her approaching martyrdom in terms of a gladiatorial contest with an Egyptian (the devil). She was stripped and rubbed with oil, "as is the custom before a contest," "and I became a man" (3.2).[14]

The compiler's account of the martyrdom relates how the new Christians "proceeded from the prison into the amphitheatre, as if into an assembly, joyous and of brilliant countenance" (6.1).

Perpetua . . . was tossed [by a very fierce cow], and fell on her loins; and when she saw her tunic torn from her side, she drew it over her as a veil for her thigh rather mindful of her modesty than her suffering. . . . [W]hen she saw Felicitas crushed, she approached and gave her her hand, and lifted her up. And both of them stood together . . . (6.3).

The Christians were then individually dispatched by the sword.

Washington: University Press of America, 1981): 1-32; Alvyn Petersen, "Perpetua—Prisoner of Conscience," *VC* 41 (1987): 139-153.

   [14]See David M. Scholer, " 'And I Was A Man': The Power and Problem of Perpetua," *Daughters of Sarah* 15.5 (1989): 10-14. The philosophical background and early Christian development are explored by Kerstin Aspegren and Rene Kieffer, *The Male Woman: A Feminine Ideal in the Early Church* (Uppsala, Almqvist & Wiksell, 1990): 133-139.

Perpetua, that she might taste more pain, being pierced between the ribs, cried out loudly, and she herself placed the wavering right hand of the youthful gladiator to her throat. Possibly such a woman could not have been slain unless she herself had willed it, because she was feared by the impure spirit (6.4).

The "trembling hand of the young gladiator" (Musurillo) speaks eloquently of the moral dilemma the persecution of Christians posed.

In martyrdom, women equalled or excelled men in the "manly" virtues of courage and endurance. The blood of female martyrs was part of the seed from which Christians multiplied (Tertullian, *Apol.* 50), and so women contributed to the victory of Christianity over paganism.

3. *Women as Monastics/Ascetics*

Asceticism had deep roots in second and third-century Christianity. It became institutionalized in the monasticism of the fourth century. When martyrdom ceased with the triumph of Christianity in the fourth century, those who chose the interior martyrdom of ascetic self-denial were exalted as the spiritual heroes and heroines off the church, the "real" Christians. Women often gained recognition in the early Christian texts for breaking with tradition and adopting a celibate lifestyle. Celibacy gave women a freedom from a male dominated world of family and home and, in accord with ancient ideas, provided a closer communication with the divine. Asceticism may be seen as the path to women's liberation in the early church.[15]

---

[15]Elizabeth A. Clark, "Ascetic Renunciation and Feminine Advancement: A Paradox of Late Ancient Christianity," *ATR* 63 (1981): 240-257 (reprinted in the next cited work, pp. 175-208). She takes note of this while also sketching the ambivalence of the Church Fathers about the female sex (cursed as the source of temptation and sin yet honored as models of celibate dedication to God) in "Devil's Gateway and Bride of Christ: Women in the Early Christian World,"

Second-century apologists[16] in contrasting Christian sexual morality with paganism took note of the number of Christians, male and female, who chose to live continent lives. The phenomenon was noted by the pagan Galen.[17] Even writers defending marriage against its rejection by heretics saw continence as superior.[18] Although virgins may have been identified as a separate group already by Ignatius in the early second century,[19] the earliest asceticism seems to have been practiced individually and privately. There is no evidence of virgins living together in separate communities before the third century, but small group living arrangements earlier are not to be ruled out. Communities of celibate women did apparently precede those of men.[20] Organized monastic communities of women in the fourth century gave women opportunities for leadership and administration not often available in the larger society.

Ascetic Piety and Women's Faith: Essays on the Late Ancient Christianity (Lewiston: Edwin Mellen, 1986): 23-60, esp. 25-29, 42-52. See also the introduction to her collection of texts on *Women in the Early Church* (Wilmington: Michael Glazier, 1983): 15-25. Most of these texts are from the fourth century. For a discussion of the earlier period, see Jo Ann McNamara, *A New Song: Celibate Women in the First Three Christian Centuries* (New York: Institute for Research in History, 1983); on the general theme, see *idem*, "Sexual Equality and the Cult of Virginity in Early Christian Thought," *Feminist Studies* 3 (1967): 145-158. Cf. a different view in T. K. Seim, "Ascetic Autonomy? New Perspectives on Single Women in the Early Church," *ST* 43 (1989): 125-140.

[16]Justin, *1 Apology* 15, 29; Athenagoras, *Plea* 33.

[17]Richard Walzer, *Galen on Jews and Christians* (London: Oxford University, 1949): 15.

[18]Especially as applied to second marriages (Tertullian, *Exhortation to Chastity*; *On Monogamy*; *On Modesty*). See Origen's evaluation of virginity as the foremost sacrifice one could offer to God (*Commentary on Romans* 9). Clement of Alexandria has the most favorable comments about marriage among early Christian authors, placing it and celibacy on the same level as pertains to salvation (*Miscellanies* 3).

[19]*Smyrn.* 13, but included in the order of widows, for which see below; see Pol., *Phil.* 5.

[20]Athanasius, *Life of Antony* 3.

A special kind of living arrangement spawned by the ascetic impulse in the early church was "spiritual marriage," in which a man and woman (unmarried) lived in the same house as brother and sister.[21] The practice gave the woman the protection of a man in the house and was designed to provide mutual support and encouragement to the spiritual life. We know about the practice from those who warned of its dangers, even where there were the best of intentions. Cyprian, bishop of Carthage in the mid-third century, knew of couples that slept in the same bed and yet the woman claimed to be a virgin; he instructed that such be separated.[22] A few years later the bishop of Antioch, Paul of Samosata (condemned for faulty Christology by synods in 264 and 268), left himself open to suspicion and gossip by keeping spiritual sisters in his household.[23] The fullest invective against the threat to celibacy and the danger of scandal to outsiders from "spiritual marriage" comes in two treatises by John Chrysostom (late fourth century), one directed against the men and one against the women.[24]

In the second century the strongest advocacy within the Christian movement of a life of asceticism comes from the apocryphal Acts. As in the Hellenistic novels, similar in literary genre to the apocryphal Acts, the women are sexually attractive and inflame the desires of men, must experience great trials to protect their chastity, and are delivered by a divine power through a man who does not treat them as a sex object. The reader of the *Acts of Paul*, *Acts of John*, *Acts of Thomas*, and others gains the impression that the

---

[21]The practice has not received much study in recent literature, but see Rosemary Rader, *Breaking Boundaries: Male/Female Friendship in the Early Christian Communities* (New York: Paulist, 1983): 62-71, and Elizabeth A. Clark, "John Chrysostom and the Subintroductae," *CH* 46 (1977): 171-185.

[22]*Epistle* 4; see Pseudo-Cyprian, *De singularitate clericorum*; Pseudo-Clement, *Two Epistles on Virginity* 1.10-13; 2.1-5; *Epistle of Titus*.

[23]Eusebius, *Church History* 7.30.12-14.

[24]See Elizabeth A. Clark, *Jerome, Chrysostom, and Friends: Essays and Translations* (New York: Edwin Mellen, 1979): 158-348.

gospel invitation was "Repent and separate from your spouse and you will be saved." The conversion stories follow a consistent literary pattern. Names are given of women, usually wealthy and prominent, who, under the influence of the teaching of the apostles, refused to marry their betrothed or refused further sexual relations with their husbands and experienced persecution for their rejection of traditional female sociosexual roles. Although we cannot now verify the historicity of these persons, undeniable is the appeal to sexual continence as implicit within the Christian message. The life of chastity becomes a means for women to be freed from social structures based on their sexuality.[25] Women are so prominent in the apocryphal Acts, not only as ascetics but also as devoted followers of the apostles, as teachers, and as miracle workers, that some have thought that these works were written by and/or for women, even specifying the setting as groups of widows.[26]

Tertullian indicated that among the "heretics" women took a more prominent role than in the mainstream churches: "For they are bold enough to teach, to dispute, to enact exorcisms, to undertake cures—it may be even to baptize."[27] Gnostics are his probable target, and Gnostic influence is suspected in some of the apocryphal Acts. The publication of the Gnostic writings from Nag Hammadi in Egypt[28] has

---

[25]For this paragraph, see Ross S. Kraemer, "The Conversion of Women to Ascetic Forms of Christianity," *Signs* 6 (1980): 298-307; see also V. Burrus, *Chastity as Autonomy: Women in the Stories of the Apocryphal Acts* (Lewiston: Edwin Mellen, 1987).

[26]Stevan L. Davies, *The Revolt of the Widows: The Social World of the Apocryphal Acts* (Carbondale: Southern Illinois University, 1980); Dennis MacDonald, ed., *The Apocryphal Acts of the Apostles, Semeia* 38 (1986), esp. 43-52 on the composition of the *Acts of Thecla* and 101-135 on women in the apocryphal Acts.

[27]*On Prescription Against Heretics* 41; trans. by Peter Holmes in ANF, 3.263.

[28]English translation in James Robinson, ed., *The Nag Hammadi Library* (rev. ed.; San Francisco: Harper, 1988).

stimulated interest in women in Gnosticism.[29] There is an ambivalence about the feminine in these writings. Female figures are prominent in the Gnostic mythology, but a strain of antifemininity also runs through the texts,[30] and "even when the feminine is highly valued, it is often done so at the expense of real sexuality."[31] Women may have had a prominent role in Gnosticism, but it is difficult to go from these mythological texts to a sociological description of Gnostic sects. Although there were libertine Gnostics,[32] the Nag Hammadi texts represent the ascetic alternative, and the observations on the significance of asceticism for women in other texts would apparently apply to women in ascetic Gnostic circles as well.

Literature on virginity began to appear in the third century,[33] and became a flood in the fourth.[34] Moreover, collections of stories about hermits and ascetics of the fourth and fifth centuries and collections of their sayings put us on firmer historical ground about the names and the actual attitudes and the teachings of the champions of Christian asceticism in its classical period. The sayings of three women (Theodora, Sarah, and Syncletica) are included in the *Sayings of the Desert Fathers*, and nineteen of the sixty-eight histories of hermits and monks in *Lausiac History* of Palladius concern women. Some of the greatest examples of female asceticism are known from the correspondence of John Chrysostom and Jerome with admired and admiring

---

[29]Karen King, ed., *Images of the Feminine in Gnosticism* (Philadelphia: Fortress, 1988).

[30]Frederik Wisse, "Flee Femininity: Antifemininity in the Gnostic Texts and the Question of Social Milieu," *ibid.*, 297-307.

[31]King, *ibid.*, xvii.

[32]James E. Goehring, "Libertine or Liberated: Women in the So-called Libertine Gnostic Communities," *ibid.*, 329-344.

[33]Cyprian, *On the Dress of Virgins*; Pseudo-Clement, *Two Epistles on Virginity*.

[34]See Clark, *Women in the Early Church*, esp. chap. 3, and Rader, *Breaking Boundaries*, 72-110. Notable is Methodius, *Symposium* (ca. 300) because it presents the speeches in favor of virginity as spoken by women.

female associates in their work: Olympius (John Chrysostom), Eustochium, and others (mentioned below— Jerome).

An early ascetic discipline in which women took a lead was pilgrimage. The conversion of Constantine and the travels of his mother, Helena, to identify the historical sites of the faith opened the way for a steady stream of pilgrims to the Holy Land. The most famous of these pilgrims, and author of the most informative account, was Egeria, an ascetic woman from southern Gaul or northern Spain who made a journey to the Sinai and Palestine at the turn of the fourth to the fifth century.

4. *Women as Missionaries*

Missionary work is pilgrimage in reverse and often involves suffering and an ascetic discipline. Clement of Alexandria (*Miscellanies* 3.6.53) refers to wives of apostles assisting in missionary work as the means through which the gospel reached the women's quarters of households. Representative of early female missionaries is a woman from the apocryphal Acts—Thecla, who could as well be treated as representative of asceticism or martyrdom.

According to the *Acts of Paul and Thecla* (part of the larger *Acts of Paul*), Thecla was converted to Paul's message, "You must fear one single God only, and live chastely" (9).[35] Thamyris, an important man in Iconium to whom she was engaged, brought charges before the governor against Paul. Paul was released after a scourging, but the governor condemned Thecla to be burned for refusing to marry Thamyris. A thunderstorm quenched the fire, however, and Thecla was saved. She said to Paul, "I will cut my hair short and follow thee wherever thou goest" (25). At Antioch a certain Alexander tried to force his attentions on

---

[35]The translation is from E. Hennecke and W. Schneemelcher, *New Testament Apocrypha* (trans. R. Mcl. Wilson; Philadelphia: Westminster, 1965): 2.355. On Thecla, see Aspegren, *The Male Woman*, 99-114, 158-164.

Thecla, and when she refused, for a second time she was brought before a governor and condemned to death, this time by fighting wild beasts. There was a pit full of water in the arena, and Thecla jumped in and baptized herself "in the name of Jesus Christ" (34). The beasts would not touch her, and eventually the governor released her.

Paul commissioned Thecla, "Go and teach the word of God!" (41). This section of the *Acts* concludes, "after enlightening many with the word of God she slept with a noble sleep" (43).

The most successful woman missionary of the ancient church was Nino, "the apostle of Georgia."[36] She was a slave from Cappadocia whose miraculous healing abilities brought her to the attention of the queen of Georgia. Nino healed her in the name of Christ. Eventually the king was converted and built a church. Nino's influence brought about the conversion of the country of Georgia to Orthodox Christianity from the top down.

5. *Women as Ministers*

Women performed many serving functions in the early church. Organization was given to their work through the orders of widows and deaconesses.

Many references to widows in early Christian literature are to women who had lost their husbands and were in need of charity. Some early passages may reflect the existence of a special order of widows.[37] Such may be implied by

---

[36]The subject of the inaugural address at the Ninth International Conference of Patristic Studies at Oxford, 1983, by Fairy von Lilienfeld was "St. Nino, Apostle and Illuminator of Georgia." I have not seen the articles (in English) about her in the *Journal of the Moscow Patriarchate* 11 (1985): 77-82 and 3 (1986): 49-56.

[37]See 1 Timothy 5:3ff. C. H. Turner, "Ministries of Women in the Primitive Church: Widow, Deaconess and Virgin in the First Four Christian Centuries," *Catholic and Apostolic* (ed. H. N. Bate; London:

Ignatius' words about "virgins who are called widows."[38]
Hermas refers to a woman named Grapte whose task was to
instruct the widows and orphans (*Visions* 2.4.3). The
association of widows and orphans here and in some other
texts may be due not to the fact that these were the principal
classes of needy persons but to the practice of the church in
supporting widows to care for orphan children.[39] We are on
firmer ground with the *Apostolic Tradition* of Hippolytus,
who says about ordination of church offices,

> When a widow is appointed she is not ordained but she
> shall be chosen by name. . . . Let the widow be
> instituted by word only and (then) let her be reckoned
> among the (enrolled) widows. But she shall not be
> ordained, because she does not offer the oblation nor
> has she a (liturgical) ministry. But ordination is for the
> clergy on account of their (liturgical) ministry. But the
> widow is appointed for prayer, and this is (a function)
> of all (Christians) (11).[40]

Hippolytus gives separate treatment to the Virgins: "(The
Virgin is not appointed but voluntarily separated and
named.) A Virgin does not have an imposition of hands,
for personal choice alone is that which makes a Virgin"
(13). From the mid-third century the Pseudo-Clementines
have Peter, when he established a church, not only ordaining

Mowbray, 1931): 316-351; B. B. Thurston, *The Widows—A Women's
Ministry in the Early Church* (Minneapolis: Fortress, 1989).

[38]*Smyrn.* 13. J. B. Lightfoot understands this as referring to
widows who by purity of life were really virgins rather than to virgins
incorporated into the order of widows—*Apostolic Fathers* 2.2 (London:
Macmillan, 1885): 323-24. On the other hand, Tertullian, *On the
Veiling of Virgins* 9, knows "that in a certain place a virgin of less
than twenty years of age has been placed in the order of widows." This
may be a clue as to how the order of widows in the New Testament
became Virgins later, viz., the widows had to remain unmarried and
soon those who had not married took the same vow.

[39]See Lucian, *The Passing of Peregrinus* 12.

[40]I follow the translation of Gregory Dix, *The Apostolic
Tradition of St. Hippolytus* (London: SPCK, 1968): 20-21.

a bishop, presbyters, and deacons, but also instituting the order of widows (*Recog.* 6.15; *Hom.* 11.36).

The fullest discussion of the order of widows in the Ante-Nicene literature occurs in chapters 14 and 15 of the *Didascalia*, from Syria in the third century.[41] The description, qualifications, duties, and warnings closely follow 1 Timothy 5, except that the minimum age is set at fifty. The appointed widows' responsibility was primarily to pray, but they were also to engage in benevolence and to fast, pray for, lay hands upon, and visit the sick. They were forbidden to teach and to preside at baptisms, a prohibition applying to all women, although as explained below deaconesses did assist at baptisms of women.[42]

Somewhat later the *Apostolic Church Order* distinguishes two types of work for widows:

Three widows shall be appointed, two to persevere in prayer for all those who are in temptation, and for the reception of revelations where such are necessary, but one to assist the women visited with sicknesses, she must be ready for service, discreet, communicating what is necessary to the presbyters, not avaricious, not given to much love of wine, so that she may be sober and capable of performing the night services, and other loving service if she will (5).[43]

The widows who are not able to go out and be actively involved are to stay home and spend their time in prayer; a widow able still to be active visits the sick and cares for the needy. This document seems to reject female deacons (8).

---

[41]R. H. Connolly, *Didascalia Apostolorum* (Oxford: Clarendon, 1929).

[42]Tertullian concurred in objecting to women baptizing (*On Baptism* 17; *On the Veiling of Virgins* 9), but there are reports of women among the Montanists baptizing (Cyprian, *Epistle* 74.10).

[43]A. Harnack, *Sources of the Apostolic Canons* (London: Black, 1895): 19-21.

Deaconesses[44] appear to have succeeded the order of widows, at least in the eastern church.[45] "Women servants" (*ministrae*) among the Christians are referred to by Pliny the Younger in the early second century (*Epistle* 10.96.8.). At the end of the century Clement of Alexandria understood the "women" of 1 Timothy 3:11 as "women deacons."[46] Only later was the word deaconess (*diakonissa*) coined for the special order of female servants of the church.

The first description we have of deaconesses occurs in the *Didascalia* 16, where they are discussed with deacons, separately from widows but less extensively. The bishop is instructed to choose and appoint helpers, "a man for the performance of the most things that are required, but a woman for the ministry of women." The deaconess could enter the women's quarters, where a man could not go, "to visit those who are sick, and to minister to them that of which they have need, and to bathe those who have begun to recover from sickness." Also, the pre-baptismal anointing (according to the Syrian rite) of the body of women was to be done by the deaconess, the bishop only anointing the head. A man pronounced the invocation of the divine names while the baptizand stood in the water. "[W]hen she who is being baptized has come up from the water, let the deaconess receive her, and teach and instruct her how the seal of baptism ought to be (kept) unbroken in purity and holiness." The fact that the Lord was ministered to by women justified the appointment of women deacons to perform things "needful and important."

Although women were denied public preaching and liturgical functions, including baptism, there were many opportunities for women to serve, e.g., private teaching.

---

[44] A. G. Martimort, *Deaconesses: An Historical Study* (San Francisco: Ignatius, 1986).

[45] *Canons of Basil* 24, "A widow put into the catalogue of widows, that is, a deaconess."

[46] *Miscellanies* 3.6.53; or does he mean the widows of 1 Timothy 5:9-11?

6. *Women as Mentors*

Women in their capacities as wives, mothers, ascetics, missionaries, and ministers have already been observed teaching in various home and private settings, in spite of a feeling by many that women could not be trusted to teach.

There had been many places where women functioned as teachers and prophets in New Testament times, and the attempted revival of prophecy in the second-century Montanist movement gave women once more a prominent speaking ministry. Although the presence of Priscilla and Maximilla in the company of Montanus caused some raised eyebrows, the church's objections against the Montanists were not to its having female as well as male prophets but to their manner of prophesying (in ecstasy) and to the content of their messages.[47] The setting in which they did their prophesying is not clear. Even in Montanism there was no regular practice of women speaking in church. Tertullian relates that a woman who had visions during the assembly reported their contents privately after the dismissal.[48]

The most noteworthy examples of learned women who served as mentors of others come from the fourth century.[49] I select for comment here from the Greek east Gorgonia, sister of Gregory of Nazianzus, and from the Latin west Paula, close associate of Jerome.

---

[47]Eusebius, *Church History* 5.16-18; Epiphanius, *Panarion* 48. See all the relevant texts now conveniently classified in Ronald E. Heine, *The Montanist Oracles and Testimonia* (Macon: Mercer University Press, 1989).

[48]*On the Soul* 9. For celebrating the eucharist and baptizing, see Cyprian, *Epistle* 74.10; Didymus the Blind, *Trinity* 3.41.3; Epiphanius, *Panarion* 49.2).

[49]I discussed Macrina the Younger (Gregory of Nyssa, *Life of Macrina*), whom Gregory calls "teacher" (*On the Soul and the Resurrection*), and Marcella (Jerome, *Letter* 127), with whom Jerome discussed scholarly questions, in *Early Christians Speak*, 231-232, 234-235.

Gregory of Nazianzus celebrated the virtues of
Gorgonia in his oration for her funeral (*Oration* 8). She was
married, the mother of three daughters, and won her
husband, her children, and her grandchildren for the Lord.
In addition to modeling the virtues of modesty, hospitality,
self-denial, and charity, her intellect made her a mentor of
others, even outside her family.

> What could be keener than the intellect of her who was
> recognized as a common advisor not only by those of
> her family . . . but even by all men round about, who
> treated her counsels and advice as a law not to be
> broken? What more sagacious than her words? What
> more prudent than her silence? . . . Who had a fuller
> knowledge of the things of God, both from the Divine
> oracles, and from her own understanding? But who
> was less ready to speak, confining herself within the
> due limits of women? [She surpassed]not only
> women, but the most devoted of men, by her
> intelligent chanting of the psalter, her converse with
> and unfolding and apposite recollection of the divine
> oracles, her bending of her knees which had grown
> hard and almost taken root in the ground . . . (11,
> 13).[50]

Thus, in Gregory's words, she demonstrated "that the
distinction between male and female is one of body and not
of soul" (14).

Paula came from a noble and wealthy family in Rome,
tracing her ancestry to the Gracchi and Scipios, while her
husband was of the Julian family. She bore five children,
one of whom, Eustochium, shared her combination of
learning and asceticism and succeeded her in the direction of
her monastery at Bethlehem. On her husband's death, Paula
adopted a life of chastity and service to the Lord. Jerome
praised her as a model of ascetic piety, commending her

---

[50]Translation by C. G. Browne and J. E. Swallow in NPNF,
Second Series, VII: 241-242.

humility, self-restraint, patience, and perseverance.[51] Especially noteworthy was her liberality to a fault, so that she died leaving her daughter with a debt.   She gave generously to the poor and built twin monasteries at Bethlehem, one for men and one for women, where she settled after a pilgrimage to the east. Jerome commended her administration of the monastery, where she was a mentor of the women under her charge, giving instruction, correction, and encouragement.   She financed Jerome's studies and writings, but she was more than a patron of the learning of others.   Already knowing Greek as well as her native Latin, she learned Hebrew, succeeding so well that she could chant the Psalms in Hebrew and speak the language without a trace of Latin pronunciation. She studied with Jerome to the point that she was able publicly to refute heresy.

Conclusion

Except in some heretical and schismatic groups, the churches in the early patristic period evidence prohibitions on women speaking in the assembly and serving in leadership positions of bishop/presbyter or presiding at liturgical functions.   On the other hand, in ministering functions women were actively involved and exercised leadership responsibilities in a variety of other ways.

Although the quantity of information from the early church about women is not as great as we would like, there is much that can be learned. The interest in women's studies in recent years has brought to the surface much more than previously was generally recognized.   A story can be presented, if still in rough draft. This brief survey will indicate something of the scope and direction the available material provides.   Women in no way played only insignificant roles in the unfolding drama of early Christianity.

---

[51]Jerome, *Letter* 108.

Scripture

Classical Works

Alexis
  Pythagorean Woman 81

Antye
  Palatine Anthology 54, 58
    6.312: 54
    7.190: 54
    7.486: 58
    7.490, 649: 58

Appain
  Bella Civillia
    4.33: 72

Apuleis
  Metamorphoses
    9.14: 90
    11.10: 204

Aristotle
  de Generation Animalium
    1.20: 48
    2.1: 48
    4.3: 48
  Men.
    71e-73e: 74
  Nichomachean Ethics
    1160b:74
  Politica
    7.14.6: 57
    1254b, 1259a, 1260a: 74
    1254: 243
  Oeconomica
    1.3: 49
  Thes.
    837: 206

Arrian
  Anabasis
    4.13.4-6: 87

Athanasius
  Life of Antony
    3: 503
Aulus Gellius 88

Cicero 56

Brutus
  58.211: 56
De Oratoria
  1.183, 238: 64
Divinatione
  1.199.37, 38: 86
Epistulae ad Familiares
  8.7.2: 64
Oratio pro L. Flacco
  71-72: 61
Epistuale ad Atticum
  1.13: 88
Orationes Phillipicae
  2.28, 69: 64

Cornelius Nepos
  Praefatio
    6-7:41

Corpus inscriptionum iudaicarum
    19: 126
    315: 123
    400: 123
    496: 123
    523: 23
    581: 123
    590: 123
    597: 123
    619: 126
    639: 123
    696: 123
    731c: 123
    738: 512
    756: 123
    762: 126
    763: 126
    776: 126
    1007: 123
    1514: 123

Corpus Inscriptionum Latinarum
  $I^3$581: 90

Demosthenes
  30.7: 59

Jewish Sources

Early Christian Sources

Modern Authors